CRIMINOLOGY
The Shorter Version

CRIMINOLOGY
The Shorter Version
THIRD EDITION

Freda Adler

Distinguished Professor of Criminal Justice
School of Criminal Justice, Rutgers University

Gerhard O. W. Mueller

Distinguished Professor of Criminal Justice
School of Criminal Justice, Rutgers University

William S. Laufer

Associate Professor of Legal Studies
Wharton School, University of Pennsylvania

Boston, Massachusetts   Burr Ridge, Illinois   Dubuque, Iowa
Madison, Wisconsin   New York, New York   San Francisco, California   St. Louis, Missouri

McGraw-Hill

A Division of The **McGraw·Hill** Companies

CRIMINOLOGY
The Shorter Version

Copyright © 1998, 1995, by The McGraw-Hill Companies, Inc. All rights reserved. Printed in the United States of America. Except as permitted under the United States Copyright Act of 1976, no part of this publication may be reproduced or distributed in any form or by any means, or stored in a data base or retrieval system, without the prior written permission of the publisher.

Acknowledgments appear on pages 373–378, and on this page by reference.

This book is printed on acid-free paper.

2 3 4 5 6 7 8 9 0 DOW DOW 9 0 9 8

ISBN 0-07-000512-5

This book was set in New Caledonia by The Clarinda Company.
The editors were Marge Byers and Nancy Blaine;
the text designer was Joseph A. Piliero;
the production supervisors were Louise Karam and Kathryn Porzio.
The photo editor was Barbara Salz.
The cover designer was Joan Greenfield.
Project Supervision was done by The Total Book.
R. R. Donnelley & Sons Company was printer and binder.

Cover painting: "White Haired Girl" by Jane Dickson.

Library of Congress Cataloging-in-Publication Data

Adler, Freda.
    Criminology : the shorter version / Freda Adler, Gerhard O. W.
Mueller, William S. Laufer.—3rd ed.
      p. cm.
    Includes bibliographical references and index.
    ISBN 0-07-000512-5
    1. Criminology. I. Mueller, Gerhard O. W. II. Laufer, William S.
III. Title.
HV6025.A35   1997
364—DC21   97-12515
                                              CIP

http://www.mhhe.com

ABOUT THE AUTHORS

FREDA ADLER is Distinguished Professor of Criminal Justice at Rutgers University, School of Criminal Justice. She received her B.A. in sociology, her M.A. in criminology, and her Ph.D. in sociology from the University of Pennsylvania. Teaching since 1968, Dr. Adler has taught subjects that include criminology, statistics, research methods, and international comparative criminology. She has served as criminological advisor to the United Nations, as well as to federal, state, and foreign governments. Her published works include ten books as author or co-author, eight books as editor, and over seventy journal articles. She has served on the editorial boards of the *Journal of Research in Crime and Delinquency, Criminology,* and the *Journal of Criminal Justice.* Presently, Dr. Adler is editorial consultant to the *Journal of Criminal Law and Criminology* and co-editor of *Advances in Criminological Theory.* She served as President of the American Society of Criminology (November 1994–1995).

GERHARD O. W. MUELLER is Distinguished Professor of Criminal Justice at Rutgers University, School of Criminal Justice. He studied law and sociology in Europe and America, earning his J.D. degree from the University of Chicago. He went on to receive his L.L.M. degree from Columbia University. He was awarded the degree of Dr. Jur. (h.c.) by the University of Uppsala, Sweden. His teaching in criminal law, criminal procedure, criminology, criminal justice, and comparative criminal justice, begun in 1953, was partially interrupted between 1974 and 1982, when, as Chief of the United Nations Crime Prevention and Criminal Justice Branch, he was responsible for all of the United Nations' programs dealing with problems of crime and justice worldwide. Professor Mueller has been a member of the faculties of the University of Washington, West Virginia University, New York University, and the National Judicial College, with visiting appointments and lectureships at universities and institutes in the Americas, Western and Eastern Europe, Africa, Asia, and Australia. His published works include some 50 authored or edited books and 260 scholarly articles.

WILLIAM S. LAUFER is Associate Professor of Legal Studies at the Wharton School of the University of Pennsylvania. Dr. Laufer received his B.A. in social and behavioral sciences at The Johns Hopkins University, his J.D. at Northeastern University School of Law, and his Ph.D. at Rutgers University School of Criminal Justice. Teaching since 1987, he has taught such subjects as criminological theory, corporate and white-collar crime, and business ethics. Dr. Laufer's research has appeared in law reviews and a wide range of criminal justice, legal, and psychology journals, such as the *Journal of Research in Crime and Delinquency, Law and Human Behavior,* and the *Journal of Personality and Social Psychology.* He is co-editor of the *Handbook of Psychology and Law, Personality Theory, Moral Development and Criminal Behavior,* and *Crime, Values and Religion.* Dr. Laufer is co-editor of *Advances in Criminological Theory,* with Freda Adler.

TO OUR CHILDREN AND GRANDCHILDREN

Mark J. Adler and Susan B. Weinstock-Adler with
    David S. Adler and Daniel Adler
Jill E. Adler-Donkersloot and Willem H. F. A.
    Donkersloot
Nancy D. Adler-Knijff and Robert F Knijff

Mark H. Mueller and Constance Sobol Mueller with
    Nicolai Alexander and John Joseph Mueller
Marla L. Mueller and Lawrence Frederick Bentley
Monica R. Mueller
Matthew A. Mueller and Martha Sullivan Mueller
    with Lauren Elizabeth, Stephen William, and
    Anna Lisette Mueller

Hannah M. Laufer

CONTENTS IN BRIEF

	List of Boxes	xvii
	Preface	xix
PART I	**UNDERSTANDING CRIMINOLOGY**	**1**
CHAPTER 1	**An Overview of Criminology**	**2**
CHAPTER 2	**Measuring Crime and Criminal Behavior Patterns**	**18**
CHAPTER 3	**Schools of Thought throughout History**	**46**
PART II	**EXPLANATIONS OF CRIME AND CRIMINAL BEHAVIOR**	**67**
CHAPTER 4	**Psychological and Biological Perspectives**	**68**
CHAPTER 5	**Strain and Cultural Deviance Theories**	**97**
CHAPTER 6	**The Formation of Subcultures**	**123**
CHAPTER 7	**Social Control Theory**	**147**
CHAPTER 8	**Targets and Victims of Crime**	**167**
CHAPTER 9	**Alternative Explanations of Crime: Labeling, Conflict, and Radical Theories**	**187**
PART III	**TYPES OF CRIME**	**209**
CHAPTER 10	**The Concept of Crime**	**210**
CHAPTER 11	**Violent Crimes**	**230**
CHAPTER 12	**Crimes against Property**	**263**
CHAPTER 13	**Organizational Criminality**	**284**
CHAPTER 14	**Drug-, Alcohol-, and Sex-Related Crime**	**312**
CHAPTER 15	**Comparative Criminology**	**342**
	Glossary	367
	Photo Credits	373
	Illustration and Text Credits	375
	Name Index	379
	Subject Index	391

CONTENTS

List of Boxes xvii
Preface xix

PART I
UNDERSTANDING CRIMINOLOGY
1

CHAPTER 1
An Overview of Criminology
2

Key Terms 3
What Is Criminology 6
The Making of Laws 7
 Deviance 7
 The Concept of Crime 8
 The Consensus and Conflict Views of Law
  and Crime 9
The Breaking of Laws 11
Society's Reaction to the Breaking of Laws 12
 Criminology and the Criminal Justice System 14
 The Global Approach to the Breaking of Laws 14
Research Informs Policy 14
BOXES
 Criminological Focus: Fairy Tales and Crime 10
 At Issue: Obituary for Tupac Amaru Shakur
  (1971–1996) 12
 Window to the World: The New Terrorism 15
Review 16 / Notes 17

CHAPTER 2
Measuring Crime and Criminal Behavior Patterns
18

Key Terms 19
Measuring Crime 20
 Methods of Collecting Data 21
 Ethics and the Researcher 23
The Nature and Extent of Crime 24
 Police Statistics 24
 Victimization Surveys 27
 Self-Report Surveys 27

Measuring Characteristics of Crime 29
 Crime Trends 29
 Locations and Times of Criminal Acts 31
 Severity of Crime 33
Measuring Characteristics of Criminals 34
 Age and Crime 35
 Gender and Crime 39
 Social Class and Crime 41
 Race and Crime 42
BOXES
 Window to the World: Measuring World Crime 26
 At Issue: Stalking: An Unrecorded Crime 30
 Criminological Focus: Criminologists versus
  the NYPD 34
Review 43 / Notes 43

CHAPTER 3
Schools of Thought throughout History
46

Key Terms 47
Classical Criminology 49
 The Historical Context 49
 Cesare Beccaria 50
 Jeremy Bentham's Utilitarianism 52
 The Classical School: An Evaluation 52
Positivist Criminology 53
Biological Determinism: The Search
 for Criminal Traits 53
 Lombroso, Ferri, Garofalo: The Italian School 54
 A Return to Biological Determinism 57
Psychological Determinism 60
 Pioneers in Criminal Psychology 60
 Psychological Studies of Criminals 60
Sociological Determinism 61
 Adolphe Quételet and André Michel Guerry 61
 Gabriel Tarde 61
 Émile Durkheim 61
Historical and Contemporary Criminology:
 A Time Line 62

BOXES

Window to the World: *Stone Age Crime
and Social Control* **48**
Criminological Focus: *The Mismeasure of Man* **54**
At Issue: *Somatotyping: A Physique for Crime?* **58**
Review 64 / Notes 64

PART II
EXPLANATIONS OF CRIME AND
CRIMINAL BEHAVIOR
67

CHAPTER 4
Psychological and Biological Perspectives
68

Key Terms **69**
Psychology and Criminality **71**
Psychological Development 71
Moral Development 72
Maternal Deprivation and Attachment Theory 73
Learning Aggression and Violence 77
Personality 80
Mental Disorders and Crime **81**
Biology and Criminality **84**
Modern Biocriminology 84
Genetics and Criminality 84
The Controversy over Violence and Genes 86
The IQ Debate 87
Biochemical Factors 88
Neurophysiological Factors 91
Crime and Human Nature **91**
Criticisms of Biocriminology 92
An Integrated Theory 92
BOXES
At Issue: *The Crime of Parricide* **76**
Window to the World: *Censoring TV Violence* **78**
Criminological Focus: *Myths of the Insanity
Defense* **82**
Review 92 / Notes 93

CHAPTER 5
Strain and Culture Deviance Theories
97

Key Terms **98**
The Interconnectedness of Sociological Theories **99**
Anomie: Émile Durkheim **99**
The Structural-Functionalist Perspective 99
Anomie and Suicide 100
Strain Theory **100**
Merton's Theory of Anomie 102
Modes of Adaptation 103
Tests of Merton's Theory 104

Evaluation: Merton's Theory 106
Institutional Imbalance and Crime 106
General Strain Theory 107
Theory Informs Policy 107
Cultural Deviance Theories **109**
The Nature of Cultural Deviance 109
Social Disorganization Theory 110
Tests of Social Disorganization Theory 113
Evaluation: Social Disorganization Theory 114
Theory Informs Policy 114
Differential Association Theory 115
Tests of Differential Association Theory 116
Evaluation: Differential Association Theory 116
Theory Informs Policy 117
Culture Conflict Theory 117
BOXES
Window to the World:
A Social System Breaks Down **101**
At Issue: *Social Disorganization in Los Angeles* **112**
Criminological Focus:
Culture Conflict in Waco, Texas **118**
Review 119 / Notes 120

CHAPTER 6
The Formation of Subcultures
123

Key Terms **124**
The Function of Subcultures **125**
**Subcultural Theories of Delinquency
and Crime** **125**
The Middle-Class Measuring Rod 125
Corner Boy, College Boy, Delinquent Boy 126
Tests of Cohen's Theory 128
Evaluation: Cohen's Theory 128
Delinquency and Opportunity **129**
Tests of Opportunity Theory 130
Evaluation: Differential Opportunity 131
The Subculture of Violence **132**
Tests of the Subculture of Violence 132
Evaluation: The Subculture of Violence Theory 133
Focal Concerns: Miller's Theory **134**
Tests of Miller's Theory 135
Evaluation: Miller's Theory 135
Gangs of the 1990s **136**
Guns and Gangs 137
Female Delinquent Subcultures **138**
Early Research 138
Recent Studies 138
Middle-Class Delinquency **140**
Explanations 142

Theory Informs Policy 142
   MOBY 142
   Other Programs 142
   Getting Out: Gang Banging or the Morgue 144
BOXES
   At Issue: *The Tagger Subculture* 127
   Criminological Focus: *The Girls in the Gang* 139
   Window to the World: *America's Changing
     Ethnic Gangs* 141
Review 144 / Notes 144

CHAPTER 7
Social Control Theory
147

Key Terms 148
What Is Social Control? 149
Theories of Social Control 150
   The Microsociological Perspective: Hirschi 150
   Social Bonds 150
   Empirical Tests of Hirschi's Theory 153
   Evaluation: Hirschi's Social Control Theory 153
Social Control and Drift 155
Personal and Social Control 156
   Failure of Control Mechanisms 156
   Stake in Conformity 157
Containment Theory 158
   Empirical Tests of Containment Theory 159
   Evaluation: Containment Theory 159
Integrated Theories 160
   Developmental Theories 160
   Multiple Control Factors 161
   General Theories 161
Theory Informs Policy 161
   Family 163
   School 163
   Neighborhood 163
BOXES
   At Issue: *Respect for Authority: Carjacking* 154
   Criminological Focus:
     Out of Control: School Violence 156
   Window to the World:
     Nations with Low Crime Rates 162
Review 164 / Notes 164

CHAPTER 8
Targets and Victims of Crimes
167

Key Terms 168
Theories of Crime 169
   Environmental Criminology 169
   Rational-Choice Perspective 171

   Routine-Activity Approach 172
Theories of Victimization 174
   Lifestyle Theories 175
   Repeat Victimization 176
   Hot Spots of Crime 176
   Geography of Crime 177
   Interrelatedness of Theories 177
**Preventing Crimes against Places, People,
   and Valuable Goods** 177
   Situational Crime Prevention 177
   Displacement 184
BOXES
   Window to the World: *Decresting the Lovebug,
     Worldwide* 173
   Criminological Focus: *Defensive Space: Bumps,
     Barriers, and Barricades* 178
   At Issue: *Why Wait for a Million-Dollar Civil
     Liability Suit When You Can Have CPTED
     for Peanuts?* 183
Review 184 / Notes 184

CHAPTER 9
Alternative Explanations of Crime: Labeling, Conflict,
and Radical Theories
187

Key Terms 187
Labeling Theory 189
   The Origins of Labeling Theory 190
   Basic Assumptions of Labeling Theory 190
   Labeling in the 1960s 191
   Empirical Evidence for Labeling Theory 192
   Evaluation: Labeling Theory 193
Conflict Theory 195
   The Consensus Model 195
   The Conflict Model 196
   Conflict Theory and Criminology 196
   Empirical Evidence for the Conflict Model 199
Radical Theory 199
   The Intellectual Heritage of Marxist
     Criminology 199
   Engels and Marx 199
   Willem Adriaan Bonger 200
   Georg Rusche and Otto Kirchheimer 200
   Radical Criminology from the 1970s to the 1990s 201
   Evaluation: Marxist Criminological Theory 202
   Emerging Explanations 204
BOXES
   Criminological Focus: *On Being Sane
     in Insane Places* 194
   At Issue: *The Rights of the Poorest* 197

Window to the World: *Criminal Law in an Age
of Ethnic Diversity*   203
Review 205 / Notes 205

PART III
TYPES OF CRIMES
209

CHAPTER 10
The Concept of Crime
210

Key Terms   *211*
The Ingredients of Crime   **212**
   The Seven Basic Requirements   212
   The Act Requirement   212
   The Legality Requirement   213
   The Harm Requirement   215
   The Causation Requirement   215
   Mens Rea: The "Guilty Mind" Requirement   215
   The Concurrence Requirement   216
   The Punishment Requirement   217
The Defenses: Excuses   **217**
   The Insanity Defense   217
   Guilty but Mentally Ill   220
   The Intoxication Defense   220
   Infancy   220
   Mistake of Fact   221
   Mistake or Ignorance of Law   221
The Defenses: Justifications   **221**
   Duress   221
   Necessity   222
   Public Duty   222
   Self-Defense, Defense of Others,
     Defense of Property   222
Attempt and Accessoryship   **227**
Typologies of Crime   **227**
BOXES
   Criminological Focus: *Thirty-Eight Witnesses*   **214**
   Window to the World: *Necessity at Sea*   **223**
   At Issue: *The Battered Woman Self-Defense
     and the Penal Codes*   **224**
Review 228 / Notes 228

CHAPTER 11
Violent Crimes
230

Key Terms   *231*
Homicide   **232**
   Murder   232
   Manslaughter   233

   The Extent of Homicide   233
   The Nature of Homicide   234
   A Cross-National Comparison of Homicide Rates   237
Assault   **237**
Family-Related Crimes   **241**
   Spouse Abuse   242
   Child Abuse   243
   Abuse of the Elderly   245
Rape and Sexual Assault   **245**
   Characteristics of the Rape Event   246
   Who Are the Rapists?   246
   Rape and the Legal System   247
   Community Response   247
Robbery   **248**
   Characteristics of Robbers   248
   The Consequences of Robbery   248
Kidnapping and Terrorism   **249**
   Kidnapping   249
   Terrorism   249
Violence and Gun Control   **255**
   The Extent of Firearm-Related Offenses   255
   Youth and Guns   255
   Controlling Handgun Use   256
   The Gun-Control Debate   257
BOXES
   Window to the World: *Assassinations around
     the Globe*   **239**
   Criminological Focus: *"An Epidemic
     of Hate Crimes?"*   **252**
   At Issue: *Vipers in the Desert*   **254**
Review 258 / Notes 258

CHAPTER 12
Crimes against Property
263

Key Terms   *264*
Larceny   **265**
   The Elements of Larceny   265
   The Extent of Larceny   265
   Who Are the Thieves?   266
   Shoplifting   267
   Art Theft   268
   Motor Vehicle Theft   268
   Boat Theft   268
Fraud   **271**
   Obtaining Property by False Pretenses   271
   Confidence Games and Frauds   272
   Check Forgery   272
   Credit Card Crimes   272
   Insurance Fraud   273

**High-Tech Crimes: Concerns for Today
and Tomorrow**   **273**
  Characteristics of High-Tech Crimes   274
  Crime on the Internet: Types of Crime   275
  Characteristics of the High-Tech Criminal   277
  The Criminal Justice Problem   277
Burglary   **279**
Fencing: Receiving Stolen Property   **279**
Arson   **281**
Comparative Crime Rates   **282**
BOXES
  At Issue: *"Follow This Car! I'm Being Stolen!"*   **269**
  Window to the World: *Crime on the Oceans:
    Whose Problem?*   **270**
  Criminological Focus: *When New Global
    Technology Meets Old Local Laws*   **278**
Review 282 / Notes 282

CHAPTER 13
Organizational Criminality
284

Key Terms   *285*
Defining White-Collar Crime   **286**
  Crimes Committed by Individuals   288
  Types of White-Collar Crimes   288
Corporate Crime   **292**
  Theories of Corporate Liability   293
  Governmental Control of Corporations   293
  Investigating Corporate Crime   294
  Environmental Crimes   295
  Curbing Corporate Crime   297
Organized Crime   **299**
  The History of Organized Crime   299
  The Structure and Impact of Organized Crime   302
  The New Ethnic Diversity in Organized Crime   305
BOXES
  Criminological Focus: *Corporate Crime—
    Who Are the Victims?*   **287**
  At Issue: *Dangerous Ground:
    The World of Hazardous Waste Crime*   **298**
  Window to the World: *The Business
    of Organized Crime*   **300**
Review 306 / Notes 306

CHAPTER 14
Drug-, Alcohol-, and Sex-Related Crime
312

Key Terms   *313*
Drug Abuse and Crime   **313**
  The History of Drug Abuse   315
  The Extent of Drug Abuse   317
  Patterns of Drug Abuse   317
  Crime-Related Activities   319

  The International Drug Economy   320
  Drug Control   324
Alcohol and Crime   **325**
  The History of Legalization   325
  Crime-Related Activities   326
Sexual Morality Offenses   **328**
  "Deviate Sexual Intercourse by Force
    or Imposition"   329
  Prostitution   329
  Pornography   331
BOXES
  Criminological Focus: *The Small World
    of Crack Users*   **320**
  At Issue: *Gambling: "Injurious to the Morals"*   **326**
  Window to the World: *Global Sexual Slavery:
    Women and Children*   **332**
Review 336 / Notes 336

CHAPTER 15
Comparative Criminology
342

Key Terms   *343*
What Is Comparative Criminology?   **344**
  The Definition of Comparative Criminology   344
  The History of Comparative Criminology   345
  The Goals of Comparative Research   346
**Engaging in Comparative Criminological
Research**   **346**
  Preparatory Work   346
  Comparative Research   349
  The Special Problems of Empirical
    Research   351
Theory Testing   **352**
  Validation of Major Theories   352
  The Socioeconomic Development
    Perspective   352
Practical Goals   **353**
  Learning from Others' Experiences   353
  Developing International Strategies   353
  Globalization versus Ethnic Fragmentation   362
BOXES
  Criminological Focus: *Cross-Cultural Research:
    Smoking One's Way into Cheyenne
    Culture*   **350**
  Window to the World: *Transnational Criminality:
    And Now They Deal in Human Body Parts!*   **359**
  At Issue: *BCCI: International Fraud*   **361**
Review 362 / Notes 363
Glossary   367
Photo Credits   373
Illustration and Text Credits   375
Name Index   379
Subject Index   391

LIST OF BOXES

Criminological Focus
Fairy Tales and Crime
Criminologists versus the NYPD
The Mismeasure of Man
Myths of the Insanity Defense
Culture Conflict in Waco, Texas
The Girls in the Gang
Out of Control: School Violence
Defensive Space: Bumps, Barriers, and Barricades
On Being Sane in Insane Places
Thirty-Eight Witnesses
"An Epidemic of Hate Crimes?"
When New Global Technology Meets Old Local
    Laws
Corporate Crime—Who Are the Victims?
The Small World of Crack Users
Cross-Cultural Research: Smoking One's Way into
    Cheyenne Culture

At Issue
Obituary for Tupac Amaru Shakur (1971–1996)
Stalking: An Unrecorded Crime
Somatotyping: A Physique for Crime?
The Crime of Parricide
Social Disorganization in Los Angeles
The Tagger Subculture
Respect for Authority: Carjacking

Why Wait for a Million-Dollar Civil Liability Suit
    When You Can Have CPTED for Peanuts?
The Rights of the Poorest
The Battered Woman Self-Defense and the Penal
    Codes
Vipers in the Desert
"Follow This Car! I'm Being Stolen!"
Dangerous Ground: The World of Hazardous Waste
    Crime
Gambling: "Injurious to the Morals"
BCCI: International Fraud

Window to the World
The New Terrorism
Measuring World Crime
Stone Age Crime and Social Control
Censoring TV Violence
A Social System Breaks Down
America's Changing Ethnic Gangs
Nations with Low Crime Rates
Decresting the Lovebug, Worldwide
Criminal Law in an Age of Ethnic Diversity
Necessity at Sea
Assassinations around the Globe
Crime on the Oceans: Whose Problem?
The Business of Organized Crime
Global Sexual Slavery: Women and Children
Transnational Criminality: And Now They Deal in
    Human Body Parts!

PREFACE

Criminology is a young discipline—the term "criminology" is barely a century old. But in those hundred years criminology has emerged as a major social and behavioral science. Criminology's contributions are essential for dealing with a crime problem in our society that many people consider intolerable. Problems as vital and urgent as those addressed in this book are also challenging and exciting. We invite teachers and students to join us in traveling along criminology's path, exploring its domain and mapping out its future in the twenty-first century, which is just about upon us.

THE THIRD EDITION

The previous editions of this book were so well received by students and teachers that, in updating this edition, we chose not to depart from the existing structure and approach. The third edition's most noteworthy innovations are intended to address the challenges of the twenty-first century.

To keep up with technology, we have provided:

- An Internet Exercise at the end of each chapter that asks the student to access the Internet to gain further and more detailed information on relevant topics (web sites are given).
- A new section (in Chapter 12) called "High-Tech Crimes: Concerns for Today and Tomorrow" that includes such subjects as crime on the Internet, computer network break-ins, industrial espionage, software piracy, child pornography, mail bombing, password sniffers, and credit card fraud.
- A discussion of the new high-tech criminal and his or her detection.

To focus attention on the newly emerging situational crime prevention theories and their victimological significance, we have added a new chapter (Chapter 8: "Targets and Victims of Crime") that includes rational choice, routine activity, and crime prevention through environmental design. This chapter also includes an expanded discussion of victimization: lifestyle theories, repeat victimization, hot spots of crime, geography of crime.

To cover the rapid globalization that affects America's local and transnational crime problems, including terrorism, drug trafficking, international fraud, illegal migration, and international gang activities, we have expanded and updated the coverage of this area.

The ever-changing panorama of criminality has prompted us to emphasize such new developments as antigovernment militias, children as perpetrators and victims of crime, the spread of ethnic gangs, hate crimes (including the torching of houses of worship), and media attention to the involvement of celebrities in crime. Statistical information, research literature, and policy changes are current to the moment the book went to press.

ORGANIZATION

As in previous editions, this edition has four parts (three parts if you have chosen the shorter version). Part I presents an overview of criminology and describes the vast horizon of this science. It explains techniques for measuring the amount and characteristics of crime and criminals. It also traces the history of criminological thought through the era that witnessed the formation of the major schools of criminology: classicism and positivism (eighteenth and nineteenth centuries).

Part II includes explanations of crime and criminal behavior on the basis of the various theories developed in the twentieth century. Among the subjects covered are theories that offer biological, psychological, sociological, sociopolitical, and integrated explanations. We have added a new chapter to Part II: Chapter 8, "Targets and Victims of Crime," where we discuss why offenders choose to commit one offense rather than another at a given time and place. Coverage of research by radical, socialist, and feminist criminologists has been updated.

Part III covers the various types of crimes from a legal and sociological perspective. The familiar street crimes, such as homicide and robbery, are assessed, as are other criminal activities such as high-tech crime that have been highlighted by researchers only in recent years. The chapter on comparative criminology has been expanded and updated in light of the growing research in the field. It is also an area that will have more and more practical and policy implications in the future.

Part IV, "A Criminological Approach to the Criminal Justice System," includes an explanation of the component parts and the functioning of the system. It explains contemporary criminological research on how the people who run the system operate it, the decision-making processes of all participants, and the interaction of all the system components.

SPECIAL FEATURES

In our effort to provide the student with a pleasurable learning experience and the instructor with a teaching tool that is at once dynamic and effective, we have included a number of special features:

- *Explaining Criminal Behavior.* We highlight the evolution and interrelationships of theories that explain criminal behavior to make them part of students' own experience rather than an academic exercise.
- *Theory Informs Policy.* We demonstrate the interrelatedness of theory, policy, and practice. The theory chapters, for example, include "Theory Informs Policy" sections that enable the student to appreciate the practical significance of theoretical work. In the criminal justice chapters, we present the system within the context of contemporary theory and research.
- *Boxes.* A thematic box program provides a springboard for class participation and critical thinking. Every chapter contains three boxes, one on each of three themes:

- "Criminological Focus" boxes provide an analysis of selected cases and research areas, such as girls in gangs, victims of corporate crime, school violence, the debate between criminologists and the police concerning decreasing crime rates, and the conflict at Waco, Texas.
- "At Issue" boxes contain selected problems that constitute new or continuing challenges to criminologists, such as the tagger subculture, the growth of militia groups, stalking, and battered women.
- "Window to the World" boxes highlight the international dimensions of crime and criminological study, such as the business of organized crime, global sexual slavery, new forms of terrorist acts, and measuring world crime.

Each box has the same format, with text, illustrations, tables, discussion questions, and sources.

- *Victimology.* Additional emphasis is given to another new constituent area of criminology, victimology, which also has a global aspect today, when once again entire ethnic groups have become victims of genocide.
- *Looking to the Future.* The topics and examples we have chosen for the boxes, for the chapter openings, and for the text itself are all current developments, new discoveries, or continuing problems. They include the criminological significance of the recent discovery of Oetzi, the 5300-year-old ice man, as well as crime on the Internet. They reach as far as the Amazon, where an ancient culture is being threatened with extinction, and as near as our own hometowns, where neo-Nazi skinheads are a violent and growing threat to democracy.

As in the previous editions, we have endeavored not only to reflect developments and change, but to anticipate them on the basis of trend data. The authors look forward to the challenges of the twenty-first century, when those who study criminology with this text may be decision makers, researchers, or planners of a future as free from crime as possible.

TWO VERSIONS

Recent developments in the criminology curriculum have created a need for two books, not just one; so for this edition we again have two versions of the text: the full version and a shorter one. Many schools retain the traditional criminology course, which includes criminological coverage of criminal justice. For such programs, *Criminology, Third Edition,* is the ideal text. For schools that have expanded their offerings by adding an introductory course in criminal justice, thus freeing instructors from having to cover this subject matter in a criminology course, *Criminology: The Shorter Version* is more appropriate, since it omits Part IV ("A Criminological Approach to the Criminal Justice System"). We hope these two versions will make using the text easier for instructors, and we would appreciate their comments and suggestions.

PEDAGOGICAL AIDS

Working together closely and cooperatively, the authors and the editors have developed a format for the text that is both readable and attractive: Photographs, tables, and figures, in addition to the boxes, highlight and amplify the text coverage. Chapter outlines, lists of key terms, chapter review sections, the Glossary and the Internet Exercises help make the book user-friendly. The Instructor's Manual, Test Bank, and computerized Test Banks (Windows and Mac versions) have been prepared by Kenrick S. Thompson, Northern Michigan University.

IN APPRECIATION

We greatly acknowledge the assistance and support of a number of dedicated professionals. We thank Professor Marvin E. Wolfgang, of the University of Pennsylvania, for his helpful and generous suggestions and comments. At Rutgers University, the librarian of the N.C.C.D./Criminal Justice Collection, Phyllis Schultze, has been most helpful in patiently tracking and tracing sources. We thank Pro-

fessor Sesha Kethineni, Illinois State University, for her tireless assistance on the first edition, and Deborah Leiter-Walker for her help on the second. Gratitude also extends to the many Rutgers University A.B.D.s who have valiantly contributed their labors to all editions. These include Susanna Cornett, Dory Dickman, Lisa Maher, Susan Plant, Mangai Natarajan, Dana Nurge, Sharon Chamard, Marina Myhre, Diane Cicchetti, Emmanuel Barthe, and Illya Lichtenberg, as well as Peter Heidt. Our appreciation to Kerry Dalip and Nhung Tran from the University of Pennsylvania for their work on revising the text. Joan Schroeder has done a superb job of word processing for all editions; we could not have produced the book without her.

We owe a special debt to the team at McGraw-Hill: to Editorial Director Phil Butcher and sponsoring editors Marge Byers and Nancy Blaine for their encouragement and support; to development editor Jeannine Ciliotta, whose ideas and suggestions helped shape this new edition; to Kate Scheinman of The Total Book for efficiently and expertly turning manuscript into bound book and to our copy editor Judy Duguid, who gently fine-tuned our prose. We are also grateful to Joe Piliero, the designer, and to Barbara Salz, photo researcher for giving the book its visual appeal.

Many academic reviewers (listed facing title page) offered invaluable help in planning and drafting chapters. We thank them for their time and thoughtfulness and for the wisdom they brought from their teaching and research.

A combined total of over 70 years of teaching criminology provides the basis for the writing of *Criminology, Third Edition.* We hope the result is a text that is intellectually provocative, factually rigorous, and scientifically sound and that offers a stimulating learning experience for the student.

Freda Adler
Gerhard O. W. Mueller
William S. Laufer

CRIMINOLOGY
The Shorter Version

PART I

Understanding Criminology

Criminology is the scientific study of the making of laws, the breaking of laws, and society's reaction to the breaking of laws. Sometimes these laws are arrived at by consensus; sometimes they are imposed by those in power. Today, the people of the entire world have certain common interests. As a result, criminological research and crime-prevention strategies are becoming globalized, even though the reach of laws may not yet be global. Nationally and internationally, criminological research has become influential in policy making. (Chapter 1).

Criminologists have adopted methods of study from all the social and behavioral sciences. Like all scientists, criminologists measure. They assess crime over time and place, and they measure the characteristics of criminals and crimes (Chapter 2).

Throughout history, thinkers and rulers have written about crime and criminals and the control of crime. Yet the term "criminology" is little more than a century old, and the subject has been of scientific interest for only two centuries. Two schools of thought contributed to modern criminology: the classical school, associated predominantly with Cesare Beccaria (eighteenth century), which focused on crime, and the positivist school, associated with Cesare Lombroso, Enrico Ferri, and Raffaele Garofalo (nineteenth and early twentieth centuries), which focused on criminals (Chapter 3). Contemporary American criminology owes much to these European roots.

CHAPTER 1

An Overview
of Criminology

What Is Criminology?

The Making of Laws

Deviance

The Concept of Crime

The Consensus and Conflict Views of Law and Crime

The Breaking of Laws

Society's Reaction to the Breaking of Laws

Criminology and the Criminal Justice System

The Global Approach to the Breaking of Laws

Research Informs Policy

Review

Notes

Special Features

CRIMINOLOGICAL FOCUS: Fairy Tales and Crime

AT ISSUE: Obituary for Tupac Amaru Shakur (1971–1996)

WINDOW TO THE WORLD: The New Terrorism

Key Terms

consensus model
conflict model
crime
criminology
deviance

Criminologists study crime from a broad scientific perspective, in an effort to understand its causes and, ultimately, its prevention. They are not, as most of the world learned during O.J. Simpson's televised trial, the scientists who engage in crime scene investigations. (The people who do that are called criminalists or forensic scientists.) There has been another popular misunderstanding, namely that criminologists are only, or at least primarily, interested in street crime as it affects our lives and our fears, largely as a result of media portrayal. It is true that criminologists are very much concerned with murders, robberies, burglaries, and thefts. But consider for a moment that while all of America's thieves (excluding automobile thieves) cause us a loss of $4 billion annually, a single rogue trader on the international market may cause losses of billions. So criminologists must extend their focus beyond street crime and include other criminal activities that may be less visible, but may cause far greater harm to human beings all over the globe.

• Let us begin with a few select wealthy investment bankers and traders in trouble with the law. Ivan F. Boesky was convicted of insider trading scams committed in the 1980s, went to prison, and paid a $100 million fine. Marc Rich was indicted (60 counts) for trading with the enemy and tax fraud in 1983 and fled to Switzerland. Nicholas W. Leeson, rogue trader and financier is alleged to have caused $1.3 billion in bank losses. He sits in a Singapore prison. Michael R. Milken paid $1 billion in fines and restitution and spent 2 years in prison for financial fraud. Martin A. Siegel pled guilty to conspiracy and tax evasion and paid $9 million in fines. Toshihide Iguchi of the New York branch of Daiwa Bank, after being convicted of bank fraud in the amount of $1.1 billion, is in prison. Criminologists are interested in the crimes these traders and bankers have committed. They are also interested in their deviance and in the sense of the trust they have breached.

When criminologists are interested in the punishments imposed upon these criminals (and whether the punishments work), they are also interested in the reactions of their families and their colleagues (punishments beyond the law). Nearly all the traders mentioned have lost their respected status on Wall Street and have been barred from trading. All but one have lost their spouses through divorce. Criminologists are interested in the controls and sanctions, legal or social, that guard the safety of our money and financial institutions.

The crimes we have described—financial and tax fraud—belong to an area known as white-collar crime. Much research has been conducted to understand why middle- and upper-class people commit crimes that affect broad sectors of the population. Criminologists are called upon by industry and government to measure, describe, and explain white-collar and corporate crime and to assist in devising strategies to prevent and control future offending.

• On June 6, 1993, the Taiwan-registered "rust-bucket" freighter *Golden Venture* grounded on the beach at Rockaway in New York City. The ship's captain and 12-man crew, with 281 "passengers," jumped overboard in 6-foot swells, as the ship creaked and rolled in the surf. Six died in the effort to swim ashore. Most of the others were rounded up by officers of the U.S. Coast Guard, the Immigration and Naturalization Service, and the New York City police.

By now the Coast Guard has identified or intercepted 40 of the many rust buckets that ferry an estimated 100,000 illegal Chinese immigrants to U.S. shores every year, for fees of between $20,000 and $30,000. The "lucky ones" must pay off these fees to gang enforcers through years of slavery in sweatshops or massage parlors. Chinese gang killings keep increasing.

Scholars of many disciplines are concerned with the causes and control of illegal migrations. Criminologists are expert at studying the criminal exploitation of human desires and ambitions, the organizational structure of the large and pervasive syndicates that resort to many kinds of crime in order to enrich themselves at the expense of individual victims and the public at large. Criminologists also study the links between alien, drug, arms, and contraband smuggling, and their impact on social structures and, indeed, on world peace.

• Neil Maddox, age 11, died young. He happened to get in the way of a drive-by shooting in his Chicago neighborhood. In the slang of the drug gangs, such a child is just another "mushroom," like the mushrooms of the Super Mario Brothers game that pop up, seemingly out of nowhere, into the line of fire. But the human mushrooms are either innocent bystanders, caught in a crossfire, or individuals simply wiped out for fun or revenge. Figures are hard to come by, since crime statistics do not record "mushroom killings." Before 1985 the term "mushroom children" did not even exist. By 1989 it was estimated that there were 28, and by now well over 100 such children have been killed. And the number keeps rising.

Criminologists are interested in the vast, intertwined problems of drug-related crime and violence, of the causes of addiction within society, and of the impact of drug abuse on the quality of life. They are attempting to sort out the ramifications of the drug culture in search of feasible and socially acceptable solutions, inside and outside the criminal justice system.

• In 1989, news photographs depicted the supertanker *Exxon Valdez* aground in Prince William Sound, Alaska, exuding oil through a rupture in its hull. This caused North America's largest ecological disaster. (The captain was eventually convicted on a misdemeanor charge.) Tankers have run aground before and since the *Exxon Valdez* disaster. On February 15, 1996, the tanker *Sea Empress* ran aground off Wales, spilling 20 million gallons of oil, far exceeding the *Exxon Valdez* spillage. In all probability the cause was once again human error (Table 1.1). But criminologists have many questions. How can we prevent such disasters from happening in the future? Should corporations like Exxon be held criminally liable for the acts of their employees? What sanctions are appropriate?

Criminologists study the criminal sanctions used against individuals and corporations. How can human and corporate behavior be controlled to safeguard the environment? Are new laws likely to provide greater protection against negligence and error? How much will new measures cost, and are they cost-beneficial? To do such studies, criminologists develop research questions, select the most appro-

TABLE 1.1 Some Major Marine Oil Spills			
Tanker	**Gallons**	**Date**	**Location**
Amoco Cadiz	68 million	March 16, 1978	Off Brittany, France
Torrey Canyon	36 million	March 18, 1967	Isles of Scilly, U.K.
Braer	25 million	Jan. 5, 1993	Off Garths Ness, near Scotland
Nova	21 million	Dec. 6, 1985	Arabian Gulf
Sea Empress	20 million	Feb. 15, 1996	Milford Haven, Wales
Exxon Valdez	11 million	March 24, 1989	Prince William Sound, Alaska

Source: AP/Carl Fox, data from *Golub's Oil Pollution Bulletin*, table published in *Albuquerque Journal*, Feb. 20, 1996, p. 6.

priate methods, and then assemble and analyze the results.

• After a long civil war in the former Yugoslavia, the guns are now silent. U.N. peacekeeping troops are patrolling the former battlegrounds, and a U.N. international war crimes tribunal has issued indictments and begun trials on charges of genocide, war crimes, and massive criminal violations of human rights, including "ethnic cleansing" through at least 21,000 murders (by at least 5000 perpetrators) and tens of thousands of rapes. These international crimes were rooted in deep-seated ethnic hatred and bigotry, whipped up by political opportunists.

Let us ask a challenging question: Are we in America free from ethnic hatred and bigotry? Far from it! Hate groups are on the increase, advocating white supremacy or black power and vowing death to those who oppose them, including government itself. Between January 1995 and September 1996, there have been 102 suspicious fires at black churches, 122 at white churches, 6 at synagogues, and 2 at mosques. While insurance fraud and vandalism account for some of the incidents, racial hatred appears to account for the majority.

Here, too, criminologists are searching for answers, not just those to be found in criminal sanctions, but also those of peaceful conflict resolution and education.

• On July 17, 1996, TWA flight 800 exploded in the air, off the coast of Long Island. Five months later all indications pointed to an explosion somewhere in the midsection of the 747 jumbo jet which brought it down with a loss of 230 lives. But was this explosion a crime, similar to the act of terrorism that had destroyed Pan Am flight 103, over Lockerbie, Scotland, on December 21, 1988, with a loss of 270 lives? After a police investigation extending to 50 countries, two Lybians have been indicted for the Pan Am terrorist attack. As yet, despite a judgment by the International Court of Justice against Lybia, and sanctions imposed by the U.N. Security Council, Lybia has refused to extradite the suspects for trial in either the United States or Scotland. A U.S. court has awarded $300 million in damages in favor of the victims' families, to be paid by the insurers of the now-defunct Pan Am.

People in Italy, France, Germany, and Ireland, as well as in Asia, Latin America, and the Middle East, have long been familiar with terrorism; many have dealt with it successfully. For Americans, terrorism at home is something new and shocking. The number of terrorist acts, whether domestic or foreign, has been increasing to the point where we have had nearly 2500 terrorist bombings annually since 1992, including, most recently, the bomb blast at Centennial Olympic Park in Atlanta, Georgia, on July 26, 1996 (Figure 1.1).

Terrorism poses a particular challenge to criminologists. Who are the terrorists? What prompts them to commit what types of terrorist crimes against whom, and when? What measures can be adopted to prevent terrorism, a crime that can cripple an economy and destroy a government? What international strategies can be adopted to deal with this form of crime?

FIGURE 1.1 Bombings in the United States.
Source: Bureau of Alcohol, Tobacco and Firearms.

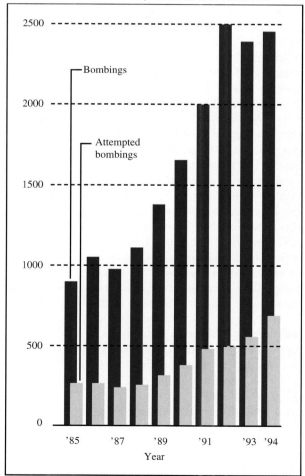

Having surveyed the broad spectrum of criminologists' interests, it is now necessary to define criminology, to delineate its place among the sciences, and to describe its major areas of concern: the making of laws, the breaking of laws, and society's reaction to the breaking of laws. We turn first to history.

WHAT IS CRIMINOLOGY?

In the Middle Ages human learning was commonly divided into four areas: law, medicine, theology, and philosophy. Universities typically had four faculties, one for each of these fields. Imagine a young person in the year 1392—a hundred years before Columbus came ashore in America—knocking at the portal of a great university with the request: "I would like to study criminology. Where do I sign up?" A stare of disbelief would have greeted the student, because the word had not yet been coined. Cautiously the student would explain: "Well, I'm interested in what crime is, and how the law deals with criminals." The university official might smile and say: "The right place for you to go is the law faculty. They will teach you everything there is to know about the law."

The student might feel discouraged. "That's a lot more than I want to know about the law. I really don't care about inheritance laws and the law of contracts. I just want to study all about crime and criminality. For example, why are certain actions considered wrong or evil in the first place, and . . ." The official would interrupt: "Then you must go to the faculty of theology. They know all there is to know about good and evil, heaven and hell." The student might persist. "But could they teach me what it is about the human body and mind that could cause some people and not others to commit crime?" "Oh, I see," the official would say. "You really should study medicine." "But, sir, medicine probably is only part of what I need to know, and really only part of medicine seems relevant. I want to know all there is to know about . . ." And then would come the official's last attempt to steer the student in the right direction: "Go and study philosophy. They'll teach you all there is to know!"

For centuries, all the knowledge the universities recognized continued to be taught in these four faculties. It was not until the eighteenth and nineteenth centuries that the natural and social sciences became full-fledged disciplines. In fact, the science of criminology has been known as such for only a little more than a century.

In 1885 the Italian law professor Raffaele Garofalo coined the term "criminology" (in Italian, *criminologia*).[1] The French anthropologist Paul Topinard used it for the first time in French (*criminologie*) in 1887.[2] "Criminology" aptly described and encompassed the scientific concern with the phenomenon of crime. The term immediately gained acceptance all over the world, and criminology became a subject taught at universities. Unlike their predecessors in 1392—or even in 1892—today's entering students will find that teaching and learning are distributed among 20 or 30 disciplines and departments. And criminology or criminal justice is likely to be one of them.

Criminology is a science, an empirical science. More particularly, it is one of the social, or behavioral, sciences. It has been defined in various ways by its scholars. The definition provided in 1934 by Edwin H. Sutherland, one of the founding scholars of American criminology, is widely accepted:

> **Criminology** is the body of knowledge regarding crime as a social phenomenon. It includes within its scope the process of making laws, of breaking laws, and of reacting toward the breaking of laws. . . . The objective of criminology is the development of a body of general and verified principles and of other types of knowledge regarding this process of law, crime, and treatment or prevention.[3]

This definition suggests that the field of criminology is narrowly focused on crime, yet broad in scope. By stating as the objective of criminology the "development of a body of general and verified principles," Sutherland mandates that criminologists, like all other scientists, collect information for study and analysis in accordance with the research methods of modern science. As we shall see in Chapter 3, it was in the eighteenth century that the first persons conducted serious investigations into criminal behavior, but the investigators were not engaged in empirical research although they based their conclusions on factual information. It was only in the nineteenth century that criminologists systematically gathered facts about crime and criminals and then evaluated their data in a scientific manner.

Among the first researchers to analyze empirical data (facts, statistics, and other observable information) in a search for the causes of crime was Cesare

Lombroso (1835–1909) of Italy (Chapter 3). His biologically oriented theories influenced American criminology at the turn of the twentieth century. At that time the causes of crime were thought to rest within the individual: Criminal behavior was attributed to feeblemindedness and "moral insanity." From then on, psychologists and psychiatrists played an important role in the study of crime and criminals.

By the 1920s other scholars saw the great influx of immigrants, with their alien ways of behaving, as the cause of crime. The search then moved to cultural and social interpretations. Crime was explained not only in terms of the offender but also in terms of social, political, and economic problems.

In increasing numbers, sociologists, political scientists, legal scholars, and economists have entered the arena of criminology. Architects too have joined the ranks of criminologists in an effort to design housing units that will be relatively free from crime. Engineers are working to design cars that are virtually theftproof. Pharmacologists play a role in alleviating the problem of drug addiction. Satellites put into space by astrophysicists can help control the drug trade. Specialists in public administration work to improve the functioning of the criminal justice system. Educators have been enlisted to prepare children for a life as free from delinquency as possible. Economists and social workers are needed to help break the cycle of poverty and crime. Biologists and endocrinologists have expanded our understanding of the relationship between biology and deviant behavior. Clearly, criminology is a discipline composed of the accumulated knowledge of many other disciplines. Criminologists acknowledge their indebtedness to all contributing disciplines, but they consider theirs a separate science.

In explaining what is meant by Sutherland's definition—"making laws," "breaking laws," and "reacting toward the breaking of laws"—we will use a contemporary as well as an historical perspective on these processes, and a global as well as a local focus.

THE MAKING OF LAWS

Conjure up a picture of a crowded supermarket just after working hours when most people are simply anxious to get home from a busy day. The checkout counters have long lines of carts overflowing with groceries. One counter—an express line—takes "ten items only." You have fifteen, but you get in line anyway. People behind you in the line stare. Your behavior is not acceptable. You are a "nonconformist," a deviant.

Deviance

Criminologists use the term **deviance** to describe behavior that violates social norms, including laws. The customary ways of doing everyday things (like not exceeding the posted limit of items at supermarket express lines) are governed by norms other than laws. More serious deviant behavior, like taking someone else's property, is governed by laws. Criminologists are interested in all social norms and in how

What is the response when an angry baseball player spits at an umpire? Baltimore Orioles second baseman Roberto Alomar is restrained by manager Davey Johnson after being ejected from a game with the Toronto Blue Jays, September 27, 1996. Three days later, the umpires voted not to work until Alomar was suspended.

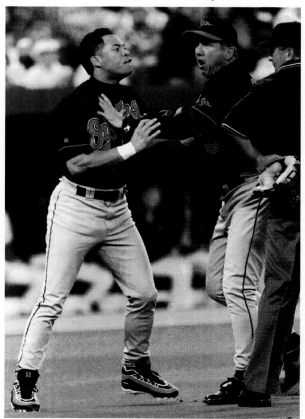

society reacts to success or failure of compliance.[4] They are interested in what society does when customary ways of doing things no longer prove effective in controlling conduct perceived as undesirable. New Yorkers concerned over the problem of dog droppings provide an example.

Disciplined city dwellers had always observed the custom of curbing their dogs. Street signs warned them to do this. But as more and more dog owners failed to comply, New Yorkers decided that the cleanliness of the sidewalks was an important issue. Laws were enacted making it an offense not to clean up after one's dog. In Beijing, China, and Reykjavik, Iceland, dogs have been severely restricted or banned from the city altogether.

The difference between crime and other forms of deviance is subject to constant change, and it may vary from one state or country to another and from one time to another. What yesterday was only distasteful or morally repugnant may today be illegal. Criminologists are therefore interested in all norms that regulate conduct. Making something that is distasteful into a crime may be counterproductive and detrimental to the social order. If everything deviant (inconsistent with the majority's norms) were to be made criminal, society would become very rigid. The more rigid a society, the more behavior defined as violating social norms is prohibited by law.

Jack D. Douglas and Frances C. Waksler have presented the continuum of deviance as a funnel (Figure 1.2). This funnel consists of definitions ranging from the broadest (a "feeling that something is vaguely wrong, strange, peculiar") to the narrowest (a "judgment that something is absolutely evil"). Somewhere between these two extremes, deviant behavior becomes criminal behavior. But the criminologist's interest in understanding the process begins at the earliest point—when a behavior is first labeled deviant.[5]

Although criminologists are interested in all deviant behavior—even that of no interest to the law—their primary interest is in criminal behavior, that which violates the law. So let us examine what crime is.

The Concept of Crime

A **crime** is any human conduct that violates a criminal law and is subject to punishment. What leads a society to designate some deviant behavior as crimes and leave other wrongs to be settled by private or civil remedies? For centuries, "natural law" philosophers, believing in the universal rightness and wrongness of certain human behavior, have held the view that some forms of behavior are innately criminal and that all societies condemn them equally. Homicide and theft were thought to be among these.

This notion is no longer supported. Raffaele Garofalo, who gave our discipline its name, defended the concept of "natural crime," by which he meant behavior that offends basic moral sentiments, such as respect for the property of others and revulsion against infliction of suffering. Nevertheless, he admit-

Most inclusive

   I. Feeling that something is vaguely wrong, strange, peculiar

   II. Feelings of dislike, repugnance

   III. Feeling that something violates values or rules

   IV. Feeling that something violates moral values or moral rules

   V. Judgment that something violates values or rules

   VI. Judgment that something violates moral values or moral rules

   VII. Judgment that something violates morally legitimate misdemeanor laws

  VIII. Judgment that something violates morally legitimate felony laws

   IX. Judgment that something violates moral human nature

   X. Judgment that something is absolutely evil

Least inclusive

FIGURE 1.2 The funnel of deviance.
Source: Adapted from Jack D. Douglas and Frances C. Waksler, *The Sociology of Deviance* (Boston: Little, Brown, 1982), p. 11.

The Code of Hammurabi, king of ancient Babylonia, is the oldest legal code we have. The 8.2-foot carving, found in Iran in 1902, is now on display in the Louvre in Paris.

ted that although we might think such crimes as murder and robbery would be recognized by all existing legal systems, "a slight investigation seems to dispel this idea."[6]

Garofalo was right. The earliest codes, including the Babylonian Code of Hammurabi (about 1750 B.C.) and the Roman Law of the Twelve Tables (451–450 B.C.), do not list homicide or ordinary theft as crimes. Problems like these were settled without resort to punishment. But all early societies imposed punishment for acts detrimental to their own existence: treason. Other crimes depended on their socioeconomic needs (destroying a bridge was a crime among the Incas; stealing a beehive was a crime among the ancient Germanic tribes; stealing a horse or a blanket was one among American Plains Indians).

The question poses itself: Who in a society decides—and when and under what circumstances—which acts that are already considered deviant in that society should be elevated to the level of gross deviance or crime, subject to punishment?

The Consensus and Conflict Views of Law and Crime

In the traditional interpretation of the historical development of legal systems, and of criminal justice in particular, lawmaking is an accommodation of interests in a society, whether that society is composed of equals (as in a democracy) or of rulers and ruled (as in absolute monarchies), so as to produce a system of law and enforcement to which everybody basically subscribes. This is the **consensus model.** According to this view, certain acts are deemed so threatening to the society's survival that they are designated crimes. If the vast majority of a group shares this view, we can say the group has acted by consensus.

The model assumes that members of society by and large agree on what is right and wrong and that law is the codification of social values, a mechanism of control which settles disputes that arise when some individuals stray too far from what is considered to be acceptable behavior. In the words of the famous French sociologist Émile Durkheim, "We can . . . say that an act is criminal when it offends strong and defined states of the collective conscience."[7] Consensus theorists view society as a stable entity in which laws are created for the general good. Laws function to reconcile and to harmonize most of the interests that most of us accept, with the least amount of sacrifice.

Some criminologists view the making of laws in a society from a different theoretical perspective. In their interpretation, known as the **conflict model,** the criminal law expresses the values of the ruling class in a society, and the criminal justice system is a means of controlling the classes without power. Conflict theorists claim that a struggle for power is a far more basic feature of human existence than is consensus. It is through power struggles that various interest groups manage to control lawmaking and law enforcement. Accordingly, the appropriate object of criminological investigation is not the violation of laws but the conflicts within society.

Traditional historians of crime and criminal justice do not deny that throughout history there have

CRIMINOLOGICAL FOCUS

FAIRY TALES AND CRIME

Have you ever wondered about the wolf who accosts Little Red Riding Hood as she makes her way through the forest to her grandmother's house? Later he devours both Grandma and Little Red Riding Hood. Who is that wolf who speaks like a man?

THE WOLF-OUTLAW

Scholarly research suggests that he is a wolf of the two-legged variety— a convicted criminal banished to the woods. Fairy tales embody ancient folk wisdom and law. Before there were written legal codes, law was transmitted orally from generation to generation. The Red Riding Hood fairy tale reflects a time when the punishment for the most serious crimes was to be a wolf. Like the four-legged variety, the offender was banished from human society and condemned to the forest, there to live or die among the four-legged

wolves, shunned or hunted like one of them.

The ancient European tribes, ever on the move, could not rely on prisons as punishment for offenders. Outlawry seemed to be the perfect solution, and the wolf provided a model.

Imprisonment as a punishment for crime does not appear in any of the Grimms' fairy tales, another accurate reflection of historical fact: German principalities began to use imprisonment only in the fourteenth century, and the tales collected by the Grimm brothers generally predated that period.

CATALOGS OF CRIME AND PUNISHMENT

Fairy tales are rich in criminological lore. Every category of crime and the punishments that were in vogue in the early Middle Ages appear in the Grimms' tales. Death by fire was the punishment of choice for witchcraft, as in "Hansel and Gretel," where the witch is incinerated in her own stove. Murderers were drowned, burned, or banished to the forest, and grand larceny was punished by hanging, as in the fairy tale "The Master-Thief" (although the ruler commuted the sentence). Petty larceny was punished corporally, and impersonation and involuntary servitude, as in "Cinderella," were punished by blinding, a penalty German tribes regarded as very severe. Tarring also appeared as a punishment for serious crimes, both in the fairy tales and in law documents from the period.

In the fairy tale "The Twelve Brothers," perverting justice and attempting to cause an innocent person

to be executed was punished by being boiled in oil into which vipers were thrown, the most unusual penalty that appears in the Grimms' collection. But it, too, reflects historical fact; a similar punishment is recorded in early Roman law.

PSYCHOLOGICAL TREATISES

These tales can tell us about more than just types of crimes and punishments. The author of a research report entitled "The Criminal Element in German Folk Tales," published in 1910, used a criminological psychology approach to analyze the Grimms' tales and those collected by others. This report uncovered "every conceivable criminal motivation, from base greed to the grossest form of psychopathology." Perhaps fairy tales would be useful "required reading" for students of criminology.

Source
Gerhard O. W. Mueller, "The Criminological Significance of the Grimms' Fairy Tales," in *Fairy Tales and Society: Illusion, Allusion, and Paradigm*, ed. Ruth B. Bottigheimer (Philadelphia: University of Pennsylvania Press, 1986), pp. 217–227.

Questions for Discussion
1. What might be the modern equivalent of fairy tales in terms of an unofficial recording of the types of crimes and punishments in use today?
2. The Grimms' fairy tales provide information about European crime and punishment. Is there any similar source of information about early forms of crime and punishment in North America?

been conflicts that needed resolution. Traditionalists claim that differences have been resolved by consensus, while conflict theorists claim that the dominant group has ended the conflicts by imposing its will.

This difference in perspective marks one of the major criminological debates today, as we shall see in Chapter 9. It also permeates criminological discussion of who breaks the criminal laws and why.

THE BREAKING OF LAWS

Sutherland's definition of criminology includes the task of investigating and explaining the process of breaking laws. This may seem simple if viewed from a purely legal perspective. A prosecutor is not interested in the fact that hundreds of people are walking on Main Street. But if one of those hundreds grabs a woman's purse and runs away with it, the prosecutor is interested, provided the police have brought the incident to the prosecutor's attention. What alerts the prosecutor is the fact that a law has been broken, that one of those hundreds of people on Main Street has turned from a law-abiding citizen into a lawbreaker. This event, if detected, sets in motion a legal process that ultimately will determine whether someone is indeed a lawbreaker.

Sutherland, in saying that criminologists have to study the process of lawbreaking, had much more in mind than determining whether or not someone has violated the criminal law. He was referring to the process of breaking laws. That process encompasses a series of events, perhaps starting at birth or even earlier, which result in the commission of crime by some individuals and not by others.

Let us analyze the following rather typical scenario: In the maximum security unit of a midwestern penitentiary is an inmate we will call Jeff. He is one of three robbers who held up a check-cashing establishment. During the robbery, another of the robbers killed the clerk. Jeff has been sentenced to life imprisonment, which in his case means he will have to serve at least another 25 years on a felony murder conviction.

Born in an inner-city ghetto, Jeff was the third child of an unwed mother. He had a succession of temporary "fathers." By age 12 he had run away from home for the first time, only to be brought back to his mother, who really did not care much whether he returned or not. He rarely went to school because, he said, "all the guys were bigger." At age 16, after failing two grades, Jeff dropped out of school completely and hung around the streets of his deteriorated, crime-ridden neighborhood. He had no job. He had no reason to go home, since usually no one was there.

One night he was beaten up by members of a local gang. He joined a rival gang for protection and soon began to feel proud of his membership in one of the toughest gangs in the neighborhood. Caught on one occasion tampering with parking meters and on another trying to steal a car radio, he was sentenced to 2 months in a county correctional institution for boys. By the age of 18 he had moved from petty theft to armed robbery.

Many people reading the story of Jeff would conclude that he deserves what is coming to him and that his fate should serve as a warning to others. Other people would say that with his background, Jeff did not have a chance. Some may even marvel at Jeff's ability to survive at all in a very tough world.

To the criminologist, popular interpretations of Jeff's story do not explain the process of breaking laws in Sutherland's terms. Nor do these interpretations explain why people in general break a certain law. Sutherland demanded scientific rigor in researching and explaining the process of breaking laws. As we will see later in the book (Parts II and III), scientists have thoroughly explored the stories of Jeff and of other lawbreakers. They ask: Why are some people prone to commit crime and others not? There is no agreement on the answer as yet. Researchers have approached the question from different perspectives. Some have examined delinquents (juvenile offenders) and criminals from a biological perspective in order to determine whether some human beings are constitutionally more prone to yield to opportunities to commit criminal acts. Are genes to blame? Hormones? Diet? Others have explored the role played by moral development and personality. Is there a criminal personality? (These questions are discussed in Chapter 4.)

Most contemporary criminologists look to such factors as economic and social conditions, which can produce strain among social groups and lead to lawbreaking (Chapter 5). Others point to subcultures committed to violent or illegal activities (Chapter 6). Yet another argument is that the motivation to commit crime is simply part of human nature. So some criminologists examine the ability of social groups and institutions to make their rules effective (Chapter 7).

Other scholars have researched the question of why people who are inclined to break laws engage in particular acts at particular times. They have demonstrated that opportunity plays a great role in the decision to commit a crime. Opportunities are suitable targets inadequately protected. In these circumstances, all that is required for a crime to be committed is a person motivated to offend. These claims are made by criminologists who explain crime in terms of two perspectives, called routine activities and rational choice (Chapter 8).

AT ISSUE

OBITUARY FOR TUPAC AMARU SHAKUR (1971–1996)

Don't shed a tear for me nigga, I
  ain't happy here
I hope they bury me and send me
  to my rest
headlines reading 'murdered to
  death'
my last breath.(1)
From Tupac's "If I Die 2nite"

At 4:03 P.M. on September 13, 1996, Tupac Amaru Shakur, rapper and actor, died at the University of Nevada Medical Center, in Las Vegas. The cause of death: gunshot wounds received 6 days earlier in a drive-by shooting. Tupac Shakur, known as 2Pac, was 25 years old.(2)

If you had been assigned to write Tupac Shakur's obituary, how would you have captured the contradiction of his artistic achievement and self-destructive life? The gangsta rapper Tupac was a sensitive poet and film actor with an innocent, endearing smile. His records were making millions of dollars. He was also a violent, abusive alcoholic. Tupac was a sweet and kind mother's boy. He was also a frightening street thug, a former drug dealer, and a convicted rapist. He was a product of the Marin Public Housing project—an impoverished group of buildings called "the jungle" by many residents.(3)

How would you have explained the unnerving convergence of violent rap and street crime that marked his death? Tupac made light of urban "gangsta" violence in rap, and died in the middle of the night from a flurry of gangland gunfire that had the look and feel of a well-choreographed music video. He challenged his own death in lyrics and song: "I heard a rumor I died/ murdered in cold blood, dramatized/pictures of me in my final state, you know how I cried."(4) In an ultimate pairing of life and art, two of the gunshots fired on that fateful Saturday night hit Tupac's *thug life* tattoo, causing the internal bleeding that took his life.

In just five years, from 1991 to 1996, Tupac released four solo albums: *2Pacalypse Now* (1991), *Strictly 4 My Ni*Gaz* (1993), *Me Against the World* (1995), and *All Eyez on Me* (1996); he also appeared in five films: *Juice* (1991), *Poetic Justice* (1993), *Above the Rim* (1994), *Gang Related* (1996), and *Gridlock* (1996). During the same five years, he was also

• charged with beating a video director in LA (5 days in jail)

• Charged with threatening another rapper with a baseball bat (charges dropped)
• Arrested in Atlanta for allegedly shooting two off-duty cops (charges dropped)
• Charged in the sexual abuse of a fan in a NYC hotel room; convicted by a jury and sentenced
• Arrested on charges of gun and marijuana possession in LA
• Shot five times in a midtown NYC recording studio (crime unsolved)
• Jailed for 8 months (serving sentence for sexual abuse conviction)
• Sentenced to 120 days for probation violations in NY and LA (freed pending appeal)

Now, put aside the contradictions of achievement and self-destruction that mark Tupac Shakur's life and death. Forget the unnerving convergence of life and art. Instead, consider how you would have captured the real meaning of Tupac Shakur's success. How would you have explained our attraction to and fascination with Dr. Dre, Eazy-E, Snoop Doggy Dog, Tha Dogg Pound, Run-DMC, and Outkast? What does the rise of gangsta rap say about the way in which we define artistic and commercial success; the image that is

---

The findings of other scholars tend to show that lawbreaking depends less on what the offender does than on what society, including the criminal justice system, does to the offender (Chapter 9). This is the perspective of the labeling, conflict, and radical theorists, who have had great influence on criminological thinking since the 1970s.

SOCIETY'S REACTION TO THE BREAKING OF LAWS

Criminologists' interest in understanding the process of breaking a law (or any social norm) is tied to understanding society's reaction to deviance. The study of reactions to lawbreaking demonstrates that society has always tried to control or prevent norm breaking.

In the Middle Ages, the wayfarer entering a city had to pass the gallows, on which the bodies of criminals swung in the wind. Wayfarers had to enter through gates in thick walls, and the drawbridges were lowered only during the daylight hours; at nightfall the gates were closed. In front of the town hall, stocks and pillory warned dishonest vendors and pickpockets. Times have changed, but perhaps less than we think. Today penitentiaries and jails dot the countryside. Teams of work-release convicts work along

fashioned of ghetto life and young black males; the commercial exploitation of black artistic talent; and our fear of and fascination with criminal violence?

Following his death, one music critic and friend noted, "It would be easy to cull the meaning of Tupac's short and turbulent life from his lyrics. If you listened hard enough, the sketchy outline of his soul revealed itself. His lyrics were a series of bloody, open sores, summing up the trials of Black boys reared in crack-crazed neighborhoods everywhere. With his mix of tough guy charisma and true ghetto flavor, Tupac captivated a nation with songs that possessed a defiant spirit almost unrivaled in modern pop music."(5)

Criminologists must look long and hard at the chronology of Tupac's life, and ask some difficult questions about why the nation is so captivated with the art form of what it fears most—street violence. Why it is that we comfortably buy and sell images of disintegrating ghetto life and urban violence, but show so little willingness to address the stark reality of urban poverty and crime?

Writing Tupac's obituary is no easy task. The same may be said of the killing of Biggie Smalls.

Sources
1. Frank Williams, "The Living End," *The Source*, November 1996, p. 103.
2. Kevin Powell, "The Short Life and Violent Death of Tupac Shakur: Bury Me Like a G," *Rolling Stone*, Oct. 31, 1996, p. 40.
3. Michael Marriott, "Shots Silence Angry Voice Sharpened by the Streets," *New York Times*, Sept. 16, 1996, p. A1.
4. Tupac Shakur, "Ain't Hard to Find."
5. Williams, p. 106.

Questions for Discussion
1. In what ways can you argue that rap music results in exploitation?
2. Was the killing of Christopher Wallace (the notorious B.I.G.) a revenge for Tupac's death?

Rapper Tupac Shakur at the MTV Music Video Awards in New York, shortly before his death from gunshot wounds in Las Vegas on September 13, 1996.

highways under guard. Signs proclaim "Drug-Free School Zone," and decals on doors announce "Neighborhood Crime Watch." Police patrol cars are as visible as they are audible.

These overt signs of concern about crime provide us with only a surface view of the apparatus society has created to deal with lawbreaking; they tell us little of the research and policy making that have gone into the creation of the apparatus. Criminologists have done much of the research on society's reaction to the breaking of laws, and the results have influenced policy making and legislation aimed at crime control. The research has also revealed that society's reaction to lawbreaking has often been irrational, arbitrary, emotional, politically motivated, and counterproductive.

Research on society's reaction to the breaking of laws is more recent than research on the causes of crime. It is also more controversial. For some criminologists, the function of their research is to assist government in the prevention or repression of crime. Others insist that such a use of science only supports existing power structures that may be corrupt. The position of most criminologists is somewhere in between. Researchers often discover inhumane and arbitrary practices and provide the data base and the ideas for a humane, effective, and efficient criminal justice system.

Criminology and the Criminal Justice System

The term "criminal justice system" is relatively new. It became popular only in 1967, with the publication of the report of the President's Commission on Law Enforcement and Administration of Justice, *The Challenge of Crime in a Free Society*. The discovery that various ways of dealing with lawbreaking form a system was itself the result of criminological research. Research into the functioning of the system and its component parts, as well as into the work of functionaries within the system, has provided many insights over the last few decades.

Scientists who study the criminal justice system are frequently referred to as "criminal justice specialists." This term suggests a separation between criminology and criminal justice. In fact, the two fields are closely interwoven. Their origins, however, do differ. Criminology has its roots in European scholarship, though it has undergone refinements, largely under the influence of American sociology. Criminal justice is a recent American innovation. Scholars of both disciplines use the same scientific research methods. They have received the same rigorous education, and they pursue the same goals. Both fields rely on the cooperation of many other disciplines, including sociology, psychology, political science, law, economics, management, and education.

The two fields are distinguished by a difference in focus. Criminology generally focuses on scientific studies of crime and criminality, whereas criminal justice focuses on scientific studies of decision-making processes, operations, and such justice-related concerns as the efficiency of police, courts, and corrections systems, the just treatment of offenders, the needs of victims, and the effects of changes in sentencing philosophy.

The United States has well over 50 criminal justice systems—those of the 50 states and of the federal government, the District of Columbia, Puerto Rico, Guam, the U.S. Virgin Islands, American Samoa, the Commonwealth of the Northern Mariana Islands, Palau, the Panama Canal Zone, and the military. They are very similar: All are based on constitutional principles and on the heritage of the common law. All were designed to cope with the problem of crime within their territories, on the assumption that crime is basically a local event calling for local response. Crimes that have an interstate or international aspect are under the jurisdiction of federal authorities, and such offenses are prosecuted under the federal criminal code.

The Global Approach to the Breaking of Laws

Until fairly recently there was rarely any need to cooperate with foreign governments, as crime had few international connections. This situation has changed drastically: Crime, like life itself, has become globalized, and responses to lawbreaking have inevitably extended beyond local and national borders. In the first 3½ decades after World War II, from 1945 until the late 1970s, the countries of the world gradually became more interdependent. Commercial relations among countries increased. The jet age brought a huge increase in international travel and transport. Satellite communications facilitated intense and continuous public and private relationships.

Beginning in the 1980s, the internationalization of national economies accelerated sharply, and with the collapse of Marxism in Eastern Europe in the 1990s, a global economy is being created. These developments, which turned the world into what has been called a "global village," have also had considerable negative consequences. As everything else in life became globalized, so did crime. Transnational crimes, those that violate the laws of more than one country, suddenly boomed. Among these are drug trafficking, commercial fraud, environmental offenses, and the smuggling of aliens. Then there are the truly international crimes—those that are proscribed by international law—such as "crimes against the peace and security of mankind," "genocide," and "war crimes." But even many apparently purely local crimes now have international dimensions, whether they are local drug crime or handgun violence. In view of the rapid globalization of crime, we devote an entire chapter (Chapter 15) to the international dimensions of criminology. In addition, a "Window to the World" box in each chapter explores the international implications of various topics.

RESEARCH INFORMS POLICY

Skeptics often ask: With so many criminologists at work in the United States, and so many studies conducted over the last half century, why do we have so

WINDOW TO THE WORLD

THE NEW TERRORISM

For years people living in the United States were unconcerned about terrorism. That was a danger that lurked overseas, even though American interests and targets had been struck by terrorists. This complacency changed abruptly in February 1993 with the bombing of the World Trade Center in New York City by foreign terrorists working out of Jersey City, New Jersey. (The defendants in that case have been convicted.) But that was not the end of it: A conspiracy to destroy the U.N. headquarters and the FBI offices in New York, as well as the Hudson River tunnels, was uncovered in time, and the conspirators are now in prison. And there was still more to come: a conspiracy to blow up simultaneously 12 U.S. airliners in the Pacific (these conspirators have been convicted); the bombing of the federal building in Oklahoma City in April

1995 (two defendants are on trial); the destruction of a U.S. military residence in Dharan, Saudi Arabia in June 1996; the explosion of a bomb at Centennial Olympic Park in Atlanta, Georgia, during the 1996 Summer Olympics; the destruction of Pan Am flight 103 over Scotland in December 1988, with a loss of 270 lives, for which two Lybians have been indicted but are beyond the jurisdiction of the United States.

There used to be categorizations of terrorism in terms of political versus profit motive, foreign versus domestic, and so on. These lines have become blurred. The profit motive seems to have disappeared. While there may still be a purely domestic form of terrorism, for example that perpetrated by fanatics and by cult-like private "militias" who see the government as an enemy, most terrorism appears to have an international base and is directed against the United States. In particular, Is-

Terrorism against the United States at home. Oklahoma City, Oklahoma, April 19, 1995: A truck bomb explodes outside the Federal Building, killing 168 Americans and seriously wounding many others.

Terrorism against the United States abroad. Dharan, Saudi Arabia, June 25, 1996: A truck bomb explodes outside a U.S. residential building, killing 19 Americans and seriously wounding many others.

lamic fundamentalist terrorists, who view the United States (largely because of its support for Israel) as the archenemy—or Satan—are increasingly identified with attacks against U.S. targets, even within the United States.

There was a time when terrorists enjoyed the support, both financial and material, of some Communist governments. That support no longer exists. Very few countries can be counted among the supporters of current terrorist groups, and certainly none of these would support America's own terror-oriented "militias."

In 1993—before most of the terrorist events discussed here took place—a meeting of over 200 counterterrorism experts and Pentagon officials concluded:

WINDOW TO THE WORLD *(continued)*

[T]hat the proliferation of ethnic and regional conflicts will spawn new radical movements, leading inevitably to new terrorism. "We're going to see a global increase in anarchy," says one Defense Department analyst. Some at the meeting worried about what they term "mass terrorism," like the ethnic cleansing rife in Bosnia. Others were more concerned about what they are calling "single issue" terrorism, attacks by radicals who share no ideology, only the hatred for a particular enemy."(1)

The assessment of the 200 experts may have been appropriate. As for mass terrorism, while the threat in Europe (Bosnia-Herzegovina) has been checked, it continues in Africa (Rwande and Burundi). As for single-issue terrorism—and that is the terrorism we are experiencing in America—"the hatred for a particular enemy," namely the U.S. government, is held in common by foreign and domestic terrorists.

Source

1. Douglas Waller, "Counterterrorism: Victim of Success?"

Newsweek, July 5, 1993, pp. 22–23.

Questions for Discussion

1. International terrorism is a criminal activity that can involve an almost limitless number of specific crimes, individuals, and countries. How would you devise a strategy to combat it at the national and international levels?
2. How would you go about studying trends in terrorism and its impact on society and the economy?

---

much crime, why is some of it increasing, and why do new forms of crime emerge constantly? There are several answers. Crime rates go up and down. At the moment, and through the mid-1990s, crime has actually been decreasing. The popular perception that the crime problem is increasing, rests on a fear of crime that is fueled by media portrayals. Obviously, the various elements of the mass media are very competitive, and such competitiveness determines the focus on crime. That is what sells newspapers and TV programs.[8] Politicians, in turn, seek security in office by catering to public perceptions of crime, rather than its reality.[9] They therefore propose and enact measures that respond to popular demands, and that often are more symbolic than result-oriented.[10] At the moment, this means ever harsher and more punitive measures for dealing with the crime problem.

Few criminologists believe that at this time there is enough research to justify such an approach. In fact, some criminological research demonstrates the futility of escalating punishments and often points to measures of quite a different nature as more promising, more humane, and more cost-beneficial. So why do criminologists not make themselves heard?[11] The answer is that criminologists are social scientists, and not politicians. Criminologists are not voted into Congress or to the presidency or a governorship. Yet, criminologists have served on virtually every federal and state commission dealing with problems of crime or criminal justice. But just as the Pentagon cannot

declare war, criminologists cannot dictate national or state crime-control policies. They can, however, provide pertinent research findings that inform national policy making.[12] Recently, for example, the attorney general of the United States asked criminologists to formulate policy recommendations based on their research findings in areas such as delinquency prevention, drug control, global crime, youth violence, and violence against women.[13] In subsequent chapters that deal with the causes of crime we continue this discussion under the heading "Theory Informs Policy."

REVIEW

Very little happens on earth that does not concern criminology. Yet criminology, as a science, is only a century old. Edwin H. Sutherland provided the most widely accepted definition: "The body of knowledge regarding crime as a social phenomenon. It includes within its scope the process of making laws, of breaking laws, and of reacting toward the breaking of laws."

Criminologists study behavior that violates all social norms, including laws. They distinguish between two conflicting views of the history of criminal law: the consensus view, which regards lawmaking as the result of communal agreement about what is to be prohibited, and the conflict view, according to which laws are imposed by those with power over those without power.

The breaking of laws (the subject to which much of this book is devoted) is not merely a formal act that may lead to arrest and prosecution, but an intricate process by which some people violate some laws under some circumstances. Many disciplines contribute to understanding the process of breaking laws or other norms, but as yet there is no consensus on why people become criminals. Society has always reacted to lawbreaking, although the scientific study of lawbreaking is of very recent origin. Today criminologists analyze the methods and procedures society uses in reacting to crime; they evaluate the success or failure of such methods; and on the basis of their research, they propose more effective and humane ways of controlling crime.

Criminologists have discovered that the various agencies society has created to deal with lawbreaking constitute a system that, like any other system, can be made more efficient. Research on the system depends on the availability of a variety of data, especially statistics. The gathering and analysis of statistics on crime and criminal justice are among the primary tasks of criminologists. The effectiveness of their work depends on reliable data. The province of criminology today is the entire world: Every aspect of life, including crime, has become increasingly globalized in recent years as a result of both rapid advances in technology and economic integration.

Criminology is a politically sensitive discipline. Its findings inform public policy. While criminologists cannot dictate what the branches of government—the legislative, the judicial, and the executive—should do about crime, their research findings are being used increasingly in making governmental decisions.

NOTES

1. Raffaele Garofalo, *Criminologia* (Naples, 1885), published in English as *Criminology*, trans. Robert W. Millar (Boston: Little, Brown, 1914; rpt., Montclair, N.J.: Patterson Smith, 1968).

2. Paul Topinard, "L'Anthropologie criminelle," *Revue d'anthropologie*, **2** (1887).

3. Edwin H. Sutherland, *Principles of Criminology*, 2d ed. (Philadelphia: Lippincott, 1934), originally published as *Criminology*, 1924.

4. Some legal scholars argue that criminologists should study only lawbreaking. See Paul W. Tappan, *Crime, Justice and Correction* (New York: McGraw-Hill, 1960).

5. Jack D. Douglas and Frances C. Waksler, *The Sociology of Deviance* (Boston: Little, Brown, 1982).

6. Garofalo, *Criminologia*, p. 5.

7. Émile Durkheim, *Rules of Sociological Method*, trans. S. A. Solaway and J. H. Mueller (Glencoe, Ill.: Free Press, 1958), p. 64.

8. See Rick Marin and Peter Katel, "Miami's Crime Time Live," *Newsweek*, June 20, 1994, pp. 71–72.

9. See David C. Anderson, "Expressive Justice Is All the Rage— Fired by Occasional 'Willie Horton' Crimes, the Public Insists: Let the Punishment Fit the Rage," *New York Times Magazine*, Jan. 15, 1995, pp. 36–37; Wendy Kaminer, *It's All the Rage: Crime and Culture* (Reading, Mass.: Addison-Wesley, 1995).

10. Nancy E. Marion, *A History of Federal Crime Control Initiatives, 1960–1993* (Westport, Conn.: Praeger, 1994); Nancy E. Marion, "Symbolism and Federal Crime Control Legislation: 1960–1990," *Journal of Crime and Justice*, **17** (1994): 69–91.

11. Samuel H. Pillsbury, "Why Are We Ignored? The Peculiar Place of Experts in the Current Debate about Crime and Justice," *Criminal Law Bulletin*, **31**(4) (1995): 305–336.

12. Jerome H. Skolnick, "What to Do about Crime—The American Society of Criminology 1994 Presidential Address," *Criminology*, **33** (1995): 1–15; Freda Adler, "Our American Society of Criminology, the World, and the State of the Art—The American Society of Criminology 1995 Presidential Address," *Criminology*, **34** (1995): 1–9.

13. *Critical Criminal Justice Issues: Task Force Reports to Attorney General Janet Reno* (Washington, D.C.: National Institute of Justice/American Society of Criminology, 1995).

Internet Exercise

One of the components of Sutherland's definition of criminology focuses on the making of laws. Congress, which makes federal laws, has recently passed the Violent Crime Control and Law Enforcement Act of 1994. What are the most significant provisions of that law?

Your Web Site is: **http://www.ojp.usdoj.gov/bja**

CHAPTER 2
Measuring Crime and
Criminal Behavior Patterns

Measuring Crime
       Methods of Collecting Data
       Ethics and the Researcher
The Nature and Extent of Crime
       Police Statistics
       Victimization Surveys
       Self-Report Surveys
Measuring Characteristics of Crime
       Crime Trends
       Locations and Times of Criminal Acts
       Severity of Crime
Measuring Characteristics of Criminals
       Age and Crime
       Gender and Crime
       Social Class and Crime
       Race and Crime
Review
Notes

       Special Features
         WINDOW TO THE WORLD: Measuring World Crime
         AT ISSUE: Stalking: An Unrecorded Crime
         CRIMINOLOGICAL FOCUS: Criminologists versus the NYPD

Key Terms

aging-out phenomenon
birth cohort
case study
crimes against
  property
crimes against the
  person
criminal careers
data
experiment
field experiment
hypothesis
Index crimes
longitudinal study
nonparticipant
  observation
participant
  observation
population
primary data
random sample
sample
secondary data
self-report surveys
survey
theory
variables
victimization surveys

In one of many versions of Aesop's fable about the three blind men and the elephant, a circus comes to town, and the residents of a home for the blind are invited to "experience" an elephant. When one blind man is led to the elephant, he touches one of its legs. He feels its size and shape. Another man happens to touch the tail, and still another feels the trunk. Back at their residence they argue about the nature of the beast. Says the first man, "An elephant is obviously like the trunk of a tree." "No," says the second, "it's like a rope." "You're both wrong," says the third. "An elephant is like a big snake." All three are partly right, for each has described the part of the animal he has touched.

Assessment of the nature and extent of crime often suffers from the same shortcomings as the three blind men's assessments of the elephant. Researcher A may make assessments on the basis of arrest records. Researcher B may rely on conviction rates to describe crime. Researcher C may use the number of convicts serving prison sentences. None of the researchers, however, may be in a position to assess the full nature and extent of crime; each is limited by the kinds of data he or she uses.

Questions about how crime is measured and what those measurements reveal about the nature and extent of crime are among the most important issues in contemporary criminology. Researchers, theorists, and practitioners need information in order to explain and prevent crime and to operate agencies that deal with the crime problem. It is extremely difficult, however, to gather accurate information. Because of these difficulties, it is necessary for students of criminology to understand how data are collected, what they mean, and whether they are useful. After we look at the objectives and methods of collecting information, we will consider the limitations of the three information sources criminologists most frequently use to estimate the nature and extent of crime in the United States. We then explore measurement of the characteristics of crimes and criminals.

MEASURING CRIME

There are three major reasons for measuring characteristics of crimes and criminals. First of all, researchers need to collect and analyze information in order to test theories about why people commit crime. One criminologist might record the kinds of offenses committed by people of different ages; another might count the number of crimes committed at different times of the year. But without ordering these observations in some purposeful way, without a **theory,** a systematic set of principles that explain how two or more phenomena are related, scientists would be limited in their ability to make predictions from the data they collect.

The types of data that are collected and the way they are collected are crucial to the research process. Criminologists analyze these data and use their findings to support or refute theories. In Part II we examine several theories (including the one outlined briefly here) that explain why people commit crime, and we will see how these theories have been tested.

One theory of crime causation, for example, is that high crime rates result from the wide disparity between people's goals and the means available to them for reaching those goals. Those who lack legitimate opportunities to achieve their goals (primarily, people in the lower class) try to reach them through criminal means. To test this theory, researchers might begin with the **hypothesis** (a testable proposition that describes how two or more factors are related) that lower-class individuals engage in more serious crimes and do so more frequently than middle-class individuals. (See "Social Class and Crime," later in this chapter.) Next they would collect facts, observations, and other pertinent information—called **data**—on the criminal behavior of both lower-class and middle-class individuals. A finding that lower-class persons commit more crimes would support the theory that people commit crimes because they do not have legitimate means to reach their goals.

The second objective of measurement is to enhance our knowledge of the characteristics of various types of offenses. Why are some more likely to be committed than others? What situational factors, such as time of day or type of place, influence the commission of crime? Experts have argued that this information is needed if we are to prevent crime and develop strategies to control it (Chapter 8 deals with this subject).

Measurement has a third major objective: Criminal justice agencies depend on certain kinds of information to facilitate daily operations and to anticipate future needs. How many persons flow through county jails? How many will receive prison sentences? Besides the questions that deal with the day-to-day functioning of the system (number of beds, distribution and hiring of personnel), other questions affect

President Clinton, flanked by Vice President Gore and Attorney General Reno, speaks on reducing crime through effective policing.

legislative and policy decisions. For instance, what effect does a change in law have on the amount of crime committed? Consider legislation on the death penalty. Some people claim that homicides decrease when a death penalty is instituted. Others claim that capital punishment laws make no difference. Does fear of crime go down if we put more police officers in a neighborhood? Does drug smuggling move to another entry point if old access routes are cut off? These and other potential changes need to be evaluated—and evaluations require measurement.

Methods of Collecting Data

Given the importance of data for research, policy making, and the daily operation and planning of the criminal justice system, criminologists have been working to perfect data collection techniques. Through the years these methods have become increasingly more sophisticated.

Depending on what questions they are asking, criminologists can and do collect their data in a variety of ways: through survey research, experiments, observation, and case studies. One of the most widely used methods is survey research, which is a cost-effective method of measuring characteristics of groups. Experimental studies are difficult and costly to conduct, and for this reason they are used infrequently. But they have been, and still are, an important means of collecting data on crime. Participant observation involves the direct participation of the researcher in the activities of the people who are the subjects of the research. A variation of this technique is nonparticipant observation, in which the researcher collects data without joining in the activity. Another way to collect information about crime, and especially about criminal careers, is to examine biographical and autobiographical accounts of individual offenders (the case-study method).

Data can be found in a wide variety of sources, but the most frequently used sources are statistics compiled by government agencies, private foundations, and business. Familiarity with the sources of data and the methods used to gather data will help in understanding the studies we discuss throughout this book. The facts and observations researchers gather for the purpose of a particular study are called **primary data.** Those they find in government sources, or data that were previously collected for a different investigation, are called **secondary data.**

Surveys. Most of us are familiar with surveys—in public opinion polls, marketing research, and election-prediction studies. Criminologists use surveys to obtain quantitative data. A **survey** is the systematic collection of respondents' answers to questions asked in questionnaires or interviews; interviews may be conducted face-to-face or by telephone. Generally, surveys are used to gather information about the attitudes, characteristics, or behavior of a large group of persons, who are called the **population** of the survey. Surveys conducted by criminologists measure, for example, the amount of crime, attitudes toward police or toward the sentencing of dangerous offenders, assessment of drug abuse, and fear of crime.

Instead of interviewing the total population under study, most researchers interview a representative subset of that population—a **sample.** If a sample is carefully drawn, researchers can generalize the results from the sample to the population. A sample determined by random selection, whereby each person in the population to be studied has an equal chance of being selected, is called a **random sample.**

Surveys are a cost-effective method, but they have limitations. If a study of drug use by high school students were done one time only, the finding of a relationship between drug use and poor grades would not tell us whether drug use caused bad grades, whether students with bad grades turned to drugs, or whether bad grades and drug taking resulted from some other factor, such as lack of family ties.

Experiments. The **experiment** is a technique used in the physical and biological sciences, and in the social sciences as well. An investigator introduces a change into a process and makes measurements or observations in order to evaluate the effects of the change. Through experimentation, scientists test hypotheses about how two or more **variables** (factors that may change) are related. The basic model for an experiment involves changing one variable, keeping all other factors the same (controlling them, or holding them constant), and observing the effect of that change on another variable. If you change one variable while keeping all other factors constant and then find that another variable changes as well, you may safely assume that the change in the second variable was caused by the change in the first.

Most experiments are done in laboratories, but it is possible to do them in real-world, or field, settings (hence the name **field experiment**). A field experiment was done at New Jersey's Rahway State Prison to test the hypothesis that if youngsters were shown the horrors of prison, they would not commit crimes. The object was to scare young people out of crime; consequently the project became known as "Scared Straight!" Several agencies were asked to propose male juveniles for the experiment. All were given a series of tests to determine their attitudes toward crime, punishment, prison, the police, and so forth. Afterward some of the juveniles were randomly assigned to the experimental group, which would actually go to the prison. The rest were assigned to a control group, which would not go.

After the experimental group had participated in the program, both groups were again given the same attitude tests to find out if the prison experience had changed the attitudes of the experimental group. Six months later the juvenile records of the two groups were checked to find out how many of the youths in both groups had committed crimes during the 6-month period. Had fewer of the youngsters who had supposedly been "scared straight" been arrested than those who had not made the prison visit? No, according to James Finckenauer's analysis. In fact, many more of the boys in the experimental group had been arrested than boys in the control group.[1]

Experiments in the real world are costly and difficult to carry out, but they have the advantage of increasing scientists' ability to establish cause and effect.

Participant and Nonparticipant Observation.
Researchers who engage in participant and nonparticipant observation have different goals. These methods provide detailed descriptions of life as it actually is lived—in prisons, gangs, and other settings.

Observation is the most direct means of studying behavior. Investigators may play a variety of roles in observing social situations. When they engage in **nonparticipant observation,** they do not join in the activities of the groups they are studying; they simply observe the activities in everyday settings and record what they see. Investigators who engage in **participant observation** take part in many of the activities of the groups in order to gain acceptance, but they generally make clear the purpose of their participation. Anne Campbell, a criminologist who spent 2 years as a participant observer of the lifestyles of girl gang members, explains:

My efforts to meet female gang members began with an introduction through the New York City Police Department's Gang Crimes Unit. Through one of their plain-clothes gang liaison officers, John Galea, I was introduced first to the male gang members of a number of Brooklyn gangs. On being reassured that I "only" wanted to talk to the female members, the male leaders gave their OK and I made arrangements to meet with the girls' leaders or "godmothers." At first they were guarded in their disclosures to me. They asked a lot about my life, my background and my reasons for wanting to hang out with them. Like most of us, however, they enjoyed talking about themselves and over the period of six months that I spent with each of three female gangs they opened up a good deal—sitting in their kitchens, standing on the stoops in the evenings or socializing at parties with allied gangs.[2]

Observations of groups in their natural setting afford the researcher insights into behavior and attitudes that cannot be obtained through such techniques as surveys and experiments.

Case Studies. A **case study** is an analysis of all pertinent aspects of one unit of study, such as an individual, an institution, a group, or a community. The sources of information are documents like life histories, biographies, diaries, journals, letters, and other records. A classic demonstration of criminologists' use of the case-study method is found in Edwin Sutherland's *The Professional Thief,* which is based on interviews with a professional thief.

Sutherland learned about the relationship between amateur and professional thieves, how thieves communicate, how they determine whether to trust each other, and how they network. From discussions with the thief and an analysis of his writings on topics selected by the researcher, Sutherland was able to draw several conclusions that other techniques would not have yielded. For instance, a person is not a "professional thief" unless he is recognized as such by other professional thieves. Training by professional thieves is necessary for the development of the skills, attitudes, and connections required in the "profession."[3] One of the drawbacks of the case-study method is that the information given by the subject may be biased or wrong and by its nature is limited. For these reasons it is difficult to generalize from one person's story—in this instance, to all professional thieves.

Using Available Data in Research. Besides collecting their own data, researchers often depend on secondary data collected by private and public organizations. The police, the courts, and corrections officials, for example, need to know the number of persons passing through the criminal justice system at various points in order to carry out day-to-day administrative tasks and to plan for the future. It is not always feasible to collect new data for a research project, nor is it necessary to do so when such vast amounts of relevant information are already available.

To study the relationship between crime and such a variable as income or a single-parent family, one might make use of the Uniform Crime Reports (national police statistics, discussed below), together with information found in the reports of the Bureau of the Census. Various other agencies, among them the Federal Bureau of Prisons, the Drug Enforcement Agency, the Treasury Department, and the Labor Department, are also excellent sources of statistics useful to criminologists. At the international level, U.N. world crime surveys contain information on crime, criminals, and criminal justice systems in countries on all continents.

Researchers who use available data can save a great deal of time and expense. However, they have to exercise caution in fitting data not collected for the purpose of a particular study into their research. Many official records are incomplete or the data have been collected in such a way as to make them inadequate for the research. It is also frequently difficult to gain permission to use agency data that are not available to the public because of a concern about confidentiality.

Ethics and the Researcher

In the course of their research, criminologists encounter many ethical issues. Chief among such issues is confidentiality. Consider the dilemma faced by a group of researchers in the late 1960s. In interviewing a sample of 9954 boys born in 1945, the team collected extensive self-reported criminal histories of offenses the boys had committed before and after they turned 18. Among the findings were 4 unreported homicides and 75 rapes. The researchers were naturally excited about capturing such interesting data: These findings supported the hypothesis of "hid-

den" delinquency (discussed below). More important, the researchers had feelings of grave concern. How should they handle their findings?

Should the results of these interviews be published? Could the failure of the research staff to disclose names be considered the crime of "obstructing justice"?

Does an obligation to society as a whole to release the names of the offenders transcend a researcher's obligation to safeguard a subject's confidentiality?

What is the best response to a demand by the police, a district attorney, or a court for the researcher's files containing the subjects' names?

Should criminologists be immune to prosecution for their failure to disclose the names of their subjects?

Is it possible to develop a technique that can ensure against the identification of a subject in a research file?[4]

Such questions have few clear-cut answers. When researchers encounter these problems, however, they can rely on standards for ethical human experimentation. Human-experimentation review committees at most universities and government agencies check all proposals for research projects to ensure the protection of human subjects. In addition, researchers are required to inform their subjects about the nature of the study and to obtain written and informed agreement to participate.

Despite heightened awareness of the ethical issues involved in human experimentation—particularly in correctional institutions, where coercion is difficult to avoid—the field of criminology has not yet adopted a formal code of ethics. Some members of the discipline are arguing in favor of one. Frank Hagan, for example, has suggested that the code include guidelines on honoring commitments made to respondents, avoiding procedures that might harm subjects, exercising integrity in the performance and reporting of research, and protecting confidentiality.[5] In the end, however, as Seth Bloomberg and Leslie Wilkins have noted, "the responsibility for safeguarding human subjects ultimately rests with the researcher. . . . A code of ethics may provide useful guidelines, but it will not relieve the scientist of moral choice."[6]

THE NATURE AND EXTENT OF CRIME

As we have seen, criminologists gather their information in many ways. The methods they choose depend on the questions they want to answer. To estimate the nature and extent of crime in the United States, they rely primarily on the Uniform Crime Reports, data compiled by the police; on the National Crime Victimization Survey, which measures crime through reports by victims; and on various self-report surveys, which ask individuals about criminal acts they have committed, whether or not these acts have come to the attention of the authorities.

Official statistics gathered from law enforcement agencies provide information available on the crimes actually investigated and reported by these agencies. But not all crimes appear in police statistics. In order for a criminal act to be "known to the police," the act first must be *perceived* by an individual (the car is not in the garage where it was left). It must then be *defined*, or classified, as something that places it within the purview of the criminal justice system (a theft has taken place), and it must be *reported* to the police. Once the police are notified, they classify it and often *redefine* what may have taken place before *recording* the act as a crime known to the police (Figure 2.1). Information about criminal acts may be lost at any point along this processing route, and many crimes are never discovered to begin with.

Police Statistics

In 1924 the director of the Bureau of Investigation, J. Edgar Hoover, initiated a campaign to make the Bureau responsible for gathering national statistics. With support from the American Bar Association (ABA) and the International Association of Chiefs of Police (IACP), the House of Representatives in 1930 passed a bill authorizing the Bureau (later renamed the Federal Bureau of Investigation, or FBI) to collect data on crimes known to the police. These data are compiled into reports called the Uniform Crime Reports (UCR). At present approximately 16,000 city, county, and state law enforcement agencies, which cover 97 percent of the total population, voluntarily contribute information on crimes brought to their attention. If the police verify that a crime has been committed, that crime goes into the report,

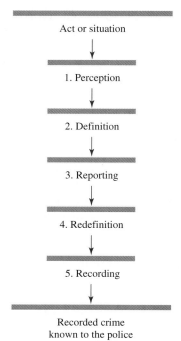

FIGURE 2.1 The process of bringing crime to the attention of police.
Source: R. F. Sparks, H. G. Genn, and D. J. Dodd, *Surveying Victims: A Study of the Measurement of Criminal Victimization, Perceptions of Crime, and Attitudes to Criminal Justice* (Chichester, England: Wiley, 1977), p. 6.

whether or not an arrest has been made. Each month, reporting agencies send data on offenses in 29 categories.

Part I and Part II Offenses. The UCR divides offenses into two major categories: Part I and Part II. Part I offenses include eight crimes, which are aggregated as **crimes against the person** (criminal homicide, forcible rape, robbery, and aggravated assault) and **crimes against property** (burglary, larceny-theft, motor vehicle theft, and arson). Collectively, Part I offenses are called **Index crimes.** Because they are serious, these crimes tend to be reported to the police more reliably than others and therefore can be used in combination as an index, or indicator, of changes over time. All other offenses, except traffic violations, are Part II crimes. Its 21 crimes include fraud, embezzlement, weapons offenses, vandalism, and simple assaults.

Crime Rates. To analyze crime data, experts frequently present them as crime rates. Crime rates are computed by the following formula:

$$\text{Crime rate} = \frac{\substack{\text{number of} \\ \text{reported crimes}}}{\text{total population}} \times 100{,}000$$

Crime rates may be computed for groups of offenses (such as the Index crimes or crimes against the person) or for specific offenses (such as homicide). If we say, for example, that the homicide rate is 10.2, we mean that there were 10.2 homicides for every 100,000 persons in the population under consideration (total U.S. population, say, or all males in the United States). Expressing the amount of crime in terms of rates shows whether an increase or a decrease in crime results from a change in the population or a change in the amount of crime committed.

In addition to data on reported crimes, the UCR includes the number of offenses "cleared by arrest." Crimes may be cleared in one of two ways: by the arrest, charging, and turning over to the courts of at least one person for prosecution, or by disposition of a case when an arrest is not possible, as when the suspect has died or fled the jurisdiction. Besides reported crimes and crimes cleared by arrest, the reports contain extensive data on characteristics of crimes (such as geographical location, time, and place), characteristics of criminals (such as gender, age, and race), and distribution of law enforcement personnel. We shall look at what these statistics reveal about the characteristics of crime and criminals in more detail later, but first we must recognize their limitations.

Limitations of the Uniform Crime Reports.

Despite the fact that the UCR is among the main sources of crime statistics, its research value has been questioned. The criticisms deal with methodological problems and reporting practices. Some scholars argue, for example, that figures on reported crime are of little use in categories such as larceny, in which a majority of crime is not reported. The statistics present the amount of crime known to law enforcement agencies, but they do not reveal how many crimes have actually been committed. Another serious limitation is the fact that when several crimes are committed in one event, only the most serious offense is

included in the UCR; the others go unreported. At the same time, when certain other crimes are committed, each individual act is counted as a separate offense. If a person robs a group of six people, for example, the UCR lists one robbery. But if a person assaults six people, the UCR lists six assaults. UCR data are further obscured by the fact that they do not differentiate between completed acts and attempted acts.

Police reports to the FBI are voluntary and vary in accuracy. In a study conducted on behalf of the Police Foundation, Lawrence Sherman and Barry Glick found that while the UCR requires that arrests be recorded even if a suspect is released without a formal charge, all 196 departments surveyed recorded an arrest only after a formal booking procedure.[7] In addition, police departments may want to improve their image by showing that their crime rate has either declined (meaning the streets are safer) or risen (justifying a crackdown on, say, prostitution).[8] New record-keeping procedures can also create significant changes (the New York robbery rate appeared to increase 400 percent in 1 year).[9] Many fluctuations in crime rates may therefore be attributable to events other than changes in the actual numbers of crimes committed.

Finally, the UCR data suffer from several omissions. Many arsons go unreported because not all fire departments report to the UCR.[10] Federal cases go unlisted. Most white-collar offenses are omitted because they are reported not to the police but to regulatory authorities, such as the Securities and Exchange Commission and the Federal Trade Commission.[11]

To deal with the limitations of the UCR, in 1986 the International Association of Chiefs of Police, the National Sheriffs' Association, and the state-level UCR programs joined forces with the FBI. A new reporting system was developed, called the National Incident-Based Reporting System (NIBRS). Reporting to the NIBRS is voluntary and coexists with the UCR. Each offense and arrest is considered an "incident," and information is recorded on victim and offender characteristics, type of property stolen, weapons used, location and time of incident, and so forth. In all, 52 items of information are collected within 22 crime categories, comprising 46 specific offenses.[12]

Some experts claim that the NIBRS will enhance the capacity for crime analysis at all jurisdictional

WINDOW TO THE WORLD

MEASURING WORLD CRIME

Crime problems do not stop at national borders. The first effort to measure world crime was based on the idea that effective international cooperation is necessary to solve global crime problems and that such cooperation is impossible without reliable data. In the mid-1970s, U.N. officials prepared questionnaires about the extent of crime, grouping offenses into a few very broad categories, and sent them to the governments of all countries. Four world crime surveys now have been published, with responses increasing with each survey. By December 1994, 100 governments had contributed to the fourth survey, though many were missing data.(1)

INCREASING PARTICIPATION

One researcher has tried to ascertain why some countries do not participate in crime surveys.(2) He discovered that crime statistics are being kept by countries accounting for the greater part of the world's population but that 48 of the world's 222 countries and other international statistical units did not participate in any of the world crime surveys. Since many of the nonparticipating countries, including China, do keep crime statistics, why do they not respond to requests for information?

Some countries are so small that their administrative staffs may not be able to cope with the requests; others are embroiled in wars, civil strife, and changes in government. They cannot keep track of crime problems. Some countries simply will not participate, perhaps because of the notion that the incidence of crime reflects negatively on their standing as a nation, or because it may affect the tourist trade, or because crime rates contradict a philosophy that crime disappears with the achievement of

national goals. Others cannot participate because there are no criminal justice statisticians to count crimes.

DIFFERENT CULTURES, DIFFERENT CRIMES

Researchers also face problems in the interpretation of world crime statistics.(3) Reported crime rates may reflect "real" rates of crime, or they may reflect the efficiency and veracity with which crimes are detected, reported, and recorded in a particular country. But these problems are almost trivial in comparison to the problem of the very real cultural and political differences among countries.

Despite all the caveats, researchers have been able to determine some very general trends in broad categories of crimes—thefts, homicides, assaults, and drug-related crimes, for example.

Sources

1. *Results of the Fourth United Nations Survey of Crime Trends and Operations of Criminal Justice* (New York: United Nations, 1994).

2. G. O. W. Mueller, *World Survey on the Availability of Criminal Justice Statistics* (Newark, N.J.: Rutgers University, 1992).

3. *Third United Nations Survey of Crime Trends, Operations of Criminal Justice Systems and Crime Prevention Strategies* (New York: United Nations, 1990).

Questions for Discussion

1. Give an example (from a newspaper, magazine, or history book) of an act that is seen as a crime in one society and not in another. Is the disparity caused by political or normative differences? Explain.

2. Countries may base their published crime rates on a variety of sources: crimes reported to the police, arrest rates, conviction rates, or imprisonment figures. Which of these data sets is most reliable, and how could countries be persuaded to report on a unified standard?

Replies to four U.N. surveys of crime trends

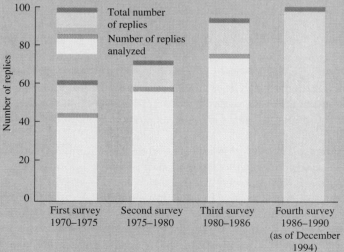

First survey 1970–1975 Second survey 1975–1980 Third survey 1980–1986 Fourth survey 1986–1990 (as of December 1994)

levels, allowing law enforcement agencies to more effectively and efficiently define their needs, justify expenditures, and allocate resources.[13] The NIBRS is a computerized system. Local agencies can download their crime data directly to state- and federal-level agencies, reducing the need for standardized reporting forms.[14] In this respect, the NIBRS seems more efficient than the more cumbersome UCR. However, the computer requirement may prove to be a stumbling block for nationwide adoption. Many smaller agencies simply cannot afford the upgrades that would allow them to participate fully in the system.

The NIBRS is a major attempt to improve the collection of crime data. But it deals only with crimes that come to the attention of the police. What about crimes that remain unreported? For what is called the "dark figure of crime," we have to rely on victimization data and self-report studies.

Victimization Surveys

Victimization surveys measure the extent of crime by interviewing individuals about their experiences as victims. The Bureau of the Census, in cooperation with the Bureau of Justice Statistics, collects information annually about persons and households that have been victimized. The report is called the National Crime Victimization Survey (NCVS). Researchers for the NCVS estimate the total number of crimes committed by asking respondents from a national sample of approximately 60,000 households, representing 135,000 persons over the age of 12 (parental permission is needed for those below 14 years old), about their experiences as victims during a specific time period. Interviewers visit (or sometimes telephone) the homes selected for the sample. Each housing unit remains in the sample for 3 years. Every 6 months 10,000 households are rotated out of the sample and replaced by a new group.

The NCVS measures the extent of victimization by rape, robbery, assault, larceny, burglary, personal theft, and motor vehicle theft. Note that two of the UCR Part I offenses—criminal homicide and arson— are not included (see Table 2.1).[15] Homicide is omitted because the NCVS covers only crimes whose victims can be interviewed. The designers of the survey also decided to omit arson, a relative newcomer to the UCR, because measuring it with some validity by means of a victimization survey was deemed to be too difficult. Part II offenses have been excluded alto-

gether because many of them are considered victimless (prostitution, vagrancy, drug abuse, drunkenness) or because victims are willing participants (gambling, con games) or do not know they have been victimized (forgery, fraud).

The survey covers characteristics of crimes such as time and place of occurrence, number of offenders, use of weapons, economic loss, and time lost from work; characteristics of victims, such as gender, age, race, ethnicity, marital status, household composition, and educational attainment; perceived characteristics of offenders, such as age, gender, and race; circumstances surrounding the offenses and their effects, such as financial loss and injury; and patterns of police reporting, such as rates of reporting and reasons for reporting and for not reporting. Recently questions have been added that encourage interviewees to discuss family violence.

Limitations of Victimization Surveys. While victimization surveys give us information about crimes that are not reported to the police, these data, too, have significant limitations. The NCVS covers crimes in a more limited way than the UCR; the NCVS includes only 7 offenses, whereas there are 8 offenses in Part I of the UCR and an additional 21 in Part II. Although the NCVS is conducted by trained interviewers, some individual variations in interviewing and recording style are inevitable, and as a result the information recorded may vary as well.

Since the NCVS is based on personal reporting, it also suffers from the fact that memories may fade over time, so some facts are forgotten while others are exaggerated. Moreover, some interviewees may try to please the interviewer by fabricating crime incidents.[16] Respondents also have a tendency to telescope events—that is, to move events that took place in an earlier time period into the time period under study. Like the UCR, the NCVS records only the most serious offense committed during an event in which several crimes are perpetrated.

Self-Report Surveys

Another way to determine the amount and types of crime actually committed is to ask people to report their own criminal acts in a confidential interview or, more usually, on an anonymous questionnaire. These investigations are called **self-report surveys.**

TABLE 2.1   How Do the Uniform Crime Reports and the National Crime Victimization Survey Differ?

	Uniform Crime Reports	National Crime Victimization Survey
Offenses measured:	Homicide Rape Robbery (personal and commercial) Assault (aggravated) Burglary (commercial and household) Larceny (commercial and household) Motor vehicle theft Arson	Rape Robbery (personal) Assault (aggravated and simple) Household burglary Larceny Personal theft Motor vehicle theft
Scope:	Crimes reported to the police in most jurisdictions; considerable flexibility in developing small-area data	Crimes both reported and not reported to police; all data are for the nation as a whole; some data are available for a few large geographical areas
Collection method:	Police department reports to FBI	Survey interviews; periodically measures the total number of crimes committed by asking a national sample of (originally) 60,000 households representing 135,000 persons over the age of 12 about their experiences as victims of crime during a specified period
Kinds of Information:	In addition to offense counts, provides information on crime clearances, persons arrested, persons charged, law enforcement officers killed and assaulted, and characteristics of homicide victims	Provides details about victims (such as age, race, sex, education, income, and whether the victim and offender were related to each other) and about crimes (such as time and place of occurrence, whether or not reported to police, use of weapons, occurrence of injury, and economic consequences)
Sponsor:	Department of Justice, Federal Bureau of Investigation	Department of Justice, Bureau of Justice Statistics

Source: Adapted from U.S. Department of Justice, Bureau of Justice Statistics. *Report to the Nation on Crime and Justice,* 2d ed. (Washington, D.C.: U.S. Government Printing Office, 1988), p. 11.

Findings of Self-Report Surveys.   Self-reports of delinquent and criminal behavior have produced several important findings since their development in the 1940s. First, they quickly refuted the conventional wisdom that only a small percentage of the general population commits crimes. The use of these measures over the last several decades has demonstrated very high rates of law-violating behavior by seemingly law-abiding people. Almost everyone, at some point in time, has broken a law.

In 1947, James S. Wallerstein and Clement J. Wyle questioned a group of 1698 individuals on whether or not they had committed any of 49 offenses that were serious enough to require a maximum sentence of not less than 1 year. They found that over 80 percent of the men reported committing malicious mischief, disorderly conduct, and larceny. More than 50 percent admitted a history of crimes

including reckless driving and driving while intoxicated, indecency, gambling, fraud, and tax evasion. The authors acknowledged the lack of scientific rigor of their study. No attempt was made to ensure a balanced or representative cross section of the individuals surveyed.[17] However, these findings do suggest that the distinction between criminals and noncriminals may be more apparent than real.

Studies conducted since the 1940s have provided a great deal more information. They suggest a wide discrepancy between official and self-report data as regards the age, race, and gender of offenders.[18] Unrecorded offenders commit a wide variety of offenses, rather than specializing in one type of offense.[19] It also appears that only one-quarter of all serious, chronic juvenile offenders are apprehended by the police. Moreover, an estimated 90 percent of all youths commit delinquent or criminal acts, primarily truancy, use of false identification, alcohol abuse, larceny, fighting, and marijuana use.[20]

From 1991 to 1993, the first International Self-Report Delinquency (ISRD) study was conducted in Finland, Great Britain, the Netherlands, Belgium, Germany, Switzerland, Portugal, Spain, Italy, Greece, the United States, and New Zealand. Each country used the same questionnaire, which had been translated into numerous languages. The studies used various sampling techniques, so the results from each country are not strictly comparable. Nonetheless, the findings support much of what is found in the self-report literature. Boys commit about twice as many offenses as girls. The peak age of offending in the participating countries is 16 to 17 years. Violence is strongly related to lower educational levels. No relationship was found between socioeconomic status and delinquency. Drug use seems related to leaving school early and unemployment. School failure is related to violent offenses.[21]

Limitations of Self-Report Surveys. Self-report surveys have taught us a great deal about criminality. But they, like the other methods of data collection, have drawbacks. The questionnaires are often limited to petty acts, such as truancy, and therefore do not represent the range of criminal acts that people may commit. Michael Hindelang, Travis Hirschi, and Joseph Weis argue that researchers who find discrepancies with respect to gender, race, and class between the results produced by official statistics and those collected by self-report methods are in fact measuring different kinds of behavior rather than different amounts of the same behavior. They suggest that if you take into account the fact that persons who are arrested tend to have committed more serious offenses and to have prior records (criteria that affect decisions to arrest), then the two types of statistics are quite comparable.[22]

Another drawback of self-reports is that most of them are administered to high school or college students, so the information they yield applies only to young people attending school. And who can say that respondents always tell the truth? The information obtained by repeated administration of the same questionnaire to the same individuals might yield different results. Many self-report measures lack validity; the data obtained do not correspond with some other criterion (such as school records) that measures the same behavior. Finally, samples may be biased. People who choose not to participate in the studies

may have good reason for not wanting to discuss their criminal activities.

Each of the three commonly used sources of data—police reports, victim surveys, and self-report surveys—adds a different dimension to our knowledge of crime. All of them are useful in our search for the characteristics of crimes, criminals, and victims.

MEASURING CHARACTERISTICS OF CRIME

Streets in Charlotte, North Carolina, with tranquil names—Peaceful Glen, Soft Wind, Gentle Breeze—have recently become killing lanes.[23] The city that had hoped to displace Atlanta as the "Queen City of the South" had 115 homicides in 1992, more than double the number it had 6 years earlier.[24] More recent figures suggest that the situation continues to grow worse and that the homicide rate is increasing at an even faster rate. Experts tie the mounting murder rate in Charlotte to drugs and the growing number of swap shops and flea markets that serve as unregulated outlets for buying guns. Most of the murders have taken place in a 26-square-mile area inhabited primarily by low-income black families.

These statistics tell us a good deal about the crime problem in Charlotte. They reveal not only a problem of drugs and illegal use of handguns, but also the number of homicides that have resulted, the changes in the homicide rate over time, the high-risk areas, and the racial and economic composition of those areas. Criminologists use these kinds of data about crimes in their research. Some investigators, for example, may want to compare drug use to crime in major cities. Others may want to explain a decrease or an increase in the crime rate in a single city (Charlotte), in a single neighborhood (the impoverished inner city), or perhaps in the nation as a whole.

Crime Trends

One of the most important characteristics of any crime is how often it is committed. From such figures we can determine crime trends, the increases and decreases of crime over time. The UCR shows that more than 13.9 million Index crimes (excluding arson) were reported to the police in 1994 (Figure 2.2a). Of the total number of Index crimes, violent crimes make up a small portion—13 percent—with a murder rate of 9.0 per 100,000. Most Index crimes

AT ISSUE

STALKING: AN UNRECORDED CRIME

Linda has bouncy auburn hair, a petite build, a shy smile, and a handgun in her purse.

She always carries the gun, even though it's illegal, just in case "he" shows up again.

It's been five years since the young, attractive, blond man stopped stalking her. She still flinches whenever she sees a pickup truck in her rearview mirror.

The man's brown truck triggered a recurring nightmare for Linda. He stalked her in it every week, and sometimes daily, for $1\frac{1}{2}$ years. He followed her to work . . . and back home again.

He parked next to her car while she shopped and waited until she came out.

Always, he stared at her with the same impassive, unsmiling look.(1)

The measurement of crime rests on a society's definitions of crime; acts cannot be recorded as crime until they have been defined as crime. In Texas in the mid-1980s, Linda's stalker was breaking no law. But by 1993, 31 states had made stalking a

crime. Most of the laws define stalking as "willful, malicious and repeated following and harassing of another person, where there is a credible threat of violence against the victim or a member of the victim's family."(2) While stalkers can be strangers, those who work with victims of stalkers say that most stalking cases grow out of "intimate relationships that have soured."(2)

STALKING AND DOMESTIC VIOLENCE

Indeed, the practice of stalking may have evolved primarily in response to laws against domestic violence, some experts feel. Restraining orders don't provide women with enough protection from abusive boyfriends or husbands, says an attorney for the National Battered Women's Law Project in New York; and before stalking was recognized as a crime, men could harass women with impunity. But now, at least in much of the United States, such harassment is a crime; yet "many of these guys know what the definition of domestic violence is and officially avoid it," the attorney explains.(3)

Defining stalking as a crime gives police a tool to use to prevent more serious crimes. When no law defines stalking as a crime, the police can do nothing about stalking complaints

except ask the stalker to stop. The problem with that, says David Beatty of the National Victim Center, is that stalking often escalates from phone calls and messages to rape, assault, or homicide. While no one knows how many of the victims had been stalked, 30 percent of the women murdered in 1990 were killed by husbands or boyfriends—the men most likely to be involved in stalking cases. Stalking laws, according to Beatty, are intended to allow the police to intervene before violence occurs.(2)

STALKING AND WOMEN'S EXPERIENCE

The definition of stalking as a crime, advocates of women's rights say, is part of the evolution of law to reflect women's problems. "Over the last 25 years . . . we have begun . . . reshaping the law in ways that are more responsive to women's experience, of giving things names, and defining them as part of a cultural pattern," comments Elizabeth Schneider, who teaches at Brooklyn Law School. "That's what happened with sexual harassment, with battering and now with stalking."(2)

Sources
1. Cheryl Laird, "Laws Confront Obsession That Turns Fear into

---

are property offenses (87 percent), and 65 percent of these property offenses are larcenies.[25]

The 1994 NCVS presents a somewhat different picture (Figure 2.2b). Though the data presented in the NCVS and the UCR are not entirely comparable because the categories differ, the number of crimes reported to the police and the number reported in the victimization survey are clearly far apart. According to the NCVS, there were over 42 million victimizations. Indeed, the NCVS reports more thefts than the total number of UCR Index offenses taken together.[26]

According to UCR data, the crime rate increased slowly between 1930 and 1960. After 1960 it began to

rise much more quickly. This trend continued until 1980 (Figure 2.3), when the crime rate rose to 5950 per 100,000. From that peak the rate steadily dropped until 1984, when there were 5031.3 crimes per 100,000. After that year the rate rose again until 1990. Then it decreased to 5374.4.[27] The NCVS also shows that the victimization rate peaked from 1979 to 1981.[28]

The gradual decline in the crime rate after 1980 is an important phenomenon that requires a bit more analysis. One important factor is the age distribution of the population. Given the fact that young people tend to have the highest crime rate, the age distribution of the population has a major effect on crime

AT ISSUE

Terror and Brings Nightmares to Life," *Houston Chronicle,* May 17, 1992, p. 1.
2. Tamar Lewin, "New Laws Address Old Problem: The Terror of a Stalker's Threat," *New York Times,* Feb. 8, 1993, p. A1.
3. Elizabeth Ross, "Problem with Men Stalking Women Spurs New

Laws," *Christian Science Monitor,* June 11, 1992, p. 6.

Questions for Discussion
1. Some civil rights advocates protest that stalking laws will violate the rights of investigative reporters who have to follow people as a part of their jobs. Do

you agree? Explain your position.
2. Just as new crimes may be defined, acts that were once considered to be crimes may become "noncrimes" as society changes. Give an example of something that once was criminal but is no longer considered to be so.

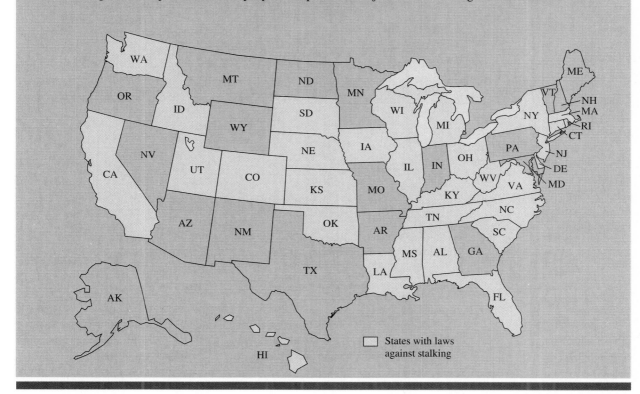

trends. After World War II, the birthrate increased sharply in what is known as the baby boom. The baby-boom generation reached its crime-prone years in the 1960s, and the crime rate duly rose. As the generation grew older, the crime rate became more stable and in the 1980s began to decline. Some researchers claim that the children of the baby boomers may very well once again expand the ranks of the crime-prone ages and that crime will once again increase.

During the period when the baby-boom generation outgrew criminal behavior, U.S. society was undergoing other changes. We adopted a get-tough crime-control policy, which may have deterred some

people from committing crimes. Mandatory prison terms permitted judges less discretion in sentencing, and fewer convicted felons were paroled. In addition, crime-prevention programs, such as Neighborhood Watch groups, became popular. These and other factors have been suggested to explain why the crime rate dropped, but we have no definitive answers.

Locations and Times of Criminal Acts

Statistics on the characteristics of crimes are important not only to criminologists who seek to know why crime occurs but also to those who want to know how

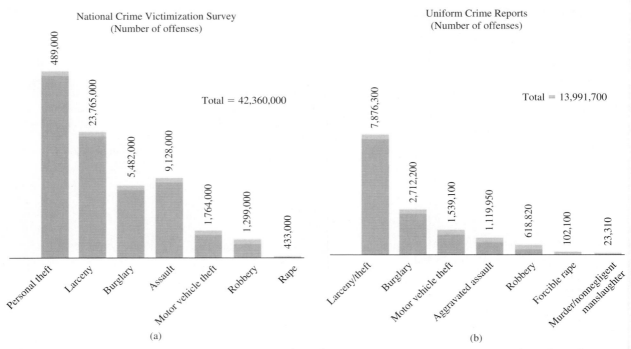

National Crime Victimization Survey
(Number of offenses)

Total = 42,360,000

489,000

23,765,000

5,482,000

9,128,000

1,764,000

1,299,000

433,000

Personal theft / Larceny / Burglary / Assault / Motor vehicle theft / Robbery / Rape

(a)

Uniform Crime Reports
(Number of offenses)

Total = 13,991,700

7,876,300

2,712,200

1,539,100

1,119,950

618,820

102,100

23,310

Larceny/theft / Burglary / Motor vehicle theft / Aggravated assault / Robbery / Forcible rape / Murder/nonnegligent manslaughter

(b)

FIGURE 2.2 National Crime Victimization Survey and Uniform Crime Reports: A comparison of number of crimes reported. (a) National Crime Victimization Survey: Total number of victimizations, 1994. (b) Uniform Crime Reports: Total number of index offenses, 1994.
Source: (a) Adapted from U.S. Department of Justice, Bureau of Justice Statistics, *Criminal Victimization 1994* (Washington D.C.: U.S. Government Printing Office, April 1996), p. 2. (b) Adapted from U.S. Department of Justice, Federal Bureau of Investigation, *Crime in the United States, 1994* (Washington D.C.: U.S. Government Printing Office, 1995), p. 58.

FIGURE 2.3 Uniform Crime Reports: Rate of all index crimes per 100,000 population, 1960–1994.
Source: U.S. Department of Justice, Federal Bureau of Investigation, *Crime in the United States, 1975; 1980; 1992; 1994* (Washington D.C.: U.S. Government Printing Office, 1976, 1981, 1993, 1995), pp. 41, 49, 58.

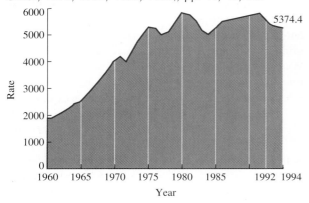

to prevent it (Chapter 8). Two statistics of use in prevention efforts are those on where crimes are committed and when.

Most crimes are committed in large urban areas rather than in small cities, suburbs, or rural areas (Figure 2.4). This pattern can be attributed to a variety of factors—population density, age distribution of residents, stability of the population, economic conditions, and the quality of law enforcement, to name but a few. The statistics for Charlotte, North Carolina, for example, show that most arrests took place in the poverty-ridden ghetto areas. The fact that the majority of those arrests were made in neighborhoods where drug dealers were visibly present on the streets fits the national picture. NCVS data tell us that the safest place to be is inside one's home; according to victims' reports, 11.7 percent of robberies and 14.4 percent of assaults were committed in their homes. The only crime that shows a significantly different pattern is rape: 37.4 percent of such attacks occurred in the victim's home or lodging.[29]

In what counties is crime most likely to occur?

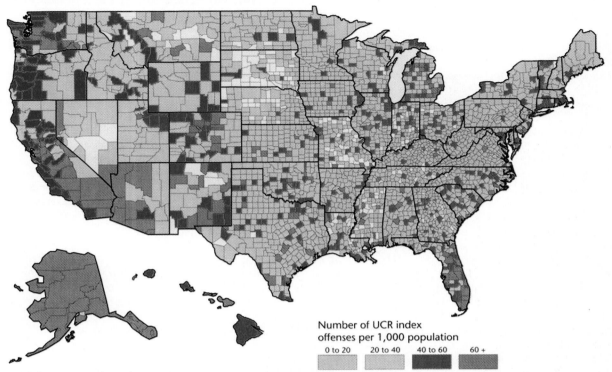

FIGURE 2.4 Number of UCR index offenses per 1000 population, by county.
Source: U.S. Department of Justice, Bureau of Justice Statistics, *Report to the Nation on Crime and Justice,* 2d ed. (Washington, D.C.: U.S. Government Printing Office, 1988), p. 18.

As for the times when crimes are committed, NCVS data reveal that over 58 percent of all violent crimes involving strangers are committed at night, between 6 P.M. and 6 A.M. Household crimes follow the same pattern: Of crimes committed within a known period, 70 percent of household larcenies and 75 percent of motor vehicle thefts are committed at night. Most personal thefts, however, are committed during the day.[30]

Nationwide crime rates also vary by season. Personal and household crimes are more likely to be committed during the warmer months of the years, perhaps because in summer people spend more time outdoors, where they are more vulnerable to crime.[31] People often leave doors and windows open when they go out in warm weather.

Severity of Crime

We have seen that crime rates vary by time and place. They also vary in people's perception of their severity.

To some extent legislation sets a standard of severity by the punishments it attaches to various crimes. But let us take a critical look at such judgments.

Do you believe that skyjacking an airplane is a more serious offense than smuggling heroin? Is forcible rape more serious than kidnapping? Is breaking into a home and stealing $1000 more serious than using force to rob a person of $10? A yes answer to all three questions conforms with the findings of the National Survey of Crime Severity, which in 1977 measured public perceptions of the seriousness of 204 events, from planting a bomb that killed 20 people to playing hooky from school.[32]

The survey, conducted by Marvin E. Wolfgang and his colleagues, found that individuals generally agree about the relative seriousness of specific crimes (Table 2.2). In ranking severity, people seem to base their decisions on such factors as the ability of victims to protect themselves, the amount of injury and loss suffered, the type of business or organization from which property is stolen, the relationship between

CRIMINOLOGICAL FOCUS

CRIMINOLOGISTS VERSUS THE NYPD

One of the biggest stories in policing circles in 1995 and 1996 was the sharp drop in the violent crime rate in cities across the country. Murder rates fell from the first 6 months of 1994 to the first 6 months of 1995: 10 percent in Washington and Detroit, 18 percent in New Orleans and Atlanta, nearly 20 percent in Chicago, and, most astonishingly, 32 percent in Houston and New York City.(1)

For some criminologists, these decreases do not necessarily represent anything more than a statistical blip. James Alan Fox, for example, observed that "It's like the Dow Jones average. What goes up must come down."(1) Others point to the stabilization of drug selling in inner cities. In business management parlance, drug markets are said to have "matured." What this translates to is fewer conflicts between rival drug dealers, and thus fewer drug-related murders. Because this type of murder accounts for so many of the homicides occurring in cities, maturation of the market could explain a significant part of the drop in murder rates. In addition, the crack "epidemic" of the 1980s has largely subsided, and there seems to have been a switch among users from cocaine to heroin. Heroin mellows users, while cocaine agitates them.(2) Demographic changes, specifically a temporary dip in the high-crime population of those aged 18 to 24, have also been used to explain the

drop.(3) Another theory is that the most dangerous criminals are now in prison. In New York State alone, the number of felons behind bars is 55,000, twice what it was 10 years ago.(2)

The most vocal critic of criminologists and their theories has been William Bratton, past police commissioner of New York City. As far as he is concerned, the reason for the drastic drop in crime in New York is a different policing strategy. Publicly taunting academics and researchers, he referred to their explanations for crime as "ducks in a row," which he vowed to knock down.(2) The crux of the debate is whether crime is something that can be controlled by the police. Criminological theory tends to discount this notion, and points instead to the breakdown of the family and community, or to other aspects of society that the police are powerless to change.

Bratton's approach was to target specific problem behaviors. What cops call the "beer and piss patrol" has become an effective way to catch more serious criminals. When stopping someone for a minor offense like public urination or public drinking, the police are able to check identification and see if the person is wanted by the authorities. Frisks are also done in these circumstances. Sophisticated crime analysis helped identify problem areas early on, before they got out of control. Beyond this, Bratton made each of his commanders personally responsible for bringing down crime rates in their

respective precincts. Anyone who couldn't perform was stripped of command.(4)

For Bratton, the reason for the drop in crime is evident, but for criminologists, it is not so clear. Evaluations of policing strategies are few and far between, so it is not easy to tell if what Bratton did has actually worked, and if so, why. Also, as Jeffrey Fagan observed, "[I]t would be a first in the history of social science for there to be a single reason for such a dramatic change in social behavior."(2)

Sources
1. Fox Butterfield, "Many Cities in U.S. Show Sharp Drop in Homicide Rate," *New York Times,* Aug. 13, 1995, p. 1.
2. Clifford Krauss, "Mystery of New York, the Suddenly Safer City," *New York Times,* July 23, 1995, p. 4A.
3. Gregory Beals and Evan Thomas, "A Crimebuster's Fall," *Newsweek,* Apr. 8, 1996, p. 42.
4. Richard Lacayo, "One Good Apple," *Time,* Jan. 15, 1996, pp. 54–55.

Questions for Discussion
1. Do you believe that police techniques for reducing the crime rate merely move the criminal behavior from one neighborhood to another, or from one state to another?
2. What role do you believe criminologists should play in police departments across the country?

---

offender and victim, and (for drug offenses) the types of drugs involved. Respondents generally agreed that violent crime is more serious than property crime. They also considered white-collar crimes, such as engaging in consumer fraud, cheating on income taxes, polluting, and accepting bribes, to be as serious as many violent and property crimes.

MEASURING CHARACTERISTICS OF CRIMINALS

Information on the characteristics of crimes is not the only sort of data analyzed by criminologists. They also want to know the characteristics of the people who commit those crimes.

Severity Score	Ten Most Serious Offenses	Severity Score	Ten Least Serious Offenses
TABLE 2.2	**How Do People Rank the Severity of Crime?**		
72.1	Planting a bomb in a public building. The bomb explodes and 20 people are killed.	1.3	Two persons willingly engage in a homosexual act.
52.8	A man forcibly rapes a woman. As a result of physical injuries, she dies.	1.1	Disturbing the neighborhood with loud, noisy behavior.
43.2	Robbing a victim at gunpoint. The victim struggles and is shot to death.	1.1	Taking bets on the numbers.
39.2	A man stabs his wife. As a result, she dies.	1.1	A group continues to hang around a corner after being told to break up by a police officer.
35.7	Stabbing a victim to death.		
35.6	Intentionally injuring a victim. As a result, the victim dies.	0.9	A youngster under 16 years old runs away from home.
33.8	Running a narcotics ring.	0.8	Being drunk in public.
27.9	A woman stabs her husband. As a result, he dies.	0.7	A youngster under 16 years old breaks a curfew law by being out on the street after the hour permitted by law.
26.3	An armed person skyjacks an airplane and demands to be flown to another country.	0.6	Trespassing in the backyard of a private home.
25.8	A man forcibly rapes a woman. No other physical injury occurs.	0.3	A person is a vagrant. That is, he has no home and no visible means of support.
		0.2	A youngster under 16 years old plays hooky from school.

Source: Adapted from Marvin E. Wolfgang, Robert Figlio, Paul E. Tracey, and Simon I. Singer, *National Survey of Crime Severity* (Washington, D.C.: U.S. Government Printing Office, 1985).

Behind each crime is a criminal or several criminals. Criminals can be differentiated by age, ethnicity, gender, socioeconomic level, and other criteria. These characteristics enable us to group criminals into categories, and it is these categories that researchers find useful. They study the various offender groups to determine why some people are more likely than others to commit crimes or particular types of crimes. It has been estimated that 14.6 million arrests were made in 1994 for all criminal offenses except traffic violations. Figure 2.5 shows how these arrests were distributed among the offenses. During the 10 years between 1985 and 1994, the number of arrests rose 20 percent. Let us take a close look at the characteristics of the persons arrested.[33]

Age and Crime

Six armed men who have been called the "over-the-hill gang" were arrested trying to rob an elegant bridge and backgammon club in midtown New York City. The robbery began at 10:25 P.M. when the men, wearing rubber gloves and ski masks and armed with two revolvers, a shotgun, and a rifle, forced the customers and employees to lie down in a back room while they loaded a nylon bag with wallets, players' money, and the club's cash box. A club worker slipped out a side door to alert police, who arrived within minutes. They surprised and disarmed one member of the gang, a 48-year-old, whom they found clutching a .22-caliber revolver. They took a .38-caliber revolver from another gang member, 41 years old.

During the scuffle with the officers, one suspect tried to escape, fell, and broke his nose. The officers then found and arrested a 40-year-old man standing in the hallway with a 12-gauge Winchester shotgun. Meanwhile, the other gang members abandoned their gloves and masks and lay down among the people they had robbed. One of the suspects, aged 72, who wore a back brace, complained of chest and back pain as police locked handcuffs on him. He was immediately hospitalized.[34]

In another case, 94-year-old "career criminal" Wesley (Pop) Honeywood, from Jacksonville, Florida, was sentenced to 7 years after he pointed an unloaded gun at another man who warned him not to

PART I OFFENSES

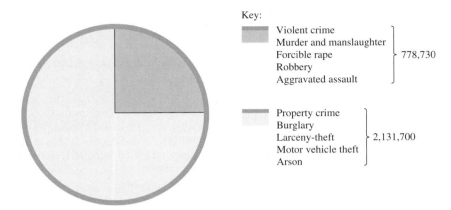

Key:

Violent crime
Murder and manslaughter
Forcible rape   } 778,730
Robbery
Aggravated assault

Property crime
Burglary
Larceny-theft   } 2,131,700
Motor vehicle theft
Arson

PART II OFFENSES

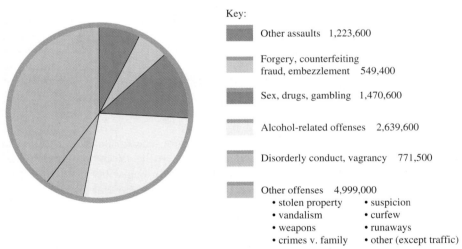

Key:

Other assaults   1,223,600

Forgery, counterfeiting
fraud, embezzlement   549,400

Sex, drugs, gambling   1,470,600

Alcohol-related offenses   2,639,600

Disorderly conduct, vagrancy   771,500

Other offenses   4,999,000
  • stolen property   • suspicion
  • vandalism   • curfew
  • weapons   • runaways
  • crimes v. family   • other (except traffic)

FIGURE 2.5 Distribution of total number of arrests, 1994 (estimated).
Source: U.S. Department of Justice, Federal Bureau of Investigation, *Crime in the United States, 1994* (Washington D.C.: U.S. Government Printing Office, 1995), p. 217.

eat grapes growing in the man's yard. Mr. Honeywood was given the option to go to a nursing home instead of prison, but he resisted, saying "If I go to jail, I may be out in a couple of years. If I go to a nursing home, I may be there the rest of my life."[35]

These cases are extraordinary for at least two reasons. First, in any given year approximately half of all arrests are of individuals under the age of 25; and second, gang membership is ordinarily confined to the young. Though juveniles (young people under 18) constitute about 8 percent of the population, they account for almost one-third of the arrests for Index crimes. Arrest rates begin to decline after age 30 and taper off to about 2 percent or less from age 50 on.[36] In fact, although people aged 65 and over constitute 12.6 percent of the population, they make up fewer than 1 percent of arrests.[37] This decline in criminal activities with age is known as the **aging-out phenomenon.** The reasons for it have sparked a lively scientific debate. Michael Gottfredson and Travis Hirschi contend there is a certain inclination to commit crimes which peaks in the middle or late teens and then declines throughout life. This relationship between crime and age does not change, "regardless of sex, race, country, time, or offense."[38]

Crime decreases with age, the researchers add, even among people who commit frequent offenses. Thus differences in crime rates found among young people of various groups, such as men and women or lower class and middle class, will be maintained throughout the life cycle. If lower-class youths are three times more likely to commit crimes than middle-class youths, for instance, then 60-year-old lower-class persons will be three times more likely to commit crimes than 60-year-old middle-class persons, though crimes committed by both lower-class and middle-class groups will constantly decline.[39] According to this argument, all offenders commit fewer crimes as they grow older because they have less strength, less mobility, and so on.

James Q. Wilson and Richard Herrnstein support the view that the aging-out phenomenon is a natural part of the life cycle.[40] Teenagers may become increasingly independent of their parents yet lack the resources to support themselves; they band together with other young people who are equally frustrated in their search for legitimate ways to get money, sex, alcohol, and status. Together they find illegitimate sources. With adulthood, the small gains from criminal behavior no longer seem so attractive. Legitimate means open up. They marry. Their peers no longer endorse lawbreaking. They learn to delay gratification. Petty crime is no longer adventurous.[41] It is at this time that the aging-out process begins for most individuals. Even the ones who continue to commit offenses will eventually slow down with increasing age.[42]

The opposing side in this debate argues that the decrease in crime rates after adolescence does not imply that the number of crimes committed by all individual offenders declines. In other words, the frequency of offending may go down for most offenders, but some chronic active offenders may continue to commit the same amount of crime over time. Why might this be so? Because the factors that influence any individual's entrance into criminal activity vary, the number and types of offenses committed vary, and the factors that eventually induce the individual to give up criminal activity vary.[43]

According to this argument, the frequency of criminal involvement, then, depends on such social factors as economic situation, peer pressure, and lifestyle; and it is these social factors that explain the aging-out phenomenon. A teenager's unemployment, for example, may have very little to do with the onset of criminal activity because the youngster is not yet in the labor force and still lives at home. Unemployment may increase an adult's rate of offending, however, because an adult requires income to support various responsibilities. Thus the relationship between age and crime is not the same for all offenders. Various conditions during the life cycle affect individuals' behavior in different ways.

Two very old inmates in the geriatric unit at Estelle Prison, Huntsville, Texas: an increasing burden for custodial care.

Two very young lawbreakers in Los Angeles: an increasing burden for custodial care.

To learn how the causes of crime vary at different ages, Alfred Blumstein and his colleagues suggest that we study **criminal careers,** a concept that describes the onset of criminal activity, the types and amount of crime committed, and the termination of such activity.[44] **Longitudinal studies** of a particular group of people over time should enable researchers to uncover the factors that distinguish criminals from noncriminals and those that differentiate among criminals in regard to the number and kinds of offenses they commit.

Those who are involved in research on criminal careers assume that offenders who commit 10 crimes may differ from those who commit 1 or 15. They ask: Are the factors that cause the second offense the same ones that cause the fourth or the fifth? Do different factors move one offender from theft to rape or from assault to shoplifting? How many persons in a **birth cohort** (a group of people born in the same year) will become criminals? Of those, how many will become career criminals (chronic offenders)?

Starting in the 1960s, researchers at the Sellin Center of the University of Pennsylvania began a search for answers. Their earliest publication, in 1972, detailed the criminal careers of 9945 boys (a cohort) born in Philadelphia in 1945. Marvin Wolfgang, Robert Figlio, and Thorsten Sellin obtained their data from school records and official police reports. Their major findings were that 35 percent of the boys had had contact with the police before reaching their eighteenth birthday; of those boys, 46 percent were one-time offenders and 54 percent were repeat offenders. Eighteen percent of those with police contact had committed five or more offenses; they represented 6 percent of the total. The "chronic 6 percent," as they are now called, were responsible for more than half of all the offenses committed, including 71 percent of the homicides, 73 percent of the rapes, 82 percent of the robberies, and 69 percent of the assaults.[45]

Research continued on 10 percent of the boys in the original cohort until they reached the age of 30. This sample was divided into three groups: those who had records of offenses only as juveniles, those who had records only as adults, and those who were persistent offenders with both juvenile and adult records. Though they made up only 15 percent of the follow-up group, those who had been chronic juvenile offenders made up 74 percent of all the arrests. Thus chronic juvenile offenders do indeed continue to break laws as adults.[46]

The boys in the original cohort were born in 1945. Researchers questioned whether the same behavior patterns would continue over the years. Criminologist Paul Tracy and his associates found the answer in a second study, which examined a cohort of 13,160 males born in 1958. The two studies show similar results. In the second cohort, 33 percent had had contact with the police before reaching their eighteenth birthday, 42 percent were one-time offenders, and 58 percent were repeat offenders. Chronic delinquents were found in both cohorts. The chronic delinquents in the second cohort, however, accounted for a greater percentage of the cohort—7.5 percent. They also were involved in more serious and injurious acts than the previous group.

The 1945 cohort study did not contain females, so no overall comparisons can be made over time. But comparing women to men in the 1958 cohort, we see significant gender differences. Of the 14,000 females in the cohort, 14 percent had had contact with the police before age 18. Among the female delinquents, 60 percent were one-time offenders, 33 percent were repeat offenders, and 7 percent were chronic offenders. Overall, female delinquency was less frequent and less likely to involve serious charges.[47]

In another longitudinal study, researchers followed about 4000 youngsters in Denver, Pittsburgh, and Rochester, New York, for 5 years, 1988 through 1992. By the age of 16, over half the youngsters admitted to committing violent criminal acts. According to Terence P. Thornberry, the principal investigator in Rochester, chronic offenders also accounted for a high percentage of all violent offenses: 15 percent of the youths in the sample were responsible for 75 percent of the acts.[48]

The policy implications of such findings are clear. If a very small group of offenders is committing a large percentage of all crime, the crime rate should go down if we incarcerate those offenders for long periods of time. Many jurisdictions around the country are developing sentencing policies to do just that, but such policies are quite controversial.

Gender and Crime

Except for such crimes as prostitution, shoplifting, and welfare fraud, males traditionally commit more crimes than females at all ages. According to the UCR for 1994, the arrest ratio is typically about 4 male offenders to 1 female offender.[49] The NCVS of 1993 reports a wider gap: For personal crimes of violence involving a single offender, 83 percent of victims perceived the gender of the offender as male.[50]

Since the 1960s, however, there have been some interesting developments in regard to gender and crime data. In 1960 females accounted for 11 percent of the total number of arrests across the country. They now account for 19 percent. And while the female arrest rate is still much lower than that of males, the rate of increase for women has risen faster than the rate for men.[51]

Self-report surveys, which show more similarities in male and female criminal activity than official reports do, find that males commit more offenses than females. However, several of these studies suggest that gender differences in crime may be narrowing. They demonstrate that the patterns and causes of male and female delinquent activity are becoming

Female gang member in action: Women criminals have traditionally been perceived as less violent than men, but the gender differences in crime may be narrowing.

more alike.[52] John Hagan and his associates agree, but only with respect to girls raised in middle-class egalitarian families in which husband and wife share similar positions of power at home and in the workplace. They argue that girls raised in lower-class, father-dominated households grow up in a "cult of domesticity" that reduces their freedom and thus the likelihood of their delinquency.[53] Researchers Merry Morash and Meda Chesney-Lind disagree. In a study of 1427 adolescents and their caretakers, they found gender differences in delinquency between girls and boys regardless of the type of family in which the youngsters were raised.[54]

Because traditionally women have had such low crime rates, the scientific community and the mass media have generally ignored the subject of female criminality. Both have tended to view female offenders as misguided children who are an embarrassment rather than a threat to society. Only a handful of the world's criminologists have deemed the subject worthy of independent study. Foremost among them was Cesare Lombroso (whom we shall meet again in Chapter 3). His book *The Female Offender* (coauthored by William Ferrero), which appeared in 1895, detailed the physical abnormalities that would predestine some girls to be criminal from birth.[55] Lombroso's findings on male criminals, however, have not stood the test of later scientific research, and his portrayal of the female criminal has been found to be similarly inaccurate.

A little over a generation later, in the 1930s, Sheldon and Eleanor Glueck launched a massive research project on the biological and environmental causes of crime, with a separate inquiry into female offenders. Their conclusions were decidedly sociological. They said, in essence, that in order to change the incidence of female criminality, there would have to be a change in the social circumstances in which females grow up.[56]

Otto Pollack shared the Gluecks' views on sociological determinants. In 1952 he proposed that female crime has a "masked character" that keeps it from being properly recorded or otherwise noted in statistical reports. Protective attitudes toward women make police officers less willing to arrest them, make victims less eager to report their offenses, make district attorneys less enthusiastic about prosecuting them, and make juries less likely to find them guilty. Moreover, Pollack noted that women's social roles as homemakers, child rearers, and shoppers furnish them with opportunities for concealed criminal activity and with victims who are the least likely to complain and/or cooperate with the police. He also argued that female crime was limited by the various psychological and physiological characteristics inherent in the female anatomy.[57]

A quarter of a century after Pollack's work, two researchers, working independently, took a fresh look at female crime in light of women's new roles in society. In 1975 Freda Adler posited that as social and economic roles of women changed in the legitimate world, their participation in crime would also change. According to this argument, the temptations, challenges, stresses, and strains to which women have been increasingly subjected in recent years cause them to act or react in the same manner in which men have consistently reacted to the same stimuli. In other words, equalization of social and economic roles leads to similar behavior patterns, both legal and illegal, on the part of both men and women. To steal a car, for example, one needs to know how to drive. To embezzle, one needs to be in a position of trust and in control of funds. To get into a bar fight, one needs to go to a bar. To be an inside trader on Wall Street, one needs to be on the inside.[58]

Rita Simon has taken a similar position. She, too, has argued that female criminality has undergone changes. But these changes, according to Simon, have occurred only in regard to certain property crimes, such as larceny/theft and fraud/embezzlement. Women are becoming more involved in these crimes because they have more opportunities to commit them. Simon hypothesizes that since the propensity of men and women to commit crime is not basically different, as more women enter the labor force and work in a much broader range of jobs, their property crime rate will continue to go up.[59]

Some criminologists have challenged the views of Adler and Simon. Many questions have been asked about the so-called new female criminal. Does she exist? If so, does she commit more crimes than the old female criminal did? What types of crimes? Is she still involved primarily in offenses against property, or has she turned to more violent offenses? Researchers differ on the answers. Some contend that the extent of female criminality has not changed through the years but that crimes committed by women are more often making their way into official statistics simply because they are more often reported and prosecuted. In other words, the days of chivalry in the criminal justice system are over.[60]

Others argue that female crime has indeed increased, but they attribute the increase to nonviolent, petty property offenses that continue to reflect traditional female gender roles.[61] Moreover, some investigators claim, the increased involvement in these petty property offenses suggests that women are still economically disadvantaged, still suffering sexism in the legitimate marketplace.[62] Other researchers support the contention of Adler and Simon that female roles have changed and that these changes have indeed led women to commit the same kinds of crimes as men, violent as well as property offenses.[63]

Though scholars disagree on the form and extent of female crime, they do seem to agree that the crimes women commit are closely associated with their socioeconomic position in society. The controversy has to do with whether or not that position has changed. In any case, the association between gender and crime has become a recognized area of concern in the growing body of research dealing with contemporary criminological issues.[64]

Social Class and Crime

Researchers agree on the importance of age and gender as factors related to crime, but they disagree strongly about whether social class is related to crime. First of all, the term "class" can have many meanings. If "lower class" is defined by income, then the category might include graduate students, unemployed stockbrokers, pensioners, welfare mothers, prison inmates, and many others who have little in common except low income. Furthermore, "lower class" is often defined by the low prestige associated with blue-collar occupations. Some delinquency studies determine the class of young people by the class of their fathers, even though the young people may have jobs quite different from those of their fathers.

Another dispute focuses on the source of statistics used by investigators. Many researchers attribute the relatively strong association between class and crime found in arrest statistics to class bias on the part of the police. If the police are more likely to arrest a lower-class suspect than a middle-class suspect, they say, arrest data will show more involvement of lower-class people in criminality whether or not they are actually committing more crimes. When Charles Tittle, Wayne Villemez, and Douglas Smith analyzed 35 studies of the relationship between social class and crime rates in 1978, they found little support for the claim that crime is primarily a lower-class phenomenon. An update of that work, which evaluates studies done between 1978 and 1990, again found no pervasive relationship.[65]

Many scholars have challenged such conclusions. They claim that when self-report studies are used for analysis, the results show few class differences because the studies ask only about trivial offenses. Delbert Elliott and Suzanne Ageton, for example, looked at serious crimes among a national sample of

Rogue trader Nicholas Leeson, who caused the collapse of Barings Bank, with his wife as he was extradited to Singapore in November 1995. He was later sentenced to six and a half years in prison for cheating on Singapore's financial futures market.

1726 young people ages 11 to 17. According to the youths' responses to a self-report questionnaire, lower-class young people were much more likely than middle-class young people to commit such serious crimes as burglary, robbery, assault, and sexual assault.[66] A follow-up study concluded that middle-class and lower-class youths differed significantly in both the nature and the number of serious crimes they committed.[67]

Controversies remain about the social class of people who commit crimes. There is no controversy, however, about the social class of people in prison. The probability that a person such as Dan Rostenkowski, former chairman of the federal House of Representatives Ways and Means Committee who was convicted for mail fraud, will get a prison sentence is extremely low. Rostenkowski does not fit the typical profile of the hundreds of thousands of inmates of our nation's jails and prisons. He is educated. Only 28 percent of prison inmates have completed high school.[68] His income was that of a high-ranking politician. The average yearly income of jail inmates who work is $5600. He had a white-collar job. Eighty-five percent of prison inmates are blue-collar workers. He committed a white-collar offense. Only 18 percent of those convicted of such offenses go to prison for more than 1 year, whereas 39 percent of the violent offenders and 26 percent of the property offenders do.[69] Finally, Dan Rostenkowski is white in a criminal justice system where blacks are disproportionately represented.

Race and Crime

Statistics on race and crime show that while blacks constitute 12 percent of the population, they account for 30 percent of all arrests for Index crimes.[70] Other statistics confirm their disproportionate representation in the criminal justice system. Fifty percent of black urban males are arrested for an Index crime at least once during their lives, compared with fourteen percent of white males. The likelihood that any man will serve time in jail or prison is estimated to be 18 percent for blacks and 3 percent for whites. Moreover, the leading cause of death among young black men is murder.[71]

These statistics raise many questions. Do blacks actually commit more crimes? Or are they simply arrested more often? Are black neighborhoods under more police surveillance than white neighborhoods?

Do blacks receive differential treatment in the criminal justice system? If blacks commit more crimes than whites, why?

Some data support the argument that there are more blacks in the criminal justice system because bias operates from the time of arrest through incarceration. Other data support the argument that racial disparities in official statistics reflect an actual difference in criminal behavior. Much of the evidence comes from the statistics of the NCVS, which are very similar to the statistics on race found in arrest data. When interviewers asked victims about the race of offenders in violent crimes, 28 percent identified the assailants as black.[72] Similarly, while self-report data demonstrate that less serious juvenile offenses are about equally prevalent among black and white youngsters, more serious ones are not: Black youngsters report having committed many more Index crimes than do whites of comparable ages.[73]

If the disparity in criminal behavior suggested by official data, victimization studies, and self-reports actually exists, and if we are to explain it, we have to try to discover why people commit crimes. A history of hundreds of years of abuse, neglect, and discrimination against black Americans has left its mark in the form of high unemployment, residence in socially disorganized areas, one-parent households, and negative self-images.[74]

In 1968, in the aftermath of the worst riots in modern American history, the National Advisory Commission on Civil Disorders alluded to the reasons blacks had not achieved the successes accomplished by other minority groups that at one time or another were discriminated against as well. European immigrants provided unskilled labor needed by industry. By the time blacks migrated from rural areas to cities, the U.S. economy was changing and soon there was no longer much demand for unskilled labor. Immigrant groups had also received economic advantages by working for local political organizations. By the time blacks moved to the cities, the political machines no longer had the power to offer help in return for votes. Though both immigrants and blacks arrived in cities with little money, all but the very youngest members of the cohesive immigrant family contributed to the family's income. As slaves, however, black persons had been forbidden to marry, and the unions they formed were subject to disruption at the owner's convenience and therefore tended to be unstable. We will have more to say about the causal factors associated with high crime rates and race in Chapters 5 and 6.

REVIEW

Researchers have three main objectives in measuring crime and criminal behavior patterns. They need (1) to collect and analyze data to test theories about why people commit crime, (2) to learn the situational characteristics of crimes in order to develop prevention strategies, and (3) to determine the needs of the criminal justice system on a daily basis. Data are collected by surveys, experiments, nonparticipant and participant observation, and case studies. It is often cost-effective to use repositories of information gathered by public and private organizations for their own purposes. The three main sources of data for measuring crime are the Uniform Crime Reports, the National Crime Victimization Survey, and self-report questionnaires. Though each source is useful for some purposes, all three have limitations.

By measuring the characteristics of crime and criminals, we can identify crime trends, the places and times at which crimes are most likely to be committed, and the public's evaluation of the seriousness of offenses. Current controversies concerning offenders focus on the relationship between crime and age throughout the life cycle, the changing role of women in crime, and the effects of social class and race on the response of the criminal justice system. Crime is an activity disproportionately engaged in by young people, males, and minorities.

NOTES

1. James O. Finckenauer, *Scared Straight and the Panacea Phenomenon* (Englewood Cliffs, N.J.: Prentice-Hall, 1982).
2. Personal communication from Anne Campbell. Based on Campbell, *The Girls in the Gang: A Report from New York City* (New York: Basil Blackwell, 1984).
3. Edwin H. Sutherland, *The Professional Thief* (Chicago: University of Chicago Press, 1937).
4. Marvin E. Wolfgang, "Ethics and Research," in *Ethics, Public Policy, and Criminal Justice*, ed. A. F. Ellison and N. Bowie (Cambridge, Mass.: Oelgeschlager, Gunn & Hain, 1982).
5. Frank E. Hagan, *Research Methods in Criminal Justice and Criminology* (New York: Macmillan, 1989), p. 358.
6. Seth A. Bloomberg and Leslie Wilkins, "Ethics of Research involving Human Subjects in Criminal Justice," *Crime and Delinquency*, **23** (1977): 435–444.
7. Lawrence Sherman and Barry Glick, "The Quality of Arrest Statistics," *Police Foundation Reports*, **2** (1984): 1–8.
8. Michael Couzens, "Getting the Crime Rate Down: Political Pressure and Crime Reporting," *Law and Society Review*, **8** (1974): 457–493.
9. President's Commission on Law Enforcement and Administration of Justice, *The Challenge of Crime in a Free Society* (Washington, D.C.: U.S. Government Printing Office, 1967), p. 25.
10. Patrick Jackson, "Assessing the Validity of Official Data on Arson," *Criminology*, **26** (1988): 181–195.
11. For a new method of describing statistics of UCR, see James J. Hennessy and Laurie Kepecs-Schlussel, "Psychometric Scaling Techniques Applied to Rates of Crime and Victimization: I. Major Population Centers," *Journal of Offender Rehabilitation*, **18** (1992): 1–80.
12. Patrick G. Jackson, "Sources of Data," in *Measurement Issues in Criminology*, ed. Kimberly L. Kempf (New York: Springer-Verlag, 1990), p. 42.
13. *Demonstrating the Operational Utility of Incident-Based Data for Local Crime Analysis* (Washington, D.C.: Bureau of Justice Statistics, 1994), p. 1.
14. Victoria L. Major, "UCR's Blueprint for the Future," *FBI Law Enforcement Bulletin*, **61** (1992): 15–21. See also Brian A. Reaves, *Using NIBRS Data to Analyze Violent Crime* (Washington, D.C.: Bureau of Justice Statistics, 1993).
15. For a comparison of victimization data with official police data, see Alfred Blumstein, Jacqueline Cohen, and Richard Rosenfeld, "Trend and Deviation in Crime Rates: A Comparison of UCR and NCS Data for Burglary and Robbery," *Criminology*, **29** (1991): 237–263; Scott Menard, "Residual Gains, Reliability, and the UCR-NCS Relationship: A Comment on Blumstein, Cohen, and Rosenfeld," *Criminology*, **30** (1992): 105–113; Alfred Blumstein, Jacqueline Cohen, and Richard Rosenfeld, "The UCR-NCR Relationship Revisited: A Reply to Menard," *Criminology*, **30** (1992): 115–124; and David McDowall and Colin Loftin, "Comparing the UCR and NSC over Time," *Criminology*, **30** (1992): 125–132. For a discussion of disparity in rape rates between UCR and NCVS, see Gary F. Jensen and Mary Altani Karpos, "Managing Rape: Exploratory Research on the Behavior of Rape Statistics," *Criminology*, **31** (1993): 363–385.
16. James Levine, "The Potential for Crime Over-reporting in Criminal Victimization Surveys," *Criminology*, **14** (1976): 307–330. See also Helen M. Eigenberg, "The National Crime Survey and Rape: The Case of the Missing Question," *Justice Quarterly*, **7** (1990): 655–672.
17. James S. Wallerstein and Clement J. Wyle, "Our Law-Abiding Law-Breakers," *Probation*, **25** (March–April 1947): 107–112.
18. Martin Gold, "Undetected Delinquent Behavior," *Journal of Research in Crime and Delinquency*, **3** (1966): 27–46; David Farrington, "Self-Reports of Deviant Behavior: Predictive and Stable?" *Journal of Criminal Law and Criminology*, **64** (1973): 99–110.
19. D. Wayne Osgood, Lloyd Johnston, Patrick O'Malley, and Jerald Bachman, "The Generality of Deviance in Late Adolescence and Early Adulthood," *American Sociological Review*, **53** (1988): 81–93.
20. Franklin Dunford and Delbert Elliott, "Identifying Career Offenders Using Self-Reported Data," *Journal of Research in Crime and Delinquency*, **21** (1983): 57–86.

21. Josine Junger-Tas, Gert-Jan Terlouw, and Malcolm W. Klein, eds., *Delinquent Behavior among Young People in the Western World* (Amsterdam: Kugler, 1994).

22. Michael Hindelang, Travis Hirschi, and Joseph Weis, *Measuring Delinquency* (Beverly Hills, Calif.: Sage, 1981).

23. Tom Squitieri, "Soaring Murder Rate 'Tears Apart' Charlotte," *USA Today,* Jan. 31, 1992, p. 6A.

24. U.S. Department of Justice, Federal Bureau of Investigation, *Crime in the United States, 1992* (hereafter cited as Uniform Crime Reports) (Washington, D.C.: U.S. Government Printing Office, 1993), p. 140; Uniform Crime Reports, 1986, p. 94.

25. Uniform Crime Reports, 1994, p. 58.

26. U.S. Department of Justice, Bureau of Justice Statistics, *Criminal Victimization, 1994* (Washington, D.C.: U.S. Government Printing Office, April 1996), p. 2.

27. Uniform Crime Reports, 1994, p. 58.

28. For a discussion of the relationship of unemployment, drugs, and family breakdown to rising crime rates, see George B. Palermo, Maurice B. Smith, John J. Di Motto, and Thomas P. Christopher, "Soaring Crime in a Midwestern American City: A Statistical Analysis," *International Journal of Offender Therapy and Comparative Criminology,* **36** (1992): 291–305.

29. U.S. Department of Justice, Bureau of Justice Statistics, *Criminal Victimization in the United States, 1993* (Washington, D.C.: U.S. Government Printing Office, May 1996), p. 67.

30. U.S. Department of Justice, Bureau of Justice Statistics, *Highlights from 20 Years of Surveying Crime Victims* (Washington, D.C.: U.S. Government Printing Office, October 1993), pp. 6–7.

31. Derral Cheatwood, "The Effects of Weather on Homicide," *Journal of Quantitative Criminology,* **11** (1995): 51–70.

32. U.S. Department of Justice, *The Severity of Crime,* Bureau of Justice Statistics Bulletin (Washington, D.C.: U.S. Government Printing Office, January 1984).

33. Uniform Crime Reports, 1994, pp. 217, 221.

34. James C. McKinley, Jr., "Six Armed Men, Aged 40–72, Held in Bungled Robbery of a Club," *New York Times,* Apr. 20, 1989, p. D6.

35. *New York Times,* Nov. 6, 1994, p. 24.

36. Uniform Crime Reports, 1992, pp. 227–228.

37. U.S. Bureau of the Census, *Statistical Abstract of the United States: 1994* (Washington, D.C.: U.S. Government Printing Office, 1994).

38. Michael Gottfredson and Travis Hirschi, "The True Value of Lambda Would Appear to Be Zero: An Essay on Career Criminals, Criminal Careers, Selective Incapacitation, Cohort Studies, and Related Topics," *Criminology,* **24** (1986): 213–234.

39. Michael Gottfredson and Travis Hirschi, "Science, Public Policy, and the Career Paradigm," *Criminology,* **26** (1988): 37–55. For a critique of Hirschi and Gottfredson's contentions, see Darrell J. Steffensmeier, Emilie Anderson Allan, Miles D. Harer, and Cathy Streifel, "Age and the Distribution of Crime," *American Journal of Sociology,* **94** (1989): 803–831. For a test of those contentions, see Sung Joon Jang and Marvin D. Krohn, "Developmental Patterns of Sex Differences in Delinquency among African American Adolescents: A Test of the Sex-Invariance Hypothesis," *Journal of Quantitative Criminology,* **11** (1995): 195–222.

40. James Q. Wilson and Richard Herrnstein, *Crime and Human Nature* (New York: Simon & Schuster, 1985), pp. 126–147.

41. Gordon Trasler, "Some Cautions for a Biological Approach to Crime Causation," in *The Causes of Crime: New Biological Approaches,* ed. Sarnoff Mednick, Terrie Moffitt, and Susan Stack (Cambridge: Cambridge University Press, 1987), pp. 7–24.

42. Charles Tittle, "Two Empirical Regularities (Maybe) in Search of an Explanation: Commentary on the Age/Crime Debate," *Criminology,* **26** (1988): 75–85.

43. Alfred Blumstein, Jacqueline Cohen, and David Farrington, "Criminal Career Research: Its Value for Criminology," *Criminology,* **26** (1988): 1–35.

44. Alfred Blumstein, Jacqueline Cohen, Jeffrey Roth, and Christy Visher, *Criminal Careers and "Career Criminals"* (Washington, D.C.: National Academy Press, 1986). On the relationship between crime and age, see Robert J. Sampson and John H. Laub, *Crime in the Making: Pathways and Turning Points through Life* (Cambridge, Mass.: Harvard University Press, 1993); Neal Shover and Carol Y. Thompson, "Age, Differential Expectations, and Crime Desistance," *Criminology,* **30** (1992): 89–104; David F. Greenberg, "The Historical Variability of the Age-Crime Relationship," *Journal of Quantitative Criminology,* **10** (1994): 361–373; Daniel S. Nagin, David P. Farrington, and Terrie E. Moffitt, "Life-Course Trajectories of Different Types of Offenders," *Criminology,* **33** (1995): 111–139; and Julie Horney, Wayne Osgood, and Ineke Haen Marshall, "Criminal Careers in the Short-Term: Intra-individual Variability in Crime and Its Relation to Local Life Circumstances," *American Sociological Review,* **60** (1995): 655–673.

45. Marvin Wolfgang, Robert Figlio, and Thorsten Sellin, *Delinquency in a Birth Cohort* (Chicago: University of Chicago Press, 1972). For a discussion of how each delinquent act was weighted for seriousness, see Thorsten Sellin and Marvin Wolfgang, *The Measurement of Delinquency* (New York: Wiley, 1964). See also Douglas A. Smith, Christy A. Visher, and G. Roger Jarjoura, "Dimensions of Delinquency: Exploring the Correlates of Participation, Frequency, and Persistence of Delinquent Behavior," *Journal of Research in Crime and Delinquency,* **28** (1990): 6–32.

46. Marvin E. Wolfgang, Terence Thornberry, and Robert Figlio, *From Boy to Man, from Delinquency to Crime* (Chicago: University of Chicago Press, 1987).

47. Paul E. Tracy, Marvin E. Wolfgang, and Robert M. Figlio, *Delinquency Careers in Two Birth Cohorts* (New York: Plenum, 1990), pp. 275–280; Paul E. Tracy, Marvin E. Wolfgang, and Robert M. Figlio, Executive Summary, *Delinquency in Two Birth Cohorts,* U.S. Department of Justice (Washington, D.C.: U.S. Government Printing Office, September 1985), pp. 5–11.

48. Terence P. Thornberry, "What's Working and What's Not Working in Safeguarding Our Children and Preventing Violence," Safeguarding Our Youth: Violence Prevention for Our Nation's Children, speech presented at Department of Education, Washington, D.C., July 20, 1993.

49. Uniform Crime Reports, 1994, p. 234.

50. *Criminal Victimization in the United States, 1993,* p. 43.

51. U.S. Department of Justice, *Report to the Nation on Crime and Justice,* 2d ed. (Washington, D.C.: U.S. Government Printing Office, 1988), p. 230.

52. Delbert Elliott and Suzanne Ageton, "Reconciling Race and Class Differences in Self-Reported and Official Estimates of Delinquency," *American Sociological Review,* **45** (1980):

95–110; and Roy L. Austin, "Recent Trends in Official Male and Female Crime Rates: The Convergence Controversy," *Journal of Criminal Justice*, **21** (1993): 447–466.

53. John Hagan, John Simpson, and A. R. Gillis, "Class in the Household: A Power Control Theory of Gender and Delinquency," *American Journal of Sociology*, **92** (1987): 788–816. See also Gary F. Jensen, John Hagan, and A. R. Gillis, "Power-Control vs. Social Control Theories of Common Delinquency: A Comparative Analysis," in *New Directions in Criminological Theory*, ed. Freda Adler and William S. Laufer (New Brunswick, N.J.: Transaction, 1993), pp. 363–398.

54. Merry Morash and Meda Chesney-Lind, "A Reformulation and Partial Test of the Power Control Theory of Delinquency," *Justice Quarterly*, **8** (1991): 347–377.

55. Cesare Lombroso and William Ferrero, *The Female Offender* (London: T. Fisher Unwin, 1895).

56. Sheldon Glueck and Eleanor T. Glueck, *Five Hundred Delinquent Women* (New York: Knopf, 1934).

57. Otto Pollack, *The Criminality of Women* (Philadelphia: University of Pennsylvania Press, 1950).

58. Freda Adler, *Sisters in Crime* (New York: McGraw-Hill, 1975), pp. 6–7.

59. Rita Simon, *The Contemporary Woman and Crime* (Rockville, Md.: National Institute of Mental Health, 1975).

60. Meda Chesney-Lind, "Female Offenders: Paternalism Reexamined," in *Women, the Courts, and Equality*, ed. Laura Crites and Winifred Hepperle (Newbury Park, Calif.: Sage, 1987).

61. Darrell J. Steffensmeier, "Crime and the Contemporary Woman: An Analysis of Changing Levels of Female Property Crimes, 1960–1975," *Social Forces*, **57** (1978): 566–584; Lee H. Bowker, *Women, Crime, and the Criminal Justice System* (Lexington, Mass.: Heath, 1978). For a description of the typical female offender, see Nancy T. Wolfe, Francis T. Cullen, and John B. Cullen, "Describing the Female Offender: A Note on the Demographics of Arrests," *Journal of Criminal Justice*, **12** (1984): 483–492.

62. Mary E. Gilfus, "From Victims to Survivors to Offenders: Women's Routes of Entry and Immersion into Street Crime," *Women and Criminal Justice*, **4** (1992): 63–89; and Sally S. Simpson and Lori Ellis, "Doing Gender: Sorting Out the Caste and Crime Conundrum," *Criminology*, **33** (1995): 47–81. For a discussion of the internalization of gender roles by female prisoners, see Edna Erez, "The Myth of the New Female Offender: Some Evidence from Attitudes toward Law and Justice," *Journal of Criminal Justice*, **16** (1988): 499–509.

63. Nanci Koser Wilson, "The Masculinity of Violent Crime—Some Second Thoughts," *Journal of Criminal Justice*, **9** (1981): 111–123; Ronald L. Simons, Martin G. Miller, and Stephen M. Aigner, "Contemporary Theories of Deviance and Female Delinquency: An Empirical Test," *Journal of Research in Crime and Delinquency*, **17** (1980): 42–57.

64. For a discussion of a unisex theory of crime, see Coramae Richey Mann, *Female Crime and Delinquency* (Tuscaloosa: University of Alabama Press, 1984). For an analysis of the relation of both gender and race to crime, see Vernetta D. Young, "Women, Race, and Crime," *Criminology*, **18** (1980): 26–34; Gary D. Hill and Elizabeth M. Crawford, "Women, Race, and Crime," *Criminology*, **28** (1990): 601–626; and Sally S. Simpson, "Caste, Class, and Violent Crime: Explaining Differences in Female Offending," *Criminology*, **29** (1991):

115–136. For a discussion of female crime in countries around the world, see Freda Adler, ed., *The Incidence of Female Criminality in the Contemporary World* (New York: New York University Press, 1984). See also Freda Adler and Rita James Simon, eds., *The Criminology of Deviant Women* (Boston: Houghton Mifflin, 1979). For other sources on the subject of female crime, see Victoria E. Brewster and M. Dwayne Smith, "Gender Inequality and Rates of Female Homicide Victimization across U.S. Cities," *Journal of Research in Crime and Delinquency*, **32** (1995): 175–190; R. Barri Flowers, *Female Crime, Criminals and Cellmates: An Exploration of Female Criminality and Delinquency* (Jefferson, N.C.: McFarland & Company, 1995); R. Emerson Dobash, Russell P. Dobash, and Lesley Noaks, eds., *Gender and Crime* (Cardiff: University of Wales Press, 1995); and Ruth Triplett and Laura B. Myers, "Evaluating Contextual Patterns of Delinquency: Gender-Based Differences," *Justice Quarterly*, **12** (1995): 59–84.

65. Charles Tittle, Wayne Villemez, and Douglas Smith, "The Myth of Social Class and Criminality: An Empirical Assessment of the Empirical Evidence," *American Sociological Review*, **43** (1978): 643–656; Charles R. Tittle and Robert F. Meier, "Specifying the SES/Delinquency Relationship," *Criminology*, **28** (1990): 271–299.

66. Elliott and Ageton, "Reconciling Race and Class Differences."

67. Delbert Elliott and David Huizinga, "Social Class and Delinquent Behavior in a National Youth Panel: 1976–1980," *Criminology*, **21** (1983): 149–177.

68. The data on socioeconomic factors come from U.S. Department of Justice, *Report to the Nation on Crime and Justice*, pp. 48–49.

69. U.S. Department of Justice, Bureau of Justice Statistics, *Annual Report, Fiscal 1986* (Washington, D.C.: U.S. Government Printing Office, April 1987), p. 39.

70. Uniform Crime Reports, 1994, p. 235. See also Gary La Free, Kriss A. Drass, and Patrick O'Day, "Race and Crime in Postwar America: Determinants of African-American and White Rates, 1957–1988," *Criminology*, **30** (1992): 157–188.

71. Joan Petersilia, "Racial Disparities in the Criminal Justice System: A Summary," *Crime and Delinquency*, **31** (1985): 15–34.

72. *Criminal Victimization in the United States, 1993*, p. 44.

73. Delbert Elliott and Harwin Voss, *Delinquency and Dropout* (Lexington, Mass.: Lexington Books, 1974).

74. Robert J. Sampson, "Urban Black Violence: The Effect of Male Joblessness and Family Disruption," *American Journal of Sociology*, **93** (1987): 348–382.

▮ Internet Exercise

The National Crime Victimization Survey tells us how many rapes, sexual assaults, other assaults, robberies, thefts, household burglaries, and motor vehicle thefts U.S. residents age 12 or older and their households experience each year. What are the most recent findings of the survey?

▮ **Your Web Site is: http://www.ojp.usdoj.gov/bja**

CHAPTER 3

Schools of Thought
throughout History

Classical Criminology

    The Historical Context

    Cesare Beccaria

    Jeremy Bentham's Utilitarianism

    The Classical School: An Evaluation

Positivist Criminology

Biological Determinism: The Search for Criminal Traits

    Lombroso, Ferri, Garofalo: The Italian School

    A Return to Biological Determinism

Psychological Determinism

    Pioneers in Criminal Psychology

    Psychological Studies of Criminals

Sociological Determinism

    Adolphe Quételet and André Michel Guerry

    Gabriel Tarde

    Émile Durkheim

Historical and Contemporary Criminology: A Time Line

Review

Notes

    Special Features

        WINDOW TO THE WORLD: Stone Age Crime and Social Control

        CRIMINOLOGICAL FOCUS: The Mismeasure of Man

        AT ISSUE: Somatotyping: A Physique for Crime?

Key Terms

anomie
atavistic stigmata
born criminal
classical school of
  criminology
eugenics
laws of imitation
phrenology
physiognomy
positivist school of
  criminology
somatotype school of
  criminology
utilitarianism

Children now love luxury. They have bad manners, contempt for authority. They show disrespect for elders. They contradict their parents, chatter before company, cross their legs and tyrannize their teachers.

The ideal condition would be, I admit, that men should be right by instinct; but since we are all likely to go astray, the reasonable thing is to learn from those who can teach.

When there is an income tax, the just man will pay more and the unjust less on the same amount of income.[1]

Criminologists traditionally consider that their field has its origins as a science in the eighteenth century, when Cesare Beccaria established what came to be known as the classical school of criminology. But when we look at what some much earlier thinkers had to say about crime, we may have to reconsider this assumption. Look again at the quotations above. The first may appear to be a modern description of delinquent youth, but Socrates made this observation over 2300 years ago. The second quotation, about instinct and learning and their association with criminality, was an observation made by Sophocles, who lived almost 2500 years ago. The final quotation, about income tax fraud, is not taken from a study of American white-collar crime: Plato voiced this insight, in his treatise *The Republic,* in the fourth century B.C.

Scholars, philosophers, and poets have speculated about the causes of crime and possible remedies since ancient times, and modern criminology owes much to the wisdom the ancient philosophers displayed. The philosophical approach culminated in the middle of the eighteenth century in the **classical school of criminology.** It is based on the assumption that individuals choose to commit crimes after weighing the consequences of their actions. According to classical criminologists, individuals have free will. They can choose legal or illegal means to get what they want; fear of punishment can deter them from committing crime; and society can control behavior by making the

WINDOW TO THE WORLD

STONE AGE CRIME AND SOCIAL CONTROL

On a fine Thursday afternoon in September 1991, vacationers from Germany, on an alpine hiking trip, spotted a head protruding from the glacial ice. They hurried to a nearby guest house and reported their find to the innkeeper, who promptly called both the Italian and the Austrian police. It became immediately apparent that this corpse was no ordinary mountain casualty. Rather, this was an ancient mountain casualty. Experts were brought in from Austrian universities, and the body was freed from its icy embrace. It was dubbed "Oetzi," after the Oetztal Alps of the discovery.

Oetzi is 5300 years old, a robust young man, 25 to 30 years old at the time of his death. Completely mummified, he was found in the position in which he had placed himself, in a crevice, probably to escape a snowstorm. He was fully dressed, in an unlined fur robe. Originally fashioned with great skill, the robe was badly repaired with sinew and plant fiber, suggesting that he could not have relied on the services of his wife or the village seamstress for some time. Oetzi had placed his equipment by his side, most of it of the best Stone Age craftsmanship. What is surprising is that he did not carry with him a ready-to-shoot bow.

Investigators determined that Oetzi was an outdoor type, a shep-

Oetzi, who was preserved in the glacial crevice in which he died.

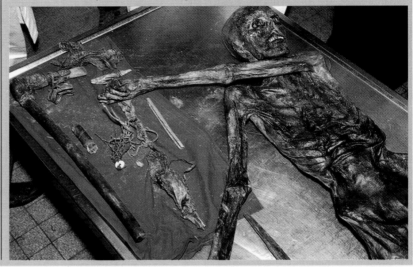

---

pain of punishment greater than the pleasure of the criminal gains.

The classical school did not remain unchallenged for long. In the early nineteenth century great advances were made in the natural sciences and in medicine. Physicians in France, Germany, and England undertook systematic studies of crimes and criminals. Crime statistics became available in several European countries. There emerged an opposing school of criminology, the **positivist school.** This school posits that human behavior is determined by forces beyond individual control and that it is possible to measure those forces. Unlike classical criminologists, who claim that people rationally choose to commit crime, positivist criminologists view criminal behavior as stemming from biological, psychological, and social factors.

The earliest positivist theories centered on biological factors, and studies of these factors dominated criminology during the last half of the nineteenth century. In the twentieth century, biological explanations were ignored (and even targeted as racist after World War II). They did not surface again until the 1970s, when scientific advances in psychology shifted the emphasis from defects in criminals' bodies to defects in their minds. Throughout the twentieth century, psychologists and psychiatrists have played a major role in the study of crime causation. A third area of positivist criminology focuses on the relation of social factors to crime. Sociological theories, developed in the second half of the nineteenth century and advanced throughout the twentieth, continue to dominate the field of criminology today.

An understanding of the foundations of modern criminology helps us to understand contemporary developments in the field. Let us begin with the developments that led to the emergence of the classical school.

herd who sought refuge in the crevice, froze to death, and was preserved for 5 millennia by permafrost and glacial ice. But what was Oetzi doing at 3210 meters (nearly 10,000 feet) above sea level on a fall day? Obviously he was not a herder since he was far above the grazing range of a herd. Nor was he a trader trying to cross the Alps in the fall. So what was he doing up there, where nothing grows and where it is hard to breathe? One possibility suggests itself on the basis of all the evidence available so far. Oetzi may have been an outlaw.

Oetzi was a Late Stone Age (Neolithic) man, likely to have come from a herding community of at most 200 persons. Robert Carneiro of the American Museum of Natural History has figured out that a community of 200 produces 20,000 one-on-one disagreement possibilities. The tasks of social control even within such a small community stagger the imagination. Oetzi may have had such interpersonal problems.

Fighting could have erupted within the community. Jealousy could be engendered about who deserves more respect as the best hunter, the best storyteller, the best healer, or the wisest person. A dispute could have happened over the distribution of food or the sharing of tools.

The evidence about Neolithic society permits us to conclude that these societies have no institution that we could compare to modern criminal justice, although they had problems that today might be referred to a criminal justice system. How were such problems solved? Minor problems were dealt with by the use of shaming, by dispute resolution, by compensation, and by sacrifices. Major unforgivable offenses led to casting out the wrongdoer: They would be declared outlaws. They had to leave camp instantly, without gathering weapons or tools, and flee to the wilderness. Oetzi fits the description of such an outlaw, literally a person cast outside the protection of the laws, the

customs, and the protection of his group, to take to the wilderness and perhaps to die there. If Oetzi was a criminal banished from his village, the punishment clearly was effective.

Source

Adapted from Gerhard O. W. Mueller and Freda Adler, "The Emergence of Criminal Justice: Tracing the Route to Neolithic Times," in *Festskrift till Jacob W. F. Sundberg*, ed. Erik Nerep and Wiweka Warnling Nerep (Stockholm: Jurisförlaget, 1993), pp. 151–170.

Questions for Discussion

1. For purposes of improving modern crime-control techniques, can we learn anything from Stone Age societies?
2. What crimes do you think might result in the banishment of one of the members of such a community?

CLASSICAL CRIMINOLOGY

In the late eighteenth to the mid-nineteenth centuries, during what is now called the neoclassical period, the classical culture of the ancient Mediterranean was rediscovered. This was also a period of scientific discoveries and the founding of new scholarly disciplines. One of these was criminology, which developed as an attempt to apply rationality and the rule of law to brutal and arbitrary criminal justice processes. The work of criminology's founders—scholars like Cesare Beccaria and Jeremy Bentham—became known as "classical" criminology.

The Historical Context

Classical criminology grew out of a reaction against the barbaric system of law, punishment, and justice that existed before the French Revolution of 1789.

Until that time, there was no real system of criminal justice in Europe. There were crimes against the state, against the church, and against the crown. Some of these crimes were specified; some were not. Judges had discretionary power to convict a person for an act not even legally defined as criminal.[2] Monarchs often issued what were called in French *lettres de cachet*, under which an individual could be imprisoned for almost any reason (disobedience to one's father, for example) or for no reason at all.

Many criminal laws were unwritten, and those that had been drafted, by and large, did not specify the kind or amount of punishment associated with various crimes. Arbitrary and often cruel sentences were imposed by judges who had unbounded discretion to decide questions of guilt and innocence and to mete out punishment. "Due process" in the modern sense did not exist. While there was some general consensus on what constituted crime, there was no real limit to the amount and type of legal sanction a court could command. Punishments included branding, burning, flogging, mutilation, drowning, banishment, and beheading.[3] In England a person might receive the death penalty for any of more than 200 offenses, including what we today call petty theft.

Public punishments were popular events. When Robert-François Damiens was scheduled to be executed on March 2, 1757, for the attempted murder of Louis XV, so many people wanted to attend the spectacle that window seats overlooking the execution site were rented for high prices. Torture to elicit confessions was common. A criminal defendant in France might be subjected to the *peine forte et dure,* which consisted of stretching him on his back and placing over him an iron weight as heavy as he could bear. He was left that way until he died or spoke. A man would suffer these torments and lose his life in order to avoid trial and therefore conviction so that his lands and goods would not be confiscated and would be preserved for his family. This proceeding was not abolished until 1772.[4]

Even as Europe grew increasingly modern, industrial, and urban in the eighteenth century, it still clung to its medieval penal practices. With prosperity came an increasing gulf between the haves and the have-nots. Just before the French Revolution, for example, a Parisian worker paid 97 percent of his daily earnings for a 4-pound loaf of bread.[5] Hordes of unemployed people begged by day and found shelter under bridges by night. One of the few ways in which the established upper class could protect itself was through ruthless oppression of those beneath it, but ruthless oppression created more problems. Social unrest grew. And as crime rates rose, so did the brutality of punishment. Both church and state became increasingly tyrannical, using violence to conquer violence.

The growing educated classes began to see the inconsistency in these policies. If terrible tortures were designed to deter crime, why were people committing even more crimes? There must be something wrong with the underlying reasoning. By the mid-eighteenth century, social reformers were beginning to suggest a more rational approach to crime and punishment. One of them, Cesare Beccaria, laid the foundation for the first school of criminology—the classical school.

Cesare Beccaria

Cesare Bonesana, Marchese di Beccaria (1738–1794), was rather undistinguished as a student. After graduating with a law degree from the University of Pavia, he returned home to Milan and joined a group of articulate and radical intellectuals. Disenchanted with contemporary European society, they organized themselves into the Academy of Fists, one of many young men's clubs that flourished in Italy at the time. Their purpose was to discover what reforms would be needed to modernize Italian society.

In March 1763 Beccaria was assigned to prepare a report on the prison system. Pietro Verri, the head of the Academy of Fists, encouraged him to read the works of English and French philosophers—David Hume (1711–1776), John Locke (1632–1704), Claude Adrien Helvétius (1715–1771), Voltaire (1694–1778), Montesquieu (1685–1755), and Jean-Jacques Rousseau (1712–1778). Another member of the academy, the protector of prisons, revealed to him the inhumanities that were possible under the guise of social control. Beccaria learned well. He read, observed, and made notes on small scraps of paper. These notes, Harry Elmer Barnes has observed, were destined to "assure to its author immortality and would work a revolution in the moral world" upon their publication in July 1764 under the title *Dei delitti e delle pene (On Crimes and Punishment).*[6] Beccaria presented a coherent, comprehensive design for an enlightened criminal justice system that was to serve the people rather than the monarchy.

The climate was right: With the publication of this small book, Cesare Beccaria became the "father of modern criminology." The controversy between the rule of men and the rule of law was at its most heated. Some people defended the old order, under which judges and administrators made arbitrary or whimsical decisions. Others fought for the rule of law, under which the decision making of judges and administrators would be confined by legal limitations. Beccaria's words provided the spark that ultimately ended medieval barbarism.

According to Beccaria, the crime problem could be traced not to bad people but to bad laws. A modern criminal justice system should guarantee all people equal treatment before the law. Beccaria's book supplied the blueprint. That blueprint was based on the assumption that people freely choose what they do and are responsible for the consequences of their behavior. Beccaria proposed the following principles:

- *Laws should be used to maintain the social contract.* "Laws are the conditions under which men, naturally independent, united themselves in society. Weary of living in a continual state of war, and of enjoying a liberty, which became of little value, from the uncertainty of its duration, they sacrificed one part of it, to enjoy the rest in peace and security."
- *Only legislators should create laws.* "The authority of making penal laws can only reside with the legislator, who represents the whole society united by the social compact."
- *Judges should impose punishment only in accordance with the law.* "[N]o magistrate then, (as he is one of the society), can, with justice inflict on any other member of the same society punishment that is not ordained by the laws."
- *Judges should not interpret the laws.* "Judges, in criminal cases, have no right to interpret the penal laws, because they are not legislators. . . . Every man hath his own particular point of view, and, at different times, sees the same objects in very different lights. The spirit of the laws will then be the result of the good or bad logic of the judge; and this will depend on his good or bad digestion."
- *Punishment should be based on the pleasure/pain principle.* "Pleasure and pain are the only springs of actions in beings endowed with sensibility. . . . If an equal punishment be ordained for two crimes that injure society in different degrees, there is nothing to deter men from committing the greater as often as it is attended with greater advantage."
- *Punishment should be based on the act, not on the actor.* "Crimes are only to be measured by the injuries done to the society. They err, therefore, who imagine that a crime is greater or less according to the intention of the person by whom it is committed."
- *The punishment should be determined by the crime.* "If mathematical calculation could be applied to the obscure and infinite combinations of human actions, there might be a corresponding scale of punishments descending from the greatest to the least."

- *Punishment should be prompt and effective.* "The more immediate after the commission of a crime a punishment is inflicted, the more just and useful it will be. . . . An immediate punishment is more useful; because the smaller the interval of time between the punishment and the crime, the stronger and more lasting will be the association of the two ideas of crime and punishment."
- *All people should be treated equally.* "I assert that the punishment of a nobleman should in no wise differ from that of the lowest member of society."
- *Capital punishment should be abolished.* "The punishment of death is not authorized by any right; for . . . no such right exists. . . . The terrors of death make so slight an impression, that it has not force enough to withstand the forgetfulness natural to mankind."
- *The use of torture to gain confessions should be abolished.* "It is confounding all relations to expect . . . that pain should be the test of truth, as if truth resided in the muscles and fibres of a wretch in torture. By this method the robust will escape, and the feeble be condemned."
- *It is better to prevent crimes than to punish them.* "Would you prevent crimes? Let the laws be clear and simple, let the entire force of the nation be united in their defence, let them be intended rather to favour every individual than any particular classes. . . . Finally, the most certain method of preventing crime is to perfect the system of education."[7]

Perhaps no other book in the history of criminology has had so great an impact. Beccaria's ideas were so advanced that Voltaire, the great French philosopher of the time, who wrote the commentary for the French version, referred to Beccaria as "brother."[8] The English version appeared in 1767; by that time, 3 years after the book's publication, it had already gone through six Italian editions and several French editions.

After the French Revolution, Beccaria's basic tenets served as a guide for the drafting of the French penal code, which was adopted in 1791. In Russia, Empress Catherine II (the Great) convened a commission to prepare a new code and issued instructions, written in her own hand, to translate Beccaria's ideas into action. The Prussian King Friedrich II (the Great) devoted his reign to revising the Prussian laws according to Beccaria's principles. Emperor Joseph II had a new code drafted for Austria-Hungary in 1787—the first code to abolish capital punishment. The impact of Beccaria's treatise spread across the Atlantic as well: It influenced the first ten amendments to the U.S. Constitution (the Bill of Rights).

Jeremy Bentham's Utilitarianism

Legal scholars and reformers throughout Europe proclaimed their indebtedness to Beccaria, but none owed more to him than the English legal philosopher Jeremy Bentham (1748–1832). Bentham had a long and productive career. He inspired many of his contemporaries, as well as criminologists of future generations, with his approach to rational crime control.

Bentham devoted his life to developing a scientific approach to the making and breaking of laws. Like Beccaria, he was concerned with achieving "the greatest happiness of the greatest number."[9] His work was governed by utilitarian principles. **Utilitarianism** assumes that all human actions are calculated in accordance with their likelihood of bringing happiness (pleasure) or unhappiness (pain). People weigh the probabilities of present and future pleasures against those of present and future pain.

Bentham proposed a precise pseudomathematical formula for this process, which he called "felicific calculus." According to his reasoning, individuals are "human calculators" who put all the factors into an equation in order to decide whether or not a particular crime is worth committing. This notion may seem rather whimsical today, but at a time when there were over 200 capital offenses, it provided a rationale for reform of the legal system.[10] Bentham reasoned that if prevention was the purpose of punishment, and if punishment became too costly by creating more harm than good, then penalties needed to be set just a bit in excess of the pleasure one might derive from committing a crime, and no higher. The law exists in order to create happiness for the community. Since punishment creates unhappiness, it can be justified only if it prevents greater evil than it produces. Thus, Bentham suggested, if hanging a man's effigy produced the same preventive effect as hanging the man himself, there would be no reason to hang the man.

Sir Samuel Romilly, a member of Parliament, met Jeremy Bentham at the home of a mutual friend. He became interested in Bentham's idea that the certainty of punishment outweighs its severity as a deterrent against crime. On February 9, 1810, in a speech before Parliament, he advocated Benthamite ideas:

> So evident is the truth of that maxim that if it were possible that punishment, as the consequence of guilt, could be reduced to an absolute certainty, a very slight penalty would be sufficient to prevent almost every species of crime.[11]

Although conservatives prevented any major changes during Romilly's lifetime, the program of legislative pressure he began was continued by his followers and culminated in the complete reform of English criminal law between 1820 and 1861. During that period the number of capital offenses was reduced from 222 to 3: murder, treason, and piracy. Gradually, from the ideals of the philosophers of the Age of Enlightenment and the principles outlined by the scholars of the classical school, a new social order was created, an order that affirmed a commitment to equal treatment of all people before the law.

The Classical School: An Evaluation

Classical criminology had an immediate and profound impact on jurisprudence and legislation. The rule of law spread rapidly through Europe and the United States. Of no less significance was the influence of the classical school on penal and correctional policy. The classical principle that punishment must be appropriate to the crime was universally accepted during the nineteenth and early twentieth centuries. Yet the classical approach had weaknesses. Critics attacked the simplicity of its argument: The responsibility of the criminal justice system was simply to enforce the law with swiftness and certainty and to treat all people in like fashion, whether the accused were paupers or nobles; government was to be run by the rule of law rather than at the discretion of its officials. In other words, the punishment was to fit the crime, not the criminal. The proposition that human beings had the capacity to choose freely between good and evil was accepted without question. There was no need to ask why people behave as they do, to seek a motive or to ask about the specific circumstances surrounding criminal acts.

During the last half of the nineteenth century, scholars began to challenge these ideas. Influenced by the expanding search for scientific explanations of behavior in place of philosophical ones, criminologists shifted their attention from the act to the actor. They argued that people did not choose of their own free will to commit crime; rather, factors beyond their control were responsible for criminal behavior.

POSITIVIST CRIMINOLOGY

During the late eighteenth century, significant advances in knowledge of both the physical and the social world influenced thinking about crime. Auguste Comte (1798–1857), a French sociologist, applied the modern methods of the physical sciences to the social sciences in his six-volume *Cours de philosophie positive (Course in Positive Philosophy)*, published between 1830 and 1842. He argued that there could be no real knowledge of social phenomena unless it was based on a positivist (scientific) approach. Positivism alone, however, was not sufficient to bring about a fundamental change in criminological thinking. Not until Charles Darwin (1809–1882) challenged the doctrine of creation with his theory of the evolution of species did the next generation of criminologists have the tools with which to challenge classicism.

The turning point was the publication in 1859 of Darwin's *Origin of Species*. Darwin's theory was that God did not make all the various species of animals in 2 days, as proclaimed in Genesis 1:20–26, but rather that the species had evolved through a process of adaptive mutation and natural selection. The process was based on the survival of the fittest in the struggle for existence. This radical theory seriously challenged traditional theological teaching. It was not until 1871, however, that Darwin publicly took the logical next step and traced human origins to an animal of the anthropoid group—the ape.[12] He thus posed an even more serious challenge to a religious tradition that maintained that God created the first human in his own image (Genesis 1:27).

The scientific world would never be the same again. The theory of evolution made it possible to ask new questions and to search in new ways for the answers to old ones. New biological theories replaced older ones. Old ideas that demons and animal spirits could explain human behavior were replaced by knowledge based on new scientific principles. The social sciences were born.

The nineteenth-century forces of positivism and evolution moved the field of criminology from a philosophical to a scientific perspective. But there were even earlier intellectual underpinnings of the scientific criminology that emerged in the second half of the nineteenth century.

BIOLOGICAL DETERMINISM: THE SEARCH FOR CRIMINAL TRAITS

Throughout history a variety of physical characteristics and disfigurements have been said to characterize individuals of "evil" disposition. In the earliest pursuit of the relationship between biological traits and behavior, a Greek scientist who examined Socrates found his skull and facial features to be those of a person inclined toward alcoholism and brutality.[13] The ancient Greeks and Romans so distrusted red hair that actors portraying evil persons wore red wigs. Through the ages cripples, hunchbacks, people with long hair, and a multitude of others were viewed with suspicion. Indeed, in the Middle Ages laws indicated that if two people were suspected of a crime, the uglier was the more likely to be guilty.[14]

The belief that criminals are born, not made, and that they can be identified by various physical irregularities is reflected not only in scientific writing but in literature as well. Shakespeare's Julius Caesar states:

Let me have men about me that are fat;
Sleek-headed men, and such as sleep o' nights.
Yond Cassius has a lean and hungry look;
He thinks too much: such men are dangerous.

Although its roots can be traced to ancient times, it was not until the sixteenth century that the Italian physician Giambattista della Porta (1535–1615) founded the school of human **physiognomy,** the study of facial features and their relation to human behavior. According to Porta, a thief had large lips and sharp vision. Two centuries later Porta's efforts were revived by the Swiss theologian Johann Kaspar Lavater (1741–1801).[15] They were elaborated by the German physicians Franz Joseph Gall (1758–1828) and Johann Kaspar Spurzheim (1776–1832), whose science of **phrenology** posited that bumps on the head were indications of psychological propensities.[16] In the United States these views were supported by the physician Charles Caldwell (1772–1853), who searched for evidence that brain tissue and cells regulate human action.[17] By the nineteenth century, the sciences of physiognomy and phrenology had intro-

CRIMINOLOGICAL FOCUS

THE MISMEASURE OF MAN

In 1981 historian, biologist, and writer Stephen Jay Gould published *The Mismeasure of Man,* a study of biased science and its social abuse. One of its reviews begins as the book itself does—with a quote from Gould's earlier work on Cesare Lombroso's 1876 *The Criminal Man:*

> "Perhaps because its bold thesis seemed so clear, simple and impeccably scientific—criminals are ignorant apes with small brains as well as a brutish physical appearance—Lombroso's book won wide assent, despite its paltry data. At criminal trials for years afterward, a 'sinister look' signaled an incorrigible miscreant. 'Theoretical ethics,' declared Lombroso, 'passes over these diseased brains, as oil does over marble, without penetrating it.'"

The review presents a brief summary: Gould brings back to

Part of the frontispiece to the atlas of Lombroso's *The Criminal Man.* Group A are German murderers; B are swindlers; C are those who declared themselves bankrupt fraudulently.

(a)   *(b)*

---

duced specific biological factors into the study of crime causation.

Lombroso, Ferri, Garofalo: The Italian School

Cesare Lombroso (1835–1909) integrated Comte's positivism, Darwin's evolutionism, and the many pioneering studies of the relation of crime to the body. In 1876, with the publication of *L'uomo delinquente (The Criminal Man),* criminology was permanently transformed from an abstract philosophy of crime control through legislation to a modern science of investigation into causes. Lombroso's work replaced the concept of free will, which had reigned for over a century as the principle that explained criminal behavior, with that of determinism. Together with his followers, the Italian legal scholars Enrico Ferri and Raffaele Garofalo, Lombroso developed a new orientation, the Italian or positivist school of criminology, which seeks explanations for criminal behavior through scientific experimentation and research.

Cesare Lombroso. After completing his medical studies, Cesare Lombroso served as an army physician, became a professor of psychiatry at the University of Turin, and later in life accepted an appointment as professor of criminal anthropology. His theory of the "born criminal" states that criminals are a lower form of life, nearer to their apelike ancestors than noncriminals in traits and dispositions. They are distinguishable from noncriminals by various **atavistic stigmata**—physical features of creatures at an earlier stage of development, before they became fully human.

He argued that criminals frequently have huge jaws and strong canine teeth, characteristics common to carnivores who tear and devour meat raw. The arm span of criminals is often greater than their height, just like that of apes, who use their forearms to pro-

CRIMINOLOGICAL FOCUS

life an astonishing rogues' gallery of once-eminent scientists, most of them committed to racial purity, a privileged elite, and the theory that class rule rests on immutable biological differences. Besides Lombroso, there is Francis Galton, a pioneer of modern statistics and the first apostle of "eugenics," a term he invented for the brave new science of breeding; Paul Broca, the French surgeon who spent a lifetime weighing brains and juggling figures to prove the superior heft of the European mind; and Samuel George Morton, a Philadelphia patrician who collected more than 1,000 skulls from all over the world, meticulously used BB's to measure the volume of each one, and then fudged the results to show that whites had bigger skulls than blacks.

Craniometry—the science of measuring skulls—seems the quaint vestige of a bygone era.

Aptitude tests, by contrast, still determine educational opportunity in our own society. Gould shows precisely how . . . scholars gathered data to suit their own assumptions. R. M. Yerkes . . . tested immigrants for "innate" intelligence by asking them multiple-choice questions like, "Crisco is a: Patent medicine, disinfectant, toothpaste, food product." H. H. Goddard, another crusading advocate of IQ testing and scientific breeding, doctored photographs of "morons"—he coined the term—to make them look demented. And then there is the case of the late Sir Cyril Burt, the doyen of British mental testing, who palmed off faked data, "patent errors and specious claims," for more than 50 years. Gould concedes that IQ testing can, in certain contexts, become a tool "for enhancing potential through proper education." But when prejudice passes for science

and bigots wield IQ as a measure of innate human limits, the results are often tragic. Between 1924 and 1972, the state of Virginia secretly sterilized more than 7,500 people—simply because they scored low on one of [these] dubious tests.(1)

Source
1. Jim Miller, book review, "The Mismeasure of Man," *Newsweek*, Nov. 9, 1981, p. 106.

Questions for Discussion
1. Alfred Binet, who first devised aptitude tests, viewed his work with caution and said that test scores should not be used as if they recorded "a fixed faculty." Why and how did IQ tests come to be misused?
2. Do you think a thesis such as that put forth by Lombroso would be accepted by the public today?

Lombroso's born criminal man and woman. Sculptures by an unknown Italian artist; commissioned by the Italian Ministry of Justice in the 1920s and now at the United Nations Interregional Crime and Justice Research Institute, Rome.

pel themselves along the ground. An individual born with any five of the stigmata is a **born criminal.** This category accounts for about a third of all offenders.

The theory became clear to Lombroso "one cold grey November morning" while he pored over the bones of a notorious outlaw who had died in an Italian prison:

> This man possessed such extraordinary agility, that he had been known to scale steep mountain heights bearing a sheep on his shoulders. His cynical effrontery was such that he openly boasted of his crimes. On his death . . . I was deputed to make the post-mortem, and on laying open the skull I found . . . a distinct depression . . . as in inferior animals.

Lombroso was delighted by his findings:

> This was not merely an idea, but a revelation. At the sight of that skull, I seemed to see all of a sudden, lighted up as a vast plain under a flaming sky the problem of the nature of the criminal—an atavistic being

who reproduces in his person the ferocious instincts of primitive humanity.[18]

Criminal women, according to Lombroso, are different from criminal men. It is the prostitute who represents the born criminal among them:

> We also saw that women have many traits in common with children; that their moral sense is different; they are revengeful, jealous, inclined to vengeance of a refined cruelty. . . . When a morbid activity of the psychical centres intensifies the bad qualities of women . . . it is clear that the innocuous semi-criminal present in normal women must be transformed into a born criminal more terrible than any man. . . . The criminal woman is consequently a monster. Her normal sister is kept in the paths of virtue by many causes, such as maternity, piety, weakness, and when these counter influences fail, and a woman commits a crime, we may conclude that her wickedness must have been enormous before it could triumph over so many obstacles.[19]

To the born criminal Lombroso added two other categories, insane criminals and criminoloids. *Insane criminals* are not criminal from birth; they become criminal as a result of some change in their brains which interferes with their ability to distinguish between right and wrong.[20] *Criminoloids* make up an ambiguous group that includes habitual criminals, criminals by passion, and other diverse types.

Most scientists who followed Lombroso did not share his enthusiasm or his viewpoint. As happens so often in history, his work has been kept alive more by criticism than by agreement. The theory that criminals were lodged on the lower rungs of the evolutionary ladder did not stand up to scientific scrutiny. But the fact that Lombroso measured thousands of live and dead prisoners and compared these measurements with those obtained from control groups (however imperfectly derived) in his search for determinants of crime changed the nature of the questions asked by the generations of scholars who came after him.

His influence continues in contemporary European research; American scientists, as the criminologist Marvin Wolfgang says, use him "as a straw man for attack on biological analyses of criminal behavior."[21] Thorsten Sellin has noted: "Any scholar who succeeds in driving hundreds of fellow-students to search for the truth, and whose ideas after half a century possess vitality, merits an honorable place in the

history of thought."[22] At his death, true to his lifetime pursuits, Lombroso willed his body to the laboratory of legal medicine and his brain to the Institute of Anatomy at the University of Turin, where for so many years the father of empirical criminology had espoused biological determinism.[23]

Enrico Ferri. The best known of Lombroso's associates was Enrico Ferri (1856–1929). Member of Parliament, accomplished public lecturer, brilliant lawyer, editor of a newspaper, and esteemed scholar, Ferri had published his first major book by the time he was 21. By age 25 he was a university professor. Although Ferri agreed with Lombroso on the biological bases of criminal behavior, his interest in socialism led him to recognize the importance of social, economic, and political determinants.

Ferri was a prolific writer on a vast number of criminological topics. His greatest contribution was his attack on the classical doctrine of free will, which argued that criminals should be held morally responsible for their crimes because they must have made a rational decision to commit these acts. Ferri believed criminals could not be held morally responsible because they did not choose to commit crimes but, rather, were driven to commit them by conditions in their lives. He did, however, stress that society needed protection against criminal acts and that it was the purpose of the criminal law and penal policy to provide that protection.

Although he advocated conventional punishments and even the death penalty for individuals he assumed would never be fit to live in society, he was more interested in controlling crime through preventive measures—state control of the manufacture of weapons, inexpensive housing, better street lighting, and so forth.

Ferri claimed that strict adherence to preventive measures based on scientific methods would eventually reduce crime and allow people to live together in society with less dependence on the penal system. Toward the end of his life he proudly admitted that he was an idealist, a statement with which generations of scholars have agreed. Though his prescription for crime reduction was overly optimistic, Ferri's importance to the development of modern criminology is undisputed. "When Enrico Ferri died on April 12, 1929," writes Thorsten Sellin, "one of the most colorful, influential figures in the history of criminology disappeared."[24]

Raffaele Garofalo. Another follower of Lombroso was the Italian nobleman, magistrate, senator, and professor of law Raffaele Garofalo (1852–1934). Like Lombroso and Ferri, Garofalo rejected the doctrine of free will and supported the position that the only way to understand crime was to study it by scientific methods. Influenced by Lombroso's theory of atavistic stigmata, in which he found many shortcomings, Garofalo traced the roots of criminal behavior not to physical features but to their psychological equivalents, which he called "moral anomalies." According to this theory, natural crimes are found in all human societies, regardless of the views of lawmakers, and no civilized society can afford to disregard them.[25]

Natural crimes, according to Garofalo, are those that offend the basic moral sentiments of probity (respect for the property of others) and piety (revulsion against the infliction of suffering on others). An individual who has an organic deficiency in these moral sentiments has no moral constraints against committing such crimes. Garofalo argued that these individuals could not be held responsible for their actions. But, like Ferri, he also emphasized that society needed protection and that penal policy should be designed to prevent criminals from inflicting harm.[26]

Influenced by Darwinian theory, Garofalo suggested that the death penalty could rid society of its maladapted members, just as the natural selection process eliminated maladapted organisms. For less serious offenders, capable of adapting themselves to society in some measure, other types of punishments were preferable: transportation to remote lands, loss of privileges, institutionalization in farm colonies, or perhaps simply reparation. Clearly, Garofalo was much more interested in protecting society than in the individual rights of offenders.

Challenges to Lombrosian Theory. Although Lombroso, Ferri, and Garofalo did not always agree on the causes of criminal behavior or on the way society should respond to it, their combined efforts marked a turning point in the development of the scientific study of crime. These three were responsible for developing the positivist approach to criminality, which influences criminology to the present day. Nevertheless, they had their critics. By using the scientific method to explore crime causation, they paved the way for criminologists to support or refute the theories they had created. The major challenge to Lombrosian theory came from the work of Charles Buckman Goring.

From 1901 until 1913 Charles Buckman Goring (1870–1919), a medical officer at Parkhurst Prison in England, collected data on 96 traits of more than 3000 convicts and a large control group of Oxford and Cambridge university students, hospital patients, and soldiers. Among his research assistants was a famous statistician, Karl Pearson. When Goring had completed his examinations, he was armed with enough data to refute Lombroso's theory of the anthropological criminal type. Goring's report to the scientific community proclaimed:

> From a knowledge only of an undergraduate's cephalic [head] measurement, a better judgment could be given as to whether he were studying at an English or Scottish university than a prediction could be made as to whether he would eventually become a university professor or a convicted felon.[27]

This evaluation still stands as the most cogent critical analysis of Lombroso's theory of the born criminal. But though Goring rejected the claim that specific stigmata identify the criminal, he was convinced that poor physical condition plus a defective state of mind were determining factors in the criminal personality.

A Return to Biological Determinism

After Goring's challenge, Lombrosian theory lost its academic popularity for about a quarter of a century. Then in 1939 Ernest Hooten (1887–1954), a physical anthropologist, reawakened an interest in biologically determined criminality with the publication of a massive study comparing American prisoners with a noncriminal control group. He concluded:

> [I]n every population there are hereditary inferiors in mind and in body as well as physical and mental deficients. . . . Our information definitely proves that it is from the physically inferior element of the population that native born criminals from native parentage are mainly derived.[28]

Like his positivist predecessors, Hooten argued for the segregation of those he referred to as the "criminal stock," and he recommended their sterilization as well.[29]

The Somatotype School. In the search for the source of criminality, other scientists, too, looked for the elusive link between physical characteristics and

SOMATOTYPING: A PHYSIQUE FOR CRIME?

One afternoon in the late 1970s, deep in the labyrinthine interior of a massive Gothic tower in New Haven, an unsuspecting employee of Yale University opened a long-locked room in the Payne Whitney Gymnasium and stumbled upon something shocking and disturbing.

Shocking, because what he found was an enormous cache of nude photographs, thousands and thousands of photographs of young men in front, rear, and side poses. Disturbing, because on closer inspection the photos looked like the record of a bizarre body-piercing ritual: sticking out from the spine of each and every body was a row of sharp metal pins.(1)

Half a generation after the "bizarre body-piercing rituals," it was a *New York Times Magazine* journalist who was shocked and disturbed, particularly so because he also had been exposed to the ritual while at Yale, and the same ritual might have been imposed upon him had he been a student at Mount Holyoke, Vassar, Smith, Princeton, or Wellesley.

The implications were mind boggling: A routine freshman procedure, supposedly aimed at assessing and improving posture, had yielded a cache of nude photographs including such luminaries as George Pataki, and George Bush. While most of the schools shredded the photographs 10 or more years ago, thousands are still being kept under lock and seal at the Smithsonian in Washington. And what does all that have to do with criminology?

Sheldon's body types: (a) mesomorphic; (b) endomorphic; (c) ectomorphic.

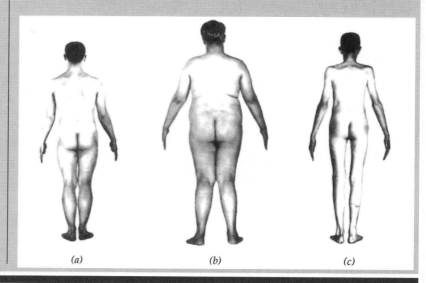

(a)   (b)   (c)

---

crime. The **somatotype school of criminology,** which related body build to behavior, became popular during the first half of the twentieth century. It originated with the work of a German psychiatrist, Ernst Kretschmer (1888–1964), who distinguished three principal types of physiques: (1) the asthenic—lean, slightly built, narrow shoulders; (2) the athletic—medium to tall, strong, muscular, coarse bones; and (3) the pyknic—medium height, rounded figure, massive neck, broad face. He then related these physical types to various psychic disorders: pyknics to manic depression, asthenics and athletics to schizophrenia, and so on.[30]

Kretschmer's work was brought to the United States by William Sheldon (1898–1977), who formulated his own group of somatotypes: the *endomorph*, the *mesomorph*, and the *ectomorph*. Sheldon's father was a dog breeder who judged animals in competition, and Sheldon worked out a point system of his own for judging humans. Thus one could actually measure on a scale from 1 to 7 the relative dominance of each body type in any given individual. People with predominantly mesomorph traits (physically powerful, aggressive, athletic physiques), he argued, tend more than others to be involved in illegal behavior.[31] This finding was later supported by Sheldon Glueck (1896–1980) and Eleanor Glueck (1898–1972), who based their studies of delinquents on William Sheldon's somatotypes.[32]

By and large, studies based on somatotyping have been sharply criticized for methodological flaws, including nonrepresentative selection of their samples (bias), failure to account for cultural stereotyping (our expectations of how muscular, physically active

AT ISSUE

In 1949 the physician William H. Sheldon reported that 200 boys living in Boston's Hayden Goodwill Inn had body builds significantly different from a control group of 4000 college students. That control group came out of the Ivy League's posture photos in the buff. The metal pins had not been inserted into the skin, but had been attached by tape.

SHELDON'S BODY TYPES

Sheldon classified physiques into three categories: mesomorphs, ectomorphs, and endomorphs. A mesomorph tends to be muscular, strong, heavy-boned, and firm; an ectomorph is fragile, thin, and delicate; and an endomorph has a predominance of soft roundness throughout the body. Sheldon used his classifications to show that body types were related to behavior, temperament, and even life expectancy.

Sheldon's 200 young males included alcoholics, mental defectives, and psychopaths, nondelinquents and criminals. He found that the criminal types were more mesomorphic.

A follow-up study of these 200 youths 30 years later identified 14 "primary criminals," individuals who had felony convictions as adults. These persistent criminals were relatively mesomorphic, compared with the others.

SOMATOTYPING: PRO AND CON

In *Crime and Human Nature* (1985), James Q. Wilson and Richard J. Herrnstein evaluated a number of studies relating physique to delinquency, including Sheldon's. They stated: "[T]he main conclusions have been confirmed wherever they have been tested, despite the initial skepticism of criminologists."(2)

Somatotyping is not without its critics. In an extensive review of Wilson and Herrnstein's conclusions, Leon J. Kamin ridicules their presentation of the topic, claiming that they completely ignore a number of studies that have appeared since 1949.(3)

Wilson and Herrnstein themselves present information that raises questions about the value of somatotyping to criminology. They cite studies in which, while the tendency toward the mesomorphic was clear, "mesomorphs could be found among the nondelinquents and ectomorphs among the delinquents." And they emphasize the difference between correlation and causation, stating clearly, "Physique does not cause crime."(1)

Sources

1. Ron Rosenbaum, "The Great Ivy League Nude Posture Photo Scandal," *New York Times Magazine,* Jan. 15, 1995, pp. 26–31, 40, 46, 55–56; quote from p. 26.
2. James Q. Wilson and Richard J. Herrnstein, *Crime and Human Nature* (New York: Simon & Schuster, 1985), p. 87.
3. Leon J. Kamin, "Crime and Human Nature," *Scientific American,* **254:** 22, February 1986.

Questions for Discussion

1. If criminals were shown conclusively to be "skewed toward the mesomorph," what use might crime prevention strategists make of such information?
2. Did Sheldon violate standards of ethics in research by utilizing nude photographs taken for other purposes?

---

people should react), and poor statistical analyses. An anthropologist summed up the negative response of the scientific community by suggesting that somatotyping was "a New Phrenology in which the bumps on the buttocks take the place of the bumps on the skulls."[33] After World War II, somatotyping seemed too close to **eugenics** (the science of controlled reproduction to improve hereditary qualities), and the approach fell into disfavor. During the 1960s, however, the discovery of an extra sex chromosome in some criminal samples (see Chapter 4) revived interest in this theory.

Inherited Criminality. During the period when some researchers were measuring skulls and bodies of criminals in their search for the physical determinants of crime, others were arguing that crim-

inality was an inherited trait passed on in the genes. To support the theory, they traced family histories. Richard Dugdale (1841–1883), for example, studied the lives of more than a thousand members of the family he called "Jukes." His interest in the family began when he found six related people in a jail in upstate New York. Following one branch of the family, the descendants of Ada Jukes, whom he referred to as the "mother of criminals," Dugdale found among the thousand of them 280 paupers, 60 thieves, 7 murderers, 40 other criminals, 40 persons with venereal disease, and 50 prostitutes.

His findings indicated, Dugdale claimed, that since some families produce generations of criminals, they must be transmitting a degenerate trait down the line.[34] A similar conclusion was reached by Henry Goddard (1866–1957). In a study of the family tree of a Revolutionary War soldier, Martin Kallikak, Goddard found many more criminals among the descendants of Kallikak's illegitimate son than among the descendants of his son by a later marriage with "a woman of his own quality."[35]

These early studies have been discredited primarily on the grounds that genetic and environmental influences could not be separated. But in the early twentieth century they were taken quite seriously. On the assumption that crime could be controlled if criminals could be prevented from transmitting their traits to the next generation, some states permitted the sterilization of habitual offenders. Sterilization laws were held constitutional by the U.S. Supreme Court in a 1927 opinion written by Justice Oliver Wendell Holmes, Jr., which included the following well-known pronouncement:

> It is better for all the world, if instead of waiting to execute degenerate offspring for crime, or to let them starve for their imbecility, society can prevent those who are manifestly unfit from continuing their kind. . . . Three generations of imbeciles are enough.[36]

Clearly the early positivists, with their focus on physical characteristics, exerted great influence. They were destined to be overshadowed, though, by investigators who focused on psychological characteristics.

PSYCHOLOGICAL DETERMINISM

On the whole, scholars who investigated criminal behavior in the nineteenth and early twentieth centuries were far more interested in the human body than in the human mind. During that period, however, several contributions were made in the area of psychological explanations of crime. Some of the earliest contributions came from physicians interested primarily in the legal responsibility of the criminally insane. Later on, psychologists entered the field and applied their new testing techniques to the study of offenders (see Chapter 4).

Pioneers in Criminal Psychology

Isaac Ray (1807–1881), acknowledged to be America's first forensic psychiatrist, was interested throughout his life in the application of psychiatric principles to the law. He is best known as the author of *The Medical Jurisprudence of Insanity*, a treatise on crim-

inal responsibility that was widely quoted and influential.[37] In it he defended the concept of "moral insanity," a disorder first described in 1806 by the French humanitarian and psychiatrist Philippe Pinel (1745–1826).[38] "Moral insanity" was a term used to describe persons who were normal in all respects except that something was wrong with the part of the brain that regulates affective responses. Ray questioned whether we could hold people legally responsible for their acts if they had such an impairment, because such people committed their crimes without an intent to do so.

Born in the same year as Lombroso, Henry Maudsley (1835–1918), a brilliant English medical professor, shared Ray's concerns about criminal responsibility. According to Maudsley, some people may be considered either "insane or criminal according to the standpoint from which they are looked at." He believed that for many persons crime is an "outlet in which their unsound tendencies are discharged; they would go mad if they were not criminals."[39] Most of Maudsley's attention focused on the borderline between insanity and crime.

Psychological Studies of Criminals

Around the turn of the twentieth century, psychologists used their new measurement techniques to study offenders. The administering of intelligence tests to inmates of jails, prisons, and other public institutions was especially popular at that time, because it was a period of major controversy over the relation of mental deficiency to criminal behavior. The new technique seemed to provide an objective basis for differentiating criminals from noncriminals.

In 1914 Henry H. Goddard (1866–1957), research director of the Vineland, New Jersey, Training School for the Retarded, examined some intelligence tests that had been given to inmates and concluded that 25 to 50 percent of the people in prison had intellectual defects that made them incapable of managing their own affairs.[40] This idea remained dominant until it was challenged by the results of intelligence tests administered to World War I draftees, whose scores were found to be lower than those of prisoners in the federal penitentiary at Leavenworth. As a result of this study and others like it, intelligence quotient (IQ) measures largely disappeared as a basis for explaining criminal behavior.

SOCIOLOGICAL DETERMINISM

During the nineteenth and early twentieth centuries, some scholars began to search for the social determinants of criminal behavior. The approach had its roots in Europe in the 1830s, the time between Beccaria's *On Crimes and Punishment* and Lombroso's *The Criminal Man*.

Adolphe Quételet and André Michel Guerry

The Belgian mathematician Adolphe Quételet (1796–1874) and the French lawyer André Michel Guerry (1802–1866) were among the first scholars to repudiate the classicists' free-will doctrine. Working independently on the relation of crime statistics to such factors as poverty, age, sex, race, and climate, both scholars concluded that society, not the decisions of individual offenders, was responsible for criminal behavior.

The first modern criminal statistics were published in France in 1827. Guerry used those statistics to demonstrate that crime rates varied with social factors. He found, for example, that the wealthiest region of France had the highest rate of property crime but only half the national rate of violent crime. He concluded that the main factor in property crime was opportunity: There was much more to steal in the richer provinces.

Quételet did an elaborate analysis of crime in France, Belgium, and Holland. After analyzing criminal statistics, which he called "moral statistics," he concluded that if we look at overall patterns of behavior of groups across a whole society, we find a startling regularity of rates of various behaviors. According to Quételet:

> We can enumerate in advance how many individuals will soil their hands in the blood of their fellows, how many will be frauds, how many prisoners; almost as one can enumerate in advance the births and deaths that will take place.[41]

By focusing on groups rather than individuals, he discovered that behavior is indeed predictable, regular, and understandable. Just as the physical world is governed by the laws of nature, human behavior is governed by forces external to the individual. The more we learn about those forces, the easier it becomes to predict behavior. A major goal of crimi-

nological research, according to Quételet, should be to identify factors related to crime and to assign to them their "proper degree of influence."[42] Though neither he nor Guerry offered a theory of criminal behavior, the fact that both studied social factors scientifically, using quantitative research methods, made them key figures in the subsequent development of sociological theories of crime causation.

Gabriel Tarde

One of the earliest sociological theories of criminal behavior was formulated by Gabriel Tarde (1843–1904), who served 15 years as a provincial judge and then was placed in charge of France's national statistics. After an extensive analysis of these statistics, he came to the following conclusion:

> The majority of murderers and notorious thieves began as children who had been abandoned, and the true seminary of crime must be sought for upon each public square or each crossroad of our towns, whether they be small or large, in those flocks of pillaging street urchins who, like bands of sparrows, associate together, at first for marauding, and then for theft, because of a lack of education and food in their homes.[43]

Tarde rejected the Lombrosian theory of biological abnormality, which was popular in his time, arguing that criminals were normal people who learned crime just as others learned legitimate trades. He formulated his theory in terms of **laws of imitation**—principles that governed the process by which people became criminals. According to Tarde's thesis, individuals emulate behavior patterns in much the same way that they copy styles of dress. Moreover, there is a pattern to the way such emulation takes place: (1) Individuals imitate others in proportion to the intensity and frequency of their contacts; (2) inferiors imitate superiors—that is, trends flow from town to country and from upper to lower classes; and (3) when two behavior patterns clash, one may take the place of the other, as when guns largely replaced knives as murder weapons.[44] Tarde's work served as the basis for Edwin Sutherland's theory of differential association, which we shall examine in Chapter 5.

Émile Durkheim

Modern criminologists take two major approaches to the study of the social factors associated with crime. Tarde's approach asks how individuals become criminal. What is the process? How are behavior patterns learned and transmitted? The second major approach looks at the social structure and its institutions. It asks how crime arises in the first place and how it is related to the functioning of a society. For answers to these questions, scholars begin with the work of Émile Durkheim (1858–1917).

Of all nineteenth-century writers on the relationship between crime and social factors, none has more powerfully influenced contemporary criminology than Durkheim, who is universally acknowledged as one of the founders of sociology. On October 12, 1870, when Durkheim was 12 years old, the German army invaded and occupied his hometown, Epinal, in eastern France. Thus at a very early age he witnessed social chaos and the effects of rapid change, topics with which he remained preoccupied throughout his life. At the age of 24 he became a professor of philosophy, and at 29 he joined the faculty of the University of Bordeaux. There he taught the first course in sociology ever to be offered by a French university.

By 1902 he had moved to the University of Paris, where he completed his doctoral studies. His *Division of Social Labor* became a landmark work on the organization of societies. According to Durkheim, crime is as normal a part of society as birth and death. Theoretically, crime could disappear altogether only if all members of society had the same values, and such standardization is neither possible nor desirable. Furthermore, some crime is in fact necessary if a society is to progress:

> The opportunity for the genius to carry out his work affords the criminal his originality at a lower level. . . . According to Athenian law, Socrates was a criminal, and his condemnation was no more than just. However, his crime, namely, the independence of his thought, rendered a service not only to humanity but to his country.[45]

Durkheim further pointed out that all societies have not only crime but sanctions. The rationale for the sanctions varies in accordance with the structure of the society. In a strongly cohesive society, punishment of members who deviate is used to reinforce the value system—to remind people of what is right and what is wrong—thereby preserving the pool of common belief and the solidarity of the society. Punishment must be harsh to serve these ends. In a large, urbanized, heterogeneous society, on the other hand, punishment is used not to preserve solidarity but rather to right the wrong done to a victim. Punishment thus is evaluated in accordance with the harm done, with the goal of restitution and reinstatement of order as quickly as possible. The offense is not considered a threat to social cohesion, primarily because in a large, complex society criminal events do not even come to the attention of most people.

The most important of Durkheim's many contributions to contemporary sociology is his concept of **anomie,** a breakdown of social order as a result of a loss of standards and values. In a society plagued by anomie (see Chapter 5), disintegration and chaos replace social cohesion.

HISTORICAL AND CONTEMPORARY CRIMINOLOGY: A TIME LINE

Classical criminologists thought the problem of crime might be solved through limitations on governmental power, the abolition of brutality, and the creation of a more equitable system of justice. They argued that the punishment should fit the crime. For over a century this perspective dominated criminology. Later on, positivist criminologists influenced judges to give greater consideration to the offender than to the gravity of the crime when imposing sentences. The current era marks a return to the classical demand that the punishment correspond to the seriousness of the crime and the guilt of the offender. Table 3.1 presents a chronology of all the pioneers in criminology we have discussed.

As modern science discovered more and more about cause and effect in the physical and social universes, the theory that individuals commit crimes of their own free will began to lose favor. The positivists searched for determinants of crime in biological, psychological, and social factors. Biologically based theories were popular in the late nineteenth century, fell out of favor in the early part of the twentieth, and emerged again in the 1970s (see Chapter 4) with studies of hormone imbalances, diet, environmental contaminants, and so forth. Since the studies of criminal responsibility in the nineteenth century centering on the insanity defense and of intelligence levels in the twentieth century, psychiatrists and psychologists have continued to play a major role in the search for the causes of crime, especially after Sigmund Freud developed his well-known theory of human personality (Chapter 4). The sociological perspective became

TABLE 3.1   Pioneers in Criminology: A Chronology

Classical Criminology

Free Will

Cesare Beccaria (1738–1794). Devised the first design for comprehensive, enlightened criminal justice system based on law

Jeremy Bentham (1748–1832). Developed utilitarian principles of punishment

Biological Determinism

Giambattista della Porta (1535–1615). Was the founder of the school of physiognomy, which is the study of facial features and their relation to human behaviors

Johann Kaspar Lavater (1741–1801). Espoused a biological approach to crime causation; developed phrenology

Franz Joseph Gall (1758–1828). Espoused a biological approach to crime causation; further developed phrenology

Charles Caldwell (1772–1853). Was a physician who searched for evidence that brain tissue and cells regulate human behavior.

Johann Kaspar Spurzheim (1776–1832). Espoused a biological approach; continued studies of phrenology

Positivist Criminology

Biological Determinism

Charles Darwin (1809–1882). Formulated theory of evolution, which changed explanations of human behavior

Cesare Lombroso (1835–1909). Saw determinism as explanatory factor in criminal behavior; posited the "born criminal"; father of modern criminology

Richard Dugdale (1841–1883). Related criminal behavior to inherited traits (Jukes family)

Raffaele Garofalo (1852–1934). Traced roots of criminal behavior to "moral anomalies" rather than physical characteristics

Enrico Ferri (1856–1929). Produced first penal code based on positivist principles; replaced "moral responsibility" with social accountability

Ernest Hooten (1887–1954). Related criminality to hereditary inferiority

Ernst Kretschmer (1888–1964). Introduced the somatotype school of criminology

William Sheldon (1898–1977). Related body types to illegal behavior

Psychological Determinism

Isaac Ray (1807–1881). Questioned whether those who were "morally insane" could be held legally responsible for their acts

Henry Maudsley (1835–1918). Pioneered criteria for legal responsibility

Henry H. Goddard (1866–1957). Related criminal behavior to intelligence (Kallikak family)

Social Determinism

Adolphe Quételet (1796–1874). Was one of the first to repudiate classical free-will doctrine; studied social determinants of behavior

Auguste Comte (1798–1857). Brought modern scientific methods from physical to social sciences

André Michel Guerry (1802–1866). Was one of the first to repudiate free-will doctrine; related crime statistics to social factors

Gabriel Tarde (1843–1904). Explained crime as learned behavior

Émile Durkheim (1858–1917). Was one of the founders of sociology; developed theory of anomie, idea that crime is "normal" in all societies

Charles Buckman Goring (1870–1919). Used empirical research to refute Lombroso's theory of criminal types

Sheldon Glueck (1896–1980) and *Eleanor Glueck (1898–1972).* Espoused primarily social causes of delinquency, but also psychological and biological explanations

popular in the 1920s and has remained the predominant approach of criminological studies. (We will examine contemporary theories in Chapters 5 through 9.)

REVIEW

In the history of criminology from ancient times to the early twentieth century, its many themes at times have clashed and at times have supported one another. There is no straight-line evolutionary track that we can follow from the inception of the first "criminological" thought to modern theories. Some scholars concentrated on criminal law and procedure, others on criminal behavior. Some took the biological route, others the psychological, still others the sociological, and the work of some investigators has encompassed a combination of factors. Toward the end of the nineteenth century a discipline began to emerge.

Tracing the major developments back in time helps us to understand how criminology grew into the discipline we know today. Many of the issues that appear on the intellectual battlefields as we approach the twenty-first century are the same issues our academic ancestors grappled with for hundreds, indeed thousands, of years. With each new clash, some old concepts died, but most were incorporated within competing doctrinal boundaries, there to remain until the next challenge. The controversies of one era become the foundations of knowledge for the next. As societies develop and are subjected to new technologies, the crime problem becomes ever more complex. So do the questions it raises. In Part II we will see how twentieth-century theorists have dealt with them.

NOTES

1. First quote: attributed to Socrates by Plato, wording unconfirmed by researchers; see *Respectfully Quoted,* ed. Suzy Platt (Washington, D.C.: Library of Congress, 1989), p. 42. Second quote: Sophocles, *Antigone,* I, 720. Third quote: Plato, *The Republic, I,* 343 d.

2. Leon Radzinowicz, *Ideology and Crime* (New York: Columbia University Press, 1966), p. 2; Marc Ancel, *Introduction to the French Penal Code,* ed. G. O. W. Mueller (South Hackensack, N.J.: Fred B. Rothman, 1960), pp. 1–2.

3. Thorsten Sellin, *Slavery and the Penal System* (New York: Elsevier, 1976); Thorsten Eriksson, *The Reformers: An Histor-*
ical Survey of Pioneer Experiments in the Treatment of Criminals (New York: Elsevier, 1976).

4. Marcello T. Maestro, *Cesare Beccaria and the Origins of Penal Reform* (Philadelphia: Temple University Press, 1973), p. 16.

5. George Rude, *The Crowd in the French Revolution* (New York: Oxford University Press, 1959), appendix.

6. Harry Elmer Barnes, *The Story of Punishment: A Record of Man's Inhumanity to Man,* 2d ed. (Montclair, N.J.: Patterson Smith, 1972), p. 99.

7. Cesare Beccaria, *On Crimes and Punishment,* 2d ed., trans. Edward D. Ingraham (Philadelphia: Philip H. Nicklin, 1819), pp. 15, 20, 22–23, 30–32, 60, 74–75, 80, 97–98, 149, 156. For a debate on the contribution of Beccaria to modern criminology, see G. O. W. Mueller, "Whose Prophet Is Cesare Beccaria? An Essay on the Origins of Criminological Theory," *Advances in Criminological Theory,* **2** (1990): 1–14; Graeme Newman and Pietro Marongiu, "Penological Reform and the Myth of Beccaria," *Criminology,* **28** (1990): 325–346; and Piers Beirne, "Inventing Criminology: The 'Science of Man,' in Cesare Beccaria's *Dei delitti e delle pene," Criminology,* **29** (1991): 777–820.

8. Marcello T. Maestro, *Voltaire and Beccaria as Reformers of Criminal Law* (New York: Columbia University Press, 1942), p. 73.

9. Jeremy Bentham, *A Fragment on Government and an Introduction to the Principles of Morals and Legislation,* ed. Wilfred Harrison (Oxford: Basil Blackwell, 1967), p. 21.

10. Barnes, *The Story of Punishment,* p. 102.

11. Quoted in Leon Radzinowicz, *A History of English Criminal Law and Its Administration from 1750,* vol. 1 (New York: Macmillan, 1948), p. 330.

12. Charles Darwin, *Origin of Species* (1854; Cambridge, Mass.: Harvard University Press, 1859); Charles Darwin, *The Descent of Man and Selection in Relation to Sex* (1871; New York: A. L. Burt, 1874).

13. Havelock Ellis, *The Criminal,* 2d ed. (New York: Scribner, 1900), p. 27.

14. Christopher Hibbert, *The Roots of Evil* (Boston: Little, Brown, 1963), p. 187.

15. Arthur E. Fink, *The Causes of Crime: Biological Theories in the United States, 1800–1915* (Philadelphia: University of Pennsylvania Press, 1938), p. 1.

16. Hermann Mannheim, *Comparative Criminology* (Boston: Houghton Mifflin, 1965), p. 213.

17. George B. Vold, *Theoretical Criminology* (New York: Oxford University Press, 1958), pp. 44–49.

18. Gina Lombroso Ferrero, *Criminal Man: According to the Classification of Cesare Lombroso,* with an Introduction by Cesare Lombroso (1911; Montclair, N.J.: Patterson Smith, 1972), pp. xxiv–xxv.

19. Cesare Lombroso and William Ferrero, *The Female Offender* (New York: Appleton, 1895), pp. 151–152.

20. Cesare Lombroso, *Crime, Its Causes and Remedies* (Boston: Little, Brown, 1918).

21. Marvin Wolfgang, "Cesare Lombroso," in *Pioneers in Criminology,* ed. Hermann Mannheim (London: Stevens, 1960), p. 168.

22. Thorsten Sellin, "The Lombrosian Myth in Criminology," *American Journal of Sociology,* **42** (1937): 898–899. For Lombroso's impact on American anthropological criminology, see

Nicole Hahn Rafter, "Criminal Anthropology in the United States," *Criminology,* **30** (1992): 525–545.

23. Wolfgang, "Cesare Lombroso."

24. Thorsten Sellin, "Enrico Ferri: Pioneer in Criminology, 1856–1929," in *The Positive School of Criminology: Three Lectures by Enrico Ferri,* ed. Stanley E. Grupp (Pittsburgh: University of Pittsburgh Press, 1968), p. 13.

25. Raffaele Garofalo, *Criminology,* trans. Robert Wyness Millar (Montclair, N.J.: Patterson Smith, 1968), pp. 4–5.

26. Marc Ancel, *Social Defense: The Future of Penal Reform* (Littleton, Colo.: Fred B. Rothman, 1987).

27. Charles B. Goring, *The English Convict: A Statistical Study* (London: His Majesty's Stationery Office, 1913), p. 145. For a critique of Goring's work, see Piers Beirne, "Heredity versus Environment," *British Journal of Criminology,* **28** (1988): 315–339.

28. E. A. Hooten, *The American Criminal* (Cambridge, Mass.: Harvard University Press, 1939), p. 308.

29. E. A. Hooten, *Crime and the Man* (Cambridge, Mass.: Harvard University Press, 1939), p. 13.

30. Ernst Kretschmer, *Physique and Character* (New York: Harcourt Brace, 1926).

31. William H. Sheldon, *Varieties of Delinquent Youth: An Introduction to Constitutional Psychiatry* (New York: Harper, 1949). See also Emil M. Hartl, Edward P. Monnelly, and Ronald D. Elderkin, *Physique and Delinquent Behavior: A Thirty-Year Follow-Up of William H. Sheldon's Varieties of Delinquent Youth* (New York: Academic Press, 1982).

32. Eleanor Glueck and Sheldon Glueck, *Unraveling Juvenile Delinquency* (Cambridge, Mass.: Harvard University Press, 1950). See also Sheldon Glueck and Eleanor Glueck, *Of Delinquency and Crime* (Springfield, Ill.: Charles C Thomas, 1974), p. 2. For a recent reanalysis of the Gluecks' data, see John H. Laub and Robert J. Sampson, "Unravelling Families and Delinquency: A Reanalysis of the Gluecks' Data," *Criminology,* **26** (1988): 355–380. For the life and work of Eleanor Touroff Glueck, see John H. Laub and Jinney S. Smith, "Eleanor Touroff Glueck: An Unsung Pioneer in Criminology," *Women in Criminal Justice,* **6** (1995): 1–22.

33. S. L. Washburn, book review, "Varieties of Delinquent Youth, An Introduction to Constitutional Psychiatry," *American Anthropologist,* **53** (1951): 561–563.

34. Richard L. Dugdale, *The Jukes: A Study in Crime, Pauperism, Disease, and Heredity,* 5th ed. (New York: Putnam, 1895), p. 8.

35. Henry H. Goddard, *The Kallikak Family: A Study in the Heredity of Feeble-Mindedness* (New York: Macmillan, 1912), p. 50.

36. *Buck v. Bell,* 274 U.S. 200, 207 (1927).

37. Isaac Ray, *The Medical Jurisprudence of Insanity* (Boston: Little, Brown, 1838).

38. Philippe Pinel, *A Treatise on Insanity* (1806; New York: Hafner, 1962).

39. Peter Scott, "Henry Maudsley," in *Journal of Criminal Law, Criminology, and Police Science,* **46** (March–April 1956): 753–769.

40. Henry H. Goddard, *The Criminal Imbecile* (New York: Macmillan, 1915), pp. 106–107.

41. Adolphe Quételet, *A Treatise on Man,* facs. ed. of 1842 ed., trans. Salomon Diamond (1835; Gainesville, Fla.: Scholars Facsimiles and Reprints, 1969), p. 97.

42. Quételet, *A Treatise on Man,* p. 103. For Quételet's influence on modern scholars, see Derral Cheatwood, "Is There a Season for Homicide?" *Criminology,* **26** (1988): 287–306.

43. Gabriel Tarde, *Penal Philosophy,* trans. R. Howell (Boston: Little, Brown, 1912), p. 252.

44. Gabriel Tarde, *Social Laws: An Outline of Sociology* (New York: Macmillan, 1907).

45. Émile Durkheim, *The Rules of Sociological Method,* ed. George E. G. Catlin (Chicago: University of Chicago Press, 1938), p. 71.

Internet Exercise

If Beccaria were alive today, how would he make a case against the death penalty?

Your Web Site is:
http://www.dnai.com/~mwood/deathpen.html

PART II

Explanations of Crime and Criminal Behavior

Having explored the history of criminology, the early explanations of criminal behavior, and the scientific methods used by criminologists, we turn now to contemporary theories and research. Current explanations of criminal behavior focus on biological, psychological, social, and economic factors. Biological and psychological theories assume that criminal behavior results from underlying physical or mental conditions that distinguish criminals from noncriminals (Chapter 4). These theories yield insight into individual cases, but they do not explain why crime rates vary from place to place and from one situation to another.

Sociological theories seek to explain criminal behavior in terms of the environment. Chapter 5 examines strain and cultural deviance theories, which focus on the social forces that cause people to engage in criminal behavior. Both theories assume that social class and criminal behavior are related. Strain theorists argue that people commit crime because they are frustrated by not being able to achieve their goals through legitimate means. Cultural deviance theorists claim that crime is learned in socially disorganized neighborhoods where criminal norms are transmitted from one generation to the next. In Chapter 6 we examine subcultures that have their own norms, beliefs, and values, which differ significantly from those of the dominant culture. Chapter 7 explains how people remain committed to conventional behavior in the face of frustration, poor living conditions, and other criminogenic factors. In Chapter 8 we explain why offenders choose to commit one offense rather than another at a given time and place. Finally, in Chapter 9 we discuss three theoretical perspectives that focus on society's role in creating criminals and defining them as such.

CHAPTER 4
Psychological and
Biological Perspectives

Psychology and Criminality
    Psychological Development
    Moral Development
    Learning Aggression and Violence
    Maternal Deprivation and Attachment Theory
    Personality
Mental Disorders and Crime
Biology and Criminality
    Modern Biocriminology
    Genetics and Criminality
    The Controversy over Violence and Genes
    The IQ Debate
    Biochemical Factors
    Neurophysiological Factors
Crime and Human Nature
    Criticisms of Biocriminology
    An Integrated Theory
Review
Notes
    Special Features
    AT ISSUE: The Crime of Parricide
    WINDOW TO THE WORLD: Censoring TV Violence
    CRIMINOLOGICAL FOCUS: Myths of the Insanity Defense

Key Terms

attachment
behavioral modeling
biocriminology
chromosomes
conditioning
cortical arousal
differential
  association-
  reinforcement
dizygotic (DZ) twins
ego
extroversion
hypoglycemia
id
minimal brain
  dysfunction (MBD)
monozygotic (MZ)
  twins
neuroticism
psychoanalytic theory
psychopathy
psychosis
psychoticism
social learning theory
superego

H eriberto Seda was a loner from birth. In a neighborhood overrun with crime, his mother tried to shield her only son from the dangers that lurked around every corner. She never let Heriberto have friends over or let him venture too far from home. Each day, Heriberto would return from school to his apartment where, in the solitude of his room, he watched television, looked at basketball trading cards, and developed a fascination with the concept of God.

In 1984, Heriberto was suspended for discharging a starter's pistol in class. A few months shy of graduation, Heriberto dropped out of Francis K. Lane High School and took to spreading the word of God on a full-time basis. He roamed the streets of his neighborhood to do "the will of God." Dressed in black, with his hair neatly restrained in a ponytail, Heriberto would emerge from his home after dark, and berate the drug dealers that conducted business in the hallways and on the streets. He preached by night and returned to the seclusion of his home by day. Here, his previously innocent hobbies had taken a sinister turn—basketball trading cards were replaced by those of serial murderers from the True Crime Series; the magazines now had a militaristic twist: *Soldier of Fortune* and mail-order catalogs for military supplies; models of boats and ships were replaced by filed-down "zip guns" and homemade pipe bombs, with a generous sprinkling of gas masks, machetes, and hundreds of rounds of ammunition.

On March 8, 1990, Heriberto embarked on the first of many shootings in his crusade to eradicate evil—to dispose of the enemies of God. During the course of the next few years, Heriberto Seda shot eight people, killing three. All his victims were vulnerable: a homeless man asleep on a park bench, a crippled factory worker on his way home, a 78-year-old man who turned his back to get his murderer a glass of water.

After several of the shootings, cryptic messages with astrological underpinnings were found nearby, scrawled on pieces of paper. Similar letters were sent to *60 Minutes* and the *New York Post*, declaring him the Zodiac, all sealed with the same trademark signa-

69

ture: an encircled cross with three sevens. This signature would prove to be his downfall.

In 1994, Heriberto Seda was arrested for illegal possession of a firearm, but the charges were dropped a few days later when the weapon was deemed inoperable for safety reasons; in no time, Heriberto was back on the streets of New York. On June 18, 1996, Heriberto shot his 18-year-old sister in the back, after an alleged dispute over her promiscuity. A 3-hour standoff with the police ensued, ending in his capture and imprisonment.

Down at the police station, Heriberto Seda gave a signed statement sealed with his trademark: an encircled cross with three sevens. This evidence, in addition to expert fingerprint analysis linking him to four of the shootings in 1990, sealed the fate of the Zodiac Killer.

In the United States, explanations of criminal behavior have been dominated by sociological theories. These theories focus on lack of opportunity and the breakdown of the conventional value system in urban ghettos, the formation of subcultures whose norms deviate from those of the middle class, and the increasing inability of social institutions to exercise control over behavior. Criminological texts have treated psychological and biological theories as peripheral, perhaps because criminology's disciplinary allegiance is to sociology. When psychological theories were first advanced to explain criminal behavior, their emphasis was largely psychoanalytic, so they

may have seemed not quantitative enough to some criminologists.[1] Others may have considered the early work of Lombroso, Goring, and Hooten too scientifically naive to be taken seriously.

Sociological theories focus on crime rates of groups that experience frustration in their efforts to achieve accepted goals, not on the particular individual who becomes a criminal. Sociological theories cannot explain how a person can be born in a slum, be exposed to family discord and abuse, never attend school, have friends who are delinquents, and yet resist opportunities for crime, while another person who grows up in an affluent suburban neighborhood in a two-parent home can end up firing a gun at the president. In other words, sociologists do not address individual differences.[2] Psychologists and biologists are interested in finding out what may account for individual differences.

It is clear that psychological, biological, and sociological explanations are not competing to answer the same specific questions. Rather, all three disciplines are searching for answers to different questions, even though they study the same act, status, or characteristic. We can understand crime in a society only if we view criminality from more than one level of analysis: why a certain individual commits a crime (psychological and biological explanations) and why some groups of individuals commit more or different criminal acts than other groups (sociological explanations).

Heriberto Seda: confessed Zodiac killer, June 1996.

Sociological theory and empirical research often ignore such factors as personality and human biology, almost as if they were irrelevant. And psychological theory often focuses on the individual, with little regard for the fact that while each one of us comes into the world with certain predispositions, from the moment we are born we interact with others in complex situations that influence our behavior.

PSYCHOLOGY AND CRIMINALITY

Psychologists have considered a variety of possibilities to account for individual differences—defective conscience, emotional immaturity, inadequate childhood socialization, maternal deprivation, poor moral development. They study how aggression is learned, which situations promote violent or delinquent reactions, how crime is related to personality factors, and the how various mental disorders are associated with criminality.

Psychological Development

The **psychoanalytic theory** of criminality attributes delinquent and criminal behavior to at least three possible causes:

- A conscience so overbearing that it arouses feelings of guilt
- A conscience so weak that it cannot control the individual's impulses
- The need for immediate gratification

Consider the case of Richard. Richard was 6 when he committed his first delinquent act: He stole a comic book from the corner drugstore. Three months before the incident his father, an alcoholic, had been killed in an automobile accident, and his mother, unable to care for the family, had abandoned the children.

For the next 10 years the county welfare agency moved Richard in and out of foster homes. During this time he actively pursued a life of crime, breaking into houses during daylight hours and stealing cars at night. By age 20, while serving a 10-year prison sentence for armed robbery, he had voluntarily entered psychoanalysis. After 2 years, Richard's analyst suggested three reasons for his criminality:

1. Being caught and punished for stealing made him feel less guilty about hating his father for dying and thus abandoning him and his mother for deliberately abandoning him.
2. Stealing did not violate his moral and ethical principles.
3. Stealing resulted in immediate gratification and pleasure, both of which Richard had great difficulty resisting.

Sigmund Freud (1856–1939), the founder of psychoanalysis, suggested that an individual's psychological well-being is dependent on a healthy interaction among the id, ego, and superego—the three basic components of the human psyche. The **id** consists of powerful urges and drives for gratification and satisfaction. The **ego** is the executive of the personality, acting as a moderator between the superego and id. The **superego** acts as a moral code or conscience. Freud proposed that criminality may result from an overactive superego or conscience. In treating patients, he noticed that those who were suffering from unbearable guilt committed crimes in order to be apprehended and punished.[3] Once they had been punished, their feelings of guilt were relieved. Richard's psychoanalyst suggested that Richard's anger over his father's death and his mother's abandonment created unconscious feelings of guilt, which he sought to relieve by committing a crime and being punished for it.

The psychoanalyst also offered an alternative explanation for Richard's persistent criminal activities: His conscience was perhaps not too strong but too weak. The conscience, or superego, was so weak or defective that he was unable to control the impulses of the id. Because the superego is essentially an internalized parental image, developed when the child assumes the parents' attitudes and moral values, it follows that the absence of such an image may lead to an unrestrained id and thus to delinquency.[4]

Psychoanalytic theory suggests yet another explanation for Richard's behavior: an insatiable need for immediate reward and gratification. A defect in the character formation of delinquents drives them to satisfy their desires at once, regardless of the consequences.[5] This urge, which psychoanalysts attribute to the id, is so strong that relationships with people are important only so long as they help to satisfy it. Most analysts view delinquents as children unable to give up their desire for instant pleasure.

The psychoanalytic approach is still one of the most prominent explanations for both normal and asocial functioning. Despite criticism,[6] three basic principles still appeal to psychologists who study criminality:

1. The actions and behavior of an adult are understood in terms of childhood development.
2. Behavior and unconscious motives are intertwined, and their interaction must be unraveled if we are to understand criminality.
3. Criminality is essentially a representation of psychological conflict.

In spite of their appeal, psychoanalytic treatment techniques devised to address these principles have been controversial since their introduction by Freud and his disciples. The controversy has involved questions about improvement following treatment and, perhaps more important, the validity of the hypothetical conflicts the treatment presupposes.

Moral Development

Consider the following moral dilemma:

> In Europe, a woman is near death from a special kind of cancer. There is one drug that the doctors think might save her. It is a form of radium that a druggist in the same town has recently discovered. The drug is expensive to make, and the druggist is charging ten times that cost. He paid $200 for the radium and is charging $2,000 for a small dose of the drug. The sick woman's husband, Heinz, goes to everyone he knows to borrow the money, but he can get together only $1,000. He tells the druggist that his wife is dying and asks him to sell the drug more cheaply or to let him pay later. The druggist says, "No, I discovered the drug and I'm going to make money from it." Heinz is desperate and considers breaking into the man's store to steal the drug for his wife.[7]

This classic dilemma sets up complex moral issues. While you may know that it is wrong to steal, you may believe that this is a situation in which the law should be circumvented. Or is it always wrong to steal, no matter what the circumstances? Regardless of what you decide, the way you reach the decision about whether or not to steal reveals much about your moral development.

The psychologist Lawrence Kohlberg, who pioneered moral developmental theory, has found that moral reasoning develops in three phases.[8] In the first, the preconventional level, children's moral rules and moral values consist of dos and don'ts to avoid punishment. A desire to avoid punishment and a belief in the superior power of authorities are the two central reasons for doing what is right. According to the theory, until the ages of 9 to 11, children usually reason at this level. They think, in effect, "If I steal, what are my chances of getting caught and being punished?"

Adolescents typically reason at the conventional level. Now individuals believe in and have adopted the values and rules of society. Moreover, they seek to uphold these rules. They think, in effect, "It is illegal to steal and therefore I should not steal, under any circumstances." Finally, at the postconventional level, individuals examine customs and social rules according to their own sense of universal human rights, moral principles, and duties. They think, in effect, "One must live within the law, but certain universal ethical principles, such as respect for human rights and for the dignity of human life, supersede the written law when the two conflict." This level of moral reasoning is generally seen in adults after the age of 20. (See Table 4.1.)

According to Kohlberg and his colleagues, most delinquents and criminals reason at the preconventional level. Low moral development or preconventional reasoning alone, however, does not result in criminality. Other factors, such as the presence or the absence of significant social bonds, may play a part. Kohlberg has argued that basic moral principles and social norms are learned through social interaction and role playing. In essence, children learn how to be moral by reasoning with others who are at a higher level of moral development.[9]

Students of Kohlberg have looked at practical applications of his theory. What would happen, for instance, if delinquents who were poor moral reasoners were exposed to individuals who reasoned at a higher level? Joseph Hickey, William Jennings, and their associates designed programs for Connecticut and Florida prisons and applied them in school systems throughout the United States. The "just-community intervention" approach involves a structured educational curriculum stressing democracy, fairness, and a sense of community. Above all, the focus is on the growth and development of moral reasoning. A series of evaluations of just-community programs has revealed significant improvement in moral development.[10]

Maternal Deprivation and Attachment Theory

In a well-known psychological experiment, infant monkeys were provided with the choice between two wire "monkeys." One, made of uncovered cage wire, dispensed milk. The other, made of cage wire covered with soft fabric, did not give milk. The infant monkeys in the experiment gravitated to the warm cloth monkey, which provided comfort and security even though it did not provide food. What does this have to do with criminality? Research has demonstrated that a phenomenon important to social development takes

TABLE 4.1 Kohlberg's Sequence of Moral Reasoning			
		Sample Moral Reasoning	
Level	**Stage**	**In Favor of Stealing**	**Against Stealing**
Level 1: Preconventional morality. At this level, the concrete interests of the individual are considered in terms of rewards and punishments.	*Stage 1: Obedience and punishment orientation.* At this stage, people stick to rules in order to avoid punishment, and there is obedience for its own sake.	If you let your wife die, you will get in trouble. You'll be blamed for not spending the money to save her, and there'll be an investigation of you and the druggist for your wife's death.	You shouldn't steal the drug because you'll be caught and sent to jail if you do. If you do get away, your conscience will bother you, thinking how the police will catch up with you at any minute.
	Stage 2: Reward orientation. At this stage, rules are followed only for one's own benefit. Obedience occurs because of rewards that are received.	If you do happen to get caught, you could give the drug back and you wouldn't get much of a sentence. It wouldn't bother you much to serve a little jail term, if you have your wife when you get out.	You may not get much of a jail term if you steal the drug, but your wife will probably die before you get out, so it won't do much good. If your wife dies, you shouldn't blame yourself; it wasn't your fault she had cancer.
Level 2: Conventional morality. At this level, moral problems are approached by an individual as a member of society. People are interested in pleasing others by acting as good members of society.	*Stage 3: "Good boy" morality.* Individuals at this stage show an interest in maintaining the respect of others and doing what is expected of them.	No one will think you're bad if you steal the drug, but your family will think you're an inhuman husband if you don't. If you let your wife die, you'll never be able to look anybody in the face again.	It isn't just the druggist who will think you're a criminal; everyone else will too. After you steal it, you'll feel bad, thinking how you've brought dishonor on your family and yourself; you won't be able to face anyone again.
	Stage 4: Authority and social-order-maintaining morality. People at this stage conform to society's rules and consider that "right" is what society defines as right.	If you have any sense of honor, you won't let your wife die just because you're afraid to do the only thing that will save her. You'll always feel guilty that you caused her death if you don't do your duty to her.	You're desperate and you may not know you're doing wrong when you steal the drug. But you'll know you did wrong after you're sent to jail. You'll always feel guilty for your dishonesty and lawbreaking.

(Continued on next page)

TABLE 4.1   Kohlberg's Sequence of Moral Reasoning (*continued*)

		Sample Moral Reasoning	
Level	Stage	In Favor of Stealing	Against Stealing
Level 3: Postconventional morality. People at this level use moral principles which are seen as broader than those of any particular society.	*Stage 5: Morality of contract, individual rights, and democratically accepted law.* People at this stage do what is right because of a sense of obligation to laws which are agreed upon within society. They perceive that laws can be modified as part of changes in an implicit social contract.	You'll lose other people's respect, not gain it, if you don't steal. If you let your wife die, it will be out of fear, not out of reasoning. So you'll just lose self-respect and probably the respect of others too.	You'll lose your standing and respect in the community and violate the law. You'll lose respect for yourself if you're carried away by emotion and forget the long-range point of view.
	Stage 6: Morality of individual principles and conscience. At this final stage, a person follows laws because they are based on universal ethical principles. Laws that violate the principles are disobeyed.	If you don't steal the drug, if you let your wife die, you'll always condemn yourself for it afterward. You won't be blamed and you'll have lived up to the outside rule of the law, but you won't have lived up to your own standards of conscience.	If you steal the drug, you won't be blamed by other people but you'll condemn yourself because you won't have lived up to your own conscience and standards of honesty.

Source: Adapted from Robert S. Feldman, *Understanding Psychology* (New York: McGraw-Hill, 1987), p. 378.

place shortly after the birth of any mammal: the construction of an emotional bond between the infant and its mother. The strength of this emotional bond, or **attachment,** will determine, or at least materially affect, a child's ability to form attachments in the future. In order to form a successful attachment, a child needs a warm, loving, and interactive caretaker.

Studies of Attachment. The psychologist John Bowlby has studied both the need for warmth and affection from birth onward and the consequences of not having it. He has proposed a theory of attachment with seven important features:

- *Specificity.* Attachments are selective, usually directed to one or more individuals in some order of preference.
- *Duration.* Attachments endure and persist, sometimes throughout the life cycle.
- *Engagement of emotion.* Some of the most intense emotions are associated with attachment relationships.

- *Ontogeny (course of development).* Children form an attachment to one primary figure in the first 9 months of life. That principal attachment figure is the person who supplies the most social interaction of a satisfying kind.
- *Learning.* Though learning plays a role in the development of attachment, Bowlby finds that attachments are the products not of rewards or reinforcements but of basic social interaction.
- *Organization.* Attachment behavior follows cognitive development and interpersonal maturation from birth onward.
- *Biological function.* Attachment behavior has a biological function—survival. It is found in almost all species of mammals and in birds.[11]

Bowlby contends that a child needs to experience a warm, intimate, and continuous relationship with either a mother or a mother substitute in order to be securely attached. When a child is separated from the mother or is rejected by her, anxious attachment

Experiments with young monkeys and surrogate mothers reveal the power of attachment in behavioral development.

results. Anxious attachment affects the capacity to be affectionate and to develop intimate relationships with others. Habitual criminals, it is claimed, typically have an inability to form bonds of affection:

> More often than not the childhoods of such individuals are found to have been grossly disturbed by death, divorce, or separation of the parents, or by other events resulting in disruption of bonds, with an incidence of such disturbance far higher than is met with in any other comparable group, whether drawn from the general population or from psychiatric casualties of other sorts.[12]

Considerable research supports the relationship between anxious attachment and subsequent behavioral problems:

- In a study of 113 middle-class children observed at 1 year and again at 6 years, researchers noted a significant relationship between behavior at age 6 and attachment at age 1.[13]
- In a study of 40 children seen when they were 1 year old and again at 18 months, it was noted that anxiously attached children were less empathetic, independent, compliant, and confident than securely attached children.[14]
- Researchers have noted that the quality of one's attachment correlates significantly with asocial preschool behavior—being aggressive, leaving the group, and the like.[15]

Family Atmosphere and Delinquency. Criminologists also have examined the effects of the mother's absence, whether because of death, divorce, or abandonment. Does her absence cause delinquency? Empirical research is equivocal. Perhaps the most persuasive evidence comes from longitudinal research conducted by Joan McCord, who has investigated the relationship between family atmosphere (such as parental self-confidence, deviance, and affection) and delinquency.

In one study, she collected data on the childhood homes of 201 men and their subsequent court records in order to identify family-related variables that would predict criminal activity. Such variables as inadequate maternal affection and supervision, parental conflict, the mother's lack of self-confidence, and the father's deviance were significantly related to the commission of crimes against persons and/or property. The father's absence was not by itself correlated with criminal behavior.[16]

Other studies, such as those by Sheldon and Eleanor Glueck and the more recent studies by Lee N. Robins, which were carried out in schools, juvenile courts, and psychiatric hospitals, suggest a moderate to strong relation between crime and childhood deprivation.[17] However, evidence that deprivation directly causes delinquency is lacking.[18]

So far we have considered psychological theories that attribute the causes of delinquency or criminality to unconscious problems and failures in moral development. Not all psychologists agree with these explanations of criminal behavior. Some argue that human behavior develops through learning. They say that we learn by observing others and by watching the responses to other people's behavior (on television or in the movies, for instance) and to our own. Social

AT ISSUE

THE CRIME OF PARRICIDE

Mark Martone was 16 when he shot his father to death. [He] remembers abuse back to age five, when he told his dad he was scared of the dark. "Oh, Jesus Christ," said the parent in disgust. Then he led the terrified boy down to the cellar, handcuffed his arms over a rafter, turned off the light and shut the door. Mark dangled in silence for hours. When Mark was nine, his father held the boy's hand over a red-hot burner as punishment for moving a book of matches on a bureau. And when he was 15, his dad, angered by a long-distance phone bill, stuck a gun in his son's mouth and "told me he was going to blow my brains out."(1)

An estimated 5.7 million children in the United States are physically, mentally, and sexually abused by their parents annually, and the problem is not lessening. Of those millions of children, maybe a few hundred each year fight back with the ultimate weapon: They kill the abusive parent. In the past such children were regarded as particularly evil, and the law reserved the most terrible forms of capital punishment for parricides. With the growing understanding of the horrors of child abuse, however, these youths are being treated with increasing sympathy. "They know what they're doing is wrong," comments a psychologist at the University of Virginia. "But they are desperate and helpless, and they don't see alternatives."(1)

The typical case involves a 16- to 18-year-old from a white middle-class family. Sons are more likely than daughters to commit murder, and the victim is more likely to be a father than a mother. While children who kill nonabusive parents usually display some sign of mental disorder, the killers of abusive parents generally are seen as well adjusted.(2)

The increasing sympathy for these teenagers has led to verdicts of not guilty by reason of self-defense or guilty of reduced charges (for example, manslaughter instead of first-degree murder). A "battered-child-syndrome" defense sometimes is successful, but the killings do not usually fit the typical idea of self-defense: Most happen when the parent is in a vulnerable position instead of in the middle of an attack on the child. But mental-health experts think that treatment is more appropriate than punishment for children who kill their abusive parents. "These kids don't need to be locked up for our protection," says one attorney and psychologist. "Some may benefit in the sense that they've been able to atone and overcome some guilt. But beyond that, it's really Draconian."(1)

CHARACTERISTICS ASSOCIATED WITH ADOLESCENT PARRICIDE OFFENDERS

1. Patterns of family violence (parental brutality and cruelty toward child and/or toward one another).
2. Adolescent's attempts to get help from others fail.
3. Adolescent's efforts to escape family situation fail (e.g., running away, thoughts of suicide, suicide attempts).
4. Adolescent is isolated from others/fewer outlets.

5. Family situation becomes increasingly intolerable.
6. Adolescent feels increasingly helpless, trapped.
7. Adolescent's inability to cope leads to loss of control.
8. Prior criminal behavior minimal or nonexistent.
9. Availability of gun.
10. Homicide victim is alcoholic.
11. Evidence to suggest dissociative state in some cases.
12. Victim's death perceived as relief to offender/family; initial absence of remorse.

Sources

1. Hannah Bloch and Jeanne McDowell, "When Kids Kill Abusive Parents," *Time,* Nov. 23, 1992.
2. Kathleen M. Heide, *Why Kids Kill Parents* (Columbus: Ohio State University Press, 1992), pp. 40–41.

Questions for Discussion

1. If you were on a jury, would you be willing to consider that what appears to be "cold-blooded murder" might have been a form of self-defense for a battered child?
2. An attorney specializing in parricide feels that such cases "open a window on our understanding of child abuse." How would you go about determining which of millions of child abuse cases are likely to lead to parricide for which a standard defense should be recognized?

Source: Excerpted from Kathleen M. Heide, *Why Kids Kill Parents* (Columbus: Ohio State University Press, 1992), table 3.1, pp. 40–41.

learning theorists reject the notion that internal functioning alone makes us prone to act aggressively or violently.

Learning Aggression and Violence

Social learning theory maintains that delinquent behavior is learned through the same psychological processes as any other behavior. Behavior is learned when it is reinforced or rewarded; it is not learned when it is not reinforced. We learn behavior in various ways: observation, direct experience, and differential reinforcement.

Observational Learning. Albert Bandura, a leading proponent of social learning theory, argues that individuals learn violence and aggression through **behavioral modeling:** Children learn how to behave by fashioning their behavior after that of others. Behavior is socially transmitted through examples, which come primarily from the family, the subculture, and the mass media.[19]

Psychologists have been studying the effects of family violence (Chapter 11) on children. They have found that parents who try to resolve family controversies by violence teach their children to use similar tactics. Thus a cycle of violence may be perpetuated through generations. Observing a healthy and happy family environment tends to result in constructive and positive modeling.

To understand the influence of the social environment outside the home, social learning theorists have studied gangs, which often provide excellent models of observational learning of violence and aggression. They have found, in fact, that violence is very much a norm shared by some people in a community or gang. The highest incidence of aggressive behavior occurs where aggressiveness is a desired characteristic, as it is in some subcultures.

Observational learning takes place in front of the television set and at the movies, as well. Children who have seen others being rewarded for violent acts often believe that violence and aggression are acceptable behaviors.[20] And today children can see a lot of violence, as Table 4.2 shows. The psychologist Leonard Eron has argued that the "single best predictor of how aggressive a young man would be when he was 19 years old was the violence of the television programs he preferred when he was 8 years old."[21]

TABLE 4.2 One Day's Body Count		
Between the hours of 6 A.M. and midnight on April 2, 1992, ABC, CBS, NBC, PBS, FOX, WDCA-Washington, Turner, USA, MTV and HBO combined aired the following carnage:		
Act	Number of Scenes	Percent of Total
Serious assaults (without guns)	389	20
Gunplay	362	18
Isolated punches	273	14
Pushing, dragging	272	14
Menacing threat with a weapon	226	11
Slaps	128	6
Deliberate destruction of property	95	5
Simple assault	73	4
All other types	28	1

Source: Harry F. Waters, "Networks under the Gun," *Newsweek,* July 12, 1993, p. 65.

There is, of course, another side to the issue of television violence. Researchers conducted a longitudinal study to assess the association between children's aggressive behavior and exposure to violence on television. Questionnaire data were collected on 3718 subjects in four time periods between 1970 and 1973. Responses were coded by exposure time and "violence weights" and compared with self-reports of violent behavior. The findings indicate that exposure to violence on television is statistically unrelated to self-reported violent behavior. The question remains open.[22]

Direct Experience. What we learn by observation is determined by the behavior of others. What we

CENSORING TV VIOLENCE

On December 19, 1996, the U.S. television industry announced a voluntary TV ratings system. All TV shows are now rated as follows:

- TV-Y, material suitable for children of all ages. Show contains little or no violence, strong language, or sexual content.
- TV-Y7, material suitable for children 7 and older.
- TV-G, material suitable for all audiences.
- TV-PG, parental guidance is suggested. Program may contain infrequent coarse language, limited violence, some suggestive sexual dialogue and situations.
- TV-14, material may be inappropriate for children under 14. Program may contain sophisticated themes, strong language, and sexual content.
- TV-M, for mature audiences only. Program may contain profane language, graphic violence, and explicit sexual content.

What prompted this unprecedented move? Many Americans had for some time been concerned about the ever-increasing amount of violence on television and its effects on children.(1)

SOCIAL CONTROL VERSUS CENSORSHIP

While many people saw the networks' plans for ratings as a disappointingly small contribution to a big problem, others began worrying about freedom of expression. Representative Edward J. Markey pushed for a plan that would require "V-block" computer chips in all new TV sets—the chip would allow parents to block all V-rated (violent) shows. "'That's getting awfully close to censorship,' frets Peggy Charren, founder of Action for Children's Television."(1)

If such warnings and "zappings" do constitute censorship, the United States is way behind other countries. In Egypt, both radio and television are owned by the state, and all broadcasts are supervised by the government.(2) In Singapore, television also is state-controlled, but a 1991 revamp of the country's film classification system was going to allow movie audiences to see for the first time "a little more sex, nudity and violence."(3) India, despite being open to satellite-dish broadcasting, was still using its government-run network in 1992 to censor the violence that occurred during religious riots across the country.(4) Indonesia's government announced in 1993 that censoring all materials citizens could watch on private and foreign networks had become "too onerous a task" for its National Film Censorship Board; it stated that the people themselves should judge what to watch and should avoid "morally unsuitable" programs, such as those containing pornography and violence.(5)

The Chinese Example

Perhaps China provides the most prominent example of the use of television for social control: "In the hands of Chinese media experts, TV

learn from direct experience is determined by what we ourselves do and what happens to us. We remember the past and use its lessons to avoid future mistakes. Thus we learn through trial and error. According to social learning theorists, after engaging in a given behavior, most of us examine the responses to our actions and modify our behavior as necessary to obtain favorable responses. If we are praised or rewarded for a behavior, we are likely to repeat it. If we are subjected to verbal or physical punishment, we are likely to refrain from such behavior. Our behavior in the first instance and our restraint in the second are said to be "reinforced" by the rewards and punishments we receive.

The psychologist Gerald Patterson and his colleagues examined how aggression is learned by direct experience. They observed that some passive children at play were repeatedly victimized by other children but were occasionally successful in curbing the attacks by counteraggression. Over time, these children learned defensive fighting, and eventually they initiated fights. Other passive children, who were rarely observed to be victimized, remained submissive.[23] Thus children, like adults, can learn to be aggressive and even violent by trial and error.

While violence and aggression are learned behaviors, they are not necessarily expressed until they are elicited in one of several ways. Albert Bandura describes the factors that elicit behavioral responses as "instigators." Thus social learning theory describes not only how aggression is acquired but also how it is instigated. Consider the following instigators of aggression:

- *Aversive instigators.* Physical assaults, verbal threats, and insults; adverse reductions in condi-

WINDOW TO THE WORLD

is both an instrument to instill terror and obedience and an educational tool," wrote *Newsday* reporter Thomas Collins after the Tiananmen Square protests. "The . . . important thing was to control and limit what a billion Chinese people would believe had happened."(6) According to Collins, the event was portrayed as follows:

> Rather than a demonstration for democratic reforms involving millions of people throughout the country, the protests were the work of a handful of "counterrevolutionaries" and "hoodlums." Instead of the massacre of hundreds, possibly thousands of students and workers, the Chinese populace is being told that the only casualties were soldiers. No students were killed.

A study of the 1991–1992 television season shows that children's programming actually features more violence than prime time shows.

	Children's Programs	Prime Time
Violent acts per hour	32	4
Violent characters	56%	34%
Characters who are victims of violence	74%	34%
Characters who are killers or who get killed	3.3%	5.7%
Characters involved in violence as perpetrators or victims	79%	47%

Source: Harry F. Waters, "Networks under the Gun," *Newsweek*, July 12, 1993, p. 64.

Sources

1. "Harry F. Waters, "Networks under the Gun," *Newsweek*, July 12, 1993, pp. 64–66.
2. "Middle East Watch Report," *Middle East News Network*, Nov. 17, 1991.
3. "Singapore: Opening Up to a Little Sex and Nudity," *Inter Press Service*, Apr. 15, 1991.
4. Molly Moore, "Satellite TV Shows Asia a World beyond Reach of State Censors," *Washington Post*, Apr. 10, 1993, p. A12.
5. "Indonesia to Revamp Film Censorship," *Straits Times*, Apr. 29, 1993, p. 13.
6. Thomas Collins, "In China, The Carnage That Never Was," *Newsday*, June 14, 1989, p. 67.

Questions for Discussion

1. Research suggests an association between children's exposure to TV violence and the likelihood that they will resolve their own conflicts by violent means. Are we then justified in censoring TV violence?
2. Suppose censorship were imposed. How could we then measure the impact of censorship on rates of violent crime?

tions of life (such as impoverishment) and the thwarting of goal-directed behavior
- *Incentive instigators.* Rewards, such as money and praise
- *Modeling instigators.* Violent or aggressive behaviors observed in others
- *Instructional instigators.* Observations of people carrying out instructions to engage in violence or aggression
- *Delusional instigators.* Unfounded or bizarre beliefs that violence is necessary or justified[24]

Differential Reinforcement. In 1965 the criminologist C. Ray Jeffery suggested that learning theory could be used to explain criminality.[25] Within one year Ernest Burgess and Ronald Akers combined Bandura's psychologically based learning theory with Edwin Sutherland's sociologically based dif-

ferential association theory (Chapter 5) to produce the theory of **differential association-reinforcement.** This theory suggests that (1) the persistence of criminal behavior depends on whether or not it is rewarded or punished, and (2) the most meaningful rewards and punishments are those given by groups that are important in an individual's life—the peer group, the family, teachers in school, and so forth. In other words, people respond more readily to the reactions of the most significant people in their lives. If criminal behavior elicits more positive reinforcement or rewards than punishment, it will persist.[26]

Social learning theory helps us understand why some individuals who engage in violent and aggressive behavior do so: They learn to behave that way. But perhaps something within the personality of a criminal creates a susceptibility to aggressive or violent models in the first place. For example, perhaps criminals are more extraverted, irresponsible, or unsocialized than noncriminals. Or perhaps criminals are more intolerant and impulsive or have lower self-esteem.

Personality

Four distinct lines of psychological research have examined the relation between personality and criminality.[27] First, investigators have looked at the differences between the personality structures of criminals and noncriminals. Most of this work has been carried out in state and federal prisons, where psychologists have administered personality questionnaires such as the Minnesota Multiphasic Personality Inventory (MMPI) and the California Psychological Inventory (CPI) to inmates. The evidence from these studies shows that inmates are typically more impulsive, hostile, self-centered, and immature than noncriminals.[28]

Second, a vast amount of literature is devoted to the prediction of behavior. Criminologists want to determine how an individual will respond to prison discipline and whether he or she will avoid crime after release. The results are equivocal. At best, personality characteristics seem to be modest predictors of future criminality.[29] Yet when they are combined with such variables as personal history, they tend to increase the power of prediction significantly.[30]

Third, many studies examine the degree to which normal personality dynamics operate in criminals. Findings from these studies suggest that the personality dynamics of criminals are often quite similar to those of noncriminals. Social criminals (those who act in concert with others), for example, are found to be more sociable, affiliative, outgoing, and self-confident than solitary criminals.[31]

Finally, some researchers have attempted to quantify individual differences between types and groups of offenders. Several studies have compared the personality characteristics of first-time offenders with those of repeat or habitual criminals. Other investigators have compared violent offenders with nonviolent offenders and murderers with drug offenders. In addition, prison inmates have been classified according to personality type.[32]

In general, research on criminals' personality characteristics has revealed some important associations. However, criminologists have been skeptical of the strength of the relationship of personality to criminality. A review of research on that relationship published in 1942 by Milton Metfessel and Constance

Lovell dismissed personality as an important causal factor in criminal behavior.[33] In 1950 Karl Schuessler and Donald Cressey reached the same conclusion.[34] Twenty-seven years later, Daniel Tennenbaum's updated review agreed with earlier assessments. He found that "the data do not reveal any significant differences between criminal and noncriminal psychology. . . . Personality testing has not differentiated criminals from noncriminals."[35]

Despite these conclusions, whether or not criminals share personality characteristics continues to be debated. Are criminals in fact more aggressive, dominant, and manipulative than noncriminals? Are they more irresponsible? Clearly, many criminals are aggressive; many have manipulated a variety of situations; many assume no responsibility for their acts. But are such characteristics common to all criminals? Samuel Yochelson and Stanton Samenow addressed these questions. In *The Criminal Personality*, this psychiatrist-psychologist team described their growing disillusion with traditional explanations of criminality.

From their experience in treating criminals in the Forensic Division of St. Elizabeth's Hospital in Washington, D.C., they refuted psychoanalysts' claims that crime is caused by inner conflict. Rather, they said, criminals share abnormal "thinking patterns" that lead to decisions to commit crimes. Yochelson and Samenow identified as many as 52 patterns of thinking common to the criminals they studied. They argued that criminals are "angry" people who feel a sense of superiority, expect not to be held accountable for their acts, and have a highly inflated self-image. Any perceived attack on their glorified self-image elicits a strong reaction, often a violent one.[36]

Other researchers have used different methods to study the association between criminality and personality. William Laufer and his colleagues conducted a review of the findings of a large sample of studies that had used the California Psychological Inventory. Their research revealed a common personality profile: The criminals tested showed remarkable similarity in their deficient self-control, intolerance, and lack of responsibility.[37]

Though studies dealing with personality correlates of criminals are important, some psychologists are concerned that by focusing on the personalities of criminals in their search for explanations of criminal behavior, investigators may overlook other important factors, like the complex social environment in which a crime is committed.[38] A homicide that began as a barroom argument between two intoxicated patrons who backed different teams to win the Super Bowl, for example, is very likely to hinge on situational factors that interact with their personalities.

Eysenck's Conditioning Theory. For over 20 years Hans J. Eysenck has been developing and refining a theory of the relationship between personality and criminality that considers more than just individual characteristics.[39] His theory has two parts. First, Eysenck claims that all human personality may be seen in three dimensions—psychoticism, extroversion, and neuroticism. Individuals who score high on measures of **psychoticism** are aggressive, egocentric, and impulsive. Those who score high on measures of **extroversion** are sensation-seeking, dominant, and assertive. High scorers on scales assessing **neuroticism** may be described as having low self-esteem, excessive anxiety, and wide mood swings. Eysenck has found that when criminals respond to items on the Eysenck Personality Questionnaire (EPQ), they uniformly score higher on each of these dimensions than do noncriminals.

The second part of Eysenck's theory suggests that humans develop a conscience through **conditioning.** From birth on we are rewarded for social behavior and punished for asocial behavior. Eysenck likens this conditioning to training a dog. Puppies are not born house-trained. You have to teach a puppy that it is good to urinate and defecate outside your apartment or house by pairing kind words and perhaps some tangible reward (such as a dog treat) with successful outings. A loud, angry voice will convey disapproval and disappointment when mistakes are made inside.

In time most dogs learn and, according to Eysenck, develop a conscience. But as Eysenck also has noted, some dogs learn faster than others. German shepherds acquire good "bathroom habits" faster than basenjis, who are most difficult to train. It is argued that the same is true of humans; there are important individual differences. Criminals become conditioned slowly and appear to care little whether or not their asocial actions bring disapproval.

Eysenck has identified two additional aspects of a criminal's poor conditionability. First, he has found that extroverts are much more difficult to condition than introverts and thus have greater difficulty in developing a conscience. Youthful offenders tend to score highest on measures of extroversion. Second, differences in conditionability are dependent on certain physiological factors, the most important of which is **cortical arousal,** or activation of the cerebral cortex.

The cortex of the brain is responsible for higher intellectual functioning, information processing, and decision making. Eysenck found that individuals who are easily conditionable and develop a conscience have a high level of cortical arousal; they do not need intense external stimulation to become aroused. A low level of cortical arousal is associated with poor conditionability, difficulty in developing a conscience, and need for external stimulation.

MENTAL DISORDERS AND CRIME

It has been difficult for psychiatrists to derive criteria that would help them decide which offenders are mentally ill. According to psychiatrist Seymour L. Halleck, the problem lies in the evolving conceptualization of mental illness. Traditionally the medical profession viewed mental illness as an absolute condition or status—either you are afflicted with **psychosis** or you are not. Should such a view concern us? Halleck suggests that it should. "Although this kind of thinking is not compatible with current psychiatric

John DuPont, heir to the DuPont fortune, who imagined himself to be the Christ Child, the Dalai Lama, and the crown prince of Russia, killed the Olympic wrestler he had hired as a coach. DuPont was found guilty but mentally ill at trial. He has been diagnosed as paranoid schizophrenic.

CRIMINOLOGICAL FOCUS

MYTHS OF THE INSANITY DEFENSE

Criminologists who study the most famous connection between mental illness and crime—the insanity defense—have had little to say over the past 20 years. Empirical research on the number of cases where the defense has been raised provides few novel insights and findings.(1) Retentionists and abolitionists occasionally renew their calls.(2) The print and television media exploit efforts to raise the insanity defense in cases of unspeakable and senseless violence.(3) National, state, and local politicians join the fray with calls for legislative reform designed to limit the use of the insanity defense."(4) Americans recoil at the image of factually guilty offenders using a defense to criminal responsibility that allows for acquittal in the face of conclusive inculpatory evidence.(5) And, some say, we are all

held prisoner by stereotypes and myths about the insanity defense.

It has been argued that the insanity defense is a prisoner of a host of myths and symbols rooted in medieval folklore and fundamentalist visions of mental illness and crime. These myths and symbols reveal our collective "punitive spirit" and "moralized aggression."(6) They reject the value of psychiatry and psychology, including psychodynamic explanations of human behavior.(7) The use of the insanity defense creates so much controversy because the public recognizes that in a few select cases the defense is necessary. At the same time, most are convinced that in virtually all cases of criminal violence some punishment is required and deserved. Reconciling the limited need for the defense with a strong desire for an exacting punishment is often too much of a challenge.

Myths about the insanity defense survive even though they are not grounded in scientific and behavioral evidence (see table). Unpacking these myths reveals four common misconceptions:

1. That those claiming the insanity defense are feigning mental illness
2. That mental illness is really different from other illness
3. That a legally insane defendant must have a different "look" or appearance from one who is sane
4. That mental illness should generally not permit an otherwise guilty person to escape punishment.(8)

Most of these myths persist because we harbor distorted assumptions about the legally insane.(9) Many are made more believable by the often distorted portrayal of the

knowledge," he writes, "it continues to exert considerable influence upon psychiatric practice. . . . As applied to the criminal, it also leads to rigid dichotomies between the 'sick criminal' and the 'normal criminal.'"[40]

Halleck and other psychiatrists, such as Karl Menninger, conceptualize mental functioning as a process.[41] Mental illness may not be considered apart from mental health—the two exist on the same continuum. At various times in each of our lives we move along the continuum from health toward illness.[42] For this reason, a diagnosis of "criminal" or "mentally ill" may overlook potentially important gradations in mental health and mental illness. This issue is perhaps no more apparent than in the insanity defense, which calls for proof of sanity or insanity and generally does not allow for gradations in mental functioning (see Chapter 10).

Estimates vary, but between 20 and 60 percent of state correctional populations suffer from a type of mental disorder that in the nineteenth century was described by the French physician Philippe Pinel as

manie sans délire ("madness without confusion"), by the English physician James C. Prichard as "moral insanity," and by Gina Lombroso Ferrero as "irresistible atavistic impulses." Today such mental illness is called **psychopathy,** sociopathy, or antisocial personality—a personality characterized by the inability to learn from experience, lack of warmth, and absence of guilt.

The psychiatrist Hervey Cleckley views **psychopathy** as a serious illness even though patients may not appear to be ill. According to Cleckley, psychopaths appear to enjoy excellent mental health; but what we see is only a "mask of sanity." Initially they seem free of any kind of mental disorder and appear to be reliable and honest. After some time, however, it becomes clear that they have no sense of responsibility whatsoever. They show a disregard for truth, are insincere, and feel no sense of shame, guilt, or humiliation. Psychopaths lie and cheat without hesitation and engage in verbal as well as physical abuse without any thought. Cleckley describes the following case:

CRIMINOLOGICAL FOCUS

Empirical Myths

Myth 1	The insanity defense is overused.
Myth 2	Use of the insanity defense is limited to murder cases.
Myth 3	There is no risk to the defendant who pleads insanity.
Myth 4	Not Guilty by Reason of Insanity (NGRI) acquittees are quickly released from custody.
Myth 5	NGRI acquittees spend much less time in custody than do defendants convicted of the same offenses.
Myth 6	Criminal defendants who plead insanity are usually faking.
Myth 7	Most insanity defense trials feature "battles of the experts."
Myth 8	Criminal defense attorneys—perhaps inappropriately—employ the insanity defense solely to "beat the rap."

mentally ill offender on television and in the newspapers.

Sources

1. Perlin, *The Jurisprudence of the Insanity Defense,* 100–132 (1994).
2. See, Morris, *Psychiatry and the Dangerous Criminal,* 41 S. Cal. L. Rev. 514 (1968); Morse, *Excusing the Crazy: The Insanity Defense Revisited,* 58 S. Cal. L. Rev. 777 (1985).
3. Id at 14–16.
4. Id at 96–97.
5. Perlin considers the *Hinkey* case as a paradigm for understanding public furor. See, Perlin supra note 1 at 14–16.
6. Id at 29
7. Id at 444. According to Perlin: "Insanity defense decision making is often irrational. It rejects empiricism, science, psychology and philosophy, and substitutes myth, stereotype, bias and distortion." Id at 387.
8. Id at 232–233.
9. See, Perlin, *Morality and Precontextuality, Psychiatry and Law: Of "Ordinary Common Sense," Heuristic Reasoning, and Cognitive Dissonance,* 19 Bull. Am. Acad. Psychiatry & L. **131** (1991).

Questions for Discussion

1. Should mentally ill offenders remain in the criminal justice system? Should they stay in the general population, for example, at state correctional facilities?
2. Can you add any more myths to this list?
3. What is the source of the public's fascination with the insanity defense?

A sixteen-year-old boy was sent to jail for stealing a valuable watch. Though apparently . . . untouched by his situation, after a few questions were asked he began to seem more like a child who feels the unpleasantness of his position. He confessed that he had worried much about masturbation, saying he had been threatened and punished severely for it and told that it would cause him to become "insane."

He admitted having broken into his mother's jewelry box and stolen a watch valued at $150.00. He calmly related that he exchanged the watch for 15 cents' worth of ice cream and seemed entirely satisfied with what he had done. He readily admitted that his act was wrong, used the proper words to express his intention to cause no further trouble, and, when asked, said that he would like very much to get out of jail.

He stated that he loved his mother devotedly. "I just kiss her and kiss her ten or twelve times when she comes to see me!" he exclaimed with shallow zeal. These manifestations of affection were so artificial, and, one would even say, unconsciously artificial, that few laymen would be convinced that any feeling, in the ordinary sense, lay in them. Nor was his mother convinced.

A few weeks before this boy was sent to jail he displayed to his mother some rifle cartridges. When asked what he wanted with them he explained that they would fit the rifle in a nearby closet. "I've tried them," he announced. And in a lively tone added, "Why, I could put them in the gun and shoot you. You would fall right over!" He laughed and his eyes shone with a small but real impulse.[43]

Psychologists also have found that psychopaths, like Hans Eysenck's extroverts, have a low internal arousal level; thus psychopaths constantly seek external stimulation, are less susceptible to learning by direct experience (they do not modify their behavior after they are punished), are more impulsive, and experience far less anxiety than nonpsychopaths about any adverse consequences of their acts.[44] Some psychiatrists consider "psychopathy" to be an artificial label for an antisocial personality.[45] To Eysenck and others, it is a major behavioral category that presents significant challenges. Eysenck sums up this view by writing that the psychopath poses the riddle of delinquency. If we could solve the riddle, then we would have a powerful weapon to fight the problem of delinquency.[46]

BIOLOGY AND CRIMINALITY

Within the last two decades, biologists have followed in the tradition of Cesare Lombroso, Raffaele Garofalo, and Charles Goring in their search for answers to questions about human behavior. Geneticists, for example, have argued that the predisposition to act violently or aggressively in certain situations may be inherited. In other words, while criminals are not born criminal, the predisposition to be violent or commit crime may be present at birth.

To demonstrate that certain traits are inherited, geneticists have studied children born of criminals but reared from birth by noncriminal adoptive parents. They wanted to know whether the behavior of the adoptive children was more similar to that of their biological parents than to that of their adoptive parents. Their findings play an important role in the debate on heredity versus environment. Other biologists, sometimes called biocriminologists, take a different approach. Some ask whether brain damage or inadequate nutrition results in criminal behavior. Others are interested in the influence of hormones, chromosomal abnormalities, and allergies. They investigate interactions between brain and behavior and between diet and behavior.

Modern Biocriminology

Biocriminology is the study of the physical aspects of psychological disorders.[47] It has been known for some time that adults who suffer from depression show abnormalities in brain waves during sleep, experience disturbed nervous system functioning, and display biochemical abnormalities. Research on depressed children reveals the same physical problems; furthermore, their adult relatives show high rates of depression as well. In fact, children whose parents suffer from depression are more than four times more likely than the average child to experience a similar illness.[48] Some researchers believe depression is an inherited condition that manifests itself in psychological and physical disturbances. The important point is that until only recently, physicians may have been missing the mark in their assessment and treat-

ment of depressed children and adults by ignoring the physiological aspects.

Criminologists who study sociology and psychology to the exclusion of the biological sciences may also be missing the mark in their efforts to discover the causes of crime. Recent research has demonstrated that crime does indeed have psychobiological aspects similar to those found in studies of depression—biochemical abnormalities, abnormal brain waves, nervous system dysfunction. There is also evidence that strongly suggests a genetic predisposition to criminality.[49]

The resurgence of interest in integrating modern biological advances, theories, and principles into mainstream criminology began two decades ago. The sociobiological work of Edward Wilson on the interrelationship of biology, genetics, and social behavior was pivotal.[50] So were the contributions of C. Ray Jeffery, who argued that a biosocial interdisciplinary model should become the major theoretical framework for studying criminal behavior.[51]

Criminologists once again began to consider the possibility that there are indeed traits that predispose a person to criminality and that these traits may be passed from parent to child through the genes. Other questions arose as well. Is it possible, for instance, that internal biochemical imbalances or deficiencies cause antisocial behavior? Could too much or too little sugar in the bloodstream increase the potential for aggression? Or could a vitamin deficiency or some hormonal problem be responsible? We will explore the evidence for a genetic predisposition to criminal behavior, the relationship between biochemical factors and criminality, and neurophysiological factors that result in criminal behavior.

Genetics and Criminality

Today the proposition that human beings are products of an interaction between environmental and genetic factors is all but universally accepted.[52] We can stop asking, then, whether nature or nurture is more important in shaping us; we are the products of both. But what does the interaction between the two look like? And what concerns are raised by reliance on genetics to the exclusion of environmental factors? Consider the example of the XYY syndrome.

The XYY Syndrome. **Chromosomes** are the basic structures that contain our genes—the biological material that makes each of us unique. Each human being has 23 pairs of inherited chromosomes. One pair determines gender. A female receives an X chromosome from both mother and father; a male receives an X chromosome from his mother and a Y from his father. Sometimes a defect in the production of sperm or egg results in genetic abnormalities. One type of abnormality is the XYY chromosomal male. The XYY male receives two Y chromosomes from his father rather than one. Approximately 1 in 1000 newborn males in the general population has this genetic composition.[53] Initial studies done in the 1960s found the frequency of XYY chromosomes to be about 20 times greater than normal XY chromosomes among inmates in maximum security state hospitals.[54] The XYY inmates tended to be tall, physically aggressive, and frequently violent.

Supporters of these data claimed to have uncovered the mystery of violent criminality. Critics voiced concern over the fact that these studies were done on small and unrepresentative samples. The XYY syndrome, as this condition became known, received much public attention because of the case of Richard Speck. Speck, who in 1966 murdered eight nurses in Chicago, initially was diagnosed as an XYY chromosomal male. However, the diagnosis later turned out to be wrong. Nevertheless, public concern was aroused: Were all XYY males potential killers?

Studies undertaken since that time have discounted the relation between the extra Y chromosome and criminality.[55] Although convincing evidence in support of the XYY hypothesis appears to be slight, it is nevertheless possible that aggressive and violent behavior is at least partly determined by genetic factors. The problem is how to investigate this possibility. One difficulty is separating the external or environmental factors, such as family structure, culture, socioeconomic status, and peer influences, from the genetic predispositions with which they begin to interact at birth.

A particular individual may have a genetic predisposition to be violent but be born into a wealthy, well-educated, loving, and calm familial environment. He may never commit a violent act. Another person may have a genetic predisposition to be rule-abiding and nonaggressive yet be born into a poor, uneducated, physically abusive, and unloving family. He may commit violent criminal acts. How, then, can we determine the extent to which behavior is genetically influ-

enced? Researchers have turned to twin studies and adoption studies in the quest for an answer.

Twin Studies. To discover whether or not crime is genetically predetermined, researchers have compared identical and fraternal twins. Identical, or **monozygotic (MZ),** twins develop from a single fertilized egg that divides into two embryos. These twins share all their genes. Fraternal, or **dizygotic (DZ),** twins develop from two separate eggs, both fertilized at the same time. They share about half of their genes. Since the prenatal and postnatal family environments are, by and large, the same, greater behavioral similarity between identical twins than between fraternal twins would support an argument for genetic predisposition.

In the 1920s a German physician, Johannes Lange, found 30 pairs of same-sex twins—13 identical and 17 fraternal pairs. One member of each pair was a known criminal. Lange found that in 10 of the 13 pairs of identical twins, both twins were criminal; in 2 of the 17 pairs of fraternal twins, both were criminal.[56] The research techniques of the time were limited, but Lange's results were nevertheless impressive.

Many similar studies have followed. The largest was a study by Karl Christiansen and Sarnoff A. Mednick which included all twins born between 1881 and 1910 in a region of Denmark, a total of 3586 pairs. Reviewing serious offenses only, Christiansen and

Separated at birth, the Mallifert twins meet accidentally.

Mednick found that the chance of there being a criminal twin when the other twin was a criminal was 50 percent for identical twins and 20 percent for same-sex fraternal twins.[57] Such findings lend support to the hypothesis that some genetic influences increase the risk of criminality.[58] A more recent American study conducted by David C. Rowe and D. Wayne Osgood reached a similar conclusion.[59]

While the evidence from these and other twin studies looks persuasive, we should keep in mind the weakness of such research. It may not be valid to assume a common environment for all twins who grow up in the same house at the same time. If the upbringing of identical twins is much more similar than that of fraternal twins, as it well may be, that circumstance could help explain their different rates of criminality.

Adoption Studies. One way to separate the influence of inherited traits from that of environmental conditions would be to study infants separated at birth from their natural parents and placed randomly in foster homes. In such cases we could determine whether the behavior of the adopted child resembled that of the natural parents or that of the adoptive parents, and by how much. Children, however, are adopted at various ages and are not placed randomly in foster homes. Most such children are matched to their foster or adoptive parents by racial and religious criteria. And couples who adopt children may differ in some important ways from other couples. Despite such shortcomings, adoption studies do help us to expand our knowledge of genetic influences on human variation.

The largest adoption study conducted so far was based on a sample of 14,427 male and female adoptions in Denmark between 1924 and 1947. The hypothesis was that criminality in the biological parents would be associated with an increased risk of criminal behavior in the child. The parents were considered criminal if either the mother or the father had been convicted of a felony. The researchers had sufficient information on more than 4000 of the male children to assess whether or not both the biological and the adoptive parents had criminal records. Mednick and his associates reported the following findings:

- Of boys whose adoptive and biological parents had no criminal record, 13.5 percent were convicted of crimes.

- Of boys who had criminal adoptive parents and noncriminal biological parents, 14.7 percent were convicted of crimes.
- Of boys who had noncriminal adoptive parents and criminal biological parents, 20 percent were convicted of crimes.
- Of boys who had both criminal adoptive parents and criminal biological parents, 24.5 percent were convicted of crimes.[60]

These findings support the claim that the criminality of the biological parents has more influence on the child than does that of the adoptive parents. Other research on adopted children has reached similar conclusions. A major Swedish study examined 862 adopted males and 913 adopted females. The researchers found a genetic predisposition to criminality in both sexes, but an even stronger one in females. An American study of children who were put up for adoption by a group of convicted mothers supports the Danish and Swedish findings on the significance of genetic factors.[61]

Results of adoption studies have been characterized as "highly suggestive" or "supportive" of a genetic link to criminality. But how solid is this link? There are significant problems with adoption studies. One is that little can be done to ensure the similarity of adopted children's environments. Of even greater concern to criminologists, however, is the distinct possibility of mistaking correlation for causation. In other words, there appears to be a significant correlation between the criminality of biological parents and adopted children in the research we have reviewed, but this correlation does not prove that the genetic legacy passed on by a criminal parent causes an offspring to commit a crime.

So far research has failed to shed any light on the nature of the biological link that results in the association between the criminality of parents and that of their children. Furthermore, even if we could identify children with a higher-than-average probability of committing offenses as adults on the basis of their parents' behavior, it is unclear what we could do to prevent these children from following the parental model.

The Controversy over Violence and Genes

At the same time that advances in research on the biological bases of violence shed new light on crime, attacks on such research are calling its usefulness into question. Government-sponsored research plans have been called racist, a conference on genetics and crime was canceled after protests, and a session on violence and heredity at a recent American Association for the Advancement of Science meeting became "a politically correct critique of the research."[62]

Few involved in such research expect to find a "violence gene"; rather, researchers are looking for a biological basis for some of the behaviors associated with violence. As one explanation put it:

> Scientists are . . . trying to find inborn personality traits that might make people more physically aggressive. The tendency to be a thrill seeker may be one such characteristic. So might "a restless impulsiveness, an inability to defer gratification." A high threshold for anxiety or fear may be another key trait. . . . such people tend to have a "special biology," with lower-than-average heart rates and blood pressure.[63]

No one yet has found any direct link between genes and violence. In fact, Sarnoff Mednick, the psychologist who conducted adoption studies of criminal behavior in Denmark found no evidence for the inheritance of violence. "If there were any genetic effect for violent crimes, we would have picked it up," says Mednick, whose study included 14,427 men.

The controversy over a genetic basis for violent behavior seems to deal less with actual research findings than with the implications of such findings. For example, Harvard psychologist Jerome Kagan predicts that in 25 years biological and genetic tests will make it possible to identify the 15 children in every 1000 who may have violent tendencies. Of those 15, only 1 will actually become violent. The ethical question, then, is what to do with this knowledge. "Do we tell the mothers of all 15 that their kids might be violent?" he asks. "How are the mothers then going to react to their children if we do that?"[64]

A recent National Academy of Science (NAS) report on violence recommended finding better ways to intervene in the development of children who could become violent, and it listed risk factors statistically linked to violence: hyperactivity, poor early grades, low IQ, fearlessness, and an inability to defer gratification, for example.[65]

What frightens those opposed to biological and genetic research into the causes of violence is the thought of how such research could be used by policy makers. If a violent personality can be shown to be genetically determined, crime-prevention strategies might try to identify "potential criminals" and to intervene before their criminal careers begin and before anyone knows if they would ever have become criminals. "Should genetic markers one day be found for tendencies . . . that are loosely linked to crime," explains one researcher, "they would probably have little specificity, sensitivity or explanatory power: most people with the markers will not be criminals and most criminals will not have the markers."[66] On the other hand, when environment—poverty, broken homes, and other problems—is seen as the major cause of violence, crime prevention takes the shape of improving social conditions rather than labeling individuals.

A middle road is proposed by those who see biological research as a key to helping criminals change their behavior. "Once you find a biological basis for a behavior, you can try to find out how to help people cope," says one such scholar. "Suppose the link is impulsivity, an inability to defer gratification. It might be you could design education programs to teach criminals to readjust their time horizon."[67]

The IQ Debate

A discussion of the association between genes and criminality would be incomplete without paying at least some attention to the debate over IQ and crime. Is an inferior intelligence inherited, and if so, how do we account for the strong relationship between IQ and criminality?

The Research Background. Nearly a century ago scientists began to search for measures to determine people's intelligence, which they believed to be genetically determined. The first test to gain acceptance was developed by a French psychologist, Alfred Binet. Binet's test measured the capacity of individual children to perform tasks or solve problems in relation to the average capacity of their peers.

Between 1888 and 1915 several researchers administered intelligence tests to incarcerated criminals and to boys in reform schools. Initial studies of the relationship between IQ and crime revealed some surprising results. The psychologist Hugo Munsterberg estimated that 68 percent of the criminals that he tested were of low IQ. Using the Binet scale, Henry H. Goddard found that between 25 and 50 percent of criminals had low IQs.[68] What could account for such different results?

Edwin Sutherland observed that the tests were poor and there were too many variations among the many versions administered. He reasoned that social and environmental factors caused delinquency, not low IQ.[69] In the 1950s the psychologist Robert H. Gault added to Sutherland's criticism. He noted particularly that it was "strange that it did not occur immediately to the pioneers that they had examined only a small sample of caught and convicted offenders."[70]

For more than a generation the question about the relationship between IQ and criminal behavior was not studied, and the early inconsistencies remained unresolved. Then in the late 1970s the debate resumed.[71] Supporters of the view that inheritance determines intelligence once again began to present their arguments. The psychologist Arthur Jensen suggested that race was a key factor in IQ differences; Richard J. Herrnstein, a geneticist, pointed to social class as a factor.[72] Both positions spurred a heated debate in which criminologists soon became involved. In 1977 Travis Hirschi and Michael Hindelang evaluated the existing literature on IQ and crime.[73] They cited the following three studies as especially important:

- Travis Hirschi, on the basis of a study of 3600 California students, demonstrated that the effect of a low IQ on delinquent behavior is more significant than that of the father's education.[74]
- Marvin Wolfgang and associates, after studying 8700 Philadelphia boys, found a strong relation between low IQ and delinquency, independent of social class.[75]
- Albert Reiss and Albert L. Rhodes, after an examination of the juvenile court records of 9200 white Tennessee schoolboys, found IQ to be more closely related to delinquency than is social class.[76]

Hirschi and Hindelang concluded that IQ is an even more important factor in predicting crime than either race or social class. They found significant differences in intelligence between criminal and noncriminal populations within like racial and socioeconomic groups. A lower IQ increases the potential for crime within each group. Furthermore, they found that IQ is related to school performance. A low IQ

ultimately results in a youngster's associating with similar nonperformers, dropping out of school, and committing delinquent acts. Hirschi and Hindelang's findings were confirmed by James Q. Wilson and Richard Herrnstein but rejected by criminologist Deborah Denno, who conducted a prospective investigation of 800 children from birth to age 17.[77] Her results failed to confirm a direct relationship between IQ and delinquency.

The Debate: Genetics or Environment?   The debate over the relationship between IQ and crime has its roots in the controversy over whether intelligence is genetically or environmentally determined. IQ tests, many people believe, measure cultural factors rather than the innate biological makeup of an individual.[78] Studies by psychologists Sandra Scarr and Richard Weinberg of black and white adopted children confirmed that environment plays a significant role in IQ development. They found that both black and white children adopted by white parents had comparable IQs and performed similarly.[79] With evidence of cultural bias and environmental influence, why not abandon the use of intelligence tests? The answer is simple: They do predict performance in school and so have significant utility. It appears that this debate will be with us for a long time to come.

Biochemical Factors

Biocriminologists' primary focus has been on the relationship between criminality and biochemical and neurophysical factors. Biochemical factors include food allergies, diet, hypoglycemia, and hormones. Neurophysical factors include brain lesions, brain wave abnormalities, and minimal brain dysfunction.

Food Allergies.   In 1993, by the time Rachel was 2 years old, she displayed a pattern of behavior that went way beyond the "terrible twos." Without warning, her eyes would glaze over, her speech became lispy, and she'd kick and hit and thrash about wildly until her mother swaddled her tightly and she fell asleep, exhausted. She even developed a "kitty-cat" routine, complete with meowing, stalking, and growling that often went on for hours.

When Rachel's sister Emma was born later that year, she nursed poorly and never slept through the night. After their mother introduced baby corn into her diet, Emma experienced severe intestinal distress, for which she was hospitalized. After a battery of medical tests proved inconclusive, she was sent home, but the symptoms continued intermittently, without apparent reason.

Last year, in desperation, Rachel and Emma, then 3 years and 15 months, were tested for food allergies. Both showed marked sensitivity to corn, wheat, sugar, preservatives, and dairy products. After eliminating those foods, Emma's health and well-being improved, and Rachel's perplexing and worrisome behavior all but disappeared.[80]

Over the last decade researchers have investigated the relation between food allergies, aggression, and antisocial behavior. In fact, since 1908 there have been numerous medical reports indicating that various foods cause such reactions as irritability, hyperactivity, seizures, agitation, and behavior that is "out of character."[81] Investigators have identified the following food components as substances that may result in severe allergic reactions:

Phenylethylamine (found in chocolate)
Tyramine (found in aged cheese and wine)
Monosodium glutamate (used as a flavor enhancer in many foods)
Aspartame (found in artificial sweeteners)
Xanthines (found in caffeine)

Each of these food components has been associated with behavioral disorders, including criminality.

Diet

- Susan had been charged with 16 offenses, including criminal damage, solvent abuse, and vehicle theft, by the time she was 13. She had no friends, showed no affection toward her parents, and frequently hit her mother. Her schoolwork deteriorated, and she played truant most days. After 6 months on a changed diet, which excluded burgers, bananas, and chocolate, the number of her offenses dropped to zero. And for the first time since she was a young child, Susan gave her mother a hug.
- Craig, 15, vandalized his home several times and committed numerous petty crimes. He was a bully and virtually impossible to teach. And his 8-year-old brother was beginning to follow in his footsteps. Both were put on a special diet, cutting out fizzy drinks and sweets, and including more green vegetables and fresh fruit. Within months,

says their mother, both were more pleasant and easier to deal with. But Craig has since quit the diet and has reoffended. The bullying and the violence have started again.
- Graham, an 11-year-old, turned from an uncontrollable delinquent into a normal, pleasant boy when pizzas, baked beans, and chocolate in his diet were replaced by fresh vegetables, coconut milk, and carrots. He became less aggressive and argumentative and, reportedly, was "happy" for the first time in his life. Graham's schoolwork improved, and he began to make friends.

Anecdotal reports, in addition to more scientific investigations, link criminality to diets high in sugar and carbohydrates, to vitamin deficiency or dependency, and to excessive food additives.

Criminologist Stephen Schoenthaler conducted a series of studies on the relation between sugar and the behavior of institutionalized offenders. In these investigations inmates were placed on a modified diet that included very little sugar. They received fruit juice in place of soda and vegetables instead of candy. Schoenthaler found fewer disciplinary actions and a significant drop in aggressive behavior in the experimental group.[82] Some individuals charged with crimes have used this finding to build a defense like that of Dan White.

In 1979, San Francisco city supervisor Dan White was on trial for the murder of his fellow supervisor, Harvey Milk, and Mayor George Moscone. White defended himself with testimony on the impact of sugar on his behavior. The testimony showed that when White was depressed, he departed from his normal, healthy diet and resorted to high-sugar junk food, including Twinkies, Coca-Cola, and chocolates. Thereafter, his behavior became less and less controllable. The jury found White guilty of manslaughter, rather than murder, due to diminished capacity. White served 5 years in prison and committed suicide after his release. His defense was promptly dubbed the "junk-food defense," "Dan White's defense," or the "Twinkie defense."

Most subsequent attempts to use the junk-food defense have failed. In a 1989 Ohio case (*Johnson*), it was ruled that the defense may not be used to establish diminished capacity. In 1990, a Cape Cod man was unsuccessful when he defended himself on a charge of stealing (and eating) 300 candy bars (*Callanan*). Nor did this defense (Twinkie and soda pop) succeed in a murder case in Ohio (*McDonald, 1988*). But in a 1987 Florida case, a defendant (*Rosenthal*) was acquitted of drunk-driving charges on evidence that consumption of chocolate mousse after half a glass of sherry caused an unusual blood sugar reaction.

Other researchers have looked for the causes of crime in vitamin deficiencies. One such study found that 70 percent of criminals charged with serious offenses in one Canadian jurisdiction had a greater-than-normal need for vitamin B6.[83] Other studies have noted deficiencies of vitamins B3 and B6 in criminal population samples.

Some investigators have examined the effects of food additives and food dyes on behavior. Benjamin Feingold has argued that between 30 and 60 percent of all hyperactivity in children may be attributable to reactions to food coloring.[84] There is additional support for this hypothesis.[85] Some studies have suggested that a diet deficient in protein may be responsible for violent aggression.

Let us look at the association between the consumption of tryptophan, an amino acid (a protein building block), and crime rates. Tryptophan is a normal component of many foods. Low levels of it have been associated with aggression and, in criminal studies, an increased sensitivity to electric shock. Anthony R. Mawson and K. W. Jacobs reasoned that diets low in tryptophan would be likely to result in higher levels of violent crime, particularly violent offenses such as homicide.

They hypothesized that because corn-based diets are deficient in tryptophan, a cross-national comparison of countries should reveal a positive relationship between corn consumption and homicide rates. Mawson and Jacobs obtained homicide data from the United Nations and the mean per capita corn intake rates of 53 foreign countries from the U.S. Department of Agriculture. They discovered that countries whose per capita rates of corn consumption were above the median had significantly higher homicide rates than countries whose diets were based on wheat or rice.[86]

Hypoglycemia. What prompted an otherwise loving father to throw his 20-month-old daughter into a nearby lake? Neighbors knew that something was amiss when they noticed 22-year-old Joe Holt climb on the roof of his duplex in a quiet Orlando suburb. Joe then proceeded to dance, touching power lines in

the course of his pantomime. No one sounded the alarm, however, until he disappeared into his lakeside apartment, returning momentarily with his daughter Ashley in his arms. The police arrived on the scene to find Joe in a state of agitation and Ashley facedown in Lake Apopka. Seated in the back of a squad car, handcuffed, the bewildered Joe had no recollection of the preceding events. When his blood was tested, he had a glucose level of 20 milligrams per deciliter of blood. The average is 80 to 120 milligrams. Joe was suffering from severe hypoglycemia. According to a sheriff's spokesman, "He had virtually no thought process."[87]

Hypoglycemia is a condition that occurs when the level of sugar in the blood falls below an acceptable range. The brain is particularly vulnerable to hypoglycemia, and such a condition can impair its function. Symptoms of hypoglycemia include anxiety, headache, confusion, fatigue, and even aggressive behavior. As early as 1943 researchers linked the condition with violent crime, including murder, rape, and assault. Subsequent studies found that violent and impulsive male offenders had a higher rate of hypoglycemia than noncriminal controls.

Consider the work of Matti Virkkunen, who has conducted a series of studies of habitually violent and psychopathic offenders in Finland. In one such study done in the 1980s he examined the results of a glucose tolerance test (used to determine whether hypoglycemia is present) administered to 37 habitually violent offenders with antisocial personalities, 31 habitually violent offenders with intermittent explosive disorders, and 20 controls. The offenders were found to be significantly more hypoglycemic than the controls.[88]

Hormones. Experiments have shown that male animals are typically more aggressive than females. Male aggression is directly linked to male hormones. If an aggressive male mouse is injected with female hormones, he will stop fighting.[89] Likewise, the administration of male hormones to pregnant monkeys results in female offspring who, even 3 years after birth, are more aggressive than the daughters of noninjected mothers.[90]

While it would be misleading to equate male hormones with aggression and female hormones with nonaggression, there is some evidence that abnormal levels of male hormones in humans may prompt criminal behavior. Several investigators have found higher levels of testosterone (the male hormone) in the blood of individuals who have committed violent offenses.[91] Some studies also relate premenstrual syndrome (PMS) to delinquency and conclude that women are at greater risk of aggressive and suicidal behavior before and during the menstrual period. After studying 156 newly admitted adult female prisoners, Katherina Dalton concluded that 49 percent of all their crimes were committed either in the premenstrual period or during menstruation.[92] Recently, however, critics have challenged the association between menstrual distress and female crime.[93]

Neurophysiological Factors

In England in the mid-1950s, a father hit his son with a mallet and then threw him out of a window, killing him instantly. Instead of pleading insanity, as many people expected him to do, he presented evidence of a brain tumor, which, he argued, resulted in uncontrollable rage and violence. A jury acquitted him on the grounds that the brain tumor had deprived him of any control over and knowledge of the act he was committing.[94] Brain lesions or brain tumors have led to violent outbursts in many similar cases. Neurophysiological studies, however, have not focused exclusively on brain tumors; they have included a wide range of investigations: MRI studies of cerebral structure, brain wave studies, clinical reports of minimal brain dysfunction, and theoretical explorations into the relationship between the limbic system and criminality.[95]

EEG Abnormalities. Sam recalled that his wife Janet looked slightly different and that the house smelled funny and he felt out of sorts. During an intimate moment in bed Janet made a funny remark, after which Sam flew into a rage, choked her, and slashed her throat. When he came to his senses, he immediately went to the police and admitted to the crime, although he had little memory of his violent acts. Can EEG tracings explain the behavior of this young U.S. Marine who had returned home on leave? Subsequent tracings were found to be abnormal—indicative of an "intermittent explosive disorder." After reviewing this evidence, the court reduced Sam's charges from first-degree murder to manslaughter.

The EEG (electroencephalogram) is a tracing made by an instrument that measures cerebral functioning by recording brain wave activity with electrodes placed on the scalp. Numerous studies that have examined the brain activity of violent prisoners reveal significant differences between the EEGs of criminals and those of noncriminals. Other findings relate significantly slow brain wave activity to young offenders and adult murderers.[96] When Sarnoff A. Mednick and his colleagues examined the criminal records and EEGs of 265 children in a birth cohort in Denmark, they found that certain types of brain wave activity, as measured by the EEG, enabled investigators to predict whether convicted thieves would steal again.[97]

When Jan Volavka compared the EEGs of juvenile delinquents with those of comparable nondelinquents, he found a slowing of brain waves in the delinquent sample, most prominently in those children convicted of theft. He concluded that thievery "is more likely to develop in persons who have a slowing of alpha frequency than in persons who do not."[98]

Minimal Brain Dysfunction. **Minimal brain dysfunction (MBD)** is classified as "attention deficit hyperactivity disorder."[99] MBD produces such asocial behavioral patterns as impulsivity, hyperactivity, aggressiveness, low self-esteem, and temper outbursts. The syndrome is noteworthy for at least two reasons. First, MBD may explain criminality when social theories fail to do so—that is, when neighborhood, peer, and familial associations do not suggest a high risk of delinquency. Second, MBD is an easily overlooked diagnosis. Parents, teachers, and clinicians tend to focus more on the symptoms of a child's psychopathology than on the possibility of brain dysfunction, even though investigators have repeatedly found high rates of brain dysfunction in samples of suicidal adolescents and youthful offenders.[100]

CRIME AND HUMAN NATURE

The criminologist Edward Sagarin has written:

> In criminology, it appears that a number of views . . . have become increasingly delicate and sensitive, as if all those who espouse them were inherently evil, or at least stupidly insensitive to the consequences of their research. . . . In the study of crime, the examples of unpopular orientations are many. Foremost is the link of crime to the factors of genes, biology, race, ethnicity, and religion.[101]

Criticisms of Biocriminology

What is it about linking biology and criminality that makes the subject delicate and sensitive? Why is the concept so offensive to so many people? One reason is that biocriminologists deny the existence of individual free will. The idea of predisposition to commit crimes fosters a sense of hopelessness. But this criticism seems to have little merit. As Diana H. Fishbein has aptly noted, the idea of a "conditioned free will" is widely accepted.[102] This view suggests that individuals make choices in regard to a particular action within a range of possibilities that is "preset" yet flexible. When conditions permit rational thought, one is fully accountable and responsible for one's actions. It is only when conditions are somehow disturbed that free choice is constricted. The child of middle-class parents who has a low IQ might avoid delinquent behavior. But if that child's circumstances changed so that he lived in a lower-class, single-parent environment, he might find the delinquent lifestyle of the children in the new neighborhood too tempting to resist.

Critics have other concerns as well. Some see a racist undertone to biocriminological research. If there is a genetic predisposition to commit crime and if minorities account for a disproportionate share of criminal activity, are minorities then predisposed to commit crime? In Chapter 2 we learned that self-reports reveal that most people have engaged in delinquent or criminal behavior. How, then, do biocriminologists justify their claim that certain groups are more prone than others to criminal behavior? Could it be that the subjects of their investigations are only criminals who have been caught and incarcerated? And is the attention of the police disproportionately drawn to members of minority groups?

How do biocriminologists account for the fact that most criminologists see the structure of our society, the decay of our neighborhoods, and the subcultures of certain areas as determinants of criminality? Are biocriminologists unfairly deemphasizing social and economic factors? (In Chapters 5 through 9 we review theories that attribute criminality to group and environmental forces.)

These issues raise a further question that is at the core of all social and behavioral science: Is human behavior the product of nature (genetics) or nurture (environment)? The consensus among social and behavioral scientists today is that the interaction of nature and nurture is so pervasive that the two cannot be viewed in isolation.

Supporters of biocriminology also maintain that recognizing a predisposition to crime is not inconsistent with considering environmental factors. In fact, some believe that predispositions are triggered by environmental factors. Even if we agree that some people are predisposed to commit crime, we know that the crime rate would be higher in areas that provide more triggers. In sum, while some people may be predisposed to certain kinds of behavior, most scientists agree that both psychological and environmental factors shape the final forms of those behaviors.

An Integrated Theory

In recent years the debate has found a new forum in integrated biocriminological theories, such as the one proposed by James Q. Wilson and Richard Herrnstein. These scholars explain predatory street crime by showing how human nature develops from the interplay of psychological, biological, and social factors. It is the interaction of genes with environment that in some individuals forms the kind of personality likely to commit crimes. The argument takes into account such factors as IQ, body build, genetic makeup, impulsiveness, ability to delay gratification, aggressiveness, and even the drinking and smoking habits of pregnant mothers.

According to Wilson and Herrnstein, the choice between crime and conventional behavior is closely linked to individual biological and psychological traits and to such social factors as family and school experiences. Their conclusion is that "the offender offends not just because of immediate needs and circumstances, but also because of enduring personal characteristics, some of whose traces can be found in his behavior from early childhood on."[103] In essence, they argue that behavior results from a person's perception of the potential rewards and/or punishments that go along with a criminal act. If the potential reward (such as money) is greater than the expected punishment (say, a small fine), the chance that a crime will be committed increases.

REVIEW

When psychologists have attempted to explain criminality, they have taken four general approaches. First, they have focused on failures in psychological development—an overbearing or weak conscience, inner conflict, insufficient moral development, and maternal deprivation, with its concomitant failure of attachment. Second, they have investigated the ways in which aggression and violence are learned through modeling and direct experience. Third, they have investigated the personality characteristics of criminals and found that criminals tend to be more impulsive, intolerant, and irresponsible than noncriminals. Fourth, psychologists have investigated the relation of criminality to such mental disorders as psychosis and psychopathy.

Biocriminologists investigate the biological correlates of criminality, including a genetic predisposition to commit crime. The XYY syndrome, though now generally discounted as a cause of criminality, suggests that aggressive and violent behavior may be at least partly determined by genetic factors. Studies of the behavior of identical and fraternal twins and of the rates of criminality among adopted children with both criminal and noncriminal biological and adoptive parents tend to support this hypothesis. Investigators have also found a strong correlation between a low IQ and delinquency. Criminologists are still debating what public policy issues are raised by the possible role of genetics in crime.

Biocriminologists' most recent and perhaps most important discovery is the relation of criminal behavior to biochemical factors (food allergies, dietary deficiencies, hormonal imbalances) and neurophysiological factors (EEG abnormalities and minimal brain dysfunction). Most scientists agree that if some people are biologically predisposed to certain behaviors, both psychological and environmental factors shape the forms of those behaviors.

NOTES

1. See Ronald Blackburn, *The Psychology of Criminal Conduct: Theory, Research, and Practice* (Chichester, England: Wiley, 1993); and Hans Toch, *Violent Men: An Inquiry into the Psychology of Violence,* rev. ed. (Washington, D.C.: American Psychological Association, 1992).

2. See, e.g., Cathy Spatz Widom, "Cycle of Violence," *Science,* **244** (1989): 160–165; and Nathaniel J. Pallone and J. J. Hennessey, *Criminal Behavior: A Process Psychology Analysis* (New Brunswick, N.J.: Transaction, 1992).

3. See, e.g., Sigmund Freud, *A General Introduction to Psychoanalysis* (New York: Liveright, 1920); and Sigmund Freud, *The Ego and the Id* (London: Hogarth, 1927).

4. August Aichhorn, *Wayward Youth* (New York: Viking, 1935).

5. Kate Friedlander, *The Psycho-Analytic Approach to Juvenile Delinquency* (New York: International Universities Press, 1947).

6. See Hans Eysenck, *The Rise and Fall of the Freudian Empire* (New York: Plenum, 1987).

7. Lawrence Kohlberg, "The Development of Modes of Moral Thinking and Choice in the Years Ten to Sixteen," Ph.D. dissertation, University of Chicago, 1958.

8. Lawrence Kohlberg, "Stage and Sequence: The Cognitive-Developmental Approach to Socialization," in *Handbook of Socialization Theory and Research,* ed. David A. Goslin (Chicago: Rand McNally, 1969).

9. Carol Gilligan has studied moral development in women—extending Kohlberg's role-taking theory of moral development. She found that moral reasoning differed in women. Women, according to Gilligan, see morality as the responsibility to take the view of others and to ensure their well-being. See Carol Gilligan, *In a Different Voice: Psychological Theory and Women's Development* (Cambridge, Mass.: Harvard University Press, 1982).

10. William S. Jennings, Robert Kilkenny, and Lawrence Kohlberg, "Moral Development Theory and Practice for Youthful Offenders," in *Personality Theory, Moral Development, and Criminal Behavior,* ed. William S. Laufer and James M. Day (Lexington, Mass.: Lexington Books, 1983). See also Daniel D. Macphail, "The Moral Education Approach in Treating Adult Inmates," *Criminal Justice and Behavior,* **15** (1989): 81–97; Jack Arbuthnot and Donald A. Gordon, "Crime and Cognition: Community Applications of Sociomoral Reasoning Development," *Criminal Justice and Behavior,* **15** (1988): 379–393; and J. E. LeCapitaine, "The Relationships between Emotional Development and Moral Development and the Differential Impact of Three Psychological Interventions on Children," *Psychology in the Schools,* **15** (1987): 379–393.

11. John Bowlby, *Attachment and Loss,* 2 vols. (New York: Basic Books, 1969, 1973). See also Bowlby's "Forty-Four Juvenile Thieves: Their Characteristics and Home Life," *International Journal of Psychoanalysis,* **25** (1944): 19–52.

12. John Bowlby, *The Making and Breaking of Affectional Bonds* (London: Tavistock, 1979). See also Michael Rutter, *Maternal Deprivation Reassessed* (Harmondsworth, England: Penguin, 1971).

13. Michael Lewis, Candice Feiring, Carolyn McGuffog, and John Jaskir, "Predicting Psychopathology in Six-Year-Olds from Early Social Relations," *Child Development,* **55** (1984): 123–136.

14. L. Sroufe, "Infant Caregiver Attachment and Patterns of Adaptation in Preschool: The Roots of Maladaption and Competence," in *Minnesota Symposium on Child Psychology,* vol. 16, ed. Marion Perlmutter (Hillsdale, N.J.: Erlbaum, 1982).

15. Alicia F. Lieberman, "Preschoolers' Competence with a Peer: Influence of Attachment and Social Experience," *Child Development,* **48** (1977): 1277–1287.

16. Joan McCord, "Some Child-Rearing Antecedents of Criminal Behavior," *Journal of Personality and Social Psychology,* **37** (1979): 1477–1486; Joan McCord, "A Longitudinal View of the Relationship between Paternal Absence and Crime," in *Abnormal Offenders, Delinquency, and the Criminal Justice System,* ed. John Gunn and David P. Farrington (London: Wiley, 1982). See also Scott W. Henggeler, Cindy L. Hanson, Charles M. Borduin, Sylvia M. Watson, and Molly A. Brunk, "Mother-Son Relationships of Juvenile Felons," *Journal of*

Consulting and Clinical Psychology, **53** (1985): 942–943; and Francis I. Nye, *Family Relationships and Delinquent Behavior* (New York: Wiley, 1958).

17. Sheldon Glueck and Eleanor T. Glueck, *Unraveling Juvenile Delinquency* (New York: Commonwealth Fund, 1950); Lee N. Robins, "Aetiological Implications in Studies of Childhood Histories Relating to Antisocial Personality," in *Psychopathic Behaviour,* ed. Robert D. Hare and Daisy Schalling (Chichester, England: Wiley, 1970); Lee N. Robins, *Deviant Children Grow Up* (Baltimore: Williams & Wilkins, 1966).

18. Joan McCord, "Instigation and Insulation: How Families Affect Antisocial Aggression," in *Development of Antisocial and Prosocial Behavior: Research Theories and Issues,* ed. Dan Olweus, Jack Block, and M. Radke-Yarrow (London: Academic Press, 1986).

19. Albert Bandura, *Aggression: A Social Learning Analysis* (Englewood Cliffs, N.J.: Prentice-Hall, 1973); Albert Bandura, "The Social Learning Perspective: Mechanism of Aggression," in *Psychology of Crime and Criminal Justice,* ed. Hans Toch (New York: Holt, Rinehart & Winston, 1979).

20. Leonard D. Eron and L. Rowell Huesmann, "Parent-Child Interaction, Television Violence, and Aggression of Children," *American Psychologist,* **37** (1982): 197–211; Russell G. Geen, "Aggression and Television Violence," in *Aggression: Theoretical and Empirical Reviews,* vol. 2, ed. Russell G. Geen and Edward I. Donnerstein (New York: Academic Press, 1983).

21. Leonard D. Eron and L. Rowell Huesmann, "The Control of Aggressive Behavior by Changes in Attitudes, Values, and the Conditions of Learning," in *Advances in the Study of Aggression,* vol. 1, ed. Robert J. Blanchard and D. Caroline Blanchard (Orlando, Fla.: Academic Press, 1984).

22. *National Television Violence Study: Executive Summary 1994–1995* (Studio City, Calif.: Mediascope, 1996); O. Wiegman, M. Kuttschreuter, and B. Baarda, "A Longitudinal Study of the Effects of Television Viewing on Aggressive and Prosocial Behaviors," *British Journal of Social Psychology,* **31** (1992): 147–164; B. S. Centerwall, "Television and Violence: The Scale of the Problem and Where to Go from Here," *Journal of the American Medical Association,* **267** (1992): 3059–3063; J. E. Ledingham, C. A. Ledingham, and John E. Richardson, *The Effects of Media Violence on Children* (Ottawa, Canada: National Clearinghouse on Family Violence, Health and Welfare, 1993); M. I. Tulloch, M. L. Prendergast, and M. D. Anglin, "Evaluating Aggression: School Students' Responses to Television Portrayals of Institutionalized Violence," *Journal of Youth and Adolescence,* **24** (1995): 95–115.

23. See Gerald R. Patterson, R. A. Littman, and W. Brickler, *Assertive Behavior in Children: A Step toward a Theory of Aggression,* monograph of the Society for Research in Child Development, no. 32 (1976).

24. Bandura, *Aggression.*

25. C. Ray Jeffery, "Criminal Behavior and Learning Theory," *Journal of Criminal Law, Criminology and Police Science,* **56** (1965): 294–300.

26. Ernest L. Burgess and Ronald L. Akers, "A Differential Association-Reinforcement Theory of Criminal Behavior," *Social Problems,* 14 (1966): 128–147. See also Reed Adams, "Differential Association and Learning Principles Revisited," *Social Problems,* **20** (1973): 458–470.

27. See D. W. Andrews and J. Stephen Wormith, "Personality and Crime: Knowledge Destruction and Construction in Criminology," *Justice Quarterly,* **6** (1989): 149–160.

28. William S. Laufer, Dagna K. Skoog, and James M. Day, "Personality and Criminality: A Review of the California Psychological Inventory," *Journal of Clinical Psychology,* **38** (1982): 562–573.

29. Richard E. Tremblay, "The Prediction of Delinquent Behavior from Childhood Behavior: Personality Theory Revisited," in *Facts, Frameworks, and Forecasts: Advances in Criminological Theory,* vol. 3, ed. J. McCord (New Brunswick, N.J.: Transaction, 1992).

30. Michael L. Gearing, "The MMPI as a Primary Differentiator and Predictor of Behavior in Prison: A Methodological Critique and Review of the Recent Literature," *Psychological Bulletin,* **36** (1979): 929–963.

31. Edwin I. Megargee and Martin J. Bohn, *Classifying Criminal Offenders* (Beverly Hills, Calif.: Sage, 1979); William S. Laufer, John A. Johnson, and Robert Hogan, "Ego Control and Criminal Behavior," *Journal of Personality and Social Psychology,* **41** (1981): 179–184; Edwin I. Megargee, "Psychological Determinants and Correlates of Criminal Violence," in *Criminal Violence,* ed. Marvin E. Wolfgang and Neil A. Weiner (Beverly Hills, Calif.: Sage, 1982); Edwin I. Megargee, "The Role of Inhibition in the Assessment and Understanding of Violence," in *Current Topics in Clinical and Community Psychology,* ed. Charles Donald Spielberger (New York: Academic Press, 1971); Edwin I. Megargee, "Undercontrol and Overcontrol in Assaultive and Homicidal Adolescents," Ph.D. dissertation, University of California, Berkeley, 1964; Edwin I. Megargee, "Undercontrolled and Overcontrolled Personality Types in Extreme Antisocial Aggression," *Psychological Monographs,* **80** (1966); Edwin I. Megargee and Gerald A. Mendelsohn, "A Cross-Validation of Twelve MMPI Indices of Hostility and Control," *Journal of Abnormal and Social Psychology,* **65** (1962): 431–438.

32. See, e.g., William S. Laufer and James M. Day, eds., *Personality Theory, Moral Development, and Criminal Behavior* (Lexington, Mass.: Lexington Books, 1983).

33. Milton Metfessel and Constance Lovell, "Recent Literature on Individual Correlates of Crime," *Psychological Bulletin,* **39** (1942): 133–164.

34. Karl E. Schuessler and Donald R. Cressey, "Personality Characteristics of Criminals," *American Journal of Sociology,* **55** (1950): 476–484.

35. Daniel J. Tennenbaum, "Personality and Criminality: A Summary and Implications of the Literature," *Journal of Criminal Justice,* **5** (1977): 225–235. See also G. P. Waldo and Simon Dinitz, "Personality Attributes of the Criminal: An Analysis of Research Studies, 1950–1965," *Journal of Research in Crime and Delinquency,* **4** (1967): 185–202; and R. D. Martin and D. G. Fischer, "Personality Factors in Juvenile Delinquency: A Review of the Literature," *Catalog of Selected Documents in Psychology,* vol. 8 (1978), ms. 1759.

36. Samuel Yochelson and Stanton Samenow, *The Criminal Personality* (New York: Jason Aronson, 1976).

37. Laufer et al., "Personality and Criminality"; Harrison G. Gough and Pamela Bradley, "Delinquent and Criminal Behavior as Assessed by the Revised California Psychological Inventory," *Journal of Clinical Psychology,* **48** (1991): 298–308.

38. See Anne Campbell and John J. Gibbs, eds., *Violent Transactions: The Limits of Personality* (Oxford: Basil Blackwell, 1986); Lawrence A. Pervin, "Personality: Current Controversies, Issues, and Direction," *Annual Review of Psychology,* **36** (1985): 83–114; and Lawrence A. Pervin, "Persons, Situations, Interactions: Perspectives on a Recurrent Issue," in Campbell and Gibbs, *Violent Transactions.*

39. See Hans J. Eysenck, *Crime and Personality* (London: Routledge & Kegan Paul, 1977); H. J. Eysenck, "Personality and Crime: Where Do We Stand?" *Psychology, Crime and Law,* **2** (1996): 143–152; Hans J. Eysenck, "Personality, Conditioning, and Antisocial Behavior," in Laufer and Day, *Personality Theory;* Hans J. Eysenck, "Personality and Criminality: A Dispositional Analysis," in *Advances in Criminological Theory,* vol. 1, ed. William S. Laufer and Freda Adler (New Brunswick, N.J.: Transaction, 1989); and Hans J. Eysenck and Gisli H. Gudjonnson, *The Causes and Cures of Crime* (New York: Plenum, 1990).

40. Seymour L. Halleck, *Psychiatry and the Dilemmas of Crime* (New York: Harper & Row, 1967); Nicholas N. Kittrie, *The Right to Be Different: Deviance and Enforced Therapy* (Baltimore, Md.: Johns Hopkins Press, 1971).

41. Karl Menninger, *The Crime of Punishment* (New York: Viking, 1968).

42. See Daniel L. Davis et al., "Prevalence of Emotional Disorders in a Juvenile Justice Institutional Population," *American Journal of Forensic Psychology,* **9** (1991): 5–17.

43. Hervey Cleckley, *The Mask of Sanity,* 5/e (St. Louis: Mosby, 1976), pp. 271–272.

44. Ibid., p. 57; Robert D. Hare, *Psychopathy: Theory and Research* (New York: Wiley, 1970); M. Philip Feldman, *Criminal Behavior: A Psychological Analysis* (New York: Wiley, 1978); William McCord and Joan McCord, *Psychopathy and Delinquency* (New York: Wiley, 1956).

45. *The American Psychiatric Association's Diagnostic and Statistical Manual of Mental Disorders,* 3d rev. ed. (DSM III-R) (Washington, D.C., 1987), classifies psychopathy as "antisocial personality." See Benjamin Karpman, "On the Need of Separating Psychopathy into Two Distinct Clinical Types: The Symptomatic and the Idiopathic," *Journal of Criminal Psychopathology,* **3** (1941): 112–137.

46. Eysenck and Gudjonnson, *The Causes and Cures of Crime.* See also Robert D. Hare, "Research Scale for the Assessment of Psychopathology in Criminal Populations," *Personality and Individual Differences,* **1** (1980): 111–119.

47. See, generally, A. J. Reiss, Jr., K. A. Klaus, and J. A. Roth, eds., *Biobehavioral Influences:* vol. 2, *Understanding and Preventing Violence,* (Washington, D.C.: National Academy Press, 1994); M. Hillbrand and N. J. Pallone, "The Psychobiology of Aggression: Engines, Measurement, Control," *Journal of Offender Rehabilitation,* **21** (1994): 1–243; J. T. Tedeschi and R. B. Felson, *Violence, Aggression, and Coercive Actions* (Washington, D.C.: American Psychological Association, 1994).

48. J. Puig-Antich, "Biological Factors in Prepubertal Major Depression," *Pediatric Annals,* **12** (1986): 867–878.

49. See, e.g., Guenther Knoblich and Roy King, "Biological Correlates of Criminal Behavior," in McCord, *Facts, Frameworks, and Forecasts;* Diana H. Fishbein, "Biological Perspectives in Criminology," *Criminology,* **28** (1990): 17–40; David Magnusson, Britt af Klinteberg, and Hakan Stattin,

"Autonomic Activity/Reactivity, Behavior, and Crime in a Longitudinal Perspective," in McCord, *Facts, Frameworks, and Forecasts;* Frank A. Elliott, "Violence: The Neurologic Contribution: An Overview," *Archives of Neurology,* **49** (1992): 595–603; L. French, "Neuropsychology of Violence," *Corrective and Social Psychiatry and Journal of Behavior Technology Methods and Therapy,* **37** (1991): 12–17; and Elizabeth Kandel and Sarnoff A. Mednick, "Perinatal Complications Predict Violent Offending," *Criminology,* **29** (1991): 519–530.

50. Edward O. Wilson, *Sociobiology: The New Synthesis* (Cambridge, Mass.: Harvard University Press, 1975).

51. C. Ray Jeffery, *Biology and Crime* (Beverly Hills, Calif.: Sage, 1979).

52. P. A. Brennan and S. A. Mednick, "Genetic Perspectives on Crime," *Acta Psychiatria Scandinavia,* **370** (1993): 19–26.

53. See Sarnoff A. Mednick, Terrie E. Moffitt, and Susan A. Stack, *The Causes of Crime: New Biological Approaches* (New York: Cambridge University Press, 1987).

54. A. A. Sandberg, G. F. Koepf, and T. Ishihara, "An XYY Human Male," *Lancet* (August 1961): 488–489.

55. Herman A. Witkin et al., "Criminality, Aggression, and Intelligence among XYY and XXY Men," in *Biosocial Bases of Criminal Behavior,* ed. Sarnoff A. Mednick and Karl O. Christiansen (New York: Wiley, 1977).

56. Johannes Lange, *Verbrechen als Schicksal* (Leipzig: Georg Thieme, 1929).

57. Cf. Gregory Carey, "Twin Imitation for Antisocial Behavior: Implications for Genetic Environment Research," *Journal of Abnormal Psychology,* **101** (1992): 18–25.

58. See Karl O. Christiansen, "A Preliminary Study of Criminality among Twins," in Mednick and Christiansen, *Biosocial Bases of Criminal Behavior.*

59. David C. Rowe and D. Wayne Osgood, "Heredity and Sociological Theories of Delinquency: A Reconsideration," *American Sociological Review,* **49** (1986): 526–540; David C. Rowe, "Genetic and Environmental Components of Antisocial Behavior: A Study of 256 Twin Pairs," *Criminology,* **24** (1986): 513–532.

60. Sarnoff A. Mednick, William Gabrielli, and Barry Hutchings, "Genetic Influences in Criminal Behavior: Evidence from an Adoption Court," in *Prospective Studies of Crime and Delinquency,* ed. K. Teilmann et al. (Boston: Kluwer-Nijhoff, 1983).

61. These and other studies are reviewed in Mednick et al., *The Causes of Crime.*

62. Hannah Bloch and Dick Thompson, "Seeking the Roots of Violence," *Time,* Apr. 19, 1993, pp. 52–53.

63. Daniel Goleman, "New Storm Brews on Whether Crime Has Roots in Genes," *New York Times,* Sept. 15, 1992, p. C1.

64. Hannah Bloch and Dick Thompson, *"Seeking the Roots of Violence."*

65. Fox Butterfield, "Study Cites Biology's Role in Violent Behavior," *New York Times,* Nov. 13, 1992, p. A7.

66. Goleman, "New Storm Brews on Whether Crime Has Roots in Genes."

67. Id.

68. Hugo Munsterberg, *On the Witness Stand* (New York: Doubleday, 1908); Henry H. Goddard, *Feeble-Mindedness: Its Causes and Consequences* (New York: Macmillan, 1914).

69. Edwin H. Sutherland, "Mental Deficiency and Crime," in *Social Attitudes,* ed. K. Young (New York: Henry Holt, 1931).

70. Robert H. Gault, "Highlights of Forty Years in the Correctional Field—and Looking Ahead," *Federal Probation,* **17** (1953): 3–4.

71. Arthur Jensen, *Bias in Mental Testing* (New York: Free Press, 1979).

72. Ibid.; Richard J. Herrnstein, *IQ in the Meritocracy* (Boston: Atlantic–Little, Brown, 1973).

73. Travis Hirschi and Michael J. Hindelang, "Intelligence and Delinquency: A Revisionist Review," *American Sociological Review,* **42** (1977): 571–586.

74. Travis Hirschi, *Causes of Delinquency* (Berkeley: University of California Press, 1969).

75. Marvin E. Wolfgang, Robert F. Figlio, and Thorsten Sellin, *Delinquency in a Birth Cohort* (Chicago: University of Chicago Press, 1972).

76. Albert J. Reiss and Albert L. Rhodes, "The Distribution of Juvenile Delinquency in the Social Class Structure," *American Sociological Review,* **26** (1961): 720–732.

77. James Q. Wilson and Richard Herrnstein, *Crime and Human Nature* (New York: Simon & Schuster, 1985); Deborah W. Denno, "Sociological and Human Developmental Explanations of Crime: Conflict or Consensus?" *Criminology,* **23** (1985): 711–740. See also Deborah W. Denno, "Victim, Offender, and Situational Characteristics of Violent Crime," *Journal of Criminal Law and Criminology,* **77** (1986): 1142–1158.

78. "Taking the Chitling Test," *Newsweek,* July 15, 1968.

79. Sandra Scarr and Richard Weinberg, "I.Q. Test Performance of Black Children Adopted by White Families," *American Psychologist,* **31** (1976): 726–739.

80. See Doris J. Rapp, *Allergies and the Hyperactive Child* (New York: Simon & Schuster, 1981).

81. Diana H. Fishbein and Susan Pease, "The Effects of Diet on Behavior: Implications for Criminology and Corrections," *Research on Corrections,* **1** (1988): 1–45.

82. Stephen Schoenthaler, "Diet and Crime: An Empirical Examination of the Value of Nutrition in the Control and Treatment of Incarcerated Juvenile Offenders," *International Journal of Biosocial Research,* **4** (1982): 25–39.

83. Heather M. Little, "Food May Be Causing Kids' Problems," *Chicago Tribune,* Oct. 29, 1995, p. 1; Abram Hoffer, "The Relation of Crime to Nutrition," *Humanist in Canada,* **8** (1975): 2–9.

84. Benjamin F. Feingold, *Why Is Your Child Hyperactive?* (New York: Random House, 1975).

85. James W. Swanson and Marcel Kinsbourne, "Food Dyes Impair Performance of Hyperactive Children on a Laboratory Test," *Science,* **207** (1980): 1485–1487.

86. Anthony R. Mawson and K. W. Jacobs, "Corn Consumption, Tryptophan, and Cross-National Homicide Rates," *Journal of Orthomolecular Psychiatry,* **7** (1978): 227–230.

87. "Toddler Dies after Being Thrown in Lake by Dad in Diabetic Seizure," *Chicago Tribune,* July 10, 1995, p. 9.

88. Matti Virkkunen, "Insulin Secretion during the Glucose Tolerance Test among Habitually Violent and Impulsive Offenders," *Aggressive Behavior,* **12** (1986): 303–310.

89. E. A. Beeman, "The Effect of Male Hormones on Aggressive Behavior in Mice," *Physiological Zoology,* **20** (1947): 373–405.

90. D. A. Hamburg and D. T. Lunde, "Sex Hormones in the Development of Sex Differences," in *The Development of Sex Differences,* ed. Eleanor E. Maccoby (Stanford, Calif.: Stanford University Press, 1966).

91. A. Booth and D. W. Osgood, "The Influence of Testosterone on Deviance in Adulthood: Assessing and Explaining the Relationship," *Criminology,* **31** (1993): 93–117; L. E. Kreuz and R. M. Rose, "Assessment of Aggressive Behavior and Plasma Testosterone of a Young Criminal Population," *Psychosomatic Medicine,* **34** (1972): 321–332; R. T. Rada, D. R. Laws, and R. Kellner, "Plasma Testosterone Levels in the Rapist," *Psychosomatic Medicine,* **38** (1976): 257–268.

92. Katharina Dalton, *The Premenstrual Syndrome* (Springfield, Ill.: Charles C Thomas, 1971).

93. Julie Horney, "Menstrual Cycles and Criminal Responsibility," *Law and Human Behavior,* **2** (1978): 25–36.

94. *Regina v. Charlson,* 1 A11. E.R. 859 (1955).

95. L. P. Chesterman et al., "Multiple Measures of Cerebral State in Dangerous Mentally Disordered Inpatients," *Criminal Behavior and Mental Health,* **4** (1994): 228–239; Lee Ellis, "Monoamine Oxidase and Criminality: Identifying an Apparent Biological Marker for Antisocial Behavior," *Journal of Research in Crime and Delinquency,* **28** (1991): 227–251.

96. H. Forssman and T. S. Frey, "Electroencephalograms of Boys with Behavior Disorders," *Acta Psychologica et Neurologia Scandinavica,* **28** (1953): 61–73; H. de Baudouin et al., "Study of a Population of 97 Confined Murderers," *Annales Medico-Psychologique,* **119** (1961): 625–686.

97. Sarnoff A. Mednick, Jan Volavka, William F. Gabrielli, and Turan M. Itil, "EEG as a Predictor of Antisocial Behavior," *Criminology,* **19** (1981): 219–229.

98. Jan Volavka, "Electroencephalogram among Criminals," in Mednick et al., *The Causes of Crime.* See also J. Volavka, *Neurobiology of Violence* (Washington, D.C.: American Psychiatric Press, 1995).

99. DSM III-R, 314.01. See also Michael Rutter, "Syndromes Attributed to 'Minimal Brain Dysfunction' in Children," *American Journal of Psychiatry,* **139** (1980): 21–33.

100. Lorne T. Yeudall, D. Fromm-Auch, and P. Davies, "Neuropsychological Impairment of Persistent Delinquency," *Journal of Nervous and Mental Disorders,* **170** (1982): 257–265; R. D. Robin et al., "Adolescents Who Attempt Suicide," *Journal of Pediatrics,* **90** (1977): 636–638.

101. Edward Sagarin, "Taboo Subjects and Taboo Viewpoints in Criminology," in *Taboos in Criminology,* ed. Sagarin (Beverly Hills, Calif.: Sage, 1980), pp. 8–9.

102. Diana H. Fishbein, "Biological Perspectives in Criminology," *Criminology,* **28** (1990): 27–40.

103. Wilson and Herrnstein, *Crime and Human Nature.* Infants develop attachment to mothers, or mother substitutes, for comfort, security, and warmth.

■ **Internet Exercise**

In this chapter you learned that maternal deprivation is related to delinquent behavior. What happens to deprived (often abused and neglected) children? Is there a cycle of violence?

■ **Your Web Site is: http://www.ncjrs.org**

CHAPTER 5
Strain and Cultural Deviance Theories

The Interconnectedness of Sociological Theories

Anomie: Émile Durkheim

    The Structural-Functionalist Perspective

    Anomie and Suicide

Strain Theory

    Merton's Theory of Anomie

    Modes of Adaptation

    Tests of Merton's Theory

    Evaluation: Merton's Theory

    Institutional Imbalance and Crime

    General Strain Theory

    Theory Informs Policy

Cultural Deviance Theories

    The Nature of Cultural Deviance

    Social Disorganization Theory

    Tests of Social Disorganization Theory

    Evaluation: Social Disorganization Theory

    Theory Informs Policy

    Differential Association Theory

    Tests of Differential Association Theory

    Evaluation: Differential Association Theory

    Theory Informs Policy

    Culture Conflict Theory

Review

Notes

    Special Features

      WINDOW TO THE WORLD: A Social System Breaks Down

      AT ISSUE: Social Disorganization in Los Angeles

      CRIMINOLOGICAL FOCUS: Culture Conflict in Waco, Texas

Key Terms

accommodate
conduct norms
cultural deviance
  theories
cultural transmission
culture conflict theory
deviance
differential association
  theory
general strain theory
social disorganization
  theory
strain theory

The early decades of the twentieth century brought major changes to American society. One of the most significant was the change in the composition of the populations of cities. Between 1840 and 1924, 45 million people—Irish, Swedes, Germans, Italians, Poles, Armenians, Bohemians, Russians—left the Old World; two-thirds of them were bound for the United States.[1] At the same time, increased mechanization in this country deprived many American farmworkers of their jobs and forced them to join the ranks of the foreign-born and the black laborers who had migrated from the South to northern and midwestern industrial centers. During the 1920s large U.S. cities swelled with 5 million new arrivals.[2]

Chicago's expansion was particularly remarkable: Its population doubled in 20 years. Many of the new arrivals brought nothing with them except what they could carry. The city offered them only meager wages, 12-hour working days in conditions that jeopardized their health, and tenement housing in deteriorating areas. Chicago had other problems as well: In the late 1920s and early 1930s it was the home of major organized crime groups, which fought over the profits from the illegal production and sale of liquor during Prohibition (as we shall see in Chapter 13).

Teeming with newcomers looking for work, corrupt politicians trying to buy their votes, and bootleggers growing more influential through sheer firepower and the political strength they controlled, Chicago also had a rapidly rising crime rate. The city soon became an inviting urban laboratory for criminologists, who began to challenge the then-predominant theories of crime causation, which were based on biological and psychological factors. Many of these criminologists were associated with the University of Chicago, which has the oldest sociology program in the United States (begun in 1892). By the 1920s these criminologists began to measure scientifically the amount of criminal behavior and its relation to the social turmoil Chicago was experiencing. Since that time, sociological theories have remained at the forefront of the scientific investigation of crime causation.

THE INTERCONNECTEDNESS OF SOCIOLOGICAL THEORIES

The psychological and biological theories of criminal behavior (Chapter 4) share the assumption that such behavior is caused by some underlying physical or mental condition that separates the criminal from the noncriminal. They seek to identify the kind of person who becomes a criminal and to find the factors that caused the person to engage in criminal behavior. These theories yield insight into individual cases, but they do not explain why crime rates vary from one neighborhood to the next, from group to group, within large urban areas, or within groups of individuals. Sociological theories seek the reasons for differences in crime rates in the social environment. These theories can be grouped into three general categories: strain, cultural deviance, and social control.[3]

The strain and cultural deviance theories formulated between 1925 and 1940 and still popular today focus on the social forces that cause people to engage in criminal activity. These theories laid the foundation for the subcultural theories we discuss in Chapter 6. Social control theories (Chapter 7) take a different approach: They are based on the assumption that the motivation to commit crime is part of human nature. Consequently, social control theories seek to discover why people do not commit crime. They examine the ability of social groups and institutions to make their rules effective.

Strain and cultural deviance theories both assume that social class and criminal behavior are related, but they differ about the nature of the relationship. **Strain theory** argues that all members of society subscribe to one set of cultural values—that of the middle class. One of the most important middle-class values is economic success. Since lower-class persons do not have legitimate means to reach this goal, they turn to illegitimate means in desperation. **Cultural deviance theories** claim that lower-class people have a different set of values that tend to conflict with the values of the middle class. Consequently, when lower-class persons conform to their own value system, they may be violating conventional or middle-class norms.

ANOMIE: ÉMILE DURKHEIM

Imagine a clock with all its parts finely synchronized. It functions with precision. It keeps perfect time. But if one tiny weight or small spring breaks down, the whole mechanism will not function properly. One way of studying a society is to look at its component parts in an effort to find out how they relate to each other. In other words, we look at the structure of a society to see how it functions. If the society is stable, its parts operating smoothly, the social arrangements are functional. Such a society is marked by cohesion, cooperation, and consensus. But if the component parts are arranged in such a way as to threaten the social order, the arrangements are said to be dysfunctional. In a class-oriented society, for example, the classes tend to be in conflict.

The Structural-Functionalist Perspective

The structural-functionalist perspective was developed by Émile Durkheim (1858–1917) before the end of the nineteenth century.[4] At the time, positivist biological theories, which relied on the search for individual differences between criminals and noncriminals, were dominant. So at a time when science was searching for the abnormality of the criminal, Durkheim was writing about the normality of crime in society. To him, the explanation of human conduct, and indeed human misconduct, lies not in the individual but in the group and the social organization. It is in this context that he introduced the term *anomie,* the breakdown of social order as a result of the loss of standards and values.[5]

Throughout his career, Durkheim was preoccupied with the effects of social change. He believed that when a simple society develops into a modern, urbanized one, the intimacy needed to sustain a common set of norms declines. Groups become fragmented, and in the absence of a common set of rules, the actions and expectations of people in one sector may clash with those of people in another. As behavior becomes unpredictable, the system gradually breaks down, and the society is in a state of anomie.

Anomie and Suicide

Durkheim illustrated his concept of anomie in a discussion, not of crime, but of suicide.[6] He suggested several reasons why suicide was more common in some groups than in others. For our purposes, we are interested in the particular form of suicide he called *anomic suicide*. When he analyzed statistical data, he found that suicide rates increased during times of sudden economic change, whether that change was major depression or unexpected prosperity. In periods of rapid change people are abruptly thrown into unfamiliar situations. Rules that once guided behavior no longer hold.

Consider the events of the 1920s. Wealth came easily to many people in those heady, prosperous years. Toward the end, through July, August, and September 1929, the New York stock market soared to new heights. Enormous profits were made from speculation. But on October 24, 1929, a day history records as Black Thursday, the stock market crashed. Thirteen million shares of stock were sold. As more and more shares were offered for sale, their value plummeted. In the wake of the crash, a severe depression overtook the country and then the world. Banks failed. Mortgages were foreclosed. Businesses went bankrupt. People lost their jobs. Lifestyles changed overnight. Many people were driven to sell apples on street corners to survive, and they had to stand in mile-long breadlines to get food to feed their families. Suddenly the norms by which people lived were no longer relevant. People became disoriented and confused. Suicide rates rose.

It is not difficult to understand rising suicide rates in such circumstances, but why would rates also rise at a time of sudden prosperity? According to Durkheim, the same factors are at work in both situations. What causes the problems is not the amount of money available but the sudden change. Durkheim believed that human desires are boundless, an "insatiable and bottomless abyss."[7] Since nature does not set such strict biological limits to the capabilities of humans as it does to those of other animals, he argued, we have developed social rules that put a realistic cap on our aspirations. These regulations are incorporated into the individual conscience and thus make it possible for people to feel fulfilled.

But with a sudden burst of prosperity, expectations change. When the old rules no longer determine how rewards are distributed among members of society, there is no longer any restraint on what people want. Once again the system breaks down. Thus, whether sudden change causes great prosperity or great depression, the result is the same—anomie.

STRAIN THEORY

A few generations after Durkheim, the American sociologist Robert Merton (1910–) also related the crime problem to anomie. But his conception differs somewhat from Durkheim's. The real problem, Merton argued, is created not by sudden social change but by a social structure that holds out the same goals to all its members without giving them equal means to achieve them. This lack of integration between what the culture calls for and what the structure permits, the former encouraging success and the latter preventing it, can cause norms to break down because they no longer are effective guides to behavior.

Merton borrowed the term "anomie" from Durkheim to describe this breakdown of the normative system. According to Merton:

> It is only when a system of cultural values extols, virtually above all else, certain common symbols of success for the population at large while its social structure rigorously restricts or completely eliminates access to approved modes of acquiring these symbols for a considerable part of the same population, that antisocial behavior ensues on a considerable scale.[8]

From this perspective, the social structure is the root of the crime problem (hence the approach Merton takes is sometimes called a *structural explanation*). *Strain theory*, the name given by contemporary criminologists to Merton's explanation of criminal behavior, assumes that people are law-abiding but when under

WINDOW TO THE WORLD

A SOCIAL SYSTEM BREAKS DOWN

In mid-1993, three young members of the Yanomami, an ancient Amazon tribal people, committed suicide—an unprecedented remedy for life's problems in a culture that forbids even talking about death. But the man and two women who took their own lives are among more than 1500 Yanomami who have died from the effects of the invasion of their lands—and culture—by gold miners.(1)

The "gold rush" began in 1987 when prospectors began cutting through swaths of the rain forest where the Yanomami have lived for perhaps 40,000 years, according to one theory. Miners built airstrips, extracted tons of gold, polluted the rivers with metal silt, and left behind "the dubious gifts of the 20th century: disease, prostitution, weapons, alcohol, denuded forests and befouled rivers."(2) While most of the deaths of the Yanomami have resulted from

A Yanomami man with the trappings of modern civilization.

malaria, the tribe also has suffered from flu, venereal disease, measles, tuberculosis, and mercury poisoning from the fish they catch in the now-polluted rivers of their lands. Others have died in direct clashes with miners. In August 1993, for example, there were allegations of a massacre in Brazil of up to 73 tribal members, including at least 10 children, by wildcat gold miners.(3)

OPERATION FREE JUNGLE

Attempts have been made to protect the Yanomami. In 1990, Operation Free Jungle employed soldiers and police to destroy airstrips, remove mining equipment, and expel prospectors. The Brazilian government created a 37,000-mile reservation for its 9000 members of the Yanomami tribe, but the 11,000 tribe members on the Venezuelan side of the border had no such reservation. In 1993, in a second major attempt to protect the tribe, Brazilian police and military evacuated 3000 miners, and Venezuelan troops seized gold miners who crossed the border into the Venezuelan Amazon region.(4)

A POOR PROGNOSIS

But the chances that the Yanomami will be able to withstand the attack on their land and culture are slim. The land contains large deposits of gold, diamonds, tin, and other minerals, and the miners typically are impoverished Brazilians fiercely determined to continue prospecting. Even if the government wants to continue its attempts to protect the area, funds to enforce protective measures are limited. "It's not enough to create a reserve when, inside, you have riches and, outside, marginalized people," says Sidney Possuelo, who is charged with protecting Brazil's indigenous peoples.(5) Already outnumbered by the miners, the Yanomami have lost 20 percent of their tribe members since this battle

began; 200 people died in 1992. And their traditional way of life has been disrupted: Hunting and fishing are increasingly difficult; alcohol and prostitution are taking their toll; miners have raped women, and they have shot children from trees.

The problems of the Yanomami are far from unique. Brazil's Indian population has fallen from 5 million to 220,000 since 1500, and the pattern has repeated itself in virtually every industrializing country. "As the pressure for minerals and timber increases, indigenous groups become more vulnerable to armed attack," stated an Amnesty International report on the Yanomami.(2)

Sources
1. Lynne Wallis, "Quiet Genocide: Miners Seeking Precious Metals Are Causing Deaths of the Yanomami," *Ottawa Citizen,* June 28, 1993, p. A6.
2. "Aid for an Ancient Tribe," *Newsweek,* Apr. 9, 1990, p. 34.
3. "Genocide in the Amazon," *Newsweek,* Aug. 30, 1993, p. 61.
4. James Brooke, "Brazil Evicting Miners in Amazon to Reclaim Land for the Indians," *New York Times,* Mar. 8, 1993, p. A4.
5. Christina Lamb, "Extermination in Eden: A Visit to Amazonia Where the Lust for Gold Threatens the Last Stone Age Tribe," *Financial Post,* Feb. 27, 1993, p. 47.

Questions for Discussion
1. As the Yanomami culture is destroyed, how would you expect the tribe's traditional ways of dealing with crime to be affected? Explain.
2. What measures might be effective in protecting indigenous peoples in all parts of the world from suffering a fate similar to that of the Yanomami?

great pressure will resort to crime. Disparity between goals and means provides that pressure.

Merton's Theory of Anomie

Merton argued that in a class-oriented society, opportunities to get to the top are not equally distributed. Very few members of the lower class ever get there. His anomie theory emphasizes the importance of two elements in any society: (1) cultural aspirations, or goals that people believe are worth striving for, and (2) institutionalized means or accepted ways to attain the desired ends. If a society is to be stable, these two elements must be reasonably well integrated; in other words, there should be means for individuals to reach the goals that are important to them. Disparity between goals and means fosters frustration, which leads to strain.

Merton's theory explains crime in the United States in terms of the wide disparities in income among the various classes. Statistics clearly demonstrate that such disparities exist. The poorest fifth of American families received less than 4 percent of all income in 1990, while the highest fifth received 46 percent of all income—more than 10 times as much.[9] A summary of Americans' incomes in 1993 shows that the median income for white families was $32,960, for black families $19,532, and for Hispanic families $22,886. Close to 40 million persons (15 percent of the country's population) live below the official poverty level.[10] Children represent almost half of this group. By race, the poverty rate was 12 percent for whites, 33 percent for blacks, and 31 percent for persons of Hispanic origin.

It is not, however, solely wealth or income that determines people's position on a social ladder that ranges from the homeless to the very, very rich who live on great estates. In 1966 Oscar Lewis described the "culture of poverty" that exists in inner-city slums. It is characterized by helplessness, apathy, cynicism, and distrust of social institutions such as schools and the police.[11] A few years later Gunnar Myrdal argued that there is a worldwide "underclass, whose members lack the education and skills necessary to compete with the rest of society."[12] And in 1987, William Julius Wilson depicted the ranks of the underclass as the "truly disadvantaged." This group of urban inner-city dwellers is at the bottom of the ladder. Basic institutions such as the school and the family have deteriorated. There is little community cohesion. The people remain isolated—steeped in their own ghetto culture and the anger and aggression that accompanies their marginal existence.[13]

The United States. In our society opportunities to move up the social ladder exist, but they are not equally distributed. A child born to a single, uneducated, 13-year-old girl living in a slum has practically no chance to move up, whereas the child of a middle-class family has a better-than-average chance of reaching a professional or business position. Yet all people in the society share the same goals. And those goals are shaped by billions of advertising dollars spent each year to spread the message that everyone can drive a sports car, take a well-deserved Caribbean vacation, and record the adventure on videotape.

The mystique is reinforced by instant lottery millionaires, superstar athletes, the earnings of Wall Street traders, and rags-to-riches stories of such people as Ray Kroc. Kroc, a high school dropout, believed that a 15-cent hamburger with a 10-cent bag of French fries could make dining out affordable for low-income

NBA star Michael Jordan, who earns millions from his athletic skills and commercial endorsements.

families; his idea spread quickly through the United States—and to 29 other countries that now have McDonald's restaurants with the familiar golden arches. Superstar athletes, like the NBA's Michael Jordan, who at age 21 had a rookie contract of $6.3 million over 7 years and is now in the $15 million to $25 million salary range per season plus $40 million in commercial endorsements, are American icons. Though Merton argued that lack of legitimate means for everyone to reach material goals like these does create problems, he also made it clear that the high rate of deviant behavior in the United States cannot be explained solely on the basis of lack of means.

India. The world has produced class systems that are more rigid than our own, and societies that place much stricter limitations on people's ability to achieve their goals, without causing the problems the United States faces. In the traditional society of India, for example, the untouchables at the bottom of the caste system are forbidden by custom (although no longer by law) even to enter the temples and schools used by those above them, while those at the top enjoy immense privileges.

All Hindu castes fall within a hierarchy, each one imposing upon its members duties and prohibitions covering both public and private life. People of high status may give food to people of lower status, for example, but may not receive food from them. One may eat in the home of a person of lower status, but the food must be cooked and served by a person of equal or higher status. Members of such a rigid system clearly face many more restraints than we do. Why, then, does India not have a very high crime rate?

The answer lies in the fact that Indians learn from birth that all people do not and cannot aspire to the same things. In the United States, the egalitarian principle denies the existence of limits to upward mobility within the social structure.[14] In reality, everyone in society experiences some pressures and strains, and the amounts are inversely related to position in the hierarchy: The lower the class, the higher the strain.

Modes of Adaptation

To be sure, not everyone who is denied access to a society's goals becomes deviant. Merton outlined five ways in which people adapt to society's goals and

TABLE 5.1 A Typology of Modes of Individual Adaptation		
Modes of Adaptation	Culture Goals*	Institutionalized Means*
Conformity	+	+
Innovation	+	−
Ritualism	−	+
Retreatism	−	−
Rebellion	±	±

*+ = acceptance; − = rejection; ± = rejection and substitution.
Source: Robert K. Merton, *Social Theory and Social Structure* (New York: Free Press, 1957), p. 140.

means. Individuals' responses (modes of adaptation) depend on their attitudes toward the cultural goals and the institutional means of attaining those goals. The options are conformity, innovation, ritualism, retreatism, and rebellion (see Table 5.1).

Merton does not tell us how any one individual chooses to become a drug pusher, for example, and another chooses to work on an assembly line. Instead, he explains why crime rates are high in some groups and low in others.

Conformity. Conformity is the most common mode of adjustment. Individuals accept both the culturally defined goals and the prescribed means for achieving those goals. They work, save, go to school, and follow the legitimate paths. Look around you in the classroom. You will see many children of decent, hardworking parents. After college they will find legitimate jobs. Some will excel. Some will walk the economic middle path. But all those who are conformists will accept (though not necessarily achieve) the goals of our society and the means it approves for achieving them.

Innovation. Individuals who choose the adaptation of innovation accept society's goals, but since they have few legitimate means of achieving them, they design their own means for getting ahead. The means may be burglary, robbery, embezzlement, or a host of other crimes. Youngsters who have no parental attention, no encouragement in school, no way to the top—no future—may scrawl their signatures on subway cars and buildings and park benches in order to achieve recognition of a sort. Such illegitimate forms of innovation are certainly not restricted to the lower classes, as evidenced by such crimes as stock manipulation, sale of defective products, and income tax evasion.

Ritualism.   People who adapt by ritualism abandon the goals they once believed to be within reach and resign themselves to their present lifestyles. They play by the rules; they work on assembly lines, hold middle-management jobs, or follow some other safe routine. Many workers have been catching a bus at the same street corner at the same hour every day for 20 years or more. They have long forgotten why, except that their jobs are where their paychecks come from. Their great relief is a 2-week vacation in the summer.

Retreatism.   Retreatism is the adaptation of people who give up both the goals (can't make it) and the means (why try?) and retreat into the world of drug addiction or alcoholism. They have internalized the value system and therefore are under internal pressure not to innovate. The retreatist mode allows for an escape into a nonproductive, nonstriving lifestyle. Some members of the antiwar movement of the 1960s opted to drop out entirely. The pressure was too great; the opportunities were unacceptable. They became addicts or followers of occult religions.

Rebellion.   Rebellion occurs when both the cultural goals and the legitimate means are rejected. Many individuals substitute their own goals (get rid of the establishment) and their own means (protest). They have an alternate scheme for a new social structure, however ill-defined. In 1981, when youths of conservative Zurich, Switzerland, grew frustrated over the establishment's rejection of their demands for a "youth house," they took to the streets, stripped naked, and threw eggs at the operagoers and at the opera house itself.

Merton's theory of how the social structure produces strain that may lead to deviant behavior is illustrated in Figure 5.1. His theory has challenged researchers for half a century.

Tests of Merton's Theory

Merton and his followers (Chapter 6) predict that the greatest proportion of crime will be found in the lower classes because lower-class people have the least opportunity to reach their goals legitimately. Many research studies designed to test the various propositions of strain theory focus on the association between social class and delinquency (an association that evokes considerable controversy). Some studies report a strong inverse relationship: As class goes up, crime rates go down. Others find no association at all between the two variables (Chapter 2).

Social Class and Crime.   The controversy over the relationship between social class and crime began when researchers, using self-report questionnaires, found more serious and more frequent delinquency among lower-class boys.[15] In Chapter 2 we saw that other researchers seriously questioned those findings.[16] When Charles Tittle and his colleagues attempted to clarify the relationship by analyzing 35 empirical studies, they concluded that "class is not now and has not been related to criminality in the recent past."[17] Among the researchers who continued to question the association was Travis Hirschi, who commented: "If socioeconomic status is unrelated to delinquency, then consistency requires that 'socioeconomic status' be removed from the dictionary of delinquency theory and research."[18]

FIGURE 5.1 Modes of deviant behavior.

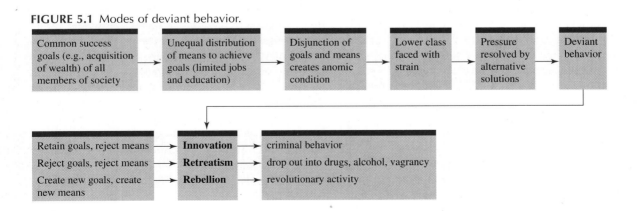

Once again there was a critical reaction. A summary of more than 100 projects concluded that "lower-class people do commit those direct interpersonal types of crime which are normally handled by the police at a higher rate than middle-class people."[19] But if low social status creates frustration that pushes people to commit crime, why don't all the people in the lowest class commit crimes, or drop out into the drug world, or become revolutionaries? Since they clearly do not, there must be some limitations to the causal relationship between crime and social class.

Terence Thornberry and Margaret Farnworth have tried to address this limitation by explaining that the problem arises with studies that make a simple connection between class and crime. The relationship, they say, is highly complex; it involves race, seriousness of the offense, education of family and offender, and many other factors.[20]

According to a number of researchers, we may be able to learn more about the relationship between social class and crime if we look closely at specific types of offenses rather than at aggregate crime (or delinquency) rates. Take homicide, for example: In two large cross-national studies, two teams of Canadian researchers explored the relationship between income inequality and national homicide rates.[21] Both teams reported results that support strain theory. When opportunities or means for success are not provided equally to all members of society (as indicated by crime rates), pressure is exerted on some members of that society to engage in deviant behavior (in this case, homicide). Further analyses by one of the teams showed that the effects of inequality on homicide may be even more pronounced in more democratic societies. The researchers commented: "Income inequality might be more likely to generate violent behavior in more democratic societies because of the coexistence of high material inequality and an egalitarian value system."[22]

David Brownfield also related social class to specific offenses, in this instance to fistfights and brawls among teenagers.[23] His information came from two sources: the Richmond Youth Study, conducted at the University of California at Berkeley, and the Community Tolerance Study, done by a team of researchers at the University of Arizona. Brownfield's analysis of questionnaires completed by 1500 white male students in California and 1300 white male students in Arizona suggests a very strong relation between poverty—as measured by unemployment and welfare assistance—and violent behavior. He concluded that the general public expresses much hostility against the "disreputable poor," a term used by David Matza to describe people who remain unemployed for a long time, even during periods of full employment.[24] In fact, Brownfield suggests, many people hold them in contempt. (He cites a *New York Times*/CBS poll that found that over half of all the respondents believed that most people on welfare could get along without it if they only tried.) This hostility causes the "disreputable poor" to build up frustration, which is made worse by the lack of such fundamental necessities as food and shelter. Such a situation breeds discontent—and violence.

John Hagan argues that youngsters who grow up in a culture where friends are delinquent, parents are criminals, and drug abuse is common, and where early experiences with delinquent activities are widespread, become "embedded" in behaviors that result in later adult unemployment. They are excluded from employment by events that begin early in life. Of course, youngsters can become equally "embedded" in a culture of middle-class values, economic stability, and early work experiences—the foundation for job stability and career success.[25]

Race and Crime. Yet another question that relates to strain theory concerns the relationship between racial inequality and violent crime. Judith and Peter Blau studied data from 125 metropolitan areas in the United States.[26] Their primary finding was that racial inequality—as measured by the difference in socioeconomic status between whites and nonwhites—is associated with the total rate of violent crime. The conclusion fits well with Merton's theory.

The Blaus argued that in a democratic society that stresses equal opportunities for individual achievement but in reality distributes resources on the basis of race, there is bound to be conflict. The most disadvantaged are precisely those who cannot change their situation through political action. In such circumstances, the frustrations created by racial inequalities tend to be expressed in various forms of aggression, such as violent crime. Several researchers have supported these findings. But not all researchers are in agreement.

John Braithwaite examined Uniform Crime Report statistics for a sample of 175 American cities. He compared the rates of violent crime with racial inequality, as measured by the incomes of black families and the incomes of all other families in his sample cities. He concluded that racial inequality does not cause specific crime problems.[27] Other researchers confirm his finding.[28] Perhaps the crucial point is not whether one actually has an equal chance to be successful but rather how one perceives one's chances. According to this reasoning, people who feel the most strain are those who have not only high goals but also low expectations of reaching them. So far, however, research has not supported this contention.[29]

Evaluation: Merton's Theory

The strain perspective developed by Merton and his followers has influenced both research and theoretical developments in criminology.[30] Yet, as popular as this theory remains, it has been questioned on a variety of grounds.[31] By concentrating on crime at the lower levels of the socioeconomic hierarchy, for example, it neglects crime committed by middle- and upper-class people. Radical criminologists (see Chapter 9), in fact, claim that strain theory "stands accused of predicting too little bourgeois criminality and too much proletarian criminality."[32]

Other critics question whether a society as heterogeneous as ours really does have goals on which everyone agrees. Some theorists argue that American subcultures have their own value systems (Chapter 6). If that is the case, we cannot account for deviant behavior on the basis of Merton's cultural goals. Other questions are asked about the theory. If we have an agreed-upon set of goals, is material gain the dominant one? If crime is a means to an end, why is there so much useless, destructive behavior, especially among teenagers?

No matter how it is structured, each society defines goals for its members. The United States is far from being the only society in which people strive for wealth and prestige. Yet, while some people in other cultures have limited means for achieving these goals, not all these societies have high crime rates. Two such societies—Japan and Switzerland—are among the most developed and industrialized in the world. Although the United States has quite a bit in common with them, it does not share their very low crime rates.[33]

Despite the many critical assessments, strain theory, as represented primarily by Merton's formulation

of anomie, has had a major impact on contemporary criminology. It dominated the delinquency research of the 1950s and 1960s. During the 1970s the theory lost its dominant position as criminologists paid increasing attention to how crime and delinquency were related to individuals' loss of attachment to their social institutions—the family, the school, or the government (see Chapter 7). Then, in the mid-1980s and continuing unabated into the 1990s, there was a resurgence of interest in empirical research and theorizing based on strain concepts.

Institutional Imbalance and Crime

In their recent book *Crime and the American Dream*, Steven Messner and Richard Rosenfeld agree with Merton that the material success goal is pervasive in American culture. In essence, the American Dream is quite clear—succeed by any means necessary, even if those means are illegitimate.[34] The American Dream, then, encourages high crime rates. Messner and Rosenfeld expand on Merton's ideas on the relationship between culture, social structure, anomie, and crime rates. High crime, they contend, is more than a matter of striving for monetary gains. It also results from the fact that our major social institutions do not have the capacity to control behavior. These institutions fail to counterbalance the ethos of the American Dream. The dominance of economic institutions manifests itself in three ways: devaluation of other institutions, their accommodation to economic institutions, and the penetration of economic norms.

- The *"devaluation"* of noneconomic roles and functions. Performance in the economic world takes precedence over performance in other institutional settings: Noneconomic functions are "devalued." Education is important, for example, only because it promises economic gains. Learning for its own sake is relatively unimportant. In the context of the family, the homeowner is more important than the homemaker. In politics, too, there is a devaluation: If a citizen does not vote, there may be mild disapproval; if an adult citizen does not work, he or she loses status.
- The *"accommodation"* of other institutions to economic needs. In situations where institutions compete, noneconomic ones **accommodate.** Family life is generally dominated by work schedules. Individuals go to school primarily to get a "good"

job. Once out of school, those who return usually do so to get a better job. In political accommodation, government strives to maintain an environment hospitable to business.

- *The "penetration" of economic norms.* Penetration of economic norms into those of other institutions is widespread. Spouses become partners in "managing" the home, businesspeople/politicians campaign for public office claiming they will "run the country like a corporation," and economic terms such as "accountability" are adopted by educators.

Messner and Rosenfeld contend that as long as there is a disproportionate emphasis on monetary rewards, the crime problem will increase. In fact, if economic opportunities increase, there may be an increase in the preoccupation with material success. Crime will decrease only when noneconomic institutions have the capacity to control behavior.[35]

Freda Adler's study of ten countries with low crime rates supports this argument. She demonstrates that where economic concerns have not "devalued" informal social control institutions such as family, community, or religion, crime rates are relatively low and stable. This finding held for nonindustrialized *and* highly industrialized societies.[36]

General Strain Theory

Sociologist Robert Agnew substantially revised Merton's theory in order to make it more broadly explanatory of criminal behavior.[37] The reformulation is called **general strain theory.** Agnew argues that failure to achieve material goals (the focal point of Merton's theory) is not the only reason for committing crime. Criminal behavior may also be related to the anger and frustration that result when an individual is treated in a way he or she does not want to be treated in a social relationship. General strain theory explains the range of strain-producing events.

- *Strain caused by failure to achieve positively valued goals.* This type of strain is based on Merton's view that lower-class individuals are often prevented from achieving monetary success goals through legitimate channels. When people do not have the money to get what they want, some of them turn to illegitimate means to get it.
- *Stress caused by the removal of positively valued stimuli from the individual.* This type of strain

results from the actual or anticipat[ed] thing or someone important in o[ne's life,] a loved one, breakup with a boy[friend,] divorce of parents, move to a new school. Crim[inal] behavior results when individuals seek revenge against those responsible, try to prevent the loss, or escape through illicit drug use.

- *Strain caused by the presentation of negative stimuli.* The third major source of strain involves stressful life situations. Adverse situations and events may include child abuse, criminal victimization, bad experiences with peers, school problems, or verbal threats. Criminal behavior in these situations may result when an individual tries to run away from the situation, end the problem, or seek revenge.[38]

According to Agnew, each type of strain increases an individual's feelings of anger, fear, or depression. The most critical reaction for general strain theory is anger, an emotion that increases the desire for revenge, helps to justify aggressive behavior, and stimulates individuals into action.

General strain theory acknowledges that not all persons who experience strain become criminals. Many are equipped to cope with their frustration and anger. Some come up with rationalizations ("don't really need it anyway"); others use techniques for physical relief (a good workout at the gym); and still others walk away from the condition causing stress (get out of the house). The capacity to deal with strain depends on personal experience throughout life. It involves the influence of peers, temperament, attitudes, and, in the case of pressing financial problems, economic resources. Recent empirical tests show preliminary support for general strain theory.[39] By broadening Merton's concepts, general strain theory has the potential to explain a wide range of criminal and delinquent behavior including aggressive acts, drug abuse, and property offenses among individuals from all classes in society.

Theory Informs Policy

Strain theory has helped us develop a crime-prevention strategy. If, as the theory tells us, frustration builds up in people who have few means for reaching their goals, it makes sense to design programs that give lower-class people a bigger stake in society.

Head Start. In the 1960s, President Lyndon Johnson inaugurated the Head Start program as part of a major antipoverty campaign. The goal of Head Start is to make children of low-income families more socially competent, better able to deal with their present environment and their later responsibilities.[40] The youngsters get a boost (or a head start) in a 1-year preschool developmental program that is intended to prevent them from dropping out of society. Program components include community and parental involvement, an 8-to-1 child/staff ratio, and daily evaluation and involvement of all the children in the planning of and responsibility for their own activities.

Since a 1-year program could not be expected to affect the remainder of a child's life, Project Follow Through was developed in an effort to provide the same opportunities for Head Start youngsters during elementary school. What began as a modest summer experience for half a million preschool children has expanded into a year-round program that provides educational and social services to millions of young people and their families. This, then, is a program clearly intended to lower stress in the group most likely to develop criminal behavior.

Some research findings do indicate that the program has had a certain measure of success. Yet successes of individual Head Start programs are unevenly distributed over the country, depending largely on program and staff quality. President Clinton, in his 1993 State of the Union Message, called Head Start "a success story" and noted that "for every dollar we invest today, we'll save $3 tomorrow."[41] But even supporters warn that Head Start's success rates can improve only if these funds are carefully aimed at program improvement, rather than enlargement.

Perry Preschool Project. Another program that tried to ameliorate the disparity between goals and means in society was the Perry Preschool Project, begun in 1962 on the south side of Ypsilanti, Michigan. Its purpose was to develop skills that would give youngsters the means of getting ahead at school and in the workplace, thereby reducing the amount and seriousness of delinquent behavior. Overall, 123 black children 3 and 4 years old participated for 2 years, 5 days a week, 2½ hours a day. The program provided a teacher for every 5 children, weekly visits by a teacher to a child's home, and a follow-up of every child annually until age 11 and thereafter at ages 14, 15, and 19.

There is little doubt about the effectiveness of the project. By age 19, the participants did better in several areas than a group that had not participated:

- Employment rates doubled.
- Rates of postsecondary education doubled.
- Teenage pregnancy was cut in half.
- The high school graduation rate was one-third higher.
- Arrest rates were 40 percent lower.[42]

Job Corps. Yet another survivor of President Johnson's War on Poverty is the federal Job Corps

FIGURE 5.2 A profile of Job Corps members. Job Corps figures are for members from July 1, 1990, to June 30, 1991.
Source: Jane Gross, "Remnant of the War on Poverty, Job Corps Is Still a Quiet Success," *New York Times,* Feb. 17, 1992, p. A14.

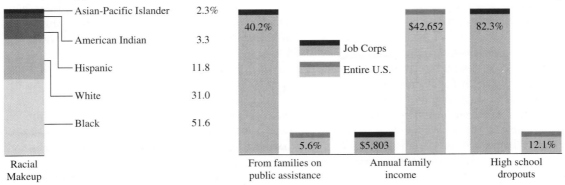

program. It aims at "the worst of the worst," as Senator Orrin Hatch of Utah said.[43] The program enables neglected teenagers—otherwise headed for juvenile detention or jail—to master work habits that they did not learn at home. In 1992, 62,000 young people were serving in the Job Corps. Most of them had enlisted on the basis of recruitment posters, like those distributed by the armed forces. The average length of stay in the corps is just short of a year, at an annual cost of $18,831. That sounds expensive, but juvenile detention costs $29,600 a year—and residential drug treatment centers cost $19,000.

Over two-thirds of former Job Corps members get jobs, and 17 percent go on to higher education. Research has shown that the Job Corps returns $1.46 for every dollar spent, because of increased tax revenue and decreased cost of welfare, crime, and incarceration. Over two-thirds of Job Corps members come from minorities; over 80 percent are high school dropouts (see Figure 5.2).

CULTURAL DEVIANCE THEORIES

The programs that emanate from strain theory attempt to give lower-class children ways to achieve middle-class goals. Programs based on cultural deviance theories concentrate on teaching middle-class values.

Strain theory attributes criminal behavior in the United States to the striving of all citizens to conform with the conventional values of the middle class, primarily financial success. Cultural deviance theories attribute crime to a set of values peculiar to the lower class. Conformity with the lower-class value system, which determines behavior in slum areas, causes conflict with society's laws. Both strain and cultural deviance theories locate the causes of crime in the disadvantageous position of those at the lowest stratum in a class-based society.

Scholars who view crime as resulting from cultural values that permit, or even demand, behavior in violation of the law are called cultural deviance theorists. The three major cultural deviance theories are social disorganization, differential association, and culture conflict. **Social disorganization theory** focuses on the development of high-crime areas in which there is a disintegration of conventional values caused by rapid industrialization, increased immigration, and urbanization. **Differential association**

theory maintains that people learn to commit crime as a result of contact with antisocial values, attitudes, and criminal behavior patterns. **Culture conflict theory** states that different groups learn different conduct norms (rules governing behavior) and that the conduct norms of some groups may clash with conventional middle-class rules.

All three theories contend that criminals and delinquents in fact do conform—but to norms that deviate from those of the dominant middle class. Before we examine the specific theories that share the cultural deviance perspective, we need to explore the nature of cultural deviance.

The Nature of Cultural Deviance

When you drive through rural Lancaster County in Pennsylvania, or through Holmes County in Ohio, or through Elkhart and Lagrange Counties in Indiana, in the midst of fertile fields and well-tended orchards, you will find isolated villages with prosperous and well-maintained farmhouses but no electricity. You will see the farmers and their families traveling in horse-drawn buggies, dressed in homespun clothes, and wearing brimmed hats. These people are Amish. Their ancestors came to this country from the German-speaking Rhineland region as early as 1683 to escape persecution for their fundamentalist Christian beliefs. Shunning motors, electricity, jewelry, and affiliation with political parties, they are a *nonconformist* community within a highly materialistic culture.

Motorcycle gangs made their appearance shortly after World War II. The Hell's Angels were the first of many gangs to be established in slum areas of cities across the country. To become a member of this gang, initiates are subjected to grueling and revolting degradations. They are conditioned to have allegiance only to the gang. Contacts with middle-class society are usually antagonistic and criminal. Motorcycle gangs finance their operations through illegal activities such as dealing drugs, running massage parlors and gambling operations, and selling stolen goods. The members' code of loyalty to one another and to their national and local groups makes the gangs extremely effective criminal organizations.

The normative systems of the Amish and the bikers are at odds with the conventional norms of the society in which they live. Both deviate from middle-class standards. Sociologists define **deviance** as any behavior that members of a social group define as violating their norms. As we can see, the concept of deviance can be applied to noncriminal acts that members of a group view as peculiar or unusual (the lifestyle of the Amish) or to criminal acts (behavior that society has made illegal). The Hell's Angels fit the expected stereotype of deviance as negative; the Amish culture demonstrates that deviance is not necessarily bad, just different.

Cultural deviance theorists argue that our society is made up of various groups and subgroups, each with its own standards of right and wrong. Behavior considered normal in one group may be considered deviant by another. As a result, those who conform to the standards of cultures considered deviant are behaving in accordance with their own norms but may be breaking the law—the norms of the dominant culture.

You may wonder whether the Hell's Angels are outcasts in the slum neighborhoods where they live. They are not. They may even be looked up to by younger boys in places where toughness and violence are not only acceptable but appropriate. Indeed, groups such as the Hell's Angels may meet the needs of youngsters who are looking for a way to be important in a disorganized ghetto that offers few opportunities to gain status.

Social Disorganization Theory

Scholars associated with the University of Chicago in the 1920s became interested in socially disorganized Chicago neighborhoods where criminal values and traditions replaced conventional ones and were transmitted from one generation to the next. In their classic work *The Polish Peasant in Europe and America*, W. I. Thomas and Florian Znaniecki described the difficulties Polish peasants experienced when they left their rural life in Europe to settle in an industrialized city in America.[44] The scholars compared the conditions the immigrants had left in Poland with those they found in Chicago. They also investigated the immigrants' assimilation.

Older immigrants, they found, were not greatly affected by the move because they managed, even within the urban slums, to continue living as they had lived in Poland. But the second generation did not grow up on Polish farms; these people were city dwellers and they were American. They had few of the old Polish traditions but were not yet assimilated into the new ones. The norms of the stable, homogeneous folk society were not transferable to the anonymous, materially oriented urban settings. Rates of crime and delinquency rose. Thomas and Znaniecki attributed this result to *social disorganization*—the breakdown of effective social bonds, family and neighborhood associations, and social controls in neighborhoods and communities. (See Figure 5.3.)

The Park and Burgess Model. Thomas and Znaniecki's study greatly influenced other scholars at the University of Chicago. Among them were Robert Park and Ernest Burgess, who advanced the study of social disorganization by introducing ecological analysis into the study of human society.[45] Ecology is the study of plants and animals in relation to each other and to their natural habitat, the place where they live and grow. Ecologists study these interrelationships, how the balance of nature continues and how organisms survive. Much the same approach is used by *social ecologists*, scholars who study the interrelationships of people and their environment.[46]

In their study of social disorganization, Park and Burgess examined area characteristics instead of

FIGURE 5.3 Social disorganization.
Source: Donald J. Shoemaker, *Theories of Delinquency*, 2d ed. (New York: Oxford University Press, 1990), p. 82.

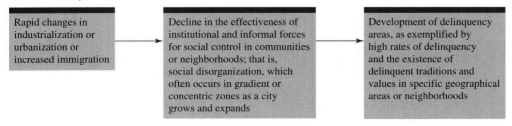

criminals for explanations of high crime rates. They developed the idea of natural urban areas, consisting of concentric zones extending out from the downtown central business district to the commuter zone at the fringes of the city. Each zone had its own structure and organization, its own cultural characteristics and unique inhabitants (Figure 5.4). Zone I, at the center, called the Loop because the downtown business district of Chicago is demarcated by a loop of the elevated train system, was occupied by commercial headquarters, law offices, retail establishments, and some commercial recreation. Zone II was the zone in transition, where the city's poor, unskilled, and disadvantaged lived in dilapidated tenements next to old factories. Zone III housed the working class, people whose jobs enabled them to enjoy some of the comforts the city had to offer at its fringes. The middle class—professionals, small-business owners, and the

managerial class—lived in Zone IV. Zone V was the commuter zone of satellite towns and suburbs.

Shaw and McKay's Work. Clifford Shaw and Henry McKay, two researchers at Chicago's Institute for Juvenile Research, were particularly interested in the model Park and Burgess had created to demonstrate how people were distributed spatially in the process of urban growth. They decided to use the model to investigate the relationship between crime rates and the various zones of Chicago. Their data, found in 55,998 juvenile court records covering a period of 33 years, from 1900 to 1933, indicated the following:

- Crime rates were differentially distributed throughout the city, and areas of high crime rates had high rates of other community problems,

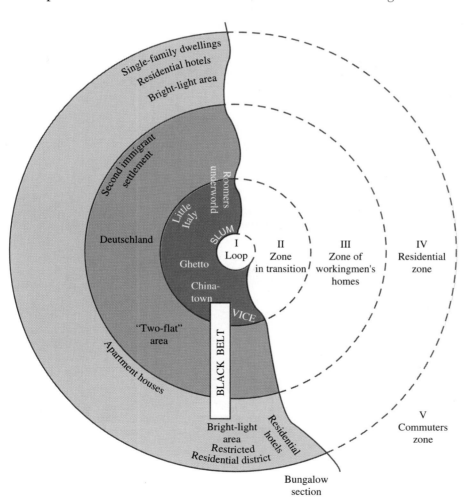

FIGURE 5.4 Park and Burgess's conception of the "natural urban areas" of Chicago.
Source: Robert E. Park, Ernest W. Burgess, and R. D. McKenzie, *The City* (Chicago: University of Chicago Press, 1925), p. 55.

SOCIAL DISORGANIZATION
IN LOS ANGELES

On April 29, 1992, Los Angeles exploded in a firestorm of riots. It was the day of the announcement of the not-guilty verdicts in the trial of the four L.A. Police Department officers accused of beating black motorist Rodney King. While the variety of crimes that were committed during the week of rioting and looting might serve as case studies for many of the explanations of criminal behavior we consider in this section, the context in which the riots occurred provides a clear example of social disorganization. We shall let excerpts from the report of a special advisory committee that assessed the event tell the story, beginning with a description of the riots:

> Crowds began to congregate in South Central Los Angeles to protest the verdicts. As these street corner protests began to grow in number and size, they first became angry and then turned violent. . . . Over the course of the next six days, the reaction escalated into a terrifying reign of violence, widespread looting, and mass destruction of property in many communities across the City. . . . The perpetrators of this violence were not confined to any single racial or ethnic classification. . . . People of all ages and gender participated in the looting. . . .

A Context for Violence

The Rodney King incident did not occur in a vacuum but within the context of the entire social, economic, and political climate of the City. In the past decade, Los Angeles has experienced rapid demographic and economic changes. The population of the City as a whole has grown by 17 percent during that period and now exceeds 3.5 million people. At the same time, the makeup of the population has shifted to 40 percent Hispanic, 37 percent Anglo, 13 percent African-American, 9 percent Asian-American, and 1 percent Native American. As the ethnic makeup of the City has changed fundamentally, so too has the economic stratification of its population. By 1990, more than 18.5 percent of Los Angeles residents were living below the poverty line.

Since its beginnings as a Spanish mission, the City has seen a steady immigration of diverse peoples. Today, the Los Angeles Unified School District consists of 700 schools with approximately 640,000 students who speak 100 different languages. This influx of people provides an enormous amount of creativity and energy . . . but the rapid growth also frustrates the development of a common civic culture. Indeed, the increasingly diverse population of Los Angeles is viewed as increasingly difficult to govern and . . . to police.

A Tinderbox Ready to Explode

The decade of the 1980s brought fewer jobs—but plenty of drugs, crime and violence—to many Los Angeles neighborhoods. Los Angeles street gangs now had crack cocaine. Like no other drug before it, crack had a devastating impact on families. . . . By early 1992, the problems of the inner city—gangs, crime, crack cocaine, poverty and homelessness, and racial and ethnic tension—had come to dominate daily life for a great many residents of Los Angeles. The struggle to preserve a sense of community in the City had begun in earnest. The City of Los Angeles had become a tinderbox ready to explode at the striking of a single match.(1)

Source
1. *The City in Crisis: A Report by the Special Advisor to the Board of Police Commissioners on the Civil Disorder in Los Angeles,* Oct. 21, 1992, pp. 11, 13, 23, 34–35, 41–42.

Questions for Discussion
1. In Los Angeles it was an unpopular jury verdict that sparked a series of violent riots. If similar riots could be caused by natural disasters, political events, or mechanical failures like blackouts, what are the implications for policy makers?
2. The report's analysis of the social climate in Los Angeles makes it sound as if the riots were almost inevitable. Why, then, was the city apparently so unprepared for the reaction of the public to the Rodney King verdicts?

such as truancy, mental disorders, and infant mortality.

- Most delinquency occurred in the areas nearest the central business district and decreased with distance from the center.
- Some areas consistently suffered high delinquency rates, regardless of the ethnic makeup of the population.
- High-delinquency areas were characterized by a high percentage of immigrants, nonwhites, and low-income families and a low percentage of homeownership.
- In high-delinquency areas there was a general acceptance of nonconventional norms, but these norms competed with conventional ones held by some of the inhabitants.[47]

Shaw and McKay demonstrated that the highest rates of delinquency persisted in the same areas of Chicago over the extended period from 1900 to 1933, even though the ethnic composition changed (German, Irish, and English at the turn of the century; Polish and Italian in the 1920s; an increasing number of blacks in the 1930s). This finding led to the conclusion that the crucial factor was not ethnicity but, rather, the position of the group in terms of economic status and cultural values. Finally, through their study of three sets of Cook County juvenile court records—1900 to 1906, 1917 to 1923, and 1927 to 1933—they learned that older boys were associated with younger boys in various offenses and that the same techniques for committing delinquent acts had been passed on through the years. The evidence clearly indicated to them that delinquency was socially learned behavior, transmitted from one generation to the next in disorganized urban areas.[48] This phenomenon is called **cultural transmission.**

Tests of Social Disorganization Theory

Social disorganization, like early strain theory, was overshadowed in the 1970s by social control theorists who turned to explanations of why people do *not* break laws in the face of poor social environments with few means of becoming successful. While these explanations still have widespread impact on the scholarly community, the 1980s and 1990s have seen a major resurgence of interest in how neighborhoods affect people's lives. Modern-day social ecologists have once again begun to focus on the interrelation-

ship between individuals and their environment. What are the consequences of rising crime rates in a neighborhood? Ralph Taylor suggests separating these consequences into three categories: psychological and social, behavioral, and economic.[49]

Psychological and Social Effects. Life in physically deteriorated neighborhoods with their rat-infested buildings, graffiti-ridden streets, trash-strewn vacant lots, boarded-up windows, and openly conducted drug selling, takes its psychological toll on residents.[50] They feel less emotional investment in their communities, mistrust their neighbors, and harbor increasing desires to "get out." Frustration mounts because they are unable to do so. Many parents are so worried about violence on their streets that they confine their youngsters to the home except for school attendance. Young people refer to this confinement as "lockdown" (a term used to describe the locking of prison cells for security reasons). This desperate move to protect their children from getting hurt physically has had harmful psychological effects. According to one professor of developmental psychology, in a world where a simple altercation can end as an assault, or even a murder,[51] these "protected" children are at a disadvantage. When they eventually go back on the streets, they don't know how to survive.

Researchers are questioning whether people living in socially disorganized neighborhoods become more fearful. The answer is, they usually do.[52] When word of victimization begins to spread, fear can reach epidemic proportions. Residents begin to stay off the streets, abandoning them to the gangs, drug sellers, and others involved in illicit activities. Fear becomes greatest in communities undergoing rapid age and racial-composition changes.[53]

Fear increases when there is a perception that the police care little about a neighborhood. Douglas Smith looked at police behavior and characteristics of 60 neighborhoods in 3 large U.S. cities (Rochester, New York; St. Louis, Missouri; Tampa/St. Petersburg, Florida). His major findings suggest that police officers are less likely to file reports of crime incidents in high-crime areas than in low-crime areas and that they are more likely to assist residents and initiate contacts with suspicious-looking people in low-crime neighborhoods.[54]

Behavioral Effects. Crime in the community generally tends to make people limit their participation in efforts to "clean up" the neighborhood. There are, however, communities that fight back with community patrols, anticrime programs, and various activities to protect children. Many would prefer to move away, but few do. Factors besides crime come into play: low income, stage of life cycle, an affordable place to live, or location of employment.[55] Those moving in usually do so because it is the only place they can find an inexpensive place to live.[56]

Economic Effects. Crime problems in a community influence assessments of property values by realtors and lenders. Research in Boston suggests that a 5 percent decrease in crime could bring in $7 million to $30 million in increased tax revenue.[57] In another investigation, researchers asked about the impact of Atlantic City casinos and the related increased crime rate on real estate in three southern New Jersey counties.[58] They found a sizable drop in house values. Those communities most accessible to Atlantic City suffered the worst economic consequences.

Middle- and working-class people tend to escape the urban ghetto, leaving behind the most disadvantaged. When you add to those disadvantaged the people moving in from outside who are also severely disadvantaged, over time these areas become places of concentrated poverty, isolated from the mainstream.

Some social ecologists argue that communities, like people, go through life cycles. Neighborhood deterioration precedes rising crime rates. When crime begins to rise, neighborhoods go from owner-occupied to renter-occupied housing, with a significant decline in the socioeconomic status of residents and an increase in population density. Later in the community life cycle, there is a renewed interest on the part of investors in buying up the cheap real estate with the idea of renovating it and making a profit (gentrification).[59]

Evaluation: Social Disorganization Theory

Though their work has made a significant impact, social ecologists have not been immune to challenges. Their work has been criticized for its focus on how crime patterns are transmitted, not on how they start in the first place. The approach has also been faulted for failing to explain why delinquents stop committing crime as they grow older, why most people in socially disorganized areas do not commit criminal acts, and

why some bad neighborhoods seem to be insulated from crime. Finally, critics claim that this approach does not come to grips with middle-class delinquency.

Clearly, however, modern criminology owes a debt to social disorganization theorists, particularly to Shaw and McKay, who in the 1920s began to look at the characteristics of people and places and to relate both to crime. There is now a vast body of research for which they laid the groundwork.

Theory Informs Policy

Theorists of the Chicago school were the first social scientists to suggest that most crime is committed by normal people responding in expected ways to their immediate surroundings, rather than by abnormal individuals acting out individual pathologies. If social disorganization is at the root of the problem, crime control must involve social organization. The community, not individuals, needs treatment. Helping the community, then, should lower its crime rate.

The Chicago Area Project. Social disorganization theory was translated into practice in 1934 with the establishment of the Chicago Area Project (CAP), an experiment in neighborhood reorganization. The project was initiated by the Institute for Juvenile Research, at which Clifford Shaw and Henry McKay were working. It coordinated the existing community support groups—local schools, churches, labor unions, clubs, and merchants. Special efforts were made to control delinquency through recreational facilities, summer camps, better law enforcement, and the upgrading of neighborhood schools, sanitation, and general appearance.[60]

In 1984 this first community-based delinquency-prevention program celebrated its fiftieth anniversary.[61] South Chicago, its largest area, remains physically very much the way it was over half a century ago. The pollution from the surrounding steel mills has been cleaned up, but the urban decay has not. Boarded-up buildings, trash-littered lots, and badly deteriorated housing still characterize the area with which Shaw and McKay were originally concerned. CAP continues to work as a self-help group, committed mainly to community treatment of juvenile delinquency. Its motto is still "Concerned people striving to make South Chicago a better place to live." It has had modest success.

Boston's Mid-City Project and Others. During the 1950s, Boston initiated the Mid-City Project, which was similar in many ways to CAP. But instead of waiting for gang members to come to community centers, workers went out into the streets to meet the gangs on their own turf. Good relationships were formed. Delinquency rates, however, stayed the same.[62] Local crime-prevention programs got a bigger boost in the 1960s, with John F. Kennedy's New Frontier and Lyndon Johnson's War on Poverty (Chapter 6).

More recently another community action project has concentrated on revitalizing a Puerto Rican slum community. Sister Isolina Ferre worked for 10 years in the violent Navy Yard section of Brooklyn, New York. In 1969 she returned to Ponce Plaza, a poverty-stricken area in Ponce, Puerto Rico, infested with disease, crime, and unemployment. The area's 16,000 people had no doctors, nurses, dentists, or social agencies. The project began with a handful of missionaries, university professors, dedicated citizens, and community members who were willing to become advocates for their neighborhood. Among the programs begun were a large community health center, Big Brother/Big Sister programs for juveniles sent from the courts, volunteer tutoring, and recreational activities to take young people off the streets. Young photographers of Ponce Plaza, supplied with a few cameras donated by friends at Kodak, mounted an exhibit at the Metropolitan Museum of Art in New York. Regular fiestas have given community members a chance to celebrate their own achievements as well.[63]

Programs based on social disorganization theory attempt to bring conventional social values to disorganized communities. They provide an opportunity for young people to learn norms other than those of delinquent peer groups. Let us see how such learning takes place.

Differential Association Theory

What we eat, what we say, what we believe—in fact, the way we respond to any situation—depends on the culture in which we have been reared. In other words, to a very large extent the social influences that people encounter determine their behavior. Whether a person becomes law-abiding or criminal, then, depends on contacts with criminal values, attitudes, definitions, and behavior patterns. This proposition underlies one of the most important theories of crime causation in American criminology—differential association.

Sutherland's Theory. In 1939 Edwin Sutherland introduced differential association theory in his textbook *Principles of Criminology*. Since then scholars have read, tested, reexamined, and sometimes ridiculed this theory, which claimed to explain the development of all criminal behavior. The theory states that crime is learned through social interaction. People come into constant contact with "definitions favorable to violations of law" and "definitions unfavorable to violations of law." The ratio of these definitions—criminal to noncriminal—determines whether a person will engage in criminal behavior.[64] In formulating this theory, Sutherland relied heavily on Shaw and McKay's findings that delinquent values are transmitted within a community or group from one generation to the next.

Sutherland's Nine Propositions. Nine propositions explained the process by which this transmission of values takes place:

1. Criminal behavior is learned.
2. Criminal behavior is learned in interaction with other persons in a process of communication. A person does not become a criminal simply by living in a criminal environment. Crime is learned by participation with others in verbal and nonverbal communications.
3. The principal part of the learning of criminal behavior occurs within intimate personal groups. Families and friends have the most influence on the learning of deviant behavior. Their communications far outweigh those of the mass media.
4. When criminal behavior is learned, the learning includes (a) techniques of committing the crime, which are sometimes very complicated, sometimes very simple, and (b) the specific direction of motives, drives, rationalizations, and attitudes. Young delinquents learn not only how to shoplift, crack a safe, pick a lock, or roll a joint but also how to rationalize and defend their actions. One safecracker accompanied another safecracker for 1 year before he cracked his first safe.[65] In other words, criminals, too, learn skills and gain experience.
5. The specific direction of motives and drives is learned from definitions of the legal codes as

favorable or unfavorable. In some societies an individual is surrounded by persons who invariably define the legal codes as rules to be observed, while in others he or she is surrounded by persons whose definitions are favorable to the violation of the legal codes. Not everyone in our society agrees that the laws should be obeyed; some people define them as unimportant. In American society, where definitions are mixed, we have a culture conflict in relation to legal codes.

6. A person becomes delinquent because of an excess of definitions favorable to violation of law over definitions unfavorable to violation of law. This is the key principle of differential association. In other words, learning criminal behavior is not simply a matter of associating with bad companions. Rather, learning criminal behavior depends on how many definitions we learn that are favorable to law violation as opposed to those that are unfavorable to law violation.

7. Differential associations may vary in frequency, duration, priority, and intensity. The extent to which associations and definitions will result in criminality is related to the frequency of contacts, their duration, and their meaning to the individual.

8. The process of learning criminal behavior by association with criminal and anticriminal patterns involves all the mechanisms that are involved in any other learning. Learning criminal behavior patterns is very much like learning conventional behavior patterns and is not simply a matter of observation and imitation.

9. While criminal behavior is an expression of general needs and values, it is not explained by those general needs and values, since noncriminal behavior is an expression of the same needs and values. Shoplifters steal to get what they want. Others work to get money to buy what they want. The motives—frustration, desire to accumulate goods or social status, low self-concept, and the like—cannot logically be the same because they explain both lawful and criminal behavior.

Tests of Differential Association Theory

Since Sutherland presented his theory more than 50 years ago, researchers have tried to determine whether his principles lend themselves to empirical measurement. James Short tested a sample of 126 boys and 50 girls at a training school and reported a consistent relationship between delinquent behavior and frequency, duration, priority, and intensity of interactions with delinquent peers.[66] In another test, researchers found that the chance of committing a delinquent act depends on whether friends commit the same act.[67] Similarly, Travis Hirschi demonstrated that boys with delinquent friends are more likely to become delinquent.[68] Research on seventh- and eighth-grade students attending Rochester, New York, public schools in the late 1980s and early 1990s shows that gang membership is strongly associated with peer delinquency and the amount of delinquency and drug use.[69] Mark Warr demonstrated that while the duration of delinquent friendships over a long period of time has a greater effect than exposure over a short period, it is recent friendships rather than early friendships that have the greatest effect on delinquency.[70]

Adults have also been the subjects of differential association studies. Two thousand residents of New Jersey, Oregon, and Iowa were asked such questions as how many people they knew personally had engaged in deviant acts and how many were frequently in trouble. They were also asked how often they attended church (assumed to be related to definitions unfavorable to the violation of law). This differential association scale correlated significantly with such crimes as illegal gambling, income tax cheating, and theft.[71]

Evaluation: Differential Association Theory

Many researchers have attempted to validate Sutherland's differential association theory. Others have criticized it. Much of the criticism stems from errors in interpretation. Perhaps this type of error is best demonstrated by the critics who ask why it is that not everyone in heavy, prolonged contact with criminal behavior patterns becomes a criminal. Take, for argument's sake, corrections officers, who come into constant contact with more criminal associations than noncriminal ones. How do they escape from learning to be law violators themselves?

The answer, of course, is that Sutherland does not tell us that individuals become criminal by associating with criminals or even by association with criminal behavior patterns. He tells us, rather, that a person becomes delinquent because of an "excess of definitions favorable to violation of law over definitions unfavorable to violation of law." The key word is "definitions." Furthermore, unfavorable definitions may be communicated by persons who are not robbers or murderers or tax evaders. They may, for example, be law-abiding parents who, over time, define certain situations in such a way that their children get verbal or nonverbal messages to the effect that antisocial behavior is acceptable.

Several scholars have asked whether the principles of differential association really explain all types of crime. They might explain theft, but what about homicide resulting from a jealous rage?[72] Why do some people who learn criminal behavior patterns not engage in criminal acts? Why is no account taken of nonsocial variables, such as a desperate need for money? Furthermore, while the principles may explain how criminal behavior is transmitted, they do not account for the origin of criminal techniques and definitions. In other words, the theory does not tell us how the first criminal became a criminal.

Differential association theory suggests there is an inevitability about the process of becoming a criminal. Once you reach the point where your definitions favorable to law violation exceed your definitions unfavorable to law violation, have you crossed an imaginary line into the criminal world? Even if we could add up the definitions encountered in a lifetime, could scientists measure the frequency, priority, duration, and intensity of differential associations?

Despite these criticisms, the theory has had a profound influence on criminology.[73] Generations of scholars have tested it empirically, modified it to incorporate psychologically based learning theory (see Chapter 4), and used it as a foundation for their own theorizing (Chapter 6). The theory has also had many policy implications.

Theory Informs Policy

If, according to differential association theory, a person can become criminal by learning definitions favorable to violating laws, it follows that programs that expose young people to definitions favorable to conventional behavior should reduce criminality. Such educational efforts as Head Start and the Perry Preschool Project have attempted to do just that. The same theory underlies many of the treatment programs for young school dropouts and pregnant teenagers.

An innovative Ohio program is trying to break the vicious cycle between poverty–welfare–school dropout–drugs–delinquency and teenage pregnancy. This program, LEAP (for learning, earning, and parenting), provides financial rewards for teenage single parents to stay in, or return to, school and deductions from the welfare checks of those who do not participate in education. A 1993 evaluation found that the program, which costs the state very little, has been moderately successful. Success appears to increase with increased counseling and aid services. Several states have instituted similar "learnfare" programs (for example, Virginia, Florida, Maryland, and Oklahoma), while others are considering this option.[74]

Recently schools in Chicago, New York, Boston, Los Angeles, Tucson, and Washington have introduced "conflict resolution" into the curriculum. These programs zero in on teaching youngsters to deal with problems nonviolently. For example, children practice how to respond when someone insults or challenges them by role-playing situations. In the Chicago area alone, 5000 students are going through this antiviolence program, which is supported by the National Institute of Mental Health.[75]

Culture Conflict Theory

Differential association theory is based on the learning of criminal (or deviant) norms or attitudes. Culture conflict theory focuses on the source of these criminal norms and attitudes. According to Thorsten Sellin, **conduct norms**—norms that regulate our daily lives—are rules that reflect the attitudes of the groups to which each of us belongs.[76] Their purpose is to define what is considered appropriate or normal behavior and what is inappropriate or abnormal behavior.

Sellin argues that different groups have different conduct norms and that the conduct norms of one group may conflict with those of another. Individuals may commit crimes by conforming to the norms of their own group if that group's norms conflict with those of the dominant society. According to this rationale, the main difference between a criminal and a noncriminal is that each is responding to different sets of conduct norms.

Examples of groups with values significantly deviating from those of the surrounding majority include Move, an Afro-American group concerned with issues like police brutality, animal rights, and African her-

CRIMINOLOGICAL FOCUS

CULTURE CONFLICT IN WACO, TEXAS

A fire swept through the headquarters of a religious cult in Waco, Texas, in April 1993, killing nearly every one of the 90 adults in the compound and all 17 children. The fire was the final event in a 3-month-long standoff between the cult and U.S. federal agents who wanted to investigate the community's stockpile of weapons. What enabled so many people to defy American law-and-order authority for so long? This was a classic case of a deviant culture clashing with the dominant one.

DIFFERENT RULES

What kind of community was it that kept so many people together in the face of attempts to impose law and

David Koresh preaching in Australia.

order from the outside—and led them all to die? The answer is simple: The cult members' rules of conduct, shaped by their religious beliefs, were different from those of the world outside the compound. David Koresh, the leader of the cult, was a key factor. Thought to be a psychopath, Koresh was described in one report as follows: "David Koresh—high school dropout, rock musician, polygamist preacher—built his church on a simple message: "If the Bible is true, then I'm Christ."(1)

As Christ, Koresh ruled over more than 100 people in the compound, keeping the men separate from the women, taking as wives anyone of his choosing (some 12 of whom bore his children), preaching long sermons to cult members, strict-

ly rationing their food, and subjecting the children to frequent and severe physical punishment in "the whipping room." Traditional family structure was disrupted; fathers never lived with families, and children were taken from their mothers by age 12.(2)

SHARED APOCALYPSE

Clearly a departure from the society they had lived in outside, all this was accepted by the cult members, who sought religious fulfillment. Koresh often told his followers that the end of the world was coming, and the raid by the federal agents probably served to strengthen his hold on the community.

Sources

1. Richard Lacayo, "Cult of Death," *Time,* Mar. 15, 1993, p. 36.
2. Sophfronia Scott Gregory, "Children of a Lesser God," *Time,* May 17, 1993, p. 54.

Questions for Discussion

1. Among the crimes that may have been committed inside the cult's compound were arson, statutory rape, child abuse, polygamy, financial fraud, and murder. When a group has obviously different conduct norms from those of the society in which its members live, should exceptions be made under the First Amendment in imposing criminal law? Where would you draw the line?
2. Could the conflict between conduct norms of deviant cultures and the rules of middle-class society be eased? Does this possibility hold any promise for crime-prevention strategies? Explain.

itage, which was located in a house on Osage Street in Philadelphia. It alienated its neighbors by loud and profanity-laced loudspeaker messages. Mutual animosity escalated. Some Move members armed them-

selves. A police officer was killed. Ultimately the police, armed with arrest warrants for some members, entered the area. The group did not surrender. The police attacked: 10,000 rounds of ammunition

MOVE members and neighbors watching their houses burn after aerial and ground attacks by the Philadelphia police, May 1985.

were fired, and a bomb was dropped from a police helicopter. All but two of the Move members died, and all the houses on the street went up in flames.

Another example—far more criminal—was the Solar Temple, founded by a former Gestapo officer, which flourished in Switzerland and Canada. This mystic cult attracted wealthy members who "donated" all their property to the cult, perhaps $93 million in all; much of it was spent for the personal benefit of two cult leaders. Cult members were heavily armed (and engaged in arms trading), in anticipation of the end of the world. Their end of the world came in the fall of 1994, when the two cult leaders murdered nearly all their followers and then committed suicide.

Sellin distinguishes between primary and secondary conflicts. *Primary conflict* occurs when norms

of two cultures clash. A clash may occur at the border between neighboring cultural areas; a clash may occur when the law of one cultural group is extended to cover the territory of another; or it may occur when members of one group migrate to another culture. In a widening gap between cultural norms and generations, Southeast Asian immigrant children are running away from home in increasing numbers. They often run into an informal nationwide network of "safe houses." No one knows how many runaways there are, but efforts estimate that at least one-third of all refugee families have had at least one child vanish for days, months, or even longer.

Secondary conflict arises when a single culture evolves into a variety of cultures, each with its own set of conduct norms. This type of conflict occurs when the homogeneous societies of simpler cultures become complex societies in which the number of social groupings multiplies constantly and norms are often at odds. Your college may make dormitory living mandatory for all freshmen, for example, but to follow the informal code of your peer group, you may seek the freedom of off-campus housing. Or you may have to choose whether to violate work rules by leaving your job half an hour early to make a mandatory class or to violate school rules by walking into class half an hour late. Life situations are frequently controlled by conflicting norms, so no matter how people act, they may be violating some rule, often without being aware that they are doing so.

In the next chapter, which deals with the formation and operation of subcultures, we will expand the discussion of the conflict of norms. We will also examine the empirical research that seeks to discover whether there is indeed a multitude of value systems in our society and, if so, whether and how they conflict.

REVIEW

Contemporary criminologists tend to divide the sociological explanation of crime into three categories: strain, cultural deviance, and social control. The strain and cultural deviance perspectives focus on the social forces that cause people to engage in deviant behavior. They assume that there is a relationship between social class and criminal behavior. Strain theorists argue that all people in society share one set of cultural values and that since lower-class persons often do not have legitimate means to attain society's goals, they may turn to illegitimate means instead. General strain theory, a revision of Merton's theory, relates criminal behavior to the anger that results when an individual is treated in a way he or she does not want to be treated in a social relationship. Cultural deviance theorists maintain that the lower class has a distinctive set of values and that these values often conflict with those of the middle class.

Cultural deviance theories—social disorganization, differential association, and culture conflict—relate criminal behavior to the learning of criminal values and norms. Social disorganization theory focuses on the breakdown of social institutions as a precondition for the establishment of criminal norms. Differential association theory concentrates on the processes by which criminal behavior is taught and learned. Culture conflict theory focuses on the specifics of how the conduct norms of some groups may clash with those of the dominant culture.

NOTES

1. Ysabel Rennie, *The Search for Criminal Man* (Lexington, Mass.: Lexington Books, 1978), p. 125.
2. James T. Carey, *Sociology and Public Affairs: The Chicago School* (Beverly Hills, Calif.: Sage, 1975), pp. 19–20.
3. See the discussion of sociological theory in Frank P. Williams III and Marilyn D. McShane, *Criminological Theory* (Englewood Cliffs, N.J.: Prentice-Hall, 1988).
4. Émile Durkheim, *The Division of Labor in Society* (New York: Free Press, 1964).
5. Émile Durkheim, *Rules of Sociological Method* (New York: Free Press, 1966).
6. Émile Durkheim, *Suicide* (Glencoe, Ill.: Free Press, 1951), pp. 241–276.
7. Ibid., p. 247.
8. Robert K. Merton, "Social Structure and Anomie," *American Sociological Review*, 3 (1938): 672–682. For a complete history of the social structure and anomie paradigm, see recent reflections of Merton in Robert K. Merton, "Opportunity Structure: The Emergence, Diffusion, and Differentiation of a Sociological Concept, 1930s–1950s," in *Advances in Criminological Theory: The Legacy of Anomie*, vol. 6, ed. Freda Adler and William S. Laufer (New Brunswick, N.J.: Transaction, 1994), pp. 3–78. Several measures of anomie have been developed. Probably the best-known indicator of anomie at the social level was formulated by Bernard Lander in a study of 8464 cases of juvenile delinquency in Baltimore between 1939 and 1942. Lander devised a measure that included the rate of delinquency, the percentage of nonwhite population in a given area, and the percentage of owner-occupied homes. According to Lander, those factors were indicative of the amount of normlessness (anomie) in a community. See Bernard Lander,

Towards an Understanding of Juvenile Delinquency (New York: Columbia University Press, 1954), p. 65.
9. U.S. Department of Commerce, Bureau of the Census, *Statistical Abstract of the United States 1990* (Washington, D.C.: U.S. Government Printing Office, 1991), table 731.
10. *1996 Information Please Almanac* (Boston: Houghton Mifflin, 1996), p. 51.
11. Oscar Lewis, "The Culture of Poverty," *Scientific American*, 215 (1966): 19–25.
12. Gunnar Myrdal, *The Challenge of World Poverty* (New York: Vintage, 1990).
13. William Julius Wilson, *The Truly Disadvantaged* (Chicago: University of Chicago Press, 1987).
14. Robert K. Merton, *Social Theory and the Social Structure* (New York: Free Press, 1957), p. 187.
15. Albert J. Reiss, Jr., and Albert L. Rhodes, "The Distribution of Juvenile Delinquency in the Social Class Structure," *American Sociological Review*, 26 (1961): 720–732. For the relationship between economic changes and crime, see Pamela Irving Jackson, "Crime, Youth Gangs, and Urban Transition: The Social Dislocations of Postindustrial Economic Development," *Justice Quarterly*, 8 (1991): 380–397.
16. F. Ivan Nye, James F. Short, and Virgil J. Olson, "Socioeconomic Status and Delinquent Behavior," *American Journal of Sociology*, 63 (1958): 381–389.
17. Charles R. Tittle, Wayne J. Villemez, and Douglas A. Smith, "The Myth of Social Class and Criminality: An Empirical Assessment of the Empirical Evidence," *American Sociological Review*, 43 (1978): 652; Charles R. Tittle and Robert F. Meier, "Specifying the SES/Delinquency Relationship by Social Characteristics of Contexts," *Journal of Research in Crime and Delinquency*, 28 (1991): 430–455.
18. Travis Hirschi, *Causes of Delinquency* (Berkeley: University of California Press, 1969), p. 67. See also Marvin D. Krohn, Ronald L. Akers, Marcia J. Radosevich, and Lonn Lanza-Kaduce, "Social Status and Deviance," *Criminology*, 18 (1980): 303–318.
19. John Braithwaite, "The Myth of Social Class and Criminality Reconsidered," *American Sociological Review*, 46 (1981): 41. See also Delbert S. Elliott and Suzanne S. Ageton, "Reconciling Race and Class Differences in Self-Reported and Official Estimates of Delinquency," *American Sociological Review*, 45 (1980): 95–110; and Michael W. Neustrom and William M. Norton, "Economic Dislocation and Property Crime," *Journal of Criminal Justice*, 23 (1995): 29–39.
20. Terence P. Thornberry and Margaret Farnsworth, "Social Correlates of Criminal Involvement: Further Evidence on the Relationship between Social Status and Criminal Behavior," *American Sociological Review*, 47 (1982): 505–518; Thomas J. Bernard, "Control Criticisms of Strain Theories: An Assessment of Theoretical and Empirical Adequacy," *Journal of Research in Crime and Delinquency*, 21 (1984): 353–372; Delbert S. Elliott and David Huizinga, "Social Class and Delinquent Behavior in a National Youth Panel," *Criminology*, 21 (1983): 149–177.
21. William R. Avison and Pamela L. Loring, "Population Diversity and Cross-National Homicide: The Effects of Inequality and Heterogeneity," *Criminology*, 24 (1986): 733–749; Harvey Krahn, Timothy F. Hartnagel, and John W. Gartrell, "Income Inequality and Homicide Rates: Cross-National Data and

Criminological Theories," *Criminology,* **24** (1986): 269–295; Richard Fowles and Mary Merva, "Wage Inequity and Criminal Activity: An Extreme Bounds Analysis for the United States, 1975–1990," *Criminology,* **34** (1996): 163–182.

22. Krahn et al., "Income Inequality," p. 288.

23. David Brownfield, "Social Class and Violent Behavior," *Criminology,* **24** (1986): 421–438.

24. David Matza, "The Disreputable Poor," in *Class, Status, and Power,* ed. Reinhard Bendix and Seymour M. Lipset (New York: Free Press, 1966). See also Chris Hale, "Unemployment and Crime: Differencing Is No Substitute for Modeling," *Journal of Research in Crime and Delinquency,* **28** (1991): 426–429.

25. John Hagan, "The Social Embeddedness of Crime and Unemployment," *Criminology,* **31** (1993): 465–492.

26. Judith R. Blau and Peter M. Blau, "The Cost of Inequality: Metropolitan Structure and Violent Crime," *American Sociological Review,* **47** (1982): 114–129. See also Steven F. Messner and Reid M. Golden, "Racial Inequality and Racially Disaggregated Homicide Rates: An Assessment of Alternative Theoretical Explanations," *Criminology,* **30** (1992): 421–446; and James A. Chambers, *Blacks and Crime: A Function of Class* (Westport, Conn.: Praeger, 1995).

27. John Braithwaite, *Inequality, Crime, and Public Policy* (London: Routledge & Kegan Paul, 1979), p. 219.

28. Robert J. Sampson, "Race and Criminal Violence: A Demographically Disaggregated Analysis of Urban Homicide," *Crime and Delinquency,* **31** (1985): 47–82.

29. Delbert Elliott and Harwin L. Voss, *Delinquency and Dropout* (Lexington, Mass.: Lexington Books, 1974); William S. Laufer, "Vocational Interests of Homeless, Unemployed Men," *Journal of Vocational Behavior,* **18** (1981): 196–201.

30. Thomas J. Bernard, "Merton versus Hirshi: Who Is Faithful to Durkheim's Heritage?" in Adler and Laufer, *Advances in Criminological Theory,* vol. 4, pp. 81–91; Nikos Passas, "Continuities in the Anomie Tradition," in Adler and Laufer, *Advances in Criminological Theory,* vol. 4, pp. 91–112; Scott Menard, "A Developmental Test of Mertonian Anomie Theory," *Journal of Research in Crime and Delinquency,* **32** (1995): 136–174.

31. Gary F. Jensen, "Salvaging Structure through Strain: A Theoretical and Empirical Critique," in Adler and Laufer, *Advances in Criminological Theory,* vol. 4, pp. 139–158; Velmer S. Burton, Jr., Francis T. Cullen, T. David Evans, and R. Gregory Dunaway, "Reconsidering Strain Theory: Operationalization, Rival Theories, and Adult Criminality," *Journal of Quantitative Criminology,* **10** (1994): 213–239.

32. Ian Taylor, Paul Walton, and Jock Young, *The New Criminology* (New York: Harper & Row, 1973), p. 107.

33. Freda Adler, *Nations Not Obsessed with Crime* (Littleton, Colo.: Fred B. Rothman, 1983).

34. Steven F. Messner and Richard Rosenfeld, *Crime and the American Dream* (Belmont, Calif.: Wadsworth, 1994).

35. Mitchell B. Chamlin and John K. Cochran, "Assessing Messner and Rosenfeld's Institutional Anomie Theory: A Partial Test," *Criminology,* **33** (1995): 411–429.

36. Freda Adler, "Synnomie to Anomie: A Macrosociological Formulation," in Adler and Laufer, *Advances in Criminological Theory,* vol. 4, pp. 271–283.

37. Robert Agnew, "Foundations for a General Strain Theory of Crime and Delinquency," *Criminology,* **30** (1992): 47–87.

38. Robert Agnew, "The Contribution of Social-Psychological Strain Theory to the Explanation of Crime and Delinquency," in Adler and Laufer, *Advances in Criminological Theory,* pp. 113–137.

39. Raymond Paternoster and Paul Mazerolle, "General Strain Theory and Delinquency: A Replication and Extension," *Journal of Research in Crime and Delinquency,* **31** (1994): 235–263; Timothy Brezina, "Adapting to Strain: An Examination of Delinquent Coping Responses," *Criminology,* **34** (1996): 39–60; Robert Agnew and Helene Raskin White, "An Empirical Test of General Strain Theory," *Criminology,* **30** (1992): 475–499.

40. R. H. McKey, L. Condelle, H. Ganson, B. J. Barrett, C. McConkey, and M. C. Planty, *Executive Summary: The Impact of Head Start on Children, Families, and Communities: Final Report of the Head Start Evaluation, Synthesis, and Utilization Project,* for U.S. Department of Health and Human Services, Administration for Children, Youth, and Families (Washington, D.C.: U.S. Government Printing Office, 1985).

41. Barbara Kantrowitz and Pat Wingert, "No Longer a Sacred Cow: Head Start Has Become a Free-Fire Zone," *Newsweek,* Apr. 12, 1993, p. 51.

42. John R. Berrueta-Clement, Lawrence J. Schweinhart, W. Steven Barnett, Ann S. Epstein, and David P. Weekart, *Changed Lives: The Effects of the Perry Preschool Program on Youths through Age 19* (Ypsilanti, Mich.: High/Scope, 1984).

43. Jane Gross, "Remnants of the War on Poverty, Job Corps Is Still a Quiet Success," *New York Times,* Feb. 17, 1992, pp. 1, 14.

44. W. I. Thomas and Florian Znaniecki, *The Polish Peasant in Europe and America* (Boston: Gorham, 1920).

45. Robert E. Park, "Human Ecology," *American Journal of Sociology,* **42** (1936): 1–15.

46. For a contemporary discussion of the human ecology approach to crime, see Rodney Stark, "Deviant Places: A Theory of the Ecology of Crime," *Criminology,* **25** (1987): 893–909.

47. Clifford R. Shaw, Frederick M. Forbaugh, Henry D. McKay, and Leonard S. Cottrell, *Delinquency Areas* (Chicago: University of Chicago Press, 1929).

48. Clifford R. Shaw and Henry D. McKay, *Juvenile Delinquency and Urban Areas* (Chicago: University of Chicago Press, 1942); see also the revised and updated edition: Clifford R. Shaw and Henry D. McKay, *Juvenile Delinquency and Urban Areas: A Study of Delinquency in Relation to Differential Characteristics of Local Communities in American Cities* (Chicago: University of Chicago Press, 1969); and Frederick M. Thrasher, *The Gang* (Chicago: University of Chicago Press, 1927).

49. Ralph B. Taylor, "The Impact of Crime on Communities," *The Annals of the American Academy,* **539** (1995): 28–45.

50. Ralph B. Taylor, Steve D. Gottfredson, and Sidney Brower, "Attachments to Place: Discriminant Validity and Impacts of Disorder and Diversity," *American Journal of Community Psychology,* **13** (1985): 525–542.

51. Michael Marriott, "Living in 'Lockdown,'" *Newsweek,* Jan. 23, 1995, p. 57.

52. Lynn Newhart Smith and Gary D. Hill, "Victimization and Fear of Crime," *Criminal Justice and Behavior,* **18** (1991):

217–239; and Randy L. LaGrange, Kenneth F. Ferraro, and Michael Supancic, "Perceived Risk of Fear of Crime: Role of Social and Physical Incivilities," *Journal of Research in Crime and Delinquency,* **29** (1992): 311–334. For research that measures safety and perceived safety resources in the context of other environmental concerns (as an alternative to measuring fear of crime), see John J. Gibbs and Kathleen J. Hanrahan, "Safety Demand and Supply: An Alternative to Fear of Crime," *Justice Quarterly,* **10** (1993): 369–394.

53. Ralph Taylor and Jeanette Covington, "Community Structural Change and Fear of Crime," *Social Problems,* **40** (1993): 374–392.

54. Douglas A. Smith, "The Neighborhood Context of Police Behavior," in *Communities and Crime,* ed. Albert J. Reiss and Michael Tonry (Chicago: University of Chicago Press, 1986), pp. 313–341; Terance D. Miethe, Michael Hughes, and David McDowall, "Social Change in Crime Rates: An Evaluation of Alternative Theoretical Approaches," *Social Forces,* **70** (1991): 165–185; E. Britt Paterson, "Poverty, Income Inequality, and Community Crime Rates," *Criminology,* **29** (1991): 755–776; Josefina Figueira-McDonough, "Community Structure and Delinquency: A Typology," *Social Service Review,* **65** (1991): 65–91; and Denise C. Gottfredson, Richard J. McNeil, and Gary D. Gottfredson, "Social Area Influence on Delinquency: A Multilevel Analysis," *Journal of Research in Crime and Delinquency,* **28** (1991): 197–226.

55. Steve J. South and Gary D. Deane, "Race and Residential Mobility: Individual Determinants and Structural Constraints," *Social Forces,* **72** (1993): 147–167.

56. See Faith Peeples and Rolf Loeber, "Do Individual Factors and Neighborhood Context Explain Ethnic Differences in Juvenile Delinquency?" *Journal of Quantitative Criminology,* **10** (1994): 141–157; and Thomas A. Petee, Gregory S. Kowlaski, and Don W. Duffield, "Crime, Social Disorganization, and Social Structure: A Research Note on the Use of Interurban Ecological Models," *American Journal of Criminal Justice,* **19** (1994): 117–132.

57. Taylor, "The Impact of Crime on Communities," p. 36.

58. Andrew J. Buck, Simon Hakim, and Ulrich Spiegel, "Casinos, Crime, and Real Estate Values: Do They Relate?" *Journal of Research in Crime and Delinquency,* **28** (1991): 288–303.

59. Robert J. Bursik and Harold G. Grosmick, *Neighborhoods and Crime* (New York: Lexington Books, 1993).

60. Solomon Kobrin, "The Chicago Area Project: 25 Years of Assessment," *Annals of the American Academy of Political and Social Science,* **332** (1959): 20–29.

61. Steven Schlossman, Goul Zellman, and Richard Shavelson, "Delinquency Prevention in South Chicago: A Fifty-Year Assessment of the Chicago Area Project," report prepared for the National Institute of Education by the Rand Corporation, May 1984, p. 1.

62. Walter Miller, "The Impact of a 'Total Community' Delinquency Control Project," *Social Problems,* **10** (1962): 168–191.

63. M. Isolina Ferre, "Prevention and Control of Violence through Community Revitalization, Individual Dignity, and Personal Self-Confidence," *Annals of the American Academy of Political and Social Science,* **494** (1987): 27–36.

64. Edwin H. Sutherland, *Principles of Criminology,* 3d ed. (Philadelphia: Lippincott, 1939).

65. William Chambliss, *Boxmen* (New York: Harper & Row, 1972).

66. James S. Short, "Differential Association as a Hypothesis: Problems of Empirical Testing," *Social Problems,* **8** (1960): 14–15; Mark Warr, "Age, Peers, and Delinquency," *Criminology,* **31** (1993): 17–40. See also Charles R. Tittle, Mary Jean Burke, and Elton F. Jackson, "Modeling Sutherland's Theory of Differential Association: Toward an Empirical Clarification," *Social Forces,* **65** (1986): 405–432; and R. Matsueda and K. Heimer, "Race, Family Structure, and Delinquency: A Test of Differential Association and Social Control Theories," *American Sociological Review,* **52** (1987): 826–840.

67. Reiss and Rhodes, "The Distribution of Juvenile Delinquency."

68. Hirschi, *Causes of Delinquency,* p. 95.

69. Beth Bjerregaard and Carolyn Smith, "Patterns of Male and Female Gang Membership," working paper no. 13, Rochester Youth Development Study (Albany, N.Y.: Hindelang Criminal Justice Research Center, 1992), p. 20. For the relationship of delinquents to their delinquent siblings, see Janet L. Lauritsen, "Sibling Resemblance in Juvenile Delinquency: Findings from the National Youth Survey," *Criminology,* **31** (1993): 387–409.

70. Warr, "Age, Peers, and Delinquency."

71. Charles Tittle, *Sanctions and Social Deviance* (New York: Praeger, 1980).

72. Clayton A. Hartjen, *Crime and Criminalization* (New York: Praeger, 1974), p. 51.

73. Ross L. Matsueda, "The Current State of Differential Association," *Crime and Delinquency,* **34** (1988): 277–306; and Craig Reinarman and Jeffrey Fagan, "Social Organization and Differential Association: A Research Note from a Longitudinal Study of Violent Juvenile Offenders," *Crime and Delinquency,* **34** (1988): 307–327.

74. Susan Chira, "A Program That Works for Teen-Age Mothers," *New York Times,* Apr. 28, 1993, p. A12.

75. Fox Butterfield, "Programs Seek to Stop Trouble Before It Starts," *New York Times,* Dec. 30, 1994, A25.

76. Thorsten Sellin, *Culture Conflict and Crime,* Bulletin 41 (New York: Social Science Research Council, 1938); Avison and Loring, "Population Diversity and Cross-National Homicide"; Mark R. Pogrebin and Eric D. Poole, "Culture Conflict and Crime in the Korean-American Community," *Criminal Justice Policy Review,* **4** (1990): 69–78; and Ira Sommers, Jeffrey Fagan, and Deborah Baskin, "The Influences of Acculturation and Familism on Puerto Rican Delinquency," *Justice Quarterly,* **11** (1994): 207–228.

▣ **Internet Exercise**

Social disorganization theory focuses on effective social bonds, family and neighborhood associations, and social controls in neighborhoods and communities. Is the association between victimization levels and neighborhoods supported by recent survey data?

▣ **Your Web Site is: http://www.ojp.usdoj.gov/bjs/**

CHAPTER 6

The Formation of Subcultures

The Function of Subcultures

Subcultural Theories of Delinquency and Crime

The Middle-Class Measuring Rod

Corner Boy, College Boy, Delinquent Boy

Tests of Cohen's Theory

Evaluation: Cohen's Theory

Delinquency and Opportunity

Tests of Opportunity Theory

Evaluation: Differential Opportunity Theory

The Subculture of Violence

Tests of the Subculture of Violence

Evaluation: The Subculture of Violence Theory

Focal Concerns: Miller's Theory

Tests of Miller's Theory

Evaluation: Miller's Theory

Gangs of the 1990s

Guns and Gangs

Female Delinquent Subcultures

Early Research

Recent Studies

Middle-Class Delinquency

Explanations

Theory Informs Policy

MOBY

Other Programs

Getting Out: Gang Banging or the Morgue

Review

Notes

Special Features

AT ISSUE: The Tagger Subculture

CRIMINOLOGICAL FOCUS: The Girls in the Gang

WINDOW TO THE WORLD: America's Changing Ethnic Gangs

Key Terms

differential
   opportunity theory
reaction formation
subculture
subculture of violence

At an evening party in the spring of 1994, several members of the Vice Lords made plans to rob a convenience store. All they needed was a car. When 17-year-old Michelle Jensen refused to hand over the keys to her Ford Escort, the boys convinced her that she had had too much to drink and promised to drive her home. On a dusty, rural road near a cornfield, one of them shot her with a sawed-off shotgun, tearing away part of her head. They then decided not to rob the convenience store because it was too crowded. Instead they went to eat hamburgers and then drove other gang members out to see the body to show that they had the nerve to kill. When asked by a sheriff's deputy if it bothered him to eat after Michelle's murder, the one who pulled the trigger replied, "No, not really. I was hungry. I wasn't even thinking about it!"[1] Davenport, Iowa, where the event took place, was in shock. The city of under 100,000 residents could not believe that big-city-style gang violence had come to the Heartland.

The number of gangs like the Vice Lords continues to grow. Twenty-three cities nationwide had known street gangs in 1961. In 1995, the National Youth Gang Center surveyed close to 2000 cities, towns, and counties and found 25,000 gangs and 652,000 gang members.[2] Gang violence, too, is on the rise. Reports about juvenile gang activities fill the files of police departments, of juvenile courts, and of adult courts as well. How did these groups get started in American society? What keeps them going?

THE FUNCTION OF SUBCULTURES

Strain theorists explain criminal behavior as a result of the frustrations suffered by lower-class individuals deprived of legitimate means to reach their goals. Cultural deviance theorists assume that individuals become criminal by learning the criminal values of the groups to which they belong. In conforming to their own group standards, these people break the laws of the dominant culture. These two perspectives are the foundation for subcultural theory, which emerged in the mid-1950s.

A **subculture** is a subdivision within the dominant culture that has its own norms, beliefs, and values. Subcultures typically emerge when people in similar circumstances find themselves isolated from the mainstream and band together for mutual support. Subcultures may form among members of racial and ethnic minorities, among prisoners, among occupational groups, among ghetto dwellers. Subcultures exist within a larger society, not apart from it. They therefore share some of its values. Nevertheless, the lifestyles of their members are significantly different from those of individuals in the dominant culture.

SUBCULTURAL THEORIES OF DELINQUENCY AND CRIME

Subcultural theories in criminology had been developed to account for delinquency among lower-class males, especially for one of its most important expressions—the teenage gang. According to subcultural theorists, delinquent subcultures, like all subcultures, emerge in response to special problems that members of the dominant culture do not face. Theories developed by Albert Cohen and by Richard Cloward and Lloyd Ohlin are extensions of the strain, disorganization, and differential association. They explain why delinquent subcultures emerge in the first place (strain), why they take a particular form (social disorganization), and how they are passed on from one generation to the next (differential association).

The explanations of delinquency developed by Marvin Wolfgang and Franco Ferracuti and by Walter Miller are somewhat different from those mentioned above. These theorists do not suggest that delinquency begins with failure to reach middle-class goals. Their explanations are rooted in culture conflict theory. The subculture of violence thesis argues that the value systems of some subcultures demand the use of violence in certain social situations. This norm, which affects daily behavior, conflicts with conventional middle-class norms. Along the same lines, Miller suggests that the characteristics of lower-class delinquency reflect the value system of the lower-class culture and that the lower-class values and norms conflict with those of the dominant culture.

Although Miller contends that the lower-class culture as a whole—not a subculture within it—is responsible for criminal behavior in urban slums, his theory is appropriate to our discussion because it demonstrates how the needs of young urban males are met by membership in a street gang. Miller's street gangs, like those of Cohen and of Cloward and Ohlin, condone violent criminal activity as one of the few means of attaining status in a slum.

The Middle-Class Measuring Rod

Albert Cohen was a student of Robert Merton and of Edwin Sutherland, both of whom had made convincing arguments about the causes of delinquency. Sutherland persuaded Cohen that differential association and the cultural transmission of criminal norms led to criminal behavior. From Merton he learned about structurally induced strain. Cohen combined and expanded these perspectives to explain how the delinquent subculture arises, where it is found within the social structure, and why it has the particular characteristics that it does.[3]

According to Cohen, delinquent subcultures emerge in the slum areas of larger American cities. They are rooted in class differentials in parental aspirations, child-rearing practices, and classroom standards. The relative position of a youngster's family in the social structure determines the problems the child will have to face throughout life.

Lower-class families who have never known a middle-class lifestyle, for example, cannot socialize their children in a way that prepares them to enter the middle class. The children grow up with poor communication skills, lack of commitment to education, and an inability to delay gratification. Schools present a particular problem. There, lower-class children are evaluated by middle-class teachers on the basis of a middle-class measuring rod. The measures are based on such middle-class values as self-reliance, good manners, respect for property, and long-range planning. By such measures, lower-class children fall far short of the standards they must meet if they are to compete successfully with middle-class children. Cohen argues that they experience status frustration and strain, to which they respond by adopting one of three roles: corner boy, college boy, or delinquent boy.

Corner Boy, College Boy, Delinquent Boy

Corner boys try to make the best of a bad situation. The corner boy hangs out in the neighborhood with his peer group, spending the day in some group activity such as gambling or athletic competition. He receives support from his peers and is very loyal to them. Most lower-class boys become corner boys. Eventually they get menial jobs and live a conventional lifestyle.

There are very few *college boys.* These boys continually strive to live up to middle-class standards, but their chances for success are limited because of academic and social handicaps.

Delinquent boys band together to form a subculture in which they can define status in ways that to them seem attainable. Cohen claims that even though these lower-class youths set up their own norms, they have internalized the norms of the dominant class and they feel anxious when they go against these norms. To deal with this conflict, they resort to **reaction formation,** a mechanism that relieves anxiety through the process of rejecting with abnormal intensity what one wants but cannot obtain. These boys turn the middle-class norms upside down, thereby making conduct right in their subculture precisely because it is wrong by the norms of the larger culture (Figure 6.1).

Consequently, their delinquent acts serve no useful purpose. They do not steal things to eat them, wear them, or sell them. In fact, they often discard or destroy what they have stolen. They appear to delight in the discomfort of others and in breaking taboos. Their acts are directed against people and property at random, unlike the goal-oriented activities of many adult criminal groups. The subculture is typically characterized by short-run hedonism, pure pleasure-seeking, with no planning or deliberation about what to do, where, or when. The delinquents hang out on the street corner until someone gets an idea; then they act impulsively, without considering the consequences. The group's autonomy is all-important. Its members are loyal to each other and resist any attempts on the part of family, school, or community to restrain their behavior.

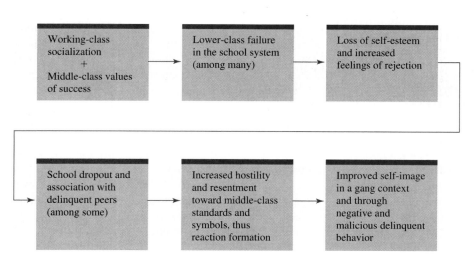

FIGURE 6.1 The process of reaction formation among delinquent boys.
Source: Donald J. Shoemaker, *Theories of Delinquency: An Examination of Explanations of Delinquent Behavior,* 3d ed. (New York: Oxford University Press, 1996), p. 107.

AT ISSUE

THE TAGGER SUBCULTURE

Commuters across the country are becoming increasingly concerned with a new form of adolescent subculture: tagger groups. Bands or "crews" of taggers engage in large-scale graffiti vandalism. Originally, taggers formed small groups that adopted a name, or "tag," and spray-painted it on buildings, fences, bridges, and even moving trains, buses, and cars. Recently tagging has become dangerous and aggressive.

A New Mexico report says that tagger problems are growing. Taggers work openly to challenge law enforcement by demonstrating that they can tag a wall by "outsmarting the cops." In one day in Albuquerque a tagger crew did an estimated $70,000 in damage. Some of the taggers said that society "owes them" and they can get back at society by making the city clean up their graffiti.(1)

Tagging is popular among middle-class suburban youths, and it is estimated that there are 30,000 crews nationwide. In Los Angeles county alone, over 600 roam affluent areas. The names of tagger groups demonstrate their objective: AAA (Against All Authority), TIK (Think I Kare), INF (Insane Family), ACK (Artistic Criminal Kings), CMC (Creating Mass Confusion), KMT (Kings Making Trouble).(2) Taggers typically wear oversized trousers, baseball caps, and hoop earrings. They even have their own vocabulary:

- *All city*—tagging any areas
- *Seek and destroy*—tag anything in sight
- *Kill* or *kill a wall*—completely cover with graffiti
- *To be crossed*—to have a tag erased by a rival tagger group
- *Slash*—cross out another tagger group's name

- *Landmark*—a prime spot where a tag will not be taken off(3)

Taggers "battle" with other taggers to see who can damage more property in a given period of time. Many now carry knives and guns along with their spray paint to use in encounters with rival groups. Tagger gang fights begin because of "dissing" or "tag banging." Tagging over another group's graffiti is considered disrespectful and requires revenge.

Experts suggest that a need for attention and recognition underlies tagging. By placing their mark in public places, taggers become known; they have an identity. Thus, tagger groups, with their specific tag, secret meeting places, designated "turf," and risk-taking activities, provide a sense of belonging and a place to have fun.

Sources
1. *New Mexico Street Gangs, 1974 Update,* New Mexico Department of Public Safety, Criminal Information and Analysis Bureau, Albuquerque, 1994, p. 12.
2. Wayne S. Wooden, *Renegade Kids, Suburban Outlaws: From Youth Culture to Delinquency* (Belmont, Calif.: Wadsworth, 1995), p. 120.
3. Ibid., pp. 118–119.

Questions for Discussion
1. Have illicit taggers learned from licit taggers, who purchase the right to place their logos and advertisements in public places? What lessons might this teach us?
2. Arrested and convicted taggers face small fines or jail sentences. What problems would have to be overcome if they were to be sentenced to remove their graffiti?

A Los Angeles tagger and his art.

Tests of Cohen's Theory

Criminological researchers generally agree that Cohen's theory is responsible for major advances in research on delinquency.[4] Among them are researchers who have found a relationship between delinquency and social status in our society (Chapter 5). Much evidence also supports Cohen's assumption that lower-class children perform more poorly in school than middle-class children.[5] Teachers often expect them to perform less ably than their middle-class students, and this expectation is one of the components of poor performance.

Researchers have demonstrated that poor performance in school is related to delinquency. When Travis Hirschi studied more than 4000 California schoolchildren, he found that youths who were academically incompetent and performed poorly in school came to dislike school. Disliking it, they rejected its authority; rejecting its authority, they committed delinquent acts (Chapter 7).[6] Delbert Elliott and Harwin Voss also investigated the relationship between school and delinquency. They analyzed annual school performance and delinquency records of 2000 students in California from ninth grade to one year after the expected graduation date. Their findings indicated that those who dropped out of school had higher rates of delinquency than those who graduated. They also found that academic achievement and alienation from school were closely related to dropping out of school.[7]

From analysis of the dropout-delinquency relationship among over 5000 persons nationwide, G. Roger Jarjoura concluded that while dropouts were more likely to engage in delinquent acts than graduates, the reason was not always simply the fact that they had dropped out. Dropping out because of a dislike for school, poor grades, or financial reasons was related to future involvement in delinquency; dropping out because of problems at home was not. Dropping out for personal reasons such as marriage or pregnancy was significantly related to subsequent violent offending.[8] All these findings support Cohen's theory. Other findings, however, do not.

In a study of 12,524 students in Davidson County, Tennessee, Albert Reiss and Albert Rhodes found only a slight relationship between delinquency and status deprivation.[9] This conclusion was supported by the research of Marvin Krohn and his associates.[10] Furthermore, several criminologists have challenged Cohen's claim that delinquent behavior is purposeless.[11] They contend that much delinquent behavior is serious and calculated, and often engaged in for profit.[12] Others have also questioned the consistency of the theory: Cohen argues that the behavior of delinquent boys is a deliberate response to middle-class opinion; yet he also argues that the boys do not care about the opinions of middle-class people.[13]

Evaluation: Cohen's Theory

Researchers have praised and criticized Cohen's work. Cohen's theory answers a number of questions left unresolved by the strain and cultural deviance theories. It explains the origin of delinquent behavior and why some youths raised in the same neighborhoods and attending the same schools do not become involved in delinquent subcultures. His concepts of status deprivation and the middle-class measuring rod have been useful to researchers. Yet his theory does not explain why most delinquents eventually become law-abiding even though their position in the class structure remains relatively fixed. Some criminologists also question whether youths are driven by some serious motivating force or whether they are simply out on the streets looking for fun.[14] Moreover, if delinquent subcultures result from the practice of measuring lower-class boys by a middle-class measuring rod, how do we account for the growing number of middle-class gangs?

Other questions concern the difficulty of trying to test the concepts of reaction formation, internalization of middle-class values, and status deprivation, among others. To answer some of his critics, Cohen, with his colleague James Short, expanded the idea of delinquent subcultures to include not only lower-class delinquent behavior but also such variants as middle-class delinquent subcultures and female delinquents.[15] Cohen took Merton's strain theory a step further by elaborating on the development of delinquent behavior. He described how strain actually creates frustration and status deprivation, which in turn foster the development of an alternative set of values that give lower-class boys a chance to achieve recognition. Since the mid-1950s Cohen's theory has stimulated not only research but the formulation of new theories.

DELINQUENCY AND OPPORTUNITY

Like Cohen's theory, the theory of differential opportunity developed by Richard Cloward and Lloyd Ohlin combines strain, differential association, and social disorganization concepts.[16] Both theories begin with the assumption that conventional means to conventional success are not equally distributed among the socioeconomic classes, that lack of means causes frustration for lower-class youths, and that criminal behavior is learned and culturally transmitted. Both theories also agree that the common solution to shared problems leads to the formation of delinquent subcultures. They disagree, however, on the content of these subcultures. As we have noted, norms in Cohen's delinquent subcultures are right precisely because they are wrong in the dominant culture. Delinquent acts are negative and nonutilitarian. Cloward and Ohlin disagree; they suggest that lower-class delinquents remain goal-oriented. The kind of delinquent behavior they engage in depends on the illegitimate opportunities available to them.

According to Cloward and Ohlin's **differential opportunity theory,** delinquent subcultures flourish in lower-class areas and take the particular forms they do because opportunities for illegitimate success are no more equitably distributed than those for conventional success. Just as means—opportunities—are unequally distributed in the conventional world, opportunities to reach one's goals are unequally distributed in the criminal world. A person cannot simply decide to join a theft-oriented gang or, for that matter, a violence-oriented one. Cloward and Ohlin maintain that the types of subcultures and of the juvenile gangs that flourish within them depend on the types of neighborhoods in which they develop (Figure 6.2).

In areas where conventional and illegitimate values and behavior are integrated by a close connection of illegitimate and legitimate businesses, *criminal gangs* emerge. Older criminals serve as role models. They teach youngsters the kinds of people to exploit, the necessary criminal skills, the importance of loyal relationships with criminal associates, and the way to make the right connections with shady lawyers, bail bondsmen, crooked politicians, and corrupt police officers. Adolescent members of criminal gangs, like adult criminals in the neighborhood, are involved in extortion, fraud, theft, and other activities that yield illegal income.

FIGURE 6.2 Factors leading to development of three types of delinquent gangs.
Source: Donald J. Shoemaker, *Theories of Delinquency: An Examination of Explanations of Delinquent Behavior,* 3rd ed. (New York: Oxford University Press, 1996), p. 115.

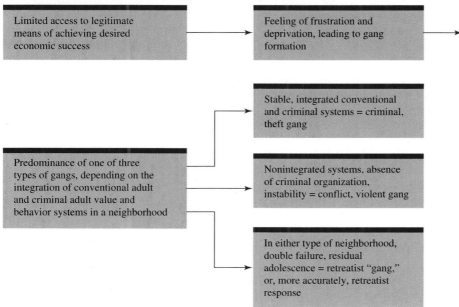

Limited access to legitimate means of achieving desired economic success → Feeling of frustration and deprivation, leading to gang formation →

Predominance of one of three types of gangs, depending on the integration of conventional adult and criminal adult value and behavior systems in a neighborhood →

Stable, integrated conventional and criminal systems = criminal, theft gang

Nonintegrated systems, absence of criminal organization, instability = conflict, violent gang

In either type of neighborhood, double failure, residual adolescence = retreatist "gang," or, more accurately, retreatist response

This type of neighborhood was described by one of its members in a classic work published in 1930:

> Stealing in the neighborhood was a common practice among the children and approved by the parents. Whenever the boys got together they talked about robbing and made more plans for stealing. I hardly knew any boys who did not go robbing. The little fellows went in for petty stealing, breaking into freight cars, and stealing junk. The older guys did big jobs like stick-ups, burglary, and stealing autos. The little fellows admired the "big shots" and longed for the day when they could get into the big racket. Fellows who had "done time" were the big shots and looked up to and gave the little fellows tips on how to get by and pull off big jobs.[17]

Neighborhoods characterized by transience and instability, Cloward and Ohlin argue, offer few opportunities to get ahead in organized criminal activities. This world gives rise to *conflict gangs,* whose goal is to gain a reputation for toughness and destructive violence. Thus "one particular biker would catch a bird and then bite off its head, allowing the blood to trickle from his mouth as he yelled 'all right!'"[18] It is the world of the warrior: Fight, show courage against all odds, defend and maintain the honor of the group. Above all, never show fear.

Violence is the means used to gain status in conflict gangs. Conventional society's recognition of the "worst" gangs becomes a mark of prestige, perpetuating the high standards of their members. Conflict gangs emerge in lower-class areas where neither criminal nor conventional adult role models exercise much control over youngsters.

A third subcultural response to differential opportunities is the formation of *retreatist gangs.* Cloward and Ohlin describe members of retreatist gangs as double failures because they have not been successful in the legitimate world and have been equally unsuccessful in the illegitimate worlds of organized criminal activity and violence-oriented gangs. This subculture is characterized by a continuous search for getting high through alcohol, atypical sexual experiences, marijuana, hard drugs, or a combination of these.

The retreatist hides in a world of sensual adventure, borrowing, begging, or stealing to support his habit, whatever it may be. He may peddle drugs or work as a pimp or look for some other deviant income-producing activity. But the income is not a primary concern; he is interested only in the next high. Belonging to a retreatist gang offers a sense of superiority and well-being that is otherwise beyond the reach of these least successful dropouts.

Not all lower-class youngsters who are unable to reach society's goals become members of criminal, conflict, or retreatist gangs. Many choose to accept their situation and to live within its constraints. These law-abiding youngsters are Cohen's corner boys.

Tests of Opportunity Theory

Cloward and Ohlin's differential opportunity theory presented many new ideas, and a variety of studies emerged to test it empirically.

The first of Cloward and Ohlin's assumptions—that blocked opportunities are related to delinquency—has mixed support. Travis Hirschi, for example, demonstrated that "the greater one's acceptance of conventional (or even quasi-conventional) success goals, the less likely one is to be delinquent, regardless of the likelihood these goals will someday be attained."[19] In other words, the youngsters who stick to hard work and education to get ahead in society are the least likely to become delinquent, no matter what their real chances of reaching their goals. John Hagedorn disagrees. In late 1992 and early 1993, he conducted interviews with 101 founding members of 18 gangs in Milwaukee. His conclusion: "Most of those we were trying to track appeared to be on an economic merry-go-round, with continual movement in and out of the secondary labor market. Although their average income from drug sales far surpassed their income from legal employment, most Milwaukee male gang members apparently kept trying to find licit work."[20] There is also evidence that both gang and nongang boys believe the middle-class values of hard work and scholastic achievement to be important. Gang boys, however, are more ready to approve of a wide range of behaviors, including aggressive acts and drug use.[21]

The second assumption of differential opportunity theory—that the type of lower-class gang depends on the type of neighborhood in which it emerges—has also drawn the attention of criminologists. Empirical evidence suggests that gang behavior is more versatile and involves a wider range of criminal and noncriminal acts than the patterns outlined by Cloward and Ohlin. Ko-lin Chin's research on New York gangs in 1993 demonstrates that Chinese gangs are engaged in extortion, alien smuggling, heroin trafficking, and the running of gambling establishments and houses of prostitution.[22] A recent report from the Denver Youth Survey showed that while the most frequent form of illegal activity is fighting with other gangs, gang members are also involved in robberies, joyriding, assaults, stealing, and drug sales.[23]

Research does, however, support Cloward and Ohlin's argument that "criminal gangs" emerge in areas where conventional and illegitimate behavior are integrated by a close connection with illegitimate and legitimate businesses. Chinatowns in America, for example, are social, economic, political, and cultural units.[24] All types of organizations, including those that dominate illegal activities, play an important role in the maintenance of order in the community. The illegitimate social order has control of territorial rights, gambling places, heroin trafficking, alien smuggling, and loan-sharking. The illegal order defines who is in control of particular restaurants, retail shops, garment factories, and the like. Business owners pay a "membership fee" for protection. Adult criminals maintain control of youth gang members by threatening to exclude them from work that pays well. They also resolve conflicts, provide recreational facilities, loan money, and give the young gang members a chance to climb the illegitimate career ladder within the criminal organization. Gang activities are closely supervised by their leaders, who work with the adult crime groups. Elaborate initiation rites are conducted by an adult the youngsters call "uncle"—the link between the gang and the adult sponsoring organization.

Gang members (1015) from California, Illinois, Iowa, Michigan, and Ohio also reported having a variety of legal and illegal income sources, collective gang "treasuries," and mostly adult leaders.[25] Their businesses include dance clubs, billiard halls, and stereo, liquor, jewelry, grocery, cellular phone/beeper, and auto repair shops. They also sell illegal goods: $268 for a 9-mm Glock semiautomatic pistol, $42 for a box of cartridges, $882 for 1 ounce of cocaine, and $155 for a stolen 12-gauge shotgun.[26] These gangs operate somewhat like a union for the underground economy. Members attend meetings, pay dues, follow rules, have their own language, and make collective expenditures (for guns, funerals, attorneys).

Evaluation: Differential Opportunity Theory

For three decades criminologists have reviewed, examined, and revised the work of Cloward and Ohlin.[27] One of the main criticisms is that their theory is class-oriented. If, as Cloward and Ohlin claim, delinquency is a response to blocked opportunities, how can we explain middle-class delinquency? Another question arises from contradictory statements. How can delinquent groups be nonutilitarian, negativistic, and malicious (Cohen)—and also goal-oriented and utilitarian? Despite its shortcomings,

however, differential opportunity theory has identified some of the reasons why lower-class youngsters may become alienated. Cloward and Ohlin's work has also challenged researchers to study the nature of the subcultures in our society. Marvin Wolfgang and Franco Ferracuti have concentrated on one of them—the subculture of violence.

THE SUBCULTURE OF VIOLENCE

Like Cohen, and like Cloward and Ohlin, Marvin Wolfgang and Franco Ferracuti turned to subcultural theory to explain criminal behavior among lower-class young urban males. All three theories developed by these five researchers assume the existence of subcultures made up of people who share a value system that differs from that of the dominant culture. And they assume that each subculture has its own rules or conduct norms that dictate how individuals should act under varying circumstances. The three theories also agree that these values and norms persist over time because they are learned by successive generations. The theories differ, however, in their focus.

Cohen and Cloward and Ohlin focus on the origin of the subculture, specifically culturally induced strain. The major thrust of Wolfgang and Ferracuti's work is on culture conflict. Furthermore, the earlier theories encompass all types of delinquency and crime; Wolfgang and Ferracuti concentrate on violent crime. They argue that in some subcultures behavior norms are dictated by a value system that demands the use of force or violence.[28] Subcultures that adhere to conduct norms conducive to violence are referred to as **subcultures of violence.**

Violence is not used in all situations, but it is frequently an expected response. The appearance of a weapon, a slight shove or push, a derogatory remark, or the opportunity to wield power undetected may very well evoke an aggressive reaction that seems uncalled for to middle-class people. Fists rather than words settle disputes. Knives or guns are readily available, so confrontations can quickly escalate. Violence is a pervasive part of everyday life. Child-rearing practices (hitting), gang activities (street wars), domestic quarrels (battering), and social events (drunken brawls) are all permeated by violence.

Violence is not considered antisocial. Members of this subculture feel no guilt about their aggression. In fact, individuals who do not resort to violence may be reprimanded. The value system is transmitted from generation to generation, long after the original reason for the violence has disappeared. The pattern is very hard to eradicate.

When Wolfgang and Ferracuti described population groups that are likely to respond violently to stress, they posed a powerful question to the criminal justice system. How does one go about changing a subcultural norm? This question becomes increasingly significant with the merging of the drug subculture and the subculture of violence.

Tests of the Subculture of Violence

Howard Erlanger, using nationwide data collected for the President's Commission on the Causes and Prevention of Violence, found no major differences in attitudes toward violence by class or race. Erlanger concluded that though members of the lower class show no greater approval of violence than middle-class persons do, they lack the sophistication necessary to settle grievances by other means.[29] The subculture of violence thesis has also generated a line of empirical research that looks at regional differences in levels of violent crime.

The South (as you will see in Chapter 11) has the highest homicide rate in the country. Some researchers have attributed this high rate to subcultural values.[30] They argue that the southern subculture of violence has its historical roots in an exaggerated defense of honor by southern gentlemen, mob violence (especially lynching), a military tradition, the acceptance of personal vengeance, and the widespread availability and use of handguns.[31]

The problem with many of these studies is that it is difficult to separate the effects of economic and social factors from those of cultural values. Several researchers have sought to solve this problem. Colin Loftin and Robert Hill, for example, using a sophisticated measure of poverty, found that economic factors, not cultural ones, explained regional variation in homicide rates.[32] Similarly, others suggest that high homicide rates and gun ownership may have a great deal to do with socioeconomic conditions, especially racial inequality in the South.[33] (See Figure 6.3.)

Researchers who support the subculture of violence thesis point to statistics on characteristics of homicide offenders and victims: Lower class, inner-city black males are disproportionately represented in the FBI's Uniform Crime Reports. In addition:

THE PRICE OF POVERTY TODAY

Low-income assistance, including food and housing, excluding medical care	Billions $120
Cost of police and corrections*	$50
Additional gain to GNP if poor were fully employed	$60
Total	$230

*Assumes most crime is linked to poverty.

The Growing Disadvantage of the Poor

(a)

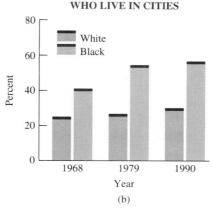

PERCENTAGE OF POOR WHO LIVE IN CITIES

(b)

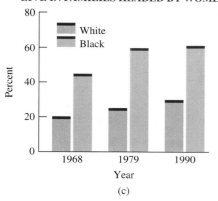

PERCENTAGE OF POOR WHO LIVE IN FAMILIES HEADED BY WOMEN

(c)

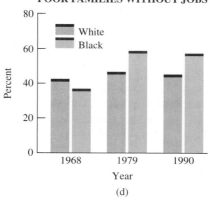

PERCENTAGE OF HEADS OF POOR FAMILIES WITHOUT JOBS

(d)

FIGURE 6.3 The social costs of poverty and crime: Being poor often means living in a decaying urban center in a single-parent family whose head does not have a job. *Source: Business Week,* May 18, 1992, pp. 40–41.

- The majority of the offenders are young, most in their twenties but many in their late teens.
- Typically the offender and the victim know each other.
- The offender and the victim are usually in the same age group and of the same race.[34]

Furthermore, in a study of 556 males interviewed at age 26, 19 percent of the respondents, all inner-city males, reported having been shot or stabbed. These victimizations were found to be highly correlated with both self-reported offenses and official arrest statistics. In fact, the best single predictor of committing a violent act was found to be whether or not the individual had been a victim of a violent crime. Though most people in the dominant society who are shot or stabbed do not commit a criminal act in response, it appears that many inner-city males alternate the roles of victim and offender in a way that maintains the values and attitudes of a violent subculture.[35]

Evaluation: The Subculture of Violence Theory

Though empirical evidence remains inconclusive, the subculture of violence theory is supported by the distribution of violent crime in American society.[36] The number of gangs and the violence associated with their activities are growing.[37] Jeffrey Fagan noted that "drug use is widespread and normative" among gangs.[38] Gang warfare, which takes the lives of innocent bystanders in ghetto areas, is a part of life in most of the impoverished, densely populated neighborhoods in such major cities as Los Angeles, New York, Chicago, Miami, Washington, D.C., and Atlanta and in smaller disintegrating urban centers as well.

For example, over the 3 years between 1985 and 1988, Jamaican "posses"—gangs transplanted from Kingston, Jamaica, to the United States—have been involved in 1400 homicides.[39]

Though not all persons in these subcultures follow the norm of violence, it appears that a dismaying number of them attach less and less importance to the value of human life and turn increasingly to violence to resolve immediate problems and frustrations. (We return to this issue later in the chapter.)

FOCAL CONCERNS: MILLER'S THEORY

All the theorists we have examined thus far explain criminal and delinquent behavior in terms of subcultural values that emerge and are perpetuated from one generation to the next in lower-class urban slums. Walter Miller reasons differently. According to Miller:

> In the case of "gang" delinquency, the cultural system which exerts the most direct influence on behavior is that of the lower-class community itself—a long-established, distinctively patterned tradition with an integrity of its own—rather than a so-called "delinquent subculture" which has arisen through conflict with middle-class culture and is oriented to the deliberate violation of middle-class norms.[40]

To Miller, juvenile delinquency is not rooted in the rejection of middle-class values; it stems from lower-class culture, which has its own value system. This value system has evolved as a response to living in slums. Gang norms are simply the adolescent expression of the lower-class culture in which the boys have grown up. This lower-class culture exists apart from the middle-class culture, and it has done so for generations. The value system, not the gang norms, generates delinquent acts.

Miller has identified six focal concerns, or areas, to which lower-class males give persistent attention: trouble, toughness, smartness, excitement, luck, and autonomy. Concern over *trouble* is a major feature of lower-class life. Staying out of trouble and getting into trouble are daily preoccupations. Trouble can get a person into the hands of the authorities, or it can result in prestige among peers. Lower-class individuals are often evaluated by the extent of their involvement in activities such as fighting, drinking, and sexual misbehavior. In this case, the greater the involvement or the

more extreme the performance, the greater the prestige or "respect" the person commands.

These young men are almost obsessively concerned with *toughness;* the code requires a show of masculinity, a denial of sentimentality, and a display of physical strength. Miller argues that this concern with toughness is related to the fact that a large proportion of lower-class males grow up in female-dominated households and have no male figure from whom to learn the male role. They join street gangs in order to find males with whom they can identify.

Claude Brown's classic 1965 autobiography, *Manchild in the Promised Land,* illustrates the concerns about trouble and toughness among adolescents growing up in an urban slum:

> My friends were all daring like me, tough like me, dirty like me, ragged like me, cursed like me, and had a great love for trouble like me. We took pride in being able to hitch rides on trolleys, buses, taxicabs and in knowing how to steal and fight. We knew that we were the only kids in the neighborhood who usually had more than ten dollars in their pockets. . . . Somebody was always trying to shake us down or rob us. This was usually done by the older hustlers in the neighborhood or by storekeepers or cops. . . . We accepted this as a way of life.[41]

Another focal concern is *smartness*—the ability to gain something by outsmarting, outwitting, or conning another person. In lower-class neighborhoods youngsters practice outsmarting each other in card games, exchanges of insults, and other trials. Prestige is awarded to those who demonstrate smartness.

Many aspects of lower-class life are related to another focal concern, the search for *excitement.* Youngsters alternate between hanging out with peers and looking for excitement, which can be found in fighting, getting drunk, and using drugs. Risks, danger, and thrills break up the monotony of their existence.

Fate, particularly *luck,* plays an important role in lower-class life. Many individuals believe that their lives are subject to forces over which they have little control. If they get lucky, a rather drab life could change quickly. Common discussions center on whether lucky numbers come up, cards are right, or dice are good. Brown recalls:

> After a while [Mama] settled down, and we stopped talking about her feelings, then somebody came upstairs and told her she had hit the numbers. We just

forgot all about her feelings. I forgot about her feelings. Mama forgot about her feelings. Everybody did. She started concentrating on the number. This was the first time she'd had a hit in a long time. They bought some liquor. Mama and Dad started drinking: everyone started making a lot of noise and playing records.[42]

Miller's last focal concern, *autonomy*, stems from the lower-class person's resentment of external controls, whether parents, teachers, or police. This desire for personal freedom is expressed often in such terms as "No one can push me around" and "I don't need nobody."[43]

According to Miller, status in every class is associated with the possession of qualities that are valued. In the lower class the six focal concerns define status. It is apparent that by engaging in behavior that affords status by these criteria, many people will be breaking the laws of the dominant society (Figure 6.4).

Tests of Miller's Theory

An obvious question is whether in our urban, heterogeneous, secular, technologically based society any isolated pockets of culture are still to be found. The pervasiveness of mass advertising, mass transit, and mass communication makes it seem unlikely that an entire class of people could be unaware of the dominant value system. Empirical research on opportunity theory has found that lower-class boys share the conventional success goals of the dominant culture. This finding suggests that the idea of isolation from the dominant system does not fit with reality. Empirical research has also found, however, that while gang boys may support middle-class values, they are willing to deviate from them. If an opportunity arises to gain prestige in a fight, gang boys are willing to take the chance that their act will not result in punishment.

Most empirical tests of values question young people on their attachment to middle-class values.

Stephen Cernovich expanded this type of research by investigating attachment to lower-class focal concerns.[44] He found that toughness, excitement, trouble, and pleasure-seeking were related to self-reported delinquency in all classes. His findings also showed that boys of all classes were committed to delayed gratification, hard work, and education. Cernovich concluded that it is values, rather than class, that are associated with delinquency.

Evaluation: Miller's Theory

Criminologists have been disturbed by Miller's assumption that the lower-class lifestyle is generally focused on illegal activity. In making such an assumption, they say, Miller disregards the fact that most people in the lower class do conform to conventional norms. Moreover, some criminologists ask, if lower-class boys are conforming to their own value system, why would they suffer guilt or shame when they commit delinquent acts?[45]

Perhaps the best support for Miller's ideas is found in qualitative, rather than quantitative, accounts of life in a lower-class slum. In our discussion of cultural deviance and subcultural theories we noted that the values and norms that define behavior in these areas do not change much over time or from place to place. Successive generations have to deal with the same problems. They typically share similar responses. Angela D'Arpa-Calandra, a former probation officer who now directs a Juvenile Intensive Supervision program, says she recently walked into a New York courtroom and "saw a mother and grandmother sitting with the 14-year-old offender. 'I had the grandmother in criminal court in 1963,' D'Arpa-Calandra says. 'We didn't stop it there. The grandmother was 14 when she was arrested. The mother had this child when she was 14. It's like a cycle we must relive.'"[46]

FIGURE 6.4 The relationship between delinquency and lower-class focal concerns.
Source: Donald J. Shoemaker, *Theories of Delinquency: An Examination of Explanations of Delinquent Behavior,* 3d ed. (New York: Oxford University Press, 1996), p. 122.

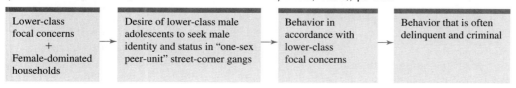

| Lower-class focal concerns + Female-dominated households | → | Desire of lower-class male adolescents to seek male identity and status in "one-sex peer-unit" street-corner gangs | → | Behavior in accordance with lower-class focal concerns | → | Behavior that is often delinquent and criminal |

Violence and police raids are part of everyday life in many inner-city housing projects.

By and large, descriptions of life in poverty-stricken areas, whether written by people who have lived in them or by people who have studied them, reveal dreary routine, boredom, constant trouble, and incessant problems with drugs, alcohol, and crime. As the father tells his son in Eugene O'Neill's autobiographical play *Long Day's Journey into Night*, "There was no damned romance in our poverty."[47] There still isn't. In 1993, the *New York Times* ran a series of profiles of youth in poverty:

> Derrick White rides through the crumbling asphalt roads of the Hurt Village housing project where he played tag among the steel clotheslines and shot baskets through bent and wobbly hoops. He passes the trash bins where men with black plastic bags mine for cans to sell to a recycling center. He passes the "dope track," where he saw a friend shot in the neck and killed.
>
> Beyond the project he passes the supermarket that refused him a job interview because, he believes, his address marks him as a project kid.[48]

GANGS OF THE 1990s

In Los Angeles:

> Right before the Uprising happened in '92, it was one week before Easter. I was at a hamburger stand on Fifty-fifth and Figuera. . . . A little girl walked up to

me, she was about five years old, and she handed me a flyer. On the flyer it said, "Let's have a no-killing weekend for Easter. From twelve o'clock midnight Friday to twelve o'clock midnight Saturday, let's have a no-killing weekend."[49] [Q-Bone, a Crip member from South Central L.A.]

In Atlanta:

> A young gang member was charged with murdering two infants after he threw a Molotov cocktail into the apartment of their 18-year-old mother, who was quarreling with another woman who was a friend of the gang.[50]

In St. Paul:

> Five children were killed by a firebomb intended to intimidate their older brother who had seen a gang murder.[51]

In Chicago:

> On Tuesday afternoon, a 10-year-old boy riding his bike in front of his home was caught in a gang crossfire and killed. A few days before, a 3-year-old boy sitting in his mother's lap in the family car was partly blinded when a bullet from a gang firefight struck him in the head.[52]

The new subculture that emerged in the 1980s and continues in the 1990s combines violence, which has become more vicious than in earlier years, with big business in drug trafficking (Figure 6.5).[53] It is estimated that one gang alone, the Eight Trey Gang-

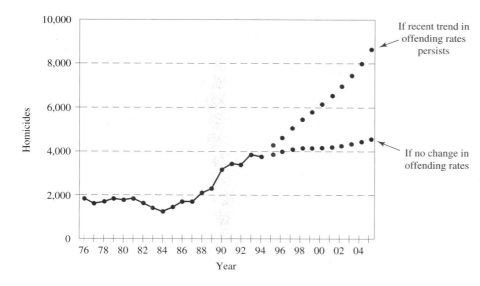

FIGURE 6.5 Forecast of homicide offenders, ages 14–17.
Source: FBI, Supplementary Homicide Reports, and Census Bureau, Current Population Survey, and Population Projections of US.

ster Crips, distributed hundreds of kilos of crack and cocaine worth over $10 million on the streets of Los Angeles and five other cities, as far east as Birmingham, Alabama, and Atlanta. The FBI reports that this network is only one of perhaps a hundred more operating across the country.[54] Rival gangs kill for more than simply turf. In cities around the world teenagers are driving BMWs with Uzi submachine guns concealed under the driver's seat and thousands of dollars in their pockets so that they can make bail at any moment. Movies like *Colors, American Me,* and *Boyz in the Hood* provide models for their activities.

Guns and Gangs

It is estimated that between 50 and 70 percent of gang members own or have access to weapons. In fact, gangs often judge each other by their firepower. Their arsenal of weapons includes sawed-off rifles and shotguns, semiautomatic weapons like the Uzi and the AK-47, all types of handguns, body armor, and explosives.[55] Gangs have "treasuries" to buy the sophisticated weapons that are now used on the street for resolving conflicts, for demonstrating bravery, for self-defense, and for protecting turf. (See Figure 6.6.)

The National Center for Juvenile Justice reports that[56]:

* From 1985 through 1992 nearly 17,000 persons under 18 were murdered in the United States (Table 6.1).
* More than half of juvenile homicide victims are killed with firearms.

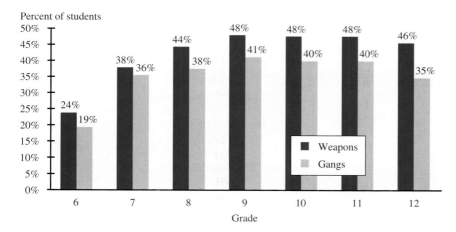

FIGURE 6.6 Almost half of high school students reported weapons in their schools in 1993, and about 40 percent reported gangs.
Data Source: National Center for Education Statistics. (1994). School safety and discipline component. *National household education survey of 1993* [machine-readable data file.] In *Juvenile Offenders and Victims: 1996 Update on Violence,* Office of Juvenile Justice and Delinquency Prevention, February 1996, p. 7 [National survey of sixth through twelfth grade].

TABLE 6.1   Juvenile Homicides, 1985–1992

Year	Number of Homicides
1985	1605
1986	1753
1987	1738
1988	1955
1989	2184
1990	2339
1991	2610
1992	2595

Source: Juvenile Offenders and Victims: A Focus on Violence, Office of Juvenile Justice and Delinquency Prevention, Department of Justice, May 1995, p. 18.

- The firearm homicide death rate for teens ages 15 to 19 increased 61 percent between 1979 and 1989, from 6.9 to 11.1 deaths per 100,000. Nonfirearm homicides decreased.
- The juvenile arrest rate for weapons violations increased 75 percent between 1987 and 1992.

Use of guns rather than knives and clubs turns violent events into life-and-death situations; gangs battle gangs in a kind of street guerrilla warfare. Drive-by shootings, in particular, have become a favored method of operation (see Table 6.2). A "drive-by" involves members of one gang driving into a rival gang's turf to shoot at someone, followed by a high-speed escape. Gang members take great pride in this hit-and-run technique. Often these encounters occur spontaneously, but they easily spiral into planned events. The sequence may be the following:

> A gang member shoots a rival gang member during an argument. The surviving rival or his friends get a gun and conduct a drive-by on the initial instigator or members of his gang at their home(s). During this retaliatory strike, a friend, family member or gang member is killed or seriously wounded. The original instigatory gang now views itself as the "passive victim" and sets

out to get back at the new aggressor. This spiral which, in real time, can result in several drive-by shootings or other murders within a few hours, can and often does lead to protracted gang wars.[57]

Some drive-bys are for "fun," some for defending gang honor, and others to get rid of competition in the drug business.

FEMALE DELINQUENT SUBCULTURES

Traditionally, gang membership has been primarily limited to young, inner-city males. Theoretical and empirical studies in this area therefore focused on that population. Little was known about female subcultures until recently.

Early Research

In one of the few early studies, done in 1958, Albert Cohen and James Short suggested that female delinquent subcultures, like their male counterparts, were composed of members who had been frustrated in their efforts to achieve conventional goals (respectability, marriage, status). The girls had drifted into a subculture that offered them substitute status, albeit outside legitimate society. Drug use and prostitution became all but inevitable. Since the research that led to this finding was conducted among mostly lower-class black females, Cohen and Short admitted that their findings probably could not be generalized to all female delinquent subcultures.[58]

Recent Studies

Twenty-six years after these tentative findings, Anne Campbell published the first major work on the lifestyle of female gang members in New York. She

TABLE 6.2   Violent Gang Confrontations in Los Angeles County, 1989–1991

	1989	1990	1991
Gang vs. gang confrontations	1,040	1,752	3,698
Drive-by shootings	N/A*	N/A*	2,371
Incidents with moderate to serious injuries	818	1,426	5,155
Total violent felonies	15,953	17,673	19,598

*Not collected prior to 1991
Source: LASD, Safe Streets Bureau, Gang Activity Reports—Cumulative Countywide Totals
In John P. Sullivan and Martin E. Silverstein, "The Disaster within Us: Urban Conflict and Street Gang Violence in Los Angeles," *A Journal of Gang Research,* **2** (Summer 1995): 11–30, p. 21.

CRIMINOLOGICAL FOCUS

THE GIRLS IN THE GANG

Psychologist Anne Campbell studied female gangs in New York City and published her findings in her 1984 book, *The Girls in the Gang*. She summarizes some of her observations here:

All the girls in the gang come from families that are poor. Many have never known their fathers. Most are immigrants from Puerto Rico. As children the girls moved from apartment to apartment as they were evicted or burned out by arsonists. Unable to keep any friends they managed to make and alienated from their mothers, whose lack of English restricted their ability to control or understand their daughters' lives, the girls dropped out of school early and grew up on the streets. In the company of older kids and street-corner men, they graduated early into the adult world. They began to use drugs and by puberty had been initiated into sexual activity. By fifteen many were pregnant. Shocked, their mothers tried to pull them off the streets. Some sent their daughters back to relatives in Puerto Rico while they had their babies. Abortion was out of the question in this Catholic world.

Those who stayed had "spoiled their identity" as good girls. Their reputations were marred before they ever reached adulthood. On the streets, among the gang members, the girls found a convenient identity in the female gang. Often they had friends or distant relatives who introduced them as "prospects." After a trial period, they could undertake the initiation rite: they had to fight an established member nominated by the godmother. What was at issue was not winning or losing but demonstrating "heart," or courage. Gangs do not welcome members who join only to gain protection. The loyalty of other gang members has to be won by a clear demonstration of willingness to "get down," or fight.

Paradoxically, the female gang goes to considerable lengths to control the sexual behavior of its members. Although the neighborhood may believe they are fast women, the girls themselves do not tolerate members who sleep around. A promiscuous girl is a threat to the other members' relationships with their boyfriends. Members can take a boyfriend from among the male gang members (indeed, they are forbidden to take one from any other gang) but they are required to be monogamous. A shout of "Whore!" is the most frequent cause of fistfights among the female members.

On the positive side, the gang provides a strong sense of belonging and sisterhood. After the terrible isolation of their lives, the girls acquire a ready-made circle of friends who have shared many of their experiences and who are always willing to support them against hostile words or deeds by outsiders. Fighting together generates a strong sense of camaraderie and as a bonus earns them the reputation of being "crazy." This reputation is extremely useful in the tough neighborhoods where they live. Their reputation for carrying knives and for solidarity effectively deters outsiders from challenging them. They work hard at fostering their tough "rep" not only in their deeds but in their social talk. They spend hours recounting and embroidering stories of fights they have been in. Behind all this bravado it is easy to sense the fear they work so hard to deny. Terrified of being victims (as many of them have already been in their families and as newcomers in their schools), they make much of their own "craziness"—the violent unpredictability that frightens away anyone who might try to harm them.(1)

Source
1. Written by Anne Campbell. Adapted from Anne Campbell, *The Girls in the Gang* (New York: Basil Blackwell, 1984).

Questions for Discussion
1. How similar are Campbell's female gangs to the male gangs described in this chapter? Are there any significant differences?
2. Would you expect female gangs to become as involved in criminal activity as male gangs? Why or why not?

California's All-Girl Asian-American Gangs, 1993. All-girl gangs exist in major cities throughout the United States. California's all-girl gangs in 1993 included these Asian-American groups:

Sisters 4 Life
Sacramento Bad Girls
Pretty in Yellow
Best Side Posse
Lady Rascal Gangsters
National Color Girls
Koreatown Crazy Chicas
West Coast Ladies
Southside Scissors

spent 2 years with three gangs: one Hispanic (the Sex Girls), one black (the Five Percent Nation), and one racially mixed (the Sandman Ladies). Campbell's findings demonstrate that girls, like boys, join gangs for mutual support, protection, and a sense of belonging. They, too, gain status by living up to the value system of their gang. Campbell also noted that these youngsters will probably end up, as their mothers have, living on welfare assistance in a ghetto apartment. Men will come and go in their lives, but after their gang days the women feel they have lost their support group and are constantly threatened by feelings of isolation."[59]

Between 10 and 25 percent of gang members nationwide are female. In major cities the number is higher. Among 214 wards of the state of California in 1990, 32 percent were gang members, ages 14–21.[60] Among them they had 289 arrests. All but 3 of the women had been arrested for a violent crime—22 murders, 31 armed robberies, and 31 assaults with a deadly weapon.

Many of the female gangs are affiliates of male gangs, often offering support for the young men they refer to as their "homeboys." Initiation rites for females involve either a "jump-in, jump-out" in which they are beaten by four or five gang members or a "sex-in, sex-out" in which they have sexual relations with all male members.[61] Some female affiliate gangs, however, have their own initiation rites (which mimic male ceremonies but are usually much less violent) and their own gang colors. A strong allegiance exists among each gang's members. For many of these youngsters the gang takes the place of a family. Shorty, a member of Los Angeles's Tiny Diablas, had no family except a grandmother, who had given up on trying to control her. Shorty's mother, who had been a gang member, abandoned her at an early age. Her father overdosed on heroin and was identified by a tattoo of Shorty's name. Her aunt had a teardrop tattoo next to her eye, to signify 1 year in jail; her uncle had two teardrops. Such family ties are not unusual among gang members.[62]

Not all female gangs have male affiliates. In a study of crack sales and violence among gangs in San Francisco, researchers interviewed members of an all-female group, the Potrero Hill Posse (PHP).[63] This independent group was formed in the mid-1980s when the females realized that their gang-affiliated boyfriends were not distributing the profits and labor of their crack sales fairly. The PHP young women run "rock houses" (outlets for crack sales, lent by tenants who receive a small quantity of crack in return), procure other women to provide sex to male customers, and engage in a major shoplifting business that fills orders placed by people who do not want to pay retail prices.

Gang members rely on the gang for assistance ("Nobody will mess with me . . . because they know that I got back-up. I got back-up. I got my homegirls behind me. And whatever goes down with me, they are going to have to take up with them") and for status ("It [membership] means being bad, being tough, and being able to walk without . . . you know, everybody just respects me because they know I am one of the Potrero Hill Posse girls").[64]

Overall, according to 1992 gang research done as part of the Rochester Youth Development Study, the extent and nature of female participation has changed considerably over the last few decades. The findings show increased participation in gangs (in this study, about equal to that of males) and in gang-related activities, including serious delinquent acts and drug abuse.[65]

MIDDLE-CLASS DELINQUENCY

In Tucson, Arizona, a white middle-class teenager wearing gang colors died, a victim of a drive-by shooting as he stood with black and Hispanic members of the Bloods gang.

At Antelope Valley High School in Lancaster, California, about 50 miles north of Los Angeles, 200 students threw stones at a policeman who had been called to help enforce a ban on the gang outfits that have become a fad on some campuses. . . .

A member of the South Bay Family gang in Hermosa Beach, a 21-year-old surfer called Road Dog, who said his family owned a chain of pharmacies, put it this way: "This is the 90's, man. We're the type of people who don't take no for an answer. If your mom says no to a kid in the 90's, the kid's just going to laugh." He and his friends shouted in appreciation as another gang member lifted his long hair to reveal a tattoo on a bare shoulder: "Mama tried."[66]

Most people think of gangs as synonymous with inner-city slums, low-income housing projects, "turf wars," and a membership that often comes into conflict with law enforcement. But now gang lifestyle is moving to suburbia.[67] Affluent youngsters are joining established gangs such as the Crips and the Bloods or

WINDOW TO THE WORLD

AMERICA'S CHANGING ETHNIC GANGS

Irish, Italian, and Puerto Rican inner-city gangs have been replaced or augmented by gangs reflecting the new waves of immigrants to America, who seek the protection and group loyalty that gang membership traditionally was thought to have provided.

Most Mexican gang members, for example, are migrants from rural areas where gangs do not exist. At home they had family support. That support all but vanishes when they find themselves in the ghetto neighborhoods of American cities. Other Latin American and Caribbean cultures are also represented in the American gang structure. Jamaican gangs, specializing in the drug and weapons trade, are known for their violence. Asian gangs, among them Vietnamese, Korean, Cambodian, Laotian, and Chinese, have sprung up on both coasts and in the middle of the country. Other groups hail from the Pacific Islands. The Tongan Crips gangsters and Sons of Samoa, demonstrating their macho values, have spread fear in once quiet, pastoral Utah. The Vietnamese have established a reputation as "house-breakers"; they burglarize the homes of other, wealthier Vietnamese immigrants.

Chinese gangs have been the greatest surprise for American law enforcement. Traditionally, Chinese-Americans were considered particularly law-abiding. This picture changed drastically with the easing of immigration restrictions that allowed larger numbers of younger Chinese from the mainland, as well as Taiwan and Hong Kong, into the country. These new arrivals have formed gangs.

Chinese gangs, although small in number (an estimated 2000 members nationwide), engage in the smuggling of illegal Chinese immigrants by the tens of thousands annually. Often these immigrants are enslaved until the transportation fee has been paid off. They also engage in major heroin trafficking and "protection" of the gambling clubs popular in Chinese communities. Their main business is extortion. Their strength, and tradition of ferocious violence, derives from their affiliation with Chinese secret societies known as Triads.

The end of the cold war and the collapse of the Soviet Union have opened new windows of opportunity for Russian entrepreneurs—legal and illegal. A thriving Russian colony in Brighton Beach, New York, is the seat of Russian gangs as ruthless as those of any other ethnic origin. They smuggle gold and Russian army surplus—often passing it off as high-grade Japanese products. They deal in bootlegged gasoline. They use extortion and murder to strengthen their operations. Some of the gang leaders are experienced criminals with long histories of economic offenses in Russia. Russians call them "thieves-in-law."

Gangs made up of immigrant Albanians and former Yugoslavians have been committing burglaries along the East Coast since the early 1990s. Their targets are retail shops, banks, and automated teller machines. They specialize in supermarket safes because these stores generally have a great deal of cash on hand. Their techniques are highly sophisticated, not the run-of-the-mill break and enter. The burglars rarely carry guns; every detail is carefully planned (oxygen tanks may be brought for their safe-cracking torches); and they are equipped with an arsenal of tools, gloves, and walkie-talkies. Often they cut phone lines to set off alarms, wait until the police come and go, and then strike.

Some gangs have ties to their mother countries; others are independent. Some are national; others are strictly local. Some have memberships of young adults; others, of teenagers. Some are involved in the sale and use of drugs and arms; others are geared primarily toward survival in tough neighborhoods. Indeed, if ethnic gangs have any common characteristic beyond a membership of a single ethnic group, it is probably the diversity of patterns of formation and operation. That diversity is likely to continue as the country's ever-changing immigrant populations result in the emergence of new gangs.

Questions for Discussion
1. Dealing with gangs may require infiltrating them. What if there are no young police officers from the gangs' ethnic groups? What else can be done?
2. Are there ways of dealing with ethnic gangs outside the criminal justice system? What of the role of elders, who are highly respected in many ethnic cultures?

forming their own gangs, sometimes referred to as yuppie gangs.[68] Their activities can be as harmless as adhering to a particular dress code or as violent as a drive-by shooting. Experts have identified several types of suburban gangs.[69]

Delinquent Gangs. Delinquent gangs are similar to most inner-city gangs. Criminal activities include physical assaults, theft, burglary, and distribution of illegal drugs. The members seek money, peer recognition, the thrill of high-risk behavior, or even protection: "If you want to be able to walk the mall, you have to know you've got your boys behind you."[70] They typically adopt hand signals used by inner-city gangs.

Hate Gangs. These gangs, such as skinheads, attach themselves to an ideology that targets racial and ethnic groups. Physical assaults and even murder are justified by their belief system. Their numbers are growing rapidly. In 1988 there were 1000 to 1500 skinheads operating in 12 states. By June 1993, the number was close to 3500, spread across 40 states.[71] According to the FBI, 2232 hate crimes were committed by neo-Nazis, skinheads, and other right-wing extremist groups in 1993. Due to the difficulties in gathering hate crime statistics, this number is considered only a small percentage of the actual figure.[72]

Satanic Gangs. These groups are affiliated with the controversial satanic cults. Their practices include the worship of specific gods, desecration of graveyards, use of a Ouija board to predict the future, ritualistic drug consumption, animal sacrifice, various witchcraft and pagan rituals, and submission to sexual abuse or pain. The common element for these gangs is heavy-metal music. One heavy-metal group KISS stands for Kids (or Knights) in Satan's Service.[73] Members can be identified by their dress: metal-spiked wrist cuffs, belts, anti-Christian items, and T-shirts labeled with heavy-metal band names such as Iron Maidens, Venom, Judas Priest, and Dio.[74]

Explanations

Most explanations of middle-class delinquency are extensions of subcultural explanations of lower-class delinquency. Albert Cohen, for example, suggested that changes in the social structure have weakened the value traditionally associated with delay of gratification.[75] Some criminologists say that a growing number of middle-class youngsters no longer believe that the way to reach their goals is through hard work and delayed pleasure. They prefer profits from a quick drug sale or shoplifting goods that attract them. Behavior has become more hedonistic and more peer-oriented. While most of this youth subculture exhibits nondelinquent behavior, sometimes the pleasure-seeking activities have led to delinquent acts. Bored and restless, these youngsters seek to break the monotony with artificial excitement and conspicuous

indulgence: fast cars, trendy clothes, alcohol, drugs, and sexual activity. Experts note that many affluent gang members come from broken, unstable, or extremely dysfunctional homes. Their problems stem from divorce, separation, physical or sexual abuse, or a drug- or alcohol-addicted parent.[76]

THEORY INFORMS POLICY

Subcultural theory assumes that individuals engage in delinquent or criminal behavior because (1) legitimate opportunities for success are blocked and (2) criminal values and norms are learned in lower-class slums. The theory was translated into action programs during the 1960s. Two presidents, John F. Kennedy and Lyndon Johnson, directed that huge sums of money be spent on programs to help move lower-class youths into the social mainstream.

MOBY

The best-known program, Mobilization for Youth (MOBY), was based on opportunity theory.[77] It provided employment, social services, teacher training, legal aid, and other crime-prevention services to an area on New York's Lower East Side. The cost was over $12 million. MOBY ultimately became highly controversial. Many people accused it of being too radical, especially when neighborhood participants became involved in rent strikes, lawsuits charging discrimination, and public demonstrations. News of the conflict between supporters and opponents, and between the staff and the neighborhood it served, reached Congress, which made it clear that the point of the project was to reduce delinquency, not to reform society.

Little was done to evaluate the program's success. The project was eventually abandoned, and the commission that had established it ceased to exist. The political climate had changed, and federal money was no longer available for sweeping social programs. However, MOBY's failure does not disprove the opportunity theory on which it was based.

Other Programs

Many other programs based on subcultural theory have attempted to change the attitudes and behavior of ghetto youngsters who have spent most of their lives learning unconventional street norms. Change is accomplished by setting up an extended-family environment for high-risk youths, one that provides positive role models, academic and vocational training, strict rules for behavior, drug treatment, health care, and other services. For many youths these programs provide the first warm, caring living arrangement they have ever had. One such program is the House of Umoja (a Swahili word for "unity") in Philadelphia.

At any given time about 25 black male teenage offenders live together as "sons" of the founder, Sister Fattah. Each resident signs a contract with Umoja obligating himself to help in the household, become an active part of the family group, study, and work in one of the program's businesses (a restaurant, a moving company, a painting shop) or elsewhere. By many measures this program is successful. In 1972 a newly elected mayor threatened, "All gang members have ten days to turn their guns in to the nearest firehouse, after which time we [the police] will kick your door in and take them."[78] Umoja responded by calling a meeting of representatives of all gangs. More than 5000 youths from 75 gangs showed up. The result was a 60-day truce, and during those 60 days no one died in gang warfare.

Programs similar to Umoja exist throughout the country; they include Argus in New York's South Bronx; Violent Juvenile Offender Research and Development programs in Chicago, Dallas, New Orleans, Los Angeles, and San Diego; and Neighborhood Anticrime Self-Help programs in Baltimore, Newark, Cleveland, Boston, Miami, and Washington, D.C. All have the same mission: to provide a bridge from a delinquent subcultural value system to a conventional one.[79]

Other means have been used to break up delinquent subcultures. Street workers, many of them former gang members (called OGs, for "original gangsters"), serve as a "street-smart diplomatic corps" in many of the poorest ghettos in the country.[80] In Los Angeles, where gang members control many streets, the OGs work for the Community Youth Gang Service (a government-funded agency). Five nights a week more than 50 of these street workers cover the city, trying to settle disputes between rival gangs and to discourage nonmembers from joining them. They look for alternatives to violence, in baseball matches, fairs, and written peace treaties. During a typical evening the street workers may try to head off a gang fight:

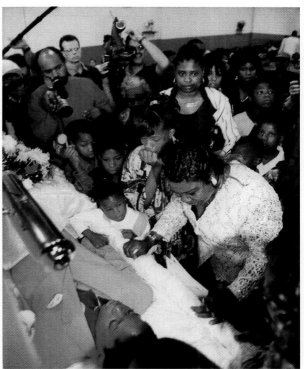

Grandmother says goodbye to her 11-year-old grandson, a suspect in the shooting death of a 14-year-old girl, who was himself then killed execution-style: Chicago, September 1994.

Parton [street worker]: Hey, you guys, Lennox is going to be rollin' by here. . . .

Ms. Diaz [street worker]: You with your back to the street, homeboy. They goin' to be lookin' for this car, some burgundy car.

Boy: If they want to find me, they know where I'm at.

Ms. Diaz: I'm tellin' you to be afraid of them. There are some girls here. You better tell them to move down the street. . . . We are goin' back over there to try to keep them there. Don't get lazy or drunk and not know what you're doin'. I know you don't think it's serious, but if one of your friends gets killed tonight, you will.

Boy: It's serious, I know.

Ms. Diaz: We're goin' to keep them in their 'hood, you just stay in yours for a while.

Boy: All right.[81]

After 2 hours of negotiation, the fight was called off. There was plenty of work left for the team. They would continue the next day to help the gang members find jobs.

Getting Out: Gang Banging or the Morgue

The most difficult problem that counselors and street workers face is the power of gangs over their members. Gangs, through loyalty and terror, make it almost impossible for members to quit. Many gang members would gladly get out, but any move to leave leads to gang banging or the morgue. A Wichita, Kansas, group, the church-sponsored Project Freedom, has created an "underground railroad," a network of local contacts that leads families with gang members to anonymity and freedom out of state.[82]

Gangs, once a local problem, have become a national concern. The federal antigang budget goes primarily to police and prosecution. In 1992 the Department of Justice spent $500 million on law enforcement, while the Department of Health and Human Services spent $40 million on prevention programs over a 3-year period.[83] Experts agree that unless we put more money into educational and socioeconomic programs, there is little likelihood that America's gang problems will lessen as we enter the twenty-first century.

REVIEW

In the decade between the mid-1950s and mid-1960s, criminologists began to theorize about the development and content of youth subcultures and the gangs that flourish within them. Some suggested that lower-class males, frustrated by their inability to meet middle-class standards, set up their own norms by which they could gain status. Often these norms clashed with those of the dominant culture. Other investigators have refuted the idea that delinquent behavior stems from a rejection of middle-class values. They claim that lower-class values are separate and distinct from middle-class values and that it is the lower-class value system that generates delinquent behavior.

Gangs of the 1990s show increasing violence and reliance on guns. They are involved in large profit-making activities such as drug distribution. The number of homicides is rising.

Explanations of female delinquent subcultures and middle-class delinquency are an extension of subcultural explanations of lower-class delinquency. While the theories of reaction formation, the subculture of violence, and differential opportunity differ in some respects, they all share one basic assumption—that delinquent and criminal behaviors are linked to the values and norms of the areas where youngsters grow up.

NOTES

1. Don Terry, "Killed by Her Friends, Sons of the Heartland," *New York Times,* May 18, 1994, p. B22 (first part A1).
2. Malcolm W. Klein, "Preliminary Report Delivered to the National Youth Gang Symposium, Dallas, TX, June 20, 1996," *The American Street Gang: Its Nature, Prevalence and Control* (New York: Oxford University Press, 1995), pp. 38–39. For how gangs spread, see John A. Laskey, "Gang Migration: The Familial Gang Transplant Phenomenon," *Journal of Gang Research,* **3** (1996): 1–15; and Cheryl L. Maxon, "Investigating Gang Migration: Contextual Issues for Intervention," *Gang Journal,* **1** (1993): 1–8.
3. Albert K. Cohen, *Delinquent Boys: The Culture of the Gang* (Glencoe, Ill.: Free Press, 1955).
4. E.g., James F. Short, Jr., and Fred L. Strodtbeck, *Group Process and Gang Delinquency* (Chicago: University of Chicago Press, 1965).
5. Kenneth Polk and Walter B. Schafer, eds., *School and Delinquency* (Englewood Cliffs, N.J.: Prentice-Hall, 1972); Alexander Liazos, "School, Alienation, and Delinquency," *Crime and Delinquency,* **24** (1978): 355–370.
6. Travis Hirschi, *Causes of Delinquency* (Berkeley: University of California Press, 1969).
7. Delbert S. Elliott and Harwin L. Voss, *Delinquency and Dropout* (Lexington, Mass.: Lexington Books, 1974).
8. G. Roger Jarjoura, "Dropping Out of School Enhances Delinquent Involvement? Results from a Large-Scale National Probability Sample," *Criminology,* **31** (1993): 149–172.
9. Albert J. Reiss and Albert L. Rhodes, "Deprivation and Delinquent Behavior," *Sociological Quarterly,* **4** (1963): 135–149.
10. Marvin Krohn, R. L. Akers, M. J. Radosevich, and L. Lanza-Kaduce, "Social Status and Deviance," *Criminology,* **18** (1980): 303–318.
11. Mark Warr, "Organization and Instigation in Delinquent Groups," *Criminology,* **34** (1996): 11–37.
12. David F. Greenberg, "Delinquency and the Age Structure of Society," *Contemporary Crisis,* **1** (1977): 189–223.
13. John I. Kitsuse and David C. Dietrick, "Delinquent Boys: A Critique," *American Sociological Review,* **24** (1959): 208–215.
14. David J. Bordua, "Delinquent Subcultures: Sociological Interpretations of Gang Delinquency," *Annals of the American Academy of Political and Social Science,* **338** (1961): 119–136.
15. Albert K. Cohen and James F. Short, Jr., "Research in Delinquent Subcultures," *Journal of Social Issues,* **14** (1958): 20–37.
16. Richard A. Cloward and Lloyd E. Ohlin, *Delinquency and Opportunity* (Glencoe, Ill.: Free Press, 1960).
17. Clifford R. Shaw, *The Jack-Roller* (Chicago: University of Chicago Press, 1930), p. 54.
18. James R. David, *Street Gangs* (Dubuque, Iowa: Kendall/Hunt, 1982).
19. Hirschi, *Causes of Delinquency,* p. 227.
20. John M. Hagedorn, "Homeboys, Dope Fiends, Legits, and New Jacks," *Criminology,* **32** (1994): 197–219.

21. James Short, Ramon Rivera, and Ray Tennyson, "Perceived Opportunities, Gang Membership, and Delinquency," *American Sociological Review*, **30** (1965): 56–57.

22. Lecture by Ko-lin Chin, Rutgers University, Nov. 22, 1993. See also K. Chin, *Chinese Subculture and Criminality: Nontraditional Crime Groups in America*, Criminology and Penology Series, vol. 29 (Westport, Conn.: Greenwood, 1990); Mark Warr, "Organization and Instigation in Delinquent Groups," *Criminology*, **34** (1996): 11–37; Kevin M. Thompson, David Brownfield, and Ann Marie Sorenson, "Specialization Patterns of Gang and Nongang Offending: A Latent Structure Analysis," *Journal of Gang Research*, **3** (1996): 25–35.

23. Finn-Aage Esbensen and David Huizinga, "Gangs, Drugs, and Delinquency in a Survey of Urban Youth," *Criminology*, **31** (1993): 565–587; Terence P. Thornberry, Marvin D. Krohn, Alan J. Lizotte, and Deborah Chard-Wierschem, "The Role of Juvenile Gangs in Facilitating Delinquent Behavior," *Journal of Research in Crime and Delinquency*, **30** (1993): 55–87; Malcolm Klein, Cheryl L. Maxson, and Lea C. Cunningham, "'Crack,' Street Gangs, and Violence," *Criminology*, **29** (1991): 623–650.

24. K. Chin and J. Fagan, "Social Order and Gang Formation in Chinatown," in *Advances in Criminological Theory*, vol. 6, ed. Freda Adler and William S. Laufer (New Brunswick, N.J.: Transaction, 1994).

25. George W. Knop, Edward D. Tromanhauser, James G. Houston, et al., *The Economics of Gang Life: A Task Force Report of the National Gang Crime Research Center* (Chicago: National Crime Research Center, 1995).

26. Ibid., p. ii.

27. John P. Hoffman and Timothy Ireland, "Cloward and Ohlin's Strain Theory Reexamined: An Elaborated Theoretical Model," in Adler and Laufer, *Advances in Criminological Theory*, vol. 6.

28. Marvin E. Wolfgang and Franco Ferracuti, *The Subculture of Violence* (London: Tavistock, 1967).

29. Howard S. Erlanger, "The Empirical Status of the Subcultures of Violence Thesis," *Social Problems*, **22** (1974): 280–292. See also Sandra Ball-Rokeach, "Values and Violence: A Test of the Subculture of Violence Thesis," *American Sociological Review*, **38** (1973): 736–749. For the relationship of the thesis to routine activities, see Leslie W. Kennedy and Stephen W. Baron, "Routine Activities and a Subculture of Violence: A Study on the Street," *Journal of Research in Crime and Delinquency*, **30** (1993): 88–112.

30. William G. Doerner, "A Regional Analysis of Homicide Rates in the United States," *Criminology*, **13** (1975): 90–101.

31. Jo Dixon and Alan J. Lizotte, "Gun Ownership and the Southern Subculture of Violence," *American Journal of Sociology*, **93** (1987): 383–405.

32. Colin Loftin and Robert Hill, "Regional Subculture of Violence: An Examination of the Gastril-Hackney Thesis," *American Sociological Review*, **39** (1974): 714–724.

33. Judith Blau and Peter Blau, "Metropolitan Structure and Violent Crime," *American Sociological Review*, **47** (1982): 114–129. For a study that examines the subculture of violence thesis as it relates to three groups—blacks, Hispanics, and American Indians—see Donald J. Shoemaker and J. Sherwood Williams, "The Subculture of Violence and Ethnicity," *Journal of Criminal Justice*, **15** (1987): 461–472.

34. Wolfgang and Ferracuti, *The Subculture of Violence*, pp. 258–265. See also Marvin E. Wolfgang, *Patterns in Criminal Homicide* (Philadelphia: University of Pennsylvania Press, 1958); and Franco Ferracuti, "La personalità dell' omicida," *Quaderni di Criminologia Clinica*, **4** (1961): 419–456.

35. Marvin E. Wolfgang, Robert M. Figlio, and Thorsten Sellin, *Delinquency in a Birth Cohort* (Chicago: University of Chicago Press, 1972); Simon I. Singer, "Victims of Serious Violence and Their Criminal Behavior: Subcultural Theory and Beyond," *Violence and Victims*, **1** (1986): 61–70. See also Neil Alan Weiner and Marvin E. Wolfgang, "The Extent and Character of Violent Crime in America, 1969–1982," in *American Violence and Public Policy*, ed. Lynn Curtis (New Haven, Conn.: Yale University Press, 1985), pp. 17–39.

36. Steven Messner, "Regional and Racial Effects on the Urban Homicide Rate: The Subculture of Violence Revisited," *American Journal of Sociology*, **88** (1983): 997–1007.

37. Scott H. Decker, "Collective and Normative Features of Gang Violence," *Justice Quarterly*, **13** (1996): 243–264.

38. Jeffrey Fagan, "The Social Organization of Drug Use and Drug Dealing among Urban Gangs," *Criminology*, **27** (1989): 633–666.

39. Joseph B. Treaster, "Jamaica's Gangs Take Root in U.S.," *New York Times*, Nov. 13, 1988, p. 15.

40. Walter B. Miller, "Lower-Class Culture as a Generating Milieu of Gang Delinquency," *Journal of Social Issues*, **14** (1958): 5–19.

41. Claude Brown, *Manchild in the Promised Land: A Modern Classic of the Black Experience* (New York: New American Library, 1965), p. 22.

42. Ibid., p. 129.

43. Miller, "Lower-Class Culture."

44. Stephen A. Cernovich, "Value Orientations and Delinquency Involvement," *Criminology*, **15** (1978): 443–458.

45. Gresham Sykes and David Matza, "Techniques of Neutralization: A Theory of Delinquency," *American Sociological Review*, **22** (1957): 664–673.

46. Barbara Kantrowitz, "Wild in the Streets," *Newsweek*, Aug. 2, 1993, p. 46.

47. Eugene O'Neill, *Long Day's Journey into Night*, in *Great Scenes from the World Theater*, ed. James L. Steffenson, Jr. (New York: Avon, 1965), p. 199.

48. Peter T. Kilborn, "Finding a Way: The Quest of Derrick, 19," *New York Times*, Apr. 22, 1993, p. 1.

49. Yusef Jah and Sister Shah' Keyah, *Uprising: Crips and Bloods Tell the Story of American Youth in the Crossfire* (New York: Scribner, 1995).

50. Fox Butterfield, "Police Find Pattern of Arson by Gangs," *New York Times*, Oct. 29, 1994, p. 7.

51. Ibid.

52. Don Terry, "A Fight for Peace on Chicago's Streets," *New York Times*, Apr. 4, 1994, A8.

53. Jeffrey Fagan, "The Political Economy of Drug Dealing among Urban Gangs," in *Drugs and the Community*, ed. Robert Davis, Arthur Lurigio, and Dennis Rosenbaum (Springfield, Ill.: Charles C Thomas, 1993), pp. 19–54.

54. John Bonfante, "Entrepreneurs of Crack," *Time*, Feb. 27, 1995, p. 22.

55. Beth Bjerregaard and Alan J. Lizotte, "Gun Ownership and Gang Membership," *The Journal of Criminal Law and Crimi-*

nology, **86** (1995): 37–58; Alan J. Lizotte, James M. Tesoriero, Terence P. Thornberry, and Marvin D. Krohn, "Patterns of Adolescent Firearms Ownership and Use," *Justice Quarterly,* **11** (1994): 51–74.

56. Howard N. Snyder and Melissa Sickmund, *Juvenile Offenders and Victims: A Focus on Violence,* Office of Juvenile Justice and Delinquency Prevention, U.S. Department of Justice, May 1995, pp. 18, 20, 21. See also Alfred Blumstein, "Youth Violence, Guns, and the Illicit-Drug Industry," *The Journal of Criminal Law and Criminology,* **86** (1995): 10–36.

57. John P. Sullivan and Martin E. Silverstein, "The Disaster within Us: Urban Conflict and Street Gang Violence in Los Angeles," *Journal of Gang Research,* **2** (1995): 11–30 (p. 28).

58. Cohen and Short, "Research in Delinquent Subcultures."

59. Anne Campbell, *The Girls in the Gang* (New York: Basil Blackwell, 1984), p. 267.

60. Jill Leslie Rosenbaum, "A Violent Few: Gang Girls in the California Youth Authority," *Journal of Gang Research,* **3** (1996): 17–23.

61. *New Mexico Street Gangs, 1994: Update* (Albuquerque: New Mexico Department of Public Safety, 1994).

62. Seth Mydans, "Life in Girls' Gang: Colors and Bloody Noses," *New York Times,* Jan. 29, 1990, pp. 1, 20.

63. David Lauderback, Joy Hansen, and Dan Waldorf, "'Sisters Are Doin' It for Themselves': A Black Female Gang in San Francisco," *Gang Journal,* **1** (1992): 57–72.

64. Ibid., p. 67.

65. Beth Bjerregaard and Carolyn Smith, *Rochester Youth Development Study: Patterns of Male and Female Gang Membership,* working paper no. 13 (Albany, N.Y.: Hindelang Criminal Justice Research Center, 1992).

66. Seth Mydans, "Not Just the Inner City: Well-to-Do Join Gangs," *New York Times,* Apr. 10, 1990, p. A10.

67. C. Ronald Huff, ed., *Gangs in America* (Newbury Park, Calif.: Sage, 1990).

68. Mydans, "Not Just the Inner City."

69. Dan Korem, *Suburban Gangs: Affluent Rebels* (Richardson, Tex.: International Focus, 1994).

70. As quoted in Mydans, "Not Just the Inner City."

71. Korem, *Suburban Gangs.*

72. Mark S. Hamon, *American Skinheads* (Westport, Conn.: Praeger, 1993), p. 12.

73. Wayne S. Wooden, *Renegade Kids, Suburban Outlaws: From Youth Culture to Delinquency* (Belmont, Calif.: Wadsworth, 1995), p. 190.

74. "L.A. Style: A Street Gang Manual of the Los Angeles County Sheriff's Department," in *The Modern Gang Reader,* ed. Malcolm W. Klein, Cheryl L. Maxson, and Jody Miller (Los Angeles: Roxbury, 1995).

75. Albert K. Cohen, "Middle-Class Delinquency and the Social Structure," in *Middle-Class Delinquency,* ed. E. W. Vaz (New York: Harper & Row, 1967), pp. 207–221.

76. Korem, *Suburban Gangs,* p. 50.

77. J. Robert Lilly, Francis T. Cullen, and Richard A. Ball, *Criminological Theory: Context and Consequences* (Newbury Park, Calif.: Sage, 1989), pp. 78–80.

78. Quoted in David Fattah, "The House of Umoja as a Case Study for Social Change," *Annals of the American Academy of Political and Social Science,* **494** (1987): 37–41.

79. Lynn A. Curtis, Preface to "Policies to Prevent Crime: Neighborhood, Family, and Employment Strategies," *Annals of the American Academy of Political and Social Science,* **494** (1987).

80. Robert Reinhold, "In the Middle of L.A.'s Gang Warfare," *New York Times Magazine,* May 22, 1988, p. 31.

81. Ibid., p. 70.

82. Jon D. Hull, "No Way Out," *Time,* Aug. 17, 1992, p. 40.

83. *Time,* June 15, 1992, p. 37.

▓ **Internet Exercise**

You have learned in this chapter that there has been a dramatic increase in the number of gangs across the country. Do partnerships between gang members, community agencies, and schools reduce gang violence?

▓ **Your Web Site is:**
   http://www.harbour.com/crimprev/youth/

CHAPTER 7
Social
Control Theory

What Is Social Control?

Theories of Social Control

      The Microsociological Perspective: Hirschi

      Social Bonds

      Empirical Tests of Hirschi's Theory

      Evaluation: Hirschi's Social Control Theory

Social Control and Drift

Personal and Social Control

      Failure of Control Mechanisms

      Stake in Conformity

Containment Theory

      Empirical Tests of Containment Theory

      Evaluation: Containment Theory

Integrated Theories

      Developmental Theories

      Multiple Control Factors

      General Theories

Theory Informs Policy

      Family

      School

      Neighborhood

Review

Notes

      Special Features

        AT ISSUE: Respect for Authority: Carjacking

        CRIMINOLOGICAL FOCUS: Out of Control: School Violence

        WINDOW TO THE WORLD: Nations with Low Crime Rates

Key Terms

attachment
belief
commitment
conformity
containment theory
direct control
drift
indirect control
internalized control
involvement
macrosociological
   studies
microsociological
   studies
social control theory
synnomie

In William Golding's novel *Lord of the Flies,* a group of boys are stranded on an island far from civilization. Deprived of any superior authority—all the grown-ups, their parents, their teachers, the government, that have until now determined their lives—they begin to decide on a structure of government for themselves. Ralph declares:

> "We can't have everybody talking at once. We'll have to have 'Hands up' like at school. . . . Then I'll give him the conch."
>
> "Conch?"
>
> "That's what this shell is called. I'll give the conch to the next person to speak. He can hold it when he's speaking!" . . .
>
> Jack was on his feet.

"We'll have rules!" he cried excitedly. "Lots of rules!"[1]

But do rules alone guarantee the peaceful existence of the group? Who and what ensure compliance with the rules? Social control theorists study these questions.

Strain theories, as we noted, study the question of why some people violate norms, for example, by committing crimes. Social control theorists are interested in learning why people conform to norms. Control theorists take it for granted that drugs can tempt even the youngest schoolchildren; that truancy can lure otherwise good children onto a path of academic failure and lifetime unemployment; that petty fighting, petty theft, and recreational drinking are attractive features of adolescence and young adulthood.

A scene from a film version of *Lord of the Flies:* Young boys cast away on an uninhabited island soon invent their own social rules and social controls.

They ask why people conform in the face of so much temptation and peer pressure. The answer is that juveniles and adults conform to the law in response to certain controlling forces in their lives. They become criminals when the controlling forces are weak or absent.

WHAT IS SOCIAL CONTROL?

What are those controlling forces? Think about the time and energy you have invested in your school, your job, your extracurricular activities. Think about how your academic or vocational ambition would be jeopardized by persistent delinquency. Think about how the responsibility of homework has weighed you down, setting limits on your free time. Reflect on the quality of your relationships with your family, friends, and acquaintances and on how your attachment to them has encouraged you to do right and discouraged you from doing wrong.

Social control theory focuses on techniques and strategies that regulate human behavior and lead to conformity, or obedience to society's rules—the influences of family and school, religious beliefs, moral values, friends, and even beliefs about government. The more involved and committed a person is to conventional activities and values and the greater the attachment to parents, loved ones, and

friends, the less likely that person is to violate society's rules and to jeopardize relationships and aspirations.

The concept of social control emerged around the turn of the century in a volume by E. A. Ross, one of the founders of American sociology. According to Ross, belief systems, rather than specific laws, guide what people do and universally serve to control behavior. Since that time, the concept has taken on a wide variety of meanings. Social control has been conceptualized as representing practically any phenomenon that leads to conformity. The term is found in studies of laws, customs, mores, ideologies, and folkways describing a host of controlling forces.[2]

Is there danger in defining social control so broadly? It depends on your perspective. To some sociologists, the vagueness of the term—its tendency to encompass almost the entire field of sociology—has significantly decreased its value as a concept.[3] To others, the value of social control lies in its representation of a mechanism by which society regulates its members. According to this view, social control defines what is considered deviant behavior, what is right or wrong, and what is a violation of the law.

Theorists who have adopted this orientation consider laws, norms, customs, mores, ethics, and etiquette to be forms of social control. Donald Black, a sociologist of law, noted: "Social control is found whenever people hold each other to standards, explicitly or implicitly, consciously or not: on the street, in prison, at home, at a party."[4]

If an example would help, consider that as recently as 20 years ago there were no legal restrictions, norms, or customs regulating the smoking of cigarettes in public places. The surgeon general's declaration in 1972 that secondhand smoke poses a health hazard ushered in two decades of controls over behavior that not too long ago was considered sociable—if not sophisticated and suave.

At present most states have laws restricting or banning smoking in public places. Los Angeles recently became the thirty-second city in California to outlaw smoking in all its restaurants.[5] Laws, norms, customs, and etiquette relating to smoking exert strong controls over this behavior.

THEORIES OF SOCIAL CONTROL

Why is social control conceptualized in such different ways? Perhaps because social control has been examined from both a macrosociological and a microsociological perspective. **Macrosociological studies** explore formal systems for the control of groups:

- The legal system, laws, and particularly law enforcement
- Powerful groups in society
- Social and economic directives of governmental or private groups

These types of control can be either positive—that is, they inhibit rule-breaking behavior by a type of social guidance—or negative—that is, they foster oppressive, restrictive, or corrupt practices by those in power.[6]

The microsociological perspective is similar to the macrosociological approach in that it, too, explains why people conform. **Microsociological studies,** however, focus on informal systems. Researchers collect data from individuals (usually by self-report methods), are often guided by hypotheses that apply to individuals as well as groups, and frequently make reference to or examine a person's internal control system.

The Microsociological Perspective: Hirschi

Travis Hirschi has been the spokesperson of the microsociological perspective since the publication of

his *Causes of Delinquency* in 1969. He is not, however, the first scholar to examine the extent of individual social control and its relationship to delinquency. In 1957 Jackson Toby introduced the notion of individual "commitment" as a powerful determining force in the social control of behavior.[7] Eight years later Scott Briar and Irving Piliavin extended Toby's thesis by advancing the view that the extent of individual commitment and conformity plays a role in decreasing the likelihood of deviance. They noted that the degree of an adolescent's commitment is reflected in relationships with adult authority figures and with friends and is determined in part by "belief in God, affection for conventionally behaving peers, occupational aspirations, ties to parents, desire to perform well at school, and fear of material deprivations and punishments associated with arrest."[8]

Briar and Piliavin were not entirely satisfied with control dimensions alone, however, and added another factor: individual motivation to be delinquent. This motivation may stem from a person's wish to "obtain valued goods, to portray courage in the presence of, or to belong to, peers, to strike out at someone who is disliked, or simply to get his kicks."[9]

Hirschi was less interested in the source of an individual's motivation to commit delinquent acts than in the reasons why people do not commit such acts. He claimed that social control theory explains conformity and adherence to rules, not deviance. It is thus not a crime-causation theory in a strict sense but a theory of prosocial behavior used by criminologists to explain deviance.

Social Bonds

Hirschi posited four social bonds that promote socialization and conformity: attachment, commitment, involvement, and belief. The stronger these bonds, he claimed, the less likelihood of delinquency.[10] To test this hypothesis, he administered a self-report questionnaire to 4077 junior and senior high school students in California (see Table 7.1) that measured both involvement in delinquency and the strength of the four social bonds. Hirschi found that weakness in any of the bonds was associated with delinquent behavior.

Attachment. The first bond, **attachment,** takes three forms: attachment to parents, to school (teachers), and to peers. According to Hirschi, youths who have formed a significant attachment to a parent

TABLE 7.1   Items from Travis Hirschi's Measure of Social Control

1. In general, do you like or dislike school?
   A. Like it
   B. Like it and dislike it about equally
   C. Dislike it
2. How important is getting good grades to you personally?
   A. Very important
   B. Somewhat important
   C. Fairly important
   D. Completely unimportant
3. Do you care what teachers think of you?
   A. I care a lot
   B. I care some
   C. I don't care much
4. Would you like to be the kind of person your father is?
   A. In every way
   B. In most ways
   C. In some ways
   D. In just a few ways
   E. Not at all
5. Did your mother read to you when you were little?
   A. No
   B. Once or twice
   C. Several times
   D. Many times, but not regularly
   E. Many times, and regularly
   F. I don't remember
6. Do you ever feel that "there's nothing to do"?
   A. Often
   B. Sometimes
   C. Rarely
   D. Never

Source: Travis Hirschi, *Causes of Delinquency* (Berkeley: University of California Press, 1969).

refrain from delinquency because the consequences of such an act might jeopardize that relationship. The bond of affection between a parent and a child thus becomes a primary deterrent to criminal activities.[11] Its strength depends on the depth and quality of parent-child interaction. The parent-child bond forms a path through which conventional ideals and expectations can pass. This bond is bolstered by:

- The amount of time the child spends with parents, particularly the presence of a parent at times when the child is tempted to engage in criminal activity
- The intimacy of communication between parent and child
- The affectional identification between parent and child[12]

Next Hirschi considered the importance of the school. As we saw in Chapter 6, Hirschi linked inability to function well in school to delinquency through the following chain of events: academic incompetence leads to poor school performance; poor school performance results in a dislike of school; dislike of school leads to rejection of teachers and administrators as authorities. The result is delinquency. Thus attachment to school depends on a youngster's appreciation for the institution, perception of how he or she is received by teachers and peers, and level of achievement in class.

Hirschi found that attachment to parents and school overshadows the bond formed with peers:

> As was true for parents and teachers, those most closely attached to or respectful of their friends are least likely to have committed delinquent acts. The relation does not appear to be as strong as was the case for parents and teachers, but the ideas that delinquents are unusually dependent upon their peers, that loyalty and solidarity are characteristic of delinquent groups, that attachment to adolescent peers fosters nonconventional behavior, and that the delinquent is unusually likely to sacrifice his personal advantage to the "requirements of the group" are simply not supported by the data.[13]

Commitment.   Hirschi's second group of bonds consists of **commitment** to or investment in conventional lines of action—that is, support of and participation in social activities that tie the individual to the society's moral or ethical code. Hirschi identified a number of stakes in conformity or commitments: vocational aspirations, educational expectations, educational aspirations.

Many programs and institutions currently strive to nurture and encourage such aspirations. One such institution is the Pioneer Academy of Electronics, established soon after the 1992 riots in South-Central Los Angeles. Founded on "academic rigor, real work opportunities, decision-making responsibilities, a teacher who serves as a mentor, and a peer group that reinforces positive behavior," the Pioneer Academy gives inner-city high school students an opportunity to immerse themselves in something other than everyday gang activity. The academy's commitment to providing one-on-one interaction and training has changed the aspirations and work ethic of its students. Gilbert Ybarra, a prospective graduate, attests to its positive impact. Before enrollment in the academy, Gilbert opted for play over work, an attitude that was reflected in his high school grades and attendance. Soon thereafter, he was a proud and confident leader among his peers, excelling in his vocational pursuits, and aspiring to be the first in his family to attend college.[14]

Though Hirschi's theory is at odds with the competing theories of Albert Cohen and Richard Cloward and Lloyd Ohlin (Chapter 6), Hirschi provided empirical support for the notion that the greater the aspiration and expectation, the more unlikely delinquency becomes. Also, "students who smoke, those who drink, and those who date are more likely to commit delinquent acts; . . . the more the boy is involved in adult activities, the greater his involvement in delinquency."[15]

Involvement. Hirschi's third bond is **involvement,** or preoccupation with activities that promote the interests of society. This bond is derived from involvement in school-related activities (such as homework) rather than in working-class adult activities (such as smoking and drinking). A person who is busy doing conventional things has little time for deviant activities.

With this premise in mind, several regional schools will soon be following the example set by Parrot Middle School in Southwest Florida. Parrot Middle School currently offers its students an invaluable service. As part of an after-school program that provides counseling and tutoring services, students have been given the opportunity to participate in a diverse range of recreational courses, including martial arts, gymnastics, home economics, computer basics, and art. The program is designed to provide constructive pastimes for youths formerly left unsupervised during the interim between the end of the school day and that of the typical workday.[16]

Belief. "This type of prejudice insults me as an individual, but I am helpless because I can't vote. Then again, it's not as if any of the new legislation is affecting me, right? Why should I have any say in my own life? After all, I'm just a teen."

Jeff Lofvers's sentiments reflect much of Florida's teenage population. As of July 1, 1996, the state of Florida enacted a curfew restricting late-night driving for all licensed drivers under the age of 18. Between the hours of 11 P.M. and 6 A.M., 16-year-olds cannot

Commitment and Conformity: The U.S. Women's Gymnastic Team wins a gold in the team competition at the 1996 Olympics in Atlanta, Georgia.

legally drive, unless accompanied by a licensed driver at least 21 years old. The same applies to 17-year-olds between 1 A.M. and 6 A.M. "It amazes me that my friends and I can walk around town as late as we want, yet we're not allowed to be safely locked in our cars past 11 P.M.," protested one angry teen. And another's defiant response when asked to comment on the anticipated effectiveness of this law? "[I]f they (legislators) are trying to trap us in our homes, it won't work."[17]

The last of the bonds, **belief,** consists of assent to the society's value system. The value system of any society entails respect for its laws and for the people and institutions that enforce them. The results of Hirschi's survey lead to the conclusion that if young people no longer believe laws are fair, their bond to society weakens, and the probability that they will commit delinquent acts increases.[18]

Empirical Tests of Hirschi's Theory

Hirschi's work has inspired a vast number of studies. We can examine only a small selection of some of the more significant research.

Michael Hindelang studied rural boys and girls in grades 6 through 12 on the East Coast. His self-report delinquency measure and questionnaire items were very similar to those devised by Hirschi. Hindelang found few differences between his results and those of Hirschi. Two of those differences, however, were significant. First, he found no relationship between attachment to mother and attachment to peers. Hirschi had observed a positive relationship (the stronger the attachment to the mother, the stronger the attachment to peers). Second, involvement in delinquency was positively related to attachment to peers.[19] Hirschi had found an inverse relationship (the stronger the attachment to peers, the less the involvement in delinquency).

In another study, criminologists administered a self-report questionnaire to 3056 male and female students in three midwestern states. The researchers were critical of Hirschi's conceptualization of both commitment and involvement, finding it difficult to understand how he separated the two. Serious involvement, they argued, is quite unlikely without commitment. They combined commitment and involvement items and ended up with only three bonds: attachment, commitment, and belief.[20]

The study related these bonds to alcohol and marijuana use, use of strong drugs, minor delinquent behavior, and serious delinquent behavior. The results suggested that strong social bonds were more highly correlated with less serious deviance than with such delinquent acts as motor vehicle theft and assault. Also, the social bonds were more predictive of deviance in girls than in boys. Moreover, criminologists who conducted this study noticed that the commitment bond (now joined with involvement) was more significantly correlated with delinquent behavior than were attachment and belief.

Other researchers administered questionnaires to 2213 tenth-grade boys at 86 schools, seeking to answer three questions: First, are Hirschi's four bonds distinct entities? Second, why did Hirschi name only four bonds? Third, why were some factors that are related to educational and occupational aspiration (such as ability and family socioeconomic status) omitted from his questionnaire? The researchers constructed new scales for measuring attachment, commitment, involvement, and belief. They used a self-report measure to assess delinquency. These researchers found little that is independent or distinctive about any of the bonds.[21]

Robert Agnew provided the first longitudinal test of Hirschi's theory by using data on 1886 boys in the tenth and eleventh grades. Eight social control scales (parental attachment, grades, dating index, school attachment, involvement, commitment, peer attachment, and belief) were examined at two periods in relation to two self-report scales (one measuring total delinquency and the other measuring seriousness of delinquency). Agnew found the eight control scales to be strongly correlated with the self-reported delinquency, but the social control measures did little to predict the extent of future delinquency reported at the second testing. Agnew concluded that the importance of Hirschi's control theory has probably been exaggerated.[22]

Evaluation: Hirschi's Social Control Theory

While social control theory has held a prominent position in criminology for several decades, it is not without weaknesses. For example, social control theory seeks to explain delinquency, not adult crime. It concerns attitudes, beliefs, desires, and

AT ISSUE

RESPECT FOR AUTHORITY: CARJACKING

In his attempts to explain the links between respect for authority and criminal behavior, Travis Hirschi quoted developmental psychologist Jean Piaget: "Respect is the source of the law."(1) Hirschi went on to explain:

> "Insofar as the child respects (loves and fears) his parents, and adults in general, he will accept their rules. Conversely, insofar as this respect is undermined, the rules will tend to lose their obligatory character. . . . Lack of respect for the police presumably leads to lack of respect for the law."(1)

Certainly many criminals seem to lack respect for the police, for law, and for their victims. Carjackers provide a good example. The armed theft of cars from drivers, *carjacking* was defined as a violent crime in 1992, when the director of the FBI announced that carjacking was be-

coming such a serious problem nationwide that it warranted full attention from his bureau.(2) The nation was appalled by a 1992 case in which a Maryland woman was killed when carjackers threw her from her car and then dragged her, tangled in

a seat belt, for nearly 2 miles. The carjackers tossed her 22-month-old daughter—in her car seat—into the road, and she was rescued unharmed. But in an example of the extreme lack of respect for authority shown by carjackers, that shocking

Having fatally shot a driver during an apparent carjacking, this 16-year-old and his partner were caught when they crashed a stolen pickup head-on into a sheriff's patrol car in southwestern Indiana.

behaviors that, though deviant, are often characteristic of adolescents. This is unfortunate because there has long been evidence that social bonds are also significant explanatory factors in postadolescent behavior.[23]

Questions also have been raised about the bonds. Hirschi claims that antisocial acts result from a lack of affective values, beliefs, norms, and attitudes that inhibit delinquency. But these terms are never clearly defined.[24] Critics have also faulted Hirschi's work for other reasons:

- Having too few questionnaire items that measure social bonds
- Failing to describe the chain of events that results in defective or inadequate bonds
- Creating an artificial division of socialized versus unsocialized youths

- Suggesting that social control theory explains why delinquency occurs, when in fact it typically explains no more than 50 percent of delinquent behavior and only 1 to 2 percent of the variance in future delinquency.[25]

Despite the criticisms, Hirschi's work has made a major contribution to criminology. The mere fact that a quarter century of scholars have tried to validate and replicate it testifies to its importance.

Furthermore, research using and extending Hirschi's constructs has become increasingly sophisticated. Recent research coming from the Rochester Youth Development Study, for example, has considered not only the role of weakened bonds to family and school in promoting delinquency but the role of delinquent behavior in attenuating the strength of these very bonds. Criminologists have refined

incident—far from slowing other carjackers—was followed by seven more carjackings in a single day in the Washington area.

Nearly a year after this 1992 incident in Maryland, carjacking was once again the most talked about crime in the nation. This time, the father of basketball star Michael Jordan was killed in a carjacking in South Carolina. The murder of Jordan was followed by the carjacking death of two Japanese college students in a parking lot in San Pedro California in 1994.(4)

How has carjacking become such a problem? Two scholars, Tod W. Burke and Charles E. O'Rear, offered their theories in a 1993 article.(3) The crime is an outgrowth of simple car theft, which has become less simple as car manufacturers increasingly attempt to prevent theft by providing steering-column locks, sophisticated alarm systems, and tracking devices for stolen vehicles. When the vehicle is occupied, however, such devices are likely to be disengaged, so carjackers specialize in accosting drivers at stop signs, in

gas stations, on highway entrance ramps, and in "bump and rob" simulated accidents.

The theory suggested by Burke and O'Rear, and supported by Hirschi's ideas about respect for authority, is the "brazen theory":

The "brazen theory" is based upon the arrogance and self-confidence of the suspects, who tend to believe they are invincible and that their weapons will speak for themselves. Furthermore, with minimal chances of police apprehension and a firm belief that they will beat the system if caught, they consider the risk is worthwhile and cost-effective. . . .

Of 70,000 vehicles stolen in Los Angeles during one recent reporting period, more than 4188 were stolen "by fear or force," and assailants used handguns, knives, blunt instruments, machetes, simulated guns, and even a broken bottle.(3) Thumbing their noses at authority, carjackers continue to plague the nation with an average of 35,000 attempted

or successful carjackings each year.(4)

Sources

1. Travis Hirschi, *Causes of Delinquency* (Berkeley: University of California Press, 1969), pp. 30, 202.
2. "FBI Forms Unit to Battle 'Carjacking,'" *New York Times*, Sept. 16, 1992, p. A21.
3. Tod W. Burke and Charles E. O'Rear, "Armed Carjacking: A Violent Problem in Need of a Solution," *Police Chief*, January 1993, pp. 18–24.
4. John L. Mitchell, "Suspect Arraigned in Carjacking Death," *Los Angeles Times*, April 16, 1996, p. B1.

Questions for Discussion

1. Could the "brazen theory" be used to account for other crimes besides carjacking? Explain.
2. What approaches to preventing carjacking might serve to increase the amount of respect potential carjackers feel for the police and the law?

Hirschi's constructs so that the effects of social control on delinquency, as well as the effects of delinquency on social control, are considered.[26]

SOCIAL CONTROL AND DRIFT

In the 1960s David Matza developed a different perspective on social control that explains why some adolescents drift in and out of delinquency. According to Matza, juveniles sense a moral obligation to be bound by the law. A "bind" between a person and the law, something that creates responsibility and control, remains in place most of the time. When it is not in place, the youth may enter into a state of **drift,** or a period when he or she exists in a limbo between convention and crime, responding in turn to the demands

of each, flirting now with one, now with the other, but postponing commitment, evading decision. Thus, the person drifts between criminal and conventional actions.[27]

If adolescents are indeed bound by the social order, how do they justify their delinquent acts? The answer is that they develop techniques to rationalize their actions. These techniques are defense mechanisms that release the youth from the constraints of the moral order:

- Denial of responsibility ("It wasn't my fault; I was a victim of circumstances.")
- Denial of injury ("No one was hurt, and they have insurance, so what's the problem?")
- Denial of the victim ("Anybody would have done the same thing in my position—I did what I had to do given the situation.")

CRIMINOLOGICAL FOCUS

OUT OF CONTROL: SCHOOL VIOLENCE

Law enforcement and public-health officials describe a virtual "epidemic" of youth violence in the last five years, spreading from the inner cities to the suburbs. "We're talking about younger and younger kids committing more and more serious crimes," says Indianapolis Prosecuting Attorney Jeff Modisett. "Violence is becoming a way of life."(1)

Much of that violence is occurring inside the nation's schools. Consider these statistics:

An estimated 2.7 million crimes occur on or near school campuses every year.(2)
One-quarter of the nation's large urban school districts use metal detectors to search for weapons on students.(3)
One student in five reports carrying a weapon of some sort and one in twenty a gun.(3)

In some schools, like this Newark, New Jersey, high school, students are electronically frisked for weapons upon entering the building.

Almost 60 percent of sixth- through twelfth-graders say they could get a handgun if they wanted one, and one-third of those said they could get a handgun within an hour.(1)

And consider these individual cases: In New Orleans, a third-grad-

er recently took a .357 magnum to school. In Dartmouth, Massachusetts, three teenagers fatally stabbed another student in a social studies class. An argument over a book bag in another school led a 14-year-old to open fire with his 9-mm semiautomatic pistol, killing a student and

---

- Condemnation of the condemner ("I bet the judge and everyone on the jury has done much worse than what I was arrested for.")
- Appeal to higher loyalties ("My friends were depending on me and I see them every day— what was I supposed to do?")[28]

Empirical support for drift theory has not been clear. Some studies show that delinquents consider these rationalizations valid,[29] while other research suggests that they do not. Later investigations also demonstrate that delinquents do not share the moral code or values of nondelinquents.[30]

PERSONAL AND SOCIAL CONTROL

Over the last 40 years support has increased for the idea that both social (external) and personal (internal)

control systems are important forces in keeping individuals from committing crimes. In other words, Hirschi's social bonds and Matza's drift paradigm may not be enough by themselves to explain why people do not commit crimes.

Failure of Control Mechanisms

Albert J. Reiss, a sociologist, was one of the first researchers to isolate a group of personal and social control factors. According to Reiss, delinquency is the result of (1) a failure to internalize socially accepted and prescribed norms of behavior; (2) a breakdown of internal controls; and (3) a lack of social rules that prescribe behavior in the family, the school, and other important social groups.

To test these notions, Reiss collected control-related data on 1110 juvenile delinquents placed on probation in Cook County (Chicago), Illinois. He

CRIMINOLOGICAL FOCUS

wounding a teacher, neither of whom had been involved in the dispute.

What happened to the days when throwing a spitball or an eraser got students into big trouble? Experts say that students are growing up with violence—one survey of inner-city children showed that 43 percent of 7- to 19-year-olds have seen a homicide.(2) And the decay of social support systems worsens the problem. One reporter summed up the situation this way:

> In this heightened atmosphere of violence, normal rules of behavior don't apply. As traditional social supports—home, school, community—have fallen away, new role models take their place. "It takes an entire village to raise a child, but the village isn't there for the children anymore," says Modisett.(1)

A 5-year study of 4000 students allowed criminologist Terence Thornberry to identify a number of risk factors, any of which increase the likelihood that students will become delinquent. The list includes exposure to child abuse and maltreatment, spouse abuse, violent behavior, and poverty and parents who began having children when they were teenagers or who are unemployed, on welfare, or poorly educated.(1) The availability of weapons is another essential ingredient. Law enforcement officials say that 80 to 90 percent of the guns used by students come from their parents.(3)

Thornberry says that the best solution to school violence is to eliminate risk factors—and that prevention programs need to begin very early. A California program that starts with third-graders trains students to resolve conflicts without violence. Other people claim the problem should be solved by limiting the availability of handguns—not just in schools but in society as a whole. One advocate expressed his concern about schools bearing the responsibility for such control: "The school setting is almost impossible to police without tyrannical dictatorship. At what point do we create such a hostile environment that these are no longer schools?"(3)

Sources
1. Barbara Kantrowitz, "Wild in the Streets," *Newsweek,* Aug. 2, 1993, pp. 40–47.
2. Mary Jo Nolin, Elizabeth Davies, and Kathryn Chandler, "Student Victimization at School," *Journal of School Health,* Vol. 66, 1996, p. 216.
3. Tom Morganthau, "It's Not Just New York . . . ," *Newsweek,* Mar. 9, 1992, pp. 25–29.

Questions for Discussion
1. Some states have passed legislation making parents responsible for their children's crimes if the crimes are committed with the parents' guns. Do you think such laws will result in safer schools?
2. Do the problems of school violence change your position on gun control? Explain.

examined three sources of information: (1) a diverse set of data on such variables as family economic status and moral ideals and/or techniques of control by parents during childhood; (2) community and institutional information bearing on control, such as residence in a delinquency area and homeownership; and (3) personal control information, such as ego or superego controls, from clinical judgments of social workers and written psychiatric reports. Reiss concluded that measures of both personal and social control seem "to yield more efficient prediction of delinquent recidivism than items which are measures of the strength of social control."[31]

Stake in Conformity

Imagine that your earliest childhood memory conjures up the sound of splintering wood as the police break down your front door, and the image of your grandmother being led away in handcuffs. You are 4 years old. What impact would such an image have on you? What if your formative years were spent in an impoverished urban environment where your mother and grandmother sold heroin out of your living room, your closest friends were high school dropouts with criminal records, and your adolescent confrontations did not involve the school bully demanding your lunch money, but rather the neighborhood drug dealer stopping by to settle overdue debts? Where would you be today?

Six years after the publication of Reiss's study, Jackson Toby proposed a different personal and social control model. Toby discussed the complementary role of neighborhood social disorganization and an individual's own stake in conformity. He agreed that the social disorganization of the slums explains why some communities have high crime rates while others do not: In slums both the community and the family are powerless to control members' behavior. Thieves and hoodlums usually come from such neighborhoods. But a great many law-abiding youngsters come from slums as well. Toby questioned how a theory that explained group behavior could account for individual differences in response to a poor environment. In other words, how can the theory of social disorganization explain why only a few among so many slum youths actually commit crimes?[32]

According to Toby, the social disorganization approach can explain why one neighborhood has a much higher crime rate than another, but not why one particular individual becomes a hoodlum while another does not. What accounts for the difference is a differing stake in **conformity,** or correspondence of behavior to society's patterns, norms, or standards. One person may respond to conditions in a "bad" neighborhood by becoming hostile to conventional values, perhaps because he or she knows that the chances for legitimate success are poor. Another person in the same neighborhood may maintain his or her stake in conformity and remain committed to abiding by the law. Toby reminds us that when we try to account for crime in general, we should look at both group-level explanations (social disorganization) and individual-level explanations (stake in conformity).

CONTAINMENT THEORY

A broad analysis of the relationship between personal and social controls is found in Walter Reckless's presentation of containment theory.[33] **Containment theory** assumes that for every individual there exists a containing external structure and a protective internal structure, both of which provide defense, protection, or insulation against delinquency.

According to Reckless, *outer containment,* or the structural buffer that holds the person in bounds, can be found in the following components:

- A role that provides a guide for a person's activities
- A set of reasonable limits and responsibilities
- An opportunity for the individual to achieve status
- Cohesion among members of a group, including joint activity and togetherness
- A sense of belongingness (identification with the group)
- Identification with one or more persons within the group
- Provisions for supplying alternative ways and means of satisfaction (when one or more ways are closed)[34]

Inner containment, or personal control, is ensured by:

- A good self-concept
- Self-control
- A strong ego
- A well-developed conscience
- A high frustration tolerance
- A high sense of responsibility

Reckless suggests that the probability of deviance is directly related to the extent to which internal pushes (such as a need for immediate gratification, restlessness, and hostility), external pressures (such as poverty, unemployment, and blocked opportunities), and external pulls are controlled by one's inner and outer containment. The primary containment factor is found in self-concept, or the way one views oneself in relation to others, and to the world as well. A strong self-concept, coupled with some additional inner controls (such as a strong conscience and sense of responsibility), plus outer controls, makes delinquency highly unlikely.

Table 7.2 shows how the probability of deviance changes as an individual's inner and outer containment weakens. But why is it important to examine inner and outer controls simultaneously? Consider

TABLE 7.2   The Probability of Deviance as Indicated by Inner and Outer Containment*

Outer Containment (Social Control)	Inner Containment (Personal Control)	
	Strong	**Weak**
Strong	+ +	+ −
Weak	+ −	− −

*+ + = very low; + − = average; − − = very high.
Source: Adapted from Walter C. Reckless, "A Non-Causal Explanation: Containment Theory," *Excerpta Criminologia,* **2** (1962): 131–132.

John, a college freshman, who had extensive community ties and strong family attachments and was valedictorian of his high school class. He also was a dealer in cocaine. All efforts to explain John's drug selling would prove disappointing if measures of social control were used alone. In other words, according to Hirschi's social control theory, John should be a conformist—he should focus his efforts on becoming a pharmacist or teacher. Containment theory, on the other hand, would be sensitive to the fact that John, while socially controlled and bonded by external forces, had a poorly developed self-concept, had an immature or undeveloped conscience, and was extremely impulsive. In short, he was driven to selling drugs as a result of a poor set of inner controls.

The idea that both internal and external factors are involved in controlling behavior has interested a number of scholars. Francis Ivan Nye, for example, developed the notion that multiple control factors determine human behavior. He argued that **internalized control,** or self-regulation, was a product of guilt aroused in the conscience when norms have been internalized. **Indirect control** comes from an individual's identification with noncriminals and a desire not to embarrass parents and friends by acting against their expectations.

Nye believes that social control involves "needs satisfaction," by which he means that control depends on how well a family can prepare the child for success at school, with peers, and in the workplace. Finally, **direct control,** a purely external control, depends on rules, restrictions, and punishments.[35]

Other researchers have looked at direct controls in different ways. Parental control, for example, may depend on such factors as a broken home, the mother's employment, and the number of children in the family; such factors indicate some loss of direct control. Once again we find mixed results. Some studies indicate very little relationship between a broken home and delinquency, except for minor offenses such as truancy and running away.[36] The same can be said about the consequences of a mother's employment and family size.[37] A national study of 1886 males concluded, however, that direct parental control as measured by strictness and punitiveness is indeed correlated with delinquent behavior, and the study warned us not to dismiss this fact lightly. But the question remains open.[38]

Empirical Tests of Containment Theory

"Not when you're 15 and live in a crowded apartment with seven siblings, all younger than 6. Not when your mom has no job, is coming off drugs and belongs to the same gang as you, your drug-addicted dad, and all your relatives belong to. Not when you have to dress so carefully for the trip to class each day, because one mistake could kill. Does Calvin Klein know his logo means "Crips Killer" in Southeast L.A.? Green means you deal drugs. The wrong belt buckle or shoelace knot is big trouble if you meet rival gangs on your way."[39]

How can a child living in this neighborhood grow up to be a good, law-abiding citizen? How is he or she protected from the crime-producing influences lurking around each corner? To answer these questions, Reckless and his associates had high school teachers in a high-crime neighborhood nominate boys they believed would neither commit delinquent acts nor come into contact with police and juvenile court.

The 125 "good boys" scored high on a social responsibility test and low on a delinquency-proneness test. These boys avoided trouble, had good relations with parents and teachers, and had a good self-concept. They thought of themselves as obedient. Reckless concluded that nondelinquent boys follow conventional values even in bad neighborhoods if they maintain a positive self-image. It is this positive self-image that protects them. In a follow-up study the research team compared "good boys" with those nominated by teachers as "bad boys" (those they believed were headed for trouble). The good boys scored better on parental relation, self-image, and social responsibility tests. Far more of the bad boys had acquired police and juvenile court records.[40]

Evaluation: Containment Theory

Containment theory, like Hirschi's social control theory, has received significant criticism.[41] The most damaging has come from Clarence Schrag, who contends that the terminology used is vague and poorly defined, that the theory is difficult to test empirically, and that the theory fails to consider why some poorly contained youths commit violent crimes while others commit property crimes.[42] These criticisms are not easy to answer. And because little empirical research has been done to test the findings of Reckless and his colleagues over the intervening 30 years, there is little evidence of the validity of containment theory.

INTEGRATED THEORIES

Over the past several years a number of attempts have been made to reconceptualize social control theory through the technique of *theoretical integration*—a technical term for the joining, merging, and testing of different theoretical hypotheses and propositions.[43] As Table 7.3 reveals, theoretical criminologists have relied on social control theory to propose developmental, multifactor, and general theories of crime.

Developmental Theories

All developmental theories share one thing in common: explanations for why offending starts (onset), why it continues (continuance), why it becomes more frequent or serious (escalation), and why, inevitably, it stops (desistance). Rather than focusing exclusively on childhood, adolescence, young adulthood, or adulthood, these theories consider each developmental period in relation to the life span of an offender. In an extension of Hirschi's theory to the "life course," for example, Robert J. Sampson and John H. Laub found that family, school, and peer attachments were most strongly associated with delinquency from childhood to adolescence (through age 17).[44] From the transition to young adulthood through the transition to middle adulthood, attachment to work (job stability) and family (marriage) appears most strongly related to crime causation. Sampson and Laub found evidence that these positive personal and professional relationships build a "social capital" in otherwise vulnerable individuals that significantly inhibits deviance over time.

Another life-course integrated theory combines control with learning theory (Chapter 4). Terence Thornberry argues that the potential for delinquency begins with the weakening of a person's bonds to the conventional world (parents, school, and accepted values). For this potential to be realized, there must be a social setting in which to learn delinquent values. In this setting, delinquents seek each other out and form common belief systems. There is nothing static about this kind of learning. Criminality, according to Thornberry, is a function of a dynamic social process that changes over time.[45]

Finally, David Farrington's work with the data from the Cambridge Study of Delinquent Development reveals different explanations for the general tendency to engage in crime (long-term variables) over time, as well as the influences that prompt an individual, at any given time, to engage in crime (short-term variables) (Table 7.3). The former include

TABLE 7.3 Integrated Social Control Theories	
Theories	**Sample Hypotheses**
Life-course theories:	
Farrington	A combination of multiple personal (e.g., impulsivity), social (e.g., poor parental supervision), and environmental factors (e.g., low income) are associated with crime over the course of a lifetime.
Thornberry	Crime is a function of a dynamic social process that is determined by learning variables (e.g., association with delinquent peers), boundary variables (e.g., attachment and commitment to conventional activities), as well as social class, race, and gender.
Laub and Sampson	Crime causation must be viewed developmentally—in the context of the turning points in a criminal career.
Multifactor theories:	
Weis	Crime results from an interaction between diminished social controls and influences from delinquent peers.
Elliott	Delinquency is traced to strain, weakened social bonds, and deviant subcultures.
General theories:	
Gottfredson and Hirschi	Individual differences in crime commission may be attributed to levels of self-control.

impulsivity, low empathy, and belief systems favorable to law violation. The latter consider momentary opportunities and situationally induced motivating factors, such as alcohol consumption and boredom.[46]

Multiple Control Factors

Multiple control factor theories integrate a criminological theory, such as differential association, with a number of social controls. For example, Delbert Elliott and his colleagues have integrated the social bonds of Hirschi's theory of social control with strain theories. These researchers suggest that limited or blocked opportunities and a subsequent failure to achieve cultural goals would weaken or even destroy bonds to the conventional or social order. In other words, even if someone establishes strong bonds in childhood, a series of negative experiences in school, in the community, and at home, along with blocked access to opportunity, would be likely to lead to a weakening of those social bonds. As strain weakens social bonds, the chance of delinquency increases.[47]

Joseph Weis has proposed a social development model of crime which is an elegant integration of social control and social learning theory. He proposes that delinquency is minimized when youth who are at risk to commit crime have the opportunity to engage in conforming activities, and are rewarded for doing so. Consistent reinforcement maximizes the social bonds which, in turn, diminish associations with delinquent peers and reduce crime.[48]

General Theories

In *A General Theory of Crime*, Michael Gottfredson and Travis Hirschi propose a new model of personal and social control—one designed to explain an individual's propensity to commit crime.[49] Gottfredson and Hirschi claim that their model, unlike earlier conceptualizations, explains the tendency to commit all crimes, from crimes of violence such as robbery and sexual assault to white-collar offenses such as mail fraud and federal securities violations.[50]

This "general theory" of propensity to commit crimes, shown in Figure 7.1, assumes that offenders have little control over their own behavior and desires. When the need for momentary pleasure and immediate gratification outweighs long-term interests, crime occurs. In short, crime is a function of poor self-control.

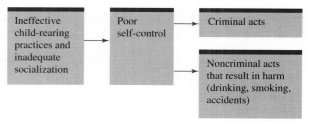

FIGURE 7.1 The Gottfredson-Hirschi self-control model. Gottfredson and Hirschi's model assumes that poor self-control is an intervening variable that explains all crime, as well as differences in crime rates, by age, gender, and race.

What leads to poor self-control? Inadequate socialization and poor child-rearing practices, coupled with poor attachment, increase the probability of impulsive and uncontrolled acts. According to Gottfredson and Hirschi, individuals with low self-control also tend to be involved in noncriminal events that result in harm, such as drinking, smoking, and most types of accidents including auto crashes, household fires, and unwanted pregnancies.

Evidence in support of this theory is mixed. In their analysis of interviews and breathalyzer tests, one study found a definite association between self-control and DUI.[51] Equivocal results, however, were obtained by other researchers who examined interview data from a sample of college students, high school students, adults from Oklahoma City, residents of a Canadian province, and residents of a large southwestern U.S. city.[52] Additional research will establish the usefulness of this general theory of crime.[53]

It is important to remember that all the integrated theories share one common variable—the social bonds that are at the foundation of social control theory. The ingredients of social control theory have been used quite effectively over the last decade as building blocks in the development and refinement of integrated criminological theories.

THEORY INFORMS POLICY

Social control theory tells us that people commit crimes when they have not developed adequate attachments, have not become involved in and committed to conventional activities, and have not internalized the rules of society (or do not care about

WINDOW TO THE WORLD

NATIONS WITH LOW CRIME RATES

Most criminologists devote their efforts to learning why people commit crime and why there is so much crime. A few have looked at the question from the opposite perspective: In places with little crime, what accounts for the low crime rate? Using the United Nations' first World Crime Survey (1970–1975), Freda Adler studied the two countries with the lowest crime rates in each of five general cultural regions of the world(1):

Western Europe: Switzerland and the Republic of Ireland
Eastern Europe: The former German Democratic Republic (East Germany) and Bulgaria
Arab countries: Saudi Arabia and Algeria
Asia: Japan and Nepal
Latin America: Costa Rica and Peru(2)

This is an odd assortment of countries. They seem to have little in common. Some are democratic, others authoritarian. Some are republics, others monarchies. Some were ruled by dictators, others by communal councils. Some are rural, others highly urbanized. Some are remote and isolated; others are in the political mainstream. Some are highly religious, some largely atheistic. Some have a very high standard of living, others a very low one. What explains their common characteristic of low crime rates?

Investigations slowly revealed a common factor in all ten countries: each appeared to have an intact social control system, quite apart from whatever formal control system (law enforcement) it had. Here are brief descriptions of the types of social control systems identified:

Western Europe: Switzerland fostered a strong sense of belonging to and participating in the local community.(3) The family was still strong in the Republic of Ireland, and it was strengthened by shared religious values.
Eastern Europe: The German Democratic Republic involved all youths in communal activities, organized by groups and aimed at having young people excel for the glory of self and country. In Bulgaria, industrialization focused on regional industry centers so that the workers would not be dislodged from their hometowns, which served as continuing social centers.
The Arab countries: Islam continued to be strong as a way of life and exercised a powerful influence on daily activities, especially in Saudi Arabia. Algeria had, in addition, a powerful commitment to socialism in its postindependence era, involving the citizens in all kinds of commonly shared development activities.
Asia: Nepal retained its strong family and clan ties, augmented by councils of elders that oversaw the community and resolved problems. Highly industrialized Japan had lost some of the social controls of family and kinship, but it found a substitute family in the industrial community, to which most Japanese belonged: Mitsubishi might now be the family that guided one's every step.
Latin America: Costa Rica spent all the funds that other governments devoted to the military on social services and social development,

caring for and strengthening its families. Peru went through a process of urbanization in stages: village and family cohesion marked the lives of people in the countryside, and this cohesion remained with the people as they migrated from Andean villages to smaller towns and then to the big city, where they were received by and lived surrounded by others from their own hometowns.

The study concluded that **synnomie,** a term derived from the Greek *syn* meaning "with" and *nomos* meaning "norms," marked societies with low crime rates.

Sources

1. United Nations, *Report of the Secretary General on Crime Prevention and Control,* A/32/199 (popularly known as the First U.N. World Crime Survey) (New York: United Nations, 1977).
2. Freda Adler, *Nations Not Obsessed with Crime* (Littleton, Colo.: Fred B. Rothman, 1983).
3. Marshall B. Clinard, *Cities with Little Crime: The Case of Switzerland* (Cambridge, Mass.: Cambridge University Press, 1978).

Questions for Discussion

1. People in the United States work in factories, live in family groups, go to church, and join youth groups. Why do these institutions not function effectively as forms of social control to keep the crime rate low?
2. How could government or community decision makers use the information presented by this study to help solve crime problems in the United States?

them). Efforts to prevent crime must therefore include the teaching of conventional values. It is also necessary to find ways to strengthen individual bonds to society, commitment to the conventional order, and involvement in conventional activities. One way is to strengthen the institutions that socialize people and continue to regulate their behavior throughout life—the family, the school, and the workplace.[54]

Family

In the early 1980s an experimental school-based parent training program opened in Seattle, Washington, as part of a delinquency-prevention project. First-graders in six schools were assigned to an experimental classroom or a control classroom. The parents of those in the experimental group were given training, and the parents of the children in the control group were not.

The major premise of the experiment was that a child's bond to a family is crucial. To develop this bond, parents learned to provide opportunities that would help the child participate and succeed in a social unit such as the school (by demonstrating good study habits, for example) and to reinforce conformity or punish violations of the group's norms. Preliminary results suggest that such a training program decreases children's aggressiveness and increases parental skills.[55]

School

A program called PATHE (Positive Action Through Holistic Education) operated in four middle schools and three high schools of Charleston County, South Carolina, between 1980 and 1983. Its object was to reduce delinquency by strengthening students' commitment to school and attachment to conforming members—in other words, by bonding young people to the conventional system.

PATHE brought together students, school staff, and community members to plan and implement a program designed to foster a better school climate (encourage more open discussion), improve academic skills, and prepare students for careers. The results of the program were higher grades, better attendance, fewer dropouts, and increased commitment to education.[56]

Neighborhood

Historically church and family have helped to protect and maintain the social order in neighborhoods, to instill a sense of pride and comfort in residents. This is no longer the case in many areas. The neighborhood as an institution of informal social control has been very much weakened. Various agencies have tried to reverse this trend: Between 1981 and 1986 programs to prevent juvenile crime were implemented through neighborhood-based organizations in Chicago, Dallas, Los Angeles, New York, New Orleans, and San Diego. These federally funded programs sought to reduce crime by strengthening neighborhood cohesion. Each program assessed the needs of residents and then set up crisis intervention centers, mediation (between youngsters and school, family, or police and between warring gangs), youth training, supervision programs, and family support systems.

Within the first 3 years, serious juvenile crime decreased in three of the target areas.[57] Hundreds of such community crime-prevention projects around the country have been organized by government agencies, private persons, and religious groups.[58] They have made a local impact, but they have not been able to change the national crime rate. The most successful models, however, may offer a plan for crime prevention on a broader, perhaps even a national, scale.

As our understanding of control theory evolves, so will our appreciation of the effects of control interventions. If nothing else, it is fair to say that social control programs and interventions are proliferating and may be found in every state. Here are just a few examples:

Homebuilders (Tacoma, Washington). A family preservation program that seeks to keep at-risk children at home[59]

Families First (Michigan). A program that strengthens vulnerable families[60]

S.W.E.A.T. Team (Bridgeport, Connecticut). A project that employs teenagers to create new activities for children who may be tempted into joining gangs or selling drugs[61]

Learnfare (Ohio, Virginia, Florida, Maryland, and Oklahoma). Programs that provide financial and social support for teenage welfare mothers who attend school[62]

REVIEW

The term "social control" has taken on a wide variety of meanings. In general, it describes any mechanism that leads to conformity to social norms. Mainstream studies of social control take one of two approaches. Macrosociological studies focus on formal systems of social control. Most contemporary criminological research takes the microsociological approach, which focuses on informal systems. Travis Hirschi's social control theory has had a long-lasting impact on the scholarly community. Hirschi identified four social bonds that promote adherence to society's values: attachment, commitment, involvement, and belief. The stronger these bonds, Hirschi claimed, the less the likelihood of delinquency.

According to the containment theory of Walter Reckless, every person has a containing external structure (a role in a social group with reasonable limits and responsibilities and alternative means of attaining satisfaction). In addition, each individual has a protective internal structure that depends on a good self-concept, self-control, a well-developed conscience, a tolerance for frustration, and a strong sense of responsibility.

Most investigators today believe that personal (inner) controls are as important as social (external) controls in keeping people from committing crimes. Albert Reiss found that personal controls reinforce social controls. Jackson Toby stressed the importance of a stake in conformity in keeping a person from responding to social disorganization with delinquent behavior. Recent efforts to integrate social control theories with other theories have resulted in developmental, multifactor, and general theories of crime. All share one common variable—the social bonds that constitute social control theory.

As part of an effort to reduce delinquency, a variety of programs at the local and regional levels help parents, schools, and neighborhood groups develop social controls.

NOTES

1. William Golding, *Lord of the Flies* (New York: Coward-McCann, 1954), p. 31.
2. Jack P. Gibbs, "Social Control, Deterrence, and Perspectives on Social Order," *Social Forces,* **56** (1977): 408–423. See also Freda Adler, *Nations Not Obsessed with Crime* (Littleton, Colo.: Fred B. Rothman, 1983).
3. Travis Hirschi, *Causes of Delinquency* (Berkeley: University of California Press, 1969).
4. Donald J. Black, *The Behavior of Law* (New York: Academic Press, 1976), p. 105. See Allan V. Horwitz, *The Logic of Social Control* (New York: Plenum, 1990), for an exceptional evaluation of Black's work.
5. Joseph Perkins, "Smoke Signals Taxes, Harsh Rules Go Too Far in Crusade to Snuff Out Habit," *San Diego Union-Tribune,* Mar. 12, 1993, p. B7; editorial, "Smoke Clouds the Political Air in California's City of Angels," *Washington Times,* July 17, 1993, p. C2.
6. Nanette J. Davis and Bo Anderson, *Social Control: The Production of Deviance in the Modern State* (New York: Irvington, 1983); S. Cohen and A. Scull, eds., *Social Control and the State* (New York: St. Martin's Press, 1983).
7. Jackson Toby, "Social Disorganization and Stake in Conformity: Complementary Factors in the Predatory Behavior of Hoodlums," *Journal of Criminal Law, Criminology, and Police Science,* **48** (1957): 12–17.
8. Scott Briar and Irving Piliavin, "Delinquency, Situational Inducements, and Commitment to Conformity," *Social Problems,* **13** (1965): 41.
9. Ibid., p. 36.
10. Hirschi, *Causes of Delinquency.*
11. See John Bowlby, *Attachment and Loss,* 2 vols. (New York: Basic Books, 1969, 1973); John Bowlby, "Forty-Four Juvenile Thieves: Their Characteristics and Home Life," *International Journal of Psychoanalysis,* **25** (1944): 19–25; and John Bowlby, *The Making and Breaking of Affectional Bonds* (London: Tavistock, 1979).
12. Hirschi, *Causes of Delinquency.*
13. Ibid., p. 145.
14. June Gross, "Successful Program Shows Difficulty of Job Training," *Los Angeles Times,* Apr. 22, 1996, p. 1.
15. Hirschi, *Causes of Delinquency.*
16. Teresa D. Brown, "School Adds After-School Fun," *St. Petersburg Times,* Jan. 12, 1995, p. 3.
17. Jeff Lofvers, "I Don't Understand Why Teens Get Such a Bad Rap," *Orlando Sentinel,* June 5, 1996, p. A13.
18. Hirschi, *Causes of Delinquency,* p. 55.
19. Michael J. Hindelang, "Causes of Delinquency: A Partial Replication and Extension," *Social Problems,* **20** (1973): 471–487.
20. Marvin D. Krohn and James L. Massey, "Social Control and Delinquent Behavior: An Examination of the Elements of the Social Bond," *Sociological Quarterly,* **21** (1980): 529–544.
21. Michael D. Wiatrowski, David Griswold, and Mary K. Roberts, "Social Control Theory and Delinquency," *American Sociological Review,* **46** (1985): 525–541.
22. Robert Agnew, "Social Control Theory and Delinquency: A Longitudinal Test," *Criminology,* **23** (1985): 47–61. See also Scott Menard, "Demographic and Theoretical Variables in the Age-Period-Cohort Analysis of Illegal Behavior," *Journal of Research in Crime and Delinquency,* **29** (1992): 178–199; Stephen A. Cernovich and Peggy C. Giordano, "School Bonding, Age, Race, and Delinquency," *Criminology,* **30** (1992): 261–291; Kimberly L. Kempf, "The Empirical Status of Social Control Theory," in *New Directions in Criminological Theory,* ed. Freda Adler and William S. Laufer (New Brunswick, N.J.: Transaction, 1993), pp. 143–185; Marc LeBlanc and Aaron

Caplan, "Theoretical Formalization, a Necessity: The Example of Hirschi's Bonding Theory," in Adler and Laufer, *New Directions in Criminological Theory*, pp. 237–336; and Orlando Rodriguez and David Weisburd, "The Integrated Social Control Model and Ethnicity: The Case of Puerto Rican American Delinquency," *Criminal Justice and Behavior*, **18** (1991): 464–479.

23. Kimberly K. Leonard and S. H. Decker, "The Theory of Social Control: Does It Apply to the Very Young?" *Journal of Criminal Justice*, **22** (1994): 89–105; Karen S. Rook, "Promoting Social Bonding: Strategies for Helping the Lonely and Socially Isolated," *American Psychologist*, **39** (1984): 1389–1407.

24. Milton Rokeach, *The Nature of Human Values* (New York: Free Press, 1973).

25. See Donald J. Shoemaker, *Theories of Delinquency: An Examination of Explanations of Delinquent Behavior*, 2d ed. (New York: Oxford University Press, 1990), pp. 172–207, for an evaluation of social control theory.

26. Terence P. Thornberry, "Toward an Interactional Theory of Delinquency," *Criminology*, **25** (1987): 863–891.

27. David Matza, *Delinquency and Drift* (New York: Wiley, 1964), p. 21.

28. Gresham Sykes and David Matza, "Techniques of Neutralization: A Theory of Delinquency," *American Sociological Review*, **22** (1957): 664–670. For a more recent look at techniques of neutralization, see John Hamlin, "The Misplaced Role of Rational Choice in Neutralization Theory," *Criminology*, **26** (1988): 425–438.

29. Richard A. Ball, "An Empirical Exploration of Neutralization Theory," *Criminologica*, **4** (1966): 103–120. See also N. William Minor, "The Neutralization of Criminal Offense," *Criminology*, **18** (1980): 103–120.

30. Robert Gordon, James F. Short, Jr., D. Cartwright, and Fred L. Strodtbeck, "Values and Gang Delinquency: A Study of Street Corner Groups," *American Journal of Sociology*, **69** (1963): 109–128.

31. Albert J. Reiss, "Delinquency as the Failure of Personal and Social Controls," *American Sociological Review*, **16** (1951): 206.

32. Toby, "Social Disorganization," p. 137.

33. Walter C. Reckless, "A New Theory of Delinquency and Crime," *Federal Probation*, **25** (1961): 42–46; Walter C. Reckless, Simon Dinitz, and E. Murray, "Self-Concept as an Insulator against Delinquency," *American Sociological Review*, **21** (1956): 744–746; Frank R. Scarpitti, Ellen Murray, Simon Dinitz, and Walter C. Reckless, "The Good Boy in a High Delinquency Area: Four Years Later," *American Sociological Review*, **25** (1960): 555–558. See also K. Heimer and R. L. Matsueda, "Role-Taking, Role Commitment, and Delinquency: A Theory of Differential Social Control," *American Sociological Review*, **59** (1994): 365–390.

34. Walter C. Reckless, "A Non-causal Explanation: Containment Theory," *Excerpta Criminologia*, **2** (1962): 131–132.

35. Francis Ivan Nye, *Family Relationships and Delinquent Behavior* (New York: Wiley, 1958).

36. L. Edward Wells and Joseph H. Rankin, "Broken Homes and Juvenile Delinquency: An Empirical Review," *Criminal Justice Abstracts*, **17** (1985): 249–272.

37. Mary Reige, "Parental Affection and Juvenile Delinquency in Girls," *British Journal of Criminology*, **12** (1972): 55–73;

Lawrence Rosen, "Family and Delinquency: Structure or Function?" *Criminology*, **23** (1985): 553–573.

38. L. Edward Wells and Joseph H. Rankin, "Direct Parental Controls and Delinquency," *Criminology*, **26** (1988): 263–285. See also Douglas Smith and Raymond Paternoster, "The Gender Gap in Theories of Deviance: Issues and Evidence," *Journal of Research in Crime and Delinquency*, **24** (1987): 140–172; and John Hagan, A. R. Gillis, and John Simpson, "The Class Structure of Gender and Delinquency: Toward a Power-Control Theory of Common Delinquent Behavior," *American Journal of Sociology*, **90** (1985): 1151–1178. See Joan McCord, "Some Child-Rearing Antecedents of Criminal Behavior in Adult Men," *Journal of Personality and Social Psychology*, **36** (1979): 1477–1486. For an examination of the family backgrounds of female offenders, see Jill Leslie Rosenbaum, "Family Dysfunction and Female Delinquency," *Crime and Delinquency*, **35** (1989): 31–44.

39. Betti Jane Levine, "Tender Mercies: They Traded Their Humanity for a Life in Crime," *Los Angeles Times*, June 21, 1996, p. 1.

40. Reckless et al., "Self-Concept as an Insulator"; Scarpitti et al., "The Good Boy in a High Delinquency Area."

41. Gary F. Jensen, "Delinquency and Adolescent Self-Conceptions: A Study of the Personal Relevance of Infraction," *Social Problems*, **20** (1972): 84–103.

42. Clarence Schrag, *Crime and Justice American Style* (Washington, D.C.: U.S. Government Printing Office, 1971), pp. 82–89.

43. Alan Liska, Marvin D. Krohn, and Steven F. Messner, "Strategies and Requisites for Theoretical Integration in the Study of Crime and Deviance," in *Theoretical Integration in the Study of Deviance and Crime: Problems and Prospects*, ed. S. F. Lessner, M. D. Krohn, and A. Liska (New York: SUNYA, 1989), p. 4. See also R. J. Hepburn, "Testing Alternative Models of Delinquency Causation," *Journal of Criminal Law and Criminology*, **67** (1977): 450–460; T. Ross Matsueda, "Testing Control Theory and Differential Association: A Causal Modeling Approach," *American Sociological Review*, **47** (1982): 489–497; and Frank S. Pearson and Neil A. Weiner, "Toward an Integration of Criminological Theories," *Journal of Criminal Law and Criminology*, **76** (1985): 116–150.

44. Robert J. Sampson and John H. Laub, *Crime in the Making: Pathways and Turning Points through Life* (Cambridge, Mass.: Harvard University Press, 1993). R. J. Sampson and J. H. Laub, "Understanding Variability in Lives through Time: Contributions of Life-Course Criminology," *Studies on Crime and Crime Prevention*, **4** (1995): 143–158.

45. Terence P. Thornberry, A. J. Lizotte, and M. D. Krohn, "Delinquent Peers, Beliefs, and Delinquent Behavior: A Longitudinal Test of Interactional Theory," *Criminology*, **32** (1994): 47–83; Terence P. Thornberry, Alan J. Lizotte, Marvin D. Krohn, Margaret Farnsworth, and Sung Juon Jung, "Testing Interactional Theory: An Examination of Reciprocal Causal Relationships among Family, School, and Delinquency," *Journal of Criminal Law and Criminology*, **82** (1991): 3–35; See also Madeline G. Aultman and Charles F. Wellford, "Toward an Integrated Model of Delinquency Causation: An Empirical Analysis," *Sociology and Social Research*, **63** (1979): 316–317.

46. D. S. Nagin and D. P. Farrington, "The Onset and Persistence of Offending," *Criminology*, **30** (1992): 501–524; D. S. Nagin

and D. P. Farrington, "The Stability of Criminal Potential from Childhood to Adulthood," *Criminology,* **30** (1992): 235–260, D. P. Farrington, "Explaining the Beginning, Progress, and Ending of Antisocial Behavior from Birth to Adulthood," *Advances in Criminological Theory,* **3** (1992): 253–286.

47. Delbert S. Elliott, Suzanne S. Ageton, and R. J. Canter, "An Integrated Theoretical Perspective on Delinquent Behavior," *Journal of Research in Crime and Delinquency,* **16** (1979): 3–27; S. Menard and Delbert S. Elliott, "Delinquent Bonding, Moral Beliefs, and Illegal Behavior: A Three Wave Panel Model," *Justice Quarterly,* **11** (1994): 173–188.

48. David J. Hawkins and Joseph G. Weis, "The Social Development Model: An Integrated Approach to Delinquency Prevention," *Journal of Primary Prevention,* **6** (1985): 73–97.

49. Michael R. Gottfredson and Travis Hirschi, *A General Theory of Crime* (Stanford, Calif.: Stanford University Press, 1990); Michael Gottfredson and Travis Hirschi, "A Propensity-Event Theory of Crime," in *Advances in Criminological Theory,* vol. 1, ed. W. Laufer and F. Adler (New Brunswick, N.J.: Transaction, 1989); B. J. Arneklev, H. G. Grasmick, and C. R. Tittle, "Low Self-Control and Imprudent Behavior," *Journal of Quantitative Criminology,* **9** (1993): 225–247; D. Brownfield and A. M. Sorenson, "Self Control and Juvenile Delinquency: Theoretical Issues and an Empirical Assessment of Selected Elements of a General Theory of Crime," *Deviant Behavior,* **14** (1993): 243–264; T. Hirschi and M. Gottfredson, "Commentary: Testing the General Theory of Crime," *Journal of Research in Crime and Delinquency,* **30** (1993): 47–54.

50. Travis Hirschi and Michael Gottfredson, "The Significance of White-Collar Crime for a General Theory of Crime," *Criminology,* **27** (1989): 359–371; Darrell Steffensmeier, "On the Causes of 'White Collar' Crime: An Assessment of Hirschi and Gottfredson's Claim," *Criminology,* **27** (1989): 345–358.

51. Carl Keane, Paul S. Maxim, and James J. Teevan, "Drinking and Driving, Self-Control, and Gender: Testing a General Theory of Crime," *Journal of Research in Crime and Delinquency,* **30** (1993): 30–46.

52. See, e.g., A. Sorenson and D. Brownfield, "Adolescent Drug Use and a General Theory of Crime: An Analysis of a Theoretical Integration," *Canadian Journal of Criminology,* **37** (1995): 19–37; J. J. Gibbs and D. Giever, "Self-Control and Its Manifestations among University Students: An Empirical Test of Gottfredson and Hirschi's General Theory," *Justice Quarterly,* **12** (1995): 231–255; Harold G. Grasmick, Charles R. Tittle, and Robert J. Bursik, Jr., "Testing the Core Empirical Implications of Gottfredson and Hirschi's General Theory of Crime," *Journal of Research in Crime and Delinquency,* **30** (1993): 5–29; Travis Hirschi and Michael Gottfredson, "Commentary: Testing the General Theory of Crime," *Journal of Research in Crime and Delinquency,* **30** (1993): 47–54; S. L. Miller and C. Burack, "A Critique of Gottfredson and Hirschi's General Theory of Crime: Selective (In) Attention to Gender and Power Positions," *Women and Criminal Justice,* **4** (1993); M. L. Benson and E. Moore, "Are White-Collar and Common Offenders the Same? An Empirical and Theoretical Critique of a Recently Proposed General Theory of Crime," *Journal of Research in Crime and Delinquency,* **29** (1992): 251–272.

53. Don Weatherburn, "On the Quest for a General Theory of Crime," *Australian and New Zealand Journal of Criminology,* **26** (1993): 35–46.

54. See W. Timothy Austin, "Crime and Custom in an Orderly Society: The Singapore Prototype," *Criminology,* **25** (1987): 279–294; J. M. Day and William S. Laufer, eds., *Crime, Values, and Religion* (Norwood, N.J.: Ablex, 1987); and Freda Adler and William S. Laufer, "Social Control and the Workplace," in *US-USSR Approaches to Urban Crime Prevention,* ed. James Finckenauer and Alexander Yakovlev (Moscow: Soviet Academy of State and Law, 1987).

55. David J. Hawkins, Richard F. Catalano, Gwen Jones, and David Fine, "Delinquency Prevention through Parent-Training: Results and Issues from Work in Progress," in *From Children to Citizens:* vol. 3, *Families, Schools, and Delinquency Prevention,* ed. James Q. Wilson and Glenn C. Loury (New York: Springer Verlag, 1987), pp. 186–204.

56. Denise C. Gottfredson, "An Empirical Test of School-Based Environmental and Individual Interventions to Reduce the Risk of Delinquent Behavior," *Criminology,* **24** (1986): 705–731.

57. Jeffrey Fagan, "Neighborhood Education, Mobilization, and Organization for Juvenile Crime Prevention," *Annals of the American Academy for the Advancement of Political and Social Sciences,* **494** (1987): 54–70.

58. For an examination of community social control, see David Weisburd, "Vigilantism as Community Social Control: Developing a Quantitative Criminological Model," *Journal of Quantitative Criminology,* **4** (1988): 137–153.

59. "Fostering the Family: An Intensive Effort to Keep Kids with Parents," *Newsweek,* June 22, 1992, p. 64.

60. Ibid.

61. George Judson, "Fighting Temptations of Summer: Bridgeport Puts Teenagers to Work Helping Other Youths," *New York Times,* Aug. 22, 1992, p. B1.

62. Susan Chirn, "A 'Learnfare' Program Offers No Easy Lessons," *New York Times,* Apr. 28, 1993, p. A12.

▓ Internet Exercise

Hirschi identified four social bonds that promote socialization: attachment, commitment, involvement, and belief. How do the programs and resources of the Omega Boys Club promote a commitment to conventional lines of action?

▓ Your Web Site is: **http://www.street-soldiers.org/**

CHAPTER 8
Targets and
Victims of Crime

Theories of Crime

    Environmental Criminology

    Rational-Choice Perspective

    Routine-Activity Approach

Theories of Victimization

    Lifestyle Theories

    Repeat Victimization

    Hot Spots of Crime

    Geography of Crime

    Interrelatedness of Theories

Preventing Crimes against Places, People, and Valuable Goods

    Situational Crime Prevention

    Displacement

Review

Notes

    Special Features

        WINDOW TO THE WORLD: Decresting the Lovebug, Worldwide

        CRIMINOLOGICAL FOCUS: Defensive Space

        AT ISSUE: Why Wait for a Million-Dollar Civil Liability Suit?

Key Terms

displacement
rational choice
routine activity
target hardening
theories of crime
theories of
  victimization

Riverside, California:

After an hour-long sexual assault during which she thought she was about to die, the 24-year-old Moreno Valley woman testified she turned to her attacker and asked: "Do you think God loves me?"

She then testified that she asked him to tell her mother she loved her if she died.

But she survived to testify in Riverside Superior Court to what police and a prosecutor called one of the most brutal rape cases they ever investigated.

Thursday, Edward Frank Ross, 35, of Moreno Valley, was convicted under the state's tough sexual predator law of six rape and sexual assault counts, including a torture allegation, that could bring an 82-year prison term plus two consecutive life terms.

Deputy District Attorney Tim Schaaf called the Aug. 1, 1995 attack one of the worst he had prosecuted.

"She spent over an hour with this monster," Schaaf said after the eight men and four women returned a verdict following 90 minutes of deliberations. . . .

Although the attack was so violent she was near death from loss of blood, the woman wrapped herself in a sheet and ran from her Moreno Valley apartment in the pre-dawn hours searching for help from a neighbor, Schaaf said. She testified the suspect warned that he would return with his friends.[1]

Arvada, Colorado:

For the second time in two weeks, the Sizzler Steak House . . . has been held up by the same man. In each case, the robber claimed to be armed with a .357 Magnum revolver, demanded money and got an undisclosed amount of cash. No weapon was seen during the March 25 holdup or in the latest incident Monday night, police said.

The robber was described as a "scruffy" white male in his mid-30s to early-40s, about 6 feet tall and 160 pounds, with blondish-brown hair and glasses. He may be a suspect in several other robberies . . . spokeswoman Susan Rossi said.[2]

Paramus, New Jersey:

A group of car thieves using a limousine as a workshop to make keys for stealing cars . . . would remove a lock cylinder from a car they wanted, go into the limo and file a master key to fit the lock. . . . [T]hey keep working the key and tune it until it fits. They insert the key into the ignition and take off . . . . The most common vehicles stolen have been trucks—not cars—sport-utility vehicles with six-cylinder engines and four-wheel drive, including the Mitsubishi Montero and two Toyota models, the Land Cruiser and 4Runner. . . . Just about any Honda and the Toyota Camry top the thieves' list of desirable passenger cars. . . . The location of Garden State Plaza is enticing. . . . The plaza provides three escape routes, Route 4, Route 17, and the Garden State Parkway.[3]

Here we have three different types of crime, committed in three different jurisdictions—California, Colorado, and New Jersey—involving three different types of harm: non-consensual intercourse, the taking of property by force and violence, and the loss of automobiles. The prosecutors in these jurisdictions will know what to do. They will identify these crimes under their respective penal codes as sexual assault, robbery, and larceny, respectively, and they will file charges accordingly. But the criminologist, looking more deeply into these crime scenarios, will consider something in addition, something seemingly not of interest to the law, namely that each of the three crimes occurs at a specific time, at a specific place. The presence of an offender is only one of the necessary components: crimes require many conditions that are independent of the offender, such as the availability of a person to be assaulted or of goods to be stolen.

The three scenarios enable us to see how, up to the actual moment of the crime, the events were a part of everyday life: People sleep in their homes; cars break down, sometimes at odd hours; stores are open for business; and people own Hondas, which must be parked when not being driven. To understand crime, it is necessary to find out how offenders view the scenes and situations around them as they exercise an option to commit a crime.

In other chapters we have focused on factors explaining why individuals and groups engage in criminal behavior. These theories of criminality, Michael Gottfredson and Travis Hirschi point out, explain why some people are more likely than others to commit crimes.[4] In recent years, however, some criminologists have focused on why offenders choose to commit one offense rather than another at a given time and place. These explanations are called **theories of crime.** They identify conditions under which those who are prone to commit crime will in fact do so. Current criminological research shows that both a small number of victims and a small number of places experience a large amount of all crime committed. Crimes are events. Criminals choose their targets. Certain places actually attract criminals. Certain lifestyles increase people's chances of being victimized. Although victims of crime rarely are to blame for their victimization, they frequently play a role in the crimes that happen to them. **Theories of victimization** explain why this happens.

In this chapter we discuss theories of crime and theories of victimization. We will demonstrate how various environmental, opportunity, and victimization theories are interrelated. We will also explore the prevention of crimes against people, places, and valuable goods, presenting current criminological research. In this discussion we include situational crime prevention, diffusion of benefits, routine precautions, and the theoretical and practical implications of focusing on the victims and targets of crime.

THEORIES OF CRIME

Among the theories of crime, three distinct approaches have been identified: environmental criminology, the rational-choice perspective, and the routine-activity approach. These theories of crime are sometimes called opportunity theories because they analyze the various situations that provide opportunities for specific crimes to occur.

Environmental Criminology

Environmental criminologists examine the location of a specific crime and the context in which it occurred in order to understand and explain crime patterns. They ask: Where and when did the crime occur? What are the physical and social characteristics of the crime site? What movements bring offender and target together at the crime site? Environmental criminologists want to know how physical "location in time and space" interacts with the offender, the target/victim, and the law that makes the crime an illegal act.[5]

Contrary to the established criminological theories that explain criminal motivation, environmental criminology begins with the assumption that some people are criminally motivated. Through mapping crimes on global, country, state, county, city, or site-specific levels, like a particular building or plot of land, environmental criminologists can see crime patterns. They then relate these crime patterns to the number of targets; to the offender population; to the location of routine activities such as work, school, shopping, or recreation; to security; and to traffic flow.

Mapping crimes and analyzing the spatial crime patterns is not new (Chapter 3). In the nineteenth century, Guerry examined the spatial patterning of crime through his comparison of conviction rates in different regions in France.[6] Quetelet tried to establish links between seasonal differences and the probability of committing crime. He found, for instance, that property crimes increase in the winter months in France, whereas "the violence of the passions predominating in summer, excites to more frequent personal collisions" and a rise in crimes against persons (Chapter 3).[7] Contemporary research takes a more focused, crime-specific approach.

Burglars and Burglary. Criminologists are increasingly interested in the factors that go into a decision to burglarize: the location or setting of the building, the presence of guards or dogs, the type of burglar alarms and external lighting, and so forth. Does a car in the driveway or a radio playing music in the house have a significant impact on the choice of home to burglarize? George Rengert and John Wasilchick conducted extensive interviews with suburban burglars in an effort to understand their techniques. They found significant differences with respect to several factors[8]:

- *The amount of planning* that precedes a burglary. Professional burglars plan more than do amateurs.
- The extent to which a burglar engages in *systematic selection of a home.* Some burglars examine the obvious clues, such as presence of a burglar alarm, a watchdog, mail piled up in the mailbox, newspapers on a doorstep. More experienced burglars look for subtle clues, for example, closed windows coupled with air conditioners that are turned off.
- The extent to which a burglar pays *attention to situational cues.* Some burglars routinely choose a corner property because it offers more avenues of escape, has fewer adjoining properties, and offers visibility.

Rengert and Wasilchick have also examined the use of time and place in burglary (Figure 8.1). Time is a critical factor to burglars, for three reasons:

- They must minimize the time spent in targeted places so as not to reveal their intention to burglarize.
- Opportunities for burglary occur only when a dwelling is unguarded or unoccupied, that is, during daytime. (Many burglars would call in sick so often that they would be fired from their legitimate jobs; others simply quit the job because it interfered with their burglaries.)
- Burglars have "working hours"; that is, they have time available only during a limited number of hours (if they have a legitimate job).

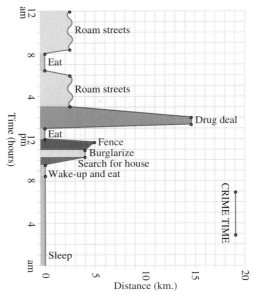

FIGURE 8.1 Crime day of burglar #26.
Source: George Rengert and John Wasilchick, *Suburban Burglary: A Time and a Place for Everything* (Springfield, Ill.: Charles C Thomas Publisher, 1985), p. 35.

Before committing their offenses, burglars take into account familiarity with the area, fear of recognition, concern over "standing out" as somebody who does not belong, and the possibility (following some successful burglaries) that a particular area is no longer cost-beneficial. Season, too, plays an important role. One experienced burglar stated that because neighborhoods are populated with children in the summer, he opted for winter months: "The best time to do crime out here is between 8:00 and 9:00 [A.M.]. All the mothers are taking the kids to school. I wait until I see the car leave. By the time she gets back, I've come and gone."[9]

Recent research demonstrates how important it is for burglars to have prior knowledge of their targets. They obtain such knowledge by knowing the occupants, by being tipped off about the occupants, or by observing the potential target.[10] Some burglars even obtain jobs that afford them the opportunity of observing their potential victims' daily activities; others gain access to the interior of a house, search for valuable goods, and steal them at a later date.

Robbers and Robberies. Robbers who target business establishments are interested in some of the same factors that concern burglars. Perpetrators carefully examine the location of the potential robbery, the potential gain, the capability of security personnel, the possibility of intervention by bystanders, and the presence of guards, cameras, and alarms.[11]

Criminologists have found that potential victims and establishments can do quite a bit to decrease the likelihood of being robbed. Following a series of convenience-store robberies in Gainesville, Florida, in 1985, a city ordinance required store owners to clear their windows of signs that obstructed the view of the interior, to position cash registers where they would be visible from the street, and to install approved electronic cameras. Within a little over a year, convenience-store robberies had decreased 64 percent.[12] We will return to this discussion later in this chapter.

Rational-Choice Perspective

The **rational-choice** perspective, developed by Ronald Clarke and Derek Cornish, draws from classical utilitarian notions of the calculations of pleasure and pain and from traditional economic choice theory.[13] According to this perspective, a "likely" offender decides to commit a specific crime (the "choice" aspect) in order to satisfy his or her needs. This goal-oriented or "purposive" behavior is marked by a rough calculation of the risks, efforts, and rewards of committing that particular offense (the "rational" element). Rational choice implies a limited sense of rationality. The "rational" offender may have only limited knowledge of the costs and benefits of engaging in a specific crime, or may not be completely able to accurately process information (e.g., the offender is under the influence of alcohol or drugs).

According to the rational-choice perspective, most crime is neither extraordinary nor the product of a deranged mind. Most crime is quite ordinary and committed by reasoning individuals who decide that the chances of getting caught are low and the possibilities for a relatively good payoff are high. Since the rational-choice perspective treats each crime as a specific event and focuses on analyzing all of its compo-

nents, it looks at crime in terms of an offender's decision to commit a *specific* offense at *a particular* time and place.

A variety of attributes or characteristics structure the likely offender's decision to commit the crime in question. These attributes are called *choice structuring properties*. With the emphasis of rational-choice theory on analyzing each crime on a crime-specific basis, each particular type of crime has its own set of choice structuring properties (Figure 8.2). Those for sexual assault differ from those for computer crime, and those for burglary differ from those for theft. Nevertheless, these properties tend to fall into the same seven categories. Thus, a potential thief, before committing a theft, is likely to consider the following aspects (categories):

- The number of targets and their accessibility
- Familiarity with the chosen method (for example, fraud by credit card)
- The monetary yield per crime
- The expertise needed
- The time required to commit the act

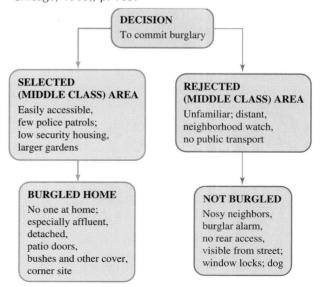

FIGURE 8.2 Event model (*example:* burglary in a middle-class suburb).
Source: Adapted from Ronald V. Clarke and Derek B. Cornish, "Modeling Offenders' Decisions: A Framework for Research and Policy," *Crime and Justice,* vol. 6, ed. Michael Tonry and Norval Morris (Chicago: University of Chicago, 1985), p. 169.

- The physical danger involved
- The risk of apprehension

Characteristics fall into two distinct sets: those of the offender and those of the offense. The offender's characteristics include specific needs, values, learning experiences, and so on. The characteristics of the offense include the location of the target and the potential yield. According to rational-choice theory, involvement in crime depends on a personal decision made after one has weighed available information.

Rational-choice theory, unlike traditional theories, is not concerned with strategies of overall crime prevention. (It leaves those problems to others.) Rather, it is concerned with reducing the likelihood that any given offense will be committed by somebody "involved" in criminal activity. This theory, therefore, has its greatest potential in developing strategies to frustrate perpetrators and to prevent them from committing a crime then and there. It has its greatest challenge in demonstrating that such prevention will not lead to the commission of the intended crime later on, or to the commission of other crimes (displacement). We turn to both of these issues shortly.

Routine-Activity Approach

According to Lawrence Cohen and Marcus Felson, a crime can occur only if there is someone who intends to commit a crime (likely offender), something or someone to be victimized (a suitable target), and no other person present to prevent or observe the crime (the absence of a capable guardian) (Figure 8.3).[14] This explanation is called the **routine-activity** approach. It does not explore the factors that influence the offender's decision to commit a crime. Instead, Cohen and Felson focus on the "routine" or

daily activities of people, such as going to work, pursuing recreation, running errands, and the like. It is through routine activities that offenders come into contact with suitable victims and targets.

The routine-activity approach began with an analysis of crime rate increases in the post-World War II era (1947 to 1974), when socioeconomic conditions had improved in America. The increase raised a puzzling question, since the general public (and some criminologists) expected crime rates to decrease with an increase in prosperity. But the authors of the routine-activity approach demonstrated that certain technological changes and alterations in the work force created new crime opportunities. They referred to increases in female participation in the labor force, out-of-town travel, automobile usage, and technological advances as factors that account for higher risks of predatory victimization. Further advances in technology create further opportunities for the commission of crime. For example, as television sets, VCRs, personal and laptop computers, and CD players have become more common and lighter to carry, they have become attractive targets for thieves and burglars. The chance that a piece of property will become the target of a theft is based on the value of the target and its weight.[15] One need only compare the theft of washing machines and of electronic goods. Although both washing machines and electronic goods (like television sets, laptop computers, and compact disc players) are expensive, washing machines are so heavy that their value is estimated at $4 per pound, compared with roughly $400 per pound for a laptop computer. And, of course, cellular phones have increasingly been subject to theft, for resale, for unauthorized telephone use, and for facilitating other crimes. Thus, cellular phones, as useful as they

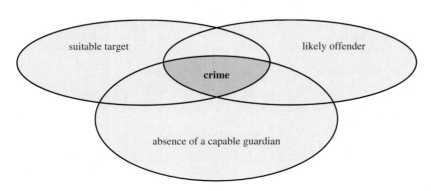

FIGURE 8.3 Components of a criminal event: The model of the routine-activity approach.

WINDOW TO THE WORLD

DECRESTING THE LOVEBUG, WORLDWIDE

It happened long before rational choice and routine activities had been created. Environmental design and situational crime prevention had yet to be invented. Yet there were Volkswagen beetles the world over.

By 1961 the Volkswagen Company had produced more than 4 million of these cars, fondly known as lovebugs, according to a popular movie of that time. Close to 1 million were being driven in America, and the rest all over the world. On their hoods, these cars had the distinctive crest of the town of their manufacture: Wolfsburg.

It so happens that soon after the beetles reached the American market they lost their crests. Research conducted in 1961 established that 80 percent of the beetles in the United States had been decrested. The question naturally arose: Who did it (and why)? Police statistics were useless, since VW owners did not feel inclined to report a loss amounting to a little over $3, even though some cars had body damage (the result of removal) many times that amount. Nor did VW owners report the loss to their insurance companies—the value being below the deductible.

The researchers got the help of industry. VW of America made available its sales figures for replacement crests. These figures, statistically analyzed, showed an amazing pattern: The crest thefts started in the east and traveled west within a little over 2 years. The thefts also traveled from the outer perimeters of cities to the suburbs (in less time).

Research established that decrestings were highest in the neighborhood of junior high schools. In collaboration with junior high school administrators and police officials, it was learned that many students had

amassed quantities of VW crests (but not those of other motor vehicles). Some were wearing them as necklaces; others had presented them to girlfriends.

Further statistical analysis showed that the fad—for that is what it seemed to be—had spread all over the world—except Brazil. It turned out that VW beetles manufactured in Brazil were not adorned with the

Wolfsburg crest, but the totally different crest of São Paolo, which apparently was not attractive to pubescent males.

A copy of the research report was sent to the VW company. Now everybody knows how reluctant VW was to change its lovebug. But it did: Within a few months the beetles rolled off VW's assembly line without the crest, but with a slightly

WINDOW TO THE WORLD *(continued)*

longer chrome strip. Problem solved, no more decrestings, no more body damage to the hood.

Source
Gerhard O. W. Mueller, *Delinquency and Puberty: Examination of a Juvenile Delinquency Fad* (New

York: Criminal Law Education and Research Center, 1971; Fred B. Rothman & Co., Distr.).

Questions for Discussion
1. Which of the theories discussed in this chapter best explains the decresting of VW beetles?

2. What can and should manufacturers of any product do at the design stage to prevent their product from becoming the targets (or instruments) of crime?

are in helping potential crime victims in feeling more secure, are also used increasingly by drug dealers, who use them to reduce the risk of their calls being traced.[16] It may be concluded that technological developments help society run more smoothly, but they also create new targets for theft, make old targets more suitable, or create new tools for criminals to use in committing their crimes. As people's daily work and leisure activities change with time, the location of property and personal targets also changes.

The logic of the routine-activity argument is straightforward: Routine patterns of work, play, and leisure time affect the convergence in time and place of motivated offenders, suitable targets, and the absence of guardians. If one component is missing, crime is not likely to be committed. And if all components are in place and one of them is strengthened,

crime is likely to increase. Even if the proportions of motivated offenders and targets stay the same, changes in routine activities alone—for example, changes of the sort we have experienced since World War II—will raise the crime rate by multiplying the opportunities for crime. This approach has helped explain, among other things, rates of victimization for specific crimes, rates of urban homicide, and "hot spots"—areas that produce a disproportionate number of calls to police.[17]

THEORIES OF VICTIMIZATION

Although the victim is mentioned in both theories of crime and theories of criminality, direct consideration of the role that victims play in the criminal event has been of secondary significance. As a result of the

New York City police brass in the commissioner's "war room" at One Police Plaza, where crime incidents are mapped and traced and then reviewed in high-level meetings like this one to develop intervention strategies.

"missing victim" in basic criminology, theories of victimization have recently been developed for the purpose of understanding crime from the victim's perspective, or with the victim in mind.

The history of victims in criminology can be traced to Hans von Hentig's first article on the subject of victims, in 1941, in which he postulated that crime was an "interaction of perpetrator and victim."[18] Von Hentig, a highly respected scientist, had been a victim of Nazi persecution. It was that experience that made him focus on the significance of the victim. By carefully gathering and analyzing information, he demonstrated that tourist resorts were attractive to criminals who wanted to prey on unsuspecting vacationers. Von Hentig, through his book *The Criminal and His Victim*, published in 1948, founded the criminological subdiscipline of victimology, which examines the role played by the victim in a criminal incident.[19] Nevertheless, it must be acknowledged that the term "victimology" is a year older than von Hentig's book. The term was coined in 1947 by the Romanian lawyer Beniamin Mendelsohn, in a lecture before the Romanian Psychiatric Association in Bucharest, entitled "New Bio-Psycho-Social Horizons: Victimology."[20] In 1948, Frederic Wertham, an American psychiatrist, first used the term "victimology" in America.[21]

According to Canadian criminologist Ezzat Fattah, "von Hentig insisted that many crime victims contribute to their own victimization be it by inciting or provoking the criminal or by creating or fostering a situation likely to lead to the commission of the crime."[22] Thus, the entire event is regarded as crucial, because criminal behavior involves both the action of the offender and interaction between offender and victim. Nor is it tenable to regard "criminals and victims . . . as different as night and day," because there is an undeniable link between offending and victimization.[23] Many offenders are victimized repeatedly, and victims are frequently offenders.

Such findings may be deemed highly controversial in a time when victims' rights groups have been active, and successful, in securing rights for victims of crimes. It must be understood, however, that *guilt* is not shared by offender and victim. Criminal guilt belongs to the perpetrator of a crime—and it must be proved at trial beyond a reasonable doubt. The victim is free of guilt. Victimology, however, can demonstrate how potential victims, by acting differently, can decrease the risk of being victimized.[24]

We turn now to a discussion of the dominant victimological theories.

Lifestyle Theories

A *lifestyle theory of victimization* was developed by Michael Hindelang, Michael Gottfredson, and James Garofalo in 1978. It posits that because of changing roles (working mother versus homemaker) and schedules (a child's school calendar), people lead different lifestyles (work and leisure activities). These differences are related to differences in the number of situations that have high victimization risks.[25] The kinds of people someone associates with, such as coworkers, friends, and sexual partners, also affect victimization rates. For instance, if someone has a drug dealer or an insider trader as a friend, the chances of that person being victimized are higher than if he or she associates only with law-abiding people. (The similarity of the lifestyle theory of victimization and the routine-activities approach is quite apparent.)

The lifestyle theory of victimization centers on a number of specific propositions that outline the essence of the theory and signal directions for future research[26]:

Proposition 1:
   The probability of suffering a personal victimization is directly related to the amount of time that a person spends in public places (e.g., on the street, in parks, etc.), and particularly in public places at night.

Proposition 2:
   The probability of being in public places, particularly at night, varies as a function of lifestyle.

Proposition 3:
   Social contacts and interactions occur disproportionately among individuals who share similar lifestyles.

Proposition 4:
   An individual's chances of personal victimization are dependent upon the extent to which the individual shares demographic characteristics with offenders [such as young urban males].

Proposition 5:
   The proportion of time that an individual spends among nonfamily members varies as a function of lifestyle.

Proposition 6:
   The probability of personal victimization, particularly personal theft, increases as a function of the proportion

of the time that an individual spends among nonfamily members [such as a young man who works a double shift at a factory versus a middle-aged woman who stays home to take care of an elderly parent].

Proposition 7:
Variations in lifestyle are associated with variations in the ability of individuals to isolate themselves from persons with offender characteristics [being able to leave high-crime urban areas for sheltered suburbs].

Proposition 8:
Variations in lifestyle are associated with variations in the convenience, the desirability, and vincibility of the person as a target for a personal victimization [people who pass within the view of offenders, seem to have what the offender wants, appear unable to resist, or would probably not report the crime to the police].

Both the lifestyle theory of victimization and the routine-activity approach present some basic guidelines for reducing one's chances of victimization. And just as these theories themselves tend to embody common sense, so do the preventive measures derived from them. For instance, people in American society are told not to drive while intoxicated, not to smoke or abuse alcohol or drugs, and not to eat too much greasy food. All these messages are intended to reduce the risks of dying in a motor vehicle accident, or from lung or liver cancer, or from an overdose, or from a heart attack. Although public-service messages designed to protect health may not always be heeded, people do not see them as "blaming the victim." Similarly, messages to prevent criminal victimization, like not walking alone and not frequenting deserted or unfamiliar places late at night, should not be viewed as overly restrictive and intrusive, or as blaming victims who did not heed the advice. The messages directed at preventing victimization are based on theory and research and merely promote living and acting responsibly to ensure a more crime-free existence.

Repeat Victimization

Not unlike the lifestyle theory of victimization, theories of repeat victimization also focus on the specific characteristics of situations in order to determine which factors account for the initial, as well as for repeat, victimization.[27] Theories of repeat victimization, also called multiple victimization, dispel the myth that crime is uniformly distributed. Research

shows that a small number of people and places account for a large amount of the crimes committed. For example, an analysis of the British Crime Survey (a victimization survey) from 1982 to 1992 found that between 24 and 38 percent of all victims of property and personal crime experienced five or more such offenses in a little over a year.[28]

The research literature on repeat victimization is increasing rapidly. A recent study of police calls for service from 34 fast-food restaurants in San Antonio, Texas, from 1990 to 1992 found that fast-food restaurants had the greatest chance of repeat police calls for service within one week of the last call. Thereafter, the number of calls decreases as the time between calls increases.[29] Similar findings have been made in research on the repeat risks of burglary.[30] Risks of a repeat burglary are highest immediately after a previous burglary. In their analysis of repeat victimization for crimes ranging from the repeated physical and sexual abuse of children to repeated credit card fraud, researchers concluded that the rational-choice theory of offender decision making is useful in understanding repeat victimization. Offenders choose targets based on the knowledge they gained in the previous victimization about the risks and rewards of a particular offense.[31]

Formulating strategies to deal with repeat victimizations would certainly be cost-beneficial. Resources could be concentrated on relatively few targets. Unhappily, police recording systems are not designed to keep track of repeat victimizations. To overcome this problem, several innovative researchers have created their own databases, starting a whole new line of research, called *hot-spots* research.

Hot Spots of Crime

In 1989, Lawrence Sherman, Patrick Gartin, and Michael Buerger published the results of a study that immediately excited the profession. They had analyzed 911 calls for police assistance in Minneapolis, Minnesota, for the period December 15, 1985, to December 15, 1986. After plotting the more than 320,000 calls on a map, they discovered that 3 percent of the addresses and intersections in the city were the subject of 50 percent of the calls received.[32]

They also found that certain types of crime were committed in specific places—for example, all auto thefts at 2 percent of all places. The researchers conclude that attempts to prevent victimization should be focused not on victims, but rather on the places themselves by making them less vulnerable to crime. Change places, not people! We should identify neighborhood hot spots, reduce social disorder and physical "incivilities," and promote housing-based neighborhood stabilization.[33]

Geography of Crime

Recently new research based on the idea of hot spots has come into existence. It is labeled "geography of crime." Researchers found that more crime occurs around high schools[34] and blocks with bars,[35] liquor stores,[36] the city center,[37] and abandoned buildings.[38] Higher crime in areas that border high schools and bars is readily explainable: High schools contain a highly crime-prone age group. Bars attract, among others, offenders.[39] Abandoned buildings that are open and unsecured attract illegal users. In city centers there are more opportunities to commit crime and generally fewer social controls in place.

A study on the vulnerability of ports and marinas to vessel and equipment theft found that the proximity of a port or marina to a high-crime area is significant in predicting boat theft.[40] Research on drug markets in Jersey City, New Jersey, shows that areas with illicit drug markets account for a disproportionate amount of arrests and calls for police service.[41] In sum, the discovery that a large amount of crime occurs at a small number of places, and that such places have distinct characteristics, has led criminologists to explain crime in terms of not only who commits it, but also where it is committed.[42]

Interrelatedness of Theories

Environmental criminology, the rational-choice perspective, and the routine-activity approach focus on the interaction between the victim (or target), the offender, and the place. Recently there has been an integration of these theories of crime with theories of victimization.[43] For example, one study using the lifestyle theory of victimization and the routine-activity approach explores how drinking routines are linked with victimization.[44] It found that alcohol contributed to victimization by making potential victims less able to protect themselves (more suitable targets). Motivated offenders also knew where to find their targets (in bars). Although the evidence on the relationship between alcohol, lifestyle, and increased risks of victimization is not conclusive, this research represents an important attempt at testing the interaction of lifestyle and routine-activity theories.

A further study on the relationship of alcohol and risks of victimization focuses specifically on the "suitable target" portion of routine-activity theory as it relates to sexual assault against women on college campuses.[45] It found that women who were sexually victimized went out more often and drank more when they were out than other women. Moreover, many of the women surveyed had experienced "uncomfortable advances in a bar or restaurant" or "on the street" or had "received obscene or threatening phone calls." In sum, by successfully combining theories of crime, like routine-activity theory, with lifestyle theory, situational factors (e.g., alcohol), and place considerations (e.g., bars and college settings) to examine victimization rates, criminological research has added a new dimension to explaining crime.[46]

PREVENTING CRIMES AGAINST PLACES, PEOPLE, AND VALUABLE GOODS

Situational crime prevention seeks to protect places, people, and valuable goods from victimization. It is rooted in the 1971 work of C. Ray Jeffery's "crime prevention through environmental design" (CPTED)[47] and in Oscar Newman's concept of "defensible space."[48] CPTED posits that environments can be altered, often at little expense, so as to decrease victimizations. *Defensible space* refers to improved architectural designs, particularly of public housing, in order to provide increased security. Design can enhance surveillance, reduce offenders' escape possibilities, and give residents a feeling of ownership that encourages them to protect their own space.[49] CPTED and defensible space have converged with rational choice and routine activity to form a new approach called *situational crime prevention*.

Situational Crime Prevention

Rational-choice theory provides the foundation for designing situational-crime-prevention techniques and their classification (Table 8.1). Situational crime prevention consists of the knowledge of how, where,

CRIMINOLOGICAL FOCUS

DEFENSIVE SPACE: BUMPS, BARRIERS, AND BARRICADES

Architect Oscar Newman, renowned for his 1972 book *Defensible Space,* jumped at the opportunity to rescue the Five Oaks neighborhood in Dayton, Ohio, from rising crime rates and the prospects of becoming a ghetto. After the residents of Five Oaks decided to apply his crime-prevention strategies to the entire community and not just the worst areas, streets were closed, and barriers and speed bumps were erected. Crime rates dropped. The barriers and street closures reduced community traffic by 67 percent. Total crimes went down 26 percent, and violent crimes, 50 percent. Ray Reynolds, Dayton's urban-development chief, expected crime to rise elsewhere (displacement); no such increase occurred. Oscar Newman then directed his attention to "work the same magic in Seattle and elsewhere, [although] all concerned concede that Dayton has found no panacea, that it has merely demonstrated that a determined and energized community with

some good ideas can make a dent in crime."(1)

Evidence that "defensible space" works to prevent crime can be found throughout the criminological literature. Research on the interrelationship between traffic flow and crime has demonstrated that property crime is high near streets that are easily accessible and frequently traveled, as contrasted with quiet, out-of-the-way streets. When offenders pursue their own daily activities—on the way to work or recreation—they, too, travel on accessible through streets, where they note potential targets. Criminologists also have determined that outsider-perpetrators favor through streets which permit an easy escape. The most obvious solution is to alter the flow of traffic by creating road barriers and cul-de-sacs.(2)

A recent evaluation of the impact of street closures and barricades on crime in the city of Miami Shores indicates that burglaries, larcenies, and auto thefts decreased in Miami Shores from the 1986–1987 period to the 1991–1992 period. The rates

of robberies and aggravated assault did not change during those years.(3)

In the north of London, street closures served to transform a notorious red-light district "into a tranquil residential area in less than two years."(4) Tranquil and low-crime neighborhoods have been similarly created through defensible space techniques in Atlanta, Georgia, and Richmond, Virginia.(5)

The question remains whether the bumps, barriers, and barricades themselves have cut down on unwelcome visits from would-be offenders, or whether the redesigned communities have created a real sense of community with a spirit of mutual protection. Obviously, while these successful experiments demonstrate the value of techniques in changing or altering street networks in urban and suburban settings, more research is needed to arrive at more universally applicable strategies.

Sources
1. Ellis Cose, "Drawing Up Safer Cities. Design: How a Communi-

---

and when to implement a specific measure that will alter a particular situation in order to prevent a crime from occurring. The routine-activity approach also aims at situational crime prevention by reducing the opportunities for likely offenders to commit crimes. Techniques include protecting suitable targets (making them less suitable) and increasing the presence of capable guardians. Measures such as steering column locks, vandal-resistant construction, enhanced street lighting, and improved library checkout systems demonstrably decrease opportunities for crime. These are **target-hardening** techniques.

Rational-choice theorists have recently reviewed their situational-crime-prevention techniques. They have added aspects of the offender's *perception* of a crime opportunity to the catalog of relevant factors, as well as adding the element of guilt or shame (Table 8.2).[50] The addition of the category of "perception" of opportunity was self-evident. After all, offenders act

only in accordance with what they perceive. The addition of a category called "inducing guilt or shame," on the other hand, is a significant expansion of rational choice. It has been adopted from Sykes and Matza's "techniques of neutralization" (Chapter 7).[51] Such techniques include the installation of signs saying "shoplifting is stealing" or other measures calculated to prevent common crimes by increasing the personal and social cost in terms of shaming—especially after being caught in the act. For instance, if a high school student is leaving the school library with friends and the library checkout system detects a copy of *Rolling Stone* in his bookbag (a magazine that is not allowed to leave the library), two things are expected to happen. First, the librarian will make the student surrender the magazine. Second, the student may be so embarassed by having the librarian search his bookbag while his friends stand by that he will not try to steal anything from the library again.

CRIMINOLOGICAL FOCUS

ty Divided Conquers Crime,"
Newsweek, July 11, 1994, p. 57.
2. Daniel J. K. Beavon, P. L. Brantingham, and P. J. Brantingham, "The Influence of Street Networks on the Patterning of Property Offenses, in *Crime Prevention Studies,* vol. 2, ed. Ronald V. Clarke (Monsey, N.Y.: Criminal Justice Press, 1994), pp. 115–148.
3. Randall Atlas and William G. LeBlanc, "The Impact on Crime of Street Closures and Barricades: A Florida Case Study," *Security Journal,* **5** (1994): 140–145.
4. Roger Matthews, "Developing More Effective Strategies for Curbing Prostitution," *Security Journal,* **1** (1990): 182–187.
5. Ralph B. Taylor and Adele V. Harrell, *Physical Environment and Crime,* for National Institute of Justice (Washington, D.C.: U.S. Government Printing Office, 1996).

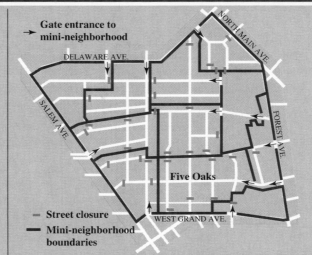

Source: Ellis Cose, "Drawing Up Safer Cities. Design: How a Community Divided Conquers Crime," *Newsweek,* July 11, 1994, p. 57.

Questions for Discussion
1. If street closures and barricades lead to lower crime rates in a community, is it because the barriers have restricted access to criminals and outsiders or because they have restored a sense of community to the residents?

2. Is it fair to provide for street closures and barriers only in high-income and middle-class neighborhoods? What about high-crime ghetto neighborhoods?

There are a number of successful examples of situational crime prevention. For example, situational-crime-prevention techniques have been successfully implemented to prevent crime at Disney World, to stop auto theft, to deter robberies at convenience stores, and to lessen crime in parking facilities.

The Phantom Crime Prevention at Disney World. Disney World, home of Donald Duck, Mickey and Minnie Mouse, Goofy, and their friends, provides us with an example of environmental/situational crime prevention. Illegal behavior is successfully controlled, yet in an environment that does not have the sterile, fortress-like appearance so often associated with security. How has this been accomplished?[52]

The intricate web of security and crowd control (not visible to the untrained eye) starts at the parking lot with advice to lock your car and remember that you have parked at a particular lot, for example,

"Donald Duck 1." With friendly greetings of "have a good time," watchful eyes surround visitors on the rubber-wheeled train into never-never land. Crowd control is omnipresent, yet unobtrusive. Signs guide you through the maze of monorails, rides, and attractions. Physical barriers prevent injury and regulate the movement of adults and children alike. Mickey Mouse and Goofy monitor movements. Flower gardens, pools, and fountains are pretty to look at; they also direct people toward particular locations. Yet with all these built-in control strategies, few visitors realize the extent to which their choices of movement and action are limited.

Situational Prevention: Auto Theft. Let us return to the car theft scenario at the beginning of this chapter to illustrate how action research works in the case of car theft.[53] First, the Paramus Police Department collected information on the specific

TABLE 8.1   Sixteen Techniques of Situational Prevention

Increasing Perceived Effort	Increasing Perceived Risks	Reducing Anticipated Rewards	Inducing Guilt or Shame

1. *Target hardening:*
    Slug rejector device
    Steering locks
    Bandit screens
	5. *Entry/exit screening:*
	    Automatic ticket gates
	    Baggage screening
	    Merchandise tags
		9. *Target removal:*
		    Removable car radio
		    Women's refuges
		    Phonecard
			13. *Rule setting:*
			    Harassment codes
			    Customs declaration
			    Hotel registrations

2. *Access control:*
    Parking lot barriers
    Fenced yards
    Entry phones
	6. *Formal surveillance:*
	    Burglar alarms
	    Speed cameras
	    Security guards
		10. *Identifying property:*
		    Property marking
		    Vehicle licensing
		    Cattle branding
			14. *Strengthening moral condemnation:*
			    "Shoplifting is stealing"
			    Roadside speedo-meters
			    "Bloody-idiots drink and drive"

3. *Deflecting offenders:*
    Bus stop placement
    Tavern location
    Street closures
	7. *Surveillance by employees:*
	    Pay phone location
	    Park attendants
	    CCTV systems
		11. *Reducing temptation:*
		    Gender-neutral phone lists
		    Off-street parking	

4. *Controlling facilitators:*
    Credit card photo
    Caller-ID
    Gun controls
	8. *Natural surveillance:*
	    Defensible space
	    Street lighting
	    Cab driver ID
		12. *Denying benefits:*
		    Ink merchandise tags
		    PIN for car radios
		    Graffiti cleaning
			15. *Controlling disin-hibitors:*
			    Drinking age laws
			    Ignition interlock
			    Server intervention

			16. *Facilitating compli-ance:*
			    Improved library checkout
			    Public lavatories
			    Trash bins

Source: Ronald V. Clarke and Ross Homel, "A Revised Classification of Situational Crime Prevention Techniques," in *Crime Prevention at a Crossroads,* ed. Steven P. Lab (Cincinnati, Ohio: Anderson, in press).

TABLE 8.2   Ten Factors Considered by Commercial Burglars in Suburban Philadelphia

1. *Revenues generated by burglary:*
    Is there a high "pay-off"?
	5. *Shopping mall:*
	    Is the target in a mall?
	    Malls and large retail stores are ideal targets
		8. *Exterior lighting:*
		    How dark is the area around the target?

2. *Chances of being caught:*
    Can I get away with it?
	6. *Concentration of businesses:*
	    Are there other businesses around? The more commercial establishments around, the greater the likelihood of burglary.
		9. *Length of time the establishment has been in business:*
		    Is this a new store?
		    New commercial establishments are prime targets

3. *Location of target:*
    Is the target near a major road or thoroughfare? Commercial burglars like remote targets.
	7. *Burglar alarm:*
	    Is there a visible alarm or alarm sign?
		10. *Retail store:*
		    Is the target retail?
		    Retail is perferred over wholesale.

4. *Corner lot:* Is the target at the corner? Corner properties are easier to get into and out of.		

Source: Simon Hakim and Yochanan Shachmurove, "Spatial and Temporal Patterns of Commercial Burglaries: The Evidence Examined," *American Journal of Economics and Sociology,* 1996, **55,** pp. 443–456.

Even Goofy is part of the Disney crime prevention and control strategy, making Disneyland and Disney World some of the safest locations in America.

models and makes of the cars stolen, as well as the particular locations of the thefts. The Toyota Land Cruiser, Toyota 4Runner, and Mitsubishi Montero were the sport-utility vehicles preferred by the thieves, while any Honda and the Toyota Camry were the favored cars. Second, information provided by the Highway Loss Data Institute (see Table 8.3) indicated that some of these makes and models are the most targeted vehicles for theft not only in malls in Bergen County, New Jersey, but throughout the nation.

With this information, situational-crime-prevention practitioners analyze the vehicles and the specific situational factors that lead to their being targeted for theft. They then devise measures to block the oppor-

tunities that give rise to the theft of these particular vehicles, e.g., side window panels that are particularly vulnerable, or key codes in the gas tank compartment (the thief simply writes down the key code and gets a replacement of the "lost" car key).[54]

Devising situational prevention measures, however, is usually not as easy as suggesting to a car manufacturer that the key code be placed in a more secure place. It is important that a researcher also analyze the type of offenders who are stealing specific types of cars (Table 8.4).

Convenience Stores.   One of the most successful crime-prevention studies was the Tallahassee Con-

TABLE 8.3   Theft Losses of 1992–1994 Model Utility Vehicles and Two-Door Cars, based on an average rate of 100

Utility Vehicle	Theft Rate	Two-Door Car	Theft Rate
Toyota Land Cruiser	1729	Honda Prelude	318
GMC T15Jimmy 2-door 4×4	1023	Honda Civic Coupe	139*
Toyota 4Runner 4-door 4×4	498[†]	Honda Accord	111
Ford Explorer 2-door 4×4	60	Mercury Topaz	24
Ford Explorer 4-door	74	Mazda 323	34
Suzuki Sidekick 4-door 4×4	83	Toyota Tercel	37

*Although the Honda Civic Coupe has a high theft rate of 139, the Pontiac Sunbird convertible and the Chrysler LeBaron convertible ranked higher, with theft rates of 159 and 145, respectively.

[†]Similarly, the Nissan Pathfinder 4-door 4×4 and the Chevrolet T10 Blazer 2-door 4×4 both ranked higher than the Toyota 4Runner 4-door 4×4, with theft rates of 602 and 583, respectively.

Source: Highway Loss Data Institute, *Injury Collision and Theft Losses by Make and Model* (Arlington, Va.: Highway Loss Data Institute, 1995).

TABLE 8.4   Typologies of Frequent Auto Theft Offenders

Acting-out joyrider:
- Most emotionally disturbed of the offenders—derives status from having his peers think he is crazy and unpredictable
- Engages in outrageous driving stunts—dangerous to pursue—possesses a kamikaze attitude
- Vents anger via car—responsible for large proportion of the totaled and burned cars
- Least likely to be deterred—doesn't care what happens

Thrill-seeker:
- Heavily into drugs—doing crime is a way to finance the habit—entices others to feel the "rush" of doing crime
- Engages in car stunts and willful damage to cars, but also steals them for transportation and to use in other crimes
- Steals parts for sale in a loosely structured friendship network
- Thrill-seeking behavior likely to be transferred to other activities and might be directed to legitimate outlets

Instrumental offender:
- Doing auto theft for the money—most active of the offenders (5 or more cars a week) but the smallest proportion of the sample—connected to organized theft operations
- Rational, intelligent—does crimes with least risk—may get into auto theft from burglary—thinks about outcomes
- Doing crime while young offender status affords them lenient treatment—indicate that they will quit crime at age eighteen

Source: Zachary Fleming, Patricia Brantingham, and Paul Brantingham, "Exploring Auto Theft in British Columbia," in *Crime Prevention Studies,* vol. 3, ed. Ronald V. Clarke (Monsey, N.Y.: Criminal Justice Press, 1994), p. 62.

THE FAR SIDE   By GARY LARSON

Inconvenience stores

venience Store Study. In fact, it launched CPTED. It had long been known that convenience stores, like the 7-Eleven shops, had been prime robbery targets. Researchers studied the vulnerability of these stores in great detail, assessing risks as well as losses, in terms of lives and property. The researchers recommended that stores have two or more clerks on duty, post "limited cash" signs, increase exterior lighting, and restrict escape routes and potential hiding places for robbers. The study led to the passage of the Florida Convenience Store Security Act (1990), which made certain security measures mandatory.[55] Convenience store robberies in Florida have dropped by two-thirds.

Parking Facilities.[56]   Parking garages are said to be dangerous places: Individuals are alone in a large space, there are many hiding places, the amount of valuable property (cars and their contents) is high, they are open to the public, an offender's car can go unnoticed, and lighting is usually poor. Yet statistics indicate that because of the small amount of time and the relatively limited number of trips that each person takes to and from parking facilities, an individual's chances of being raped, robbed, or assaulted in a parking facility are very low. Nevertheless, the fear of victimization in these facilities is high. Efforts to

AT ISSUE

WHY WAIT FOR A MILLION-DOLLAR CIVIL LIABILITY SUIT WHEN YOU CAN HAVE CPTED FOR PEANUTS?

The store, part of a small chain, was located in a quasi-residential area next to a park near a two-lane highway. The cashier station was located in the rear of the store, adjacent to a doorway that led to a rear storage room where there was a desk and a safe. Posters and advertisements covered the front windows, and the only outside lighting came from a street light across the road.

One night, two men recently released from a state prison held up the store. After forcing the cashier into the rear storage room and making her open the safe, they shot her. As the men were preparing to leave, two people entered the store: a female employee coming to work at the shift change and a young man coming in to make a purchase while his date and another couple waited in the car outside. Seeing the two people enter, the gunman concealed his weapon behind his back and announced that the store was closed. "It can't be," the employee replied. "I work here!" With that, the man revealed his gun, forced the woman and the young man to the rear of the store, and shot them. Both died.

Although the families of the two murdered employees could not sue the employer under workman's compensation laws, the father of the slain young man sued the store, charging that the store failed to provide adequate security:

- The cashier should not have been alone in such an isolated store.
- The counter was located in the rear of the store, which made it difficult for anyone outside to see what was happening within.
- The posters on the windows further isolated the cashier.

- There was no drop safe, which would have removed the incentive for the robbery.
- The second cashier's failure to recognize the threat when she was told by the gunman that the store was closed indicated a failure on the part of store owners to provide proper security training.

Several of these factors involved environmental design: the lighting, the posters, and the location of the cash register. In an interview, which was used as a basis for expert testimony, one of the perpetrators reported that he canvassed the area looking for the "right store" and that he had rejected several because they were brightly lit, the cashier's station was toward the front of the store, and there were no posters to interfere with the view from the parking lot.

This case did not go to trial; it was settled for a substantial sum after expert testimony was submitted. Its usefulness as an example lies in the fact that the criminals acknowledged the importance of environmental design in deciding to strike at this particular store.(1)

Under English common law "landowners had no legal duty to prevent criminal assaults on visitors to their property, and no legal liability could befall them."(2) Tort law, in most jurisdictions in the United States, employs a "totality of the circumstances" test. In deciding whether a civil liability case has merit, judges now examine such factors "as the nature of the business, its surrounding locale, the lack of customary security precautions as an invitation to crime, and the experience of the particular landowner at other locations."(3) The risks of civil liability are high. When life is lost, millions of dollars may be at stake. This is where CPTED comes in. In-

creasingly, criminologists are analyzing the links between crime-prevention measures according to CPTED factors, which can be instituted at low cost before a criminal event, and civil liability.

Research indicates that the chance of a lawsuit is positively related to two factors: (1) the classification of a place as high or low risk and (2) its financial resources. Investment in crime prevention is driven by the expected costs of a lawsuit. Unhappily, high-risk places that have little or no financial resources do not expect to be sued and therefore implement fewer crime-prevention measures. But many low-risk places that have more financial resources with which to compensate victims and/or to install crime-prevention or security measures are sued more often.(4)

When companies decide to pursue crime-prevention measures, considerations of a lawsuit might seem like a far-fetched idea with few real implications. But large damage awards have become a real threat to many American businesses. Businesses are well advised to consider the low-cost CPTED principles.

Sources

1. Corey L. Gordon and William Brill, "The Expanding Role of Crime Prevention through Environmental Design in Premises Liability," for National Institute of Justice (Washington, D.C.: U.S. Government Printing Office, 1996), p. 4.
2. Ibid., p. 1.
3. Ibid., p. 3.
4. John Eck, "Do Premise Liability Suits Promote Business Crime Prevention?" paper presented at the Business and Crime Prevention Conference, an International Seminar Sponsored by the National Institute of Justice and Rutgers,

improve conditions include better lighting, stairways and elevators that are open to the air or glass-enclosed, ticket-booth personnel monitoring drivers exiting and entering, color-coded signs designating parking areas, elimination or redesign of public restrooms, panic buttons and emergency phones, closed-circuit television, and uniformed security personnel.

Displacement

One important question concerning crime-prevention measures remains. What will happen, for example, if these measures do prevent a particular crime from being committed? Will the would-be offender simply look for another target? Crime-prevention strategists have demonstrated that **displacement**—the commission of a quantitatively similar crime at a different time or place—does not always follow. German motorcycle helmet legislation demonstrates the point. Due to a large number of accidents, legislation that required motorcyclists to wear helmets was passed and strictly enforced. It worked: Head injuries decreased. But there were additional, unforeseen consequences. Motorcycle theft rates decreased dramatically.[57] The risks of stealing a motorcycle became too high because a would-be offender could not drive it away without wearing a helmet. At this point researchers expected to see a rise in the numbers of cars or bikes stolen. They did not. In other words, there was very little displacement. Of course, some offenders will look for other crime opportunities, but many others will quit for some time, perhaps forever.

REVIEW

This chapter focuses on theories of crime. These theories, which assume that there are always people motivated to commit crime, try to explain why crimes

are being committed by a particular offender against a particular target. They analyze opportunities and environmental factors that prompt a potential perpetrator to act.

We discussed the three most prominent theories of crime: environmental criminology, the rational-choice perspective, and the routine-activity approach. We noted that they have merged somewhat, particularly insofar as all these theories aim at preventing victimization by altering external conditions that are conducive to crime.

Theories of victimization view crime as the dynamic interaction of perpetrators and victims (at a given time and place). Here too the aim is to find ways for potential victims to protect themselves. Research into lifestyles, repeat victimization, hot spots, and geography of crime has vast implications for crime control in entire cities or regions. Theories of crime and victimization are interrelated.

NOTES

1. Marlowe Churchill, "Jury Finds Man Guilty of One-Hour Sex Attack," *The Press-Enterprise,* July 26, 1996, B3.
2. "Suburban Digest," *The Denver Post,* Apr. 10, 1996, p. B-2.
3. Daniel Sforza, "Thieves Favor Giant Malls When Shopping for Cars," *The Record,* June 26, 1996, pp. A1, A20.
4. Michael Gottfredson and Travis Hirschi, "A Propensity-Event Theory of Crime," in *Advances in Criminological Theory,* vol. 1, ed. William S. Laufer and Freda Adler (New Brunswick, N.J.: Transaction, 1989), pp. 57–67.
5. Paul J. Brantingham and Patricia L. Brantingham, "Introduction: The Dimensions of Crime," in *Environmental Criminology,* ed. Brantingham and Brantingham (Prospect Heights, Ill.: Waveland, 1991), p. 8.
6. André M. Guerry, *Essai sur la Statistique Morale de la France* (Paris: Crochard, 1833).
7. Adolphe Quetelet, *A Treatise on Man* (Edinburgh: Chambers, 1842), reprinted excerpt Adolphe Quetelet, "Of the development of the propensity to crime," in *Criminological Perspectives: A Reader,* ed. John Muncie, Eugene McLaughlin, and Mary Langan (Thousand Oaks, Calif.: Sage, 1996), p. 19.

8. George Rengert and John Wasilchick, *Suburban Burglary: A Time and a Place for Everything* (Springfield, Ill.: Charles C Thomas, 1985).

9. Paul F. Cromwell, James N. Olson, and D'Aunn Webster Avary, *Breaking and Entering: An Ethnographic Analysis of Burglary* (Newbury Park, Calif.: Sage, 1991), pp. 45–46.

10. Richard T. Wright and Scott H. Decker, *Burglars on the Job: Streetlife and Residential Break-Ins* (Boston: Northeastern University Press, 1994), pp. 63–68.

11. Philip J. Cook, *Robbery in the United States: An Analysis of Recent Trends and Patterns*, U.S. Department of Justice (Washington, D.C.: U.S. Government Printing Office, 1983).

12. Wayland Clifton, Jr., *Convenience Store Robbery in Gainesville, Florida* (Gainesville, Fla.: Gainesville Police Department, 1987), p. 15.

13. Ronald Clarke and Derek Cornish, "Modeling Offenders' Decisions: A Framework for Research and Policy," in *Crime and Justice*, vol. 6, ed. Michael Tonry and Norval Morris (Chicago: University of Chicago Press, 1985), pp. 147–185; Derek B. Cornish and Ronald V. Clarke, eds., *The Reasoning Criminal* (New York: Springer Verlag, 1986); Jeremy Bentham, *On the Principles and Morals of Legislation* (New York: Kegan Paul, 1789) [reprinted 1948]; Gary S. Becker, "Crime and Punishment: An Economic Approach," *Journal of Political Economy*, **76** (1968): 169–217.

14. Lawrence E. Cohen and Marcus Felson, "Social Change and Crime Rate Trends: A Routine Activity Approach," *American Sociological Review*, **44** (1979): 588–608.

15. Marcus Felson, *Crime and Everyday Life: Insights and Implications for Society* (Thousand Oaks, Calif.: Pine Forge Press, 1994), pp. 20–21, 35.

16. Mangai Natarajan, "Telephones as Facilitators of Drug Dealing," paper presented at the Fourth International Seminar on Environmental Criminology and Crime Analysis, July 1995, Cambridge, England.

17. Lawrence W. Sherman, Patrick R. Gartin, and Michael E. Buerger, "Hot Spots of Predatory Crime: Routine Activities and the Criminology of Place," *Criminology*, **27** (1989): 27–55; Ronald V. Clarke and Patricia M. Harris, "A Rational Choice Perspective on the Targets of Automobile Theft," *Criminal Behaviour and Mental Health*, **2** (1992): 25–42. See also the following articles in Ronald V. Clarke and Marcus Felson, eds., *Routine Activity and Rational Choice, Advances in Criminological Theory*, vol. 5 (New Brunswick, N.J.: Transaction, 1993); Raymond Paternoster and Sally Simpson, "A Rational Choice Theory of Corporate Crime," pp. 37–58; Richard W. Harding, "Gun Use in Crime, Rational Choice, and Social Learning Theory," pp. 85–102; Richard B. Felson, "Predatory and Dispute-Related Violence: A Social Interactionist Approach," pp. 103–125; Nathaniel J. Pallone and James J. Hennessy, "Tinderbox Criminal Violence: Neurogenic Impulsivity, Risk-Taking, and the Phenomenology of Rational Choice," pp. 127–157; Max Taylor, "Rational Choice, Behavior Analysis, and Political Violence," pp. 159–178; Pietro Marongiu and Ronald V. Clarke, "Ransom Kidnapping in Sardinia, Subcultural Theory and Rational Choice," pp. 179–199; Bruce D. Johnson, Mangai Natarajan, and Harry Sanabria, "'Successful' Criminal Careers: Toward an Ethnography within the Rational Choice Perspective," pp. 201–221.

18. Hans von Hentig, "Remarks on the Interaction of Perpetrator and Victim," *Journal of Criminal Law and Criminology*, **31** (1941): 303–309.

19. Hans von Hentig, *The Criminal and His Victim* (New Haven, Conn.: Yale University, 1948).

20. See Beniamin Mendelsohn, "The Origin of the Doctrine of Victimology," in *Victimology*, ed. Israel Drapkin and Emilio Viano (Lexington, Mass.: Lexington Books, 1974), pp. 3–4.

21. Frederic Wertham, *The Show of Violence* (Garden City, N.Y.: The Country Life Press, 1948), p. 259.

22. Ezzat A. Fattah, "Victims and Victimology: The Facts and the Rhetoric," *International Review of Victimology*, **1** (1989): 44–66, at p. 44.

23. Ezzat A. Fattah, "The Rational Choice/Opportunity Perspective as a Vehicle for Integrating Criminological and Victimological Theories," in Clarke and Felson, *Routine Activity and Rational Choice*, pp. 230–231.

24. Fattah, "Victims and Victimology: The Facts and the Rhetoric," p. 54.

25. Michael J. Hindelang, Michael R. Gottfredson, and James Garofalo, *Victims of Personal Crime: An Empirical Foundation for a Theory of Personal Victimization* (Cambridge, Mass.: Ballinger Publishing Company, 1978), p. 245.

26. Hindelang, Gottfredson, and Garofalo, *Victims of Personal Crime*, pp. 251–265.

27. Alan Trickett, Dan Ellingworth, Tim Hope, and Ken Pease, "Crime Victimization in the Eighties: Changes in Area and Regional Inequality," *British Journal of Criminology*, **35** (1995): 343–359; Graham Farrell, "Preventing Repeat Victimization," in Michael Tonry and David P. Farrington, *Building a Safer Society: Strategic Approaches to Crime Prevention, Crime and Justice*, vol. 19 (Chicago: University of Chicago Press, 1995), pp. 469–534.

28. Dan Ellingworth, Graham Farrell, and Ken Pease, "A Victim Is a Victim Is a Victim? Chronic Victimization in Four Sweeps of the British Crime Survey," *British Journal of Criminology*, **35** (1995): 360–365.

29. William Spellman, "Once Bitten, Then What? Cross-Sectional and Time-Course Explanations of Repeat Victimization," *British Journal of Criminology*, **35** (1995): 366–383.

30. Natalie Polvi, Terah Looman, Charlie Humphries, and Ken Pease, "The Time-Course of Repeat Burglary Victimization," *British Journal of Criminology*, **31** (1991): 411–414.

31. Graham Farrell, Coretta Phillips, and Ken Pease, "Like Taking Candy: Why Does Repeat Victimization Occur?" *British Journal of Criminology*, **35** (1995): 384–399.

32. Lawrence W. Sherman, Patrick R. Gartin, and Michael E. Buerger, "Hot Spots of Predatory Crime: Routine Activities and the Criminology of Place," *Criminology*, **27** (1989): 27–55.

33. Robert J. Sampson, "The Community," in *Crime*, ed. James Q. Wilson and Joan Petersilia (San Francisco: ICS Press, 1995), pp. 193–216.

34. Dennis W. Roncek and Donald Faggiani, "High Schools and Crime: A Replication," *Sociological Quarterly*, **26** (1985): 491–505.

35. Dennis W. Roncek and Pamela A. Maier, "Bars, Blocks, and Crimes Revisited: Linking the Theory of Routine Activities to the Empiricism of 'Hot Spots,'" *Criminology*, **29** (1991): 725–753.

36. Richard L. Block and Carolyn R. Block, "Space, Place and Crime: Hot Spot Areas and Hot Places of Liquor-Related Crime," in *Crime and Place: Crime Prevention Studies,* vol. 4, ed. John E. Eck and David Weisburd (Monsey, N.Y.: Criminal Justice Press; Washington, D.C.: The Police Executive Research Forum, 1995), pp. 145–183.

37. Per-Olof Wikström, "Preventing City-Center Street Crimes," in Tonry and Farrington, *Building a Safer Society,* vol. 19, pp. 429–468.

38. William Spellman, "Abandoned Buildings: Magnets for Crime?" *Journal of Criminal Justice,* **21** (1993): 481–495.

39. Dennis W. Roncek and Ralph Bell, "Bars, Blocks, and Crimes," *Journal of Environmental Systems,* **11** (1981): 35–47; Roncek and Faggiani, "High Schools and Crime."

40. Jeffrey Peck, G. O. W. Mueller, and Freda Adler, "The Vulnerability of Ports and Marinas to Vessel and Equipment Theft," *Security Journal,* **5** (1994): 146–153.

41. David Weisburd and Lorraine Green with Frank Gajewski and Charles Bellucci, Jersey City Police Department, "Defining the Street Level Drug Market," in *Drugs and Crime: Evaluating Public Policy Initiatives,* ed. Doris Layton MacKenzie and Craig Uchida (Newbury Park, Calif.: Sage, 1994), pp. 61–76.

42. Lawrence W. Sherman, "Hot Spots of Crime and Criminal Careers of Places," in Eck and Weisburd, *Crime and Place,* pp. 35–52.

43. See Fattah, "The Rational Choice/Opportunity Perspectives as a Vehicle for Integrating Criminological and Victimological Theories," in Clark and Felson, *Routine Activity and Rational Choice,* pp. 225–258.

44. James R. Lasley, "Drinking Routines/Lifestyles and Predatory Victimization: A Causal Analysis," *Justice Quarterly,* **6** (1989): 529–542.

45. Martin D. Schwartz and Victoria L. Pitts, "Exploring a Feminist Routine Activities Approach to Explaining Sexual Assault," *Justice Quarterly,* **12** (1995): 9–31.

46. Robert F. Meier and Terance D. Miethe, "Understanding Theories of Criminal Victimization," in *Crime and Justice: A Review of Research,* vol. 17, ed. Michael Tonry (Chicago: University of Chicago Press, 1993), pp. 459–499; Richard Titus, "Bringing Crime Victims Back into Routine Activities Theory/Research," paper presented at Fourth International Seminar on Environmental Criminology and Crime Analysis, July 1995, Cambridge, England.

47. C. Ray Jeffery, *Crime Prevention through Environmental Design* (Beverly Hills, Calif.: Sage, 1971).

48. Oscar Newman, *Defensible Space: Crime Prevention through Urban Design* (New York: Macmillan, 1972).

49. Ronald V. Clarke, "Introduction," *Situational Crime Prevention: Successful Case Studies,* ed. Ronald V. Clarke (New York: Harrow and Heston, 1992), pp. 3–36.

50. Ronald V. Clarke and Ross Homel, "A Revised Classification of Situational Crime Prevention Techniques," in *Crime Prevention at a Crossroads,* ed. Steven P. Lab (Cincinnati: Anderson, in press).

51. Gresham M. Sykes and David Matza, "Techniques of Neutralization: A Theory of Delinquency," *American Sociological Review,* **22** (1957): 664–670; Harold G. Grasmick and Robert J. Bursik, "Conscience, Significant Others, and Rational Choice," *Law and Society Review,* **34** (1990): 837–861; John Braithwaite, *Crime, Shame and Reintegration* (Cambridge: Cambridge University, 1989).

52. Clifford D. Shearing and Phillip C. Stenning, "From the Panopticon to Disney World: The Development of Discipline," in *Perspectives in Criminal Law: Essays in Honour of John L. J. Edwards,* ed. Anthony N. Doob and Edward L. Greenspan (Aurora: Canada Law Book, 1984), pp. 335–349.

53. See Ronald V. Clarke, "Introduction," in Clarke, *Situational Crime Prevention,* p. 5.

54. Kim Hazelbaker, paper presented at the Business and Crime Prevention Conference, an International Seminar Sponsored by the National Institute of Justice and Rutgers, State University of New Jersey, New Brunswick, N.J., 1996.

55. Ronald D. Hunter and C. Ray Jeffery, "Preventing Convenience Store Robbery through Environmental Design," in Clarke, *Situational Crime Prevention,* pp. 194–204.

56. All information for this section abstracted from Mary S. Smith, *Crime Prevention through Environmental Design in Parking Facilities,* Research in Brief, for National Institute of Justice (Washington, D.C.: U.S. Government Printing Office, 1996).

57. Patricia Mayhew, Ronald V. Clarke, and David Elliott, "Motorcycle Theft, Helmet Legislation and Displacement," *Howard Journal of Criminal Justice,* **28** (1989): 1–8.

▓ **Internet Exercise** ════════════

You learned in this chapter that the risk of being burglarized can be greatly reduced by taking steps to make your home more difficult to enter. What steps would you take?

▓ **Your Web Site is:**
http://www.state.ga.us/ga.inscommission/burglar.htm.

CHAPTER 9

Alternative Explanations of Crime:
Labeling, Conflict, and Radical Theories

Labeling Theory
The Origins of Labeling Theory
Basic Assumptions of Labeling Theory
Labeling in the 1960s
Empirical Evidence for Labeling Theory
Evaluation: Labeling Theory

Conflict Theory
The Consensus Model
The Conflict Model
Conflict Theory and Criminology
Empirical Evidence for the Conflict Model

Radical Theory
The Intellectual Heritage of Marxist Criminology
Engels and Marx
Willem Adriaan Bonger
Georg Rusche and Otto Kirchheimer
Radical Criminology from the 1970s to the 1990s
Evaluation: Marxist Criminological Theory
Emerging Explanations

Review

Notes

Special Features
CRIMINOLOGICAL FOCUS: On Being Sane in Insane Places
AT ISSUE: The Rights of the Poorest
WINDOW TO THE WORLD: Criminal Law

Key Terms
conflict theory
consensus model
due process
equal protection
labeling theory
penologists
radical criminology
social interactionists

Each era of social and political turmoil has produced profound changes in people's lives. Perhaps no such era was as significant for criminology as the 1960s. A society with conservative values was shaken out of its complacency when young people, blacks, women, and other disadvantaged groups demanded a part in the shaping of national policy. They saw the gaps between philosophical political demands and reality: Blacks had little opportunity to advance; women were kept in an inferior status; old politicians made wars in which the young had to die. Rebellion broke out, and some criminologists joined it.

These criminologists turned away from theories that explained crime by characteristics of the offender or of the social structure. They set out to demonstrate that individuals become criminals because of what people with power, especially those in the criminal justice system, do. Their alternative explanations largely reject the consensus model of crime, on which all earlier theories rested. The new theories not only question the traditional explanations of the creation and enforcement of criminal law but blame that law for the making of criminals. (See Table 9.1.)

It may not sound so radical to assert that unless an act is made criminal by law, no person who performs that act can be adjudicated a criminal. The exponents of contemporary alternative explanations of crime grant that much. But they also ask: Who makes these laws in the first place? And why? Is breaking such laws the most important criterion for being a criminal? Are all people who break these laws criminals? Do all members of society agree that those singled out by the criminal law to be called "criminals" are criminals and that others are not?

TABLE 9.1   Comparison of Four Criminological Perspectives

Perspective	Origin of Criminal Law	Causes of Criminal Behavior	Focus of Study
Traditional/ consensus	Laws reflect shared values.	Psychological, biological, or sociological factors	Psychological and biological factors (Chap. 4); unequal opportunity (Chap. 5); learning criminal behavior in disorganized neighborhoods (Chap. 5); subculture values (Chap. 6); social control (Chap. 7).
Labeling	Those in power create the laws, decide who will be the rule breakers.	The process that defines (or labels) certain persons as criminals.	Effects of stigmatizing by the label "criminal"; sociopolitical factors behind reform legislation; origin of laws; deviant behavior (Chap. 9).
Conflict	Powerful groups use laws to support their interests.	Interests of one group do not coincide with needs of another.	Bias and discrimination in criminal justice system; differential crime rates of powerful and powerless; development of criminal laws by those in power; relationship between rulers and ruled (Chap. 9).
Radical (Marxist)	Laws serve interests of the ruling class.	Class struggle over distribution of resources in a capitalist system.	Relationship between crime and economics; ways in which state serves capitalist interests; solution to crime problem based on collapse of capitalism (Chap. 9).

LABELING THEORY

The 1950s was a period of general prosperity and pride for Americans. Yet some social scientists, uneasy about the complacency they saw, turned their attention to the social order. They noted that some of the ideals the United States had fought for in World War II had not been achieved at home. Human rights existed on paper but were often lacking in practice. It was clear that blacks continued to live as second-class citizens. Even though the Fourteenth Amendment to the Constitution guaranteed blacks equal rights, neither the law of the country nor the socioeconomic system provided them with equal opportunities.

Nowhere was this fact more apparent than in the criminal justice system. Social scientists and liberal lawyers pressed for change, and the Supreme Court, under Chief Justice Earl Warren, responded. In case after case the Court found a pervasive influence of rules and customs that violated the concepts of **due process,** under which a person cannot be deprived of life, liberty, or property without lawful procedures, and **equal protection,** under which no one can be denied the safeguards of the law. The result of hundreds of Supreme Court decisions was that both black and white citizens now were guaranteed the right to counsel in all criminal cases, freedom from self-incrimination, and other rights enumerated in the first ten amendments to the Constitution. Nevertheless, a great deal of social injustice remained.

In this social climate, a small group of social scientists, known as *labeling theorists,* began to explore how and why certain acts were defined as criminal or, more broadly, as deviant behavior and others were not, and how and why certain people were defined as criminal or deviant. These theorists viewed criminals not as inherently evil persons engaged in inherently wrong acts but, rather, as individuals who had had criminal status conferred upon them by both the criminal justice system and the community at large.

Viewed from this perspective, criminal acts themselves are not particularly significant; the social reaction to them, however, is. Deviance and its control involve a process of social definition in which the response of others to an individual's behavior is the key influence on subsequent behavior and on individuals' views of themselves. The sociologist Howard S. Becker has written:

> Deviance is not a quality of the act the person commits, but rather a consequence of the application by others of rules and sanctions to an "offender." The deviant is one to whom that label has successfully been applied; deviant behavior is behavior that people so label.[1]

In focusing on the ways in which social interactions create deviance, **labeling theory** declares that the reaction of other people and the subsequent effects of those reactions create deviance. Once it becomes known that a person has engaged in deviant acts, he or she is segregated from conventional society, and a label ("thief," "whore," "junkie") is attached to the transgressor. This process of segregation creates "outsiders" (as Becker called them), or outcasts from society, who begin to associate with others like themselves.[2]

As more people begin to think of these people as deviants and to respond to them accordingly, the deviants react to the response by continuing to engage in the behavior society now expects of them. Through this process their self-images gradually change as well. So the key factor is the label that is attached to an individual: "If men define situations as real, they are real in their consequences."[3]

The Origins of Labeling Theory

The intellectual roots of labeling theory can be traced to the post-World War I work of Charles Horton Cooley, William I. Thomas, and George Herbert Mead. These scholars, who viewed the human self as formed through a process of social interaction, were called **social interactionists.** In 1918 Mead compared the impact of social labeling to "the angel with the fiery sword at the gate who can cut one off from the world to which he belongs."[4]

Labeling separates the good from the bad, the conventional from the deviant. Mead's interest in deviance focused on the social interactions by which an individual becomes a deviant. The person is not just a fixed structure whose action is the result of certain factors acting upon it. Rather, social behavior develops in a continuous process of action and reac-

tion.[5] The way we perceive ourselves, our self-concept, is built not only on what we think of ourselves but also on what others think of us.

Somewhat later, the historian Frank Tannenbaum (1893–1969) used the same argument in his study of the causes of criminal behavior. He described the creation of a criminal as a process: Breaking windows, climbing onto roofs, and playing truant are all normal parts of the adolescent search for excitement and adventure. Local merchants and others who experience these activities may consider them a nuisance or perhaps even evil. This conflict is the beginning of the process by which the evil act transforms the transgressor into an evil individual. From that point on, the evil individuals are separated from those in conventional society. Given a criminal label, they gradually begin to think of themselves as they have been officially defined.

Tannenbaum maintained that it is the process of labeling, or the "dramatization of evil," that locks a mischievous boy into a delinquent role ("the person becomes the thing he is described as being"). Accordingly, "the entire process of dealing with young delinquents is mischievous insofar as it identifies him to himself and to the environment as a delinquent person."[6] The system starts out with a child in trouble and ends up with a juvenile delinquent.

Basic Assumptions of Labeling Theory

In the 1940s the sociologist Edwin Lemert elaborated on Tannenbaum's discussion by formulating the basic assumptions of labeling theory.[7] He reminded us that people are constantly involved in behavior that runs the risk of being labeled delinquent or criminal. But although many run that risk, only a few are so labeled. The reason, Lemert contended, is that there are two kinds of deviant acts: primary and secondary.[8]

Primary deviations are the initial deviant acts that bring on the first social response. These acts do not affect the individual's self-concept. It is the *secondary deviations,* the acts that follow the societal response to the primary deviation, that are of major concern. These are the acts that result from the change in self-concept brought about by the labeling process.[9] The scenario goes somewhat like this:

1. An individual commits a simple deviant act (primary deviation)—throwing a stone at a neighbor's car, for instance.

2. There is an informal social reaction: The neighbor gets angry.
3. The individual continues to break rules (primary deviations)—he lets the neighbor's dog out of the yard.
4. There is increased, but still primary, social reaction: The neighbor tells the youth's parents.
5. The individual commits a more serious deviant act—he is caught shoplifting (still primary deviation).
6. There is a formal reaction: The youth is adjudicated a "juvenile delinquent" in juvenile court.
7. The youth is now labeled "delinquent" by the court and "bad" by the neighborhood, by his conventional peers, and by others.
8. The youth begins to think of himself as "delinquent"; he joins other unconventional youths.
9. The individual commits another, yet more serious, deviant act (secondary deviation)—he robs a local grocery store with members of a gang.
10. The individual is returned to juvenile court, has more offenses added to his record, is cast out further from conventional society, and takes on a completely deviant lifestyle.

According to Lemert, secondary deviance sets in after the community has become aware of a primary deviance. Individuals experience "a continuing sense of injustice, which [is] reinforced by job rejections, police cognizance, and strained interaction with normals."[10] In short, deviant individuals have to bear the stigma of the "delinquent" label, just as English and American convicts, as late as the eighteenth century, bore stigmas, in the form of an M for murder or a T for thief, burned or cut into their bodies to designate them as persons to be shunned.[11] Once such a label is attached to a person, a deviant or criminal career has been set in motion. The full significance of labeling theory was not recognized, either in Europe or in the United States, until political events provided the opportunity.[12]

Labeling in the 1960s

The 1960s witnessed a movement among students and professors to join advocacy groups and become activists in the social causes that rapidly were gaining popularity on college campuses across the nation, such as equal rights for minorities, liberation for women, and peace for humankind. The protests took many forms—demonstrations and rallies, sit-ins and teach-ins, beards and long hair, rock music and marijuana, dropping out of school, burning draft cards.

Arrests of middle-class youths increased rapidly; crime was no longer confined to the ghettos. People asked whether arrests were being made for behavior that was not really criminal. Were the real criminals the legislators and policy makers who pursued a criminal war in Vietnam while creating the artificial crime of draft card burning at home? Were the real criminals the National Guardsmen who shot and killed campus demonstrators at Kent State University? Labeling theorists made their appearance and provided answers. The sociologist Kai Erickson has put it well:

> Deviance is not a property inherent in certain forms of behavior; it is a property conferred upon these forms by audiences which directly or indirectly witness them. The critical variable in the study of deviance, then, is the social audience rather than the individual actor, since it is the audience which eventually determines whether or not any episode or behavior or any class of episodes is labeled deviant.[13]

Edwin Schur, a leading labeling theorist of the 1960s, elaborated Erickson's explanation:

> Human behavior is deviant to the extent that it comes to be viewed as involving a personally discreditable departure from a group's normative expectation, and it elicits interpersonal and collective reactions that serve to "isolate," "treat," "correct," or "punish" individuals engaged in such behavior.[14]

Schur also expanded on Lemert's secondary deviance with his own concept of "secondary elaboration," by which he meant that the effects of the labeling process become so significant that individuals who want to escape from their deviant groups and return to the conventional world find it difficult to do so. Schur points to members of the gay and drug cultures.[15] The strength of the label, once acquired, tends to exclude such people permanently from the mainstream culture.[16] Schur found that involvement in activities that are disapproved of may very well lead to more participation in deviance than one had originally planned, and so increase the social distance between the person labeled deviant and the conventional world.[17]

The labeling theorists then asked: Who makes the rules that define deviant behavior, including

Kent State University protestor grieving over body of fellow student shot and killed by National Guardsmen, Ohio, 1970.

crime? According to Howard Becker, it is the "moral entrepreneurs"—the people whose high social position gives them the power to make and enforce the social rules by which members of society have to live. By making the rules that define the criminal, Becker argues, certain members of society create outsiders.

The whole process thus becomes a political one, pitting the rule makers against the rule breakers. Becker goes even further, suggesting that people can be labeled simply by being falsely accused. As long as others believe that someone has participated in a given deviant behavior, that individual will experience negative social reaction. People can also suffer the effects of labeling when they have committed a deviant act that has not been discovered. Since most people know how they would be labeled if they were caught, these secret deviants may experience the same labeling effects as those who have been caught.[18]

Empirical Evidence for Labeling Theory

Empirical investigations of labeling theory have been carried out by researchers in many disciplines using a variety of methodologies. One group of investigators arranged to have eight sane volunteers apply for admission to various mental hospitals. In order to get themselves admitted, the subjects claimed to be hearing voices, a symptom of schizophrenia. Once admitted to the hospital, however, they behaved normally. The experiences of these pseudopatients clearly reveal the effects of labeling.

Doctors, nurses, and assistants treated them as schizophrenic patients. They interpreted the normal everyday behavior of the pseudopatients as manifestations of illness. An early arrival at the lunchroom, for example, was described as exhibiting "oral aggressive" behavior; a patient seen writing something was referred to as a "compulsive note-taker." Interestingly enough, none of the other patients believed the pseudopatients were insane; they assumed they were researchers or journalists. When the subjects were discharged from the hospital, it was as schizophrenics "in remission."

The findings support criminological labeling theory. Once the sane individuals were labeled schizophrenic, they were unable to eliminate the label by acting normally. Even when they supposedly had recovered, the label stayed with them in the form of "schizophrenia in remission," which implied that future episodes of the illness could be expected.[19]

Researchers have also looked at how labels affect people and groups with unconventional lifestyles, whether prohibited by law or not—"gays," "public drunks," "junkies," "strippers," "streetwalkers."[20] The results of research, no matter what the group, were largely in conformity: "Once a _____, always a _____." Labeling by adjudication may have lifelong consequences. Richard Schwartz and Jerome Skolnick, for example, found that employers were reluctant to hire anyone with a court record even though the person had been found not guilty.[21]

The criminologist Anthony Platt has investigated how certain individuals are singled out to receive labels. Focusing on the label "juvenile delinquent," he shows how the social reformers of the late nineteenth century helped create delinquency by establishing a special institution, the juvenile court, for the processing of troubled youths. The Chicago society women who lobbied for the establishment of juvenile courts may have had the best motives in trying to help immigrants' children who, by their standards, were out of control. But by getting the juvenile court established, they simply widened the net of state agencies empowered to label some children as deviant.

The state thus aggravated the official problem of juvenile delinquency, which until then had been a neighborhood nuisance handled by parents, neighbors, priests, the local grocer, or the police officer on the street. Juvenile delinquency, according to Platt, was invented. Through its labeling effect it contributed to its own growth.[22]

The criminologist William Chambliss also studied the question of the way labels are distributed. Consider the following description:

> Eight promising young men [the Saints]—children of good, stable, white upper-middle-class families, active in school affairs, good pre-college students—were some of the most delinquent boys at Hanibal High

School. . . . The Saints were constantly occupied with truancy, drinking, wild driving, petty theft and vandalism. Yet not one was officially arrested for any misdeed during the two years I observed them.

> This record was particularly surprising in light of my observations during the same two years of another gang of Hanibal High School students, six lower-class white boys known as the Roughnecks. The Roughnecks were constantly in trouble with police and community even though their rate of delinquency was about equal with that of the Saints.[23]

What accounts for the different responses to these two groups of boys? According to Chambliss, the crucial factor is the social class of the boys, which determined the community's reaction to their activities. The Roughnecks were poor, outspoken, openly hostile to authority, and highly visible because they could not afford cars to get out of town. Their behavior was discovered, processed, and punished. The Saints, on the other hand, had reputations for being bright, they acted apologetic when authorities confronted them, they held school offices, they played on athletic teams, and they had cars to get them out of town so that their delinquent acts would not be noticed. Their behavior went undiscovered, unprocessed, and unpunished.

Up to this point, the contentions of labeling theorists and the evidence they present provide a persuasive argument for the validity of labeling theory. But despite supportive scientific evidence, labeling theory has been heavily criticized.

Evaluation: Labeling Theory

Critics ask: Why is it that individuals, knowing they might be labeled, get involved in socially disapproved behavior to begin with? Most labeled persons have indeed engaged in some act that is considered morally or legally wrong.[24] According to the sociologist Ronald Akers, the impression is sometimes given that people are passive actors in a process by which the bad system bestows a derogatory label, thereby declaring them unacceptable, or different, or untouchable.[25] Critics suggest that the labels may identify real behavior rather than create it. After all, many delinquents have in fact had a long history of deviant behavior, even though they have never been caught and stigmatized. These critics question the overly active role labeling theory has assigned to the

CRIMINOLOGICAL FOCUS

ON BEING SANE IN INSANE PLACES

Psychologist D. L. Rosenhan reported the results of an experiment in which sane volunteers were admitted to psychiatric hospitals after complaining that they had been hearing voices. Length of hospitalization for the volunteers, who stopped "hearing voices" and said they felt fine as soon as they were admitted, ranged from 7 to 52 days, with an average length of 19 days. In this passage, Rosenhan describes how one patient was viewed:

As far as I can determine, diagnoses were in no way affected by the relative health of the circumstances of a pseudopatient's life. Rather, the reverse occurred: the perception of his circumstances was shaped entirely by the diagnosis. A clear example of such translation is found in the case of a pseudopatient who had had a close relationship with his mother but was rather remote from his father during his early childhood. During adolescence and beyond, however, his father became a close friend, while his relationship with his mother cooled. His present relationship with his wife was characteristically close and warm. Apart from occasional angry exchanges, friction was minimal. The children had rarely been spanked. Surely there is nothing especially pathological about such a history. Indeed, many readers may see a similar pattern in their own experiences, with no markedly deleterious consequences. Observe, however, how such a history was translated

in the psychopathological context, this from the case summary prepared after the patient was discharged.

"This white 39-year-old male . . . manifests a long history of considerable ambivalence in close relationships, which begins in early childhood. A warm relationship with his mother cools during his adolescence. A distant relationship to his father is described as becoming very intense. Affective stability is absent. His attempts to control emotionality with his wife and children are punctuated by angry outbursts and, in the case of the children, spankings. And while he says that he has several good friends, one senses considerable ambivalence embedded in those relationships also. . . ."(1)

The facts of the case were unintentionally distorted by the staff to achieve consistency with a popular theory of the dynamics of a schizophrenic reaction. Nothing of an ambivalent nature had been described in relations with parents, spouse, or friends. To the extent that ambivalence could be inferred, it was probably not greater than is found in all human relationships. It is true the pseudopatient's relationships with his parents changed over time, but in the ordinary context that would hardly be remarkable—indeed, it might very well be expected. Clearly, the meaning ascribed to his verbalizations (that is, ambivalence, affective instability) was determined by the diagnosis: schizophrenia. An entirely different meaning would have been ascribed if it were known that the man was "normal."

A psychiatric label has a life and an influence of its own. Once the impression has been formed that the patient is schizophrenic, the expectation is that he will continue to be schizophrenic. When a sufficient amount of time has passed, during which the patient has done nothing bizarre, he is considered to be in remission and available for discharge. But the label endures beyond discharge, with the unconfirmed expectation that he will behave as a schizophrenic again. Such labels, conferred by mental health professionals, are as influential on the patient as they are on his relatives and friends, and it should not surprise anyone that the diagnosis acts on all of them as a self-fulfilling prophecy. Eventually, the patient himself accepts the diagnosis, with all of its surplus meanings and expectations, and behaves accordingly.

Source

1. D. L. Rosenhan, "On Being Sane in Insane Places," *Science*, **179** (1973): 253–254.

Questions for Discussion

1. The hospital staff assumed the sane volunteers were schizophrenic, while 35 of 118 hospital patients in one experiment voiced their suspicions about the pseudopatients' insanity. What accounts for that difference in perception?

2. Have you ever been in a situation in which you felt you had been labeled unfairly or incorrectly and were suffering the consequences? Describe what happened.

community and its criminal justice system and the overly passive role it has assigned to offenders.

Some criminologists also question how labeling theory accounts for individuals who have gone through formal processing but do not continue deviant lifestyles. They suggest that punishment really does work as a deterrent.[26] The argument is that labeling theorists are so intent on the reaction to behavior that they completely neglect the fact that someone has defied the conventions of society.[27] The criminologist Charles Wellford reminds us that, by and large, offenders get into the hands of authorities because they have broken the law. Furthermore, the decisions made about them are heavily influenced by the seriousness of their offenses. He concludes:

> The assumption that labels are differentially distributed, and that differential labelling affects behavior, is not supported by the existing criminological research. In sum, one should conclude that to the degree that these assumptions can be taken to be basic to the labelling perspective, the perspective must be seriously questioned; and criminologists should be encouraged to explore other ways to conceptualize the causal process of the creation, perpetuation, and intensification of criminal and delinquent behavior.[28]

While most critics believe that labeling theorists put too much emphasis on the system, others of a more radical or Marxist persuasion believe that labeling theorists have not gone far enough. They claim that the labeling approach concentrates too heavily on "nuts, sluts, and perverts," the exotic varieties of deviants who capture public imagination, rather than on "the unethical, illegal and destructive actions of powerful individuals, groups, and institutions of our society."[29] We will look at this argument more closely in a moment.

Empirical evidence that substantiates the claims of labeling theory has been modest. All the same, the theory has been instrumental in calling attention to some important questions, particularly about the way defendants are processed through the criminal justice system. Labeling theorists have carried out important scientific investigations of that system which complement the search of mainstream criminologists for the causes of crime and delinquency.

Some of the criticism of labeling theory can best be countered by one of its own proponents. Howard Becker explains that labeling is intended not as a theory of causation but, rather, as a perspective, "a way of looking at a general area of human activity, which

expands the traditional research to include the process of social control."[30] Labeling theory has provided this perspective; it has also spawned further inquiry into the causes of crime.

CONFLICT THEORY

Labeling theorists are as well aware as mainstream criminologists that some people make rules and some break them. Their primary concern is the consequences of making and enforcing rules. One group of scholars has carried this idea further by questioning the rule-making process itself. They claim that a struggle for power is a basic feature of human existence. It is by means of such power struggles that various interest groups manage to control lawmaking and law enforcement.[31] To understand the theoretical approach of these conflict theorists, we must go back to the traditional approach, which views crime and criminal justice as arising from communal consensus.

The Consensus Model

Sometimes members of a society consider certain acts so threatening to community survival that they designate these acts as crimes. If the vast majority of a group's members share this view, the group has acted by consensus. This is the **consensus model** of criminal lawmaking. The model assumes that members of society by and large agree on what is right and wrong and that law is the codification of these agreed-upon social values. The law is a mechanism to settle disputes that arise when individuals stray too far from what the community considers acceptable.

In Durkheim's words, "We can . . . say that an act is criminal when it offends strong and defined states of the collective conscience."[32] Consensus theorists view society as a stable entity in which laws are created for the general good. The laws' function is to reconcile and to harmonize most of the interests that most members of a community cherish, with the least amount of sacrifice.[33]

Deviant acts not only are part of the normal functioning of society but in fact are necessary, because when the members of society unite against a deviant, they reaffirm their commitment to shared values. Durkheim captured this view:

> We have only to notice what happens, particularly in a small town, when some moral scandal has been com-

mitted. They stop each other on the street, they visit each other, they seek to come together to talk of the event and to wax indignant in common. From all the similar impressions which are exchanged, for all the temper that gets itself expressed, there emerges a unique temper, more or less determinate according to the circumstances, which is everybody's without being anybody's in particular. That is the public temper.[34]

Societies in which citizens agree on right and wrong and the occasional deviant serves a useful purpose are scarce today. Such societies could be found among primitive peoples at the very beginning of social evolution. By and large, consensus theory recognizes that not everyone can agree on what is best for society. Yet consensus theory holds that conflicting interests can be reconciled by means of law.[35]

The Conflict Model

With this view of the consensus model, we can understand and evaluate the arguments of the conflict theorists. In the 1960s, while labeling theorists were questioning why some people were designated as criminals, another group of scholars began to ask who in society has the power to make and enforce the laws. Conflict theory, already well established in the field of sociology, thus became popular as an explanation of crime and justice as well.

Like labeling theory, **conflict theory** has its roots in rebellion and the questioning of values. But while labeling theorists and traditional criminologists focused on the crime and the criminal, including the labeling of the criminal by the system, conflict theorists questioned the system itself. The clash between traditional and labeling theorists, on the one hand, and conflict theorists, on the other, became ideological.

Conflict theorists asked: If people agree on the value system, as consensus theorists suggest, why are so many people in rebellion, why are there so many crimes, so many punitive threats, so many people in prison? Clearly conflict is found everywhere in the world, between one country and another, between gay rights and antigay groups, between people who view abortion as a right and others who view it as murder, between suspects and police, between family members, between neighbors. If the criminal law supports the collective communal interest, why do so many people deviate from it?

Conflict theorists answered that, contrary to consensus theory, laws do not exist for the collective good; they represent the interests of specific groups that have the power to get them enacted.[36] The key concept in conflict theory is power. The people who have political control in any given society are the ones who are able to make things happen. They have power. Conflict theory holds that the people who possess the power work to keep the powerless at a disadvantage. The laws thus have their origin in the interests of the few; these few shape the values, and the values, in turn, shape the laws.[37]

It follows that the person who is defined as criminal and the behavior that is defined as crime at any given time and place mirror the society's power relationships. The definitions are subject to change as other interests gain power. The changing of definitions can be seen in those acts we now designate as "victimless" crimes. Possession of marijuana, prostitution, gambling, refusing to join the armed forces—all have been legal at some times, illegal at others. We may ask, then, whether any of these acts is inherently evil. The conflict theorist would answer that all are *made* evil when they are so designated by those in power and thus defined as crimes in legal codes.

The legal status of victimless crimes is subject to change. But what about murder, a crime considered evil in all contemporary societies? Many conflict theorists would respond that the definition of murder as a criminal offense is also rooted in the effort of some groups to guard their power. A political terrorist may very well become a national hero.

Conflict theorists emphasize the relativity of norms to time and place: Capital punishment is legal in some states, outlawed in others; alcohol consumption is illegal in Saudi Arabia but not in the United States. Powerful groups maintain their interests by making illegal any behavior that might be a threat to them. Laws thus become a mechanism of control, or "a weapon in social conflict."[38]

Conflict Theory and Criminology

The sociologist George Vold (1896–1967) was the first theorist to relate conflict theory to criminology. He argued that individuals band together in groups because they are social animals with needs that are best served through collective action. If the group serves its members, it survives; if not, new groups form to take its place. Individuals constantly clash as they try to advance the interests of their particular group over those of all the others. The result is that

AT ISSUE

THE RIGHTS OF THE POOREST

The poorest and least powerful have had little influence on the making of laws and on society's reaction to the breaking of laws. Somehow, the poorest have to survive in a society on which they have no apparent impact. In recent years court cases in New York have served as the battleground over what for some is a basic question of survival: Do the poor have a constitutional right to beg?

YES-NO-YES: COURT RULINGS

Yes, said New York federal district court judge Leonard Sand in January 1990, they have a right to panhandle in subway cars.(1) His ruling was overturned by the federal court of appeals in May of the same year, thus denying citizens the right to beg in the New York City subway system.(2) In 1993, when the question concerned the rights of the poor to beg in city streets and public parks, a federal court of appeals decided in favor of the poor.(3)

What did the justices consider in their efforts to decide whether beggars are criminals? Sand's novel ruling stated that panhandling is a form of free speech protected by the First Amendment. "A true test of one's commitment to constitutional principles," he wrote, "is the extent to which recognition is given to the rights of those in our midst who are the least affluent, least powerful and least welcome."(1) The case he decided grew out of attempts by the Metropolitan Transit Authority (MTA) to crack down on panhandling in New York City subway cars and stations. The Legal Action Center for the Homeless had filed a class action against the MTA on behalf of homeless panhandlers.

The court of appeals, in reversing the decision of the district court, criticized the lower court for overlooking the concerns of the MTA's millions of riders. It said that "whether intended as so, or not, begging in the subway often amounts to nothing less than assault, creating in the passengers the apprehension of imminent danger."(2)

CRITICAL COMMENTARY

Judge Sand's ruling created a spate of mostly virulent comments focusing on the judiciary's right to rule on the conduct of those dispossessed of power. One critic, Jill Adler, responded to these attacks:

Judges as the ultimate guardians and interpreters of the Constitution have been charged with the duty of insuring that its fundamental guarantees such as freedom of speech and assembly are not abridged by the government. In this capacity they may sometimes be required to make unpopular decisions.

It is at least arguable that panhandling or begging is a form of symbolic speech—if only because it may be the only avenue of expression open to those society has shunned. Time, place, and manner restrictions, while undoubtedly an important protection for the community, can also be a convenient means of ignoring constitutional guarantees. They will not, however, make the homeless disappear.(4)

Watch for the U.S. Supreme Court to consider this issue soon.

Sources
1. 729 F. Supp. 341 (S.D.N.Y. 1990).
2. 903 F. 2d 146 (2d Cir. 1990).
3. Docket No. 92-9127, United States Court of Appeals for the Second Circuit, July 29, 1993.
4. Andrea Sachs, *Time,* Feb. 12, 1990, p. 55; Jill Adler, *International Herald Tribune*, Feb. 15, 1990, p. 9.

Questions for Discussion
1. Begging has been regulated throughout history in the United States, and some 25 states currently have statutes that limit or ban begging. What do you suppose the U.S. Supreme Court will do to these statutes?
2. Do you agree that subway begging should be viewed as different from begging on the street?

society is in a constant state of conflict, "one of the principal and essential social processes upon which the continuing ongoing of society depends." For Vold, the entire process of lawmaking and crime control is a direct reflection of conflict between interest groups, all trying to get laws passed in their favor and to gain control of the police power.[39]

The sociologist Ralf Dahrendorf and the criminologist Austin Turk are major contemporary contributors to the application of conflict theory to criminology. To Dahrendorf, the consensus model of society is utopian. He believes that enforced constraint, rather than cooperation, binds people together. Whether society is capitalist, socialist, or feudal, some people have the authority and others are subject to it. Society is made up of a large number of interest groups. The interests of one group do not always coincide with the needs of another—unions and management, for instance.

Conflict: Pro-choice advocates confront right to life supporters over the explosive issue of abortion.

Dahrendorf argues that social change is constant, social conflicts are ever-present, disintegration and change are ongoing, and all societies are characterized by coercion of some people by others. The most important characteristics of class, he contends, are power and authority. The inequities remain for him the lasting determinant of social conflict. Conflict can be either destructive or constructive, depending on whether it leads to a breakdown of the social structure or to positive change in the social order.[40]

Austin Turk has continued and expanded this theoretical approach. "Criminality is not a biological, psychological, or even behavioral phenomenon," he says, "but a social status defined by the way in which an individual is perceived, evaluated, and treated by legal authorities." Criminal status is defined by those he calls the "authorities," the decision makers. Criminal status is imposed on the "subjects," the subordinate class. Turk explains that this process works so that both authorities and subjects learn to interact as performers in their dominant and submissive roles. There are "social norms of dominance" and "social norms of deference." Conflict arises when some people refuse to go along and they challenge the authorities. "Law breaking, then, becomes a measure of the stability of the ruler/ruled relationship."[41] The people who make the laws struggle to hold on to their power, while those who do not make laws struggle to do so.

People with authority use several forms of power to control society's goods and services: police or war power, economic power, political power, and ideological power (beliefs, values).[42] The laws made by the "ins" to condemn or condone various behaviors help shape all social institutions—indeed, the entire culture. Where education is mandatory, for example, the people in power are able to maintain the status quo by passing on their own value system from one generation to the next.[43]

History seems to demonstrate that primitive societies, in their earliest phases of development, tend to be homogeneous and to make laws by consensus. The more a society develops economically and politically, the more difficult it becomes to resolve conflict situations by consensus. For an early instance of criminal lawmaking by the conflict model, we can go back to 1530, when King Henry VIII of England broke away from the Roman Catholic church because the pope refused to annul Henry's marriage to Catherine of Aragon so that he could marry Anne Boleyn. Henry confiscated church property and closed all the monasteries. Virtually overnight, tens of thousands of people who had been dependent on the monasteries for support were cast out, to roam the countryside in search of a living. Most ended up as beggars. This huge army of vagrants posed a burden on and danger to the establishment. To cope with the problem, Parliament revived the vagrancy laws of 1349, which prohibited the giving of aid to vagrants and beggars. Thus the powerful, by controlling the laws, gained control over the powerless.[44]

Empirical Evidence for the Conflict Model

Researchers have tested several conflict theory hypotheses, such as those pertaining to bias and discrimination in the criminal justice system, differential crime rates of powerful and powerless groups, and the intent behind the development of the criminal law. The findings offer mixed support for the theory.

Alan Lizotte studied 816 criminal cases in the Chicago courts over a 1-year period to test the assumption that the powerless get harsher sentences. His analysis relating legal factors (such as the offense committed) and extralegal factors (such as the race and job of the defendant) to length of prison sentence pointed to significant sentencing inequalities related to race and occupation.[45] When Freda Adler studied the importance of nonlegal factors in the decision making of juries, she found that the socioeconomic level of the defendants significantly influenced their judgment.[46]

While these and similar studies tend to support conflict theory by demonstrating class or racial bias in the administration of criminal justice, others, unexpectedly, show an opposite bias.[47] When we evaluate the contribution of conflict theory to criminological thought, we must keep in mind Austin Turk's warning that conflict theory is often misunderstood. The theory does not, he points out, suggest that most criminals are innocent or that powerful persons engage in the same amount of deviant behavior as do powerless persons or that law enforcers typically discriminate against people without power. It does acknowledge, however, that behaviors common among society's more disadvantaged members have a greater likelihood of being called "crime" than the activities in which the more powerful typically participate.[48]

Conflict theory does not attempt to explain crime; it simply identifies social conflict as a basic fact of life and as a source of discriminatory treatment by the criminal justice system of groups and classes that lack the power and status of those who make and enforce the laws. Once we recognize this, we may find it possible to change the process of criminalizing people, to provide greater justice. Conflict theorists anticipate a guided evolution, not a revolution, to improve the existing criminal justice system.

RADICAL THEORY

While labeling and conflict theorists were developing their perspectives, social and political conditions in the United States and Europe were changing rapidly and drastically. The youth of America were deeply disillusioned about a political and social structure that had brought about the assassinations of John F. Kennedy, Robert Kennedy, and Martin Luther King, Jr., the war in Vietnam, and the Watergate debacle. Many looked for radical solutions to social problems, and a number of young criminologists searched for radical answers to the nation's questions about crime and criminal justice. They found their answers in Marxism, a philosophy born in similar social turmoil a century earlier.

The Intellectual Heritage of Marxist Criminology

The major industrial centers of Europe suffered great hardships during the nineteenth century. The mechanization of industry and of agriculture, heavy population increases, and high rates of urbanization had created a massive labor surplus, high unemployment, and a burgeoning class of young urban migrants forced into the streets by poverty. London is said to have had at least 20,000 individuals who "rose every morning without knowing how they were to be supported through the day or where they were to lodge on the succeeding night, and cases of death from starvation appeared in the coroner's lists daily."[49] In other cities conditions were even worse.

Engels and Marx

It was against this background that Friedrich Engels (1820–1895) addressed the effects of the Industrial Revolution. A partner in his father's industrial empire, Engels was himself a member of the class he attacked as "brutally selfish." After a 2-year stay in England, he documented the awful social conditions, the suffering, and the great increase in crime and arrests. All these problems he blamed on one factor—competition. In *The Condition of the Working Class in England,* published in 1845, he spelled out the association between crime and poverty as a political problem:

> The earliest, crudest, and least fruitful form of this rebellion was that of crime. The working man lived in poverty and want, and saw that others were better off than he. . . . Want conquered his inherited respect for the sacredness of property, and he stole.[50]

Though Karl Marx (1818–1883) paid little attention to crime specifically, he argued that all aspects of social life, including laws, are determined by economic organization. His philosophy reflects the economic despair that followed the Industrial Revolution. In his *Communist Manifesto* (1848) Marx viewed the history of all societies as a documentation of class struggles: "Freeman and slave, patrician and plebeian, lord and serf, guildmaster and journeyman, in a word, oppressor and oppressed, stood in constant opposition to one another."[51]

Marx went on to describe the most important relationship in industrial society as that between the capitalist bourgeoisie, who own the means of production, and the proletariat, or workers, who labor for them. Society, according to Marx, has always been organized in such a hierarchical fashion, with the state representing not the common interest but the interests of those who own the means of production. Capitalism breeds egocentricity, greed, and predatory behavior; but the worst crime of all is the exploitation of workers. Revolution, Marx concluded, is the only means to bring about change, and for that reason it is morally justifiable.

Many philosophers before Marx had noted the link between economic conditions and social problems, including crime. Among them were Plato, Aristotle, Virgil, Horace, Sir Thomas More, Cesare Beccaria, Jeremy Bentham, André Guerry, Adolphe Quételet, and Gabriel Tarde (several of whom we met in Chapter 3). But none of them had advocated revolutionary change. And none had constructed a coherent criminological theory that conformed with economic determinism, the cornerstone of the Marxist explanation that people who are kept in a state of poverty will rebel by committing crimes. Not until 1905 can we speak of Marxist criminology.

Willem Adriaan Bonger

As a student at the University of Amsterdam, Willem Adriaan Bonger (1876–1940) entered a paper in a competition on the influence of economic factors on crime. His entry did not win; but its expanded version, *Criminality and Economic Conditions*, which appeared in French in 1905, was selected for translation by the American Institute of Criminal Law and Criminology. Bonger wrote in his preface, "[I am] convinced that my ideas about the etiology of crime will not be shared by a great many readers of the American edition."[52] He was right. Nevertheless, the book is considered a classic and is invaluable to students doing research on crime and economics.

Bonger explained that the social environment of primitive people was interwoven with the means of production. People helped each other. They used what they produced. When food was plentiful, everyone ate. When food was scarce, everyone was hungry. Whatever people had, they shared. People were subordinate to nature. In a modern capitalist society, people are much less altruistic. They concentrate on production for profit rather than for the needs of the community. Capitalism encourages criminal behavior by creating a climate that is less conducive to social responsibility. "We have a right," argued Bonger, "to say that the part played by economic conditions in criminality is predominant, even decisive."[53]

Willem Bonger died as he had lived, a fervent antagonist of the evils of the social order. An archenemy of Nazism and a prominent name on Hitler's list of people to be eliminated, he refused to emigrate even when the German army was at the border. On May 10, 1940, as the German invasion of Holland began, he wrote to his son: "I don't see any future for myself and I cannot bow to this scum which will now overmaster us."[54] He then took his own life. He left a powerful political and criminological legacy. Foremost among his followers were German socialist philosophers of the progressive school of Frankfurt.

Georg Rusche and Otto Kirchheimer

Georg Rusche and Otto Kirchheimer began to write their classic work at the University of Frankfurt. Driven out of Germany by Nazi persecution, they continued their search in exile in Paris and completed it at Columbia University in New York in 1939. In *Punishment and the Social Structure* they wrote that punishments had always been related to the modes of production and the availability of labor, rather than to the nature of the crimes themselves.

Consider galley slavery. Before the development of modern sailing techniques, oarsmen were needed to power merchant ships; as a result, galley slavery was a punishment in antiquity and in the Middle Ages. As sailing techniques were perfected, galley slavery was no longer necessary, and it lost favor as a sanction. By documenting the real purposes of punishments through the ages, Rusche and Kirchheimer made **penologists,** who study the penal system, aware that severe and cruel treatment of offenders had more to do with the value of human life and the needs of the economy than with preventing crime.

The names Marx, Engels, Bonger, and Rusche and Kirchheimer were all but forgotten by mainstream criminologists of the 1940s and 1950s, perhaps because of America's relative prosperity and conservatism during those years. But when tranquillity turned to turmoil in the mid-1960s, the forgotten names provided the intellectual basis for American and European radical criminologists, who explicitly stated their commitment to Marxism.

Radical Criminology from the 1970s to the 1990s

Radical criminology (also called critical, new, and Marxist criminology) made its first public appearance in 1968, when a group of British sociologists organized the National Deviancy Conference (NDC), a group of more than 300 intellectuals, social critics, deviants, and activists of various persuasions. What the group members had in common was a basic disillusion with the criminological studies being done by the British Home Office which they believed was system-serving and "practical." They were concerned with the way the system controlled people rather than with traditional sociological and psychological explanations of crime. They shared a respect for the interactionist and labeling theorists but believed these theorists had become too traditional. Their answer was to form a new criminology based on Marxist principles.

The conference was followed by the publication in 1973 of *The New Criminology*, the first textual formulation of the new radical criminology. According to its authors, Ian Taylor, Paul Walton, and Jock Young, it is the underclass, the "labor forces of the industrial society," that is controlled through the criminal law and its enforcement, while "the owners of labor will be bound only by a civil law which regulates their competition between each other." The economic

institution, then, is the source of all conflicts. Struggles between classes always relate to the distribution of resources and power, and only when capitalism is abolished will crime disappear.[55]

About the time that Marxist criminology was being formulated in England, it was also developing in the United States, particularly at the School of Criminology of the University of California at Berkeley, where Richard Quinney, Anthony Platt, Herman and Julia Schwendinger, William Chambliss, and Paul Takagi were at the forefront of the movement. These researchers were also influenced by interactionist and labeling theorists, as well as by the conflict theories of Vold, Dahrendorf, and Turk.

Though the radical criminologists share the central tenet of conflict theory, that laws are created by the powerful to protect their own interests, they disagree on the number of forces competing in the power struggle. For Marxist criminologists, there is only one dominating segment, the capitalist ruling class, which uses the criminal law to impose its will on the rest of the people in order to protect its property and to define as criminal any behavior that threatens the status quo.[56] The leading American spokesperson for radical criminology is Richard Quinney. His earliest Marxist publications appeared in 1973: "Crime Control in Capitalist Society" and "There's a Lot of Us Folks Grateful to the Lone Ranger."[57]

The second of these essays describes how Quinney drifted away from capitalism, with its folklore myths embodied in individual heroes like the Lone Ranger. He asserts that:

> The state is organized to serve the interests of the dominant economic class, the capitalist ruling class; that criminal law is an instrument the state and the ruling class use to maintain and perpetuate the social and economic order; that the contradictions of advanced capitalism . . . require that the subordinate classes remain oppressed by whatever means necessary, especially by the legal system's coercion and violence; and that only with the collapse of capitalist society, based on socialist principles, will there be a solution to the crime problem.[58]

In *Class, State, and Crime*, Quinney proclaims that "the criminal justice movement is . . . a state-initiated and state-supported effort to rationalize mechanisms of social control. The larger purpose is to secure a capitalist order that is in grave crisis, likely in its final stage of development."[59] Quinney challenges criminologists to abandon traditional ways of thinking about causation, to study what could be rather than what is, to question the assumptions of the social order, and to "ultimately develop a Marxist perspective."[60]

Marxist theory also can be found in the writings of other scholars who have adopted the radical approach to criminology. William Chambliss and Robert Seidman present their version in *Law, Order, and Power*:

> Society is composed of groups that are in conflict with one another and . . . the law represents an institutionalized tool of those in power (ruling class) which functions to provide them with superior moral as well as coercive power in conflict.[61]

The comment that if, in the operation of the criminal justice system by the powerful, "justice or fairness happen to be served, it is sheer coincidence."[62]

To Barry Krisberg, crime is a function of privilege. The rich create crimes to distract attention from the injustices they inflict on the masses. Power determines which group holds the privilege, defined by Krisberg as that which is valued by a given social group in a given historical time.[63] Herman and Julia Schwendinger warn that because of:

> the inherent antagonisms built into the capitalist system, all laws generally contradict their stated purpose of producing justice. Legal relations maintain patterns of individualism and selfishness and in so doing perpetuate a class system characterized by anarchy, oppression, and crime.[64]

Anthony Platt, in a forceful attack on traditional criminology, has even suggested it would not be "too farfetched to characterize many criminologists as domestic war criminals" because they have "serviced domestic repression in the same way that economics, political science, and anthropology have greased the wheels and even manufactured some of the important parts of modern imperialism."[65]

He suggests that traditional criminology serves the state through research studies that purport to "investigate" the conditions of the lower class but in reality only prove, with their probes of family life, education, jobs, and so on, that the members of the lower class are in fact less intelligent and more criminal than the rest of us. Platt claims that these inquiries, based as they are on biased and inaccurate data, are merely tools of the middle-class oppressors.

A number of other areas have come under the scrutiny of Marxist criminologists.[66] They have studied how informal means of settling disputes outside courts actually extend the control of the criminal justice system by adjudicating cases that are not serious enough for the courts; how juvenile court dispositions are unfairly based on social class; how sentencing reform has failed to benefit the lower class; how police practices during the latter half of the nineteenth century were geared to control labor rather than crime; how rape victims are made to feel guilty; how penitentiary reform has benefited the ruling class by giving it more control over the lower class; and how capitalist interests are strengthened by private policing.[67]

Evaluation: Marxist Criminological Theory

Critiques of Marxist criminology range from support for the attention the approach calls to the crimes of the powerful to accusations that it is nothing more than a revival of the Robin Hood myth, in which the poor steal from the rich in order to survive.[68] By far the most incisive criticism is that of the sociologist Carl Klockars, who points out that the division of society into social classes may have a beneficial effect, contrary to Marxist thought. Standards, he argues, are created by some people to inspire the remainder of society. In present-day America, Klockars claims, poverty has lost some of its meaning because luxuries and benefits are spread out over classes. To him, ownership and control of industry are two different things. Anyone who buys a share of stock, for example, can be an owner, while control is handled by bureaucrats who may or may not be owners.[69]

Class Interests versus Interest Groups. Klockars attacks Marxists for focusing exclusively on class interests and ignoring the fact that society is made up of many interest groups. This Marxist bias has yielded results that are untrustworthy and predictable, ignore reality, explain issues that are self-evident (some businesspeople are greedy and corrupt), and do not explain issues that are relevant (why socialist states have crime).[70]

Not without a note of sympathy, Richard Sparks summed up the criticism when he said:

> Marxist criminologists tend to be committed to praxis and the desire for radical social reform; but this commitment is not entailed by the scientific claims which Marxists make, and it has sometimes led to those claims being improperly suspect.[71]

WINDOW TO THE WORLD

CRIMINAL LAW IN AN AGE OF ETHNIC DIVERSITY

Hardly a region in the world is free from ethnic conflict. We live in an age of ethnicity and of a drive, often by force of arms, to break nation-states up into ethnic states. What does this have to do with criminal law? A great deal.

It has been the practice of nation-states to adopt a single penal code that governs everyone, regardless of ethnic group. But such a policy can lead to problems for law enforcement and criminal justice: A penal code written and imposed by a distant "central authority" that is itself of one particular ethnic group may not be effective with another group far from the seat of government. Everywhere in the world, ethnic groups are fighting for greater autonomy; they want to be governed by laws of their own making, compatible with their own customs and traditions.

THE CASE OF THE FORMER SOVIET UNION

The dissolution of the Soviet Union provides a good example of the importance of ethnicity in the formulation of criminal law. On January 1, 1992, the once-mighty Soviet Union ceased to exist as a nation. It had been the largest country in the world—2½ times the size of the United States—with nearly 300 million people of over 100 nationalities.

The three Baltic nations, Lithuania, Latvia, and Estonia, annexed by the Soviet Union in 1939, regained their independence in 1991. All the other former Soviet republics followed suit, although nine republics have joined in a loose-knit federation.

To some extent, the central authorities of the Soviet Union had made allowances for ethnic diversity. The Soviet Penal Code of 1953 imposed only its General Part on the entire U.S.S.R., with its Special Part, which defined the various crimes and punishments, reserved for variations among the republics.(1)

VICE BECOMES VIRTUE

What happens now that the various republics are independent? The three Baltic states, whose populations are not Slavic, are in the process of resurrecting their pre-1939 national penal codes. The predominantly Islamic republics (Kazakhstan, Uzbekistan, Turkmenistan, and Kyrgyzstan) had long been unhappy with a Russian-inspired penal code and are now searching for something more compatible with their traditions. The countries with predominantly Christian traditions, including Belarus, Ukraine, Moldova, Georgia, and Armenia, also want to shed the Russian imprint. And Russia itself is rapidly discarding the Soviet features of its penal code. For example, a law of 1961 made it criminal for persons to "avoid socially useful work, derive unearned income from

the exploitation of land plots, automobiles, or housing, or commit other anti-social acts which enable them to lead a parasitic way of life."(2) What was a vice and a crime has now become a virtue: Today people are encouraged to exploit land plots, automobiles, or housing and to derive "unearned income" from investments.

Penal codes, to be respected, must conform to the cultural norms of a society; otherwise, the people addressed will not comply readily, and the police and courts will have a difficult time enforcing the codes.

Sources
1. Harold J. Berman and James W. Spindler, *Soviet Criminal Law and Procedure* (Cambridge, Mass.: Harvard University Press, 1966), pp. 15–16.
2. Edict of the Presidium of the Supreme Soviet of the RSFSR of May 4, 1961, as quoted in Berman and Spindler, p. 9.

Questions for Discussion
1. Some crimes, like murder, robbery, or arson, seem to be so universal that they should be included in all penal codes. Right or wrong?
2. What makes for the severity of the various crimes defined in a penal code? Is there agreement on severity within a country or between countries?

Opposition to the new criminology follows many paths, but the most popular, in one way or another, is concerned with its oversimplification of causation by the exclusive focus on capitalism.[72] Critics also attack Marxist criminologists for their assertion that even by studying crime empirically, criminologists are supporting the status quo. That puts Marxist criminologists on the defensive, because if they are not ideologically in a position to expose their theories to empirical research or are unwilling to do so, their assertions will remain just that—assertions with no proof.[73]

Collapse of the Economic Order. Even sharper criticism of Marxist theory can be anticipated in the wake of the collapse of the Marxist economic order in the Soviet Union, Poland, Czechoslovakia, Hungary, the German Democratic Republic, Bulgaria, Albania, and Romania, as well as in countries in Africa and Latin America.[74] Many East European criminologists are no longer quoting Marx in their publications, which tend increasingly to focus on the classical rule-of-law concept. But Quinney has never seen the conditions in those countries as representative of Marxism. According to him, a true Marxist state has not yet been attained, but the ideal is worth pursuing.[75]

To the credit of radical criminologists, it must be said that they have encouraged their more traditional colleagues to look with a critical eye at all aspects of the criminal justice system, including the response of

As the Marxist socioeconomic order was toppled, so was the statue of the founder of the KGB, Felix Dzerzhinsky, at the Moscow headquarters.

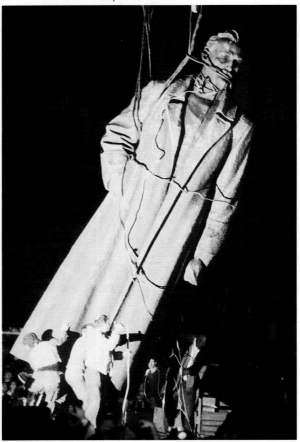

the system to both poor and rich offenders. Their concern is the exercise of power. They ask: Whose power? On whose behalf? For whose benefit? What is the legitimacy of that power? And who is excluded from the exercise of power, by whom, and why? Criminologists have had to address all these questions. Many may not have changed their answers, but the fact that the questions have been raised has ensured clearer answers than had been offered before.

Emerging Explanations

Over the last decade a number of important critical perspectives have emerged that are worthy of attention. These perspectives include radical feminist theory, left realism, and peacemaking criminology.

Radical Feminist Theory. One significant limitation to critical and Marxist work is an almost exclusive focus on crime committed by males. This limitation has been addressed only recently by both radical and socialist (Marxist) feminists. The former find the cause of crime in women to be male aggression, as well as men's attempts to control and subordinate women. The latter view female crime in terms of class, gender, and race oppression.[76]

Research by both radical and socialist feminists has revealed important insights into our conceptualization of law, social control, power relationships, and crime-causation theory. They include:

- Reframing the way in which rape is conceptualized (see Chapter 14)
- Acknowledging the fact that the way in which criminologists conceive of and define violence is male-centered
- Uncovering the relationship between male power, female economic dependency, and battery (for example, spouse abuse)
- Revealing the powerful effect of gender on justice processing[77]

Left Realism. Another critical perspective is left realism.[78] This school of thought emerged over the last decade as a response to the perception that radical criminologists (called "radical idealists" by left realists) place far too much weight on the evils of elite deviance, largely ignoring the fact that the disenfranchised lower classes are persistently victimized by street crime. Radical idealists, it is argued, have developed only weak crime-control strategies. Left realists, on the other hand, recognize street crime as an inevitable outcome of social and political deprivation. They seek a crime-control agenda, capable of being implemented in a capitalist system, that will protect the more vulnerable members of the lower classes from crime, and the fear of crime. The latter, according to left realists, has given conservative right-wing politicians a green light to promote a repressive law-and-order agenda.

Peacemaking Criminology. The most recently articulated critical perspective, peacemaking, promotes the idea of peace, justice, and equality in society. The current obsession with punishment and the war on crime suggests an orientation to criminology that only encourages violence. Peacemakers suggest that mutual aid, mediation, and conflict resolution, rather than coercive state control, are the best means to achieve a harmonious, peaceful society.[79] In short, peacemaking criminology advocates humanistic, nonviolent, and peaceful solutions to crime.

REVIEW

Labeling theory, conflict theory, and radical theory offer alternative explanations of crime, in the sense that they do not restrict their inquiry to individual characteristics or to social or communal processes. These three theories examine the impact of lawmaking and law enforcement processes on the creation of offenders. The labeling and conflict theories, as critical as they are of the existing system of criminal justice, envisage a system made more just and equitable by reform and democratic processes; radical theory demands revolutionary change. With long historical antecedents, all three theories gained prominence in the 1960s and early 1970s, during an era of rebellion against social, political, and economic inequities.

Labeling theory does not presume to explain all crime, but it does demonstrate that the criminal justice system is selective in determining who is to be labeled a criminal. It explains how labeling occurs, and it blames the criminal justice system for contributing to the labeling process and, therefore, to the crime problem.

Conflict theory goes a step beyond labeling theory in identifying the forces that selectively decide in the first place what conduct should be singled out for condemnation—usually, so it is claimed, to the detriment of the powerless and the benefit of the powerful.

Radical theory singles out the relationship between the owners of the means of production and the workers under capitalism as the root cause of crime and of all social inequities. Radical theory demands the overthrow of the existing order, which is said to perpetuate criminality by keeping the oppressed classes under the domination of the capitalist ruling class.

All three theories have adherents and opponents. Research to demonstrate the validity of the theories has produced mixed results. More important, all these theories have challenged conventional criminologists to rethink their approaches and to provide answers to questions that had not been asked before.

NOTES

1. Howard S. Becker, *Outsiders: Studies in the Sociology of Deviance* (New York: Macmillan, 1963), p. 9.
2. For an excellent discussion of how society controls deviance, see Nicholas N. Kittrie, *The Right to Be Different* (Baltimore: Johns Hopkins University Press, 1972).
3. William I. Thomas, *The Unadjusted Girl* (1923; New York: Harper & Row, 1967).
4. George Herbert Mead, "The Psychology of Punitive Justice," *American Journal of Sociology,* **23** (1918): 577–602. See also Charles Horton Cooley, "The Roots of Social Knowledge," *American Journal of Sociology,* **32** (1926): 59–79.
5. Herbert Blumer, "Sociological Implications of the Thought of George Herbert Mead," in *Symbolic Interactionism,* ed. Blumer (Englewood Cliffs, N.J.: Prentice-Hall, 1969), pp. 62, 65, 66.
6. Frank Tannenbaum, *Crime and the Community* (Boston: Ginn, 1938), p. 27.
7. Edwin M. Lemert, *Social Pathology* (New York: McGraw-Hill, 1951).
8. Edwin M. Lemert, *Human Deviance, Social Problems, and Social Control* (Englewood Cliffs, N.J.: Prentice-Hall, 1967), chap. 3.
9. Lemert, *Social Pathology,* pp. 75–76.
10. Lemert, *Human Deviance,* p. 46. See also Albert K. Cohen, *Deviance and Control* (Englewood Cliffs, N.J.: Prentice-Hall, 1966), pp. 24–25.
11. Erving Goffman, *Stigma: Notes on the Management of Spoiled Identity* (Englewood Cliffs, N.J.: Prentice-Hall, 1963).
12. Gerhard O. W. Mueller, "Resocialization of the Young Adult Offender in Switzerland," *Journal of Criminal Law and Criminology,* **43** (1953): 578–591, at p. 584.

13. Kai T. Erickson, "Notes on the Sociology of Deviance," in *The Other Side: Perspectives on Deviance,* ed. Howard S. Becker (New York: Free Press, 1964), p. 11.

14. Edwin Schur, *Labeling Deviant Behavior* (New York: Harper & Row, 1971), p. 21.

15. Edwin M. Schur, *Crimes without Victims* (Englewood Cliffs, N.J.: Prentice-Hall, 1965).

16. M. Ray, "The Cycle of Abstinence and Relapse among Heroin Addicts," *Social Problems,* **9** (1961): 132–140.

17. David Matza, *Becoming Deviant* (Englewood Cliffs, N.J.: Prentice-Hall, 1969), pp. 44–53.

18. Becker, *Outsiders,* pp. 18, 20.

19. D. L. Rosenhan, "On Being Sane in Insane Places," *Science,* **179** (1973): 250–258. See also Bruce G. Link, "Understanding Labeling Effects in the Area of Mental Disorders: An Assessment of the Effects of Expectations of Rejection," *American Sociological Review,* **52** (1987): 96–112; and Anthony Walsh, "Twice Labeled: The Effect of Psychiatric Labeling on the Sentencing of Sex Offenders," *Social Problems,* **37** (1990): 375–389.

20. Carol Warren and John Johnson, "A Critique of Labeling Theory from the Phenomenological Perspective," in *Theoretical Perspectives on Deviance,* ed. J. D. Douglas and R. Scott (New York: Basic Books, 1973), p. 77; James P. Spradley, *You Owe Yourself a Drunk: An Ethnography of Urban Nomads* (Boston: Little, Brown, 1979), p. 254.

21. Richard D. Schwartz and Jerome H. Skolnick, "Two Studies of Legal Stigma," *Social Problems,* **10** (1962): 133–138.

22. Anthony Platt, *The Child Savers* (Chicago: University of Chicago Press, 1969). For a further discussion of the effects of stigmatization by the criminal justice system, see Charles W. Thomas and Donna M. Bishop, "The Effect of Formal and Informal Sanctions on Delinquency: A Longitudinal Comparison of Labeling and Deterrence Theories," *Journal of Criminal Law and Criminology,* **75** (1984): 1222–1245.

23. William J. Chambliss, "The Saints and the Roughnecks," *Society,* **11** (1973): 24–31.

24. Walter R. Gove, "Deviant Behavior, Social Intervention, and Labeling Theory," in *The Uses of Controversy in Sociology,* ed. Lewis A. Coser and Otto N. Larsen (New York: Free Press, 1976), pp. 219–227; Ross L. Matsueda, "Reflected Appraisals, Parental Labeling, and Delinquency: Specifying a Symbolic Interactionist Theory," *American Journal of Sociology,* **97** (1992): 1577–1611.

25. Ronald L. Akers, "Problems in the Sociology of Deviance," *Social Forces,* **46** (1968): 455–465.

26. Ronald L. Akers, *Deviant Behavior: A Social Learning Approach,* 2d ed. (Belmont, Calif.: Wadsworth, 1977); David Ward and Charles R. Tittle, "Deterrence or Labeling: The Effects of Informal Sanctions," *Deviant Behavior,* **14** (1993): 43–64.

27. Jack P. Gibbs, "Conceptions of Deviant Behavior: The Old and the New," *Pacific Sociological Review,* **9** (Spring 1966): 9–14.

28. Charles Wellford, "Labelling Theory and Criminology: An Assessment," *Social Problems,* **22** (1975): 343; Charles F. Wellford and Ruth A. Triplett, "The Future of Labeling Theory: Foundations and Promises," in *Advances in Criminological Theory,* vol. 4, ed. Freda Adler and William S. Laufer (New Brunswick, N.J.: Transaction, 1993).

29. Alexander Liazos, "The Poverty of the Sociology of Deviance: Nuts, Sluts, and Perverts," *Social Problems,* **20** (1972): 103–120.

30. Howard S. Becker, "Labelling Theory Reconsidered," in *Outsiders: Studies in the Sociology of Deviance,* rev. ed., ed. Becker (New York: Free Press, 1973), pp. 177–208. See also Schur, *Labeling Deviant Behavior,* for an excellent review of labeling theory.

31. Compare this perspective with the emerging notion of criminology as peacemaking; see Harold E. Pepinsky and Richard Quinney, eds., *Criminology as Peace-Making* (Bloomington: University of Indiana Press, 1991).

32. Émile Durkheim, *The Division of Labor in Society* (New York: Free Press, 1947), p. 80.

33. Roscoe Pound, "A Survey of Social Interests," *Harvard Law Review,* **57** (1943): 1–39 at p. 39.

34. Durkheim, *The Division of Labor in Society,* p. 102.

35. Roscoe Pound, *An Introduction to the Philosophy of Law* (Boston: Little, Brown, 1922), p. 98.

36. Richard Quinney, *Crime and Justice in Society* (Boston: Little, Brown, 1969), pp. 26–30.

37. William Chambliss, "The State, the Law, and the Definition of Behavior as Criminal or Delinquent," in *Handbook of Criminology,* ed. Daniel Glaser (Chicago: Rand McNally, 1974), pp. 7–44.

38. Austin Turk, "Law as a Weapon in Social Conflict," *Social Problems,* **23** (1976): 276–291.

39. George Vold, *Theoretical Criminology* (New York: Oxford University Press, 1958), pp. 204, 209.

40. Ralf Dahrendorf, *Class and Class Conflict in Industrial Society* (Stanford, Calif.: Stanford University Press, 1959). See also Ralf Dahrendorf, "Out of Utopia: Toward a Reorientation of Sociological Analysis," *American Journal of Sociology,* **64** (1958): 127.

41. Austin Turk, *Criminality and Legal Order* (Chicago: Rand McNally, 1969), pp. 25, 33, 41–42, 48. See also Thomas O'Reilly-Fleming et al., "Issues in Social Order and Social Control," *Journal of Human Justice,* **2** (1990): 55–74.

42. Austin Turk, *Political Criminality: The Defiance and Defense of Authority* (Beverly Hills, Calif.: Sage, 1982), p. 15.

43. Turk, "Law as a Weapon."

44. William J. Chambliss, "A Sociological Analysis of the Law of Vagrancy," *Social Problems,* **12** (1966): 67–77. For an opposing view on the historical development of criminal law, see Jeffrey S. Adler, "A Historical Analysis of the Law of Vagrancy," *Criminology,* **27** (1989): 209–229; and a rejoinder to Adler: William J. Chambliss, "On Trashing Criminology," ibid., pp. 231–238.

45. Alan Lizotte, "Extra-Legal Factors in Chicago's Criminal Courts: Testing the Conflict Model of Criminal Justice," *Social Problems,* **25** (1978): 564–580. See also Kathleen Daly, "Neither Conflict nor Labeling nor Paternalism Will Suffice: Intersections of Race, Ethnicity, Gender, and Family in Criminal Court Decisions," *Crime and Delinquency,* **35** (1989): 136–168; and Elizabeth Comack, ed., "Race, Class, Gender and Justice," *Journal of Human Justice,* **2** (1990): 1–124.

46. Freda Adler, "Socioeconomic Variables Influencing Jury Verdicts," *New York University Review of Law on Social Change,* **3** (1973): 16–36. See also Martha A. Myers, "Social Back-

ground and the Sentencing Behavior of Judges," *Criminology,* **26** (1988): 649–675.

47. Celesta A. Albonetti, Robert M. Hauser, John Hagan, and Ilene H. Nagel, "Criminal Justice Decision-Making as a Stratification Process: The Role of Race and Stratification Resources in Pretrial Release," *Journal of Quantitative Criminology,* **5** (1989): 57–82.

48. Austin Turk, "Law, Conflict, and Order: From Theorizing toward Theories," *Canadian Review of Sociology and Anthropology,* **13** (1976): 282–294.

49. Georg Rusche and Otto Kirchheimer, *Punishment and Social Structure* (New York: Columbia University Press, 1939), p. 93.

50. Friedrich Engels, *"To the Working Class of Great Britain," Introduction to The Condition of the Working Class in England (1845),* in Karl Marx and Friedrich Engels, *Collected Works,* vol. 4 (New York: International Publishers, 1974), pp. 213–214, 298.

51. Karl Marx and Friedrich Engels, *The Communist Manifesto* (1848; New York: International Publishers, 1979), p. 9.

52. Willem Adriaan Bonger, *Criminality and Economic Conditions,* trans. Henry P. Horton (Boston: Little, Brown, 1916).

53. Ibid., p. 669.

54. J. M. Van Bemmelen, "Willem Adriaan Bonger," in *Pioneers in Criminology,* ed. Hermann Mannheim (London: Stevens, 1960), p. 361.

55. Ian Taylor, Paul Walton, and Jock Young, *The New Criminology: For a Social Theory of Deviance* (London: Routledge & Kegan Paul, 1973), pp. 264, 281. See also Jock Young, "Radical Criminology in Britain: The Emergence of a Competing Paradigm," *British Journal of Criminology,* **28** (1988): 159–183.

56. Gresham Sykes, "The Rise of Critical Criminology," *Journal of Criminal Law and Criminology,* **65** (1974): 206–213.

57. Richard Quinney, "Crime Control in Capitalist Society: A Critical Philosophy of Legal Order," *Issues in Criminology,* **8** (1973): 75–95; Richard Quinney, "There's a Lot of Us Folks Grateful to the Lone Ranger: Some Notes on the Rise and Fall of American Criminology," *Insurgent Sociologist,* **4** (1973): 56–64.

58. Richard Quinney, "Crime Control in Capitalist Society," in *Critical Criminology,* ed. Ian Taylor, Paul Walton, and Jock Young (London: Routledge & Kegan Paul, 1975), p. 199.

59. Richard Quinney, *Class, State, and Crime: On the Theory and Practice of Criminal Justice,* 2d ed. (New York: David McKay, 1977), p. 10.

60. Richard Quinney, *Critique of Legal Order: Crime Control in a Capitalist Society* (Boston: Little, Brown, 1974), pp. 11–13.

61. William Chambliss and Robert Seidman, *Law, Order, and Power* (Reading, Mass.: Addison-Wesley, 1971), p. 503.

62. Ibid., p. 504.

63. Barry Krisberg, *Crime and Privilege: Toward a New Criminology* (Englewood Cliffs, N.J.: Prentice-Hall, 1975).

64. Herman Schwendinger and Julia Schwendinger, "Delinquency and Social Reform: A Radical Perspective," in *Juvenile Justice,* ed. Lamar Empey (Charlottesville: University of Virginia Press, 1979), pp. 246–290.

65. Elliot Currie, "A Dialogue with Anthony M. Platt," *Issues in Criminology,* **8** (1973): 28.

66. Steven F. Messner and Marvin D. Krohn, "Class, Compliance Structures, and Delinquency: Assessing Integrated Structural-Marxist Theory," *American Journal of Sociology,* **96** (1990): 300–328.

67. Lance H. Selva and Robert M. Bohm, "A Critical Examination of the Informalism Experiment in the Administration of Justice," *Crime and Social Justice,* 29 (1987): 43–57; Timothy Carter and Donald Clelland, "A Neo-Marxian Critique, Formulation, and Test of Juvenile Dispositions as a Function of Social Class," *Social Problems,* **27** (1979): 96–108; David Greenberg and Drew Humphries, "The Co-optation of Fixed Sentencing Reform," *Crime and Delinquency,* **26** (1980): 216–225.

68. Jackson Toby, "The New Criminology Is the Old Sentimentality," *Criminology,* **16** (1979): 516–526; Jim Thomas and Aogan O'Maolchatha, "Reassessing the Critical Metaphor: An Optimistic Revisionist View," *Justice Quarterly,* **6** (1989): 143–171; David Brown and Russell Hogg, "Essentialism, Radical Criminology and Left Realism," *Australian and New Zealand Journal of Criminology,* **25** (1992): 195–230.

69. Carl B. Klockars, "The Contemporary Crises of Marxist Criminology," *Criminology,* **16** (1979): 477–515.

70. Ibid.

71. Richard F. Sparks, "A Critique of Marxist Criminology," in *Crime and Justice: An Annual Review of Research,* ed. Norval Morris and Michael Tonry (Chicago: University of Chicago Press, 1980), p. 159.

72. Milton Mankoff, "On the Responsibility of Marxist Criminology: A Reply to Quinney," *Contemporary Crisis,* **2** (1978): 293–301.

73. Austin T. Turk, "Analyzing Official Deviance: For Nonpartisan Conflict Analysis in Criminology," in *Radical Criminology: The Coming Crisis,* ed. James A. Inciardi (Beverly Hills, Calif.: Sage, 1980), pp. 78–91. See also Sykes, "The Rise of Critical Criminology," p. 212.

74. Philip L. Reichel and Andrzej Rzeplinski, "Student Views of Crime and Criminal Justice in Poland and the United States," *International Journal of Comparative and Applied Criminal Justice,* **13** (1989): 65–81.

75. Quinney, *Class, State, and Crime,* p. 40.

76. Meda Chesney-Lind, "Feminism and Criminology," *Justice Quarterly,* **5** (1988): 497–538; Pat Carlen, "Women, Crime, Feminism, and Realism," *Social Justice,* **17** (1990): 106–123.

77. Sally Simpson, "Feminist Theory, Crime and Justice," *Criminology,* **27** (1989): 605–632; Meda Chesney-Lind, "Judicial Enforcement of the Female Sex Role: The Family Court and the Female Delinquent," *Issues in Criminology,* **8** (1973): 51–69.

78. Martin D. Schwartz and Walter S. DeKeseredy, "Left Realist Criminology: Strengths, Weaknesses and the Feminist Critique," *Crime, Law and Social Change,* **15** (1991): 51–72; John Lowman and Brian D. MacLean, eds., *Realist Criminology: Crime Control and Policing in the 1990s* (Ontario: University of Toronto Press, 1990); Walter S. DeKeseredy and Martin D. Schwartz, "British and U.S. Left Realism: A Critical Comparison," *International Journal of Offender Therapy and Comparative Criminology,* **35** (1991): 248–262.

79. Pepinsky and Quinney, eds., *Criminology as Peacemaking;* Richard Quinney, "Socialist Humanism and the Problem of

Crime," *Crime, Law and Social Change,* **23** (1995): 147–156; Robert Elias et al., Special Issue, "Declaring Peace on Crime," *Peace Review: A Transnational Quarterly,* **6** (1994): 131–254.

▩ **Internet Exercise**

You learned in this chapter that some scholars question the rule-making process in our society. They claim that a struggle for power is a basic feature of human existence. Many of these scholars belong to the Critical Criminology Division of the American Society of Criminology. What are its purposes?

▩ **Your Web Site is:**
http://sun.soci.niu.edu/~critcrim/

PART III

Types of Crimes

The word "crime" conjures up many images: mugging and murder, cheating on taxes, and selling crack. Penal codes define thousands of different crimes. But all crimes have certain elements in common. All are human acts in violation of law, committed by an actor who acted with a criminal intent to cause a specified harm. The various legal defenses to crime are based on the defendant's alleging that one of the required elements was missing (Chapter 10).

After analyzing the common ingredients of all crimes, we examine specific types of crime: violent crime (Chapter 11); crime against property (Chapter 12); white-collar, corporate, and organized crime (Chapter 13); and crime related to drug and alcohol trafficking and consumption and to sexual mores (Chapter 14). All these types of crime are explained in terms of legal and criminological perspectives. Their occurrence, frequency, and pervasiveness are also discussed in comparison with the occurrence of crime in other parts of the world. Chapter 15, which is concerned with comparative criminology, includes a discussion of international and transnational crimes.

CHAPTER 10
The Concept
of Crime

The Ingredients of Crime

The Seven Basic Requirements
The Act Requirement
The Legality Requirement
The Harm Requirement
The Causation Requirement
Mens Rea: The "Guilty Mind" Requirement
The Concurrence Requirement
The Punishment Requirement

The Defenses: Excuses

The Insanity Defense
Guilty but Mentally Ill
The Intoxication Defense
Infancy
Mistake of Fact
Mistake or Ignorance of Law

The Defenses: Justifications

Duress
Necessity
Public Duty
Self-Defense, Defense of Others, Defense of Property

Attempt and Accessoryship
Typologies of Crime
Review
Notes

Special Features

CRIMINOLOGICAL FOCUS: Thirty-Eight Witnesses
WINDOW TO THE WORLD: Necessity at Sea
AT ISSUE: The Battered Woman Self-Defense and the Penal Codes

Key Terms

accomplices
criminal attempt
felonies
mens rea
misdemeanors
principals
strict liability
torts
violations

Police in Richmond, California, have an ironclad case against three burglars who had entered the Bermudez family's home and absconded with a tricycle. The ringleader also attacked the only witness to the burglary, beating and kicking him, cracking his skull, and leaving him for dead. In early May 1996, the three were arraigned on charges of having committed burglary. The ringleader was also charged with attempted murder.

What is unusual about the case is that the ringleader is 6 years old, and his companions are 2-year-old twins. The "witness" was a 1-month-old baby! The ringleader obviously is a bad kid, so neighbors concluded. He had unlawfully entered the Bermudez home before; he held a grudge against the Bermudez family; he had harassed other kids in the neighborhood.

Now the three are charged with burglary; and the ringleader, whom his public defender has dubbed a "munchkin," has been charged with attempted murder as well. Journalists, neighbors, and at least some officials are all aflutter: charges of attempted murder and burglary against children that young? "The judicial system has few guidelines for dealing with such youthful *offenders*," wrote *Time*.[1] Are there too "few" guidelines?

211

This is where the concept of crime becomes relevant. Were crimes committed? What is it that makes a crime? Which crimes were committed?

In trying to answer these questions, we must begin by looking at the law, here the criminal code of the state of California, which defines what is considered a crime in California. This will not get us too far.[2] Codes, for the most part, do not contain theoretical propositions. It is scholars who, over time, have worked out the basics of the concept of crime as these inhere in all the different types of crime defined in criminal codes.

THE INGREDIENTS OF CRIME

We begin by examining that part of criminal law that deals with the common legal ingredients, or elements, found in all crimes. With few exceptions, if any one of these elements is not present, no crime has been committed. All the defenses available to a person charged with a crime allege that at least one of these elements is not present.

The Seven Basic Requirements

The American criminal law scholar Jerome Hall has developed the theory that a human event, in order to qualify as a crime, must meet seven basic requirements[3]:

1. The act requirement
2. The legality requirement
3. The harm requirement
4. The causation requirement
5. The mens rea requirement
6. The concurrence requirement
7. The punishment requirement[4]

The Act Requirement

Law scholars have long agreed that one fundamental ingredient of every crime is a human act. In this context, what is an "act"? Suppose a sleepwalker, in a trance, grabs a stone and hurls it at a passerby, with lethal consequences. The law does not consider this event to be an act; before any human behavior can qualify as an act, there must be a conscious interaction between mind and body, a physical movement that results from the determination or effort of the actor. Thus the Model Penal Code (MPC), which the American Law Institute proposed to legislatures in 1962, says that the following behaviors are not voluntary acts:

- A reflex or convulsion
- A bodily movement that occurs during unconsciousness or sleep
- Conduct that occurs during hypnosis or results from hypnotic suggestion
- A bodily movement that is not determined by the actor, as when somebody is pushed by another person[5]

Free Will? This formula gives the impression that the law is based on "free will," the idea that people are accountable only if they freely choose to do something and then consciously do it. But scientists and lawyers have yet to discover an individual who is completely free to make choices. All of us have been molded by factors beyond our control, and our choices are to some extent conditioned by internal and external factors and forces. It is only when choices are overpoweringly influenced by forces beyond our control, such as the case of the sleepwalking stone thrower, that the law will consider behavior irrational and beyond its reach.

Act versus Status. The criminal law, in principle, does not penalize anyone for a status or condition. Suppose the law made it a crime to be more than 6 feet tall or to have red hair. Or suppose the law made it a crime to be a member of the family of an army deserter or to be of a given religion or ethnic background. That was exactly the situation in the Soviet Union under Stalin's penal code, which made it a crime to be related to a deserter from the Red Army. It was also the situation in Hitler's Germany, where in effect it was a crime to be Jewish, and it was punishable by death.

There is thus more to the act requirement than the issue of a behavior's being voluntary and rational: There is the problem of distinguishing between act and status. A California law made it a criminal offense, subject to a jail term, to be a drug addict. In *Robinson v. California* the U.S. Supreme Court held that statute to be unconstitutional. By making a status or condition a crime, the statute violated the Eighth Amendment to the U.S. Constitution, which prohibits "cruel and unusual punishments." Addiction, the

Court noted, is a condition, an illness, much like leprosy or venereal disease. Even babies born of addict mothers are addicts. Said the Court: "Even one day in prison would be cruel and unusual punishment for the 'crime' of having a common cold."[6]

In a subsequent case, *Powell v. Texas*, the Supreme Court backed away from its recognition of the act requirement.[7] A Texas statute had made it a crime to be drunk in public. Powell was a chronic alcoholic, prosecuted for being in a public place while drunk. The defense argued that chronic alcoholics cannot refrain from drinking. If they are homeless, they cannot help being in public places. The Supreme Court, however, upheld Powell's conviction, in essence saying that he had not been punished for being a chronic alcoholic but for doing something—for going to a public place in an intoxicated state. This ruling is considered by many to be inconsistent with the *Robinson* decision.

Failure to Act. The act requirement has yet another aspect. An act requires the interaction of mind and body. If only the mind is active and the body does not move, we do not have an act: Just thinking about punching someone in the nose is not a crime (Figure 10.1). We are free to think. But if we carry a thought into physical action, we commit an act, which may be a crime.

Then there is the problem of omission, or failure to act. If the law requires that convicted sex offenders register with the police, and such a person decides not to fill out the registration form, that person is guilty of a crime by omission. But he has acted! He told his hand not to pick up that pen, not to fill out the form. Inaction may be action when the law clearly spells out what one has to do and one decides not to do it.

The law in most U.S. states imposes no duty to be a good Samaritan, to offer help to another person in distress. The Kitty Genovese case is a well-known example. Not one of her 38 neighbors was a good Samaritan. The law requires action only if one has a legal duty to act. Lifeguards, for example, are contractually obligated to save bathers from drowning; parents are obligated by law to protect their children; law enforcement officers and firefighters are required to rescue people in distress; baby-sitters must protect babies in their care from harm. In addition, the law imposes a duty to continue rescue operations on anybody who, though not required to

© 1962 The Saturday Evening Post

FIGURE 10.1 Has a crime been committed? Is walking on the grass prohibited by law, subject to punishment? Did the actor commit the act by actually walking on the grass, or did he merely have a criminal intent to do so? Perhaps the actor is incapable of forming a legally relevant intent because he is too young to do so!

do so, has voluntarily come to the aid of a person in need.

The Legality Requirement

Marion Palendrano was charged with, among other things, being a "common scold" because she disturbed "the peace of the neighborhood and of all good and quiet people of this State." Mrs. Palendrano moved that the charge be dismissed, and the Superior Court of New Jersey agreed with her, reasoning:

1. Such a crime cannot be found anywhere in the New Jersey statute books. Hence there is no such crime, although, long ago, the common law of England may have recognized such a crime.
2. "Being a common scold" is so vague a concept that to punish somebody for it would violate constitutional due process: "We insist that laws give the person of ordinary intelligence a reasonable

CRIMINOLOGICAL FOCUS

THIRTY-EIGHT WITNESSES

On March 27, 1964, the *New York Times* printed the following story:

For more than half an hour thirty-eight respectable, law-abiding citizens in Queens watched a killer stalk and stab a woman in three separate attacks in Kew Gardens.

Twice the sound of their voices and the sudden glow of their bedroom lights interrupted him and frightened him off. Each time he returned, sought her out and stabbed her again. Not one person telephoned the police during the assault; one witness called after the woman was dead.

That was two weeks ago today. But Assistant Chief Inspector Frederick M. Lussen, in charge of the borough's detectives and a veteran of twenty-five years of homicide investigations, is still shocked.

(1) Where she parked her car.
(2) Place of initial attack.
(3) Place of second attack.
(4) Place of third attack.

He can give a matter-of-fact recitation of many murders. But the Kew Gardens slaying baffles him—not because it is a murder, but because the "good people" failed to call the police.

"As we have reconstructed the crime," he said, "the assailant had three chances to kill this woman during a thirty-five-minute period. He returned twice to complete the job. If we had been called when he first attacked, the woman might not be dead now."

This is what the police say happened beginning at 3:30 a.m. in the staid, middle-class, tree-lined Austin Street area:

Twenty-eight-year-old Catherine Genovese, who was called Kitty by almost everyone in the neighborhood, was returning home from her job as manager of a bar in Hollis. She parked her red Fiat . . . turned off the lights of her car, locked the door and started to walk the 100 feet to the entrance of her apartment . . . Miss Genovese noticed a man at the far end of the lot . . . She halted. Then, nervously, she headed up Austin Street . . . where there is a call box to the 102d Police Precinct in nearby Richmond Hill.

She got as far as a street light in front of a bookstore before the man grabbed her. She screamed. Lights went on in the ten-story apartment house . . . which faces the bookstore. Windows slid open and voices punctured the early-morning stillness.

Miss Genovese screamed: "Oh, my God, he stabbed me! Please help me! Please help me!"

From one of the upper windows in the apartment house, a man called down: "Let that girl alone!"

The assailant looked up at him, shrugged and walked down Austin Street . . . Miss Genovese struggled to her feet.

Lights went out. The killer returned to Miss Genovese [and] stabbed her again.

"I'm dying!" she shrieked. "I'm dying!"

Windows were opened again, and lights went on in many apartments. The assailant got into his car and drove away. Miss Genovese staggered to her feet. It was 3:35 a.m.

The assailant returned. By then, Miss Genovese had crawled to the back of the building . . . The killer . . . saw her slumped on the floor at the foot of the stairs. He stabbed her a third time—fatally.

It was 3:50 by the time the police received their first call from a man who was a neighbor of Miss Genovese. In two minutes they were at the scene.

It was 4:25 a.m. when the ambulance arrived for the body of Miss Genovese. It drove off. "Then," a solemn police detective said, "the people came out."(1)

Source
1. Excerpted from A. M. Rosenthal, *Thirty-Eight Witnesses* (New York: McGraw-Hill, 1964).

Questions for Discussion
1. Could the Kitty Genovese case have happened in the 1990s? Why or why not?
2. Excuses offered by the witnesses for not calling the police when they first heard screams included "I was tired," "We were afraid," "I didn't want my husband to get involved," and "I don't know." Would you have called the police?

opportunity to know what is prohibited, so that he may act accordingly," ruled the court.[8]

If we want a person to adhere to a standard, the person has to know what that standard is. Thus we have the ancient proposition that only conduct that has been made criminal by law before an act is committed can be a crime; in Latin, this is known as the maxim *nullum crimen sine lege* ("no crime without law"). Police, prosecutors, and courts are not interested in the billions of acts human beings engage in unless such acts have previously been defined by law as criminal. The law is interested only in an act (*actus*) that is *reus*, in the sense of guilty, evil, and prohibited. Additionally, as Marion Palendrano's case demonstrates, when the law has made some behavior a crime, the language defining it must be clear enough to be understood.

The Harm Requirement

Every crime has been created to prevent something bad (a given harm) from happening. Murder is prohibited because we don't want people to be killed. Arson and theft are prohibited because we want people to be secure in their possessions. This detrimental consequence that we are trying to avoid is called *harm*. If the specified harm has not been created by the defendant's act, the crime is not complete. Just think of would-be assassin John W. Hinckley, Jr., who tried to kill President Reagan. He shot Reagan, but the president did not die. The harm envisioned by the law against murder had not been accomplished. (Hinckley could have been found guilty of attempted murder, but he was acquitted by reason of insanity.)

Sometimes the harm is less drastic than a dead person or a burned house. Pooper-scooper laws (you must clean up after your dog) are designed to prevent the harm of dirty streets and sidewalks. In the case of drunk-driving statutes, the harm is not of a physical nature. It consists of the grave danger to the public which driving while intoxicated constitutes. (If the drunk driver kills someone, a more serious charge is brought.)

From a criminological perspective, most crimes are grouped by the harm that each entails. Offenses against the person involve harm to an individual, and offenses against property involve damage to property or loss of its possession.

The Causation Requirement

What is the act of hitting a home run? Of course it is a hit that allows a batter to run to first, second, and third base and then back to home plate. Actually it is much more complicated than that. It starts with the decision to swing a bat, at a certain angle, with a particular intensity, in a specific direction, in order to cause a home run. Suppose that at a San Diego Padres home game, the batter hits a ball unusually high into the air. A passing pelican picks it up, flies off with it, and then drops it into the bleachers. Has the batter hit a home run? We doubt it.

It's the same in crime. Causation requires that the actor achieve the result (the harm) through his or her own effort. Suppose that A, in an effort to kill B, wounds him and that B actually dies when the ambulance carrying him to the hospital collides with another vehicle. Despite B's death, A did not succeed in her personal attempt to kill B. Thus the act of murder is incomplete, although A may be guilty of an attempt to kill. The causation requirement, then, holds that a crime is not complete unless the actor's conduct necessarily caused the harm without interference by somebody else, and that it is the proximate cause of the act.[9]

Mens Rea: The "Guilty Mind" Requirement

Every crime, according to tradition, requires **mens rea,** a "guilty mind." Let us examine the case of Ms. Lambert. She was convicted in Los Angeles of an offense created by city ordinance: having lived in the city without registering with the police as a person previously convicted of a crime. Ms. Lambert had no idea that Los Angeles had such a registration requirement. Nor could she possibly have known that she was required to register. She appealed all the way to the U.S. Supreme Court, and she won. Said the Court: "Where a person did not know [of the prohibition] (s)he may not be convicted consistent with due process."[10]

Of course, to blame Ms. Lambert for violating the Los Angeles city ordinance would make no sense. Ms. Lambert had no notion that she was doing something wrong by living in Los Angeles and not registering herself as a convicted person. The potential of blame that follows a choice to commit a crime is meant to be a powerful incentive to do the right thing and avoid doing the wrong thing. That is the function of mens rea. (We will return to Ms. Lambert later on.)

With Ms. Lambert's case we have reached a fundamental point: No one can be guilty of a crime unless he or she acted with the knowledge of doing something wrong. This principle always has existed. It is implicit in the concept of crime that the perpetrator know the wrongfulness of the act. It is not required that the perpetrator know the penal code or have personal feelings of guilt. It is enough that the perpetrator knows that he or she had no right to do what he or she did and decided to do it anyway.[11]

In a 1994 landmark decision, a sharply divided U.S. Supreme Court has once again expressed its adherence to the mens rea–guilty mind requirement. A married couple, the Ratzlefs, had made cash transactions (to pay a gambling debt) which they should have reported to the Internal Revenue Service. They honestly did not know of their obligation to report—the law had only recently been amended. Prior law required only banks to report.[12] But the majority reached this conclusion only because Congress had used the word "wilful" in defining the crime. That was good enough for Justice Ruth Bader Ginsburg to conclude that Congress wanted to subject to punishment only those who failed to report, knowing that not to report was wrong. The dissent, in an opinion by Justice Harry A. Blackmun, argued that "wilful" means no more than willing to act (or to omit, as in this case). Yet if that were so, can one conceive of any act that is not wilful by definition? And if that is so, then Congress would have used a self-evident term to describe the act. The controversy over whether "wilfulness" is part of the act requirement, or signals a significant component of the mens rea–knowledge-of-wrongfulness requirement, has led some scholars to argue that the centuries-old distinction between *actus reus* and *mens rea* is meaningless and should be abandoned.[13] It does not seem so. The mind has two functions to perform when it comes to the commission of a crime: First, the mind must be on the job when it comes to committing an act; second, the mind must entertain the notion of wrongfulness—and that is mens rea— for otherwise it is not alerted to the threat of punishment.

Anyone who violently attacks another person, takes another's property, invades another's home, forces intercourse, or forges a signature on someone else's check knows rather well that he or she is doing something wrong. All these examples of mens rea entail an intention to achieve harm or a knowledge that the prohibited harm will result. For some crimes, however, less than a definite intention suffices: reckless actions by which the actors consciously risk causing a prohibited harm (for example, the driver who races down a rain-slicked highway or the employer who sends his employees to work without safety equipment, knowing full well that lives are thereby being endangered).

Strict liability is an exception to the mens rea requirement. There is a class of offenses for which legislatures or courts require no showing of criminal intent or mens rea. For these offenses, the fact that the actor makes an innocent mistake and proceeds in good faith does not affect criminal liability. Such offenses are called strict-liability offenses, and they crept into our law with the Industrial Revolution. Most of them involve conduct subject to regulation, conduct that threatens the public welfare as a whole. Strict-liability offenses range all the way from distributing adulterated food to passing a red light. Typically these offenses are subject to small penalties only, but in a few cases substantial punishments can be and have been imposed.[14]

The efficacy of strict criminal liability is very much in doubt. Vast numbers of persons being found guilty who had no idea of doing something wrong— and in precisely the kind of minor cases which affect the largest portion of the population—can only lead to disrespect for the law.[15]

The Concurrence Requirement

The concurrence requirement states that the criminal act must be accompanied by an equally criminal mind. Suppose a striker throws a stone at an office window in order to shatter it, and a broken piece of glass pierces the throat of a secretary, who bleeds to death. Wanting to damage property deserves condemnation, but of a far lesser degree than wanting to kill. Act and intent did not concur in this case, and the striker should not be found guilty of murder. The law has created many exceptions to the concurrence requirement, one of which, the felony murder rule, we discuss in Chapter 11.

The Punishment Requirement

The last ingredient needed to constitute a crime is that of punishment. An illegal act coupled with an evil mind (criminal intent or mens rea) still does not constitute a crime unless the law subjects it to a punishment. If a sign posted in the park states "Do not step on the grass" and you do it anyway, have you committed a criminal offense? Not unless there is a law that subjects that act to punishment. Otherwise it is simply an improper or inconsiderate act.

The punishment requirement, more than any of the others, helps us differentiate between crimes (which are subject to punishments) and **torts,** civil wrongs for which the law does not prescribe punishment but merely grants the injured party the right to recover damages.

The nature and severity of punishments also help us differentiate between grades of crime. Most penal codes recognize three degrees of severity: **Felonies** are severe crimes, subject to punishments of a year or more in prison or to capital punishment. **Misdemeanors** are less severe crimes, subject to a maximum of 1 year in jail. (For crimes of both grades, fines can also be imposed as punishments.) **Violations** are minor offenses, normally subject only to fines.

THE DEFENSES: EXCUSES

When we turn to the various defenses recognized by law, we discover that each defense simply claims that one or more of the seven basic constituent elements of the crime does not exist. In other words, what at first glance may indicate that a crime was committed—a dead body or a burned building—may turn out not to be a crime after all because, for example, the perpetrator lacked criminal intent or the law granted the actor the right to do what he or she did so that the "illegality" is absent.

A recent analysis by legal scholar and defense counsel Alan Dershowitz demonstrated that in recent years clever defense attorneys have worked 53 new defenses into the legal vocabulary, such as the "black rage defense" or the "everyone-does-it" defense.[16] None of these is a proper legal defense, though all may conjure up pity and compassion. For, to repeat, a defense, technically, simply argues the absence of one or more of the seven constituent elements of crime.

The Insanity Defense

On March 30, 1981, a young man stood in front of the Hilton Hotel in Washington, D.C., and mixed with the crowd that had assembled to greet President Reagan. As the president and his entourage left the hotel, the young man drew a revolver and fired several shots, wounding the president, White House Press Secretary James Brady, a secret service agent, and a District of Columbia police officer.[17] All survived, but Brady was permanently disabled.

The young man turned out to be John W. Hinckley, Jr., who had become fascinated with the actress Jodie Foster. She had appeared in a movie that featured a deranged taxi driver who armed himself and killed a political candidate. Hinckley seemed to follow this script: He believed his only hope of winning Miss Foster's admiration lay in killing the president. Hinckley pleaded not guilty by reason of insanity. That plea amounts to saying: "Whatever happened, I am not guilty because I suffered from a mental illness that made me incapable of committing the crime you have charged me with."

In its modern form, the insanity defense was formulated by the House of Lords, following a case that was not very different from Hinckley's. Daniel M'Naghten was obsessed by the idea that the prime minister, Sir Robert Peel, wanted to destroy the liberties of English subjects. In 1829, when Peel was home secretary, with responsibility for security and

John W. Hinckley, Jr., who attempted to assassinate President Reagan in March 1981, holds a pistol to his head in this self-portrait. His defense of insanity at his trial was successful.

internal affairs, he created a police force, and in the 1830s and 1840s he used the police to suppress public dissent. M'Naghten joined a campaign against Sir Robert. As a consequence of these activities, he became convinced that Sir Robert was spying on and persecuting him. When M'Naghten could no longer stand the pressure of his obsession, he traveled to London and loitered around 10 Downing Street, the prime minister's official residence.

M'Naghten's opportunity came on Friday, January 20, 1843. He shot into the back of the person he thought was Sir Robert. The victim was actually the prime minister's private secretary, Edward Drummond. A few days later Drummond died of the gunshot wounds. The trial of Daniel M'Naghten became a cause célèbre (a notorious case), and aristocratic ladies and gentlemen were frequently in attendance at court.[18] M'Naghten was acquitted by reason of insanity.[19]

The M'Naghten Test. After M'Naghten's acquittal the question of insanity was debated in the House of Lords, which is also England's highest court. It formulated the now famous M'Naghten rules:

> The jurors ought to be told in all cases that every man is to be presumed to be sane, and to possess a sufficient degree of reason to be responsible for his crimes, until the contrary is proved to their satisfaction; and that, to

establish a defense on the ground of insanity, it must be clearly proved that, at the time of the committing of the act, the party accused was labouring under such a defect of reason, from disease of the mind, as not to know the nature and quality of the act he was doing; or if he did know it, that he did not know he was doing what was wrong.[20]

This test of insanity can be reduced to the following formula. As a result of mental illness, the accused either:

1. Did not know the nature and quality of his act; that is, the voluntary act requirement was not fulfilled.

Or:

2. Did not know that the act was wrong; that is, the mens rea requirement was not fulfilled.

In either case there can be no crime.[21]

The debate about the M'Naghten test has raged for a century and a half. Some courts have misunderstood the test, believing that the only criterion for insanity was whether the defendant knew the difference between right and wrong. They called it the "right-wrong test." Others thought a test that focuses only on what a person knows fails to capture the complexity of the human mind and its processes.

The trial of Daniel McNaughten, whose name is perpetuated in the famous rules on murders by lunatics

M'Naghten, obsessed with the idea that Sir Robert Peel was destroying the liberty of Englishmen by creating a police force, stalked Sir Robert but killed his secretary by mistake. He was acquitted of murder by reason of insanity.

The Irresistible Impulse Test.   Imagine a case in which the defendant "knows" perfectly well what he or she is doing and understands that what he or she is doing is wrong. But the defendant contends that somehow he or she lost control over his or her actions; that is, he or she lost the power to choose between right and wrong. Some process in his or her mind compelled him or her to do what he or she did. To deal with that kind of situation, some American courts in the second half of the nineteenth century added another component to the M'Naghten rules: If as a result of mental illness the accused was unable to control his or her actions, then he or she must be acquitted. Such loss of self-control has been called an "irresistible impulse."[22]

The Durham or Product Test.   Judge David Bazelon's opinion in *Durham v. United States* in 1954 developed a new insanity test, partly based on an old New Hampshire case.[23] Under the Durham rule, the defendant was to be acquitted if the crime was the product of mental disease or defect. As soon as the defendant introduced some evidence of disease or defect, the prosecution had to prove the contrary beyond a reasonable doubt. Of all the tests, Durham has met with the most criticism and resistance from the legal community. In order to be acquitted by reason of insanity under the Durham formulation, a defendant simply had to introduce "some" evidence that the crime charged was a "product of" mental illness; that is, a mental disease or defect had the effect of producing the crime. It then became virtually impossible for the prosecution to disprove the "some evidence" and the resulting "product."

The Durham or "product" test allowed the medical profession to determine what was included among mental diseases or defects. The list of diseases and defects grew longer and longer. Ultimately the U.S. Court of Appeals for the District of Columbia, in *United States v. Brawner,* abolished the Durham test in favor of the American Law Institute (A.L.I.) test.[24] Today the Durham test is used in only one jurisdiction: Maine.

The A.L.I. Test.   The Model Penal Code of the American Law Institute (1962) includes an insanity test that incorporates features of the M'Naghten rules and irresistible impulse. Under this test:

[A] person is not responsible for criminal conduct if at the time of such conduct as a result of mental disease or defect he lacks substantial capacity either to appreciate the criminality [wrongfulness] of his conduct or to conform his conduct to the requirements of law.[25]

The special feature of this compromise is that the test leads to an acquittal when the defendant lacks "substantial capacity," whereas M'Naghten is frequently understood as requiring a total lack of capacity. The A.L.I. test is now used in about half of the American states.

The New Federal Test.   Let us return to the Hinckley case. The acquittal of Hinckley by reason of insanity caused the same kind of public outcry that M'Naghten's acquittal had caused nearly a century and a half earlier. At the time of the Hinckley case, the District of Columbia was using the A.L.I. test. In reaction to Hinckley's acquittal, Congress for the first time debated what the insanity defense should be for the federal courts, just as the House of Lords in 1843 had discussed the same question following M'Naghten's acquittal.

Congress came to the conclusion that the defendant should be acquitted by reason of insanity if "at the time of the commission of the act the defendant, as a result of a severe mental disease or defect, was unable to appreciate the nature and quality or wrongfulness of his act."[26] The new federal test returned to the idea that mental illness, if severe enough, cancels a defendant's criminal act (appreciating the nature and quality) or criminal intent (appreciating the wrongfulness of the act).

The insanity defense is actually so rare that the debate on it is of more academic interest than practical significance. Defendants evaluated for insanity at the Colorado State Hospital in the early 1980s, for example, represented only 0.03 percent of all persons arrested in Colorado, and those ultimately acquitted by reason of insanity amounted to only 0.007 percent of all persons arrested.[27] Despite the statistical infrequency of the insanity defense, some legislatures have abolished it and others are planning to do so, out of fear that no matter how few such defendants may be, a "guilty" one might go free. When a Montana prisoner claimed that the abolition of the insanity defense is unconstitutional, the Supreme Court refused to hear the case, thereby allowing the states to abolish the insanity defense.[28]

Guilty but Mentally Ill

A growing number of states have found yet another way to deal with troublesome insanity cases. They have added to the three available verdicts—guilty, not guilty, not guilty by reason of insanity—a fourth one: guilty but mentally ill (in some states, guilty but insane). This somewhat illogical verdict is considered appropriate when a defendant suffers from a mental disease that is not severe enough to warrant acquittal by reason of insanity. It acknowledges the defendant's guilt, and at the same time recognizes as a mitigating factor the presence of a significant but not disabling mental disorder. In practice it permits a guilty verdict for a defendant who, by reason of insanity, has acted without the requisite criminal intent.

Both the abolition of the insanity defense and the verdict "guilty but insane" have two negative consequences: (1) Those who by virtue of mental illness could not formulate the requisite criminal intent are nevertheless condemned as "guilty"; (2) mentally ill persons wind up in prison, rather than psychiatric care facilities which would be far better able to treat them successfully.[29] As might have been expected, the combination of a finding of criminal guilt, but also of insanity, has led to considerable confusion for jurors; nor have acquittals been reduced.[30]

The Intoxication Defense

Can anything other than mental illness affect the mind to such an extent that the accused does not have the required guilty mind or could not fulfill the act requirement? The most prominent example is intoxication, whether by alcohol or by drugs.

In colonial times, the Puritans were extremely averse to excusing the actions of those who drank to excess. In fact, drunkenness itself was an offense. But over time, and as the composition of the population changed, American law changed. The clearest example is "involuntary" intoxication. Suppose that, after taking a prescription drug, a person becomes so disoriented and confused that she loses the capacity to act rationally or to form a criminal intent. Suppose that she then commits a crime. All courts would acquit an involuntarily intoxicated defendant who lacked the capacity to form the required guilty mind. But such cases are extremely rare.

Let us now look at situations in which a perpetrator is voluntarily intoxicated. This is a common prob-

lem (as we shall see in Chapter 14). According to a 1991 study of state prison inmates, 49 percent of all inmates were under the influence of drugs, alcohol, or both drugs and alcohol at the time they committed their offense.[31] These figures tell us that alcohol and drugs play an important role in crime. They do not tell us much about the role an intoxicant may have played in any given case. Among those who have acted while under the influence of drugs, we find addicts who have committed offenses to pay for their habits. We also know that most persons who have committed crimes after drinking alcohol are likely to have experienced a lowering of inhibitions induced by the alcohol they drank. These perpetrators might not have acted violently had they not been under the influence of alcohol.

Voluntary intoxication is recognized in most states as a defense of sorts. Occasionally it may exonerate a defendant if it negates mens rea, but most often it merely reduces the degree of crime charged—from murder in the first degree to murder in the second degree, for example. It is as if the law has retained its original Puritan imprint: Drunkenness is bad, and people who drink and violate the law do not deserve much leniency.

Infancy

The common law recognized early on that children of tender age cannot "act" in any meaningful way. (Commonly, children below 1 year of age cannot even walk.) Nor can they form "criminal intent" (or mens rea) in any meaningful way. Tantrums may show anger, but they are not a sensible indication of intent to inflict harm. When it comes to causing death or near death, it is questionable whether an infant understands the meaning of death. It would be futile to take young children before a court in order to determine, in each case, whether they had "acted" with the requisite criminal intent. Infants should be recognized as beyond the reach of the criminal law, and left to the custody and care of parents or guardians.

The common law drew the line at age 7, by inventing the defense of "infancy." This age coincides, generally, with beginning school and thus socialization. Under common law the upper limit of infancy was drawn at age 14: Those 14 and older were subject to full adult criminal liability. Again, this age generally coincided with the end of public schooling and entrance into the adult world of work. The period between 7 and 14 was divided into two phases: From 7 to 10½ children were presumed to be incapable of forming a (meaningful, adultlike) criminal intent—but in specific cases the prosecution was allowed to prove the contrary. From 10½ to 14 children were presumed to be capable of forming a criminal intent, but it might be established, on the child's behalf, that this particular child was too immature to form a criminal intent.

In the "munchkin" case with which we started this chapter, the common law simply would not have allowed an inquiry into whether the child could "act" or form a criminal intent. The munchkin, no matter how nasty a little character he may be, was deemed beyond the reach of the criminal law.

Mistake of Fact

A restaurant patron goes to the coatrack to retrieve his raincoat. He verifies the manufacturer's label, takes the coat, and departs. Another patron, obviously agitated, jumps up and grabs the coat taker. "You stole my coat!" he shouts. The first man is greatly embarrassed. It turns out that the coat is not his. But is he a thief?

To be a thief, as we shall see in Chapter 12, one has to intend to deprive someone else of his or her property. That is the mens rea requirement. In this instance, did the first patron intend to deprive the owner of his property? No. He is not a thief, because he had no awareness of wrongdoing. That is the essence of the defense of mistake of fact. If there is no mens rea, there is no crime.[32]

Mistake or Ignorance of Law

At this point let us return to Ms. Lambert. Recall that Ms. Lambert had no idea she was doing something wrong when she failed to register as an ex-convict in Los Angeles. Yet a jury convicted her, and the court fined her $250. But does it make any sense to punish Ms. Lambert for what she did, or rather for what she didn't do? What conceivable purpose could punishment possibly serve under these circumstances?

It is clear that she had no mens rea—no guilty mind—and thus did not commit a crime. But her mistake was not one of fact. Rather, she acted under ignorance of law, and ignorance of the law is no defense, according to an ancient common law maxim.

It will be recalled that in the extreme circumstances of Ms. Lambert's case, the Supreme Court ultimately granted her a defense of ignorance of law, and it recognized ignorance of law even in the far less extreme Ratzlaf case.

Obviously the idea that ignorance or mistake of law is no defense made good sense when the criminal law was restricted to crimes such as clubbing somebody over the head or slaughtering somebody's else's cow. People could not claim they did not know that what they had done was forbidden. But times have changed, and who now can know all the laws? Even attorneys often have to do extensive research to find out if and how something is covered by criminal law. And if we all were to refrain from doing anything until we had legal advice, life would come to a standstill. Yet most courts perpetuate the fiction that "everybody is presumed to know the law."

THE DEFENSES: JUSTIFICATIONS

All the defenses discussed so far have one common ingredient: They simply negate the existence of the crime charged because the defendant, in effect, alleges that as a result of some internal or external condition, his or her mind did not participate in the behavior, so he or she did not commit the required act or form the guilty mind. In the next group of defenses the defendant fulfills all the act and intent requirements, and still the law does not impose criminal liability: The act is no longer prohibited by law, since the law itself gives the actor permission to act in exceptional situations.[33]

Duress

A robber approaches a bank teller with the following demand: "Your money or your life!" A simple choice. The teller probably reaches into the drawer and hands over the cash. Is the teller guilty of larceny or embezzlement? It is not her money. Her job as a teller does not give her the right to steal, to give away, or to embezzle funds entrusted to her.

To deal with such situations, the law has established the defense of duress:

> It is . . . [a] defense that the actor engaged in the conduct charged to constitute an offense because he was coerced to do so by the use of, or a threat to use,

unlawful force against his person or the person of another, which a person of reasonable firmness in his situation would have been unable to resist.[34]

This defense applies when the actor has done something the law prohibits. The bank teller took money entrusted to her and gave it to someone else. She was not authorized to do so. All the elements of a crime are there. But the teller had no choice. And that is precisely the point. The law recognizes that we cannot be expected to yield our lives, our limbs, the safety of our relatives, our houses, or our property when we are confronted by a criminal threat that forces us to violate a law. But there is a general requirement that the evil that threatens the actor ("Your money or your life!") and the evil created by the actor (handing over the bank's cash) be commensurate, that is, not out of proportion.

Necessity

As a general rule, necessity is a defense to a criminal charge when one has violated a law in the reasonable belief that the act was necessary to avoid an imminent and greater harm. Suppose two hikers are surprised by a snowstorm. They stumble upon a vacation cottage. Under the rule of necessity, they may break into and enter the cottage and use its provisions to stay alive.

If the necessity defense is to apply, the paramount threat must emanate from a force other than a human aggressor. The cause is, as it has been called, an "act of God"—a storm, a fire, a shipwreck. (If the source of the threat is a human aggressor, the defense is duress.)[35]

The question that has caused the most trouble is whether the defense of necessity ever permits the taking of an innocent life. Courts in England and the United States have reached contrasting solutions. English law does not permit the taking of an innocent life, even under dire necessity. American law permits the taking of innocent lives under certain conditions. A person who has fulfilled all legal obligations may sacrifice innocent human life, by random-lot selection, in order to save more lives.

Public Duty

Jus is the Latin word for law. Thus *justifications* are instances in which the law itself has created a counterlaw. The law prohibits an act; the counterlaw commands or authorizes it (see Table 10.1).

By far the most frequent justification defense is use of force in law enforcement. Law enforcement officers may use as much force as necessary, for example, to effect an arrest, but no more. The use of deadly force is subject to severe restrictions. Law enforcement officers who use more force than necessary are likely to be committing a criminal offense, such as assault and battery, or a civil rights violation under federal law, as was demonstrated by the federal conviction of the officers who beat Rodney King in Los Angeles.

Self-Defense, Defense of Others, Defense of Property

On the Saturday before Christmas in 1984, Bernhard H. Goetz entered a subway car at the IRT station at Seventh Avenue and 14th Street in Manhattan. He sat down close to four young men in their late teens. One of them offered a "How are ya"; then he approached Goetz and asked for $5. At that point Goetz pulled out a .38-caliber revolver and shot all four youths (one in the back).[36]

TABLE 10.1   Law Prohibitions and Counterlaw Justifications

Law Prohibitions	Counterlaw Justifications
The law prohibits the taking of life (criminal homicide).	The counterlaw requires execution of a convict sentenced to capital punishment.
	The counterlaw permits the shooting of a fleeing felon who is armed and constitutes a threat to life.
The law prohibits the taking of property (as in larceny).	The counterlaw allows impoundment of an illegally parked car.
The law prohibits the seizure of a person (as in false imprisonment or kidnapping).	The counterlaw requires the arrest of a suspect on probable cause.

WINDOW TO THE WORLD

NECESSITY AT SEA

Two cases of lives sacrificed to save others after a shipwreck show the difference between the American and English approaches to necessity as a defense. The descriptions below are from *Outlaws of the Ocean*.(1)

THE AMERICAN CASE

The American packet [passenger vessel] *William Brown* was en route from Liverpool to Philadelphia with a shipload of 65 Scottish and Irish immigrants when she struck an iceberg on April 19, 1841, 250 miles southeast of Race, Newfoundland. She sank rapidly in a howling nor'easter . . . . The first mate and eight sailors manned the longboat, filling it with thirty-two passengers. Even while the longboat was shoving off, they saw the *William Brown* go down, with the remaining passengers screaming, praying, and disappearing in the waves. . . . The first mate managed to keep the longboat afloat, but the seas and wind grew worse. The sea cock plug was lost, and the boat took on more and more water. The crew bailed as much as they could. The first mate shouted to his fellow sailors, "This work won't do. Help me, God. Men, go to work." Finally, the sailors obeyed, throwing a number of passengers overboard, being careful not to separate husband from wife, or mother from child. By such action the longboat was saved, and all still aboard were rescued by a passing vessel.

Holmes, one of the sailors, was tried on a murder charge and found guilty of manslaughter, but only because, as the court said, he had failed to exercise his duties toward passengers by throwing some of them overboard indiscriminately rather than by casting lots. . . . Unlike English law, American law recognizes the defense of necessity in taking of innocent lives on the high seas under extreme conditions.°

THE ENGLISH CASE

[T]hree shipwrecked sailors had been adrift in an open boat in the doldrums of the equatorial Atlantic. Their predicament had lasted for weeks. They had neither food nor water. They were delirious and the end appeared near, especially for the cabin boy, who was about to expire. In phantasmagoric exasperation, Dudley and Stephens killed the cabin boy and ate his flesh. This enabled them to survive for another few days until they were rescued by a passing vessel. The Court of Kings Bench convicted them of murder. Innocent human life must never be taken even to save one's own life, and even under the most dire necessity. . . . As Chief Justice Lord Coleridge stated: "We are often compelled to set up standards we cannot reach ourselves, and to lay down rules which we could not ourselves satisfy."†

Dudley and Stephens' [capital] sentences were commuted to the misdemeanor range, six months imprisonment.

Source

1. G. O. W. Mueller and Freda Adler, *Outlaws of the Ocean: The Complete Book of Contemporary Crime on the High Seas* [New York: Hearst Marine Books (William Morrow), 1985], pp. 217–218.

Questions for Discussion

1. What other defenses might have applied in these cases? Self-defense? Public duty? Duress? Why or why not?
2. Which view of necessity as a defense do you support, the American or the British? Explain your position.

*United States v. Holmes, I Wall Jr. I, 26 Fed. Cas. 360 (U.S. Cir. Ct., E.D. Pa., 1842).

†*Regina v. Dudley and Stephens*, 14 Q.B.D. 273 (1884).

The crew of the vessel *Mignonette* in an open lifeboat after the loss of the ship, from sketches by Mr. Stephens, mate, who survived by killing and eating the cabin boy.

AT ISSUE

THE BATTERED WOMAN SELF-DEFENSE AND THE PENAL CODES

The law is very strict when it comes to the application of force in self-defense. The Model Penal Code decrees: "The use of force upon or toward another person is justifiable when the actor believes that such force is immediately necessary for the purpose of protecting himself against the use of unlawful force by such other person on the present occasion."(1)

In recent years an increasing number of women abused by their mates have resorted to deadly force. The law has treated such women leniently in some respects, harshly in others. To begin with, the standard of law is phrased in terms of "protecting himself." How will courts translate the "protecting himself" standard, based on centuries of experience with male self-defense, into a "protecting herself" standard? Lenore E. Walker's study of the battered woman syndrome permitted her to conclude:

Occasionally (less than 15 percent of all homicides) a woman will kill her abuser while trying to defend herself or her children.

Sometimes, she strikes back during a calm period, knowing that the tension is building towards another acute battering incident,

Minouche Kandel, attorney for the California Coalition of Battered Women in Prison, holds up the clemency petition for imprisoned women who have killed their batterers. News conference May 7, 1996, San Francisco.

Few cases have ignited as much controversy as the Goetz case. Some people saw Goetz as an avenging angel, the city dweller who constantly suffers from crime and the fear of crime. Others labeled him a vigilante. Or was he simply the meek underdog, as his appearance suggested, trying to defend himself against yet another attack on the subway? He could have been any one of those. Goetz was charged with attempted murder, assault, and illegal possession of a weapon. In legal terms, the case simply raised the question of the right to use force, even deadly force, in self-defense, as well as the extent to which the defense still exists if the actor is mistaken about the actual threat that confronts him.

It is safe to say that in most states a person can use as much force as is reasonably necessary to defend himself or herself against what appears to be an immediate threat of violence by another, as long as

the following four elements are present:

- The person must have an "honest and reasonable belief" that the force is necessary.
- The person must believe that the harm threatened will be immediately forthcoming.
- The harm threatened must be unlawful.
- The force used must be reasonable—only as much as appears necessary under the circumstances.[37]

Let us return to the Goetz case. Did Goetz find himself in a life-threatening situation? We will never know. As it turned out, some of his victims had criminal records. They carried no firearms, only screwdrivers, which they said they used to pilfer vending machines. Objectively, it appears that Goetz was in no immediate physical danger. What, then, went on in his mind? He had earlier been the victim of a brutal

AT ISSUE

where this time she may die. When examining the statistics, we find that more women than men are charged with first or second degree murder. There seems to be a sexist bias operating in which the courts find it more difficult to see justifiable or mitigating circumstances for women who kill. The now classic Broverman et al. (1970) studies demonstrated that the kinds of behaviors and emotions expressed when committing an aggressive act will be viewed as normal for men but not for women. On the other hand, a woman's violence is more likely to be found excusable, if her insanity under the law can be demonstrated. Any changes in the insanity laws will probably have the greatest impact on women and other assault victims who reach a breaking point and no longer appreciate the wrongfulness of their action and/or can no longer refrain from an overpowering impulse to survive.

In most states' criminal codes, self-defense is defined as the jus-

tifiable commission of a criminal act by using the least amount of force necessary to prevent imminent bodily harm which needs only to be reasonably perceived as about to happen. The perception of how much force is necessary must also be reasonable. Such a definition works against women because they are not socialized to use physical force, are rarely equal to a man in size, strength, or physical training, and may have learned to expect more injury with inadequate attempts to repel a man's attack. Thus, some courts have ruled it would be reasonable for a woman to defend herself with a deadly weapon against a man armed only with the parts of his body he learned to use as a deadly weapon. Courts also have been allowing evidence to account for the cumulative effects of repeated violence in self-defense and diminished-capacity assertions. Expert witness testimony has been admitted in many states to help explain the reasonableness of such perceptions.(2)

It would be rash to conclude that the penal codes need immediate reform to protect women who kill in perceived self-defense. But it is reasonable to expect that penal code reformers review the entirety of penal codes to see that men and women are covered and protected equally, with particular consideration of contemporary life situations.

Sources
1. American Law Institute, Model Penal Code, sec. 3.04.
2. Lenore E. Walker, *The Battered Woman Syndrome* (New York: Springer Publishing Company, Inc., 1984), pp. 142–143.

Questions for Discussion
1. Should the difference between men and women in the way threats of violence are perceived be taken into account in self-defense cases?
2. How should the constant threat of violence a battered woman experiences be interpreted in terms of the law's "present occasion" requirement for self-defense?

mugging in similar circumstances. Like many other subway riders, he feared the predators who seemed to be ever present beneath the streets.

The defense made a strong case that Goetz was in fear of his life. The legal question was whether he should be judged by a subjective standard (whether he felt in fear of his life) or by an objective standard (whether *a reasonable person* in the same situation would have been in fear of his or her life). The jury resolved this issue by acquitting him of all charges except one: illegal possession of a handgun. But in a subsequent civil suit against Goetz by the paralyzed victim, with a far lesser proof requirement, a jury awarded a multimillion-dollar civil damage award. Alas, in 1996, Goetz was adjudicated a bankrupt.

The right to use reasonable force, and if necessary deadly force, extends to the defense of others. In most jurisdictions, a defender can use as much force

on behalf of another as he or she could have used in self-defense. Of course, such defenders must reasonably believe that if they were in the other person's position, they would have the right to defend themselves, and the amount of force used must be necessary. Some states require, in addition, that the person being assisted must also have the right to use force, regardless of the defender's perception.

The law views the protection of property and human life differently (Table 10.2). With few exceptions, the right of self-defense is far more extensive than the right of defense of property. The general rule in this area is that nondeadly force may be used, typically after some request has been made to desist, when it is necessary to stop an intrusion. When there is some indication that the intruder intends to commit a felony on the premises, and a warning to desist has been issued and ignored, deadly force may be used.

TABLE 10.2   Justifiable Use of Deadly Force Even if Life Is Not Threatened*

State	Deadly Force May Be Justified		
	To Protect Dwelling	**To Protect Property**	**Against Specific Crime**
Alabama	Yes	No	Arson, burglary, rape, kidnapping, robbery
Alaska	Yes	No	Actual commission of felony
Arizona	Yes	No	Arson, burglary, kidnapping, aggr. assaults
Arkansas	Yes	No	Felonies (defined by statute)
California	Yes	No	Unlawful or forcible entry
Colorado	Yes	No	Felonies
Connecticut	Yes	No	Any violent crime
Delaware	Yes	No	Felonious activity
District of Columbia	Yes	No	Felony
Florida	Yes	No	Forcible felony
Georgia	Yes	Yes	Actual commission of a forcible felony
Hawaii	Yes	Yes	Felonious property damage, burglary, robbery, etc.
Idaho	Yes	Yes	Felonious breaking and entering
Illinois	Yes	Yes	Forcible felony
Indiana	Yes	No	Unlawful entry
Iowa	Yes	Yes	Breaking and entering
Kansas	Yes	No	Breaking and entering, incl. attempts
Kentucky	No	No	—
Louisiana	Yes	No	Unlawful entry, incl. attempts
Maine	Yes	No	Criminal trespass, kidnapping, rape, arson
Maryland	No	No	—
Massachusetts	No	No	—
Michigan	Yes	No	Case-by-case basis
Minnesota	Yes	No	Felony
Mississippi	Yes	—	Felony, including attempts
Missouri	No	No	—
Montana	Yes	Yes	Any forcible felony
Nebraska	Yes	No	Unlawful entry, kidnapping, rape
Nevada	Yes	—	Actual commission of felony
New Hampshire	Yes	—	Felony
New Jersey	Yes	No	Burglary, arson, robbery
New Mexico	Yes	Yes	Any felony
New York	Yes	No	Burglary, arson, kidnapping, robbery, incl. attempts
North Carolina	Yes	No	Intending to commit a felony
North Dakota	Yes	No	Any violent felony
Ohio	—	—	—
Oklahoma	Yes	No	Felony within a dwelling
Oregon	Yes	—	Burglary in a dwelling, incl. attempts
Pennsylvania	Yes	—	Burglary or criminal trespass
Rhode Island	Yes	—	Breaking or entering
South Carolina	No	No	—
South Dakota	Yes	—	Burglary, incl. attempts
Tennessee	Yes	No	Felony
Texas	Yes	No ~~yes~~	Burglary, robbery, or theft at night
Utah	Yes	—	Felony
Vermont	Yes	—	Forcible felony
Virginia	No	No	—
Washington	No	No	—
West Virginia	Yes	No	Any felony
Wisconsin	No	No	—
Wyoming	No	No	—

*All states allow ultimate recourse to deadly force when life is in immediate danger.
Source: U.S. Department of Justice, Report to the Nation on Crime and Justice, 2d ed. (Washington, D.C.: U.S. Government Printing Office, 1988).

ATTEMPT AND ACCESSORYSHIP

The doctrines pertaining to defenses are not the only doctrines of criminal law used to determine criminal charges. Foremost among the remaining doctrines is the one pertaining to attempted crimes. What should the law do to someone who tries to commit a crime but does not succeed? Under early common law, attempts to commit crimes were not considered crimes, because the actus reus was not completed. But a person who tries to complete a crime surely has the same mens rea and thus the same culpability as one who succeeds. Should the would-be perpetrator be treated differently just because he or she did not succeed? In 1784, it was decided in England that an attempt to commit a felony was indeed a crime.[38] That case laid the foundation for our present conceptualization of **criminal attempt:** "an act or omission constituting a substantial step in a course of conduct planned to culminate in the commission of a crime."[39]

The common law also created a sophisticated system for determining the liability of all persons involved in the commission of a crime. When, where, and how the various parties could be prosecuted, and the use of evidence at trial, depended on the type of participation.

Today most states recognize only **principals** (all persons who commit an offense by their own conduct) and **accomplices** (all those who aid the perpetrator). That system has not solved all the problems, because the line between committing a crime and aiding in its commission is a fine one. Though principals and accomplices are usually considered equally culpable, in practice judges often impose lighter sentences on accomplices.

TYPOLOGIES OF CRIME

The general term "crimes" covers a wide variety of different types of crimes with their own distinct features. Murder and arson, for example, both are crimes. They have the same seven general elements, including a criminal intent (mens rea) and a harm element. But these elements take different forms in different crimes. In murder the criminal intent takes the form of intending to kill another human being wrongfully, while in arson the intent is that of wrongfully burning the property of another. Lawyers and criminologists have searched for a system of grouping the many types of crimes into coherent, rational categories, for ease of understanding, of learning, and of finding them in the law books and for purposes of studying them from both a legal and a criminological perspective. Such categorizations are called *typologies.*

Here are some examples: The ancient Romans classified their crimes as those against the gods and those against other human beings. As late as the eighteenth century, some English lawyers simply listed crimes alphabetically. The French of the early nineteenth century created a typology with three categories: serious crimes (which we would call felonies), medium serious crimes (which we would call misdemeanors), and crimes of a petty character (which we would call violations). The more serious crimes were grouped into categories based on the harm those crimes entailed, such as harm against life, against physical integrity, against honor, against property, and so on.

Nowadays the French categorization is generally accepted worldwide, although lawyers and criminologists may differ on the desirability of lumping various crime types together into categories. Lawyers, after all, may be much more interested in the procedural consequences that flow from the categorizations, while criminologists may be much more concerned with criminological implications for studying different types of perpetrators and devising schemes of crime prevention.

There are also political considerations in devising a typology. For example, the criminal codes of the former communist countries had large categories of political crimes, which were given the most prominent place in those codes. They included many crimes that in Western democracies are grouped in other categories, such as property crimes or crimes against the person, or that may have no counterpart at all.

The typology we have chosen for this book seeks to accommodate both the established legal typology—for example, that used in the Model Penal Code—and the criminological objectives that are so important for the study of crime from a sociological and behavioral perspective. These categories are:

- Violent crimes
- Crimes against property
- Organizational criminality
- Drug-, alcohol-, and sex-related crimes

We discuss these categories in the following chapters.

REVIEW

All crimes can be easily understood if we learn what it is that all crimes have in common. Based on the analysis of Anglo-American common law, scholars have discovered that all crimes are characterized by seven general principles (sometimes called ingredients or elements). Thus, a crime needs (1) an act *(actus)* that (2) is in violation of law *(reus)*, that (3) causes (4) the harm identified by the law, and that is committed with (5) criminal intent (mens rea, or a guilty mind). In addition, (6) the criminal act must concur with the guilty mind, and (7) the act must be subject to punishment.

Defenses to crime simply negate the existence of one of the seven basic elements, usually the mens rea (as in mistake of fact and insanity), sometimes even the act itself (as in some insanity defenses), and sometimes the unlawfulness of the act (as in justification defenses). These defenses have been grouped into excuses and justifications.

Additional propositions of law explain why and when offenders may incur criminal liability when they try to commit a crime but do not succeed (attempts), and how liability is imposed when several persons act jointly or help each other (accessoryship).

Crimes are usually grouped into categories by severity or type of harm (typologies).

NOTES

1. Anastasia Toufexis and J. Howard Green, "From the Fists of Babes—Can a Six-Year-Old Be Prosecuted for Attempted Murder? A Tragic Beating Tests the Limits of Law," *Time,* May 6, 1996, p. 38; Nadine Joseph, "Just 'A Little Munchkin'—Did a Boy, 6, Try to Kill a Baby?" *Newsweek,* May 6, 1996, p. 38.

2. Paul H. Robinson, "Are Criminal Codes Irrelevant?" *Southern California Law Review,* **68** (1994): 159–202.

3. The Anglo-American concept of crime was developed by a long line of distinguished legal scholars, as discussed in G. O. W. Mueller, *Crime, Law, and the Scholars* (London: Heinemann; Seattle: University of Washington Press, 1969).

4. Jerome Hall, *General Principles of Criminal Law,* 2d ed. (Indianapolis: Bobbs-Merrill, 1960).

5. American Law Institute, Model Penal Code, sec. 2.01(1). The American Law Institute, dedicated to law reform, is an association of some of the most prestigious American lawyers. Between 1954 and 1962 this group sought to codify the best features of the penal codes of the various states. The resultant Model Penal Code (MPC) has had considerable influence on law reform in many states, and has been adopted nearly in full by New Jersey and Pennsylvania. We shall have frequent occasion to refer to the MPC as "typical" American criminal law. See also Gerhard O. W. Mueller, "The Public Law of Wrongs—Its Concepts in the World of Reality," *Journal of Public Law,* **10** (1961): 203–260; Michael Moore, *Act and Crime—The Philosophy of Action and Its Implications for Criminal Law* (Oxford: Clarendon Press, 1993).

6. *Robinson v. California,* 370 U.S. 660 (1962).

7. *Powell v. Texas,* 392 U.S. 514 (1968).

8. *State v. Palendrano,* 120 N.J. Super. 336, 293 A. 2d 747 (1972).

9. G. O. W. Mueller, "Causing Criminal Harm," in *Essays in Criminal Science,* ed. Mueller (South Hackensack, N.J.: Fred B. Rothman, 1961), pp. 167–214.

10. *Lambert v. California,* 355 U.S. 225 (1957). This decision must be approached with care. It does not stand for the proposition that ignorance of the law is an excuse. The Supreme Court was very careful to limit the scope of its decision to offenses by omission of adherence to regulations not commonly known, when the defendant in fact did not know—and had no means of knowing—of the prohibition.

11. G. O. W. Mueller, "On Common Law Mens Rea," *Minnesota Law Review,* **42** (1958): 1043–1104, at p. 1060.

12. *Ratzlaf v. U.S.,* 510 U.S. 135, 114 S. Ct. 655 (1994).

13. See Paul H. Robinson, "Should the Criminal Law Abandon the Actus Reus–Mens Rea Distinction?" in *Action and Value in Criminal Law,* ed. Stephen Shute, John Gardner, and Jeremy Harder (Oxford: Clarendon Press, 1993), pp. 187–211.

14. Wayne R. LaFave and Austin W. Scott, Jr., *Criminal Law* (St. Paul, Minn.: West, 1983), p. 222.

15. H. Lowell Brown, "Vicarious Criminal Liability of Corporations for the Acts of Their Employees and Agents," *Loyola Law Review,* **41** (1995): 279, 328–329.

16. Alan M. Dershowitz, *The Abuse Excuse and Other Cop-Outs, Sob Stories, and Evasions of Responsibility* (Boston: Little, Brown, 1994).

17. Peter W. Low, John Calvin Jeffries, Jr., and Richard J. Bonnie, *The Trial of John W. Hinckley, Jr.* (Mineola, N.Y.: Foundation Press, 1986).

18. Richard Moran, *Knowing Right from Wrong: The Insanity Defense of Daniel McNaughten* (New York: Free Press, 1981), is a fascinating discussion of the M'Naghten case. See also Bernard L. Diamond, "Isaac Ray and the Trial of Daniel M'Naghten," *American Journal of Psychiatry,* **112** (1956): 651–656.

19. In general, see Ralph Slovenko, *Psychiatry and Criminal Culpability* (New York: John Wiley, 1995); Michael L. Perlin, *The Jurisprudence of the Insanity Defense* (Durham, N.C.: Carolina Academic Press, 1994); Finbarr McAuley, *Insanity, Psychiatry and Criminal Responsibility* (Dublin: Round Hall Press, 1993; comparative in coverage).

20. *Daniel M'Naghten's Case,* 10 C.F. 200, 210–211, 8 Eng. Rep. 718, 722–723 (1843).

21. G. O. W. Mueller, "M'Naghten Remains Irreplaceable: Recent Events in the Law of Incapacity," *Georgetown Law Journal,* **50** (1961): 105–119. The literature on the law of insanity is extensive. Noteworthy recent works include Donald H. J. Herfmann, *The Insanity Defense: Philosophical, Historical, and Legal Perspectives* (Springfield, Ill.: Charles C Thomas, 1983); and Michael S. Moore, *Law and Psychiatry: Rethinking*

the Relationship (New York: Cambridge University Press, 1984).

22. See *Parsons v. State*, 81 Ala. 577, 2 So. 854 (1887).

23. *Durham v. United States*, 214 F. 2d 862 (D.C. Cir. 1954); *States v. Pike*, 49 N.H. 399 (1869).

24. *United States v. Brawner*, 471 F. 2d 696 (D.C. Cir. 1972).

25. Model Penal Code, sec. 4.01.

26. 18 U.S. Code, sec. 17.

27. Richard A. Pasewark, Richard Jeffrey, and Stephen Bieber, "Differentiating Successful and Unsuccessful Insanity Plea Defendants in Colorado," *Journal of Psychiatry and Law,* **15** (1987): 55–82, at p. 65, covering the period July 1, 1980, to June 30, 1983.

28. *Cowan v. Montana*, 114 S. Ct. 1371 (Mem) (1994).

29. Henrik Belfrage, "Variability in Forensic-Psychiatric Decisions—Evidence for a Positive Crime Prevention Effect with Mentally Disordered Violent Offenders?" *Studies on Crime and Crime Prevention,* **4** (1995): 119–124.

30. Kurt M. Bumby, "Reviewing the Guilty but Mentally Ill Alternative: A Case of the Blind 'Pleading' the Blind," *Journal of Psychiatry and Law,* **2** (1993): 191–220.

31. Bureau of Justice Statistics, *Survey of State Prison Inmates, 1991* (Washington D.C.: U.S. Department of Justice, Office of Justice Programs, 1993), p. 26.

32. Paul H. Robinson, *Fundamentals of Criminal Law* (Boston: Little, Brown, 1988), pp. 287 ff.

33. On the disputed distinction between excuses and justifications, see Michael Louis Corrado, ed., *Justification and Excuse in the Criminal Law* (New York: Garland, 1994).

34. Basically, the defense is not available if the actor was at fault by placing himself in the situation: Model Penal Code, sec. 2.09(1).

35. Model Penal Code, Tentative Draft no. 8 (Philadelphia: American Law Institute, 1958), pp. 5–10.

36. For a fascinating legal and factual analysis of the case, see George P. Fletcher, *A Crime of Self-Defense: Bernhard Goetz and the Law on Trial* (New York: Free Press, 1988).

37. Suzanne Unisacke, *Permissible Killing: The Self-Defence Justification of Homicide* (Cambridge: Cambridge University Press, 1994).

38. *Rex v. Scofield* (1784 Cald. 402).

39. Model Penal Code, sec. 5.01(1) (c).

Internet Exercise

Consider that voluntary intoxication is rarely used as a defense in the criminal law. What percentage of persons arrested test positive for drugs or alcohol? You may be surprised.

Your Web Site is:

http://www.ojp.usdoj.gov/bjs/spectps.html

Homicide

    Murder

    Manslaughter

    The Extent of Homicide

    The Nature of Homicide

    A Cross-National Comparison of Homicide Rates

Assault

Family-Related Crimes

    Spouse Abuse

    Child Abuse

    Abuse of the Elderly

Rape and Sexual Assault

    Characteristics of the Rape Event

    Who Are the Rapists?

    Rape and the Legal System

    Community Response

Robbery

    Characteristics of Robbers

    The Consequences of Robbery

Kidnapping and Terrorism

    Kidnapping

    Terrorism

Violence and Gun Control

    The Extent of Firearm-Related Offenses

    Youth and Guns

    Controlling Handgun Use

    The Gun-Control Debate

Review

Notes

    Special Features

        WINDOW TO THE WORLD: Assassinations around the Globe

        CRIMINOLOGICAL FOCUS: "An Epidemic of Hate Crimes?"

        AT ISSUE: Vipers in the Desert

Key Terms

aggravated assault
assault
battery
felony murder
homicide
involuntary
  manslaughter
justifiable homicide
kidnapping
malice aforethought
manslaughter
mass murder
murder
negligent homicide
rape
robbery
serial murder
simple assault
sociopath
stranger homicide
terrorism
victim precipitation
voluntary
  manslaughter

To millions of Americans few things are more pervasive, more frightening, more real today than violent crime and the fear of being assaulted, mugged, robbed, or raped. The fear of being victimized by criminal attack has touched us all in some way. People are fleeing their residences in cities to the expected safety of suburban living. Residents of many areas will not go out on the street at night. Others have added bars and extra locks to windows and doors in their homes. Bus drivers in major cities do not carry cash because incidents of robbery have been so frequent. In some areas local citizens patrol the streets at night to attain the safety they feel has not been provided. . . .

There are numerous conflicting definitions of criminal violence as a class of behavior. Police, prosecutors, jurists, federal agents, local detention officials, and behavioral scientists all hold somewhat different viewpoints as to what constitute acts of violence. All would probably agree, however, as the police reports make abundantly clear, that criminal violence involves the use of or the threat of force on a victim by an offender.[1]

The penal law defines types of violent crime, and each is distinguished by a particular set of elements. We concentrate on criminological characteristics: the frequency with which each type of violent crime is committed, the methods used in its commission, and its distribution through time and place. We also examine the people who commit the offense and those who are its victims. If we can determine when, where, and how a specific type of crime is likely to be committed, we will be in a better position to reduce the incidence of that crime by devising appropriate strategies to prevent it.

We begin with homicide, since the taking of life is the most serious harm one human being can inflict on another. Serious attacks that fall short of homicide are assaults of various kinds, including serious sexual assault (rape) and the forceful taking of property from another person (robbery). Other patterns of violence are not defined as such in the penal codes but are so important in practice as to require separate discussion. Family-related violence and terrorism, both of which encompass a variety of crimes, fall into this category.

HOMICIDE

Homicide is the killing of one human being by another. Some homicides are sanctioned by law. In this category of **justifiable homicide,** we find homicides committed by law enforcement officers in the course of carrying out their duties (see Chapter 10), homicides committed by soldiers in combat, and homicides committed by a homeowner who has no recourse other than to kill an intruder who threatens the lives of family members. Criminologists are most interested in *criminal homicides—* unlawful killings, without justification or excuse. Criminal homicides are subdivided into three separate categories: murder, manslaughter, and negligent homicide.

Murder

At common law, **murder** was defined as the intentional killing of another person with **malice aforethought.** Courts have struggled with an exact definition of "malice." To describe it, they have used such terms as "evil mind" and "abandoned and malignant heart." Actually, malice is a very simple concept. It is the defendant's awareness that he or she had no right to kill but intended to kill anyway.[2]

Originally the malice had to be "aforethought": The person had to have killed after some contemplation, rather than on the spur of the moment. The concept eventually became meaningless because some courts considered even a few seconds sufficient to establish forethought. The dividing line between planned and spur-of-the-moment killings disappeared. But many legislators believed contemplation was an appropriate concept, because it allowed us to distinguish the various types of murder. They reintroduced it, calling it "premeditation and deliberation." A premeditated, deliberate, intentional killing became murder in the first degree; an intentional killing without premeditation and deliberation became murder in the second degree.

States that had the death penalty reserved it for murder in the first degree. Some state statutes listed particular means of committing murder as indicative of premeditation and deliberation, such as killing by poison or by lying in wait. More recently the charge of murder in the first degree has been reserved for the killing of a law enforcement officer or of a corrections officer and for the killing of any person by a prisoner serving a life sentence. Among the most serious forms of murder is *assassination,* the killing of a head of state or government or of an otherwise highly visible figure.

A special form of murder, **felony murder,** requires no intention to kill. It requires, instead, the intention to commit some other felony, such as robbery or rape, and the death of a person during the commission of, or flight from, that felony. Even accomplices are guilty of felony murder when one of their associates has caused a death. For example, while A and B are holding up a gas station attendant, A fires a warning shot, and the bullet ricochets and kills a passerby. Both A and B are guilty of felony murder. The rule originated in England centuries ago, when death sentences were imposed for all felonies, so it made no difference whether a perpetrator actually intended to kill or merely to rob. Most states today apply the felony murder rule only when the underlying felony is a life-endangering one, such as arson, rape, or robbery.

Manslaughter

Manslaughter is the unlawful killing of another person without malice. Manslaughter may be either voluntary or involuntary.

Voluntary Manslaughter. **Voluntary manslaughter** is a killing committed intentionally but without malice—for example, in the heat of passion or in response to strong provocation. Persons who kill under extreme provocation cannot make rational decisions about whether they have a right to kill or not. They therefore act without the necessary malice.[3]

Just as passion, fright, fear, or consternation may affect a person's capacity to act rationally, so may drugs or alcohol. In some states a charge of murder may be reduced to voluntary manslaughter when the defendant was so grossly intoxicated as not to be fully aware of the implications of his or her actions. All voluntary-manslaughter cases have one thing in common: The defendant's awareness of the unlawfulness of the act was dulled or grossly reduced by shock, fright, consternation, or intoxication.

Involuntary Manslaughter. A crime is designated as **involuntary manslaughter** when a person has caused the death of another unintentionally but recklessly by consciously disregarding a substantial and unjustifiable risk that endangered another person's life. Many states have created an additional category, **negligent homicide**, to establish criminal liability for grossly negligent killing in situations where the offender assumed a lesser risk.

Manslaughter plays an increasingly prominent role in our society, with its high concentrations of population, high-tech risks, and chemical and even nuclear dangers. The reach of the crime of involuntary manslaughter was clearly demonstrated in the 1942 Coconut Grove disaster in Boston, in which 491 people perished because of a nightclub owner's negligence in creating fire hazards. The nightclub was overcrowded, it was furnished and decorated with highly flammable materials, and exits were blocked.

The court ruled that a reasonable person would have recognized the risk. If the defendant is so "stupid" as not to have recognized the risk, he is nevertheless guilty of manslaughter.[4]

The Extent of Homicide

Social scientists who look at homicide have a different perspective from that of the legislators who define such crimes. Social scientists are concerned with rates and patterns of criminal activities.

Homicide Rates in the United States Today. The American murder rate always has been high. It reached a peak in 1980 and has been declining erratically since then. In 1994, our population of close to 260 million experienced 23,310 murders and nonnegligent homicides (as reported to the police), or 9.0 per 100,000 of the population.[5] This rate is not equally distributed over the whole country: Murder rates are higher in the southern and western states (11 and 9 per 100,000, respectively) than in the northeastern and midwestern states (7 and 8 per 100,000, respectively).[6]

Your chance of becoming a murder victim is much higher if you are male than if you are female: Of all murder victims, 78 percent are male, 22 percent female. Age plays a role—nearly half of all murder victims are between the ages of 20 and 34; and so does race—47 percent of all murder victims are white, 51 percent are black, and the remaining 2 percent are of other ethnic origins.[7]

Ninety-four percent of the black murder victims were slain by black offenders, and 84 percent of the white murder victims were killed by white offenders. Intentional criminal homicide apparently is an intraracial crime. But it is not an intragender crime. The data show that males were most often killed by males (88 percent); nine out of ten female victims were murdered by males.[8]

Homicide Rates over Time. Researchers have asked what happens to homicide rates over time when the composition of the population changes. What is the effect, for example, of a change in the racial composition of a city? Roland Chilton, using data on offenses committed in Chicago between 1960 and 1980 and census data for those years, found that about 20 percent of the total increase in homicide rates could be explained by increases in the nonwhite male population.[9] The same correlation is found in most major cities in the United States. Chilton argues that the problem will remain because of the poverty and demoralization of the groups involved. We can even expect that it will get worse if municipal governments are unable to improve the schools, reduce unemployment, and extend social services.

In a 1996 article, "Work," sociologist William Julius Wilson explains why America's ghettos have descended into "ever-deeper poverty and misery." According to him:

> For the first time in the 20th century, a significant majority of adults in many inner-city neighborhoods are not working in a typical week. Inner cities have always featured high levels of poverty, but the current levels of joblessness in some neighborhoods are unprecedented. For example, in the famous black-belt neighborhood of Washington Park on Chicago's South Side, a majority of adults had jobs in 1950; by 1990, only 1 in 3 worked in a typical week. High neighborhood joblessness has a far more devastating effect than high neighborhood poverty. A neighborhood in which people are poor but employed is different from a neighborhood in which people are poor and jobless. Many of today's problems in the inner-city neighborhoods—crime, family dissolution, welfare—are fundamentally a consequence of the disappearance of work.[10]

Until conditions change, what has been poignantly referred to as "the subculture of exasperation" will continue to produce a high homicide rate among nonwhite inner-city males.[11] Coramae Mann has found that although black women make up about 11 percent of the female population in the United States, they are arrested for three-fourths of all homicides committed by females. She argues that given such a disproportionate involvement in violent crime, one has to question whether the subculture of exasperation alone is entirely responsible.[12] But so few studies have been done on the subject that we cannot reach any definitive conclusion. Other investigators agree that homicide rates cannot be explained solely by such factors as poverty; the rates are also significantly associated with cultural approval of a resort to violence.

The Nature of Homicide

Let us take a closer look at killers and their victims and see how they are related to each other. In the 1950s Marvin Wolfgang studied homicide situations, perpetrators, and victims in the Philadelphia area. Victims and offenders were predominantly young black adults of low socioeconomic status. The offenses were committed in the inner city; they occurred primarily in the home of the victim or offender, on weekends, in the evening hours, and among friends or acquaintances.

Building on the pioneering work of Hans von Hentig,[13] Wolfgang found that many of the victims had actually initiated the social interaction that led to the homicidal response, in a direct or subliminal way. He coined the term **victim precipitation** for such instances, which may account for as many as a quarter to a half of all intentional homicides. In such cases it is the victim who, by insinuation, bodily movement, verbal incitement, or the actual use of physical force, initiates a series of events that results in his or her own death. For example:

> During an argument in which a male called a female many vile names, she tried to telephone the police. He grabbed the phone from her hands, knocked her down, kicked her, and hit her with a tire gauge. She ran to the kitchen, grabbed a butcher knife, and stabbed him in the stomach.[14]

Recent studies have provided additional insight into the patterns of homicide. Robert Silverman and Leslie Kennedy demonstrated that gender relationships, age, means of commission of the act, and location vary with relational distance, from closest relatives (lovers, spouses) to total strangers.[15]

Margaret Zahn and Philip Sagi have developed a model that distinguishes among homicides on the basis of characteristics of victims, offenders, location, method of attack, and presence of witnesses. They conclude that all these characteristics and variables serve to differentiate four categories of homicides: (1) those within the family, (2) those among friends and acquaintances, (3) stranger homicides associated with felonies, and (4) stranger homicides not associated with felonies.[16]

Stranger Homicides. The rate of **stranger homicide**—a killing in which killer and victim have had no known previous contact—has not varied between 1977 (13.4 percent) and 1992 (13 percent).[17] Marc Riedel, however, found these stranger homicide rates to be considerably understated. The true figures, according to Riedel, ranged from 14 to 29 percent.[18] Furthermore, the impact of stranger homicides on the quality of urban life—especially the fear of crime they engender—is far greater than their relatively small numbers would suggest.[19]

Relatives and Acquaintances. Almost half of all homicides occur among relatives and acquaintances (40 percent of the relationships are unknown).[20] Of these homicides, those in which women killed their mates have received particular attention. Criminologists take special interest in the factors behind such crimes.[21] Researchers have found a high incidence of long-term abuse suffered by women who subsequently kill their mates.[22] They also suggest that mate homicides are the result of a husband's efforts to control his wife and the wife's efforts to retain her independence.[23]

Some recent trends are also noteworthy: an increase in women who kill in domestic encounters, more planned killings, and less acceptance of self-defense as a motive in such cases.[24] Children are also at risk of death at the hands of family members. In most murders of a child under age 15, a family member killed the child, while murder victims aged 15 to 17 are more likely to be killed by an acquaintance of the victim or by someone unknown to the law enforcement authorities.[25] One investigator found that in the 5- to 9-year age group, black boys had the highest homicide fatality rate: 25 per 100,000 (3.7 times higher than the rate for white boys). High rates of child homicide persist in low-income areas.[26] Once again, many observers blame the subculture of exasperation.

Young and Old Perpetrators. Not surprisingly, the very young and the elderly have low homicide rates. In 1994, 379 homicide charges were placed against youngsters under 15, but this figure does not include the number of homicides in which the young killers were dealt with by juvenile courts or welfare agencies. Of the 18,497 persons of all ages arrested for homicide in 1994, 3102 were under 18. The elderly, too, are underrepresented among killers. People age 55 and older accounted for only 2.3 percent of all murders in 1994.[27]

Homicide without Apparent Motive. In most homicides, the killer has a motive or a reason for killing the victim. Popular fiction tells us that detectives tend to consider a case solved if they can establish the motive. But research shows that in a substantial number of murders, the motive remains unclear. The "unmotivated" murderers are a puzzle—and they constitute 25 percent of all homicide offenders.

Though in most respects the killers without motive are similar to those who kill for a reason, they are more likely to have "(1) no history of alcohol abuse; (2) a recent release from prison; (3) claims of amnesia for the crime; (4) denial of the crime; and (5) a tendency to exhibit psychotic behavior following the crime and to be assessed not guilty of the crime due to mental illness."[28]

Mass and Serial Murders. Criminological researchers have paid special attention to two types of murder that are particularly disturbing to the community: **serial murder,** the killing of several victims over a period of time, and **mass murder,** the killing of multiple victims in one event or in very quick succession. Between 1970 and 1993 U.S. police knew of approximately 125 cases of multiple homicides. The literature on the subject is enormous.[29] Some recent serial murderers have become infamous.

Theodore "Ted" Bundy, law student and former crime commission staff member, killed between 19 and 36 young women in the northwestern states and Florida. David Berkowitz, the "Son of Sam," killed 6 young women in New York. Douglas Clark, the "Sunset Strip killer," killed between 7 and 50 prostitutes in Hollywood. The "Green River killer" of Seattle may have killed more than 45 victims. In the Midwest, Jeffrey Dahmer preserved, and took Polaroid photographs of, the mutilated body parts of his 11 to 17 victims; and on Long Island, Joel Rifkin collected souvenirs—a shoe, an earring, a driver's license—from the more than 13 streetwalkers he claimed as his victims.

In just one week in June 1996, two men, both suspected of being serial killers, were captured in New York City. Heriberto Seda, 28, lived a largely solitary life, except for those moments when he would emerge from the apartment he shared with his mother and sister. In two separate crime waves (in 1990, then again during 1992 and 1993), the self-proclaimed Zodiac Killer allegedly shot eight people, killing three (Chapter Four). Larry Stevens, 31, who also lived with his mother, would allegedly trick old people into letting him into their homes. He would beat them or throw them down stairs, and then rob them. He is suspected of killing at least two elderly persons.[30]

Comedian Bill Cosby discusses the murder of his son, Ennis, in an interview with CBS news anchor Dan Rather. Ennis was shot and killed in Los Angeles on January 16, 1997.

In 1991, the worst mass murder in U.S. history took place in a Texas café. An unemployed young man drove his pickup through the restaurant's glass window and opened fire with a semiautomatic pistol, leaving 22 dead. James Huberty walked into a McDonald's in California and killed 20 people. Colin Ferguson boarded a train where he killed 6 and wounded 17 in the Long Island massacre of 1993. In 1996, Thomas Hamilton entered a school in Dunblane, Scotland; shot and killed 16 kindergarten students and their teacher; and wounded 12 others.[31]

Recently, there has been an increase in mass murders in the workplace. San Franciscan failed businessman Gian Luigi Ferri, who blamed lawyers for his problems, burst into the thirty-fourth-floor law office where he had been a client and, with two pistols, killed eight persons working in the firm. Disgruntled employee Paul Calder returned 8 months after being fired to kill three and wound two at a Tampa insurance company. The U.S. Postal Service, where 38 employees died violently between 1986 and 1993, is now looking into ways to reduce employer-employee tension, especially when layoffs are imminent.[32]

It is popularly believed that multiple murderers are mentally ill; their offenses, after all, are often quite bizarre. In many such cases psychiatrists have indeed found severe pathology.[33] Yet juries are reluctant to find these offenders not guilty by reason of insanity. Albert Fish, who cooked and ate the children he murdered, died in the electric chair.[34] Edmund Kemper, who killed hitchhikers as well as his own mother (he used her head as a dartboard), received a life term.[35]

The criminologists Jack Levin and James Fox do not agree with the hypothesis that all mass and serial murderers are mentally diseased (for example, psychotic) and therefore legally insane or incompetent. On the contrary, they say, serial killers are **sociopaths,** persons who lack internal controls, disregard common values, and have an intense desire to dominate others. But psychological characteristics alone cannot explain the actions of these people. They are also influenced by the social environment in which they function: the openness of our society, the ease of travel, the availability of firearms, the lack of external controls and supervision, and the general friendliness and trust of Americans in dealing with each other and with strangers.[36]

Levin and Fox suggest that the recent increase in mass and serial murders, despite a general decline in the murder rate, is to some extent attributable to the publicity given to mass murders and the resulting copy-cat phenomenon, the repetition of a crime as a result of the publicity it receives.[37] When one person killed at random by poisoning Tylenol capsules with cyanide, others copied the idea. This phenomenon has prompted experts to recommend that the media cooperate with the criminal justice system when the circumstances demand discretion.[38] Yet cooperation may be hard to achieve when media help is needed to alert the public to a health hazard (as in the Tylenol cases). In any event, the First Amendment's guarantee of freedom of the press does not permit controls.

Gang Murder. Up to this point we have dealt largely with homicides committed by single offenders. But what about homicides by gangs of offenders? Are there any differences between the two types? On the basis of an analysis of data contained in 700 homicide investigation files, researchers found that "gang homicides differ both qualitatively and quantitatively from nongang homicides. Most distinctly, they differ with respect to ethnicity [more likely to be intraethnic], age [gang killers are 5 years younger], number of participants [2½ times as many participants], and relationship between the participants [gang killers are twice as likely not to know their victims]."[39] But similarities can also be seen. The causes of gang homicides, like those of single offenders, are often attributable to social disorganization, economic inequality, and deprivation.[40]

Since the 1950s the nature of gang murder has changed dramatically. As we discuss in Chapter 6, besides the major increase in killings, gang homicides have also gotten more brutal. Drive-by and crossfire shootings of intended victims and innocent bystanders are no longer uncommon. In Brooklyn, New York, all three brothers in one family fell victim to street violence. Motives also have changed through the years. Once, gang wars, with a few related homicides, took place over "turf," territory that members protected, with knives, rocks, or metal chains as weapons. Now the wars are over drugs, and the weapons are assault rifles and semiautomatic guns.[41]

A Cross-National Comparison of Homicide Rates

The criminal homicides we have been discussing are those committed in the United States. By comparing homicide rates in this country with those of other countries, we can gain a broader understanding of that crime. In the World Crime Survey ending with the year 1990 the United Nations revealed that the average rate of intentional homicide for developed (industrialized Western) countries was 4.5 per 100,000.[42]

The survey figures demonstrated that by comparison with the other developed countries, the United States was not doing well: Its homicide rate was 9.0 per 100,000 population, the highest among industrialized Western countries. Figure 11.1 shows that the United States is the leader in homicide rates.[43]

One cross-national study found a moderate association between inequality of income and rate of homicide. It likewise revealed a relationship between a youthful population and the homicide rate. The analysis, the study concluded, "suggests that homicide rates are higher in poorer countries, more culturally diverse countries, in countries which spend less on

defense, in less democratic societies, and in countries where fewer young people are enrolled in school."[44] Another researcher who compared the homicide rates in 76 countries with the rate in the United States found that when he took into consideration the differences in the age and sex distributions of the various populations, the United States had a higher rate than all but 15 countries,[45] most of which were experiencing civil war or internal strife.

A comparison of homicide rates with historical and socioeconomic data from 110 nations over a 5-year period led researchers to the following conclusions:

- Combatant nations experience an increase in homicides following cessation of hostilities (violence has come to be seen as a legitimate means of settling disputes).
- The largest cities have the highest homicide rates; the smallest have the lowest homicide rates; but, paradoxically, as a city grows, its homicide rate per capita does not.
- The availability of capital punishment does not result in fewer homicides and in fact often results in more; abolition of capital punishment decreases the homicide rate.[46]

We have seen that murder rates are not distributed equally among countries or within a single country, or even within neighborhoods (Figure 11.2). As noted earlier, in the United States homicide rates tend to be higher in the West and the South.[47] A greater proportion of males, young people, and blacks are perpetrators and victims of homicide, which tends to be committed against someone the killer knows, at or near the home of at least one of the persons involved, in the evening or on a weekend. Gang murders are increasing dramatically. A number of experts have found that homicides are related to the everyday patterns of interactions in socially disorganized slum areas.[48]

ASSAULT

The crimes of homicide and serious assault share many characteristics. Both are typically committed by young males, and a disproportionate number of arrestees are members of minority groups. Assault victims, too, often know their attackers. Spatial and

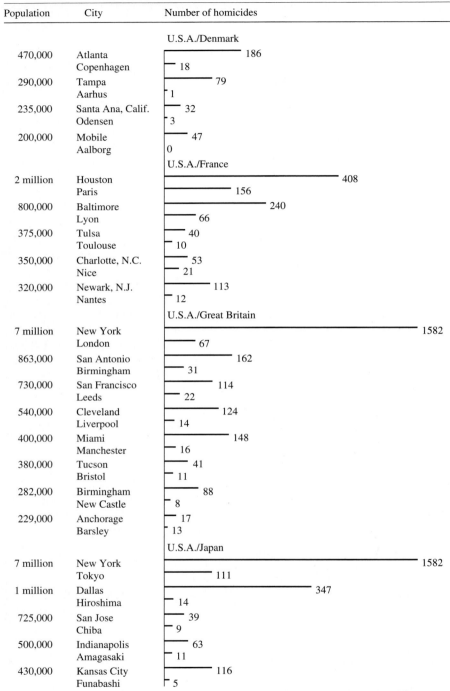

Population	City	Number of homicides
		U.S.A./Denmark
470,000	Atlanta	186
	Copenhagen	18
290,000	Tampa	79
	Aarhus	1
235,000	Santa Ana, Calif.	32
	Odensen	3
200,000	Mobile	47
	Aalborg	0
		U.S.A./France
2 million	Houston	408
	Paris	156
800,000	Baltimore	240
	Lyon	66
375,000	Tulsa	40
	Toulouse	10
350,000	Charlotte, N.C.	53
	Nice	21
320,000	Newark, N.J.	113
	Nantes	12
		U.S.A./Great Britain
7 million	New York	1582
	London	67
863,000	San Antonio	162
	Birmingham	31
730,000	San Francisco	114
	Leeds	22
540,000	Cleveland	124
	Liverpool	14
400,000	Miami	148
	Manchester	16
380,000	Tucson	41
	Bristol	11
282,000	Birmingham	88
	New Castle	8
229,000	Anchorage	17
	Barsley	13
		U.S.A./Japan
7 million	New York	1582
	Tokyo	111
1 million	Dallas	347
	Hiroshima	14
725,000	San Jose	39
	Chiba	9
500,000	Indianapolis	63
	Amagasaki	11
430,000	Kansas City	116
	Funabashi	5

FIGURE 11.1 Number of homicides in U.S. cities and in cities of comparable size in four other industrialized nations, 1988.
Source: The Police Chief, March 1988, pp. 36–37.

WINDOW TO THE WORLD

ASSASSINATIONS AROUND THE GLOBE

Since earliest times the fate of nations and world history have been affected by assassinations. Assassinations were so common in ancient Rome that it became forbidden to carry daggers into the Senate. That did not keep Gaius Julius Caesar's assassins from stabbing him to death in 44 B.C.; their weapons were stilichos, pencil-like tools used to write on wax tablets.

Assassinations are just as likely to occur in politically stable countries as in countries with turmoil, in both developed and developing countries. Is there an effective deterrent? Our penal codes treat the assassination of a head of state or government as a category of homicide distinct from, or higher than, ordinary murder. The Federal Criminal Code, Title 18 U.S. Code 1751, imposes the death penalty for the assassination of the president of the United States, the president-elect, other potential successors, and specially appointed executive staff members. The United States has had more than its share of assassinations. Abraham Lincoln was killed in 1865, and American presidents and political leaders have remained favorite targets: James A. Garfield, 1881; William McKinley, 1901; John F. Kennedy, 1963; Senator Robert F. Kennedy, 1968; Dr. Martin Luther King, Jr., 1968. Presidents Theodore Roosevelt, Franklin Delano Roosevelt, Harry S Truman, Richard Nixon, Gerald Ford, and Ronald Reagan and Governor George C. Wallace of Alabama have all been

the targets of attempted assassinations.

In the last 20 years the number of assassinations around the world appears to have increased. In 1975 President Richard Ratsimandraua of Madagascar, King Faisal of Saudi Arabia, and President Sheik Mujibur Rahman of Bangladesh were assassinated; in 1976 Nigerian head of state General Murtala Ramat Mohammed and Chilean foreign minister Orlando Letelier; in 1977 President Marien Ngouabi of the Congo; in 1978 former Iraqi premier Abdul Razak Al-Naif and former Italian premier Aldo Moro; in 1979 Lord Mountbatten and South Korean president Park Chung Hee; in 1980 Liberian president William R. Tolbert and former Nicaraguan president Anastasio Somoza Debayle; in 1981 Egyptian president Anwar El-Sadat; in 1982 Lebanese president-elect Bishir Gemayel; in 1983 Philippine opposition leader Benigno Acquino; in 1984 Indian prime minister Indira Gandhi; in 1986 Swedish prime minister Olof Palme; in 1988 Lebanese premier Rashid Karami; and in 1992 Indian prime minister Rajiv Gandhi. In the first 4 months of 1993, Sri Lanka's former minister Lalith Athulathmudali, African National Congress leader Chris Hani, Palestinian official Hussein Salem, and Bosnia-Herzegovina's deputy prime minister Hakija Turajlik were assassinated. Many more assassinations of political leaders have occurred around the world, and hundreds more have been attempted but did not succeed.

What prompts people to kill national leaders? Obviously some as-

sassins are psychologically disturbed. Several recent American assassins fall into this category: Lee Harvey Oswald, who has been identified as the killer of President Kennedy; President Ford's two would-be assassins; and John Hinckley, who tried to kill President Reagan. But some assassins act for political, idealistic reasons, such as the Puerto Rican nationalists Oscar Collazo and Griselio Torresola, who tried to kill President Truman.

Are all political assassins bad? The citizens of the former Federal Republic of Germany commemorate July 20, the day on which Colonel Count Klaus von Stauffenberg in 1944 detonated a bomb in Adolf Hitler's bunker. That was to be the last of 43 attempted assassinations of Hitler, who committed suicide less than a year later—but not before Colonel von Stauffenberg and more than 200 co-conspirators had been summarily tried by Nazi courts and hanged.

Source

James F. Kirkham, Sheldon G. Levy, and William J. Crotty, *Assassinations and Political Violence* (Washington, D.C.: U.S. Government Printing Office, 1969).

Questions for Discussion

1. Do you think assassination should be considered such a serious crime that insanity not be allowed as a defense?
2. Can you think of anything that might serve (or currently serves) as an effective deterrent to would-be assassins?

temporal distributions are also quite comparable. Assault rates, like those of homicide, are highest in urban areas, during the summer months, in the evening hours, and in the South.

Though the patterns are the same, the legal definitions are not. A murder is an act that causes the death of another person and that is intended to cause death. An **assault** is an attack on another person that

Since last December,* 10 people have been killed on or near Beekman Avenue, a short but extraordinary violent street in the Mott Haven section of the Bronx. The police say drugs were involved in all of the cases except the shooting on Jan. 3, for which they have no suspected motive.

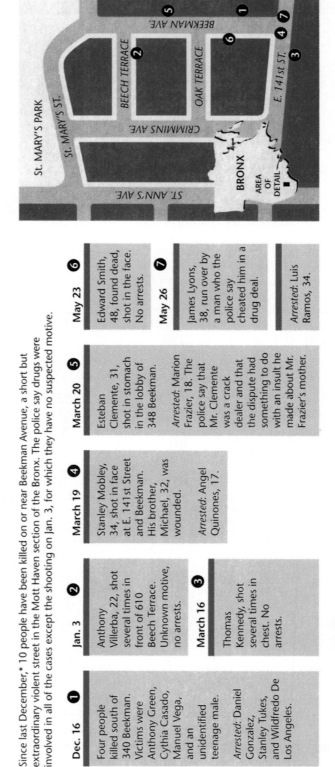

Dec. 16 ❶

Four people killed south of 340 Beekman. Victims were Anthony Green, Cythia Casado, Manuel Vega, and an unidentified teenage male.

Arrested: Daniel Gonzalez, Stanley Tukes, and Wildfredo De Los Angeles.

Jan. 3 ❷

Anthony Villerba, 22, shot several times in front of 610 Beech Terrace. Unknown motive, no arrests.

March 16 ❸

Thomas Kennedy, shot several times in chest. No arrests.

March 19 ❹

Stanley Mobley, 34, shot in face at E. 141st Street and Beekman. His brother, Michael, 32, was wounded.

Arrested: Angel Quinones, 17.

March 20 ❺

Esteban Clemente, 31, shot in stomach in the lobby of 348 Beekman.

Arrested: Marion Frazier, 18. The police say that Mr. Clemente was a crack dealer and that the dispute had something to do with an insult he made about Mr. Frazier's mother.

May 23 ❻

Edward Smith, 48, found dead, shot in the face. No arrests.

May 26 ❼

James Lyons, 38, run over by a man who the police say cheated him in a drug deal.

Arrested: Luis Ramos, 34.

*December 1991 to October 1992.

FIGURE 11.2 A deadly neighborhood.
Source: New York Times, Oct. 11, 1992, p. 85.

240

is made with apparent ability to inflict injury and that is intended to frighten or to cause physical harm. (An attack that results in touching or striking the victim is called a **battery.**) Modern statutes usually recognize two types of assault: A **simple assault** is one that inflicts little or no physical hurt; a felonious assault, or **aggravated assault,** is one in which the perpetrator inflicts serious harm on the victim or uses a deadly weapon.

Criminologists have looked closely at situations in which assaults are committed. One researcher identified six stages of a confrontational situation that leads to an assault:

1. One person insults another.
2. The insulted person perceives the significance of the insult, often by noting the reactions of others present, and becomes angry.
3. The insulted person contemplates a response: fight, flight, or conciliation. If the response chosen is a fight, the insultee assaults the insulter then and there. If another response is chosen, the situation advances to stage 4.
4. The original insulter, now reprimanded, shamed, or embarrassed, makes a countermove: fight or flight.
5. If the choice is a fight, the insulter assaults (and possibly kills) the insultee.
6. The "triumphant" party either flees or awaits the consequences (for example, police response).[49]

We can see that crucial decisions are made at all stages, and that the nature of the decisions depends on the context in which they are made. At stage 1, nobody is likely to offer an insult in a peaceful group or situation. At stage 2, the witnesses to the scene could respond in a conciliatory manner. (Let us call this a conflict-resolution situation.) At stage 3, the insulted person could leave the scene with dignity. (A confrontational person would call it flight; a conflict-resolution-minded person would call it a dignified end to a confrontational situation.) Stage 4 is a critical stage, since it calls for a counterresponse. The original aggressor could see this as the last chance to avoid violence and withdraw with apologies. That would be the end of the matter. In a confrontational situation, however, the blows will be delivered now, if none have been dealt already.

A similar pattern was proposed by James Tedeschi and Richard Felson, who developed a theory of aggression as instrumental behavior—that is, goal-oriented behavior carried out intentionally with the purpose of obtaining something. This is a different way of thinking about aggression. For years, criminologists and psychologists have generally accepted that aggression (and the violence that often goes with it) happens when a person reaches a "breaking point." There is little premeditation or thought given to some aggressive or violent behavior. But for Tedeschi and Felson, all aggression occurs after the person has thought about it first, even though these thoughts may be disorganized or illogical and may last for just a fraction of a second.[50]

The National Crime Victimization Survey estimates that 6,650,000 simple assaults were committed in 1994. Assault is the most common of all violent crimes reported to the police. The number of aggravated assaults has risen in recent years, reaching 2,478,000 in 1994.[51] These figures, however, grossly underestimate the real incidence. Many people involved in an assault consider the event a private matter, particularly if the assault took place within the family or household. Consequently, until quite recently little was known about family-related violence. But the focus of recent research is changing that situation rapidly.

FAMILY-RELATED CRIMES

In 1962 five physicians exposed the gravity of the "battered child syndrome" in the *Journal of the American Medical Association.*[52] When they reviewed X-ray photographs of patients in the emergency rooms of 71 hospitals across the country over the course of a year, they found 300 cases of child abuse, of which 11 percent resulted in death and over 28 percent in permanent brain damage. Shortly thereafter, the women's movement rallied to the plight of the battered wife and, somewhat later, to the personal and legal problems of wives who were raped by their husbands.[53]

In the 1960s and 1970s various organizations, fighting for the rights of women and children, exposed the harm that results from physical and psychological abuse in the home. They demanded public action. They created public awareness of the extent of the problem. Psychologists, physicians, anthropologists, and social scientists, among others, increasingly focused attention on the various factors that enter into episodes of domestic violence. Such factors include the sources of conflict, arguments, physical attacks, injuries, and temporal and spatial elements.

Within three decades family violence, the "well-kept secret," has come to be recognized as a major social problem.[54] Family violence shares some of the characteristics of other forms of violence, yet the intimacy of marital, cohabitational, or parent-child relationships sets family violence apart. The physical and emotional harm inflicted in violent episodes tends to be spread over longer periods of time and to have a more lasting impact on all members of the living unit. Moreover, such events tend to be self-perpetuating.

Spouse Abuse

Media celebrity and former star athlete O. J. Simpson was convicted in 1989 of assaulting his wife, Nicole Brown Simpson. He served no time in prison, nor was he required to undergo counseling. On June 13, 1994, Nicole Brown Simpson and her friend Ronald Goldman were found lying dead in pools of their own blood, victims of a vicious knife attack. O. J. Simpson was accused of their murder. Following a lengthy, highly publicized and much-discussed trial, O. J. Simpson was found not guilty by a jury of his peers. The verdict had a wide-reaching impact on various aspects of the criminal justice system. It also made abused women fear for their lives. Concerned that a man who was a convicted batterer could be found not guilty of killing his ex-wife, despite what was perceived by many as convincing evidence, they wondered if they could eventually share the same fate as Nicole Brown Simpson.[55]

The Extent of Spouse Abuse. In a national sample of 6002 households, Murray A. Straus and Richard J. Gelles found that about one of every six couples experiences at least one physical assault during the year.[56] While both husbands and wives perpetrate acts of violence, the consequences of their acts differ.[57] Men, who more often use guns, knives, or fists, inflict more pain and injury. About 60 percent of spousal assaults consist of minor shoving, slapping, pushing; the other 40 percent are considered severe: punching, kicking, stabbing, choking.[58]

Researchers agree that assaultive behavior within the family is a highly underreported crime. Data from the National Crime Victimization Survey indicate:

- One-half of the incidents of domestic assault are not reported.
- The most common reason given for failure to report a domestic assault to the police was that the victim considered the incident a private matter.
- Victims who reported such incidents to the police did so to prevent future assaults.
- Though the police classified two-thirds of the reported incidents of domestic violence as simple assaults, half of them inflicted bodily injury as serious as or more serious than the injuries inflicted during rapes, robberies, and aggravated assaults.[59]

The Nature of Spouse Abuse. Before we can understand spouse abuse, we need information about abusers. Some experts have found that interpersonal violence is learned and transmitted from one generation to the next.[60] Studies demonstrate that children who are raised by aggressive parents tend to grow up to be aggressive adults.[61] Other researchers have demonstrated how stress, frustration, and severe psychopathology take their toll on family relationships.[62] A few researchers have also explored the role of body chemistry; one investigation ties abuse to the tendency of males to secrete adrenaline when they feel sexually threatened.[63]

The relationship between domestic violence and the use of alcohol and drugs has also been explored. Abusive men with severe drug and alcohol problems are more likely to abuse their wives or girlfriends when they are drunk or high and to inflict more injury.[64]

Several studies of other societies demonstrate cultural support for the abuse of women. Moroccan researcher Mohammed Ayat reported that of 160 battered women, about 25 percent believed that a man who does *not* beat his wife must be under some magic spell; 8 percent believed that such a man has a weak personality and is afraid of his wife; 2 percent believed that he must be abnormal; and another 2 percent believed that he doesn't love her or has little interest in her.[65] Wife beating, then, appears to be accepted as a norm by over one-third of the women studied—women who are themselves beaten. It even appears to be an expected behavior. In fact, in a study of 90 cultures, spouse beating was rare or nonexistent in only 15.[66]

Spouse abuse has often been attributed to the imbalance of power between male and female partners. According to some researchers, the historical view of wives as possessions of their husbands persists even today.[67] Until recently, spousal abuse was perceived as a problem more of social service than of criminal justice.[68] Police responding to domestic disturbance calls typically do not make an arrest unless the assailant is drunk, has caused serious injury, or has assaulted the officers. Take, for example, the case of *Thurman v. Torrington.* Tracey Thurman had repeatedly requested police assistance because she feared her estranged husband. Even after he threatened to shoot her and her son, the police merely told her to get a restraining order. Eventually, the husband attacked Thurman, inflicting multiple stab wounds that caused paralysis from the neck down and permanent disfigurement. The police had delayed in responding to her call on that occasion, and the city of Torrington, Connecticut, was held liable for having failed to provide her with equal protection of the laws. In the suit that followed, Ms. Thurman was awarded $2.3 million in damages.[69]

The Thurman case is rare. The majority of assault incidents within the family either are unreported to the police or, if reported, are classified as simple assaults. By and large, the victims of family violence—those who are willing to look for help—have turned to crisis telephone lines and to shelters for battered women (safe havens that first appeared in the early 1970s to provide legal, social, and psychological services).

Whether informal interventions are as effective as the criminal justice system, however, is a matter of controversy.[70] In a study conducted some years ago, the Minneapolis Domestic Violence Experiment, three types of action were taken: (1) The batterer was arrested, (2) the partners were required to separate for a designated period of time, and (3) a mediator intervened between the partners. Over a 6-month period the offenders who were arrested had the lowest recidivism rate (10 percent), those who were required to separate had the highest (24 percent), and those who submitted to mediation fell in between (19 percent).[71] More recently, a 1991 study revealed that neither short-custody arrests for domestic violence in inner-city areas nor longer-term arrests are effective in curbing domestic violence, especially in the long run.[72] Questions on the subject of spouse

abuse still far outnumber answers. Personal, ethical, and moral concerns make the issue highly sensitive. Researchers, however, are seeking answers.

Child Abuse

Spouse abuse is closely related to child abuse. One-half to three-quarters of men who batter women also beat their children, and many sexually abuse them as well. Children are also injured as a result of reckless behavior on the part of their fathers while the latter are abusing their mothers. In fact, the majority of abused sons over 14 suffer injuries trying to protect their mothers.[73]

The Extent of Child Abuse. It is very difficult to measure the extent of child abuse. Battering usually takes place in the home, and the child victims rarely notify the police. Edna Erez and Pamela Tontodonato found that the parental abuse that is reported often involves serious physical encounters.[74] Most of the available data on the extent of child abuse come from the National Incidence Study (NIS), sponsored by the National Center on Child Abuse and Neglect, and from official reports compiled by the American Humane Association (AHA).

The NIS collected information on child maltreatment (abuse and neglect) from hospitals, police, courts, schools, and child protection agencies in a randomly selected sample of 26 counties in 10 states during 1979 and 1980. These data—which covered reported cases only—yielded the following nationwide estimates:

- 5.7 children per 1000 under age 18 are physically, sexually, or emotionally abused annually (physically abused children make up the largest category: 3.4 per 1000).
- 5.3 children per 1000 under age 18 are neglected annually.[75]

The mid-1980 AHA National Study of Child Abuse and Neglect Reporting estimated, from cases reported to official child protection agencies across the country, that 30.6 children per 1000 are maltreated (physically abused, emotionally abused, sexually abused, or neglected) annually.[76]

The estimates yielded by these two large surveys are obviously far apart. Part of the increase that occurred in the 5-year period may be due to better reporting, part to greater public awareness, and part to differences in the surveys themselves. Nevertheless, even the figure of 30.6 per 1000 is considered a low estimate of the actual number of battered children in our society.[77] Moreover, we know very little about these children, except that most of them are between 12 and 17 years old, that girls are more likely to be abused than boys, and that low-income families are disproportionately represented in the official statistics.[78]

The Nature of Child Abuse. When child abuse first began to be investigated in the early 1960s, the investigators were predominantly physicians, who looked at the psychopathology of the abusers. They discovered that a high proportion of abusers suffered from alcoholism, drug abuse, mental retardation, poor attachment, low self-esteem, or sadistic psychosis. Later the search for causes moved in other directions. Some researchers pointed out that abusive parents did not know how to discipline children or, for that matter, even how to provide for basic needs, such as nutrition and medical attention. Claims have been made that abusers have themselves been abused; to date, however, the evidence in regard to this hypothesis is mixed.[79]

The list of factors related to child abuse is long. We know, for example, that the rate of child abuse in lower-class families is high. This finding is probably related to the fact that low-income parents have few resources for dealing with the stress to which they are subjected, such as poor housing and financial problems. When they cannot cope with their responsibilities, they may become overwhelmed. The rate of child abuse may also be related to the acceptance of physical responses to conflict situations in what has been termed the "subculture of violence" (Chapter 6). Moreover, since child abuse among poor families is likely to be handled by a public agency, these cases tend to appear in official statistics.

Some researchers have found that formal action—arrest and prosecution—is the most effective means for limiting repeat offenses in the case of battered wives. The situation seems to be different when children are involved. Several advocates for children oppose any involvement of the criminal justice system. They believe that the parent-child attachment remains crucial to the child's development, and they fear that punishment of parents can only be detrimental to the child's need for a stable family environment. Only in the most extreme cases would they separate children from parents and place them in shelters or in foster homes. The preference is to prevent child abuse by other means, such as self-help groups (Parents Anonymous), baby-sitting assistance, and crisis phone lines.

Toys and flowers surround the coffin of 6-year-old Elisa Izquierdo, whose 29-year-old mother was charged with murder and endangering the welfare of a child, Brooklyn, New York, November 1995.

The results of various types of intervention are characterized by the title of a 1986 report on child maltreatment: "Half Full and Half Empty."[80] Rates of repeated abuse are high; yet some families have had positive results, and advances have been made in identifying the best treatment for various types of problems. But though our understanding of the problem has indeed increased, we need to know a great deal more about the offense before we can reduce its occurrence.[81]

Abuse of the Elderly

Abuse of the elderly has become an area of special concern to social scientists. The population group that is considered to be elderly is variously defined. The majority of researchers consider 65 the age at which an individual falls into the category "elderly." As health care in the United States has improved, longevity has increased. The population of elderly people has grown larger over the decades: from 4 percent of the total population in 1900 to 12.6 percent in the 1990s.[82] Every day 1000 more people join the ranks. It is estimated that by the year 2020, 20 percent of the population will be elderly.[83]

Elderly persons who are being cared for by their adult children are at a certain risk of abuse. The extent of the problem, however, is still largely unknown. The abused elderly frequently do not talk about their abuse for fear of the embarrassment of public exposure and possible retaliation by the abuser. Congressional hearings on domestic abuse estimate that between 500,000 and 2.5 million elderly people are abused annually.[84] Among the causes of such abuse are caregivers who themselves grew up in homes where violence was a way of life, the stress of caregiving in a private home rather than an institution, generational conflicts, and frustration with gerontological (old-age) problems of the care receiver, such as illness and senility.[85]

We can see that criminologists share a growing concern about family-related violence. Child abuse has received the attention of scholars for three decades. Spousal abuse has been studied for two decades. The abuse of the elderly has begun to receive attention much more recently. Family abuse is not new; our awareness of the size and seriousness of the problem is. The same could be said about yet another offense. It was not until the 1960s that women's advocates launched a national campaign on behalf of victims of rape. Since then, rape has become a major topic in criminological literature and research.

RAPE AND SEXUAL ASSAULT

The common law defined **rape** as an act of enforced intercourse by a man of a woman (other than the attacker's wife) without her consent. Intercourse includes any sexual penetration, however slight. The exclusion of wives from the crime of rape rested on several outdated legal fictions, among them the propositions that the marriage vows grant implicit permanent rights of sexual access and that spouses cannot testify against each other. Older laws universally classify rape as a sex crime. But rape has always been much more than that. It is inherently a crime of violence, an exercise of power.

Oddly, as Susan Brownmiller forcefully argues, it really started as a property crime. Men as archetypal aggressors (the penis as a weapon) subjugated women by the persistent threat of rape. That threat forced each woman to submit to a man for protection and thus to become a wife, the property of a man. Rape then was made a crime to protect one man's property—his wife—from the sexual aggressions of other men.[86] But even that view regards rape as a violent crime against the person, one that destroys the freedom of a woman (and nowadays of a man as well) to decide whether, when, and with whom to enter a sexual relationship.

Well over a thousand books, scholarly articles, and papers have been produced on the topic of rape and sexual assault since the 1960s. Much that was obscure and poorly understood has now been clarified by research generated largely by the initiatives of the feminist movement, the National Center for the Prevention and Control of Rape (NCPCR), and other governmental and private funding agencies. While most of the crimes in our penal codes have more or less retained their original form, the law on rape has changed rapidly and drastically. The name of the crime, its definition, the rules of evidence and procedure, society's reaction to it—all have changed.[87]

Americans regard rape as one of the most serious crimes. Respondents to the 1985 National Survey of Crime Severity rated the severity of forcible rape that resulted in injury requiring hospitalization as the fourteenth most serious of 204 offenses. Among the crimes considered more serious were stabbing that results in death, planting bombs in public places when life is lost, and armed robbery that results in death.[88]

Characteristics of the Rape Event

According to the Uniform Crime Reports, there were 102,100 forcible rapes in 1994. This figure represents 6 percent of the total number of violent crimes.[89] The incidence of rape dropped 7 percent between 1992 and 1994. Of all those arrested for forcible rape, 16 percent were under age 18; 44 percent were between 18 and 25 years old; and over half were white. Most rapes are committed in the summer, particularly in July. Several decades ago, Menachem Amir demonstrated that close to half of all rapes in Philadelphia from 1958 to 1965 were committed by a person known to or even friendly with the victim.[90] Recent victimization data show that the situation has not changed: 48 percent of rapes are committed by men who know their victims.[91] The offender may even be the husband, who in some states can now qualify as a rapist.

Research in this area thus far has not been extensive. One report estimates that 12 percent of wives are raped by their husbands.[92] Recent studies have focused attention on yet another form of rape in relational situations: *date rape*.[93] One study indicated that as many as 25 percent of all female college students may have experienced rape.[94] Criminologists have difficulty estimating the frequency of date rape, but in all likelihood such rape has increased significantly. It is estimated that only one-tenth of the date rapes committed are reported to the police.

There is an arrest made for all types of forcible rape in about 52 percent of the cases. Many "stranger rapists" remain at large because they commit their acts in ways that produce little tangible evidence as to their identities. They maintain a distance from the victim by not interacting with her before the attack. The serial rapist also attacks strangers, but because he finds his victims repeatedly in the same places, his behavior is more predictable and so leads to a better arrest rate.[95]

Who Are the Rapists?

Explanations of rape fall into two categories, psychological and sociocultural. While research in these areas has expanded over the last two decades, the causes of rape remain speculative.

Psychological Factors. Several experts view rapists as suffering from mental illness or personality disorders. They argue that some rapists are psychotic, sociopathic, or sadistic or feel deficient in masculinity. Most rapists show hostile feelings toward women, have histories of violence, and tend to attack strangers. They commit the offense because of anger, a drive for power (expressed as sexual conquest), or the enjoyment of maltreating a victim (sadism). Some rapists view women as sex objects whose role is to satisfy them.

Sociocultural Factors. Psychological explanations assume that men who rape are maladjusted in some way. But several studies done in the 1980s demonstrate that rapists are indistinguishable from other groups of offenders.[96] These studies generally conclude that rape is culturally related to societal norms that approve of aggression as a demonstration of masculinity (as we saw in Chapter 6) or that rape is the mechanism by which men maintain their power over women.

The social significance of rape has long been a part of anthropological literature. A cross-cultural study of 95 tribal societies found that 47 percent were rape-free, 35 percent intermediate, and 18 percent rape-prone. In the rape-prone societies women had low status and little decision-making power, and they lived apart from men. The author of this study concluded: "Violence is socially, not biologically, programmed."[97]

Despite anthropologists' traditional interest in gender relationships, it was not until the feminist movement and radical criminology focused on the subject that the relationship of rape, gender inequality, and socioeconomic status was fully articulated. Writing from the Marxist perspective, which we explore in Chapter 9, Julia and Herman Schwendinger posited that "the impoverishment of the working class and the widening gap between rich and poor" create conditions for the prevalence of sexual violence.[98] A test of this hypothesis showed that while the incidence of sexual violence was not related to ethnic inequality, it was significantly related to general income inequality.[99]

A more recent study analyzed these findings and concluded that economic inequality was not the sole determinant of violent crime in our society. Forcible rape was found to be an added "cost" of many factors, including social disorganization.[100] In sum, many factors have been associated with the crime of rape: psychological problems, social factors, and even sociopolitical factors. Some experts suggest that boys are socialized to be aggressive and dominating, that the innate male sex drive leads to rape, and that pornography encourages men to rape by making sex objects of women, degrading women, and glamorizing violence against them. Rape has been explained in such a wide variety of ways that it is extremely difficult to plan preventive strategies and to formulate crime-control policy. Moreover, it has created major difficulties in the criminal justice system.

Rape and the Legal System

The difficulties of rape prosecutions have their roots in the English common law. Sir Matthew Hale, a seventeenth-century jurist, explained in *Pleas of the Crown* (1685, 1736) how a jury was to be cautious in viewing evidence of rape: "[It] must be remembered . . . that it is an accusation easily to be made and hard to be proved, and harder to be defended, by the party accused, tho never so innocent."[101] This instruction, which so definitively protects the defendant, has until recently been a mandatory instruction to juries in the United States. Along with many other legal and policy changes, many jurisdictions have now cast it aside. The requirement of particularly stringent proof in rape cases had always been justified by the seriousness of the offense and the heavy penalties associated with it, plus the stigma attached to such a conviction.

Difficulties of Prosecution. Victims of rape have often been regarded with suspicion by the criminal justice system. The victim's testimony has not sufficed to convict the defendant, no matter how unimpeachable that testimony may have been. There had to be "corroborating evidence," such as semen, torn clothes, bruises, or eyewitness testimony.

Another major issue has been that of consent. Did the victim encourage, entice, or maybe even agree to the act? Was the attack forced? Did the victim resist? Martin Schwartz and Todd Clear sum up the reasons for such questions: "There is a widespread belief in our culture that women 'ask for it,' either individually or as a group." They compared rape victims to victims of other offenses: "Curiously, society does not censure the robbery victim for walk-

ing around with $10, or the burglary victim for keeping all of those nice things in his house, or the car theft victim for showing off his flashy new machine, just asking for someone to covet it."[102]

Because defendants in rape cases so often claim that the victim was in some way responsible for the attack, rape victims in the courtroom tend to become the "accused," required to defend their good reputations, their propriety, and their mental soundness. In sum, so many burdens are placed on the victim that no one seriously wonders why only a fraction of rapes are reported and why so few men accused of rape are convicted.

Legislative Changes. The feminist movement has had a considerable impact on laws and attitudes concerning rape in our country. The state of Michigan was a leader in the movement to reform such laws by creating, in 1975, the new crime of "criminal sexual conduct" to replace the traditional rape laws. It distinguishes four degrees of assaultive sexual acts, differentiated by the amount of force used, the infliction of injury, and the age and mental condition of the victim.

The new law is gender-neutral, in that it makes illegal any type of forcible sex, including homosexual rape. Other states have followed Michigan's lead. Schwartz and Clear have suggested that reform should go one step further. They argue that if rape were covered by the general assault laws rather than by a separate statute on sex crimes, the emphasis would be on the assault (the action of the offender) and not on the resistance (the action of the victim).

Recent legislation has also removed many of the barriers women encountered as witnesses in the courtroom. Thus in states with rape shield laws women are no longer required to disclose their prior sexual activity, and corroboration requirements have been reduced or eliminated; as noted earlier, some states have reversed two centuries of legal tradition by striking down the "marital rape exemption" so that a wife may now charge her husband with rape.[103] But law reform has limits. Unfortunately, prejudices die hard.

Community Response

Women's advocates have taken an interest not only in legislative reform but also in the community's response to the victims of rape. In 1970 the first rape-specific support project, the Bay Area Women Against Rape—a volunteer-staffed emergency phone information service—was established in Berkeley,

California.[104] By 1973, similar projects had spread throughout the country. Run by small, unaffiliated groups, they handled crises, monitored agencies (hospitals, police, courts) that came in contact with victims, educated the public about the problems of victims, and even provided lessons in self-defense.

By the late 1970s the number of these centers and their activities had increased dramatically. The mass media reported on their successes. Federal and, later, state and local support for such services rose. As the centers became more professional, they formed boards of directors, prepared detailed budgets to comply with the requirements of funding agencies, hired social workers and mental health personnel, and developed their political action component. But even with increased support, the demand for the services of rape crisis centers far outweighs the available resources.

ROBBERY

The very concept of rape has undergone rapid change. But legal and public response to another crime of violence that also involves a temporary and complete domination of the victim has not changed at all. It is defined as it always has been: **Robbery** is the taking of property from a victim by force and violence or by the threat of violence.

The Model Penal Code (Section 222.1) grades robbery as a felony of the second degree, commanding a prison term of up to 10 years. If the robber has intentionally inflicted serious physical injury or attempted to kill, the sentence may be as long as life. In reality, however, the average sentence upon conviction for one charge of robbery is 6 years.[105] In 1994 the number of robbery offenses was 618,820, the third consecutive year this number has declined, from a high of 687,730 in 1991.[106]

Offenders display weapons, mostly guns and knives, in almost half of all robberies. Since 44 percent of all robberies net the perpetrator less than $50, the overall reporting rate for robbery is only slightly higher than 50 percent. Robberies of individuals occur most frequently on the street (61.3 percent). The remaining robberies take place in parking lots and garages (14 percent), in residences (9.3 percent), in commercial buildings (5.2 percent), in transit stations or on public transportation (3.8 percent), in nightclubs, bars, or restaurants (2.7 percent), and in miscellaneous establishments (3.7 percent).[107]

Characteristics of Robbers

Criminologists have classified the characteristics of robbers as well as the characteristics of robberies. John Conklin detected four types of robbers:

- The *professional robber* carefully plans and executes a robbery, often with many accomplices; steals large sums of money; and has a long-term, deep commitment to robbery as a means of supporting a hedonistic lifestyle.
- The *opportunistic robber* (the most common) has no long-term commitment to robbery; targets victims for small amounts of money ($20 or less); victimizes elderly women, drunks, cab drivers, and other people who seem to be in no position to resist; and is young and generally inexperienced.
- The *addict robber* is addicted to drugs, has a low level of commitment to robbery but a high level of commitment to theft, plans less than professional robbers but more than opportunistic robbers, wants just enough money for a fix, and may or may not carry a weapon.
- The *alcoholic robber* has no commitment to robbery as a way of life, has no commitment to theft, does not plan his or her robberies, usually robs people after first assaulting them, takes few precautions, and is apprehended more often than other robbers.[108]

The Consequences of Robbery

Robbery is a property crime as well as a violent crime. It is the combination of the motive for economic gain and the violent nature of robbery that makes it so serious.[109] An estimated $496 million was lost as a result of robbery in 1994 alone. The value of stolen property per incident averaged $801, and the average amount of money stolen ranged from $387 (from convenience stores) to $3551 (from banks).[110] Loss of money, however, is certainly not the only consequence of robbery. The million-odd robberies that take place each year leave psychological and physical trauma in their wake, not to mention the pervasive fear and anxiety that have contributed to the decay of inner cities.

Not all criminologists agree, however, that the high level of fear is warranted. After examining trends in robbery-homicide data from 52 of the largest cities in the United States, one researcher found "little support for the fears that there is a new breed of street criminals who cause more serious injuries and deaths in robberies. Very recent trends point in the other direction. Killing a robbery victim appears to be going out of fashion."[111]

KIDNAPPING AND TERRORISM

Seizing and holding a person for ransom or reward is like robbery, in that it involves the use or threat of violence for the purpose of acquiring property illegally. Kidnapping in the form of hostage taking is frequently an element of a larger scheme that encompasses several distinct crimes of violence. The totality of such violence is called terrorism.

Kidnapping

Kidnapping as such was not recognized as a felony under English common law; it was a misdemeanor. Some forms of kidnapping were later criminalized by statute. In the eighteenth century, the most frequent form of kidnapping, according to the great legal scholar Sir William Blackstone, was stealing children and sending them to servitude in the American colonies. Other forms of kidnapping were the "crimping," or shanghaiing, of persons for involuntary service aboard ships and the abduction of women for purposes of prostitution abroad.

All these offenses have elements in common, and together they define the crime of **kidnapping:** abduction and detention by force or fraud and transportation beyond the authority of the place where the crime was committed. It was not until the kidnapping of the infant son of Charles Lindbergh in 1932 that comprehensive kidnapping legislation was enacted in the United States. In passing the federal kidnapping statute—the so-called Lindbergh Act [now 18 U.S. Code (sec.) 1201]—Congress made it a felony to kidnap and transport a victim across a state or national border. The crime was subject to the death penalty, unless the victim was released unharmed; the death penalty has since been dropped.

Terrorism

Terrorism is a resort to violence or a threat of violence on the part of a group seeking to accomplish a purpose against the opposition of constituted authority. Crucial to the terrorists' scheme is the exploitation of the media to attract attention to the cause. Many clandestine organizations around the world have sought to draw attention to their causes—the Irish Republican Army (IRA), committed to the cause of uniting the British counties of Northern Ireland with the Republic of Ireland; Islamic fundamentalists committed to the protection of Islam in its purist form against any Western influence; various Palestinian factions opposed to Israeli occupation or to any Mideast peace settlement; radical groups all over the world seeking an end to capitalism or colonialism or the imposition of one or another form of totalitarian rule.

From the outset the member states of the United Nations have been concerned about international terrorism because it endangers or takes innocent lives and jeopardizes fundamental freedoms, such as the freedom to travel and to congregate for public events. The U.N. effort to control international terrorism concentrates on removal of the underlying grievances that provoke people to sacrifice human lives, including their own, in an attempt to effect radical changes.[112] This approach to the control of terrorism is not concerned with the individual motivations of terrorists. Some of them may be highly motivated idealists; others are recruited for substantial rewards. The control effort is directed rather at the conditions that give rise to terrorism and at the removal of such conditions.

To the extent that some grievances have been reduced by political action, such as the granting of independence to colonies, terrorism has declined. But other problems remain, especially in Northern Ireland, India, Central America, Africa, and the West Bank and Gaza Strip occupied by Israel. Crimes of a terrorist nature occur virtually every day and are likely to continue wherever the underlying problems are not resolved. Terrorist activities include but are not restricted to assassinations, hostage taking, and interference with or destruction of ships, aircraft, or means of land transport (see Table 11.1). When funding by clandestine supporters is not forthcoming, terrorists have carried out robberies to finance their operations.

The Extent of Terrorism. The incidence of terrorism may seem slight in the light of overall national crime statistics, especially those of the United States. But the worldwide destructive impact of such acts is considerable. So too are the costs of increased security to combat terrorism. The airline industry alone spends $500 million a year for security.[113] After the bombing

TABLE 11.1   Terrorist Events against Americans, 1983–1996

- On October 23, 1983, a suicide terrorist in a TNT-laden truck blew up U.S. Marine Corps headquarters in Beirut, Lebanon, killing 241 marines and sailors. A second truck blew up a French paratrooper barracks 2 miles away, killing 58.
- On October 7, 1985, five hijackers seized the Italian cruiseliner *Achille Lauro*. They held some 400 persons for ransom and killed a wheelchair-bound American passenger.
- On April 2, 1986, a bomb exploded aboard TWA flight 840 at Athens airport, killing four Americans.
- On April 5, 1986, terrorists exploded a bomb in a West Berlin disco frequented by American service personnel, killing 2 and injuring 200. The incident prompted an American air strike against Libya in retaliation.
- On September 5, 1986, four Pakistani gunmen, followers of Abu Nidal, attempted to hijack a Pan Am 747 in Karachi, Pakistan. After keeping the plane on the runway overnight, the gunmen were overpowered by security; 21 passengers died.
- On December 21, 1988, terrorists exploded Pan Am flight 103, en route from Frankfurt, Germany, to New York, killing 270 passengers, crew, and people on the ground at Lockerbie, Scotland.
- On February 26, 1993, a terrorist bomb in the basement garage of the World Trade Center in New York City killed 6 people, injured over 1000 people, and caused extensive damage to the building.
- On April 19, 1995, a bomb made of fertilizer and diesel fuel exploded in front of the Murrah Federal Building in Oklahoma City, killing 168 and injuring over 600.
- On November 13, 1995, five Americans and two Indians were killed and 60 injured when a car bomb exploded near a U.S.-run military training facility in Riyahd, Saudi Arabia. Four Saudi Muslim militants were later executed for the attack.
- On June 25, 1996, in Dhahran, Saudi Arabia, a truck bomb exploded in front of a U.S. military barracks. Nineteen Americans were killed, and four hundred people were injured.
- On July 17, 1996, TWA flight 800, en route to Paris from New York City's JFK Airport, went down in a ball of fire into the ocean off Long Island. All 230 passengers and crew aboard were killed. (It appears to be a terrorist attack.)
- On July 27, 1996, during the time that Atlanta was hosting the Olympics, a homemade pipe bomb exploded at a late-night concert held in Atlanta's Centennial Park. Two people died, and scores more injured by flying shrapnel. The blast cast a pall over the Centennial Olympic Games.

Source: National Center for Health Statistics, World Health Organization, country reports, and media reports.

of the U.S. embassy complex in Beirut, Lebanon, with the loss of the lives of 241 marines and sailors, the strengthening of U.S. embassy security all over the world cost well over $3 billion.

In one year alone (1985) terrorists were responsible for:

4 letter bombs
5 barricade-hostage incidents
9 hijackings
17 specific threats
54 kidnappings
70 attempted attacks
84 armed assaults
165 bombings and arsons

Of these crimes, 12 were committed in Belgium, 14 in Chile, 29 in Colombia, 12 in Cyprus, 35 in West Germany, 12 in France, 29 in Greece, 17 in Italy, 47 in Lebanon, 10 in Peru, 18 in Portugal, 15 in Spain, 10 in the United Kingdom, and 148 in other countries that experienced fewer than 10 incidents each. Regionally, Western Europe was hardest hit (182),

followed by the Middle East (70) and South America (62). The remaining incidents were spread all over the other regions, with Asia and the Far East suffering the fewest incidents. Of the targets, 151 were political, 80 were diplomatic, 79 were economic, and the remainder were seemingly random public places, specific persons, and various facilities.[114] It is noteworthy that 31 of the 408 terrorist acts were committed on behalf of governments.

Among the most active terrorist groups were the Islamic Jihad (35 acts), the Fatah Revolutionary Council (24), the West German Red Army Faction (19), the Portuguese Popular Forces of 25 April (15), and the Chilean Manuel Rodriguez Popular Front (14). In the course of these acts of terrorism, 265 persons were killed, among them 46 Americans, 16 French, 15 British, 11 Germans, 11 Italians, 10 Israelis, and 9 staff members of international organizations. The terrorists suffered fewer deaths.

International Efforts to Control Terrorism.
Many years ago the world community agreed on three international conventions to combat terrorism:

- Convention on Offenses and Certain Other Acts Committed on Board Aircraft, signed at Tokyo on September 14, 1963
- Convention for the Suppression of Unlawful Seizure of Aircraft, signed at The Hague on December 16, 1970
- Convention for the Suppression of Unlawful Acts against the Safety of Civil Aviation, signed at Montreal on September 23, 1971

These conventions, which provide for widespread international cooperation in the prevention of airplane hijacking and the pursuit and extradition (surrender to a requesting country) of offenders, produced a dramatic drop in the number of such incidents. Subsequently, the international community agreed on two further conventions to protect diplomats, their families, and their installations:

- Convention on the Prevention and Punishment of Crimes against Internationally Protected Persons, Including Diplomatic Agents, adopted by the General Assembly of the United Nations on December 14, 1973
- International Convention against the Taking of Hostages, adopted by the General Assembly of the United Nations on December 17, 1979[115]

It appears that by 1989 several governments that had been supporting "freedom fighters" (elsewhere called terrorist groups) had grown disenchanted with the groups' exercise of arbitrary violence against uninvolved civilian targets, such as airplane passengers, and had ceased to support such groups. In addition, the end of the cold war and breakup of the Soviet bloc have deprived many of these groups of funding, and consequently they are on the decline. Rising in their stead is a new type of terrorist group, more difficult to monitor, and perhaps even more dangerous. The old-style politically motivated mayhem has been replaced with ethnically and religiously inspired violence. As the year 2000 approaches, groups focused on the idea of millennialism are expected to increase in number and dangerousness. *Millennialism* is a belief that a catastrophic war or natural disaster will land the "chosen few" in paradise.[116]

These "doomsday cults" can turn inward, leading to mass suicide or the murder of the membership. Eighty-six of David Koresh's followers at the Branch Davidian compound in Waco, Texas, died a fiery death after a lengthy siege by the FBI. It is still unclear whether the Branch Davidians set the compound on fire themselves, or if the FBI was responsible. Other groups direct their actions at outsiders. In Japan, the Aum Shinrikyo ("Supreme Truth") sect was implicated in the deadly sarin nerve gas attack on the Tokyo subway which killed 10 and injured over 5000. The leader of the sect, Shoko Asahara, preached about the end of the world, and claimed that sarin

Right-wing militia members at a Michigan training camp.

CRIMINOLOGICAL FOCUS

"AN EPIDEMIC OF HATE CRIMES?"

The media, academics, advocacy groups, and politicians have created what has been described as a "hate crime epidemic." But is the problem really as great as we have been led to believe? For example, the media can shape public opinion and reinforce the idea that there is an epidemic, through the use of these types of headlines:

- "A Cancer of Hatred Afflicts America"(1)
- "Rise in Hate Crimes Signals Alarming Resurgence of Bigotry"(2)

Books and articles are often inflammatory, argue James Jacobs and Jessica Henry.(3) The authors suggest that scholars simply assume a grave problem exists, in spite of an overwhelming lack of evidence. This can be a dangerous assumption, for the idea of hate crime divides the community and becomes a self-fulfilling prophecy. "Crime sells—so does racism, sexism, and homophobia. Garden-variety crime has become mundane."(3)

Advocacy groups representing blacks, Jews, gays and lesbians, women, and the disabled have embraced the idea of a hate crime epidemic, much of which is based on dubious statistics. For example, the 1991 Uniform Crime Reports shows only 4588 reported hate crimes, less than .039 percent of all reported crimes. Is this an epidemic?

Jacobs and Henry point out that American history shows attacks on racial and ethnic groups started from the moment European settlers arrived and made Native Americans a target. Historically, blacks, Jews,

Catholics, and recent immigrants have also been targeted. Now, in the 1990s, there is greater intolerance for this behavior, but, Jacobs and Henry say, there is no epidemic.

Yet it matters little whether the spate of hate crimes is real or merely perceived; significant developments have taken placed in consequence:

Throughout the 1980s, media reports of increasing numbers of hate-motivated crimes (also known as bias crimes) pressured states to adopt statutes dealing with such crimes. These statutes prohibit acts of ethnically or religiously based intimidation, enhance penalties for these crimes, or raise the level of the crime. In addition, many criminal justice agencies have developed programs for dealing with bias crime, and at the federal level the Hate Crimes Statistics Act of 1990 mandates that local law enforcement agencies compile data on such crimes.

As defined by the Federal Hate Crimes Statistics Act of 1990, hate crimes are crimes that show evidence of prejudice against certain group characteristics. The act mandates the collection of data that show evidence of prejudice based on race, sexual orientation, ethnicity, or religion.

Many bias crimes fall into the categories of simple assaults, vandalism, and harassment. Because these are relatively less serious crimes, they ordinarily get little attention. They can, however, have a major impact on community by increasing the level of fear and hostility between groups. So extra attention to them is warranted.

Special police, prosecutor, and victim service units have been established to deal with common crimes

that are motivated by bias. Police units in Boston and Baltimore track the activities of hate groups in order to prevent civil unrest and vigilante action.

It is often difficult to discern whether bias was the primary motivating factor in the offense or a secondary one. Sometimes bias is the reason for the crime; sometimes prejudicial slurs occur during the crime; and in some cases the crime is a response to a bias-motivated provocation. Determining when ordinary crime becomes hate crime is sometimes a subjective process.

Sources

1. Spencer Rumsey, "A Cancer of Hatred Afflicts America," *Newsday,* May 27, 1993, p. 129.
2. Benjamin J. Hubbard, "Commentary on Tolerance," *Los Angeles Times,* Apr. 4, 1993, p. B9.
3. James B. Jacobs and Jessica S. Henry, "The Social Construction of a Hate Crime Epidemic," *Journal of Criminal Law and Criminology,* **86** (1996): 366–391.

Questions for Discussion

1. Wisconsin's sentence-enhancement law was challenged by a defendant who claimed that his First Amendment (freedom of speech) rights were violated because the statute punishes offenders' bigoted beliefs and not just their acts. Do you agree with the U.S. Supreme Court decision to uphold the Wisconsin statute?
2. The FBI study found that intimidation was the most common type of hate crime, followed by vandalism and assault. Do you think these crimes are serious enough to warrant the extra attention they receive?

would be a primary weapon in the "final world war," which he claimed would begin as early as 1997.[117]

Home-Grown Terrorism. Most militias are groups whose memberships consist of white, Christian, working- and middle-class Americans whose fundamental belief is that their constitutional right to "bear arms" (protected under the Second Amendment) is threatened. Members tend to have apocalyptic, paranoid views of U.S. politics and the federal government. They believe leading Democratic politicians are "liberal elitists who betray traditional American values."[118] The movement is a collection of grassroots groups who call themselves Patriots, Militiamen, Freemen, Common-Law Advocates, and Strict Constitutionalists. Although they are often labeled "right-wing," members' backgrounds touch all points on the political spectrum. The movement is so fragmented that membership estimates are unreliable. The Southern Poverty Law Center says there are 441 paramilitary groups, and they can be found in all 50 states.[119] Some estimates are that as many as 100,000 Americans are involved (Figure 11.3).[120]

Most militia groups are nonviolent. Members have a fondness for wearing battle fatigues, participating in paramilitary maneuvers, and stockpiling firearms. Yet there are growing indications of involvement in illegal activities. The Michigan Militia Corps, for example, one of the nation's largest with an estimated membership of 10,000 to 12,000, has alleged ties to Timothy McVeigh and Terry Nichols, both charged in the Oklahoma City bombing.[121]

FIGURE 11.3 Beyond the fringe.
Source: Gregory L. Vistica, "Extremism in the Ranks," *Newsweek*, March 25, 1996, p. 36.

On the Troubling Fringes of Hate

As the army tries to figure out how many of its soldiers are tangled up in white-supremacist or milita movements, the Pentagon is worrying over an inescapable geographic fact: several major bases sit near clusters of either racist or antigovernment groups. A national view:

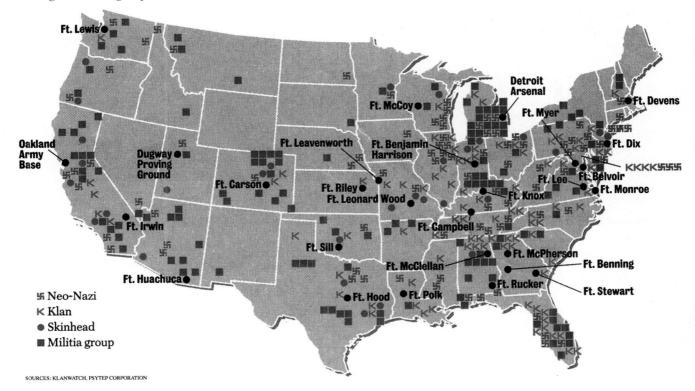

卐 Neo-Nazi
K Klan
● Skinhead
■ Militia group

SOURCES: KLANWATCH, PSYTEP CORPORATION

AT ISSUE

VIPERS IN THE DESERT

Strange things were happening in the woods. Last November agent Jose Wall of the Bureau of Alcohol, Tobacco and Firearms in Phoenix got disturbing information from people who had been through nearby Tonto National Forest. A deer hunter said he had been stopped by a group of men dressed in camouflage and armed with guns. They warned him to turn back, saying they were "security" and hinting they were with the government. The hunter didn't believe them. But something about their eyes, not to mention their weapons, made him think arguing would be imprudent. He ran into other people forced to retreat by the armed men—a Boy Scout troop. After the hunter's call, agent Wall drove out to Tonto. Near an abandoned mine, he found a crater almost big enough to swallow a car. It was recent. Someone had been using powerful explosives.(1)

In July 1996, Alcohol, Tobacco and Firearms agents uncovered a plot by members of "Team Viper" to blow up seven buildings in Phoenix, Arizona, using the same mixture of chemicals used in the Oklahoma City bombing.(1) The agents found an arsenal of two machine guns, six rifles, two pistols, grenades, fuses, blasting caps, and 56 boxes stuffed with 11,463 rounds of ammunition, as well as hundreds of pounds of the chemicals ammonium nitrate and nitromethane, which can be mixed to make a bomb.(3) Group members were charged in federal court for offenses including illegal possession of a machine gun and conspiracy to teach bombing techniques to provoke civil disorder.(2)

The Vipers are white, largely blue-collar, with no significant criminal records, and stuck in dead-end low-paying jobs. They include two janitors, a used-furniture salesman, a telephone company billing representative, an air conditioner repairman, a doughnut baker, an engineer, and a bouncer at a local topless bar. The Vipers reflect the demographics of the antigovernment paramilitary movement.(2) Indeed, the Vipers are seemingly like many Americans, although in some respects they are extremely different. One member of the group, Dean Pleasant, used to paint grenades with camouflage designs and leave them on the lawn to dry. His roommate, Randy Nelson, slept each night below a Browning machine gun he had mounted over his bed, to which he had given the name "Shirley."(2)

FBI agent Bruce Gebhardt, agent in charge of the Phoenix office, cautioned about the potential danger of a group such as the Vipers: "A lot of these individuals are copycats and wannabes. They hear the rhetoric of one and repeat it to the other. Are they really expressing their First Amendment rights? There's a line here we have to watch very closely."(3)

What may be most alarming is the ordinariness of the Vipers. An obsession with guns drew them together. This obsession is also driving some of them to devise schemes aimed at the disruption, if not the destruction, of a government based on the rule of law and the right to bear arms. Some "militias" commit serial robberies in order to finance their devious activities.(4)

Sources

1. Christopher John Farley, "A Nest of Vipers," *Time*, July 15, 1996, pp. 24–25.
2. James Brooke, "Volatile Mix in Viper Militia: Hatred Plus a Love for Guns," *New York Times*, July 5, 1996, p. 1.
3. Christopher John Farley, "A Nest of Vipers," *Time*, July 15, 1996, pp. 24–25.
4. Jo Thomas, "Bank Robbery Trial Offers a Glimpse of a Right-Wing World," *New York Times*, January 9, 1997, p. 12.

Questions for Discussion

1. What is it that makes members of groups like the Vipers feel they have a legitimate organization and a legitimate cause?
2. Where should government draw the limit on the legal possession of armament: Super rifles? Machine guns? Mortars? Heavy artillery? Tanks? Submarines?

Yet long before this bombing focused attention on the radical right, the FBI had insiders and informants tracking the Freemen of Montana. The Freemen, 13 of whom were indicted for counterfeiting and tax fraud, are reported to have posted $1 million rewards on the heads of local officials, threatened to hang local judges, and intimidated potential jurors in a case against a Freeman. Using bits of the Constitution, the Bible, and the Magna Carta, they put together a doc-

trine that says the federal government has illegally usurped the common law and power of localities. They also reject the American flag. In their own courts, the Freemen have filed multimillion-dollar "liens" against government officials, and "subpoenaed" public officials to appear before their own grand juries.

For the Freemen, their 960-acre Cranfield County, Montana, farm is sovereign territory that has its own laws, courts, and officials. They also have an armory and a bank. According to federal indictments, the bank turned over $1.8 million in phony money orders and other financial instruments. These were used in fraudulent transactions with credit card companies, mail-order houses, and banks. In 1996, 26 of the antigovernment fanatics holed up in the Freemen's enclaves. Eighty-one days, and millions of dollars later, they all left the compound. The standoff was one of the longest armed sieges in U.S. history.

VIOLENCE AND GUN CONTROL

Clearly, violence is a massive problem throughout the world. Researchers have suggested a variety of causes. Violence in the United States is frequently attributed to historical conditioning (the need of frontier people to survive in a hostile environment), social factors (poverty, inequities, and other inner-city problems), and the laxity of the criminal justice system (failure to apprehend and convict enough criminals and to imprison long enough those who are convicted). Some researchers have focused on one common element in a large proportion of violent crime: the availability of firearms in the United States.

One of the hottest and longest political and scholarly debates in our history centers on this point: Should and can Americans drastically restrict the availability of firearms, and would such controls substantially reduce the rate and severity of violent crime?

The Extent of Firearm-Related Offenses

It is difficult to be certain how many guns there are in the United States. The Bureau of Alcohol, Tobacco and Firearms estimates that from 1899 to 1993, about 223 million guns became available in this country. It is unknown how many of these guns have been seized, destroyed, or lost, or do not work properly.[122] It is estimated that currently over 100 million firearms are privately owned in the United States: 37 percent rifles, 33 percent shotguns, and 30 percent handguns.[123] Half of the handguns are so-called Saturday-night specials (defined by the Bureau of Alcohol, Tobacco and Firearms as a small weapon of .32 caliber or less with a barrel length of less than 3 inches and costing $50 or less). The supply of handguns increases by about 1.5 million each year.[124]

Approximately 13,500 of every 100,000 Americans own handguns. Compare this figure with the rates of other Western industrialized nations: Canada, 3000 in every 100,000; Austria, 3000; the Netherlands, under 500; and Great Britain, also under 500.[125] *Time* magazine devoted its issue of July 17, 1989, to "Death by Gun." Reporting on "America's toll in one typical week," a 28-page portfolio described the deaths and provided photographs of most of the victims: 464 Americans who died violently by gun during the first week of May 1989. Of these, 216 (47 percent) had shot themselves to death. Nine of the suicides killed someone else before taking their own lives. Twenty-two deaths were preventable accidents. Only 14 people were killed in self-defense. The rest of the deaths were criminal homicides.

The Federal Bureau of Investigation has reported that a handgun is used in about half of all murders and one-third of rapes and robberies. Two-thirds of police deaths in the line of duty are attributed to the use of handguns. Rates of crime involving guns are far lower in most other developed Western nations than in the United States.[126] According to the Task Force on Firearms of the National Commission on the Causes and Prevention of Violence, the rate of homicide by gun is 40 times higher in the United States than in England and Wales, and our rate of robbery by gun is 60 times higher.

The financial cost of gunshot injury and death, in terms of medical costs, lost productivity, and pain, suffering, and reduced quality of life, was estimated at $63 billion in 1992 alone. The Centers for Disease Control and Prevention estimates that between June 1, 1992, and May 31, 1993, approximately 99,000 nonfatal firearms injuries were treated in U.S. hospital emergency rooms.[127]

Youth and Guns

Three young thugs boarded a city bus in Queens yesterday, brandished guns like Wild West bandits and staged a frontier-style holdup. They strode up and down the aisle, fired shots into the roof, terrorized and robbed 22 passengers, struck a girl in the face with a gun butt and escaped with $300 in cash and fistfulls of jewelry.

The outlaws—one armed with a silver revolver and another with a pair of guns, while a third carried a book bag—made no effort to conceal their faces as they boarded the Q-85 bus at 8:30 a.m. at 140th Avenue and Edgewood Avenue in Springfield Gardens, a residential neighborhood just northeast of Kennedy International Airport.[128]

The "bandits" were three youths age 15 to 19. In a growing number of incidents across the United States, young people are using guns for robberies, gang warfare, initiation rites (drive-by shootings by wanna-be gang members), random shootings (not too long ago James Jordan, father of basketball star Michael Jordan, fell victim), and protection from their peers.[129]

Concern is mounting over the increase in adolescent illegal gun ownership and use. A study of 758 male students in inner-city high schools in California, Illinois, Louisiana, and New Jersey found that 1 in 5 had owned a gun in 1991. There was a connection between involvement in drugs and gun carrying, ownership, or use.[130] The same study sampled female students as well. One in ten female students owned a gun at some time, and roughly the same percentage carried a gun. For both sexes, the primary reason for carrying a gun was self-protection.[131]

In the decade of the 1980s, over 7150 homicides were committed by high school youths using illegal guns.[132] Research done in Seattle, Washington, found that among eleventh-grade students, 34 percent reported having access to handguns, while 6 percent reported owning a firearm. Moreover, students indicated a high rate of handgun use: 33 percent had shot someone.[133] In many cities the problem has reached a stage where high schools deploy metal detectors and use teams of security guards who make random searches of purses, backpacks, and book bags.

Why have youths turned to guns? When asked, many of them respond the way three teenagers did: "You fire a gun and you can just *hear* the power. It's like *yeah*!" or "It became cool to say you could get a gun," or "Nobody messes with you if they think you may have a gun."[134] While there are many studies on adolescent violent behavior, there are few on adolescent illegal gun use. One of the few, a recent study of ninth- and tenth-grade boys, 14- and 15-year-olds, in Rochester, New York, found that most boys who owned illegal guns had friends who owned guns; over half of the illegal gun owners were gang members; and selling drugs was a prime motivation for carrying a gun. Moreover, illegal gun ownership, friends' gun ownership, gang membership, and drug use were closely related to gun crime, street crime, and minor delinquency.[135] Illegal firearms have traditionally been used by youths in low-income urban neighborhoods. Now the problem is spreading to the suburbs.

Controlling Handgun Use

While most people agree that gun-related crime is a particularly serious part of our crime problem, there is little agreement on what to do about it. Civic organizations and police associations call for more laws prescribing mandatory sentences for the illegal purchase, possession, or use of firearms. Close to 20,000 laws that regulate firearms already exist in the United States.

A variety of methods of controlling handgun use have been tried:

- A *prohibition against carrying guns* in public seemed to be related to a drop in gun crimes in Boston[136] and a leveling off of handgun violence in Detroit.[137]

- In Kansas City, Missouri, a *police gun-confiscation program* was implemented in gun-crime "hot spots" in the target area, which had a murder rate 20 times the national average. Gun seizures in the target area increased by over 65 percent, while gun crimes decreased by 49 percent. Homicides were also significantly reduced in the target area.[138]

- Some states have passed what are referred to as *sentence-enhancement statutes:* The punishment for an offense is more severe if a person commits it under certain conditions, such as by using a gun. The Massachusetts law (1975) mandates a minimum sentence of 1 year's incarceration upon conviction for the illegal carrying of a firearm.[139] Michigan created a new offense—commission of a felony while possessing a firearm—and added a mandatory 2-year prison sentence to the sentence received for the commission of the felony itself. The state mounted a widespread publicity campaign: "One with a gun gets you two," read the billboards and bumper stickers.[140]

Sentence enhancement has been studied in six U.S. cities. Homicides committed with firearms decreased in all six after sentence-enhancement laws took effect, although the decline in homicides was large in some cities and small in others. Researchers studying sentence enhancement point out that its effectiveness is related to how closely judges follow the law. An additional 3 years in prison may deter criminals from using guns, while an additional month may not.

- A *total ban on handguns* was tried in Washington, D.C., beginning in 1976. Both gun homicides and gun suicides dropped visibly after the ban took effect, while no change occurred in homicides and suicides not committed with guns.[141]
- Some communities have tried *buy-back programs.* St. Louis, San Francisco, Philadelphia, New York, and several other cities have embarked on such programs to reduce the number of handguns in circulation in the community. Police departments buy guns, no questions asked, for $50 each. In October 1991, the St. Louis Police Department bought 5371 guns from citizens in 10 days. The Philadelphia police received 1044 guns within a 2-week period.
- *Federal legislation* has been passed in an attempt to prevent criminals from buying guns. The Brady bill, named after James Brady, White House press secretary who was injured in the 1981 assassination attempt on President Ronald Reagan, went into effect on February 28, 1994. It calls for 5-day waiting periods and background checks before handgun purchases. Further, certain groups of people, such as convicted felons, fugitives from justice, illegal aliens, juveniles, and the mentally ill, are not permitted to buy guns. Since the Brady bill has been in place, the evidence of its effectiveness in reducing gun crime is unclear. Surveys conducted by the Federal Bureau of Alcohol, Tobacco and Firearms, CBS News, and the International Association of Chiefs of Police in conjunction with Handgun Control, Inc., found that up to 45,000 convicted felons were denied handguns after they failed the background check. Supporters of the Brady bill claim this shows that fewer felons are managing to obtain handguns. Others argue that felons can still obtain handguns through illegal channels. James Q. Wilson, for example, says the real test of the Brady bill is whether "felons have been stopped from buying guns and then killing people with them." It may be too early to tell.[142]

None of these methods resulted in drastic reductions in the number of handgun-related deaths, although some led to a small decrease. As two gun-control researchers point out, the important question to be answered with regard to gun control is this: How many deaths must be prevented by a gun-control method to justify its use? Very few of the millions of people who own guns commit crimes with them, and control policies will affect legitimate owners as well as criminals. David McDowall and Alan Lizotte ask:

> Is the legitimate happiness of 10 million gun owners worth the lives of 10,000 murder victims? One murder victim? In another context, is a highly restrictive measure that would save 200 lives better than a less restrictive measure that would save 100? There is no obvious answer to these questions, and different people will draw the line in different places.[143]

Perhaps we can learn from the countries with low gun-related homicide rates. Many citizens of Switzerland and Israel, for example, have army-issue firearms at their constant disposal by virtue of citizen-army requirements, yet these weapons are rarely used for homicides. What factors control the use of handguns in these countries? Even if comparative studies come up with useful findings, some researchers believe the political problems surrounding gun control in the United States will probably continue to hinder the development of nationwide, or even statewide, gun-control policies for some time to come.

The Gun-Control Debate

The battle line on gun control appears to be clearly drawn between the opponents of regulation (including the 3 million members of the National Rifle Association, or NRA, and their supporters), on the one hand, and the advocates of control (including the 12 major law enforcement groups, the private organization Handgun Control, and three-quarters of the American public), on the other. The gun lobby likes to say that it is people who kill, not guns, so it is the people who use guns illegally who should be punished. To deter these people, gun enthusiasts say, we need to have stiffer penalties, including mandatory sentences that take these offenders off the streets.

Gun-control opponents often have bumper stickers that read, "When guns are outlawed, only outlaws will have guns." Moreover, most gun owners claim that it is their right to own firearms to protect their homes, especially when they lose confidence in the police and courts.[144] And by controlling guns, they say, the government intrudes in their private affairs. They interpret the Second Amendment to the Constitution as giving them an individual right "to keep and bear arms." Furthermore, the gun lobby maintains, people may wish to enjoy their guns as collectors or for sport and hunting.

Another argument concerns what is called the *displacement effect:* People who are deterred by gun-control legislation from using guns to commit offenses will use some other weapon to achieve their goals. Or perhaps even more violent offenses will be committed if offenders can rely on the fact that the consequences of a nonfirearm offense are less serious.

Finally, in the face of increasing random violence and a perceived inability of the police to safeguard citizens, more people are routinely carrying a gun for self-protection. In many states, it is now becoming easier to do so, as more and more jurisdictions adopt "carrying-concealed-weapons" laws.[145]

Gun-control advocates compare our extremely high homicide rate to the much lower rates of other countries with tighter gun-control laws, including our neighbor Canada. They also argue that the availability of a gun makes homicide and suicide much more probable, because it is easier to produce death with a gun than with any other weapon. Moreover, they claim, better regulation or prohibition of gun ownership is a much faster way to lessen gun-related criminality than such long-term approaches as finding remedies for social problems. Researchers are testing the claims, but thus far no definitive conclusions have been reached.

REVIEW

Murder, assaults of various kinds, rape, robbery, kidnapping—all share the common element of violence, though they differ in many ways: in the harm they cause, the intention of the perpetrator, the punishment they warrant, and other legal criteria. Social scientists have been exploring the frequency with which these crimes are committed in our society and elsewhere, their distribution through time and place, and the role played by circumstances, including the environment and behavior patterns, in facilitating or preventing them.

Such categories as mass murder, serial murder, gang murder, and date rape are shorthand designations for frequently occurring crime patterns that have not been specifically identified in penal codes. Two other patterns of crime that also are not defined as such in the penal codes have become so important that they may be considered in conjunction with the other crimes of violence: family-related crime and

terrorism. Both patterns encompass a variety of violent crimes. Recently there has been an increase in ethnically and religiously inspired violent groups who believe they are the "chosen few." Membership in antigovernment militias also grows.

The gun-control controversy demonstrates that both the definitions of crimes and the social and environmental characteristics associated with them must be studied in order to develop control and prevention strategies. Our violence-prone society will have to make serious choices if it is to reach that level of peaceful living achieved by many other modern societies.

NOTES

1. *Crimes of Violence: A Staff Report Submitted to the National Commission on the Causes and Prevention of Violence* (Washington, D.C.: U.S. Government Printing Office, December 1969), vol. 12, p. xxvii; vol. 11, p. 4.
2. G. O. W. Mueller, "Where Murder Begins," *New Hampshire Bar Journal,* **2** (1960): 214–224; G. O. W. Mueller, "On Common Law Mens Rea," *Minnesota Law Review,* **42** (1958): 1043–1104.
3. Wayne R. LaFave and Austin W. Scott, *Handbook on Criminal Law* (St. Paul, Minn.: West, 1972), pp. 572–577.
4. *Commonwealth v. Welansky,* 316 Mass. 383, N.E. 2d 902 (1944), at pp. 906–907. See G. O. W. Mueller, "The Devil May Care—Or Should We? A Reexamination of Criminal Negligence," *Kentucky Law Journal,* **55** (1966–1967): 29–49.
5. Uniform Crime Reports, 1994, p. 58.
6. Ibid., p. 14.
7. Ibid.
8. Ibid.
9. Roland Chilton, "Twenty Years of Homicide and Robbery in Chicago: The Impact of the City's Changing Racial and Age Composition," *Journal of Quantitative Criminology,* **3** (1987): 195–213. See also Carolyn Rebecca Block, *Homicide in Chicago* (Chicago: Loyola University of Chicago, 1986), p. 7; and William Wilbanks, *Murder in Miami* (Lanham, Md.: University Press of America, 1984).
10. William Julius Wilson, "Work," *New York Times Magazine,* Aug. 18, 1996, pp. 27, 28.
11. William B. Harvey, "Homicide among Young Black Adults: Life in the Subculture of Exasperation," in *Homicide among Black Americans,* ed. Darnell F. Hawkins (Lanham, Md.: University Press of America, 1986), pp. 153–171. See also Robert L. Hampton, "Family Violence and Homicide in the Black Community: Are They Linked?" in *Violence in the Black Family,* ed. Hampton (Lexington, Mass.: Lexington Books, 1987), pp. 135–156.
12. Coramae Richey Mann, "Black Women Who Kill," in Hawkins, *Homicide among Black Americans,* pp. 157–186.
13. Hans von Hentig, *The Criminal and His Victim* (New Haven, Conn.: Yale University Press, 1948).
14. Marvin E. Wolfgang, *Patterns in Criminal Homicide* (Philadelphia: University of Pennsylvania Press, 1958), p. 253. See also

Marvin E. Wolfgang, "A Sociological Analysis of Criminal Homicide," in *Studies in Homicide,* ed. Wolfgang (New York: Harper & Row, 1967), pp. 15–28.

15. Robert A. Silverman and Leslie W. Kennedy, "Relational Distance and Homicide: The Role of the Stranger," *Journal of Criminal Law and Criminology,* **78** (1987): 272–308. See also Nanci Koser Wilson, "Gendered Interaction in Criminal Homicide," in *Homicide: The Victim/Offender Connection,* ed. Anna Victoria Wilson (Cincinnati: Anderson, 1993), pp. 43–62.

16. Margaret A. Zahn and Philip C. Sagi, "Stranger Homicides in Nine American Cities," *Journal of Criminal Law and Criminology,* **78** (1987): 377–397.

17. Uniform Crime Reports, 1991, p. 14.

18. Marc Riedel, "Stranger Violence: Perspectives, Issues, and Problems," *Journal of Criminal Law and Criminology,* **78** (1987): 223–258.

19. Kenneth Polk, "Observations on Stranger Homicide," *Journal of Criminal Justice,* **21** (1993): 573–582.

20. Uniform Crime Reports, 1994, p. 14.

21. See, e.g., Colin Loftin, Karen Kindley, Sandra L. Norris, and Brian Wiersema, "An Attribute Approach to Relationships between Offenders and Victims in Homicide," *Journal of Criminal Law and Criminology,* **78** (1987): 259–271.

22. Angela Browne, "Assault and Homicide at Home: When Battered Women Kill," *Advances in Applied Social Psychology,* **3** (1986): 57–79.

23. Martin Daly and Margo Wilson, *Homicide* (New York: Aldine–De Gruyter, 1988), pp. 294–295.

24. Coramae Richey Mann, "Getting Even?: Women Who Kill in Domestic Encounters," *Justice Quarterly,* **5** (1988): 33–51.

25. Lawrence A. Greenfeld, *Child Victimizers: Violent Offenders and Their Victims* (Washington, D.C.: Bureau of Justice Statistics, 1996), p. 3.

26. Joshua E. Muscat, "Characteristics of Childhood Homicide in Ohio, 1974–1984," *American Journal of Public Health,* **78** (1988): 822–824.

27. Uniform Crime Reports, 1994, pp. 227–228.

28. William R. Holcomb and Anasseril E. Daniel, "Homicide without an Apparent Motive," *Behavioral Sciences and the Law,* **6** (1988): 429–439.

29. See Michael Newton, *Mass Murder: An Annotated Bibliography* (New York: Garland, 1988).

30. N. R. Kleinfield, "Cruelty of Strangers: 3 Men Evoke a Fearsome Trend," *New York Times,* June 23, 1996, p. 27.

31. Daniel Pedersen, "Death in Dunblane," *Newsweek,* Mar. 25, 1996, pp. 24–29.

32. See Dawn N. Castillo and E. Lynn Jenkins, "Industries and Occupations at High Risk for Work-Related Homicide," *Journal of Occupational Medicine,* **36** (1994): 125–132.

33. David Abrahamsen, *The Murdering Mind* (New York: Harper & Row, 1973).

34. Mel Heimer, *The Cannibal: The Case of Albert Fish* (New York: Lyle Stuart, 1971).

35. Margaret Cheney, *The Co-ed Killer* (New York: Walker, 1976).

36. Jack Levin and James Alan Fox, *Mass Murder: America's Growing Menace* (New York: Plenum, 1985). See also Ronald M. Holmes and Stephen T. Holmes, "Understanding Mass Murder: A Starting Point," *Federal Probation,* **56** (1992): 53–61.

37. James Alan Fox and Jack Levin, *Overkill: Mass Murder and Serial Killing Exposed* (New York: Plenum, 1994); and Philip Jenkins, "African-Americans and Serial Homicide," *American Journal of Criminal Justice,* **17** (1993): 47–60.

38. Ronald M. Holmes and James de Burger, *Serial Murder* (Newbury Park, Calif.: Sage, 1988), p. 155.

39. Cheryl L. Maxson, Margaret A. Gordon, and Malcolm W. Klein, "Differences between Gang and Nongang Homicides," *Criminology,* **23** (1985): 209–222.

40. G. David Curry and Irving A. Spergel, "Gang Homicide, Delinquency, and Community," *Criminology,* **26** (1988): 381–405.

41. Sam Howe Verhovek, "Houston Knows Murder, but This . . . ," *New York Times,* July 9, 1993, p. A8.

42. United Nations, "Results of the Fourth United Nations Survey of Crime Trends, Operation of Criminal Justice Systems and Crime Prevention Strategies," A/CONF.169/15 of 20 Dec. 1994. See also Albert J. Reiss, Jr., and Jeffrey A. Roth, eds., *Understanding and Preventing Violence* (Washington, D.C.: National Academy Press, 1993).

43. Uniform Crime Reports, 1994, p. 58.

44. Harvey Krahn, Timothy F. Hartnagel, and John W. Gartrell, "Income Inequality and Homicide Rates: Cross-National Data and Criminological Theories," *Criminology,* **24** (1986): 269–295.

45. Glenn D. Deane, "Cross-National Comparison of Homicide: Age/Sex-Adjusted Rates Using the 1980 U.S. Homicide Experience as a Standard," *Journal of Quantitative Criminology,* **3** (1987): 215–227.

46. Dane Archer and Rosemary Gartner, *Violence and Crime in Cross-National Perspective* (New Haven, Conn.: Yale University Press, 1984).

47. Candice Nelsen, Jay Corzine, and Lin Corzine-Huff, "The Violent West Reexamined: A Research Note on Regional Homicide Rates," *Criminology,* **32** (1994): 149–161.

48. See Scott H. Decker, "Exploring Victim-Offender Relationships in Homicide: The Role of Individual and Event Characteristics," *Justice Quarterly,* **10** (1993): 585–612. See also Scott H. Decker, "Reconstructing Homicide Events: The Role of Witnesses in Fatal Encounters," *Journal of Criminal Justice,* **23** (1995): 439–450.

49. David F. Luckenbill, "Criminal Homicide as a Situated Transaction," *Social Problems,* **25** (1977): 176–186. Although Luckenbill focused on homicides, the stages he identified are identical in assaults.

50. For a comprehensive, multidisciplinary review of the literature on violence, see James T. Tedeschi and Richard B. Felson, *Violence, Aggression, and Coercive Actions* (Washington, D.C.: American Psychological Association, 1994). See also Barry R. Ruback and Neil Alan Weiner, eds., *Interpersonal Violent Behaviors: Social and Cultural Aspects* (New York: Springer, 1994).

51. U.S. Department of Justice, Bureau of Justice Statistics, *Criminal Victimization, 1994* (Washington, D.C.: U.S. Government Printing Office, 1996), p. 2.

52. C. H. Kempe, F. N. Silverman, B. F. Steele, W. Droegemueller, and H. K. Silver, "The Battered-Child Syndrome," *Journal of the American Medical Association,* **181** (1962): 17–24.

53. Elizabeth Pleck, "Criminal Approaches to Family Violence, 1640–1980," in *Family Violence,* ed. Lloyd Ohlin and Michael

Tonry, vol. 2 (Chicago: University of Chicago Press, 1989), pp. 19–57.

54. For a special journal issue on the subject of family violence, see Richard J. Gelles, ed., "Family Violence," *Journal of Comparative Family Studies*, **25** (1994): 1–142.

55. Lyn Nell Hancock, "Why Batterers So Often Go Free," *Newsweek*, Oct. 16, 1995, pp. 61–62.

56. Murray A. Straus and Richard J. Gelles, "How Violent Are American Families?: Estimates from the National Family Violence Resurvey and Other Studies," in *Family Abuse and Its Consequences*, ed. Gerald T. Hotaling, David Finkelhor, John T. Kirkpatrick, and Murray A. Straus (Newbury Park, Calif.: Sage, 1988). See also Ann Goetting, *Homicide in Families and Other Special Populations* (New York: Springer Publishing Company, 1995); and Ronet Bachman, *Violence against Women: A National Crime Victimization Survey Report* (Washington, D.C.: U.S. Bureau of Justice Statistics, 1994).

57. Richard B. Felson, "Big People Hit Little People: Sex Differences in Physical Power and Interpersonal Violence," *Criminology*, **34** (1996): 433–452.

58. Straus and Gelles, "How Violent Are American Families?" p. 17.

59. Patrick A. Langan and Christopher A. Innes, *Preventing Domestic Violence against Women*, for U.S. Department of Justice, Bureau of Justice Statistics (Washington, D.C.: U.S. Government Printing Office, 1986).

60. Marvin E. Wolfgang and Franco Ferracuti, *The Subculture of Violence: Toward an Integrated Theory in Criminology* (London: Tavistock, 1967).

61. Joan McCord, "Parental Aggressiveness and Physical Punishment in Long-Term Perspective," in *Family Abuse and Its Consequences*, pp. 91–98.

62. Margery A. Cassidy, "Power-Control Theory: Its Potential Application to Woman Battering," *Journal of Crime and Justice*, **18** (1995): 1–15.

63. Donald G. Dutton, *The Domestic Assault of Women* (Boston: Allyn and Bacon, 1988), p. 15.

64. Lenore E. Walker, *The Battered Woman Syndrome* (New York: Springer Verlag, 1984); Brenda A. Miller, Thomas H. Nochajski, Kenneth E. Leonard, Howard T. Blane, Dawn M. Gondoli, and Patricia M. Bowers, "Spousal Violence and Alcohol/Drug Problems among Parolees and Their Spouses," *Women and Criminal Justice*, **1** (1990): 55–72.

65. Study conducted by Mohammed Ayat, Atiqui Abdelaziz, Najat Kfita, and El Khazouni Zineb, at the request of UNESCO and the Union of Arab Lawyers, Fez, Morocco, 1989.

66. David Levinson, *Family Violence in Cross-Cultural Perspective* (Newbury Park, Calif.: Sage, 1989).

67. Carolyn F. Swift, "Surviving: Women's Strength through Connections," in *Abuse and Victimization across the Life Span*, ed. Martha Straus (Baltimore: Johns Hopkins University Press, 1988), pp. 153–169.

68. See Christine Rasche, "Early Models for Contemporary Thought on Domestic Violence and Women Who Kill Their Mates: A Review of the Literature from 1895 to 1970," *Women and Criminal Justice*, **1** (1990): 31–53.

69. *Thurman v. Torrington*, 596 F. Supp. 1521 (1985).

70. Jeffrey Fagan, *The Criminalization of Domestic Violence: Promises and Limits* (Washington, D.C.: U.S. National Institute of Justice, 1996).

71. Lawrence W. Sherman and Richard A. Berk, "The Minneapolis Domestic Violence Experiment," *Police Foundation Reports*, **1** (1984): 1–8. See also J. David Hirschel, Ira W. Hutchinson, Charles W. Dean, and Anne-Marie Mills, "Review Essay on the Law Enforcement Response to Spouse Abuse: Past, Present and Future," *Justice Quarterly*, **9** (1992): 247–283; Cynthia Grant Bowman, "The Arrest Experiments: A Feminist Critique," *Journal of Criminal Law and Criminology*, **83** (1992): 201–208; Albert R. Roberts, "Psychosocial Characteristics of Batterers: A Study of 234 Men Charged with Domestic Violence Offenses," *Journal of Family Violence*, **2** (1987): 81–93; and Donald G. Dutton and Susan K. Golant, *The Batterer: A Psychological Profile* (New York: Basic Books, 1995); Lisa A. Frisch, "Research That Succeeds, Policies That Fail," *Journal of Criminal Law and Criminology*, **83** (1992): 209–216; David B. Mitchell, "Contemporary Police Practices in Domestic Violence Cases: Arresting the Abuser: Is It Enough?" *Journal of Criminal Law and Criminology*, **83** (1992): 241–249; Lawrence W. Sherman, Janell D. Schmidt, Dennis P. Rogan, Patrick R. Gartlin, Ellen G. Cohn, Dean J. Collins, and Anthony R. Bacich, "From Initial Deterrence to Long-Term Escalation: Short Custody Arrest for Poverty Ghetto Domestic Violence," *Criminology*, **29** (1991): 821–850.

72. Lawrence W. Sherman, Janell D. Schmidt, Dennis P. Rogan, Douglas A. Smith, Patrick R. Gartlin, Ellen G. Cohn, Dean J. Collins, and Anthony R. Bacich, "The Variable Effects of Arrest on Criminal Careers: The Milwaukee Domestic Violence Experiment," *Journal of Criminal Law and Criminology*, **83** (1992): 137–169. See also J. David Hirschel and Ira W. Hutchinson III, "Female Spouse Abuse and the Police Response: The Charlotte, North Carolina Experiment," *Journal of Criminal Law and Criminology*, **83** (1992): 73–119.

73. Joan Zorza, "The Criminal Law of Misdemeanor Domestic Violence, 1970–1990," *Journal of Criminal Law and Criminology*, **83** (1992): 46–72. See also Candace Kruttschnitt and Maude Dornfeld, "Will They Tell? Assessing Preadolescents' Reports of Family Violence," *Journal of Research in Crime and Delinquency*, **29** (1992): 136–147.

74. Edna Erez and Pamela Tontodonato, "Patterns of Reported Parent-Child Abuse and Police Response," *Journal of Family Violence*, **4** (1989): 143–159. For strategies on the investigation of child abuse, see David I. Sheppard and Patricia Zangrillo, *Improving Joint Investigations of Child Abuse: A Summary Report* (Washington, D.C.: Police Foundation, 1996).

75. K. Burgdorf, "Recognition and Reporting of Child Maltreatment," in *Findings from the National Study of the Incidence and Severity of Child Abuse and Neglect* (Washington, D.C.: National Center on Child Abuse and Neglect, 1980), p. 370.

76. American Association for Protecting Children, *Highlights of Official Child Neglect and Abuse Reporting, 1984* (Denver: American Humane Association, 1986).

77. For estimates of child maltreatment, see James Garbarino, "The Incidence and Prevalence of Child Maltreatment," in Ohlin and Tonry, *Family Violence*, pp. 219–261.

78. Mildred Daley Pagelow, "The Incidence and Prevalence of Criminal Abuse of Other Family Members," in Ohlin and Tonry, *Family Violence*, pp. 263–311.

79. Cathy Spatz Widom and M. Ashley Ames, "Criminal Consequences of Childhood Sexual Victimization," *Child Abuse and Neglect*, **18** (1994): 303–318; and Carolyn Smith and Terence

P. Thornberry, "The Relationship between Childhood Maltreatment and Adolescent Involvement in Delinquency," *Criminology,* **33** (1995): 451–481.

80. Deborah Daro, "Half Full and Half Empty: The Evaluation of Results of Nineteen Clinical Research and Demonstration Projects," *Summary of Nineteen Clinical Demonstration Projects Funded by the National Center on Child Abuse and Neglect, 1978–81* (Berkeley: University of California, School of Social Welfare, 1986).

81. See Candace Kruttschnitt and Maude Dornfeld, "Childhood Victimization, Race, and Violent Crime," *Criminal Justice and Behavior,* **18** (1991): 448–463.

82. *U.S. Bureau of the Census, Statistical Abstract of the United States: 1994* (Washington, D.C.: U.S. Government Printing Office, 1994).

83. Craig J. Forsyth and Robert Gramling, "Elderly Crime: Fact and Artifact," in *Older Offenders,* ed. Belinda McCarthy and Robert Langworthy (New York: Praeger, 1988), pp. 3–13.

84. Pagelow, "Incidence and Prevalence of Criminal Abuse," in Ohlin and Tonry, *Family Violence,* p. 267

85. Jordan I. Kosberg and Juanita L. Garcia, eds., "Elder Abuse: International and Cross-Cultural Perspectives," *Journal of Elder Abuse and Neglect,* **6** (1995): 1–197.

86. Susan Brownmiller, *Against Our Will: Men, Women, and Rape* (New York: Simon & Schuster, 1975), pp. 1–9.

87. Duncan Chappell, "Sexual Criminal Violence," in *Pathways to Criminal Violence,* ed. Neil Alan Weiner and Marvin E. Wolfgang (Newbury Park, Calif.: Sage, 1989), pp. 68–108.

88. Marvin E. Wolfgang, Robert M. Figlio, Paul E. Tracy, and Simon I. Singer, *The National Survey of Crime Severity* (Washington, D.C.: U.S. Government Printing Office, 1985).

89. Uniform Crime Reports, 1994, p. 58. For a special issue devoted to an overview of adult sexual assault, see *Journal of Social Issues,* **48** (1992): 1–195, with an Introduction by Susan B. Sorenson and Jacqueline W. White.

90. Menachem Amir, *Patterns in Forcible Rape* (Chicago: University of Chicago Press, 1977), pp. 233–234.

91. U.S. Department of Justice, Bureau of Justice Statistics, *Highlights from 20 Years of Surveying Crime Victims* (Washington, D.C.: U.S. Government Printing Office, 1993), p. 24.

92. David Finkelhor and Kersti Yllo, "Forced Sex in Marriage: A Preliminary Research Report," *Crime and Delinquency,* **28** (1982): 459–478.

93. Andrea Parrot, *Coping with Date Rape and Acquaintance Rape* (New York: Rosen, 1988).

94. M. P. Koss, C. A. Gidycz, and N. Wisniewski, "The Scope of Rape: Incidence and Prevalence of Sexual Aggression and Victimization in a National Sample of Higher Education Students," *Journal of Consulting and Clinical Psychology,* **55** (1987): 162–170.

95. James L. LeBeau, "Patterns of Stranger and Serial Rape Offending: Factors Distinguishing Apprehended and At Large Offenders," *Journal of Criminal Law and Criminology,* **78** (1987): 309–326.

96. J. Marolla and D. Scully, *Attitudes toward Women, Violence, and Rape: A Comparison of Convicted Rapists and Other Felons* (Rockville, Md.: National Institute of Mental Health, 1982).

97. Christine Alder, "An Exploration of Self-Reported Sexually Aggressive Behavior," *Crime and Delinquency,* **31** (1985):

306–331; P. R. Sanday, "The Socio-Cultural Context of Rape: A Cross-Cultural Study," *Journal of Social Issues,* **37** (1981): 5–27.

98. Julia R. Schwendinger and Herman Schwendinger, *Rape and Inequality* (Beverly Hills, Calif.: Sage, 1983), p. 220.

99. M. Dwayne Smith and Nathan Bennett, "Poverty, Inequality, and Theories of Forcible Rape," *Crime and Delinquency,* **31** (1985): 295–305.

100. Ruth D. Peterson and William C. Bailey, "Forcible Rape, Poverty, and Economic Inequality in U.S. Metropolitan Communities," *Journal of Quantitative Criminology,* **4** (1988): 99–119.

101. Matthew Hale, *History of the Pleas of the Crown,* vol. 1 (London, 1736), p. 635.

102. Martin D. Schwartz and Todd R. Clear, "Toward a New Law on Rape," *Crime and Delinquency,* **26** (1980): 129–151.

103. Cassia C. Spohn and Julie Horney, "The Impact of Rape Law Reform on the Processing of Simple and Aggravated Cases," *Journal of Criminal Law and Criminology,* **86** (1996): 861–884; Gilbert Geis, "Rape-in-Marriage: Law and Law Reform in England, the United States, and Sweden," *Adelaide Law Review,* **6** (1978): 284–303; and Joel Epstein and Stacia Langenbahn, *The Criminal Justice and Community Response to Rape* (Washington, D.C.: U.S. National Institute of Justice, 1994).

104. Janet Gornick, Martha R. Burt, and Karen J. Pittman, "Structures and Activities of Rape Crisis Centers in the Early 1980's," *Crime and Delinquency,* **31** (1985): 247–268.

105. U.S. Department of Justice, *Report to the Nation on Crime and Justice,* 2d ed. (Washington, D.C.: U.S. Government Printing Office, 1988), p. 97.

106. Uniform Crime Reports, 1994, p. 58.

107. U.S. Department of Justice, Bureau of Justice Statistics, *Criminal Victimization in the United States, 1991* (Washington, D.C.: U.S. Government Printing Office, 1992), p. 76.

108. John Conklin, *Robbery and the Criminal Justice System* (Philadelphia: Lippincott, 1972), pp. 59–78.

109. Terry L. Baumer and Michael D. Carrington, *The Robbery of Financial Institutions,* for U.S. Department of Justice (Washington, D.C.: U.S. Government Printing Office, 1986).

110. Uniform Crime Reports, 1994, p. 27.

111. Philip J. Cook, "Is Robbery Becoming More Violent?: An Analysis of Robbery Murder Trends since 1968," *Journal of Criminal Law and Criminology,* **76** (1985): 480–489.

112. Robert J. Kelly and Rufus Schatzberg, "Galvanizing Indiscriminate Political Violence: Mind-Sets and Some Ideological Constructs in Terrorism," *International Journal of Comparative and Applied Criminal Justice,* **16** (1992): 15–41; Jeffrey D. Simon, *The Terrorist Trap: America's Experience with Terrorism* (Bloomington: Indiana University Press, 1993); and Brent L. Smith and Gregory P. Orvis, "America's Response to Terrorism: An Empirical Analysis of Federal Intervention Strategies during the 1980s," *Justice Quarterly,* **10** (1993): 661–681.

113. Harvey J. Iglarsh, "Terrorism and Corporate Costs," *Terrorism,* **10** (1987): 227–230.

114. Ariel Merari, Tamar Prat, Sophia Kotzer, Anat Kurz, and Yoram Schweitzer, *Inter 85: A Review of International Terrorism in 1985* (Boulder, Colo.: Westview, 1986), p. 106.

115. Noemi Gal-Or, *International Cooperation to Suppress Terrorism* (New York: St. Martin's Press, 1985), pp. 90–96.

116. "Doomsday Cults: 'Only the Beginning,'" *Newsweek,* Apr. 3, 1995, p. 40.

117. "A Cloud of Terror and Suspicion," *Newsweek,* Apr. 3, 1995, pp. 36–41. See also Stewart A. Wright, ed., *Armageddon in Waco: Critical Perspectives on the Branch Davidian Conflict* (Chicago: University of Illinois Press, 1995).

118. For discussions of recent events that have shaped the philosophy of militias, see Alan W. Bock, *Ambush at Ruby Ridge: How Government Agents Set Randy Weaver Up and Took His Family Down* (Irvine, Calif.: Dickens Press, 1995).

119. Michael Winerip, "Ohio Case Typifies the Tensions between Militia Groups and the Law," *New York Times,* June 23, 1996, p. 1.

120. "The View from the Far Right," *Newsweek,* May 1, 1995, pp. 36–39.

121. Ibid.

122. Marianne W. Zawitz, *Guns Used in Crime* (Washington, D.C.: Bureau of Justice Statistics, 1995), p. 2.

123. James D. Wright, Peter H. Rossi, and Kathleen Daly, *Under the Gun: Weapons, Crime, and Violence in America* (New York: Aldine, 1983), p. 42.

124. Samuel Walker, *Sense and Nonsense about Crime* (Monterey, Calif.: Brooks/Cole, 1985), pp. 149–150.

125. George D. Newton, Jr., and Frank E. Zimring, *Firearms and Violence in American Life: A Staff Report Submitted to the National Commission on the Causes and Prevention of Violence* (Washington, D.C.: National Commission on the Causes and Prevention of Violence, 1969), p. 121.

126. See Martin Killias, "International Correlations between Gun Ownership and Rates of Homicide and Suicide," *Canadian Medical Association Journal,* **148** (1993): 1721–1776; Peter J. Carrington and Sharon Moyer, "Gun Availability and Suicide in Canada: Testing the Displacement Hypothesis," *Studies on Crime and Crime Prevention,* **3** (1994): 168–178.

127. Marianne W. Zawitz, *Firearm Injury from Crime* (Washington, D.C.: Bureau of Justice Statistics, 1996), p. 4.

128. Robert D. McFadden, "On a Bus in Queens, Three Bandits Stage a Frontier Robbery," *New York Times,* July 31, 1993, p. 1.

129. Alan J. Lizotte, James M. Tesoriero, Terence P. Thornberry, et al., "Patterns of Adolescent Firearms Ownership and Use," *Justice Quarterly,* **11** (1994): 51–74.

130. Joseph F. Sheley, "Drugs and Guns among Inner-City High School Students," *Journal of Drug Education,* **24** (1994): 303–321.

131. M. Dwayne Smith and Joseph F. Sheley, "The Possession and Carrying of Firearms among a Sample of Inner-City High School Females," *Journal of Crime and Justice,* **18** (1995): 109–128.

132. U.S. Public Health Service, "Weapon-Carrying among High School Students—United States, 1990," *Morbidity and Mortality Report,* **40** (1991): 681–696.

133. Charles M. Callahan and Frederick P. Rivara, "Urban High School Youth and Handguns: A School-Based Survey," *Journal of the American Medical Association,* **267** (1992): 3038–3042.

134. Jon D. Hull, "A Boy and His Gun," *Time,* Aug. 2, 1993.

135. Alan J. Lizotte, James M. Tesoriero, Terence P. Thornberry, et al., "Patterns of Adolescent Firearms Ownership and Use," *Justice Quarterly,* **11** (1994): 51–74. See also Joseph F. Sheley and James D. Wright, *In the Line of Fire: Youth, Guns, and Violence in Urban America* (Hawthorne, N.Y.: Aldine de Gruyter, 1995); Joseph F. Sheley and Victoria E. Brewer,

"Possession and Carrying of Firearms among Suburban Youth," *Public Health Reports,* **110** (1995): 18–26.

136. Glenn L. Pierce and William J. Bowers, "The Bartley-Fox Gun Law's Short-Term Impact on Crime in Boston," *Annals of the American Academy of Political and Social Science,* **455** (1981): 120–137.

137. Patrick W. O'Carroll, Colin Loftin, John B. Waller, Jr., David McDowall, Allen Bukoff, Richard O. Scott, James A. Mercy, and Brian Wiersema, "Preventing Homicide: An Evaluation of the Efficacy of a Detroit Gun Ordinance," *American Journal of Public Health,* **81** (1991): 576–581.

138. Lawrence W. Sherman, James W. Shaw, and Dennis P. Rogan, *The Kansas City Gun Experiment* (Washington, D.C.: U.S. National Institute of Justice, 1995).

139. James A. Beha II, "And Nobody Can Get You Out: The Impact of a Mandatory Prison Sentence for the Illegal Carrying of a Firearm on the Administration of Criminal Justice in Boston," *Boston University Law Review,* **57** (1977): 96–146, 289–333.

140. Colin Loftin, Milton Heumann, and David McDowall, "Mandatory Sentencing and Firearms Violence: Evaluating an Alternative to Gun Control," *Law and Society Review,* **17** (1983): 288–318.

141. Colin Loftin, David McDowall, Brian Wiersema, and Talbert J. Cottey, "Effects of Restrictive Licensing of Handguns on Homicide and Suicide in the District of Columbia," *New England Journal of Medicine,* **325** (1991): 1615–1620.

142. Fox Butterfield, "Handgun Law Deters Felons, Studies Show," *New York Times,* Mar. 12, 1995, p. 23. See also *One-Year Progress Report: Brady Handgun Violence Prevention Act* (Washington, D.C.: U.S. Bureau of Alcohol, Tobacco and Firearms, 1995).

143. David McDowall and Alan Lizotte, "Gun Control," in *Introduction to Social Problems,* ed. Craig Calhoun and George Ritzer (New York: Primis Database, McGraw-Hill, 1993).

144. John A. Arthur, "Criminal Victimization, Fear of Crime, and Handgun Ownership among Blacks: Evidence from National Survey Data," *American Journal of Criminal Justice,* **16** (1992): 121–141; Gary S. Green, "Citizen Gun Ownership and Criminal Deterrence: Theory, Research, and Policy," *Criminology,* **25** (1987): 63–81; John A. Arthur, "Gun Ownership among Women Living in One-Adult Households," *International Journal of Comparative and Applied Criminal Justice,* **18** (1994): 249–263; and Wilbur Edel, *Gun Control: Threat to Liberty or Defense against Anarchy?* (Westport, Conn.: Praeger, 1995).

145. *Concealed Carry: The Criminal's Companion. Florida's Concealed Weapons Law—A Model for the Nation?* (Washington, D.C.: Violence Policy Center, 1995).

▧ Internet Exercise

According to the UCR, serious crime declined 3 percent in 1996: Murder declined by 11 percent; robbery 8 percent; aggravated assault 6 percent; and forcible rape 3 percent. This is the fifth year in a row that reported serious crime has declined in the United States. What might account for this decline?

▧ **Your Web Site is: http://www.fbi/ucr/**

CHAPTER 12
Crimes
against Property

Larceny

    The Elements of Larceny

    The Extent of Larceny

    Who Are the Thieves?

    Shoplifting

    Art Theft

    Motor Vehicle Theft

    Boat Theft

Fraud

    Obtaining Property by False Pretenses

    Confidence Games and Frauds

    Check Forgery

    Credit Card Crimes

    Insurance Fraud

High-Tech Crimes: Concerns for Today and Tomorrow

    Characteristics of High-Tech Crimes

    Crime on the Internet: Types of Crimes

    Characteristics of the High-Tech Criminal

    The Criminal Justice Problem

Burglary

Fencing: Receiving Stolen Property

Arson

Comparative Crime Rates

Review

Notes

    Special Features

        AT ISSUE: "Follow This Car! I'm Being Stolen!"

        WINDOW TO THE WORLD: Crime on the Oceans

        CRIMINOLOGICAL FOCUS: When New Meets Old

Key Terms

arson
burglary
check forging
confidence game
false pretenses,
  obtaining property
  by
fence
fraud
high-tech crime
larceny
shoplifting

The motion picture *The Gods Must Be Crazy* introduces us to a society of happy aborigines, remote from the hustle and bustle of modern life. Such tools as they have are shared and can easily be replaced from an abundance of sticks and stones.

High up, a "noisy bird" passes over the camp of these happy people. The pilot of the noisy bird casually throws an empty Coke bottle out of the cockpit. It lands in the middle of the camp. The aborigines stare at this foreign object. They handle it delicately and then discover what a useful object it is: It holds water; it can be used for rolling dough, for hammering, for many things. Everybody needs it and wants it.

Fights ensue over who can have it. The peace and tranquillity of this little society are shattered. These people have discovered the concept of property, and they are experiencing all the troubles that go with the possession of property, including property crime.

The film has a happy ending. The aborigines finally get rid of the bottle, and life returns to normal.

We have explored some of the patterns of social interaction and the routine activities of daily life that set the stage for offenders to commit violent crimes and for other people—family members, acquaintances, strangers, airplane passengers—to become victims. We know that if we are to develop effective policies to prevent and control violent crime, we must have a thorough understanding of the characteristics of specific offenses; we need to know where, when, and how they are committed, and which individuals are most likely to commit them. The same is true for property offenses. To develop crime-prevention strategies, we need to study the characteristics that differentiate the various types of offenses which deprive people of their property.

Do such offenses as pocket-picking (pickpocketing), shoplifting, check forgery, theft by use of stolen credit cards, car theft, computer crimes, and burglary have different payoffs and risks? What kinds of resources are needed (weapons, places to sell stolen property)? Are any specific skills needed to carry out these offenses? The opportunities to commit property crime are all but unlimited. Studies demonstrate that if these opportunities are reduced, the incidence of crime is reduced as well.

The traditional property crimes are larceny (theft, or stealing); obtaining property by fraud of various sorts, including false pretenses, confidence games, forgery, and unauthorized use of credit cards; burglary, which does not necessarily involve theft; and arson, which not only deprives the owner of property but also endangers lives. New crime types are associated with high-technology equipment. We shall defer until Chapter 13 discussion of the crimes by which criminals deprive people of their property through organizational manipulations—individual white-collar crimes, corporate crimes, and activities related to organized crime.

LARCENY

Larceny (theft, stealing) is the prototype of all property offenses. It is also the most prevalent crime in our society; it includes such contemporary forms as purse-snatching, pickpocketing, shoplifting, art theft, and vehicle theft. In the thirteenth century, when Henry de Bracton set out to collect from all parts of England what was common in law—and thus common law—he learned to his surprise that there was no agreement on a concept of larceny. He found a confusing variety of ancient Germanic laws. So he did what he always did in such circumstances: He remembered what he had learned about Roman law from Professor Azo in Bologna, and simply inserted it into his new text of English law. Thus our common

law definition of larceny is virtually identical with the concept in Roman law.[1]

The Elements of Larceny

Here are the elements of **larceny** (or theft, or stealing):

A trespassory
Taking and
Carrying away of
Personal property
Belonging to another
With the intent to deprive the owner of the property permanently

Each of these elements has a long history that gives it its meaning. The first element is perhaps the easiest. There must be a trespass. "Trespass," a Norman-French term, has a variety of meanings. In the law of larceny, however, it simply means any absence of authority or permission for the taking. Second, the property must be taken: The perpetrator must exert authority over the property, as by putting a hand on a piece of merchandise or getting into the driver's seat of the targeted car.

Third, the property must be carried away. The slightest removal suffices to fulfill this element: moving merchandise from a counter, however slightly; loosening the brakes of a car so that it starts rolling, even an inch. Fourth, the property in question, at common law, has to be personal property. (Real estate is not subject to larceny.) Fifth, the property has to belong to another, in the sense that the person has the right to possess that property. Sixth, the taker must intend to deprive the rightful owner permanently of the property. This element is present when the taker (thief) intends to deprive the rightful owner of the property forever. In many states, however, the law no longer requires proof that the thief intended to deprive the owner "permanently" of the property.

The Extent of Larceny

Larceny, except for the most petty varieties, was a capital offense in medieval England.[2] Courts interpreted all its elements quite strictly—that is, in favor of defendants—so as to limit the use of capital punishment. Only once did the courts expand the reach of larceny, when they ruled that a transporter who opens a box entrusted to him and takes out some items has committed larceny by "breaking bulk." For the other forms of deceptive acquisition of property, such as embezzling funds and obtaining property by false pretenses, Parliament had to enact separate legislation.

In the United States the rate of larceny is extraordinarily high. Figure 12.1 shows the percentage change over a recent 5-year period. The UCR reported 7.8 million thefts in 1994, or a rate of 3025 for each 100,000 of the population. The NCVS figure, 23.7 million, is more than three times the UCR number, and neither figure includes automobile thefts.[3] The vast majority of thefts are, and always have been, committed furtively and without personal contact with the victims. Thefts involving personal contact—pickpocketing, purse-snatching, and other varieties of larceny—lag behind. Figure 12.2 shows the distribu-

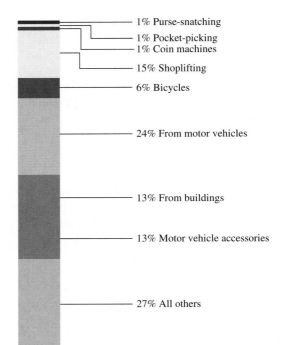

FIGURE 12.2 Distribution of larcenies known to police, 1992. (Because of rounding, percents may not add to total.)
Source: Uniform Crime Reports, 1993.

tion of all larcenies known to the police in 1994. The estimated dollar value of stolen goods to victims nationally was $4 billion.[4]

Who Are the Thieves?

Nobody knows exactly how many of the total number of thefts are committed by amateurs who lead rather conventional lives and how many are the work of professionals. According to some criminologists, the two types differ considerably.[5]

The Amateur Thief. Amateur thieves are occasional offenders who tend to be opportunists. They take advantage of a chance to steal when little risk is involved. Typically their acts are carried out with little skill, are unplanned, and result from some pressing situation, such as the need to pay the rent or a gambling debt.[6] In other words, amateurs resolve some immediate crisis by stealing. Most occasional offenders commit few crimes; some commit only one crime. Many are juveniles who do not go on to commit crimes in adulthood.

FIGURE 12.1 Percentage change in larcenies and in rate per 100,000, 1990–1994.
Source: Uniform Crime Reports, 1994.

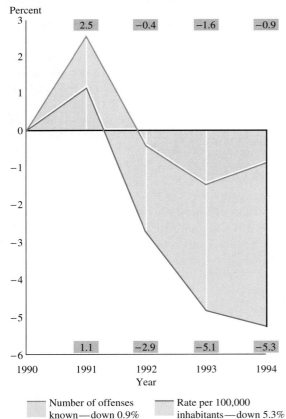

Amateur thieves do not think of themselves as professional criminals, nor are they recognized as such by those who do think of themselves as professionals. The lives of amateur thieves are quite conventional: Amateurs work, go to school, have conventional friends, and find little support or approval for their criminal behavior.

The Professional Thief. Professional thieves make a career of stealing. They take pride in their profession. They are imaginative and creative in their work and accept its risks. The most common crimes committed by professional thieves are pickpocketing, shoplifting, forgery, confidence swindling, and burglary. Professional thieves also are involved in art theft, auto vehicle theft, and fraud or theft by use of stolen or forged credit cards, among other crimes.

Thomas Bartholomew Moran, a professional thief who died in a Miami rescue mission in 1971, has been considered the best of American pickpockets. His career began in 1906, when, as a teenager, he started to pick women's purses. Under the careful guidance of Mary Kelly, a well-known pickpocket, he soon sharpened his skills until he could take wallets from pants, jeweled pins from clothing, and watches from vests without alerting the victims. He devoted his life to shoplifting, forgery, and other forms of theft. In 1912 he boarded the *Titanic*, with the intention of profiting handsomely from proximity to

> the more than 300 first-class passengers whose collective wealth exceeded $250 million. His immediate ambitions were dimmed, however, when the *Titanic* brushed an iceberg in the North Atlantic [and sank] only two hours and forty minutes later. But Moran was among the 705 passengers who managed to find space in one of the ship's twenty lifeboats, and his career in crime continued to flourish for the better part of the 59 remaining years of his life.[7]

The most influential study of professional thieves was conducted by Edwin Sutherland in 1937. Sutherland found that professional thieves share five characteristics:

1. They have well-developed technical skills for their particular mode of operation.
2. They enjoy status, accorded to them by their own subculture and by law enforcement.
3. They are bound by consensus, a sharing of values with their own peers.

4. Not only do they learn from each other, but they also protect each other.
5. They are organized, however loosely.[8]

Subsequent studies have tended to confirm Sutherland's findings.

Shoplifting

Shoplifting, the stealing of goods from retail merchants, is a very common crime; it constitutes about 15 percent of all larcenies. A recent survey in Spokane, Washington, revealed that every twelfth shopper is a shoplifter, and that men and women are equally likely to be offenders.[9] Perhaps shoplifting is so frequent because it is a low-risk offense, with a detection rate of perhaps less than 1 percent.[10] Shoppers are extremely reluctant to report shoplifters to the store management.[11] Interviews with 740 shoplifters in 50 Minneapolis stores revealed that almost half of those who expressed motivation for stealing said that they stole the merchandise because they liked it and did not have enough money to pay for it.[12]

Mary Owen Cameron found that professional shoplifters largely conform to Sutherland's five characteristics but that amateurs do not. She estimates that of all shoplifters, only 10 percent are professionals—people who derive most of their income from the sale of stolen goods.[13] A broad range of motivations may lead to shoplifting. Among amateurs, need and greed as well as opportunity may precipitate the event.[14] Some researchers point to depression and other emotional disturbances and to the use of various prescription drugs.[15]

To most people, shoplifting is a rather insignificant offense. After all, how much can be stolen? On an individual basis, usually not very much: Each shoplifter in a store takes only one item, with an average value of $11.19. All those thefts in all those stores, however, may add up to billions a year.[16] As shoplifters decrease store profits, the price of goods goes up; stepped-up security adds more to costs. Stores typically hire more and more security personnel, although it has been demonstrated that physical or electronic methods of securing merchandise are more cost-effective than the deployment of guards.[17] It is only the amateur shoplifter who is deterred by the presence of guards or store personnel, not the professional.[18]

Art Theft

At the high end of the larceny scale we find art theft. The public knows and seems to care little about art theft, yet it is as old as art itself. Looters have stolen priceless treasures from Egyptian tombs ever since they were built. As prices for antiques and for modern art soar, the demand for stolen art soars. Mexico and other countries with a precious cultural heritage are in danger of losing their treasures to gangs of thieves who destroy what they cannot take with them from historic and archaeological sites.

The International Foundation for Art Research in New York began reporting art thefts in 1976. In 1979 it had a record of 1300 stolen works. By May 1989 the number of cases on file stood at 30,000, most of them thefts of priceless and irreplaceable works by great masters. One of the most grandiose art thefts occurred on May 21, 1986, when a gang of Irish thieves invaded an estate in Ireland with commando precision and made off with 11 paintings, among them a Goya, two Rubenses, a Gainsborough, and a Vermeer.

Italy has produced some of the greatest art of Western culture. It therefore has offered the greatest opportunity for art thieves. The Italian government established an art theft office within the Carabinieri (the national police force) to deal with the problem. Every day this office receives reports on 20 to 30 art thefts, most committed by professionals. Most works stolen by professionals are not recovered. Many wind up in private collections. Works stolen for ransom are recovered more frequently, and the thieves are likely to be arrested.

Nobody knows the overall cost of art theft. Some paintings are worth $50, others $5000, others $50 million. Tens of thousands of paintings and other art objects are missing.[19]

People who commit larceny aim for places and objects that seem to offer the highest and most secure rewards. Our open, mercantile society affords an abundance of opportunities. While shoplifters need little expertise and a low level of professional connection, art thieves must have sophisticated knowledge of art and its value and good connections in the art world if they are to dispose of the items they steal. Other types of larceny, such as theft of automobiles and boats, require a moderate degree of skill—but more and more members of the general public are acquiring such skills.

Motor Vehicle Theft

Over 1.5 million motor vehicles were stolen in the United States in 1994, according to the UCR, for a total loss of more than $7.6 billion. Between 1973 and 1985, the overall loss from motor vehicle theft was $52 billion to owners, before insurance compensation and recovery of vehicles. After insurance and recovery, the loss was $16.1 billion, but even the difference ($35.9 billion) ultimately is paid by the public, largely in high insurance rates.

Motor vehicle thefts have increased steadily from 440.1 per 100,000 population in 1973 to 591 in 1994.[20] In 1994, 79 percent of the vehicles stolen were passenger cars. The clearance rate (by arrest), as distinguished from the recovery rate of vehicles, is low—about 14 percent. Many cars are stolen during July and August, when schools are not in session. Forty-four percent of car thieves are youngsters under 18. Most of their acts amount to *joyriding*, a type of larceny that lacks the element of "intent to deprive the owner of the property permanently." The thieves simply take the vehicle for momentary pleasure or transportation.

More recently young car thieves have used stolen vehicles for racing, a show of status among peers, or for the "kick" of destroying them. At the other end of the spectrum are older, professional auto thieves who steal designated cars on consignment for resale in an altered condition (with identifying numbers changed) or for disposition in "chop shops," which strip the cars for the resale value of their parts.[21]

Manufacturers of automobiles have tried to make cars more theftproof. The invention of the ignition key made it harder to steal cars. In recent years, steering-shaft locks, better door locks, and alarm systems have increased the security of protected cars. Such efforts (as we saw in Chapter 8) are examples of target hardening—that is, designing the target (the car) in such a way that it is harder to steal. Other means of providing for greater car protection include safer parking facilities. Ronald Clarke has demonstrated that parking lots with attendants experience far fewer motor vehicle thefts than unattended lots.[22]

Boat Theft

It is not our purpose to classify all larceny by the type of property stolen. We have singled out automobile theft and art theft to demonstrate the socioeconomic

---

AT ISSUE

"FOLLOW THIS CAR! I'M BEING STOLEN!"

Over 1½ million vehicles are stolen each year in the United States, and untold numbers of car radios, tape decks, CD players, and now even car computers are removed from autos. Car owners who want to protect their vehicles can spend $40 for a steering-wheel lock or several thousand dollars for a highly sophisticated antitheft system. Fears about auto theft and carjacking have driven annual sales in the auto security business to $473 million.(1)

While most antitheft devices are sold to customers for cars they already own, nearly 8 percent of 1992 cars had alarms installed before they were shipped to dealers. Strategies available for deterring car thieves include chip-encoded ignition keys, alarm systems, steering-column locks, owner-operated ignition-kill and fuel-cutoff switches, pagers that alert owners when their cars are tampered with, and remote-control headlights and interior lights to illuminate the carjacker or thief as he or she makes a getaway.(1)

LO-JACK

One of the most successful of the high-tech options for car protection may be electronic tracking systems. One such system is "Lo-Jack." A small electronic transmitter, installed in the car, is activated by police transmitters once theft of the car is reported, and a "homing signal" allows tracking computers in police cruisers to find the stolen car. A direction finder and a signal strength meter let the police know how close they are to the stolen car, thereby facilitating the search.(2)

The vice president of Lo-Jack claims that the speediest recovery of a protected car was 3 minutes; the benefit of quick recovery is that thieves do not have time to damage the car and remove valuable components. Lo-Jack began operating in New England in 1986, and car theft in Boston has declined 35 percent since then. Besides New England, the system now is in use in 200,000 cars in southern Florida, New Jersey, Michigan, most of Illinois, Los Angeles County, and northern Virginia. Nearly 5000 stolen cars have been recovered. Car owners pay $595 for the installation of the transmitter.(2)

Anticarjacking Devices

Concern that the increased sophistication of antitheft devices has increased the popularity of carjacking has led to development of anticarjacking systems. One of the "lowest-tech" approaches—but not necessarily the least effective—is the use of an inflatable dummy as a passenger in a single-occupant car. High-tech options include a setup that makes the car "die" if it is driven by someone unfamiliar with the system and remote-control alarm systems that draw attention to the escaping carjacker.

Do all the new systems and alarms significantly reduce car theft and carjacking? Probably not in cases involving professional thieves. "If he has to have that car," says an auto theft expert at an insurance company, "he'll find a way."(1) But effective deterrence may not show up in car theft statistical summaries. "The fundamental purpose of a car alarm—a vehicle security device—isn't that it prevents the car from being stolen," notes an industry official. "It's that it convinces the car thief to go steal somebody else's car."(1)

Sources
1. Tom Incantalupo, "Car Buyers Adding Some Heavy Artillery as Car Thieves Get More Aggressive," *Newsday,* Sept. 26, 1993, p. 91.
2. Eric Peters, "Anti-Car-Theft System Lo-Jack Starts in Va.; D.C., Md. Next," *Washington Times,* Aug. 13, 1993, p. G2.

Questions for Discussion
1. One criticism of Lo-Jack and similar systems is that police will focus on recovery of Lo-Jack-equipped cars and neglect other thefts, thus discriminating against those who can't afford to have the transmitter installed. Do you think this is a valid concern?
2. Should auto manufacturers be required by state or federal law to install alarm or security systems in new cars?

---

significance of these types of larceny, their dependence on the economic situation, and the challenge of changing the situational conditions that encourage people to commit them. Another type of larceny, the theft of working and pleasure boats, of little fishing skiffs and rowboats, is similarly tied to socioeconomic conditions.

No statistics were kept on boat theft in the United States before 1970. Obviously boat thefts have occurred ever since there have been boats, but such thefts attained high proportions only in the 1970s and 1980s. The FBI's National Crime Information Center started a stolen-boat file in 1969. During the first few years this service was little

WINDOW TO THE WORLD

CRIME ON THE OCEANS: WHOSE PROBLEM?

While no accurate estimates of worldwide losses from modern-day piracy are possible, knowledgeable experts think the total is probably near $250 million a year. The thieves make off with tons of cement, coffee, sugar, tomato paste, ladies' undergarments, steel, and whatever other cargo they think they can fence on shore. Even more common is the direct attack on the safe in the captain's cabin—pirates may be able to collect $50,000 in cash during a 15-minute job. In 1991 more than 120 pirate attacks were reported worldwide, and it is likely that only 40 percent of the total are reported to authorities.(1)

THE LACK OF POLICING

Unhappily, the world does not yet have an international marine enforcement agency to police the oceans. There is no one to spot a vessel dumping nuclear waste into the high seas or into an exclusive economic zone. Who can intercept arms or narcotics smugglers? Even powerful nations, like the United States, have trouble policing their own zones. The problems are much worse for small nations that cannot afford to maintain marine police forces of any size.(2) A look at the Law of the Sea Treaty map indicates that most regions affected by piracy and terrorism are in areas of notoriously underpoliced territorial waters.

THE SCOPE OF CRIME ON THE OCEANS

All these problems are magnified when we realize that piracy is only one of many crimes committed on the oceans. For example:

- Frauds in the marine shipping industry have caused severe damage to international trade and threatened the collapse of entire national economies in Africa and Latin America.
- The international drug trade uses the oceans for about half its shipments from the points of origin or manufacture to the points of distribution.
- Currently about 30,000 American boats are listed in the FBI's Stolen Boat File as having been stolen and not recovered.

Sources

1. G. O. W. Mueller and Freda Adler, *Outlaws of the Ocean* (New York: Hearst Marine Books, 1985, p. 150); Alan Farnham, "Pirates," *Fortune*, July 15, 1991, pp. 113–118.
2. Roger Villar, *Piracy Today* (London: Conway Maritime Press, 1985), p. 59.

Questions for Discussion

1. What crimes against property are committed by those who engage in maritime fraud?
2. Propose a mechanism to control property crime on the high seas. Defend your proposal.

---

known, and the number of boats listed as stolen was initially small. But by the mid-1970s, law enforcement agencies all over the country had become familiar with this service and had begun reporting the number of stolen boats in their jurisdictions. Between 1975 and 1990 the number of boats stolen and not recovered tripled, from 11,000 to over 30,000, and that number did not include boats eliminated from the file after a given expiration period (of from 1 to 5 years). After 1990, the number of boats stolen declined.

Most boat thefts, both in the water and on land, are linked to the vast increase in the number of boats in the United States. Increased boat ownership among all population groups goes hand in hand with a proliferation of skills in handling boats and outboard motors. The number of automobile thefts rose during the days when automobile ownership and driving skills increased rapidly. Now we are witnessing the same phenomenon with boats. Some of the same crime-specific approaches developed to render cars more theftproof are currently being tried to protect boats and boating equipment—registration, secret and indelible identification numbers, locking devices, alarm systems, marina guards, protection campaigns for boat owners. Already we have some indication that the choices for boat thieves are becoming more limited and that the thieves are choosing their targets with increasing care.[23]

With the exception of some brazen pickpockets, people who commit larcenies tend to avoid personal contact with their victims. Other criminals seek such contact in order to deprive victims of their property by deception.

FRAUD

Fraud is the acquisition of the property of another person through cheating or deception. In England such crimes owed their existence to the interaction of five circumstances: the advancement of trade and commerce, the inventiveness of swindlers in exploiting these economic advances, the demand of merchants for better protection, the unwillingness of the royal courts to expand the old concept of larceny, and the willingness of Parliament to designate new crimes in order to protect mercantile interests. In brief, medieval England developed a market economy that required the transport of goods by wagon trains across the country, from producer or importer to consumer. Later on, when the Crown sought to encourage settlement of colonies overseas, stock companies were created to raise money for such ventures. People with money to invest acquired part ownership in these companies in the expectation of profit.

Just as some dishonest transporters withheld some of the property entrusted to them for transport, some dishonest investment clerks used funds entrusted to them for their own purposes. Merchants suffered greatly from such losses, yet the royal courts refused to extend the definition of larceny to cover this new means of depriving owners of their property. But merchants demanded protection, and from time to time, as need arose, Parliament designated new, noncapital offenses so that the swindlers could be punished.

Obtaining Property by False Pretenses

The essence of the crime of **obtaining property by false pretenses** is that the victim is made to part with property voluntarily, as a result of the perpetrator's untrue statements regarding a supposed fact. Assume the doorbell rings. A gentleman greets you politely and identifies himself as a representative of a charitable organization, collecting money for disaster victims. On a typed list are the names of all the households in your building, with a dollar amount next to each name. Each household has supposedly contributed an average of $20. Not wanting to be considered cheap, you hand the gentleman a $20 bill. He promptly writes "$20" next to your name and thanks you.

Of course, the gentleman does not represent the charitable organization, there may not even be such a charity, there may not have been a disaster, and you

Barbara Bissel, convicted on federal mail and tax fraud charges, was sentenced to 27 months in prison on December 6, 1996. Her husband Nicholas—an ex-prosecutor in New Jersey—who was likewise convicted committed suicide before the sentencing.

may have been the first victim on his list. The man has obtained property from you by false pretenses. He has not committed a common law larceny because he did not engage in any "trespassory taking" of property.

Cheating was made a crime relatively late in history (in 1757 in England). Until that time the attitude was that people should look out for their own interests. Today obtaining property by false pretenses is a crime in all 50 states, and some states have included it in their general larceny statutes.

Confidence Games and Frauds

In an attempt to protect people from their own greed, a few fraud statutes have included a statutory offense called **confidence game.** In an effort to cover the enormous variety of confidence swindles, legislators have worded the statutory definitions somewhat vaguely. The essence of the offense is that the offender gains the confidence of the victim, induces in the victim in the expectation of a future gain, and—by abusing the trust thus created—makes the victim part with some property. In a sense, confidence games are an aggravated form of obtaining property by false pretenses.

To illustrate: A woman (A) sees a shiny object lying on the sidewalk. As she stoops to pick it up, a man (B) grabs it. A dispute ensues over who should have the "lost diamond ring." A third person (C) comes by and offers to mediate. He happens to be a jeweler, he says. C takes a jeweler's loupe out of his pocket, examines the diamond ring, and pronounces it worth $500. At this point, B generously offers his share in the ring to A for a mere $100. A pays—and gets what turns out to be a worthless object. By the time she discovers this fact, B and C are long gone.

Frauds of this sort have been with us for centuries. But frauds change with commercial developments. Some of the more prevalent fraud schemes of today would have been unimaginable a few decades ago, simply because the commercial opportunities for their occurrence had not yet been invented.

Check Forgery

Those motivated to deprive others of their property have always exploited new opportunities to do so. The invention of "instant cash," or credit, by means of a check issued by a creditable, trustworthy person provided just such new opportunities. Ever since checks were invented, they have been abused. All jurisdictions make it a criminal offense to use a counterfeit or stolen check or to pass a check on a nonexisting account, or even on one with insufficient funds, with intent to defraud. The intent may be demonstrated by the defendant's inability or unwillingness to reimburse the payee within a specified time period.

Another fraud, called **check forging,** consists of altering a check with intent to defraud. The criminologist Edwin Lemert found that most check forgers—or "hot-check artists," as they are frequently called—are amateurs who act in times of financial need or stress, do not consider themselves criminals, and often believe that nobody really gets hurt.[24]

Credit Card Crimes

Just as the introduction of checks for payment for goods and services opened up opportunities for thieves to gain illegitimate financial advantage, so did the introduction of "plastic money." There were 7 billion credit card transactions worldwide in 1991; of these, 3 billion took place in the United States. By the year 2000, the number of annual credit card transactions is expected to hit 21 billion.[25] Visa and MasterCard reported losses from credit card fraud of half a billion dollars in the United States in 1991. This type of crime increases as the volume of cards in circulation goes up. Losses from credit card crime are expected to surpass all other retailer-reported losses, such as those from bad checks, counterfeit currency, and shoplifting.

Credit card fraud during the 1980s was associated primarily with counterfeiting and lost or stolen cards. Many cards are stolen from the mails. Traffickers in stolen cards sell them for cash, with the amount based on the credit limit of the account—a $2000 credit line might bring $250.[26] The availability of new and relatively inexpensive technological equipment, however, keeps transforming the nature of the fraud. Stolen, lost, or expired credit cards are now modified with computers and encoding devices so that they appear to be valid. Totally counterfeit credit cards are also fabricated with the help of laser copiers or other duplicating techniques. And, more recently, credit card account numbers are being stolen from the Internet, where credit purchases are now possible.

The economic rewards of credit card fraud are quick and relatively easy. The risks are low. Usually merchants do not ask for personal identification; cards are issued in banks that are often in other states or countries; and authorization procedures are weak. Originally the users of stolen credit cards had the inconvenience of selling the merchandise they obtained with the cards. But when banks introduced the practice of cashing the checks of strangers as long as the transactions were guaranteed by a credit card, perpetrators gained direct access to cash and no longer had to resort to dealers in stolen goods.[27]

The banking industry has studied credit card schemes and has improved the electronic system with target-hardening responses. In 1971 Congress enacted legislation that limited the financial liability of owners of stolen credit cards to $50. Many states have enacted legislation making it a distinct offense to obtain property or services by means of a stolen or forged credit card, while others include this type of fraud under their larceny statutes.

Insurance Fraud

Insurance fraud is a major problem in the United States. Auto insurance, in particular, has been the target of many dishonest schemes. About $60 billion is paid in auto insurance claims annually. It is estimated that 10 percent of these claims are fraudulent.[28] The National Automobile Theft Bureau holds manufacturers' records on 188 million vehicles (about 95 percent of U.S. cars); its theft and loss data indicate that 15 percent of all reported thefts are fraudulent.[29] Auto insurance schemes include:

- *Staged claims.* Parts of a car are removed, reported stolen, and later replaced by the owner.
- *Owner dumping.* The car is reported stolen; it is stripped by the owner, and the parts are sold.
- *Abandoned vehicles.* The car is left in a vulnerable spot for theft; then it is reported stolen.[30]
- *Staged accidents.* No collision occurs, but an "accident scene" is prepared with glass, blood, and so forth.
- *Intended accidents.* All parties to the "accident" are part of the scheme.
- *Caused accidents.* The perpetrator deliberately causes an innocent victim in a targeted car to crash into his or her car (often in the presence of "friendly" witnesses).[31]

There are many types of insurance fraud besides that involving automobiles. One rapidly growing type involves filing fraudulent health insurance claims. Recently the Fraud Division of the New Jersey Department of Insurance staged a sting operation to catch "ghost riders," a term used to describe those who file insurance claims for injuries sustained in rides on public transportation they never took (see Figure 12.3). At some of the staged bus accidents, people falsely claiming to have been riding the bus outnumbered the undercover investigators who actually were aboard. In other cases, healthy investigators were enticed to see doctors who then treated them and billed the insurance company for the unnecessary treatments, plus others that were never provided.

Credit card crimes and insurance schemes are comparatively recent types of fraud, but they are not the last opportunities for swindlers to deprive others of their property. Computer crime, for example, is a growing concern, and technological advances continue to offer new possibilities for theft. Opportunities will always challenge the imagination of entrepreneurs—illegitimate as well as legitimate. In regard to the illegitimate entrepreneurs, the problem invariably is whether they are in violation of existing criminal laws or whether new legislation will have to be drawn up to cover their schemes.

HIGH-TECH CRIMES: CONCERNS FOR TODAY AND TOMORROW

MOSCOW (Sep 28, 1994) The Citibank Caper, a $10 million electronic break-in, may just be a taste of things to come. Post-Soviet Russia has spawned some of the world's most ruthless, daring crime gangs. It also has thousands, perhaps even tens of thousands, of idle computer programmers. . . . "This is just the beginning," Louise Shelley, an expert on Russian organized crime at American University in Washington, predicted after the Citibank case. . . . Citibank's computerized cash-management system moves up to a half-trillion dollars a day. It has extremely tight security. No one has ever penetrated the system. No one, that is, until a bespectacled young man in St. Petersburg with a laptop computer allegedly tried his hand. Bank and law enforcement officials say he hacked into the Citibank system scores of times over a five-month period from June to October 1994, using secret client codes to shuffle about $10 million into bank accounts abroad.

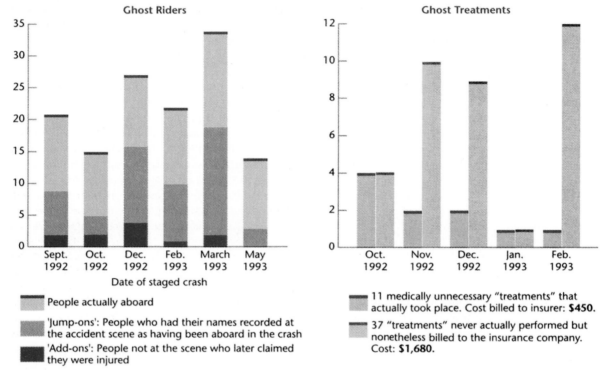

FIGURE 12.3 Ghost riders and ghost treatments: insurance sting, Fraud Division, New Jersey Department of Insurance.
Source: Peter Kerr, "'Ghost Riders' Are Target of an Insurance Sting," *New York Times,* Aug. 18, 1993, pp. A1, D2.

Although law enforcement officials say they now know—more or less—whodunit, they're still not sure how it was done. Citibank won't comment, except to say security on the cash management system was upgraded.[32]

Crimes evolve with the environments we live in. The rise of computers and other high-technology equipment has paved the way for the genesis of new crime types. These present yet another set of challenges for potential victims, law enforcement personnel, criminologists, and other criminal justice professionals.

What exactly is high-technology crime? While there may be debates over the definition of this phenomenon, it is generally agreed that **high-tech crime** involves an attempt to pursue illegal activities through the use of advanced electronic media. We shall define "high technology" as a "a form of sophisticated electronic device—computer, cellular telephone, and other digital communication—that is in common use today."[33] The new waves of computer

crime are perhaps the most illustrative examples of high-technology crime, although sophisticated credit card fraud schemes and cellular telephone scams are also modern problems. In this section, we will refer to crimes relying on modern electronic technology as "high-tech crimes."

Characteristics of High-Tech Crimes

High-tech crimes have affected the nature of property crimes by taking on a few distinct characteristics:

Role of Victims, Type of Property. Criminals engaging in high-tech crimes no longer need actual direct contact with their victims; computers equipped with modems have unlimited range, enabling offenders to victimize people thousands of miles away. The "reach" of motivated offenders has been considerably extended. Physical movement has been replaced by electronic travel.

The type of property that is stolen or affected is also very different in nature. While other property crimes (arson, vandalism, theft, larceny, burglary) victimize concrete targets, high-tech crimes involve less visible and tangible kinds of property such as information, data, and computer networks. In addition, many victims of high-tech crime realize they have been victimized only long after the crime has taken place. In most other property crimes there is often little time between the actual crime and the realization that a crime has taken place (as in cases of burglary or arson, for example).

Profits of Crime. The profits from high-tech crimes are vast. The rise in the incidence of computer crime, for example, is a testament to its efficacy and the profit to be made. The British Banking Association in London estimates the cost of computer fraud worldwide at about $8 billion a year.[34] With the increasing sophistication of equipment, computer hackers are able to steal greater amounts with greater ease, and sometimes a single act can victimize multiple people or places at once.

Detection. High-tech crime is also attractive to some individuals because they find evading detection and prosecution relatively easy. Few law enforcement agencies are equipped to detect the high-tech crimes occurring within their jurisdictions. Furthermore, since the nature of high-tech crime allows perpetrators to carry out their illegal activities without any geographic limitations, tracing high-tech criminal activity to the responsible individual is very difficult. Identifying the crime location becomes harder to do since street corners and physical space have been replaced by airwaves, cyberspace, and other electronic media. Often, by the time illegal activity has been detected, the criminals have already moved on to a new target.

Degree of Criminal Complexity. Another important aspect of high-technology crimes involves the complicated nature of the crimes being committed. Every day, new crimes are being developed and refined by highly skilled computer users. Traditional law enforcement techniques are not designed to deal with such novel and complex crimes. High-tech criminals are in a sense sophisticated criminals. Stealing credit card numbers from the Internet for illicit purposes requires a certain degree of proficiency in Internet navigation, knowledge of how to "break" into the system to commit the thefts, and, finally, experience in using the stolen credit card numbers for criminal gain—all the while avoiding detection.

International Component. Phone companies and computer network systems often advertise that using their services will allow individuals to communicate with people located at the other end of the globe. Such ease of electronic travel is appealing to high-tech criminals, who now participate in a modern phenomenon: global criminality. High-tech crimes can easily go beyond national boundaries, making them transnational crimes, a criminal activity of serious concern for targeted countries. Using a computer, a high-tech criminal can make illegal international money transfers, steal information from a computer located in another country, or diffuse illicit information (such as child pornography or terrorist propaganda) worldwide. The ability to detect and successfully deal with such criminal activities will be a major challenge for law enforcement agencies around the world.

Crime on the Internet: Types of Crime[35]

High-tech criminals have also created their own crime types. While some seek the same ends as more traditional property offenders (financial gain), modern technology allows for novel and totally new crimes.

Computer Network Break-Ins. There are two types of computer network break-ins. The first is commonly known as "hacking." It is not practiced for criminal gain, and can therefore be considered more mischievous than malicious. Nevertheless, network intrusions have been made illegal by the U.S. federal government. A hacker's reward is being able to tell peers that he or she has managed to break into a network, demonstrating superior computing ability, especially the ability to bypass security measures. Hackers, for the most part, seek entry into a computer system and "snoop around," often leaving no sign of entry. It can be likened to an individual stealthily gaining entry into another person's house, going through a few personal belongings, and carefully leaving without taking anything.

The second type of break-in is the one done for illegal purposes. A criminal might break into a large credit card company to steal card numbers, or into a network to steal data or sensitive information. Other criminal acts include computer vandalism, whereby individuals break into a system, alter its operating structure, delete important files, change passwords, or plant viruses that can destroy operating systems, software programs, and data.

Industrial Espionage.   In an age where information can create power, it should not be surprising that competing industries are very curious to know what the others are doing. "Cyber spies" can be hired to break into a competitor's computer system and gather secret information, often leaving no trace of the intrusion. Once again, these spies have such powerful technology at their disposal that they are able to target computers and information that may be thousands of miles away, making detection even more difficult.

Software Piracy.   It is estimated by the U.S. Software Publisher's Association that approximately $7.5 billion worth of American Software is illegally copied and distributed annually worldwide. Software piracy ranges from friends sharing and occasionally copying software, to international fraudulent schemes whereby software is replicated and passed on as the original product, sometimes at a lower price. The duplication process is relatively simple, and once

mastered, any software can be pirated and copies sold worldwide. Software developers are constantly trying to stay ahead of the pirates by attempting to render their software resistant to such duplication. The advent of the compact disk and digital video disk also makes casual software piracy very difficult, since few people have the technology to duplicate these disks.

Child Pornography.   The Internet provides a forum for the display of information. Some individuals, however, see this venue as a means to distribute or seek illegal information such as child pornography. Finding and downloading such material from the Internet is a simple task, even for amateur computer users. While law enforcement agencies occasionally intercept child pornography and those who engage in its dissemination over the airwaves, most offenders are never caught. Also, such material can be strategically hidden or altered to appear to be something else. "Morphing" is a practice that involves using computers to digitally alter pictures. Using such a method, an individual can superimpose two images, or cut and paste parts of one image onto another. This technique has become a tool for child pornographers to evade prosecution. They simply attach the head of an adult to a child's body, and claim the image indeed portrays an adult. Going after such offenders also becomes difficult if different countries are involved in the illegal act. Let us

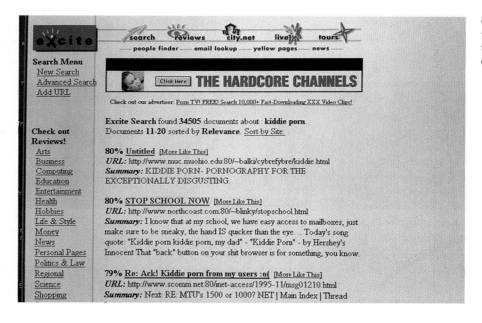

Child pornography can be found on the internet using the more popular search engines.

suppose an individual in country A posts pornographic material on the Internet, and in country A, such material is legal. If the same material is retrieved in country B (although the source is country A), where the material is considered illegal, who is to blame, and where has the crime occurred? Jurisdictional questions about information found on the Internet remain largely unresolved. They will surely become more complex with the increasing traffic of illicit information.

Mail Bombings. Computers can be used to steal money and information. They can also be used for more aggressive purposes. Like the bully told to rough up the new kid in the school yard, computers can be instructed to attack other machines. A common method is that of mail bombings. Mail bombs are the products of computer programs that instruct a computer to literally bombard another computer with information, often irrelevant electronic mail (e-mail). Mail bombs are capable of shutting down computers, and even entire networks, if the amount of information is too large for the receiving computer to digest.

Password Sniffers. Entry into a computer system often requires a password or some other form of user identification to protect the information it contains. Password sniffers are programs that carefully record the names and passwords of network users as they log in. With such confidential information, unauthorized users are able to gain unlawful access to the computer and the information it contains. Passwords can also be sold to other users for illegal purposes.

Credit Card Fraud. Computers and the Internet are used more and more to conduct business. Merchandise is ordered on-line, and payments are also made on-line. This use of credit cards is very appealing to people involved in credit card fraud. Computers can facilitate credit card fraud in two ways. First, a conventionally stolen credit card can be used to order merchandise on-line and, because no time is wasted going from store to store, a perpetrator can maximize his or her gain before the card is inactivated. Detection is also reduced since there is no physical contact with sales staff who might alert authorities should they suspect fraud. Second, credit card numbers can be stolen from the Internet as a customer is making a legitimate purchase. Programs similar to those that are designed to steal passwords from unsuspecting users are often used for this purpose. Another way of stealing credit card numbers is for offenders to access computers located in credit bureaus or financial institutions.

Characteristics of the High-Tech Criminal

While all the crimes and deviant acts discussed so far rely heavily on technology, there are still human offenders behind them. Do these people, however, resemble other property criminals, or do they have distinct characteristics? It is true that modern technology is so widespread that virtually anyone is capable of high-tech crime, but it also remains a fact that most high-tech offenders, especially computer hackers, fit a rather unique profile. These individuals are usually young (14–19 years old) white males from middle-class backgrounds. They often possess superior levels of intelligence (IQ over 120), but on a social level they tend to be withdrawn and associate mainly with peers who share their fascination for electronic gadgets and computer-related activities. Some youths also believe that they are part of a "counterculture," fighting censorship, liberating information, and challenging big business and major corporations.[36] In a way, they perceive themselves as modern-day Robin Hoods.

The Criminal Justice Problem

High-tech crimes pose a special problem to law enforcement agencies for two reasons. First, these crimes are not easily detected since the offenders can quietly commit them from any computer terminal, usually in the comfort of their own homes. Second, while a few organizations have mobilized to attack high-tech crime, most law enforcement agencies are not equipped to deal with the phenomenon: "Technology changes at an astounding rate while law enforcement techniques, which traditionally are reactionary, do not."[37] It is clear that the police forces of the future need to address this problem by concentrating on detection, and by arming themselves with the technological tools necessary to deal with it. By necessity, computer and/or Internet classes should soon find their way into police academies.

WHEN NEW GLOBAL TECHNOLOGY MEETS OLD LOCAL LAWS

Developments in technology often outpace the ability of the law to keep up: While technology rapidly creates opportunities for activities society seeks to classify as deviant, the law is often ill-equipped to address these issues. The resulting zeal on the part of legislatures to pass new laws often raises civil rights issues, such as the protections of the rights of privacy, free speech, and freedom of association. This conflict is illustrated by the stories of Jake Baker and Dave La Macchia.

Jake Baker, a student at the University of Michigan in Ann Arbor, was arrested by FBI agents on February 9, 1995 and charged with "transmitting threats across state lines." The charge came about after it was discovered that Baker had posted an erotic fantasy on the Internet in which he raped and tortured a character with the same name as one of Baker's real-life classmates. The charges were later revised to making a "threat to injure another person," but in the meantime Baker had been suspended from the University of Michigan and his story had made headlines around the world. The case raises issues beyond the legality of posting a fantasy in which a living person's name is used. Many people have expressed concern over whether Baker's civil liberties were violated when he was suspended and how much liability an individual has when posting materials to the Internet. Baker was eventually acquitted, in part because his story was determined to be "self expression" and did not constitute a threat.

• • •

Dave La Macchia was indicted by a grand jury on April 7, 1994 on charges of "conspiracy and scheme to defraud." The charges stemmed from La Macchia's involvement in the operation of a pair of bulletin board systems (BBS) at the Massachusetts Institute of Technology (MIT). The boards, called CYNOSURE I and CYNOSURE II, were allegedly used as distribution centers for illegally copied software. In this case, the law was not prepared to handle whatever crimes may have been committed. The judge ruled that there was no conspiracy and dismissed the case. If statutes were in place to address the liability taken on by a BBS operator for the materials contained on the system, situations like this might be handled more differently(1).

Local problems of the lack or inadequacy of state or federal legislation—and the consequent need to write new or amended laws—are compounded by the fact that the electronic highway does not end at state or national borders. Rather, high-tech crimes travel far and fast. Because no country can isolate itself from criminal activities, the international community must unite to combat this growing problem. Not only are countries around the globe targets of financial fraud, and of information and data theft, but entire national security systems are at risk of being jeopardized and violated.

Unfortunately, prevention of such technological crimes has not yet been properly addressed by the international community. While a few countries have begun to recognize the problem, law enforcement and effective prosecution are still in the developmental stages. In its attempt to standardize criminal justice practices around the world, the United Nations understands that the global community needs to address the issues surrounding computer and other high-tech crimes. The following are some of the problems in international cooperation in the area of computer crime and criminal law(2):

- The lack of global consensus on what types of conduct should constitute a computer-related crime
- The lack of expertise on the part of the police, prosecutors, and the courts in this field
- The inadequacy of seizure powers for investigation and access to computer systems, including the inapplicability of seizure powers to intangibles such as computerized data
- The lack of harmonization between the different national procedural laws concerning the investigation of computer-related crime
- The transnational character of many computer crimes
- The lack of extradition and mutual assistance treaties and of synchronized law enforcement mechanisms that would permit international cooperation, or the inability of existing treaties to take into account the dynamics and special requirements of computer crime investigation

Sources

1. *Jones Telecommunications and Multimedia Encyclopedia*, Drive D:\Studios, Jones Digital Century, 1996. (Found on the Internet at http://www.digitalcentury.com/encyclo/update/crime.html.)
2. *United Nations Manual on the Prevention and Control of Computer-Related Crime*, International Review of Criminal Policy (1994), nos. 43 and 44.

Questions for Discussion

1. Is it reasonable to expect different countries to agree on common standards regarding cyberspace?
2. What practices can facilitate agreement between countries?

BURGLARY

A "burg," in Anglo-Saxon terminology, was a secure place for the protection of oneself, one's family, and one's property. If the burg protects a person from larceny and assault, what protects the burg? The burghers, perhaps. But there had to be a law behind the burghers. And that was the law of burglary, which made it a crime to break and enter the dwelling of another person at night with the intention of committing a crime therein. (Of course it had to be at night, for during the day the inhabitants could defend themselves, or so it was thought.) The common law defined **burglary** as:

The breaking
And entering
Of the dwelling house
Of another person
At night
With the intention to commit a felony or larceny inside

By "breaking," the law meant any trespass (unauthorized entry), but usually one accompanied by a forceful act, such as cracking the lock, breaking a windowpane, or scaling the roof and entering through the chimney. The "entering" was complete as soon as the perpetrator extended any part of his or her body into the house in pursuit of the objective of committing a crime in the house. The house had to be a "dwelling," but that definition was extended to cover the "curtilage," the attached servants' quarters, carriage houses, and barns. The dwelling also had to be that of "another." And as we mentioned, the event had to occur at "night," between sundown and sunup.

The most troublesome element has always been the "intention to commit a felony or larceny" (even a petty or misdemeanor larceny) inside the premises. How can we know what a burglar intends to do? The best evidence of intent is what the burglar actually does inside the premises: Steal jewelry? Commit a rape? Set the house afire? Any crime the burglar commits inside is considered evidence of criminal intention at the moment the burglar broke and entered the dwelling.[38]

Today burglary is no longer limited to night attacks, although by statute the crime may be considered more serious if it is committed at night. Statutes have also added buildings other than dwellings to the definition. The UCR defines burglary simply as the unlawful entry into a structure (criminal trespass) to commit a felony or theft. The use of force to gain entry is not a required element of burglary under the UCR.

Burglary rates have declined 13 percent since 1983. Even so, in 1994, almost 2.7 million burglaries were reported to the police, with an overall loss of $3.6 billion. These crimes account for nearly a quarter of all Index offenses. Most burglaries (87 percent) are not cleared by arrests.[39]

Criminologists ask questions about the characteristics of offenders who commit burglaries and of the places that are burglarized. Neal Shover described the "good burglar" as one having competence, personal integrity, a specialty in burglary, financial success, and an ability to avoid prison.[40] Another study demonstrated that burglars are versatile, committing a wide range of offenses, but that they do specialize in burglary for short periods of time. Compared with male burglars, female burglars begin offending at a later age, more often commit burglaries with others, and have fewer contacts with the criminal justice system.[41]

Recent research on burglary asks questions not only about who is likely to commit a burglary or what distinguishes one burglar from another. As we notice in Chapter 8, criminologists are looking, for instance, at the process that leads to the burglary of a particular house in a specific neighborhood—that is, how a burglar discriminates between individual areas and targets when there are so many alternatives—and ways to make the process of burglary more difficult for any burglar.

FENCING: RECEIVING STOLEN PROPERTY

We are treating burglary as a property crime. An occasional burglar enters with the intention of committing rape, arson, or some other felony inside the building. But most burglars are thieves; they are looking for cash and for other property that can be turned into cash. Burglars and thieves depend on a network of "fences" to turn stolen property into cash.

Jonathan Wild controlled the London underworld from about 1714 until his hanging in 1725. For over 2½ centuries he has captured the imagination of historians, social scientists, and writers. Henry Fielding wrote *The Life of Mr. Jonathan Wild, the Great,* and Mack the Knife in John Gay's *Beggar's Opera* was modeled on Wild. Wild was known as a "thief-taker." Thief-takers made an occupation of capturing thieves and claiming the rewards offered for their arrest. By law, thief-takers were allowed to keep the possessions of the thieves they caught, except objects that had been stolen, which were returned to their owners.

Wild added a devious twist to his trade: He bought stolen goods from thieves and sold them back to their rightful owners. The owners paid much more than the thief could get from the usual fences, so both Wild and the thief made a considerable profit. To thieves, he was a fellow thief; to honest people, he was a legitimate citizen helping to get back their property. Playing both roles well, he ran competing fencing operations out of business, employed about 7000 thieves, and became the most famous fence of all time.[42]

A **fence** is a person who buys stolen property, on a regular basis, for resale. Fences, or dealers in stolen property, operate much like legitimate businesses: They buy and sell for profit. Their activity thrives on an understanding of the law governing the receiving of stolen property, on cooperation with the law when necessary, and on networking. The difference between a legitimate business and a fencing operation is that the channeling of stolen goods takes place in a clandestine environment (created by law enforce-ment and deviant associates) with high risks and with a need to justify one's activities in the eyes of conventional society.

Carl Klockars's *Professional Fence* and Darrell Steffensmeier's *Fence,* each focusing on the life of a particular fence, present us with fascinating accounts of this criminal business. The proprietors of such businesses deal in almost any commodity. "Oh, I done lots of business with him," said Klockars's fence, Vincent Swazzi. "One time I got teeth, maybe five thousand teeth in one action. You know, the kind they use for making false teeth—you see, you never know what a thief's gonna come up with." And many fences are quite proud of their positions in the community. Said Swazzi, "The way I look at it, this is actually my street. I mean I am the mayor. I walk down the street an' people come out the doors to say hello."[43]

Until recently it was believed that professional thieves and fences were totally interdependent and that their respective illegal activities were mutually reinforcing. Recent research, however, demonstrates a change in the market for stolen goods. D'Aunn Webster Avery, Paul F. Cromwell, and James N. Olson conducted extensive interviews with 38 active burglars, shoplifters, and their fences and concluded that it is no longer the professional fence who takes care of stolen goods but, rather, occasional receivers—otherwise honest citizens—who buy from thieves directly or at flea markets.[44] This willingness to buy

The Fulton Fish Market, New York City, was torched, with the loss of most of its records, while a police investigation into organized crime activities at the market was in progress, March 29, 1995.

merchandise that the buyers must at least suspect has been stolen may indicate that the general public is more tolerant of stealing than previous generations were.

ARSON

The crimes against property that we have discussed so far involve the illegitimate transfer of possession. The property in question is "personal property" rather than real property, or real estate. Only two types of property crime are concerned with real property. Burglary is one; the other is arson.

The common law defined **arson** as the malicious burning of or setting fire to the dwelling of another person. Modern statutes have distinguished degrees of severity of the offense and have increased its scope to include other structures and even personal property, such as automobiles. The most severe punishments are reserved for arson of dwellings, because of the likelihood that persons in the building may be injured or die.

Arson always has been viewed as a more violent crime than burglary. In comparison with burglary, however, arson is a fairly infrequent offense. A total of 102,139 arson offenses were reported in 1994. A national survey of fire departments, however, indicates that the actual number of arson incidents is likely to be far higher than the reported figure.[45]

Buildings were the most frequent targets (52 percent); 25 percent of the targets were mobile property (motor vehicles, trailers, and the like).[46] The annual estimate property loss is over $2 billion. In 1993, 560 civilian lives were lost due to suspicious fires.[47]

The seriousness of this crime is demonstrated by a series of spectacular fires set in resort hotels in such cities as San Juan, Puerto Rico (in conjunction with a labor dispute), and Las Vegas, Nevada. Although these fires were not set with the intent to kill any of the people in the buildings, many lives were lost. The inferno created by arsonists in the Du Pont Plaza Hotel in San Juan in 1987 killed 97 people. The arson at the Las Vegas Hilton caused no deaths but $14 million in damages, not including the loss of business.

While insurance fraudsters and organized-crime figures may be responsible for some of the more spectacular arsons, it is juveniles who account for the single most significant share. Consider the following statistics:

- In 1994 juveniles under age 18 accounted for about 48 percent of the arson arrests nationwide.
- Nationwide arson arrests of juveniles rose 18 percent between 1993 and 1994, while adult arrests showed a 7 percent decrease.[48]
- One of every sixteen persons arrested for arson is under age 10, and one of every four is under age 15.
- Juveniles were responsible for approximately 50 percent of the arson fires in Seattle.
- Thirty-eight percent of children in grades 1 to 8 in Rochester, New York, admitted playing with fire.[49]

Why do children set fires?[50] Recent research suggests that the motive may be psychological pain, anger, revenge, need for attention, malicious mischief, or excitement.[51] Juvenile firesetters have been classified in three groups: the playing-with-matches firesetter, the crying-for-help firesetter, and the severely disturbed firesetter.[52] Many juvenile firesetters are in urgent need of help. In response to their needs, juvenile arson intervention programs have been established in recent years.[53]

An interesting English study found that while arsonists were in many respects comparable to offenders classified as violent, they had a lower incidence of interpersonal aggression and rated themselves as less assertive than did violent offenders—perhaps because, as the study showed, arsonists were taken into care at an earlier age.[54] The motives of adult arsonists are somewhat different from those of juveniles. Though here, too, we find disturbed offenders (pyromaniacs) and people who set fires out of spite. We are also much more likely to encounter insurance fraudsters, as well as organized-crime figures who force compliance or impose revenge by burning establishments (the "torches").[55] One classification of firesetters by motive includes:

- Revenge, jealousy, and hatred
- Financial gain (mostly insurance fraud)
- Intimidation and/or extortion (often involving organized crime)
- Need for attention
- Social protest
- Arson to conceal other crimes
- Arson to facilitate other crimes
- Vandalism and accidental firesetting[56]

As arson continues to be a serious national problem, policy makers have been developing two distinct approaches for dealing with it. The offender-specific approach focuses on educational outreach in schools and the early identification of troubled children, for purposes of counseling and other assistance.[57] The offense-specific (geographic) approach focuses on places. It seeks to identify areas with a high potential for arson. The aim is to deploy arson specialists to correct problems and to stabilize endangered buildings and neighborhoods.[58]

COMPARATIVE CRIME RATES

The rates of property crime are much higher than those of the violent crime we discuss in Chapter 11. It is interesting to compare these rates for various regions of the world. If we compare the property-owning, consumer-oriented countries of the industrialized Western world with the still largely agricultural but rapidly urbanizing countries of the Third World, we note a significant discrepancy: The rate of theft per 100,000 in the developed countries was 4200, while the rate in developing countries was 600.[59]

Recall the Coca-Cola bottle that disrupted the lives of the aborigines in *The Gods Must Be Crazy*. We just may have discovered the secret of that bottle: If there is no Coke bottle, no one is going to steal it. The more property people have, especially portable property, the more opportunity other people have to make off with it. Europeans have an old saying: "Opportunity makes thieves." The foremost opportunity for theft may simply be an abundance of property.

REVIEW

Not all crimes against property are aimed at acquiring such property. A burglar invades a dwelling or other structure usually—but not necessarily—to commit a larceny inside. An arsonist endangers the existence of the structure and its occupants. Both amateurs and professionals commit property crimes of all sorts. Each new form of legitimate trade, such as the development of credit cards and computers, offers criminals new opportunities to exploit the situation for gain. It is evident that most high-tech offenders are quite sophisticated and, given the vastness of such technological wonders as the Internet, a new challenge lies ahead for social scientists and criminal justice professionals alike.

Some property-oriented crimes, as we will see in Chapter 13, depend not only on the cunning and daring of the perpetrator who targets a lone victim, but on the normal business operations of legitimate enterprises—and of illegitimate ones as well.

NOTES

1. J. W. Cecil Turner, *Kenny's Outlines of Criminal Law,* 2d ed. (Cambridge, Mass.: Cambridge University Press, 1958), p. 238.
2. Jerome Hall, *Theft, Law, and Society* (Indianapolis: Bobbs-Merrill, 1935).
3. U.S. Department of Justice, Bureau of Justice Statistics, *Criminal Victimization 1994* (Washington, D.C.: U.S. Government Printing Office, 1994), p. 1.
4. Uniform Crime Reports, 1994, p. 44.
5. See Abraham S. Blumberg, "Typologies of Criminal Behavior," in *Current Perspectives on Criminal Behavior,* 2d ed., ed. Blumberg (New York: Knopf, 1981).
6. See John Hepburn, "Occasional Criminals," in *Major Forms of Crime,* ed. Robert Meier (Beverly Hills, Calif.: Sage, 1984), pp. 73–94; and John Gibbs and Peggy Shelly, "Life in the Fast Lane: A Retrospective View by Commercial Thieves," *Journal of Research in Crime and Delinquency,* **19** (1982): 299–330, at p. 327.
7. James Inciardi, "Professional Thief," in Meier, *Major Forms of Crime,* p. 224. See also Harry King and William Chambliss, *Box Man—A Professional Thief's Journal* (New York: Harper & Row, 1972).
8. *The Professional Thief,* annotated and interpreted by Edwin H. Sutherland (Chicago: University of Chicago Press, 1937).
9. Jo-Ann Ray, "Every Twelfth Shopper: Who Shoplifts and Why?" *Social Casework,* **68** (1987): 234–239.
10. Abigail Buckle and David P. Farrington, "An Observational Study of Shoplifting," *British Journal of Criminology,* **24** (1984): 63–73.
11. Donald Hartmann, Donna Gelfand, Brent Page, and Patrice Walder, "Rates of Bystander Observation and Reporting of Contrived Shoplifting Incidents," *Criminology,* **10** (1972): 247–267.
12. P. James Carolin, Jr., "Survey of Shoplifters," *Security Management,* **36** (1992): 11–12.
13. Mary Own Cameron, *The Booster and the Snitch* (New York: Free Press, 1964). See also John Rosecrance, "The Stooper: A Professional Thief in the Sutherland Manner," *Criminology,* **24** (1986): 29–40.
14. Richard Moore, "Shoplifting in Middle America: Patterns and Motivational Correlates," *International Journal of Offender Therapy and Comparative Criminology,* **28** (1984): 53–64. See also Charles A. Sennewald and John H. Christman, *Shoplifting* (Boston: Butterworth-Heinemann, 1992).
15. Trevor N. Gibbens, C. Palmer, and Joyce Prince, "Mental Health Aspects of Shoplifting," *British Medical Journal,* **3** (1971): 612–615.

16. Roger Griffin, *Shoplifting in Supermarkets* (San Diego, Calif.: Commercial Service Systems, 1988).

17. Barry Poyner and Ruth Woodall, *Preventing Shoplifting: A Study in Oxford Street* (London: Police Foundation, 1987).

18. John Carroll and Frances Weaver, "Shoplifters' Perceptions of Crime Opportunities: A Process-Tracing Study," in *The Reasoning Criminal,* ed. Derek Cornish and Ronald V. Clarke (New York: Springer Verlag, 1986), pp. 19–38.

19. See Truc-Nhu Ho, *Art Theft in New York City: An Exploratory Study in Crime Specificity,* Ph.D. dissertation, Rutgers University, 1992; Christopher Dickey, "Missing Masterpieces," *Newsweek,* May 29, 1989, pp. 65–68.

20. Uniform Crime Reports, 1973, p. 50; 1994, p. 50.

21. See Charles McCaghy, Peggy Giordano, and Trudy Knicely Henson, "Auto Theft," *Criminology,* **15** (1977): 367–385.

22. Ronald V. Clarke, "Situational Crime Prevention: Theoretical Basis and Practical Scope," in *Crime and Justice: An Annual Review of Research,* vol. 4, ed. Michael Tonry and Norval Morris (Chicago: University of Chicago Press, 1983).

23. Jeffrey Peck, G. O. W. Mueller, and Freda Adler, "The Vulnerability of Ports and Marinas to Vessel and Equipment Theft," *Security Journal,* **5** (1994): 146–153.

24. Edwin Lemert, "An Isolation and Closure Theory of Naive Check Forgery," *Journal of Criminal Law, Criminology, and Police Science,* **44** (1953–1954): 296–307.

25. Richard Greer, "The Georgia 100," *The Atlanta Constitution,* May 19, 1996, p. 13G.

26. Barry Masuda, "Card Fraud: Discover the Possibilities," *Security Management,* **36** (1992): 71–74.

27. Pierre Tremblay, "Designing Crime," *British Journal of Criminology,* **26** (1986): 234–253.

28. Leonard Sloane, "Rising Fraud Worrying Car Insurers," *New York Times,* Nov. 16, 1991, p. 48.

29. Michael Clarke, "The Control of Insurance Fraud," *British Journal of Criminology,* **30** (1990): 1–23.

30. Sloane, "Rising Fraud Worrying Car Insurers."

31. Edmund J. Pankan and Frank E. Krzeszowski, "Putting a Claim on Insurance Fraud," *Security Management,* **37** (1993): 91–94.

32. "Citibank Caper: Harbinger of Crimes to Come?" *The News and Observer Publishing Co.,* Sept. 28, 1995.

33. Larry E. Coutorie, "The Future of High-Technology Crime: A Parallel Delphi Study," *Journal of Criminal Justice,* **23** (1995): 13–27.

34. "Survey Finds Computer Crime Widespread in Corporate America," *The News and Observer Publishing Co.,* Oct. 25, 1995.

35. Natalie D. Voss, "Crime on the Internet," *Jones Telecommunications and Multimedia Encyclopedia,* Drive D: \ Studios, Jones Digital Century (1996). (Found on the Internet at http://www.digitalcentury.com/encyclo/update/crime.html)

36. Robert W. Taylor, "Computer Crime," in *Criminal Investigation,* ed. C. R. Swanson, N. C. Chamelin, and L. Tersito (New York: Random House, 1991).

37. Coutorie, "The Future of High-Technology Crime."

38. Kenneth C. Sears and Henry Weihofen, *May's Law of Crimes,* 4th ed. (Boston: Little, Brown, 1948), pp. 307–317.

39. Uniform Crime Reports, 1994, p. 42.

40. Neal Shover, "Structures and Careers in Burglary," *Journal of Criminal Law and Criminology,* **63** (1972): 540–549.

41. Scott Decker, Richard Wright, Allison Redfern, and Dietrich Smith, "A Woman's Place Is in the Home: Females and Residential Burglary," *Justice Quarterly,* **10** (1993): 143–162.

42. Darrell Steffensmeier, *The Fence: In the Shadow of Two Worlds* (Totowa, N.J.: Rowman & Littlefield, 1986), p. 7.

43. Carl Klockars, *The Professional Fence* (New York: Free Press, 1976), pp. 110, 113.

44. D'Aunn Webster Avery, Paul F. Cromwell, and James N. Olson, "Marketing Stolen Property: Burglars and Their Fences," paper presented at the 1988 Annual Meeting of the American Society of Criminology, Reno, Nev.

45. Patrick G. Jackson, "Assessing the Validity of Official Data on Arson," *Criminology,* **26** (1988): 181–195.

46. Uniform Crime Reports, 1994, p. 50.

47. Michael J. Karter, Jr., "Fire Loss in the United States in 1993," *NFPA Journal,* **88** (1994): 59, 62, 64.

48. Uniform Crime Reports, 1994, p. 56.

49. See Rebecca K. Hersch, *A Look at Juvenile Firesetter Programs,* for U.S. Department of Justice, Office of Justice Programs, Office of Juvenile Justice and Delinquency Prevention (Washington, D.C.: U.S. Government Printing Office, May 1989), p. 1.

50. Irving Kaufman and Lora W. Heims, "A Re-evaluation of the Dynamics of Firesetting," *American Journal of Orthopsychiatry,* **31** (1961): 123–136.

51. Hersch, *A Look at Juvenile Firesetter Programs.*

52. Wayne S. Wooden and Martha Lou Berkey, *Children and Arson* (New York: Plenum, 1984), p. 3.

53. See Jessica Gaynor and Chris Hatcher, *The Psychology of Child Firesetting* (New York: Brunner/Mazel, 1987).

54. Howard F. Jackson, Susan Hope, and Clive Glass, "Why Are Arsonists Not Violent Offenders?" *International Journal of Offender Therapy and Comparative Criminology,* **31** (1987): 143–151.

55. See Wayne W. Bennett and Karen Matison Hess, *Investigating Arson* (Springfield, Ill.: Charles C Thomas, 1984), pp. 34–38.

56. John M. Macdonald, *Bombers and Firesetters* (Springfield, Ill.: Charles C Thomas, 1977), pp. 198–204.

57. See Federal Emergency Management Agency, U.S. Fire Administration, *Interviewing and Counselling Juvenile Firesetters* (Washington, D.C.: U.S. Government Printing Office, 1979).

58. Clifford L. Karchmer, *Preventing Arson Epidemics: The Role of Early Warning Strategies,* Aetna Arson Prevention Series (Hartford, Conn.: Aetna Life & Casualty, 1981).

59. "Third United Nations Survey of Crime Trends, Operations of Criminal Justice Systems and Crime Prevention Strategies," A/CONF. 144/6, July 27, 1990.

▥ Internet Exercise

Fighting high-tech crime poses many new challenges. What has the FBI done to combat computer crime?

▥ **Your Web Site is: http://www.fbi.gov/**

CHAPTER 13
Organizational Criminality

Defining White-Collar Crime

      Crimes Committed by Individuals

      Types of White-Collar Crimes

Corporate Crime

      Theories of Corporate Liability

      Governmental Control of Corporations

      Investigating Corporate Crime

      Environmental Crimes

      Curbing Corporate Crime

Organized Crime

      The History of Organized Crime

      The Structure and Impact of Organized Crime

      The New Ethnic Diversity in Organized Crime

Review

Notes

      Special Features

        CRIMINOLOGICAL FOCUS: Corporate Crime

        AT ISSUE: Dangerous Ground

        WINDOW TO THE WORLD: The Business of Organized Crime

Key Terms

bankruptcy fraud
boiler rooms
churning
consumer fraud
corporate crime
embezzlement
Federal Witness
  Protection Program
insider trading
Mafia
occupational crimes
Racketeer Influenced
  and Corrupt
  Organizations
  (RICO) Act
Sherman Antitrust Act
stock manipulation
white-collar crime

A Del Webb Corp. subsidiary paid a $1 million fine Wednesday—the largest ever in Arizona for an environmental crime—for the systematic dumping of as many as 100 truckloads of batteries and other debris into Lake Powell.

In addition, ARA Leisure Services, which took over the marina boat-renting concessions from Del Webb's Marina Operation Corp. in 1988, agreed to pay a $225,000 fine.

Both companies agreed to pay a total of $100,000 to cover investigative costs, bringing the total to more than $1.3 million.

During a press conference, Arizona Attorney General Grant Woods described the case as "one of the biggest environmental outrages in this state," "the worst form of environmental stewardship" and "an embarrassment."

Also, Woods accused National Park Service employees of "lying" in the course of a three-year investigation that found boat-related debris at five marinas on Lake Powell—one in Arizona and four in Utah. The marinas are run by concessionaires under Park Service supervision.

State investigators displayed photographs of a marina storm drain that was used to dump liquid hazardous wastes directly into the lake.

They also showed a videotape displaying all manner of debris from boats, including batteries, steering cables, flashlights, refrigerators, coolers, chairs, propellers, anchors, toilets, and barbecue grills.

"This shows a pattern of abuse and neglect of a natural Arizona jewel that went on for years," said Woods, who described the dumping from 1980 to 1990 as part of "standard operating procedure" at the marinas.[1]

              ◦ ◦ ◦

General Electric has been charged with price fixing and other monopolistic practices not only for its light bulbs, but for turbines, generators, transformers, motors, relays, radio tubes, heavy metals, and lightning arresters. At least 67 suits have been brought against General Electric by the Antitrust Division of the Justice Department since 1911, and 180 antitrust suits were brought against General Electric by private companies in the early 1960's alone. General Electric's many trips to court hardly seem to have "reformed" the company: In 1962, after 50 years' experience with General Electric, even the Justice Department was moved to comment on General Electric's proclivity for frequent and persistent involvement in antitrust violations.[2]

* * *

A Mafia boss found dead last week was involved in the 1992 murder of Cosa Nostra's enemy number one, Judge Giovanni Falcone, Italian state television channels said Sunday.

The reports said Antonino Gioe, who hanged himself with his shoelaces from the bars of his cell Thursday, was at Palermo airport when Falcone arrived there and he had apparently tipped off the Mafia commando which killed the judge minutes later.

Falcone, his wife and three bodyguards died May 23, 1992, when their armor-plated cars were blown up by a huge bomb buried under the highway between Palermo and the airport.

Falcone's murder, followed by that of his colleague Paolo Borsellino two months later, proved a major turning point in Italian politics and provoked a strong state reaction. Leading members of the Mafia were arrested after years on the run.

The reports said Gioe had killed himself because he knew the Mafia had condemned him to death for making too many mistakes. He was apparently hoping his suicide would spare his family any bloody reprisals by his former associates.

According to the reports, investigators traced a call made by Gioe on his mobile phone at Palermo airport two minutes after Falcone and his wife had landed.

The call, to a member of the Madonia clan on whose "territory" the judge was killed, ended only seconds before the killers detonated the bomb. The man Gioe was calling is also under arrest but his name has not been disclosed.

Investigators still do not know who told the Mafia Falcone was making the unannounced trip from Rome to Palermo aboard a secret service plane. The inquiry has centered around a former senior member of the intelligence service and a Sicilian MP.

Gioe, a 37-year-old Mafioso from Corleone, was being kept in solitary confinement in the same wing of Rome's maximum security jail as Salvatore "Toto" Riina, the Mafia godfather arrested last January after 23 years on the run.[3]

W hat do the crimes of the Del Webb Corporation, General Electric, and the Cosa Nostra, or Mafia, have in common? According to the criminologist Dwight Smith, white-collar, corporate, and organized crimes all involve business enterprises.[4] An offender—whether a corporation employee, the corporation itself, or a lieutenant in a Mafia family—uses a business enterprise (perhaps an insurance company, a garbage collection company, or a prostitution ring)

to profit illegally. It is the use of a legitimate or illegitimate business enterprise for illegal profit that distinguishes organizational crimes from other types of offenses. Organizational offenses are also different in another important respect. Unlike violent crimes and property offenses, which the Model Penal Code classifies quite neatly, organizational offenses are a heterogeneous mix of crimes, from homicide, fraud, and conspiracy to racketeering, gambling, and the violation of a host of federal environmental statutes.

How much white-collar crime is committed each year? What are the attributes of organized crimes? How much crime is committed by major U.S. corporations? Answers to such questions, no matter how preliminary, may provide valuable information to guide efforts to control and prevent white-collar, corporate, and organized crime.

DEFINING WHITE-COLLAR CRIME

Initial reports of a crisis in the U.S. savings and loan (S&L) industry appeared on front pages of newspapers across the country in 1989. They alleged that some savings and loan officers had ruined their institutions financially for personal profit, thereby causing the greatest amount of white-collar crime ever uncovered. Bailing out the insolvent banks may cost an estimated $300 billion to $500 billion by the year 2021.[5]

But white-collar crime is not a new phenomenon. In ancient Greece public officials reportedly violated the law by purchasing land slated for government acquisition.[6] Much of what we today define as white-collar crime, however, is the result of laws passed within the last century. For example, the Sherman Antitrust Act, passed by Congress in 1890, authorized the criminal prosecution of corporations engaged in monopolistic practices.[7] Federal laws regulating the issuance and sale of stocks and other securities were passed in 1933 and 1934. In 1940 Edwin H. Sutherland provided criminologists with the first scholarly account of white-collar crime. He defined it as crime "committed by a person of respectability and high social status in the course of his occupation."[8]

The Del Webb Corporation and General Electric cases demonstrate that Sutherland's definition is not entirely satisfactory: White-collar crime can be committed by a corporation as well as by an individual. As Gilbert Geis has noted, Sutherland's work is limited by his own definition. He has a "striking inability to dif-

CRIMINOLOGICAL FOCUS

CORPORATE CRIME—WHO ARE THE VICTIMS?

By most estimates corporate crime costs us more in human lives and in dollars than the more highly publicized, more severely punished, and far more familiar street crime. For example, it is estimated that in the United States 100,000 to 200,000 people die each year from unquestionably job-related illnesses and injuries. That is a rate five times higher than the number of people murdered by street criminals each year.(1) If you add to this the number of people who die each year from causes related to corporate "oversight," marketing, or profiteering, the rate is far higher. "All things considered," concludes sociologist Sandra Walklate, "this evidence strongly suggests that we are at far more physical risk of being victimized as a result of the activities and inactivities of business and industry than by street crime or burglary."(2)

Victims of corporate crime rarely, it seems, make their victimization known to authorities—sometimes because they don't even realize they *are* victims.(3, p. 73) In general, corporate crime not only goes unpunished; it goes unreported and even undetected. "The majority of those suffering from corporate crime remain unaware of their victimization—either not knowing it has happened to them or viewing their

'misfortune' as an accident or 'no one's fault,'" one researcher explained.(4, p. 17) "Clearly a major problem in controlling corporate crime is raising victim and public consciousness to a level where the community desires and supports a policy of more active and effective state control and regulation.(4, p. 66)

"Raising victim and public consciousness" is a problem. When victims are the public-at-large or another corporation, they do not fit our traditional picture of a victim—they are not individuals. Even when the victim is an individual, as in a case of death caused by occupational safety violations, we may not think of him or her as a victim of *crime*. Since we do not know whom in particular to blame (the offender is "depersonalized"), we tend not to blame anyone and to say it was an accident.

According to criminologist David Shichor, several scholars have suggested that social control of corporations will not occur until public opinion toward "big business" has been changed. A better understanding of corporate victimization could improve efforts to educate the public about corporate crime through publicity, "personalization of the harm," "individualization of the victim," and "personalization of the offender." The goal, says Shichor, is "to demonstrate to the public and to corporate executives that many corporate actions and business practices are often more harmful than street crimes, victimize a large number of people, undermine public trust in social institutions and deviate from social and legal norms."(3, p. 82).

Sources
1. David R. Simon and D. Stanley Eitzen, *Elite Deviance* (Boston: Allyn and Bacon, 1993), p. 40.
2. Sandra Walklate, *Victimology: The Victim and the Criminal Justice Process* (London: Unwin Hyman, 1989), p. 91.
3. David Shichor, "Corporate Deviance and Corporate Victimization: A Review and Some Elaborations," *International Review of Victimology*, **1** (1989): 67–88, at pp. 73, 82.
4. S. Box, *Power, Crime and Mystification* (London: Tavistock, 1983), pp. 17, 66.

Questions for Discussion
1. Those injured by corporations may sue the corporation for damages. When an individual is pitted against a giant corporate entity, is the likelihood of a lawsuit an incentive for the corporation to change its practices?
2. Few victims report being victimized. What strategies might induce a larger number of victims of corporate crime to report their victimization to the authorities?

---

ferentiate between the corporations themselves and their executive management personnel."[9] Other criminologists have suggested that the term "white-collar crime" not be used at all; we should speak instead of "corporate crime" and "occupational crime."[10] Generally, however, **white-collar crime** is defined as a violation of the law committed by a person or group of persons in the course of an otherwise respected and legitimate occupation or business enterprise.[11]

Just as white-collar and corporate offenses include a heterogeneous mix of corporate and individual crimes, from fraud, deception, and corruption (as in the S&L case) to pollution of the environment, victims of white-collar crime range from the savvy investor to the unsuspecting consumer. No one person or group is immune.[12] The Vatican lost millions of dollars in a fraudulent stock scheme; fraudulent charities have swindled fortunes from unsuspecting investors; and many banks have been forced into bankruptcy by losses due to deception and fraud.[13]

Crimes Committed by Individuals

As we have noted, white-collar crime occurs during the course of a legitimate occupation or business enterprise. Over time socioeconomic developments have increasingly changed the dimensions of such crimes.[14] Once, people needed only a few business relationships to make their way through life. They dealt with an employer or with employees. They dealt on a basis of trust and confidence with the local shoemaker and grocer. They had virtually no dealings with government.

This way of life has changed significantly and very rapidly during the last few decades. People have become dependent on large bureaucratic structures; they are manipulated by agents and officials with whom they have no personal relationship. This situation creates a basis for potential abuses in four sets of relations:

- Employees of large entities may abuse their authority for private gain by making their services to members of the public contingent on a bribe, a kickback, or some other favor. A corrupt employee of an insurance company, for example, may write a favorable claim assessment in exchange for half of the insurance payment.
- Taking advantage of the complexity and anonymity of a large organization, such as a corporation, employees may abuse the systems available to them or the power they hold within the structure for purposes of unlawful gain, as by embezzlement.
- Members of the public who have to deal with a large organization do not have the faith and trust they had when they dealt with individual merchants. If they see an opportunity to defraud a large organization, they may seize it in the belief that the organization can easily absorb the loss and nobody will be hurt.
- Since the relation of buyer to seller (or of service provider to client) has become increasingly less personal in an age of medical group practice, large law firms, and drugstore chains, opportunities for **occupational crimes**—crimes committed by individuals for themselves in the course of rendering a service—have correspondingly increased.

Medicare fraud, misuse of clients' funds by lawyers and brokers, substitution of inferior goods—all such offenses are occupational crimes.[15]

Types of White-Collar Crimes

White-collar crimes are as difficult to detect as they are easy to commit.[16] The detection mechanisms on which police and government traditionally rely seem singularly inadequate for this vast new body of crimes. Moreover, though people have learned through the ages to be wary of strangers on the street, they have not yet learned to protect themselves against vast enterprises. Much more scientific study has to be undertaken on the causes, extent, and characteristics of white-collar crimes before we can develop workable prevention strategies.[17]

Eight categories of white-collar offenses committed by individuals may be identified:

- Securities-related crimes
- Bankruptcy fraud
- Fraud against the government
- Consumer fraud
- Insurance fraud
- Tax fraud
- Bribery, corruption, and political fraud
- Insider-related fraud[18]

Let us briefly examine each type of crime.

Securities-Related Crimes. State and federal securities laws seek to regulate both the registration and issuance of a security and the employment practices of personnel in the securities industries. After the stock market crash on October 26, 1929, the federal government enacted a series of regulatory laws, including the Securities Act of 1933 and the Securities Exchange Act of 1934, aimed at prohibiting manipulation and deceptive practices. The 1934 act provided for the establishment of the Securities and Exchange Commission (SEC), an organization with broad regulatory and enforcement powers. The SEC is empowered to initiate civil suits and administrative actions and to refer criminal cases to the U.S. Department of Justice.

Even so, crime in the securities field remains common. Four kinds of offenses are prevalent: churning, trading on insider information, stock manipulation, and boiler-room operations.

Churning is the practice of trading a client's shares of stock frequently in order to generate large commissions. A broker earns a commission on every trade, so whether or not the stock traded increases or decreases in value, the broker makes money. Churning is difficult to prove, because brokers typically are allowed some discretion. Therefore, unless the client has given the broker specific instructions in writing, a claim of churning often amounts to no more than the client's word against the broker's.

Insider trading is the use of material, nonpublic, financial information to obtain an unfair advantage in trading securities.[19] A person who has access to confidential corporate information may make significant profits by buying or selling stock on the strength of that information. Dennis Levine, a 34-year-old managing director of the securities firm Drexel Burnham Lambert, used insider information to purchase stock for himself and others in such corporations as International Telephone and Telegraph, Sperry Corporation, Coastal Corporation, American National Resources, and McGraw Edison. After the SEC found out, Levine implicated other Wall Street executives—including Ivan Boesky, who had made millions of dollars in illegal profits.

Stock manipulation is common in the "pink sheets" over-the-counter market, in which some stocks are traded at very low prices, but it is by no means limited to such stocks. Brokers who have a stake in a particular security may make misleading or even false statements to clients to give the impression that the price of the stock is about to rise and thus to create an artificial demand for it.

Boiler rooms are operations run by stock manipulators who, through deception and misleading sales techniques, seduce unsuspecting and uninformed individuals into buying stocks in obscure and often poorly financed corporations. Significant federal legislation has been passed (Penny Stock Reform Act of 1990) to curtail these operations, but the manipulation continues.

Bankruptcy Fraud. The filing of a bankruptcy petition results in proceedings in which the property and financial obligations of an insolvent person or corporation are disposed of. Bankruptcy proceedings are governed by laws enacted to protect insolvent debtors. Unscrupulous persons have devised numerous means to commit **bankruptcy fraud**—any scam designed to take advantage of loopholes in the bank-

ruptcy laws. The most common are the "similar-name" scam, the "old-company" scam, the "new-company" technique, and the "successful-business" scam.

The *similar-name scam* involves the creation of a corporation that has a name similar to that of an established firm. The objective is to create the impression that this new company is actually the older one. If the trick is successful, the swindlers place large orders with established suppliers and quickly resell any merchandise they receive, often to fences. At the same time the swindlers remove all money and assets of the corporation and either file for bankruptcy or wait until creditors sue. Then they leave the jurisdiction or adeptly erase their tracks.

The *old-company scam* involves employees of an already established firm who, motivated by a desire for quick profits, bilk the company of its money and assets and file for bankruptcy. Such a scam is typically used when the company is losing money or has lost its hold on a market.

The *new-company scam* is much like the similar-name scam: A new corporation is formed, credit is obtained, and orders are placed. Once merchandise is received, it is converted into cash with the assistance of a fence. By the time the company is forced into bankruptcy, the architects of this scheme have liquidated the corporation's assets.

The *successful-business scam* involves a profitable corporation that is well positioned in a market but experiences a change in ownership. After the new owners have bilked the corporation of all its money and assets, the firm is forced into bankruptcy.

Fraud against the Government. Governments at all levels are victims of a vast amount of fraud, which includes collusion in bidding, payoffs and kickbacks to government officials, expenditures by a government official that exceed the budget, the filing of false claims, the hiring of friends or associates formerly employed by the government, and offers of inducements to government officials.

Consider, for example, the fall of Wedtech—a military contractor with annual sales in excess of $100 million. At one time the Wedtech Corporation was hailed as the first major employer of blacks and Hispanics in New York City's blighted South Bronx. Before its fall from grace, Wedtech was a high flier on the New York Stock Exchange. What fueled the company? As a minority-controlled business, it won defense contracts without the need to bid. But in early 1986 Wedtech lost its status as a minority business, and by the end of that year the company was in ruins.

Wedtech officials had used fraudulent accounting methods, issued false financial reports, and counted profits before they were received. Caught in the cross fire of charges was Congressman Mario Biaggi, who was later convicted of soliciting bribes in order to obtain special government support for Wedtech. Other company and government officials either pleaded guilty or were convicted.[20]

Is the Wedtech scandal an isolated case? Clearly not. In fiscal 1987 alone, the Department of Defense reported fraud amounting to $53.8 million. And this may be a conservative estimate. In response to a tip from a former Navy employee in 1987, the Federal Bureau of Investigation and the Naval Intelligence Service began a secret 2-year investigation of bribery, fraud, illegal exchanges of information, and collusion at the Pentagon that revealed widespread abuse. This investigation resulted in the issuance of 200 grand-jury subpoenas, as well as the execution of 38 search warrants in 12 states and Washington, D.C.[21]

An important step to curb government contract fraud was taken with the passage of the Major Fraud Act, signed by President Ronald Reagan in November 1988, which creates a separate offense of government contract fraud in excess of $1 million. What kinds of activities does this act cover? Federal prosecutors can seek indictments against contractors who engage in deceptive pricing or overcharging by submitting inaccurate cost and pricing data; mischarging by billing the government for improper or nonallowable charges; collusion in bidding (a conspiracy between presumed competitors to inflate bids); product substitution or the delivery of inferior, nonconforming, or untested goods; or the use of bribes, gratuities, conflicts of interest, and a whole range of techniques designed to influence procurement officials.

Clearly there is more to government-related fraud than the manipulation of contractors and consultants.[22] The Inspector General's Office in the Department of Health and Human Services reported that about $2 billion may by lost annually to fraud in the Medicare program alone.[23] Welfare fraud may amount to as much as 9 percent of the total welfare budget. Fortunately, recent studies suggest that computer programs matching welfare benefits with other information (motor vehicle licenses, voter registrations, income tax returns) may significantly reduce such fraud.

All too frequently, defense contractors and their suppliers have charged outrageous prices for parts used by the military. Senator William Roth (R-Del.) holds up a $640 toilet seat cover.

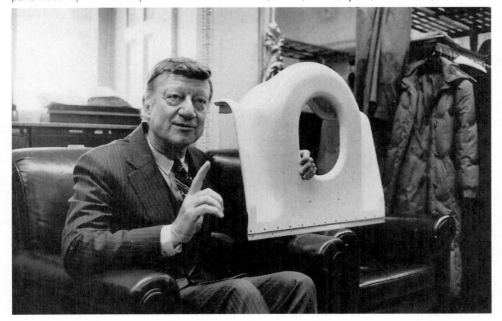

Consumer Fraud. **Consumer fraud** is the act of causing a consumer to surrender money through deceit or a misrepresentation of a material fact. Consumer frauds often appear as confidence games and may take some of the following forms:

- *Home-improvement fraud.* Consumers have been defrauded through the promise of low-cost home renovation. The homeowners give sizable down payments to the contractors, who have no plans to complete the job. In fact, contractors often leave the jurisdiction or declare bankruptcy.
- *Deceptive advertising.* Consumers are often lured into a store by an announcement that a product is priced low for a limited period of time. Once in the store, the customer is told that the product is sold out, and he or she is offered a substitute, typically of inferior quality or at a much higher price. Such schemes are known as "bait-and-switch advertising."
- *Land fraud.* Consumers are easy prey for land-fraud swindlers. Here the pitch is that a certain piece of vacation or retirement property is a worthy investment, many improvements to the property will be made, and many facilities will be made available in the area. Consumers often make purchases of worthless or overvalued land.
- *Business opportunity fraud.* The objective of business opportunity fraud is to persuade a consumer to invest money in a business concern through misrepresentation of its actual worth. Work-at-home frauds are common: Victims are told they can make big money by addressing envelopes at home or performing some other simple task. Consumers lose large sums of money investing in such ventures.

Insurance Fraud. There are many varieties of insurance fraud: Policyholders defraud insurers, insurers defraud the public, management defrauds the public, and third parties defraud insurers. Policyholder fraud is most often accomplished by the filing of false claims for life, fire, marine, or casualty insurance. Sometimes an employee of the insurance company is part of the fraud and assists in the preparation of the claim. The fraud may be simple—a false death claim—or it may become complex when multiple policies are involved.

A different type of insurance fraud is committed when a small group of people create a "shell" insurance firm without true assets. Policies are sold with no intent to pay legitimate claims. In fact, when large claims are presented to shell insurance companies, the firms disband, leaving a trail of policyholder victims. In yet another form of insurance fraud, middle- and upper-level managers of an insurance company loot the firm's assets by removing funds and debiting them as payments of claims to legitimate or bogus policyholders.[24]

Criminologists Paul Tracy and James Fox conducted a field experiment to find out how many auto-body repair shops in Massachusetts inflate repair estimates to insurance companies, and by how much. These researchers rented two Buick Skylarks with moderate damage, a Volvo 740 GLE with superficial damage, and a Ford Tempo with substantial damage. They then obtained 191 repair estimates, some with a clear understanding that the car was insured, others with the understanding that there was no insurance coverage. The results were unequivocal: Repair estimates for insured vehicles were significantly higher than those for noncovered cars. This finding is highly suggestive of fraud.[25]

Tax Fraud. The Internal Revenue Code makes willful failure to file a tax return a misdemeanor. An attempt to evade or defeat a tax, nonpayment of a tax, or willful filing of a fraudulent tax return is a felony. What must the government prove? In order to sustain a conviction, the government must present evidence of income tax due and owing, willful avoidance of payment, and an affirmative act toward tax evasion.[26] How are tax frauds accomplished? Consider the following techniques:

- *Keeping two sets of books.* A person may keep one set of books reflecting actual profits and losses and another set for the purpose of misleading the Internal Revenue Service.
- *Shifting funds.* In order to avoid detection, tax evaders often shift funds continually from account to account, from bank to bank.
- *Faking forms.* Tax evaders often use faked invoices, create fictitious expenses, conceal assets, and destroy books and records.

The IRS lacks the resources to investigate all suspicious tax forms. When the difficulty of distinguishing between careless mistakes and willful evasion is taken into account, the taxes that go uncollected each year are estimated to exceed $100 billion.[27]

Bribery, Corruption, and Political Fraud. Judges who fix traffic tickets in exchange for political favors, municipal employees who speculate with city funds, businesspeople who bribe local politicians to obtain favorable treatment—all are part of the corruption in our municipal, state, and federal governments. The objectives of such offenses vary—favors, special privileges, services, business. The actors include officers of corporations as well as of government; indeed, they may belong to the police or the courts.

Bribery and other forms of corruption are ingrained in the political machinery of local and state governments. Examples abound: Mayors of large cities attempt to obtain favors through bribes; manufacturers pay off political figures for favors; municipal officials demand kickbacks from contractors.[28] In response to the seriousness of political corruption and bribery, Congress established two crimes: It is now a felony to accept a bribe or to provide a bribe.[29] Of course, political bribery and other forms of corruption do not stop at the nation's borders. Kickbacks to foreign officials are common practice.[30]

Corruption can be found in private industry as well. One firm pays another to induce it to use a product or service; a firm pays its own board of directors or officers to dispense special favors; two or more firms, presumably competitors, secretly agree to charge the same prices for their products or services.

Insider-Related Fraud. Insider-related fraud involves the use and misuse of one's position for pecuniary gain or privilege. This category of offenses includes embezzlement, employee-related thefts, and sale of confidential information.

Embezzlement is the conversion (misappropriation) of property or money with which one is entrusted or for which one has a fiduciary responsibility. Yearly losses attributable to embezzlement are estimated at over $1 billion.[31]

Employee-related thefts of company property are responsible for a significant share of industry losses. Estimates place such losses between $4 billion and $13 billion each year. Criminologists John Clark and Richard Hollinger have estimated that the 35 percent rate of employee pilferage in some corporations results primarily from vocational dissatisfaction and a perception of exploitation.[32] And not only goods and services are taken; time and money are at risk as well. Phony payrolls, fictitious overtime charges, false claims for business-related travel, and the like are common.

Finally, in a free marketplace where a premium is placed on competition, corporations must guard against the *sale of confidential information* and trade secrets. The best insurance policy is employee loyalty. Where there is no loyalty, or where loyalty is compromised, abuse of confidential information is possible. The purchase of confidential information from employees willing to commit industrial espionage is estimated to be a multimillion-dollar business.[33]

CORPORATE CRIME

Corporate crime is a criminal act committed by one or more employees of a corporation that is attributed to the organization itself. Between January 1984 and June 1990, an average of 286 corporations were convicted each year in federal courts for offenses ranging from tax law violations to environmental crimes (see Table 13.1). The vast majority of these companies were small- to medium-size privately held corporations. In fact, between November 1, 1987, and June 30, 1995, nearly 80 percent of all corporations convicted had fewer than 100 employees. Only 4.7 percent of all convicted corporations had more than 500 employees.

One problem with corporate crime is defining it. In 1989 the supertanker *Exxon Valdez* ran aground in Prince William Sound, Alaska, spilling 250,000 barrels of oil. The spill became North America's largest ecological disaster. Prosecutors were interested in determining the liability of the captain, his officers, and his crew. But there were additional and far-reaching questions. Was the Exxon Corporation liable? If so, was this a corporate crime?

During the Great Depression thousands of unemployed people heard that there was work to be had in the little West Virginia town of Hawk's Nest, where a huge tunnel was to be dug. Thousands of people came to work for a pittance. The company set the men up in crude camps and put them to work drilling rock for the tunnel project—without masks or other safety equipment. The workers breathed in the silicon dust that filled the air. Many contracted silicosis, a chronic lung disease that leads to certain death. They died by the dozens. Security guards dragged the bodies away and buried them secretly. No one was to

TABLE 13.1 Number of Corporations Sentenced in Federal Courts, 1984–1990

Type of Offense	Year of Sentencing (Number of Offenses)							
	1984	**1985**	**1986**	**1987**	**1988**	**1989**	**1990**	**Total**
Against persons	1	0	0	0	0	0	0	1
Property	5	8	15	9	12	12	11	72
Public officials	5	4	6	4	—	6	4	29
Drugs	1	4	2	2	—	3	0	12
Racketeering	12	4	5	2	10	4	3	40
Fraud and deceit	116	94	128	105	109	82	55	689
Obscenity	0	4	1	1	—	15	8	29
Civil rights	2	1	3	2	—	0	0	8
Administration of justice	7	0	2	2	—	2	0	13
Public safety	5	3	1	0	—	2	2	13
Immigration	0	1	1	0	—	4	0	6
National defense	11	6	4	4	18	6	4	53
Food and drug laws	38	37	32	23	9	14	14	167
Environmental	10	24	17	8	28	28	21	136
Antitrust	93	70	47	68	98	58	23	457
Monetary transactions	0	0	0	0	8	5	3	16
Taxation	21	35	16	26	14	26	16	154
Other offenses	17	16	22	13	21	6	2	97
Total	344	311	302	269	328	273	173	2000

Source: United States Sentencing Committee Guidelines for Organizations, Supplementary Report, 1991, p. D10.

know. The work went on. The deaths multiplied. Who was to blame? The corporation?[34]

Theories of Corporate Liability

A *corporation* is an artificial person created by state charter. The charter provides such an entity with the right to engage in certain activities—to buy and sell certain goods or to run a railroad, for instance. The charter limits the liability of the persons who own the corporation (the shareholders) to the extent of the value of their investment (their shares). The corporation thus is an entity separate from the people who own or manage it. This convenient form of pooling resources for commercial purposes, with a view toward profiting from one's investment, has had a significant impact on the development of the United States as a commercial and industrial power. Moreover, millions of wage earners whose savings or union funds are invested in corporate stocks and bonds reap dividends from such investments in the form of income or retirement benefits.

But what if a senior official of a corporation engages in unlawful activity? Can we say that the corporation committed the crime? If so, what can be done about it?[35] Initially corporations were considered incapable of committing crimes. After all, crimes require *mens rea*, an awareness of wrongdoing. Since corporations are bodies without souls, they were deemed to be incapable of forming the requisite sense of wrongdoing. Nor could a corporation be imprisoned for its crimes. Further, corporations were not authorized to commit crimes; they were authorized only to engage in the business for which they had been chartered.

A different theory of corporate criminal liability eventually emerged when courts and legislators began to ask why corporations should not be considered "legal persons" subject to all the laws of "human persons." And so it was decided in 1909.[36] Thereafter, the theory that a corporation can be held accountable for criminal acts was widened, until the Model Penal Code broadly subjected corporations to liability for most criminal offenses, especially those that were "authorized, requested, commanded, performed or recklessly tolerated by the board of directors or by a high managerial agent acting in behalf of the corporation within the scope of his office or employment."[37]

Governmental Control of Corporations

Corporate misconduct is covered by a broad range of federal and state statutes, including the federal conspiracy laws; the Racketeer Influenced and Corrupt Organizations (RICO) Act; federal securities laws; mail-fraud statutes; the Federal Corrupt Practices

Act; the Federal Election Campaign Act; legislation on lobbying, bribery, and corruption; the Internal Revenue Code (especially as regards major tax crimes, slush funds, and improper payments); the Bank Secrecy Act; and federal provisions on obstruction of justice, perjury, and false statements.

The underlying theory is that if the brain of the artificial person (usually the board of directors of the corporation) authorizes or condones the act in question, the body (the corporation) must suffer criminal penalty. That seems fair enough, except for the fact that if the corporation gets punished—usually by a substantial fine—the penalty falls on the shareholders, most of whom had no say in the corporate decision. And the financial loss resulting from the fine may be passed on to the consumer. The counterargument, of course, is that shareholders often benefit from the illegal actions of the corporation. Thus, in fairness, they should suffer some detriment or loss when and if the corporation is apprehended and convicted.

Reliance on Civil Penalties.

Beginning in the nineteenth century, corporations were suspected of wielding monopolistic power to the detriment of consumers. The theory behind monopoly is simple: If you buy out all your competitors or drive them out of business, then you are the only one from whom people can buy the product you sell. So you can set the price, and you set it very high, for your profit and to the detriment of the consumers. The Sugar Trust was one such monopoly. A few powerful businessmen eliminated all competitors and then drove the price of sugar up, to the detriment of the public. Theodore Roosevelt fought and broke up the Sugar Trust.

In 1890 Congress passed the **Sherman Antitrust Act,** which effectively limited the exercise of monopolies.[38] The act prohibited any contract, conspiracy, or combination of business interests in restraint of foreign or interstate trade. This legislation was followed by the Clayton Antitrust Act (1914), which further curbed the ability of corporations to enrich their shareholders at the expense of the public by prohibiting such acts as price-fixing.[39] But the remedies this act provided consisted largely of splitting up monopolistic enterprises or imposing damages, sometimes triple damages, for the harm caused. In a strict sense, this was not a use of the criminal law to govern corporate misconduct.

Criminal Liability.

A movement away from exclusive reliance on civil remedies was apparent in the 1960s, when it was discovered that corporate mismanagement or negligence on the part of officers or employees could inflict vast harm on identifiable groups of victims. Negligent management at a nuclear power plant can result in the release of radiation and injury to thousands or millions of people. The marketing of an unsafe drug can cause crippling deformities in tens of thousands of bodies.[40] Violation of environmental standards can cause injury and suffering to generations of people who will be exposed to unsafe drinking water, harmful air, or eroded soil. The manufacture of hazardous products can result in multiple deaths.[41]

The problem of corporate criminal liability since the 1960s, then, goes far beyond an individual death or injury. Ultimately it concerns the health and even the survival of humankind. Nor is the problem confined to the United States. It is a global problem. It thus becomes necessary to look at the variety of activities attributable to corporations which in recent years have been recognized as particularly harmful to society.

When it comes to proving corporate criminal liability, prosecutors face formidable problems: Day-to-day corporate activity has a low level of visibility. Regulatory agencies that monitor corporate conduct have different and uncoordinated recording systems. Offending corporations operate in a multitude of jurisdictions, some of which regard a given activity as criminal, while others do not. Frequently the facts of a case are not adjudicated at a trial; the parties may simply agree on a settlement approved by the court. The accused corporation may be permitted to plead *nolo contendere* ("no contest") in return for an agreed-upon fine or settlement.

Investigating Corporate Crime

We know very little about the extent of economic criminality in the United States. There is no national data base for the assessment of corporate criminality, and corporations are not likely to release information about their own wrongdoing. The situation is worse in other countries, and worst in the developing countries of Africa south of the Sahara, where few national crime statistics are kept and where corporations are least subject to governmental control. Yet the evidence in regard to corporate crime is gradually coming in.[42]

As we noted earlier, the first American criminologist who was alert to the potential for harm in corporate conduct was Edwin Sutherland, who described the criminal behavior of 70 of the 200 largest production corporations in his 1946 book *White Collar Crime*.[43] An even more ambitious study was completed by Marshall B. Clinard and Peter C. Yeager, who investigated corporations within the jurisdiction of 25 federal agencies during 1975 and 1976. Of 477 major American corporations whose conduct was regulated by these agencies, 60 percent had violated the law. Of the 300 violating corporations, 38 (or 13 percent) accounted for 52 percent of all violations charged in 1975 and 1976, an average of 23.5 violations per firm.[44] Large corporations were found to be the chief violators, and a few particular industries (pharmaceutical, automotive) were the most likely to violate the law.

According to Clinard and Yeager, what makes it so difficult to curb corporate crime is the enormous political power corporations wield in the shaping and administration of the laws that govern their conduct. This is particularly the case in regard to multinational corporations that wish to operate in developing countries. The promise of jobs and development by a giant corporation is a temptation too great for the governments of many such countries to resist. They would rather have employment opportunities that pollute air and water than unemployment in a clean environment. Government officials in some Third World countries can be bribed to create or maintain a legal climate favorable to the business interests of the corporation, even though it may be detrimental to the people of the host country.

The work of Sutherland, Clinard and Yeager, and other traditional scholars, as well as that of a group of radical criminologists;[45] hearings on white-collar and corporate crime held by the Subcommittee on Crime of the House Judiciary Committee, under the leadership of Congressman John Conyers, Jr., in 1978; the consumer protection movement, spearheaded by Ralph Nader; and recent investigative reporting by the press have all contributed to public awareness of large corporations' power to inflict harm on large population groups.

In 1975 James Q. Wilson still considered such crime to be insignificant,[46] but more recent studies show that the public considers corporate criminality at least as serious as, if not more serious than, street crime. Marvin Wolfgang and his associates found in a national survey that Americans regard illegal retail price-fixing (the artificial setting of prices at a high level, without regard for the demand for the product) as a more serious crime than robbery committed with a lead pipe.[47] Within the sphere of corporate criminality perhaps no other group of offenses has had so great an impact on public consciousness as crimes against the environment. As we shall see, however, enforcement of major environmental statutes has been weak in the past. There is some evidence that this is changing.

Environmental Crimes

Warren D. Mooney makes life sweet—sodas, candies. His company, Liquid Sugars Inc., is the confection in Jelly Belly, the gourmet bean that everyone chewed after presidential candidate Ronald Reagan said they were his favorite.

On Friday, Mooney was indicted by the federal grand jury in Sacramento on nine felony counts, including conspiracy to pollute. Prosecutors say they are strictly enforcing the law; the defense calls it "justice run amok."

If found guilty of violating the Clean Water Act, Mooney could be sentenced to 29 years in jail and be fined $2.25 million. The company faces a fine of $4.5 million.

The indictments concluded a two-year investigation into Liquid Sugars, a company headquartered in Emeryville, managed by Mooney and accused of violating water-pollution laws at its Port of Stockton facility. The company blends sweeteners for manufacturers—its most notable client being Jelly Belly maker Herman Goelitz Candy Co. of Fairfield.

Mooney and Liquid Sugars are charged with dumping into the Stockton sewer waste water trucked from Goelitz's Fairfield facility. The waste was water contaminated with sweetener from washing down the equipment that produces exotically flavored beans—buttered popcorn, toasted marshmallow, piña colada.

Similarly, the indictment said the company trucked in waste water from a second customer, pickle-maker G. L. Mezzetta of Sonoma.

In addition to conspiracy, Liquid Sugars is charged with violating regulations imposed on industries that dump waste into sewers: four counts of dumping into the sewer waste hauled in from elsewhere, and four counts of dumping into the system waste with a pH below 5.[48]

The world's legal systems include few effective laws and mechanisms to curb destruction of the environment. The emission of noxious fumes into the air and the discharge of pollutants into the water have until recently been regarded as common law nuisances at the level of misdemeanors, commanding usually no more than a small fine. Industrial polluters could easily absorb such a fine and regard it as a kind of business tax. Only in 1969 did Congress pass the National Environmental Policy Act (NEPA). Among other things, the act created the Environmental Protection Agency (EPA). It requires environmental impact studies so that any new development that would significantly affect the environment can be prevented or controlled.

The EPA is charged with enforcing federal statutes and assisting in the enforcement of state laws enacted to protect the environment. The agency monitors plant discharges all over the country and may take action against private industry or municipal governments. Yet during the first 5 years of its existence the EPA referred only 130 cases to the U.S. Department of Justice for criminal prosecution, and only 6 of these involved major corporate offenders.[49] The government actually charged only one of the corporations, Allied Chemical, which admitted responsibility for 940 misdemeanor counts of discharging toxic chemicals into the Charles River in Virginia, thereby causing 80 people to become ill.[50]

A 1979 report of the General Accounting Office stated that the EPA inadequately monitored, inaccurately reported, and ineffectively enforced the nation's basic law on air pollution, although the agency's then chief contended that corrective action had been taken during the previous year.[51] The situation improved during the 1980s, but the environment is far from safe. Catastrophic releases of toxic and even nuclear substances, usually attributable to inadequate safeguards and human negligence, pose a particularly grave hazard, as the disasters at Bhopal in India and at Chernobyl in the former Soviet Union have demonstrated.

Enforcing Legislation. The difficulties of enforcing legislation designed to protect the environment are enormous. Consider the 250,000 barrels of oil spilled by the *Exxon Valdez* in 1989. What legislation could have prevented the disaster? Developing effective laws to protect the environment is a complex problem. It is far easier to define the crimes of murder and theft than to define acts of pollution, which are infinitely varied. A particular challenge is the separation of harmful activities from socially useful ones. Moreover, pollution is hard to quantify. How much of a chemical must be discharged into water before the discharge is considered noxious and subjects the polluter to punishment? Discharge of a gallon by one polluter may not warrant punishment, and a small

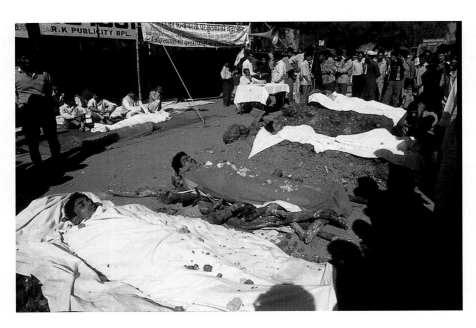

A catastrophic explosion at the Union Carbide plant in Bhopal, India, on December 2, 1984, spewed clouds of deadly gas, causing nearly 6,500 fatalities and more than 20,000 injuries.

quantity may not even be detectable. But what do we do with a hundred polluters, each of whom discharges a gallon?

Many other issues must be addressed as well. For instance, should accidental pollution warrant the same punishment as intentional or negligent pollution? Since many polluters are corporations, what are the implications of penalties that force a company to install costly antipollution devices? To cover the costs, the corporation may have to increase the price of its product, and so the consumer pays. Should the company be allowed to lower plant workers' wages instead? Should the plant be forced or permitted to shut down, thereby increasing unemployment in the community? The company may choose to move its plant to another state or country that is more hospitable.

Addressing Sensitive Issues. Fines imposed on intentional polluters have been increased so that they can no longer be shrugged off as an ordinary cost of doing business. The General Electric Company was fined $7 million and the Allied Chemical Corporation $13.2 million for pollution offenses. Fines of such magnitude are powerful incentives to corporations to limit pollution. But since many of the enterprises that are likely to pollute are in the public sector, or produce for the public sector, the public ultimately will have to pay the fine in the form of increased gas or electricity bills.[52]

In the Third World, problems of punishing and preventing pollution are enormous. Industries preparing to locate there have the power to influence governments and officials, surreptitiously and officially, into passing legislation favorable to the industry. The desire to industrialize outweighs the desire to preserve the environment. Some countries find ways to address the problem, only to relinquish controls when they prove irksome. While Japan was trying to establish its industrial dominance, for example, it observed a constitutional provision stating: "The conservation of life environment shall be balanced against the needs of economic development."[53] This provision was deleted in 1970, when Japan had achieved economic strength.

Developing Effective Legislation. U.S. legislators have several options in developing legislation to protect the environment:

- *The independent use of the criminal sanction: direct prohibition of polluting activities.* This is the way American legislators have typically tried to cope with the problem in the past. They simply made it a criminal offense to maintain a "nuisance," that is, an ongoing activity that pollutes the water, the soil, or the air.

- *The dependent-direct use of the criminal sanction: prohibition of certain polluting activities that exceed specified limits.* This is a more sophisticated legislative method. If pollution is to be kept at a low level, no one person or company can be allowed to emit more than an insignificant amount of noxious waste into the environment. This amount is fixed by administrative regulation. Anyone who exceeds the limit commits a criminal offense.

- *The dependent-indirect approach: criminal sanction reserved for firms that fail to comply with specific rulings rendered by administrative organs against violators of standards.* Under this option, polluters have already been identified by regulatory agencies, and they are now under order to comply with the agencies' requirements. If they violate these orders, a criminal punishment can be imposed.

- *The preventive use of the criminal sanction: penalties imposed for failure to install or maintain prescribed antipollution equipment.* This is the newest and most sophisticated means of regulating polluting industries. The law determines what preventive and protective measures must be taken (to filter industrial waste water, to put chemical screens on smokestacks, and so on). Any firm that fails to take the prescribed measures is guilty of a violation.[54]

In the past, legal systems relied primarily on the independent use of the criminal sanction. More recent legislation has concentrated on administrative orders and technological prevention.

Curbing Corporate Crime

Laws and regulations prescribing criminal sanctions have been passed and continue to be passed to guard the public against the dangers rooted in the power of corporate enterprise. Recently, for example, Congress passed new sentencing guidelines for corporations in federal courts. These guidelines significantly

DANGEROUS GROUND: THE WORLD OF HAZARDOUS WASTE CRIME

What kind of person would illegally dump hazardous waste into the waterways and landscapes of America? Many would guess it might be a sinister organized crime operator. Some past published works on hazardous waste crime have, in fact, described this area of crime as being synonymous with syndicate crime.

This is the introduction to criminologist Donald J. Rebovich's controversial book *Dangerous Ground: The World of Hazardous Waste Crime,* in which he reports the results of an empirical study of hazardous waste offenders in four states. (1) He continues:

Surprisingly enough, the study has found that, most commonly, the criminal dumper is an ordinary, profit-motivated businessman who operates in a business where syndicate crime activity may be present but by no means pervasive. The research uncovers a criminal world of the hazardous waste offender unlike any theorized in the past. It is a world where the intensity, duration, and methods of the criminal act will be more likely determined by the criminal opportunities available in the legitimate marketplace than by the orders of a controlling criminal syndicate.

Rebovich's portrait of hazardous waste crime replaces our ideas about midnight dumping and masked dumpers with straightforward descriptions of hazardous waste treatment/storage/disposal (TSD) facilities failing to comply with state and federal regulations:

The mark of a successful hazardous waste criminal—one who can maintain his criminal lifestyle for a lengthy duration—is his skill in effectively analyzing the potential threats to his livelihood and his versatility in adapting to those threats. For many TSD-facility operators, the serious game of working the system was played out by eluding the regulatory inspectors by capitalizing on either the inspectors' unfamiliarity with treatment apparatus or their lack of diligence in inspecting thoroughly.

TSD-facility offenders did have to contend with monitoring devices, installed by regulators, that were used to gauge volume and properties of effluents released into local sewer systems to determine compliance with existing discharge standards. The mechanisms were intended to sample effluents randomly but, in reality, offenders found the system seriously flawed and did not hesitate to seize their opportunities to work the system in a new way. . . . The tests were simply rigged to elicit a false impression

of the toxicity of the substances discharged into the sewer.

Rebovich makes this prediction:

The characteristics of future hazardous waste offenders, and the crimes that they commit, will more than likely be determined by developments in several areas external to the criminal act: (1) pressure from the general public and public interest groups for stricter enforcement, (2) legislative expansion of the scope of legal coverage, (3) redesigned enforcement, and (4) future availability of affordable disposal outlets. These areas can be seen as the components of an equation that could lead to a reduction in hazardous waste crime.

Source
1. Donald J. Rebovich, *Dangerous Ground: The World of Hazardous Waste Crime* (New Brunswick, N.J.: Transaction, 1992).

Questions for Discussion
1. Illegal hazardous waste practices may be punished by fining the company or industry. Should individuals be punished as well?
2. Some TSD-facility operators have claimed that they were forced to use illegal practices because it is economically impossible to take care of hazardous wastes under current regulations. What is your reaction to such a defense?

increased corporate sanctions, but at the same time allowed companies large reductions in fines where there was evidence of organizational due diligence— that is, implementation of effective ethics compliance programs.[55] While such laws, regulations, and guidelines may provide some disincentives for illegal acts, many governments recognize that criminal justice systems are not well prepared to deal with economic

crimes, both in terms of strategy and in terms of resources.[56] They also recognize the importance of attacking this problem at the international level, perhaps by designing strategies, standards, and guidelines that may be helpful to all governments.[57]

A disturbing thought remains: Is the imposition of criminal liability for the conduct of corporations on the corporations themselves really the best way to curb corporate misconduct? If corporations act on the decisions of their principal officers or agents, might it not be appropriate to restrict the reach of the law to these corporate actors rather than to subject the innocent and uninformed shareholders to financial loss? Why not rely more on administrative and civil proceedings? Both can and often do contain penalties that exceed those of the criminal law.

ORGANIZED CRIME

Earlier we noted that all forms of organizational criminality have in common the use of business enterprises for illegal profit. We have recognized some significant problems not only with existing definitions and conceptualizations of white-collar and corporate crime but with the criminal justice response to such offenses. Similar problems arise in efforts to deal with organized crime. It, too, depends on business enterprises. And like corporate crime, organized crime comes in so many varieties that attempts to define it precisely lead to frustration.

The difficulty of gaining access to information on organized crime has also hindered attempts to conceptualize the problems posed by this kind of law violation. Finally, law enforcement efforts have been inadequate to control the influence of organized crime. As will be evident, a greater effort must be made to uncover the nature, pattern, and extent of organized crime.

The History of Organized Crime

Organized crime had its origin in the great wave of immigrants from southern Italy (especially from Sicily) to the United States between 1875 and 1920. These immigrants came from an environment that historically had been hostile to them. Suppressed by successive bands of invaders and alien rulers dating back some 800 years before Christ, Sicily was first coveted as a strategic location between major Mediterranean trade routes by the Greeks and Phoenicians. In later centuries Roman, Byzantine, Arab, Norman, German, Spanish, Austrian, and French soldiers all laid siege and claim to Sicily. Exploited by mostly absentee landlords with their armies, Sicilians had learned to survive by relying on the strength of their own families. Indeed, these families had undergone little change since Greco-Roman times, two millennia earlier.

A traditional Sicilian family has been described as an extended family, or clan; it includes lineal relations (grandparents, parents, children, grandchildren) and lateral relations through the paternal line—uncles, aunts, and cousins as far as the bloodline can be traced. This *famiglia* is hierarchically organized and administered by the head of the family, the *capo di famiglia* (the Romans called him *pater familias*), to whom all members owe obedience and loyalty. Strangers, especially those in positions of power in state or church, are not to be trusted. The importance of the family is evident in the famous Sicilian proverb: *"La legge e' per l ricchi, La forca e' per l poveri, E la giustizie e' per l buffoni."* (The law is for the rich, the gallows are for the poor, and justice is for the fools.) For Sicilians all problems are resolved within the family, which must be kept strong. Its prestige, honor, wealth, and power have to be defended and strengthened, sometimes through alliances with more distant kin.[58]

Throughout history these strong families have served each other and Sicily. Upon migration to the United States, members of Sicilian families soon found that the social environment in their new country was as hostile as that of the old. Aspirations were encouraged, yet legitimate means to realize them were often not available. And the new country seemed already to have an established pattern for achieving wealth and power by unethical means. Many of America's great fortunes—those of the Astors, the Vanderbilts, the Goulds, the Sages, the Stanfords, the Rockefellers, the Carnegies, the Lords, the Harrimans—had been made by cunning, greed, and exploitation.

As time passed, new laws were enacted to address conspiracies in restraint of trade and other economic offenses. Yet by the time the last wave of Sicilian immigrants reached the United States, the names of the great robber barons were connected with major universities, foundations, and charitable institutions.[59] At the local level, the Sicilian immigrants found themselves involved in a system of politics in which patronage and protection were dispensed by corrupt politicians and petty hoodlums from earlier immigrant groups—German, Irish, and Jewish. The Sicilian family structure helped its members to survive in this hostile environment. It also created the organizational basis that permitted them to respond to the

WINDOW TO THE WORLD

THE BUSINESS OF ORGANIZED CRIME

Have you ever asked yourself (or anyone else) what the world's largest business is? Oil? Autos? Computers? Steel? It's none of these: Drug and arms trafficking by major crime syndicates take first and second place.(1) The United Nations estimates that the combined annual sales from organized crime ranges from $700 billion to $1000 billion annually. Trafficking in narcotics alone exceeds $300 billion each year.(2)

Much of the expansion of organized crime in recent years has been made possible by the fragile political and economic situation of developing and transitional countries. A prime example is post–cold war Russia. Enticed by the weakened judicial system, reduced law enforcement, and a susceptible bureaucracy, organized-crime groups such as the Russian and Sicilian Mafias have established a firm hold on the ex-Soviet states. Organized crime has moved in, shielded by the need for foreign capital investment. The Russian Mafia alone, with over 3 million members in 5700 gangs, controls approximately one-quarter of the commercial and retail banks, as well as tens of thousands of other legitimate businesses. Gangs traffic in everything from raw material to nuclear weapons.

The infiltration of organized crime into legitimate businesses poses a particularly significant threat to the emerging economic order of transitional economies. Politically and economically, the Mafia is becoming part of the business culture in certain markets. "Instead of being a threat to the legal order, the Mafia is becoming its rival and even its replacement. Wherever and whenever the state fails to fulfill the basic needs of its people, this creates a vacuum which the criminals can exploit."(3)

The effects of the infiltration of organized crime are unmistakable. On November 21, 1994, member states of the United Nations gathered in Naples, Italy, at the World Ministerial Conference on Organized Crime. One conclusion was very clear: "Traditionally insular and clannish, the world powers of crime—the Hong Kong–based Triads, the Cali Cartel of Columbia, the Italian Mafia, the Japanese Yakuza, the Russian Vory v. Zakonye and affiliated newcomers, and rapidly expanding West African crime groups—are now making deals with each other and taking tentative steps to maximize their operations."(4) The cooperative nature of organized crime has changed the realities of law enforcement efforts. The policing of organized crime is no longer a regional or local endeavor. To control the effects of the single largest business in the world, law enforcement efforts must also be transnational and cooperative.

Among the steps called for at the conference:

- Global assessment and regular monitoring of organized transnational crime
- New legislation, both substantive (against the crimes) and procedural (against the criminals)
- Special cooperative programs and preventive strategies
- A concerted attack on money laundering to chip away at the economic advantage of organized transnational crime and criminals

Here is why the steps are needed: Each national criminal group, as the table which follows shows, is allied with most of the others across the globe.

---

opportunity created when, on January 16, 1920, the Eighteenth Amendment to the Constitution outlawed the manufacture, sale, and transportation of alcoholic beverages.

Howard Abadinsky explains what happened:

> Prohibition acted as a catalyst for the mobilization of criminal elements in an unprecedented manner. Pre-prohibition crime, insofar as it was organized, centered around corrupt political machines, vice entrepreneurs, and, at the bottom, gangs. Prohibition unleashed an unparalleled level of competitive criminal violence and changed the order—the gang leaders emerged on top.[60]

During the early years of Prohibition, the names of the most notorious bootleggers, mobsters, and gangsters sounded German, Irish, and Jewish: Arthur Flegenheimer (better known as "Dutch Schultz"), Otto Gass, Bo and George Weinberg, Arnold Rothstein, John T. Nolen (better known as "Legs Diamond"), Vincent "Mad Dog" Coll, Waxey Gordon, Owney Madden, and Joe Rock. By the time Prohibition was repealed, Al Capone, Salvatore Luciana (better known as "Lucky Luciano"), Frank Costello, Johnny Torrio, Vito Genovese, Guiseppe Doto (better known as "Joe Adonis"), and many other Sicilians were preeminent in the underworld. They had become folk heroes and role models for young boys in the Italian ghettos, many of whom were to seek their own places in this new society.

Sicilian families were every bit as ruthless in establishing their crime empires as the earlier immi-

WINDOW TO THE WORLD

Organization	Size	Major Activities	International Ties
Colombian cartels	Hundreds of men	Drug trafficking—manage entire cycle from production to distribution	U.S. and Sicilian Cosa Nostra, Chinese Triads, Japanese Yakuza
Chinese Triads (Hong Kong and Taiwan)	150,000 in 5 groups	Drugs, usury, illegal immigration, gambling, racketeering, prostitution, money laundering	Colombian cartels, Japanese Yakuza, U.S. groups
Russian Mafia	3 million in 5700 gangs	Trafficking in everything—army weapons, nuclear materials, drugs, money laundering, prostitution, counterfeiting	Settlements in the U.S., Colombian cartels, Sicilian Cosa Nostra
Sicilian Cosa Nostra	5000 members	International drug trafficking clearinghouse, money laundering on a grand scale, arms trafficking, extortion	U.S. Cosa Nostra, Colombian cartels, Mafia families in Western Europe, Russian Mafia, Chinese Triads
U.S. Cosa Nostra	3000 soldiers in 25 families	Drug trafficking, arms, illegal gambling, prostitution, extortion, business activities	Colombian cartels, Russian Mafia, Sicilian Cosa Nostra
Japanese Yakuza	60,000 full time, 25,000 associates, in 1246 clans	Amphetamine traffic in Asia and U.S., extortion, prostitution	Chinese Triads, Colombian cartels, German groups, Russian Mafia, U.S. Cosa Nostra

Sources

1. ANSA News Agency Dossier on Organized Crime, *U.N. World Ministerial Conference on Organized Transnational Crime,* Naples, Italy, Nov. 21–23, 1994.

2. Id at 22.
3. "Russian Organized Crime," *Jane's Intelligence Review,* **8** (May 1, 1996): 195.
4. *U.N. World Ministerial Conference,* p. 6.

Questions for Discussion

1. Why is organized crime the world's largest business?
2. What efforts to control the rise of organized crime seem most promising?

grant groups had been. They were so successful in their domination of organized crime that, especially after World War II, organized crime became virtually synonymous with the Sicilian Mafia.

The term "Mafia" appears to derive from an Arabic word denoting "place of refuge." The concept, which was adopted in Sicily during the era of Arab rule, gradually came to describe a mode of life and survival. Sicilians trace the word to a tale of revenge that took place on Easter Monday, 1282. On this day, a French soldier who was part of a band of marauding foreigners raped a Sicilian woman on her wedding day. Following the assault, bands of Sicilians went to the streets of Palermo to slaughter hundreds of Frenchmen, spurred on by the screams of the young

girl's mother: "Ma fia, ma fia," ("My daughter, my daughter").[61]

Ultimately, the **Mafia** became the entirety of those Sicilian families that were loosely associated with one another in operating organized crime, both in America and in Sicily.[62] The first realistic depiction of the organization of the Mafia came with the testimony of Joseph Valachi before the Senate's McClellan Committee in 1963. Valachi, a disenchanted soldier in New York's Genovese crime family, was the first member of Italian organized crime to describe a quasi-military secret criminal syndicate. From that point on, the Mafia has also been referred to as *La Cosa Nostra,* literally translated as "this thing of ours."[63]

Despite Valachi's testimony and later revelations, some scholars still doubt the existence of a Sicilian-based American crime syndicate. To the criminologist Jay Albanese, for instance:

> [I]t is clear . . . that despite popular opinion which has for many years insisted on the existence of a secret criminal society called "the Mafia," which somehow evolved from Italy, many separate historical investigations have found no evidence to support such a belief.[64]

The Structure and Impact of Organized Crime

Americans have felt the impact of organized crime, and they have followed the media coverage of the mob wars and their victims with fascination. But little was known about the Mafia's actual structure in the United States until a succession of government investigations began to unravel its mysteries. The major investigations were conducted by the Committee on Mercenary Crimes, in 1932; the Special Senate Committee to Investigate Organized Crime in Interstate Commerce (the Kefauver Crime Committee), from 1950 to 1951; the Senate Permanent Subcommittee on Investigations (the McClellan Committee), from 1956 to 1963; President Lyndon Johnson's Commission on Law Enforcement and Administration of Justice (the Task Force on Organized Crime), from 1964 to 1967; and the President's Commission on Organized Crime, which reported to President Reagan in 1986 and 1987.[65]

The findings of these investigations established the magnitude of organized crime in the United States. It had become an empire almost beyond the reach of government, with vast resources derived from a virtual monopoly on gambling and loan-sharking, drug trafficking, pornography and prostitution, labor racketeering, murder for hire, the control of local crime activities, and the theft and fencing of securities, cars, jewels, and consumer goods of all sorts.[66] Above all, it was found that organized crime had infiltrated a vast variety of legitimate businesses, such as stevedoring (the loading and unloading of ships), the fish and meat industries, the wholesale and retail liquor industry (including bars and taverns), the vending machine business, the securities and investment business, the waste disposal business, and the construction industry.[67]

Specific legislation and law enforcement programs have allowed governmental agencies to assert some measure of control over organized crime. Cases

"I TAKE IT YOU'RE ALSO IN THE FEDERAL WITNESS-PROTECTION PROGRAM."

have been successfully prosecuted under the **Racketeer Influenced and Corrupt Organizations (RICO) Act** of 1970.[68] This statute attacks racketeering activities by prohibiting the investment of any funds derived from racketeering in any enterprise that is engaged in interstate commerce. In addition, the **Federal Witness Protection Program,** established under the Organized Crime Control Act of 1970, has made it easier for witnesses to testify in court by guaranteeing them a new identity, thus protecting them against revenge. Currently 14,000 witnesses are in the program.[69]

The information provided by the governmental commissions, in combination with scholarly research, has established that the structure of an organized crime group is similar to that of a Sicilian family. Family members are joined by "adopted" members; the family is then aided at the functional level by nonmember auxiliaries.[70] The use of military designations such as *caporegima* ("lieutenant") and "soldier" does not alter the fact that a criminal organization is rather more like a closely knit family business enterprise than like an army.[71] On the basis of testimony presented by Joseph Valachi in 1963, the commission's Task Force on Organized Crime was able to construct an organization chart of the typical Mafia, or Cosa Nostra, family (Figure 13.1).

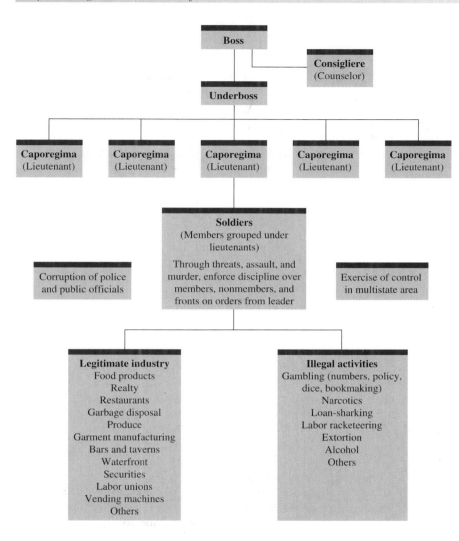

FIGURE 13.1 Organization chart of the typical Mafia family.
Source: President's Commission on Law Enforcement and Administration of Justice, *Task Force Report: Organized Crime* (Washington, D.C.: U.S. Government Printing Office, 1967), p. 9.

Relations among the various families which were formerly determined in ruthlessly fought gang wars have more recently been facilitated by a loosely formed coordinating body called "the Commission." By agreement, the country has been divided into territorial areas of jurisdiction, influence, and operation. These arrangements are subject to revision from time to time, by mutual agreement. Likewise, rules of conduct have become subject to control or regulation by the heads of the various crime families. They consider, for example, to what extent each family should enter the hard-drug market, how much violence should be used, and how each will deal with public officials and the police.[72]

Informants at the "convention" of the so-called Apalachin conspirators provided a rare opportunity to learn about the way crime families reach agreement on their operations. On November 14, 1957, 63 of the country's most notorious underworld figures were arrested in Apalachin, New York, at or near the home of Joseph M. Barbara, a well-known organized-crime figure. Participants included New York's Vito Genovese, Carlo Gambino, Paul Castellano, and Joe Bonnano. Also arrested were Florida's don, Santo Trafficante, Jr.; Sam ("Momo") Giancana of Chicago; Detroit boss Joe Zerilli; and the boss of the Buffalo rackets, Stefano Magaddino. Apparently they had congregated at Barbara's home to settle a dispute among the families, which had three weeks earlier resulted in the assassination of Mangano family boss Albert Anastasia (the Mangano family was predecessor to the largest contemporary crime family in the

United States, the Gambino crime family) and the attempted murder in May 1957 of Francesco Castiglia, better known as Frank Costello, by the current godfather of the Genovese crime family, Vincent "The Chin" Gigante.

The presence of so many out-of-state license plates on brand new Cadillacs and Lincolns in this small upstate New York town caught the attention of New York State Police Sergeant Edgar Croswell, an amateur organized-crime buff. Croswell, already somewhat suspicious of the true nature of Barbara's business dealings, put in a call to federal authorities and arranged to have a roadblock set up to guard against any of the participants leaving without being questioned. The police presence didn't go unnoticed by the gangsters, who rushed to make a quick escape back to their fiefdoms.

The comical scene of men in silk suits and fedora hats running through the forest was enough for Croswell. He caught as many as he could and placed them under arrest. None of the conspirators, however, publicly revealed the true nature of their meeting. Some suggested that, quite by coincidence, all had simply come to visit their sick friend Joe Barbara, who would die of a heart attack 2 years later.

All were indicted and convicted for refusing to answer the grand jury's questions about the true purpose of the meeting. The convictions were subsequently reversed.[73]

Certain core business matters were decided at that meeting:

- Carlo Gambino was given the leadership of the New York crime family that still bears his name, a family made famous by the more recent exploits of John Gotti.
- As a vote of confidence for Vito Genovese, Frank Costello was asked to go into semiretirement to pave the way for Genovese to take over the family that Lucky Luciano had started.
- A ban was placed on any "made man" trafficking in drugs. "If you deal, you die" was the slogan that resonated throughout organized crime as of the late 1950s. Although widely ignored, the ban still exists today.

The activities of the Mafia appear to have shifted from the once extremely violent bootlegging and street crime operations to a far more sophisticated level of criminal activity.[74] Modern organized crime

The funeral procession of Chinatown crime boss Benny Ong, August 19, 1994. Ong was the undisputed leader of New York City's Chinese gangs.

has assumed international dimensions.[75] It extends not only to international drug traffic, but also to such legitimate enterprises as real estate and trade in securities, as well as to many other lucrative business enterprises. This transition has been accomplished both by extortion and by entry with laundered money derived from illegitimate activity. It is tempting to wonder whether we may be witnessing the same kind of metamorphosis that occurred a century ago, when the robber barons became legitimate business tycoons and, ultimately, philanthropists.

The New Ethnic Diversity in Organized Crime

Organized crime is not necessarily synonymous with the Mafia. Other groups also operate in the United States. Foremost among them are the Colombian Crime families, whose brutality is unrivaled by any other organized-crime group, and Bolivian, Peruvian,

and Jamaican crime families, which since the 1970s have organized the production, transportation, and distribution within the United States of cocaine and marijuana.

Another form of organized crime, initiated by disillusioned veterans of the Korean War and reinforced by veterans of Vietnam, appears in the outlaw motorcycle gangs. Among them are the Hell's Angels, the Pagans, the Outlaws, the Sons of Silence, and the Bandidos. All are organized along military lines; all are devoted to violence; all are involved in the production and distribution of narcotics and other drugs. Many members are also involved in other criminal activities, including extortion and prostitution, trafficking in stolen motorcycles and parts, and dealing in automatic weapons and explosives.

Among other organized groups engaged in various criminal activities are Chinese gangs (see Figure 13.2), the so-called Israeli Mafia, the recently emerging Russian-Jewish Mafia, Jamaican posses, and the

FIGURE 13.2 Time line of New York City's Chinese gangs: 1960–1990.
Source: Ko-lin Chin, *Chinese Subculture and Criminality* (New York: Greenwood Press, 1990), p. 76.

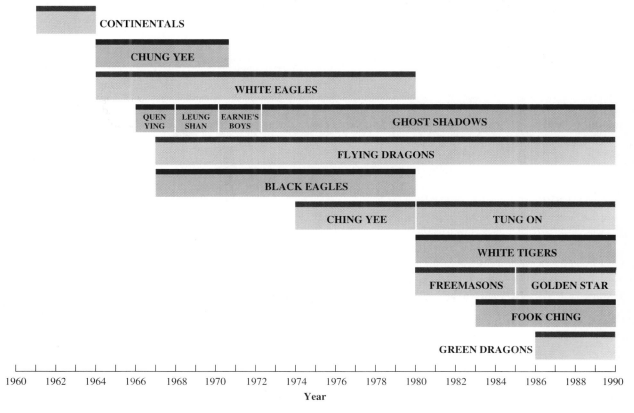

"Tattooed Men" of Japan's Yakuza, whose Yamaguchi-Gumi family alone has over 56,000 members, or nearly 20 times the number of fully initiated Italian organized-crime members in all the crews of all the families in the United States. All these groups have demonstrated potential for great social disruption.[76]

REVIEW

Organizational crimes are characterized by the use of a legitimate or illegitimate business enterprise for illegal profit. As American corporations grew in the nineteenth and twentieth centuries, they amassed much of the nation's wealth. Many corporations abused their economic power. Government stepped in to curb such abuses by legislation.

Edwin Sutherland, who provided the first scholarly insight into the wrongdoing of corporations, originated the concept of white-collar crime. Subsequent scholars have distinguished white-collar crime, committed by individuals, from corporate crime, committed by business organizations. Corporate or individual white-collar offenses include securities-related crimes, such as misrepresentation and churning; bankruptcy fraud of various kinds; fraud against the government, in particular contract and procurement fraud; consumer fraud; insurance fraud; tax fraud; bribery and political fraud; and insider-related fraud. In the twentieth century, corporations have been subjected to criminal liability for an increasing number of offenses, including common law crimes and environmental as well as other statutory offenses.

Organized crime got its start in this country when Sicilian immigrants replicated their traditional family structure in organizing criminal activities in their new home. These families and their associates were so successful in controlling bootlegging, gambling, prostitution, loan-sharking, labor racketeering, drug trafficking, and other illegal enterprises that they were able to assume control of many legitimate businesses. In recent years members of other ethnic groups—Latin Americans, Jamaicans, Russian Jews, Japanese, Chinese—have challenged the Sicilian Mafia for supremacy.

NOTES

1. Steve Yozwiak, "Big Fines for Lake Powell Dumping Exceed $1.3 Million," *Arizona Republic*, May 13, 1993, p. A1.

2. Marshall B. Clinard and Peter C. Yeager, *Corporate Crime* (New York: Free Press, 1980), pp. 59–60.

3. "Mafia Chief Tied to Crime-Busting Judge's Murder," Reuters, Aug. 1, 1993.

4. Dwight Smith, "White-Collar Crime, Organized Crime, and the Business Establishment: Resolving a Crisis in Criminological Theory," in *White Collar and Economic Crime*, ed. Peter Whickman and Timothy Dailey (Lexington, Mass.: Lexington Books, 1982).

5. Michael Binstein and Charles Bowden, *Trust Me: Charles Keating and the Missing Billions* (New York: Random House, 1993); Kitty Calavita and Henry N. Pontell, "'Other People's Money' Revisited: Collective Embezzlement in the Savings and Loan and Insurance Industries," *Social Problems*, **38** (1991): 94–112; Kitty Calavita and Henry N. Pontell, "'Heads I Win, Tails You Lost': Deregulation, Crime, and Crisis in the Savings and Loan Industry," *Crime and Delinquency*, **36** (1990): 309–341.

6. P. Renfrew, "Introduction to Symposium on White Collar Crime," *Memphis State University Law Review*, **10** (1980): 416.

7. Sally S. Simpson, "Strategy, Structure, and Corporate Crime: The Historical Context of Anticompetitive Behavior," in *Advances in Criminological Theory*, vol. 4, ed. Freda Adler and William S. Laufer (New Brunswick, N.J.: Transaction, 1993), pp. 71–93. See also Melissa Baucus and Terry Moorehead-Dworkin, "What Is Corporate Crime? It Is Not Illegal Corporate Behavior," *Law and Policy*, **13** (1991): 231–244; Ron Boostrom, *Enduring Issues in Criminology* (San Diego, Calif.: Greenhaven Press, 1995).

8. Edwin H. Sutherland, "White Collar Criminality," *American Sociological Review*, **5** (1940): 1–20.

9. Gilbert Geis, *On White Collar Crime* (Lexington, Mass.: Lexington Books, 1982), p. 9.

10. Marshall B. Clinard and Richard Quinney, *Criminal Behavior Systems*, 2d ed. (New York: Holt, Rinehart & Winston, 1982); Marshall B. Clinard, *Corporate Corruption: The Abuse of Power* (Westport, Conn.: Praeger, 1990); Gilbert Geis and Paul Jesilow, eds., "White-Collar Crime," *Annals of the American Academy of Political and Social Science*, **525** (1993): 8–169; David Weisburd, Stanton Wheeler, and Elin Waring, *Crimes of the Middle Classes: White-Collar Offenders in the Federal Courts* (New Haven, Conn.: Yale University Press, 1991); John Braithwaite, "Poverty, Power, White-Collar Crime and the Paradoxes of Criminological Theory," *Australian and New Zealand Journal of Criminology*, **24** (1991): 40–48; Frank Pearce and Laureen Snider, eds., "Crimes of the Powerful," *Journal of Human Justice*, **3** (1992): 1–124; Hazel Croall, *White Collar Crime: Criminal Justice and Criminology* (Buckingham, England: Open University Press, 1991); Stephen J. Rackmill, "Understanding and Sanctioning the White Collar Offender," *Federal Probation*, **56** (1992): 26–33; Brent Fisse, Michael Bersten, and Peter Grabosky, "White Collar and Corporate Crime," *University of New South Wales Law Journal*, **13** (1990): 1–171; Susan P. Shapiro, "Collaring the Crime Not the Criminal: Reconsidering the Concept of White-Collar Crime," *American Sociological Review*, **55** (1990): 346–365; Kip Schlegel and David Weisburd, eds., *White-Collar Crime Reconsidered* (Boston: Northeastern University Press, 1992); David Weisburd, Stanton Wheeler, Elin Waring, et al., *Crimes*

of the Middle Classes: White-Collar Offenders in the Federal Courts (New Haven, Conn.: Yale University Press, 1991); David Weisburd, Ellen F. Chayet, and Elin J. Waring, "White-Collar Crime and Criminal Careers: Some Preliminary Findings," *Crime and Delinquency,* **36** (1990): 342–355; David Weisburd, Elin Waring, and Stanton Wheeler, "Class, Status, and the Punishment of White-Collar Criminals," *Law and Social Inquiry,* **15** (1990): 223–243; Lisa Maher and Elin J. Waring, "Beyond Simple Differences: White Collar Crime, Gender and Workforce Position," *Phoebe,* **2** (1990): 44–54; John Hagan and Fiona Kay, "Gender and Delinquency in White-Collar Families: A Power-Control Perspective," *Crime and Delinquency,* **36** (1990): 391–407.

11. See James W. Coleman, *The Criminal Elite: The Sociological White-Collar Crime,* 2d ed. (New York: St. Martin's Press, 1989); and Michael L. Benson and Elizabeth Moore, "Are White-Collar and Common Offenders the Same? An Empirical and Theoretical Critique of a Recently Proposed General Theory of Crime," *Journal of Research in Crime and Delinquency,* **29** (1992): 251–272. See also Lori A. Elis and Sally S. Simpson, "Informal Sanction Threats and Corporate Crime: Additive versus Multiplicative Models," *Journal of Research in Crime and Delinquency,* **32** (1995): 399–424. For a view of white-collar offending in which the risks and rewards are considered by potential offenders, see David Weisburd, Elin Waring, and Ellen Chayet, "Specific Deterrence in a Sample of Offenders Convicted of White-Collar Crimes," *Criminology,* **33** (1995): 587–605.

12. Not only are governments at all levels victimized by corporate crimes, governments of all nations are also victimized; see Karlhans Liebl, "Developing Trends in Economic Crime in the Federal Republic of Germany," *Police Studies,* **8** (1985): 149–162. See also Jurg Gerber and Susan L. Weeks, "Women as Victims of Corporate Crime: A Call for Research on a Neglected Topic," *Deviant Behavior,* **13** (1992): 325–347; Elizabeth Moore and Michael Mills, "The Neglected Victims and Unexamined Costs of White-Collar Crime," *Crime and Delinquency,* **36** (1990): 408–418.

13. August Bequai, *White Collar Crime: A 20th-Century Crisis* (Lexington, Mass.: Lexington Books, 1978), p. 3; Linda Ganzini, Bentson McFarland, and Joseph Bloom, "Victims of Fraud: Comparing Victims of White Collar and Violent Crime," *Bulletin of the American Academy of Psychiatry and the Law,* **18** (1990): 55–63.

14. For the relationship between patterns of crimes in the savings and loan industry and those in organized crime, see Kitty Calavita and Henry N. Pontell, "Savings and Loan Fraud as Organized Crime: Toward a Conceptual Typology of Corporate Illegality," *Criminology,* **31** (1993): 519–548.

15. For an international perspective on consumer fraud, see U.S. Senate Committee on Governmental Affairs, *International Consumer Fraud: Can Consumers Be Protected?* (Washington, D.C.: U.S. Government Printing Office, 1994); Gilbert Geis, Henry N. Pontell, and Paul Jesilow, "Medicaid Fraud," in *Controversial Issues in Criminology and Criminal Justice,* ed. Joseph E. Scott and Travis Hirschi (Beverly Hills, Calif.: Sage, 1987); Maria S. Boss and Barbara Crutchfield George, "Challenging Conventional Views of White Collar Crime: Should the Criminal Justice System Be Refocused?" *Criminal Law Bulletin,* **28** (1992): 32–58. See also Richard M. Titus,

Fred Heinzelmann, and John M. Boyle, "Victimization of Persons by Fraud," *Crime and Delinquency,* **41** (1995): 54–72. For a description of fraud in an organizational setting presented from the perspective of the perpetrator, fellow employees, and the organization itself, see Steve W. Albrecht, Gerald W. Wernz, and Timothy L. Williams, *Fraud: Bringing Light to the Dark Side of Business* (Burr Ridge, Ill.: Irwin Professional Publishing, 1995).

16. For an outline of a general theory of crime causation applicable to both street crime and white-collar crime, see Travis Hirschi and Michael Gottfredson, "Causes of White-Collar Crime," *Criminology,* **25** (1987): 949–974; James W. Coleman, "Toward an Integrated Theory of White Collar Crime," *American Journal of Sociology,* **93** (1987): 406–439; and James R. Lasley, "Toward a Control Theory of White Collar Offending," *Journal of Quantitative Criminology,* **4** (1988): 347–362.

17. Donald R. Cressey, "The Poverty of Theory in Corporate Crime Research," in *Advances in Criminological Theory,* vol. 1, ed. William Laufer and Freda Adler (New Brunswick, N.J.: Transaction, 1989); for a response, see John Braithwaite and Brent Fisse, "On the Plausibility of Corporate Crime Theory," in *Advances in Criminological Theory,* vol. 2, ed. William Laufer and Freda Adler (New Brunswick, N.J.: Transaction, 1990). See also Travis Hirschi and Michael Gottfredson, "The Significance of White-Collar Crime for a General Theory of Crime," *Criminology,* **27** (1989): 359–371; and Darrell Steffensmeier, "On the Causes of 'White Collar' Crime: An Assessment of Hirschi and Gottfredson's Claims," *Criminology,* **27** (1989): 345–358.

18. Bequai, *White Collar Crime.* Bequai also includes antitrust and environmental offenses, which are corporate crimes, discussed in the next section.

19. Kenneth Polk and William Weston, "Insider Trading as an Aspect of White Collar Crime," *Australian and New Zealand Journal of Criminology,* **23** (1990): 24–38. In a report before Congress, insider trading scandals were said to have cost the securities industry nearly half a billion dollars in the early 1970s; see U.S. Congress House Select Committee on Crime, *Conversion of Worthless Securities into Cash* (Washington, D.C.: U.S. Government Printing Office, 1973). For a review of the insider trading that persists on Wall Street, see Gene G. Marcial, *Secrets of the Street: The Dark Side of Making Money* (New York: McGraw-Hill, 1995); Martin Mayer, *Nightmare on Wall Street: Salomon Brothers and the Corruption of the Marketplace* (New York: Simon & Schuster, 1993); Nancy Reichman, "Insider Trading," in Michael Tonry and Albert J. Reiss, Jr., eds., *Beyond the Law: Crime in Complex Organizations* (Chicago: University of Chicago Press, 1993).

20. For a more extensive review of the Wedtech debacle, see Mark S. Hamm, "From Wedtech and Iran-Contra to the Riots at Oakdale and Atlanta: On the Ethics and Public Performance of Edwin Meese III," *Journal of Crime and Justice,* **14** (1991): 123–147; Marilyn W. Thompson, *Feeding the Beast: How WedTech Became the Most Corrupt Little Company in America* (New York: Charles Scribner's Sons, 1990); William Power, "New York Rep. Biaggi and Six Others Indicted as Wedtech Scandal Greatly Expands," *Wall Street Journal,* June 4, 1987, p. 9.

21. Power, "New York Rep. Biaggi and Six Others Indicted as WedTech Scandal Greatly Expands." "Annual Survey of White

Collar Crime," *American Criminal Law Review*, **25** (1988): 560.

22. For a discussion of the many ways in which a person may be defrauded, see Phil Berger and Craig Jacob, *Twisted Genius: Confessions of a $10 Million Scam Man* (New York: Four Walls Eight Windows, 1995). For an Australian perspective of fraud, see M. Kapardis and A. Kapardis, "Co-regulation of Fraud Detection and Reporting by Auditors in Australia: Criminology's Lessons for Non-compliance," *Australian and New Zealand Journal of Criminology*, **28** (1995): 193–212.

23. Bequai, *White Collar Crime*, pp. 70–71.

24. For a European perspective on insurance fraud, with a particular focus on the enforcement activities in France and Belgium, see Andre Lemaitre, Rolf Lemaitre, Rolf Arnold, and Roger Litton, "Insurance and Crime," *European Journal on Criminal Policy*, **3** (1995): 7–92. For a description of insurance fraud prevalent in the American insurance industry, see Kenneth D. Myers, *False Security: Greed & Deception in America's Multibillion-Dollar Insurance Industry* (Amherst, N.Y.: Prometheus Books, 1995); Andrew Tobias, *The Invisible Banker* (New York: Washington Square Press, 1982).

25. Paul E. Tracy and James A. Fox, "A Field Experiment on Insurance Fraud in Auto Body Repair," *Criminology*, **27** (1989): 589–603.

26. Kathleen F. Brickey, *Corporate Criminal Liability*, 2 vols. (Wilmette, Ill.: Callaghan, 1984). See also Thomas Gabor, *Everybody Does It! Crime by the Public* (Toronto: University of Toronto Press, 1994). For a uniquely British perspective, see Doreen McBarnet, "Whiter Than White Collar Crime: Tax, Fraud, Insurance and the Management of Stigma," *British Journal of Sociology*, **42** (1991): 323–344.

27. Alan Murray, "IRS Is Losing Battle against Tax Evaders Despite Its New Gain," *Wall Street Journal*, Apr. 10, 1984, p. 1.

28. Ralph Salerno and John S. Tompkins, "Protecting Organized Crime," in *Theft of the City*, ed. John A. Gardiner and David Olson (Bloomington: Indiana University Press, 1984); Edwin Sutherland, *The Professional Thief* (Chicago: University of Chicago Press, 1937).

29. 18 U.S.C. [sec] 166(b) and (c).

30. Bequai, *White Collar Crime*, p. 45.

31. Ibid., p. 87. See Virginia Department of Social Services, *Report of the Financial Exploitation of Older Adults and Disabled Younger Adults in the Commonwealth* (Richmond, Va.: Senate Document no. 37, 1994). For steps to take to avoid being a victim of embezzlement, see Russell B. Bintliff, *Complete Manual of White Collar Crime Detection and Prevention* (Englewood Cliffs, N.J.: Prentice Hall, 1993). For a historic account of embezzlement in the United Kingdom from 1845 to 1929, see George Robb, *White Collar Crime in Modern England: Financial Fraud and Business Morality, 1845–1929* (Cambridge: Cambridge University Press, 1992).

32. John Clark and Richard Hollinger, *Theft by Employees in Work Organization* (Washington, D.C.: U.S. Government Printing Office, 1983).

33. Bequai, *White Collar Crime*, p. 89.

34. M. David Ermann and Richard J. Lundman, "Corporate and Governmental Deviance: Origins, Patterns, and Reactions," in *Corporate and Governmental Deviance: Problems of Organizational Behavior in Contemporary Society*, 3d ed., ed. M. David Ermann and Richard J. Lundman (New York: Oxford University Press, 1996). A school of thought holds that, unlike people, corporations have no personality, no conscience, and no shame. See, for example, Thomas Donaldson, *Corporations and Morality* (Englewood Cliffs, N.J.: Prentice-Hall, 1982); Donald R. Cressey, "The Poverty of Theory in Corporate Crime Research," in Laufer and Adler, *Advances in Criminological Theory*, vol 1. Over 100 years ago a New York court in *Darlington v. The Mayor*, 31 N.Y. 164 (1865), observed: "A corporation, as such, has no human wants to be supplied. It cannot eat, drink, or wear clothing, or live in houses." Steven Walt and William S. Laufer, "Corporate Criminal Liability and the Comparative Mix of Sanctions," in *White-Collar Crime Reconsidered*, ed. Kip Schlegel and David Weisburd (Boston: Northeastern University Press, 1992), describe corporations as being given a life and a moral personhood that clouds the distinction between crimes attributable to individuals (hourly employees, line managers, corporate officers, etc.) and those attributable to the corporate entity. John Braithwaite and Brent Fisse, "On the Plausibility of Corporate Crime Theory," in Laufer and Adler, *Advances in Criminological Theory*, vol. 2.

35. Nearly a century ago D. R. Richberg asked the question, "Should it not be the effort of all legislation dealing with corporations, to place them in as nearly as possible on a plane of equal responsibility with individuals?" D. R. Richberg, "The Imprisonment of the Corporation," *Case and Comment*, **18** (1912): 512–529. Saul M. Pilchen discovered that although notions of corporate criminal culpability have been broadened over the years, initial prosecutions under the federal sentencing guidelines for organizations generally have been limited in scope. Saul M. Pilchen, "When Corporations Commit Crimes: Sentencing under the Federal Organizational Guidelines," *Judicature*, **78** (1995): 202–206. Daniel R. Fischel and Alan O. Sykes, "Corporate Crime," *The Journal of Legal Studies*, **xxv** (1996): 319–349. Ronald L. Dixon believes, "No corporation should be unaware of these statutes or of the theories upon which criminal liability can be established. Corporations must realize that no one is immune from criminal liability, and corporate practices must reflect this fact. Ronald L. Dixon, "Corporate Criminal Liability," in *Corporate Misconduct: The Legal, Societal, and Management Issues*, ed. Margaret P. Spencer and Ronald R. Sims (Westport, Conn.: Quorum Books, 1995). For a British perspective on corporate liability, see "Great Britain, The Law Commission," in *Criminal Law: Involuntary Manslaughter: A Consultation Paper*, no. 135 (London: Her Majesty's Stationery Office, 1994). For a general overview of the corporate crime problem, see Francis T. Cullen, William J. Maakestad, and Gray Cavender, *Corporate Crime under Attack: The Ford Pinto Case and Beyond* (Cincinnati: Anderson, 1987), pp. 37–99.

36. *New York Central and Hudson River Railroad v. United States*, 212 U.S. 481 (1909); *State v. Lehigh Valley R. Co.*, 90 N.J. Law 372, 103 A. 685 (1917).

37. Model Penal Code, sec. 2.07(1) (c).

38. Sherman Antitrust Act, Act of July 2, 1890, c. 647, 26 Stat. 209, 15 U.S.C. [sec] 1-7 (1976).

39. Clayton Antitrust Act, Act of Oct. 15, 1914, c. 322, 38 Stat. 730, 15 U.S.C. [sec] 12-27 (1976); Robinson-Patman Act, Act of June 19, 1936, c. 592, [sec] 1, 49 Stat. 1526, 15 U.S.C. [sec] 13(a) (1973). See also Brickey, *Corporate Criminal Liability*.

40. Phillip Knightly, Harold Evans, Elaine Potter, and Marjorie Wallace, *Suffer the Children: The Story of Thalidomide* (New York: Viking, 1979).

41. The Ford Pinto case is fully described in Cullen et al., *Corporate Crime under Attack.* For more information on crimes against consumer safety, see Raymond J. Michalowski, *Order, Law, and Crime* (New York: Random House, 1985), pp. 334–340. For a description of corporate greed in its most vile form, see James S. Kunen, *Reckless Disregard: Corporate Greed, Government Indifference, and the Kentucky School Bus Crash* (New York: Simon & Schuster, 1994).

42. For an examination of corporate criminality in the United States and the response of the criminal justice system of America, see Spencer and Sims, *Corporate Misconduct.* See also Russell Mokhiber, *Corporate Crime and Violence: Big Business Power and the Abuse of the Public Trust* (San Francisco: Sierra Club, 1988); Susan P. Shapiro, *Wayward Capitalists: Target of the Securities and Exchange Commission* (New Haven, Conn.: Yale University Press, 1984); M. David Ermann and Richard J. Lundman, *Corporate and Governmental Deviance: Problems of Organizational Behavior in Contemporary Society,* 2d ed. (New York: Oxford University Press, 1982); Cullen et al., *Corporate Crime under Attack;* Knightly et al., *Suffer the Children;* and W. Byron Groves and Graeme Newman, *Punishment and Privilege* (New York: Harrow & Heston, 1986).

43. See Edwin Sutherland, *White Collar Crime* (1946). Sutherland had earlier published articles on the topic, including "White Collar Criminality," *American Sociological Review,* **5** (1940): 1–12, and "Is White Collar Crime 'Crime'?" *American Sociological Review,* **10** (1945): 132–139.

44. See Gary E. Reed and Peter Cleary Yeager, "Organizational Offending and Neoclassical Criminology: Challenging the Reach of a General Theory of Crime," *Criminology,* **34** (1996): 357–382; Clinard and Yeager, *Corporate Crime,* p. 116. See also Peter C. Yeager, "Analysing Corporate Offences: Progress and Prospects," *Research in Corporate Social Performance and Policy,* **8** (1986): 93–120. For similar findings in Canada, see Colin H. Goff and Charles E. Reasons, *Corporate Crime in Canada* (Scarborough, Ontario: Prentice-Hall, 1978).

45. Richard Quinney, *Critique of Legal Order: Crime Control in Capitalist Society* (Boston: Little, Brown, 1974); Richard Quinney, *Class, State, and Crime: On the Theory and Practice of Criminal Justice* (New York: David McKay, 1977); Ian Taylor, Paul Walton, and Jock Young, *The New Criminology: For a Social Theory of Deviance* (London: Routledge & Kegan Paul, 1973); William Chambliss and Robert Seidman, *Law, Order, and Power,* 2d ed. (Reading, Mass.: Addison-Wesley, 1982).

46. James Q. Wilson, *Thinking about Crime* (New York: Basic Books, 1975). For a competing school of thought, see Gilbert Geis, "Criminal Penalties for Corporate Criminals," *Criminal Law Bulletin,* **8** (1972): 377–392; Chamber of Commerce of the United States, *White Collar Crime* (Washington, D.C.: U.S. Government Printing Office, 1974); John Collins Coffee, Jr., "Beyond the Shut-Eyed Sentry: Toward a Theoretical View of Corporate Misconduct and an Effective Legal Response," *Virginia Law Review,* **63** (1977): 1099–1278; Gilbert Geis and Robert F. Meier, *White-Collar Crime: Offenses in Business, Politics, and the Professions* (New York: Free Press, 1977); Marshall B. Clinard, *Illegal Corporate Behavior* (Washington, D.C.: U.S. Government Printing Office, 1979); Miraim S. Saxon, *White-Collar Crime: The Problem and the Federal Response* (Report no. 80-84 EPW, Library of Congress, Con-

gressional Research Service, Washington, D.C., Apr. 14, 1980); Laura S. Schrager and James F. Short, Jr., "How Serious a Crime? Perceptions of Organizational and Common Crimes," in *White-Collar Crime: Theory and Research,* ed. Gilbert Geis and Ezra Stotland (Beverly Hills, Calif.: Sage Publications, 1980). Contemporary works include James W. Coleman, *The Criminal Elite: The Sociology of White-Collar Crime* (New York: St. Martin's Press, 1989); Laureen Snider, "The Regulatory Dance: Understanding Reform Processes in Corporate Crime," *International Journal of the Sociology of Law,* **19** (1991): 209–236; Kip Schlegel and David Weisburd, *White-Collar Crime: The Parallax View* (Boston: Northeastern University Press, 1993); Michael Tonry and Albert J. Reiss, *Beyond the Law: Crime in Complex Organizations* (Chicago: University of Chicago Press, 1993); Robert Tillman and Henry Pontell, "Organizations and Fraud in the Savings and Loan Industry," *Social Forces,* **73** (1995): 1439–1463.

47. Patsy Klaus and Carol Kalish, *The Severity of Crime,* Bureau of Justice Statistics Bulletin NCJ-92326 (Washington, D.C.: U.S. Government Printing Office, 1984). See also Schrager and Short, "How Serious a Crime?" Francis Cullen, B. Link, and C. Polanzi, "The Seriousness of Crime Revisited," *Criminology,* **20** (1982): 83–102; Francis Cullen, R. Mathers, G. Clark, and J. Cullen, "Public Support for Punishing White Collar Crime: Blaming the Victim Revisited," *Journal of Criminal Justice,* **11** (1983): 481–493; Richard Sparks, Hazel G. Genn, and David Dodd, *Surveying Victims* (New York: Wiley, 1977).

48. Jim Mayer, "Confection Maker Indicted in Dumping," *Sacramento Bee,* July 10, 1993.

49. Mark A. Cohen, "Environmental Crime and Punishment: Legal/Economic Theory and Empirical Evidence on Enforcement of Federal Environmental Statutes," *Journal of Criminal Law and Criminology,* **82** (1992): 1054–1108. See, for an early treatment, Timothy R. Young, "Criminal Liability under the Refuse Act of 1899 and the Refuse Act Permit Program," *Journal of Criminal Law, Criminology and Police Science,* **63** (1972): 366–376. For a global perspective on the prevention of environmental crimes, see Boon Khoo Hui, Prathan Watanavanich, Edgar Aglipay, et al., *Effective Countermeasures against Crimes Related to Urbanization and Industrialization: Urban Crime, Juvenile Delinquency and Environmental Crime* (Tokyo: Report for 1993 and Resource Material Series no. 45, UNAFEI, 1994).

50. Clinard and Yeager, *Corporate Crime,* p. 92, citing *New York Times* survey of July 15, 1979.

51. Gerhard O. W. Mueller, "Offenses against the Environment and Their Prevention: An International Appraisal," *Annals of the American Academy of Political and Social Science,* **444** (1979): 56–66.

52. Ibid., p. 60.

53. Ryuichi Hirano, "The Criminal Law Protection of Environment: General Report," Tenth International Congress of Comparative Law, Budapest, 1978. For a discussion of the problems of multinational corporations operating in developing countries, see Richard Schaffer, Beverly Earle, and Filiberto Agusti, *International Business Law and Its Environment,* 2d ed. (St. Paul, Minn.: West, 1993). For a discussion of corporate crime in Japan, see Harold R. Kerbo and Mariko Inoue, "Japanese Social Structure and White Collar Crime: Recruit Cosmos and Beyond," *Deviant Behavior,* **11** (1990): 139–154.

54. Ibid.

55. John Braithwaite, "Challenging Just Deserts: Punishing White-Collar Criminals," *Journal of Criminal Law and Criminology*, **73** (1982): 723–763; Stanton Wheeler, David Weisburd, and Nancy Boden, "Sentencing the White-Collar Offender," *American Sociological Review*, **47** (1982): 641–659. For a thoughtful analysis of corporate illegality, see Nancy Frank and Michael Lombness, *Corporate Illegality and Regulatory Justice* (Cincinnati: Anderson, 1988); Kip Schlegel, *Just Deserts for Corporate Criminals* (Boston: Northeastern University Press, 1990); and John C. Coffee, Jr., Mark A. Cohen, Jonathan R. Macey, et al., "A National Conference on Sentencing of the Corporation," *Boston University Law Review*, **71** (1991): 189–453.

56. Sally S. Simpson and Christopher S. Koper, "Deterring Corporate Crime," *Criminology*, **30** (1992): 347–375; Genevra Richardson, *Policing Pollution: A Study of Regulation and Enforcement* (Oxford: Clarendon, 1982); Albert J. Reiss and Albert D. Biderman, *Data Sources on White-Collar Law-Breaking* (Washington, D.C.: National Institute of Justice, 1980); Susan Shapiro, "Detecting Illegalities: A Perspective on the Control of Securities Violations," Ph.D. dissertation, Yale University (University Microfilms), 1980. See also Brian Widlake, *Serious Fraud Office* (London: Little, Brown, 1995).

57. Dan Magnuson, ed., *Economic Crime: Programs for Future Research* (Stockholm: National Council for Crime Prevention, 1985); Michael L. Benson, Francis T. Cullen, and William A. Maakestad, *Local Prosecutors and Corporate Crime: Final Report* (Washington, D.C.: National Institute of Justice, 1991); Michael L. Benson, Francis T. Cullen, and William J. Maakestad, "Local Prosecutors and Corporate Crime," *Crime and Delinquency*, **36** (1990): 356–372.

58. William Balsamo and George Carpozi, Jr., *Under the Clock: The Inside Story of the Mafia's First 100 Years* (Far Hills, N.J.: New Horizon Press, 1988). Some legal historians trace the appearance of organized crime in the United States to the early 1860s; see Humbert S. Nelli, "A Brief History of American Syndicate Crime," in *Organized Crime in America: Concepts and Controversies*, ed. Timothy S. Bynum (Monsey, N.Y.: Criminal Justice Press, 1987). See also Richard Gambino, *Blood of My Blood: The Dilemma of the Italian American* (Garden City, N.Y.: Doubleday, 1974), p. 3; Luigi Barzini, "Italians in New York: The Way We Were in 1929," *New York Magazine*, Apr. 4, 1977, p. 36; Howard Abadinsky, *Organized Crime*, 2d ed. (Chicago: Nelson Hall, 1985).

59. Abadinsky, *Organized Crime*, pp. 43–53.

60. Ibid., p. 91. For a description of some of the more colorful characters of the Prohibition era, see David E. Ruth, *Inventing the Public Enemy* (Chicago: University of Chicago Press, 1996); Joseph McNamara, "Dapper Bootlegger," *New York Daily News*, Oct. 15, 1995, p. 42; Charles Rappleye and Ed Becker, *All American Mafioso: The Johnny Roselli Story* (New York: Barricade Books, 1995); Mary M. Stolberg, *Fighting Organized Crime: Politics, Justice, and the Legacy of Thomas E. Dewey* (Boston: Northeastern University Press, 1995); Colin Wilson, Ian Schott, Ed Shedd, et al., *World Famous Crimes* (New York: Carroll & Graf Publishers, 1995); Jay Robert Nash, *World Encyclopedia of Organized Crime* (New York: Paragon House, 1992); Robert J. Schoenberg, *Mr. Capone: The Real and Complete Story of Al Capone* (New York: William Morrow, 1992); Robert Lacey, *Little Man: Meyer Lansky and the Gangster Life* (Boston: Little, Brown, 1991).

61. James Inciardi, *Careers in Crime* (Chicago: Rand McNally, 1975), p. 113; Norman Lewis, *The Honored Society: A Searching Look at the Mafia* (New York: Putnam, 1964), p. 25.

62. For a European perspective on the harms generated by the Sicilian Mafia, see John Follain, *A Dishonoured Society: Sicilian Mafia's Threat to Europe* (London: Little, Brown, 1995); Brian Freemantle, *The Octopus: Europe in the Grip of Organized Crime* (London: Orion Books Ltd., 1995). For a description of the Sicilian Mafia's reach into the former Soviet Union, see Werner Raith, *Das Neue Mafia-Kartell: Wie de Syndikate den Osten Erober* (The New Mafia Cartel: How the Syndicates Conquer the East) (Berlin: Rowohlt, 1994). For a global perspective, see Phil Williams and Ernesto U. Savona, "Problems and Dangers Posed by Organized Transnational Crime in the Various Regions of the World," *Transnational Organized Crime*, **1** (1995): 1–42; Louise I. Shelley, "Transnational Organized Crime: An Imminent Threat to the Nation-State?" *Journal of International Affairs*, **48** (1995): 463–489; Raimondo Catanzaro, *Men of Respect: A Social History of the Sicilian Mafia* (New York: Free Press, 1992); Pino Arlacchi, *Men of Dishonor: Inside the Sicilian Mafia* (New York: William Morrow, 1992). For a description of how the Sicilian Mafia attempted to join forces with the Colombian cocaine cartels, see William Gately and Yvette Fernandez, *Dead Ringer: An Insider's Account of the Mob's Colombian Connection* (New York: Donald I. Fine, 1994); Abadinsky, *Organized Crime*, pp. 56–62.

63. Ronald Goldfarb, *Perfect Villains, Imperfect Heros: Robert F. Kennedy's War against Organized Crime* (New York: Random House, 1995); Annelise Graebner Anderson, *The Business of Organized Crime: A Cosa Nostra Family* (Stanford, Calif.: Hoover Institution Press, 1979); Peter Maas, *The Valachi Papers* (New York: Putnam, 1968); U.S. Senate Committee on Governmental Affairs, Subcommittee on Investigations, *Organized Crime: 25 Years after Valachi* (Washington, D.C.: U.S. Government Printing Office, 1990).

64. Jay Albanese, *Organized Crime in America* (Cincinnati: Anderson, 1985), p. 25. See also Francis A. J. Ianni, *A Family Business: Kinship and Social Control in Organized Crime* (New York: Russell Sage, 1972); Joseph Albini, *The American Mafia: Genesis of a Legend* (New York: Irvington, 1971); Merry Morash, "Organized Crime," in *Major Forms of Crime*, ed. Robert F. Meier (Beverly Hills, Calif.: Sage, 1984), pp. 191–220. For a response, see Claire Sterling, *Octopus: The Long Reach of the International Sicilian Mafia* (New York: W. W. Norton & Company, 1990); Ralph Blumenthal, *Last Days of the Sicilians: At War with the Mafia* (New York: Times Books, 1988). See also Shana Alexander, *The Pizza Connection* (New York: Weidenfeld & Nicolson, 1988).

65. For a perceptive analysis of the changing focus of the two most recent commission reports, see Jay S. Albanese, "Government Perceptions of Organized Crime: The Presidential Commissions, 1967 and 1987," *Federal Probation*, **52** (1988): 58–63.

66. For a popular account of how a Sicilian Mafia associate infiltrated and almost destroyed one of the largest movie studios in Hollywood, see "The Predator: How an Italian Thug Looted MGM, Brought Credit Lyonnais to Its Knees, and Made the Pope Cry," *Fortune Magazine,* July 8, 1996, p. 128. Despite the denial of generations of Italian and Sicilian organized-crime figures concerning the trafficking of illegal narcotics, criminologists have discussed the involvement of all major American syndicates; see Peter A. Lupsha, "La Cosa Nostra in Drug Trafficking," in Bynum, *Organized Crime in America.* See also Dwight Smith, *The Mafia Mystique* (New York: Basic Books, 1975).

67. P. Beseler, Wayne Brewer, and Julienne Salzano, "Focus on Environmental Crimes," *FBI Law Enforcement Bulletin,* **64** (1995): 1–26; Joel Epstein, Theodore M. Hammett, and Laura Collins, *Law Enforcement Response to Environmental Crime,* (Washington, D.C.: U.S. National Institute of Justice, 1995). For a global perspective on environmental stability, see Norman Myers, *Ultimate Security: The Environmental Basis of Political Stability* (New York: W. W. Norton & Company, 1993). For a uniquely Italian organized-crime perspective on the illegal disposal of toxic wastes throughout the United States, see Frank R. Scarpitti and Alan A. Block, "America's Toxic Waste Racket: Dimensions of the Environmental Crisis," in Bynum, *Organized Crime in America.* For a discussion of predicting which legitimate businesses will be infiltrated by organized crime, see Jay S. Albanese, "Predicting the Incidence of Organized Crime: A Preliminary Model," in Bynum, *Organized Crime in America,* pp. 103–114.

68. Past efforts to develop civil and criminal causes of action against corporations are found in RICO legislation. See Racketeer Influenced and Corrupt Organizations (RICO) Provisions of the Organized Crime Control Act of 1970 [Act of Oct. 15, 1970, Public Law 91-452, Section 901 (a), 84 Stat. 941, 18 U.S. Code Sections 1961 through 1968, effective Oct. 15, 1970, as amended Nov. 2, 1978, Public Law 95-575, Sec. 3 (c), 92 Stat. 2465 and Nov. 6, 1978, Public Law 95-598, Sec. 314 (g), 92 Stat. 2677]. For a discussion of the pros and cons of RICO, see Donald J. Rebovich, "Use and Avoidance of RICO at the Local Level: The Implementation of Organized Crime Laws," in *Contemporary Issues in Organized Crime,* ed. Jay Albanese (Monsey, N.Y.: Criminal Justice Press, 1995).

69. Fred Montanino, "Protecting Organized Crime Witnesses in the United States," *International Journal of Comparative and Applied Criminal Justice,* **14** (1990): 123–131.

70. For a description of the contemporary leadership of New York's five Italian-American organized-crime families, see Jeffrey Goldberg, "The Mafia's Morality Crisis," *New York Magazine,* Jan. 9, 1995, p. 22. See also Donald Cressey, *Theft of the Nation* (New York: Harper & Row, 1969).

71. Abadinsky, *Organized Crime,* pp. 8–23; Donald Cressey, in President's Commission, *Task Force Report,* pp. 7–8; Gay Talese, *Honor Thy Father* (New York: World, 1971).

72. For a discussion of "Commission" membership, mores, and dispute resolution, see William F. Roemer, Jr., *Accardo: The Genuine Godfather* (New York: Donald I. Fine, 1995); Sidney Zion, *Loyalty and Betrayal: The Story of the American Mob*

(San Francisco: Collins Publishers, 1994); John H. Davis, *Mafia Dynasty: The Rise and Fall of the Gambino Crime Family* (New York: HarperCollins, 1993); Sam Giancana and Chuck Giancana, *Double Cross: The Explosive, Inside Story of the Mobster Who Controlled America* (New York: Warner Books, 1992); John Cummings and Ernest Volkman, *Goombata: The Improbable Rise and Fall of John Gotti and His Gang* (Boston: Little, Brown, 1990).

73. *United States v. Bonanno,* 180 F. Supp. 71 (S.D.N.Y. 1960), upholding the Apalachin roundup as constitutional; *United States v. Bonanno,* 177 F. Supp. 106 (S.D.N.Y. 1959), sustaining the validity of the conspiracy indictment; *United States v. Bufalino,* 285 F. 2d 408 (2d Cir. 1960), reversing the conspiracy conviction.

74. James Walston, "Mafia in the Eighties," *Violence, Aggression, and Terrorism,* **1** (1987): 13–39. For a look into organized crime's once mighty and still lingering hand on gambling in the United States, see Jay Albanese, "Casino Gambling and Organized Crime: More Than Reshuffling the Deck," in Albanese, *Contemporary Issues in Organized Crime;* Ronald A. Farrelland and Carole Case, *The Black Book and the Mob: The Untold Story of the Control of Nevada's Casinos* (Madison: University of Wisconsin Press, 1995); Nicholas Pileggi, *Casino: Love and Honor in Las Vegas* (New York: Simon & Schuster, 1995); David Johnston, *Temples of Chance: How America Inc. Bought Out Murder Inc. to Win Control of the Casino Business* (New York: Doubleday, 1992).

75. Organized-crime activities are certainly not limited to local communities. Rather, an ever-evolving organized-crime syndicate feeds off ever-increasing global opportunities; see Petrus van Duyne and Alan A. Block, "Organized Cross-Atlantic Crime: Racketeering in Fuels," *Crime, Law and Social Change,* **22** (1995): 127–147; Umberto Santino, "The Financial Mafia: The Illegal Accumulation of Wealth and the Financial-Industrial Complex," *Contemporary Crises,* **12** (1988): 203–243.

76. For a description of the damage inflicted on society by contemporary Russian organized-crime figures, see New York State Organized Crime Task Force, New York State Commission of Investigation, New Jersey State Commission of Investigation, *An Analysis of Russian-Émigré Crime in the Tri-State Region* (White Plains, N.Y.: New York State Organized Crime Task Force, June 1996); Dennis J. Kenny and James O. Finckenauer, *Organized Crime in America* (Belmont, Calif.: Wadsworth Publishing Company, 1995).

Internet Exercise

Corporate crime poses serious law enforcement investigatory problems. How much more difficult is the investigation of corporate crime in high-tech industries?

Your Web Site is:
http://www.herring.com/mag/issue22/crime.html

Drug Abuse and Crime

    The History of Drug Abuse

    The Extent of Drug Abuse

    Patterns of Drug Abuse

    Crime-Related Activities

    The International Drug Economy

    Drug Control

Alcohol and Crime

    The History of Legalization

    Crime-Related Activities

Sexual Morality Offenses

    "Deviate Sexual Intercourse by Force or Imposition"

    Prostitution

    Pornography

Review

Notes

    Special Features

        CRIMINOLOGICAL FOCUS: The Small World of Crack Users

        AT ISSUE: Gambling: "Injurious to the Morals"

        WINDOW TO THE WORLD: Global Sexual Slavery

Key Terms

money laundering
pimp
pornography
prostitution
sodomy
statutory rape

In cities across the country and around the world, people buying and selling illicit goods and services congregate in certain areas—Times Square in New York, the Ramblas district in Barcelona, St. Pauli in Hamburg—that are easily identifiable by theater marquees advertising live sex shows. Shops feature everything from child pornography to sadomasochistic slide shows; prostitutes openly solicit clients; drunks propped up in doorways clutch brown bags; drug addicts deal small amounts of whatever they can get to sell to support their habits. The friendly locals will deliver virtually any service to visitors, for a price.

The activities involved—prostitution, drunkenness, sex acts between consenting adults for money, drug use—were commonly called "victimless" crimes. Perhaps that is because it was assumed that people who engage in them rationally choose to do so and do not view themselves as victims. Often no one complains to the police about being victimized by such consensual activity. But contemporary forms of such activities and their ramifications may entail massive victimizations: How many murders are committed during drug gang wars? How many thefts are committed by addicts seeking to support their habits? How much damage is done to persons and property by drunken drivers? Does pornography encourage physical abuse? And what of the future of children sold for prostitution?

DRUG ABUSE AND CRIME

A woman arrives at the airport in Los Angeles with very few belongings, no hotel reservations, no family or friends in the United States, and a passport showing eight recent trips from Bogotá, Colombia. A patdown and strip search reveal a firm, distended abdomen, which is discovered to hold 88 balloons filled with cocaine.[1] In New York City, a heroin addict admits that "the only livin' thing that counts is the fix . . . : Like I would steal off anybody—anybody, at all, my own mother gladly included."[2] In Chicago, crack cocaine has transformed some of the country's toughest gangs into ghetto-based drug-trafficking organizations that guard their turf with automatic weapons and assault rifles.[3]

On a college campus in the Northeast a crowd sits in the basement of a fraternity house drinking beer

313

and smoking pot through the night. At a beachfront house in Miami three young professional couples gather for a barbecue. After dinner they sit down at a card table in the playroom. On a mirror, someone lines up a white powdery substance into rows about ⅛-inch wide and an inch long. Through rolled-up paper they breathe the powder into their nostrils and await the "rush" of the coke.

These incidents demonstrate that when we speak of the "drug problem," we are talking about a wide variety of conditions that stretch beyond our borders, that involve all social classes, that in one way or another touch most people's lives, and that cost society significant sums of money (Figure 14.1). The drug scene includes manufacturers, importers, primary distributors (for large geographical areas), smugglers (who transport large quantities of drugs from their place of origin), dealers (who sell drugs on the street and in crack houses), corrupt criminal justice officials, users who endanger other people's lives through negligence (train engineers, pilots, physicians), and even unborn children (Table 14.1).

FIGURE 14.1 National, state, and local spending for drug control.

	$, in thousands
Drug abuse treatment	2908.7
Corrections	2607.7
Investigations	2024
State and local assistance	1775.2
Drug abuse prevention	1591.6
Interdiction	1437.2
Prosecution	1000.9
Research and development	559.2
International	400.5
Intelligence	375.9
Other law enforcement	284.6
Regulation and compliance	98.1
Total expenditure	**$15,063.6**

1996 National Drug Control Strategy

Drug abuse treatment 18%
Corrections 17%
Investigations 13%
State and local assistance 12%
Drug abuse prevention 11%
Interdiction 10%
Prosecution 7%
Research and development 4%
Int'l. 3%
Intelligence 2%
Other law enforcement 2%
Regulation 1%

State and local spending for drug control, fiscal years 1990 and 1991

	FY 1990	FY 1991
Total	$14,075,000	$15,907,000
Justice	$11,525,000	$12,619,000
Police protection	4,035,000	4,223,000
Judicial and legal services	1,346,000	1,449,000
Corrections	6,045,000	6,827,000
Other	100,000	120,000
Health and hospitals	$2,184,000	$2,784,000
Education	$ 366,000	$ 503,000

Source: Office of National Drug Control Policy, as reported in *Fact sheet: Drug data summary.*

TABLE 14.1 Roles and Functions in the Drug Distribution Business Compared with Those in Legitimate Industry

Approximate Role Equivalents in Legal Markets	Roles by Common Names at Various Stages of the Drug Distribution Business	Major Functions Accomplished at This Level
Grower producer	Coca farmer, opium farmer, marijuana grower	Grow coca, opium, marijuana; the raw materials
Manufacturer	Collector, transporter, elaborator, chemist, drug lord	All stages for preparation of heroin, cocaine, marijuana as commonly sold
Traffickers		
Importer	Multikilo importer, mule, airplane pilot, smuggler, trafficker, money launderer	Smuggling of large quantities of substances into the U.S.
Wholesale distributor	Major distributor, investor, "kilo connection"	Transportation and redistribution of multikilograms and single kilograms
Dealers		
Regional distributor	Pound and ounce men, weight dealers	Adulteration and sale of moderately expensive products
Retail store owner	House connections, suppliers, crack-house supplier	Adulteration and production of retail-level dosage units (bags, vials, grams) in very large numbers
Assistant manager, security chief, or accountant	"Lieutenant," "muscle men," transporter, crew boss, crack-house manager/proprietor	Supervises three or more sellers, enforces informal contracts, collects money, distributes multiple dosage units to actual sellers
Sellers		
Store clerk, salesmen (door-to-door and phone)	Street drug seller, runner, juggler	Makes actual direct sales to consumer; private seller responsible for both money and drugs
Low-Level Distributors		
Advertiser, security guards, leaflet distributor	Steerer, tout, cop man, look-out, holder runner, help friend, guard, go-between	Assists in making sales, advertises, protects seller from police and criminals, solicits customers; handles drugs or money but not both
Servant, temporary employee	Run shooting gallery, injector (of drugs), freebaser, taster, apartment cleaner, drug bagger, fence, launder money	Provides short-term services to drug users or sellers for money or drugs; not responsible for money or drugs

Source: Bruce D. Johnson, Terry Williams, Kojo A. Dir, and Harry Sanabria, "Drug Abuse in the Inner City: Impact on Hard-Drug Users and the Community," in *Drugs and Crime,* vol. 13: *Crime and Justice,* ed. Michael Tonry and James Q. Wilson. (Chicago: University of Chicago Press, 1990), p. 19. © 1990 by the University of Chicago Press. All rights reserved. From U.S. Department of Justice, *Drugs, Crime and the Justice System* (Washington, D.C.: U.S. Government Printing Office, 1992).

The drug problem is further complicated by the wide diversity of substances abused, their varying effects on the mind and body, and the kinds of dependencies users develop. There is also the much-debated issue of the connection between drug use and crime—an issue infinitely more complex than the stereotype of maddened addicts committing heinous acts because either they were under the influence of drugs or they needed to get the money to support a habit. Many of the crimes we have discussed in earlier chapters are part of what has been called the nation's (or the world's) drug problem. Let us examine this problem in detail.

The History of Drug Abuse

The use of chemical substances that alter physiological and psychological functioning dates back to the

Old Stone Age.[4] Egyptian relics from 3500 B.C. depict the use of opium in religious rituals. By 1600 B.C. an Egyptian reference work listed opium as an analgesic, or painkiller. The Incas of South America are known to have used cocaine at least 5000 years ago. Cannabis, the hemp plant from which marijuana and hashish are derived, also has a 5000-year history.[5]

Since antiquity, people have cultivated a variety of drugs for religious, medicinal, and social purposes. The modern era of drug abuse in the United States began with the use of drugs for medicinal purposes. By the nineteenth century the two components of opium, which is derived from the sap of the opium poppy, were identified and given the names "morphine" and "codeine." Ignorant of the addictive properties of these drugs, physicians used them to treat a wide variety of human illnesses. So great was their popularity that they found their way into almost all patent medicines used for pain relief and were even incorporated in soothing syrups for babies (Mother Barley's Quieting Syrup and Mumm's Elixir were very popular).

During the Civil War the use of injectable morphine to ease the pain of battle casualties was so extensive that morphine addiction among veterans came to be known as the "soldier's disease."[6] By the time the medical profession and the public recognized just how addictive morphine was, its use had reached epidemic proportions. Then in 1898 the Bayer Company in Germany introduced a new opiate, supposedly a nonaddictive substitute for morphine and codeine. It came out under the trade name Heroin; yet it proved to be even more addictive than morphine.[7]

When cocaine, which was isolated from the coca leaf in 1860, appeared on the national drug scene, it too was used for medicinal purposes. (Its use to unblock the sinuses initiated the "snorting" of cocaine into the nostrils.) Its popularity spread, and soon it was used in other products: Peruvian Wine of Coca ($1 a bottle in the Sears, Roebuck catalog), a variety of tonics, and, the most famous of all, Coca-Cola, which was made with coca until 1903.[8]

As the consumption of opium products (narcotics) and cocaine spread, states passed a variety of laws to restrict the sale of these substances. Federal authorities estimated that there were 200,000 addicts in the early 1900s. Growing concern over the increase in addiction led in 1914 to the passage of the Harrison Act, designed to regulate the domestic use, sale, and transfer of opium and coca products. Though this legislation decreased the number of addicts, it was a double-edged sword: By restricting the importation and distribution of drugs, it paved the way for the drug smuggling and black-market operations that are so deeply entrenched today.

It was not until the 1930s that the abuse of marijuana began to arouse public concern. Because marijuana use was associated with groups outside the social mainstream—petty criminals, jazz musicians, bohemians, and, in the Southwest, Mexicans—a public outcry for its regulation arose.[9] Congress responded with the Marijuana Tax Act of 1937, which placed a prohibitive tax of $100 an ounce on the drug. With the passage of the Boggs Act in 1951, penalties for possession of and trafficking in marijuana (and other controlled substances) increased. Despite all the legislation, the popularity of marijuana continued.

As the drugs being used proliferated to include glue, tranquilizers (such as Valium and Librium), LSD, and many others, the public became increasingly aware of the dangers of drug abuse. In 1970 another major drug law, the Comprehensive Drug Abuse Prevention and Control Act (the Controlled Substances Act), updated all federal drug laws since the Harrison Act.[10] This act placed marijuana in the category of the most serious substances. The 1970 federal legislation made it necessary to bring state legislation into conformity with federal law. The Uniform Controlled Substances Act was drafted and now is the law in 48 states, the District of Columbia, Puerto Rico, the Virgin Islands, and Guam.

Most of the basic federal antidrug legislation has been drawn together in Title 21 of the United States Code, the collection of all federal laws. It includes many amendments passed since 1970, especially the Anti-Drug Abuse Act of 1988, which states: "It is the declared policy of the United States Government to create a drug-free America by 1995."[11]

Title 21, as amended, has elaborate provisions for the funding of national and international drug programs; establishes the Office of National Drug Control Policy, headed by a so-called drug czar; and provides stiff penalties for drug offenses. The manufacture, distribution, and dispensing of listed substances in stated (large) quantities are each subject to a prison sentence of from 10 years to life and a fine (for individuals) of from $4 million to $10 million. Even simple possession now carries a punishment of up to 1 year in prison and a $100,000 fine. Title 21, along with other recent crime-control legislation, defines many other drug crimes as well and provides for the forfeiture of any property constituting or derived from the proceeds of drug trading.

The Extent of Drug Abuse

Historically, the substance (other than alcohol) most frequently abused in the United States has been marijuana. In annual surveys, high school seniors were asked whether they ever used marijuana. Between 1975 and 1991, the percentage answering yes ranged from a high of 51 percent in 1979 to a low of 37 percent in 1991. The survey also found that in 1991 24 percent had used marijuana in the past year, and 14 percent in the past month.[12]

The most recent national household survey shows a startling increase in the rate of drug use among youths between the ages of 12 and 17. Nearly 11 percent of America's 2.2 million youths report the recent use of illegal drugs. Since 1992, drug use had escalated at a significant rate: 1995 marked an increase of up to 105 percent in marijuana use since 1992, up to a 183 percent increase in the use of LSD and other hallucinogens during this 3-year period, and a 166 percent increase in cocaine use in 1994 to 1995 alone.[13]

In the 1980s cocaine constituted the country's major drug problem. An estimated 22 million people had tried the substance, and another 4 million were using it regularly.[14] The use of heroin is much less pervasive; the number of users is estimated to be about 600,000.[15] Newer drugs on the market are crack (a derivative of cocaine) and the so-called *designer drugs*—substances that have been chemically altered in such a way that they no longer fall within the legal definition of controlled substances.[16]

It is difficult to measure how many people abuse drugs in any given period. The national household survey has shown a decline in the use of illicit drugs between 1974 and 1991 of those persons between 18 and 25 years old. The most recent data, monitoring the future, however, demonstrate that once again drug abuse among high school students is increasing (Table 14.2 and Figure 14.2).[17]

Patterns of Drug Abuse

New and more potent varieties of illicit substances, as well as increasing levels of violent crime associated with drug abuse, have led researchers to ask many

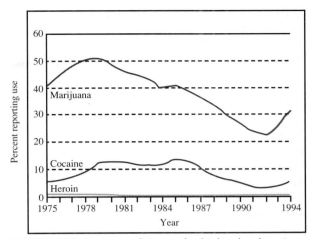

FIGURE 14.2 Past year drug use by high school seniors, by drug type, 1974 to 1995.
Source: Johnston, L., O'Malley, P., and Bachman, J. (1995). "Monitoring the Future." Washington, D.C.: National Institute on Drug Abuse.

questions about the phenomenon. Is drug abuse a symptom of an underlying mental or psychological disorder that makes some people more vulnerable than others? Some investigators argue that the addict is characterized by strong dependency needs, feelings of inadequacy, a need for immediate gratification, and lack of internal controls.[18] Or is it possible that addicts lack certain body chemicals and that drugs make them feel better by compensating for this deficit?

Perhaps the causes are environmental. Is drug abuse a norm in deteriorated inner cities, where youngsters are learning how to behave from older addicted role models? Do people escape from the realities of slum life by retreating into drug abuse?[19] If so, how do we explain drug abuse among the upper classes?

Just as there are many causes of drug abuse, there are many addict lifestyles—and the lifestyles may be linked to the use of particular substances. During the 1950s, heroin abuse began to increase markedly in the inner cities, particularly among young black and Hispanic males.[20] In fact, it was their drug of choice throughout the 1960s and early 1970s. Heroin addicts spend their days buying heroin, finding a safe place to "shoot" the substance into a vein with a needle attached to a hypodermic syringe, waiting for the euphoric feeling, or "rush," that follows the injection, and ultimately reaching a feeling of overall well-being known as a "high," which lasts about 4 hours.[21] The

TABLE 14.2   Highlights of the 1995 National Household Survey

Illicit Drug Use

- In 1995, an estimated 12.8 million Americans were current illicit drug users, meaning they had used an illicit drug in the month prior to interview. This represents no change from 1994 when the estimate was 12.6 million. The number of illicit drug users was at its highest level in 1979 when there were 25 million.

- Between 1994 and 1995, there was a continuing increase in the rate of past-month illicit drug use among youths, from 8.2 percent to 10.9 percent. The rate has doubled since 1992.

- Significant increases in past-month marijuana use (from 6.0 percent to 8.2 percent), cocaine use (from 0.3 percent to 0.8 percent), and hallucinogen use (from 1.1 percent to 1.7 percent) occurred among youths between 1994 and 1995.

- The overall number of current cocaine users did not change significantly between 1994 and 1995 (1.38 million in 1994 and 1.45 million in 1995). This is down from a peak of 5.7 million in 1985.

- There were an estimated 582,000 (0.3 percent of the population) frequent cocaine users in 1995. Frequent use, defined as use on 51 or more days during the past year, was not significantly different than in 1994 (734,000) or 1985 (781,000). However, the estimated number of occasional cocaine users (people who used in the past year but on fewer than 12 days) has sharply declined from 7.1 million in 1985 to 2.5 million in 1995.

- An estimated 2.3 million people started using marijuana in 1994. The annual number of marijuana initiates has risen since 1991.

- Despite the substantial reduction in cocaine use since 1985, there were still an estimated 530,000 Americans who used cocaine for the first time in 1994.

Alcohol Use

- In 1995, 111 million Americans age 12 and older had used alcohol in the past month (52 percent of the population). About 32 million engaged in binge drinking (5 or more drinks on at least one occasion in the past month), and about 11 million were heavy drinkers (drinking 5 or more drinks per occasion on 5 or more days in the past 30 days).

- There were no changes in rates of alcohol use between 1994 and 1995.

- About 10 million current drinkers were under age 21 in 1995. Of these, 4.4 million were binge drinkers, including 1.7 million heavy drinkers.

Cigarette Use

- An estimated 61 million Americans were current smokers in 1995. This represents a smoking rate of 29 percent. Current cigarette smoking did not change between 1994 and 1995.

- Among youths age 12–17, rates of smoking did not change between 1994 and 1995. An estimated 20 percent of youths age 12–17 (4.5 million adolescents) were current smokers in 1995.

- Current smokers are more likely to be heavy drinkers and illicit drug users than nonsmokers. Among smokers in 1995, 12.6 percent were heavy drinkers and 13.6 percent were illicit drug users. Among nonsmokers, 2.7 percent were heavy drinkers and 3.0 percent were illicit drug users.

- In 1994, about 1.5 million Americans first became daily smokers. The estimated number of new smokers per year has remained steady since the 1980s.

Women of Childbearing Age

- Overall, 7.3 percent (4.3 million) of women age 15–44 in 1995 had used an illicit drug in the past month. The corresponding rate for men age 15–44 was 11.6 percent.

- Of the 4.3 million women age 15–44 who were current illicit drug users in 1995, more than 1.6 million had children living with them, including 390,000 with at least one child under 2 years of age.

- Among women age 15–44 with no children and who were not pregnant, 9.3 percent were current illicit drug users. Only 2.3 percent of pregnant women were current drug users, which suggests that most women may reduce their drug use when they become pregnant. However, women who recently gave birth (have a child under 2 years old and are not pregnant) had a rate of use of 5.5 percent, suggesting that many women resume their drug use after giving birth.

heroin abuser's lifestyle is typically characterized by poor health, crime, arrest, imprisonment, and temporary stays in drug treatment programs.[22] Today AIDS, which is spread, among other ways, by the shared use of needles, has become the most serious health problem among heroin addicts.

During the 1960s marijuana became one of the major drugs of choice in the United States, particularly among white, middle-class young people who identified themselves as antiestablishment. Their lifestyles were distinct from those of the inner-city heroin addicts. What began as a hippie drug culture in the Haight-Ashbury area of San Francisco spread quickly through the country's college campuses.[23] In fact, a Harvard psychologist, Timothy Leary, traveled across the country in the 1960s telling students to "turn on, tune in, and drop out." Young marijuana users tended to live for the moment. Disillusioned by what they perceived as a rigid and hypocritical society, they challenged its norms through deviant behavior. Drugs—first marijuana, then hallucinogens (principally LSD), amphetamines, and barbiturates—came to symbolize the counterculture.[24]

In the 1960s and 1970s, attitudes toward recreational drug use became quite lax, perhaps as a result of the wide acceptance of marijuana.[25] By the 1980s, cocaine, once associated only with deviants, had become the drug of choice among the privileged, who watched (and copied) the well-publicized drug-oriented lifestyles of some celebrities and athletes. Typical cocaine users were well-educated, prosperous, upwardly mobile professionals in their twenties and thirties. They were lawyers and architects, editors and stockbrokers. They earned enough money to spend at least $100 an evening on their illegal recreational activities. By and large they were otherwise law-abiding, even though they knew their behavior was against the law.

The popularity of cocaine waned toward the end of the 1980s. The same is not true for crack, however, which spread to the inner-city population that had abused heroin in the latter part of the 1980s.[26] Crack is cheaper than powdered cocaine, fast-acting, and powerful. Though individual doses are inexpensive, once a person is hooked on crack, a daily supply can run between $100 and $250.

Drug addicts continually search for a new way to extend their high. In 1989 a mixture of crack and heroin, called "crank," began to be used. Crank is smoked in a pipe.[27] It is potentially very dangerous,

first, because it prolongs the brief high of crack alone and, second, because it appeals to younger drug addicts who are concerned about the link between AIDS and the sharing of hypodermic needles. The history of drug abuse suggests that crank, too, will be replaced by yet another substance that promises a better and faster high.

Crime-Related Activities

Many researchers have examined the criminal implications of addiction to heroin and, more recently, cocaine. James Inciardi found that 356 addicts in Miami, according to self-reports, committed 118,134 offenses (27,464 Index crimes) over a 1-year period.[28] A national program, Drug Use Forecasting, found that, in 1995, 51 to 83 percent of arrestees in 24 major U.S. cities had used drugs. Cocaine remains the most prevalent drug used.[29] Official statistics on "drug-related offenses" make it quite clear that street crime is significantly related to drug abuse.

The nature of the drug-crime relationship, however, is less clear. Is the addict typically an adolescent who never committed a crime before he or she became hooked but who thereafter was forced to commit crimes to get money to support the drug habit? In other words, does drug abuse lead to crime?[30] Or does criminal behavior precede drug abuse? Another possibility is that both drug abuse and criminal behavior stem from the same factors (biological, psychological, or sociological).[31] The debate continues, and many questions are still unanswered. But on one point most researchers agree: Whatever the temporal or causal sequence of drug abuse and crime, the frequency and seriousness of criminality increase as addiction increases. Drug abuse may not "cause" criminal behavior, but it does enhance it.[32]

Until the late 1970s most investigators of the drug-crime relationship reported that drug abusers were arrested primarily for property offenses. Recent scholarly literature, however, presents a different perspective. There appears to be an increasing amount of violence associated with drugs, and it may be attributable largely to the appearance of crack. Drug wars, for example, are becoming more frequent. Cities across the country have been divided into distinct turfs. Rival drug dealers settle disputes with guns, power struggles within a single drug enterprise lead

CRIMINOLOGICAL FOCUS

THE SMALL WORLD OF CRACK USERS

Interviews with crack users and dealers in Detroit in the late 1980s gave investigators "insider information" on the crack culture. The researchers' report is excerpted here:

In Detroit, distribution of crack ordinarily takes place indoors; very few sales occur on the street. . . . [T]he "dope house" or "crack house" is, by a wide margin, the primary retailing mechanism.

Anecdotal information from [our] interviews showed contrasting descriptions of sale places. Some were of the "buy, get high, and party" variety, but others were strictly (and literally) "holes in the wall." A house would have a small aperture into which the customer puts his money. A few moments pass, and then a hand materializes and deposits the crack.

"Touters" are circulating salespeople who generally are also users. The "other" category . . . generally meant, to survey respondents, users who gratuitously shared their drugs with friends. "Street" sales are generally made by "runners," "rollers," or "beepermen"—low-level retail dealers who may or may not also use the drugs they sell.

We asked the 30 respondents who admitted to dealing to characterize their own "style" of selling. Did they sell to support their own use, or mostly for profit?

Were they largely "go-betweens" (touters), often accepting drugs as payment, or a combination of touter and profit-dealer? Two-thirds of those who had sold crack most frequently chose the "user-dealer" description. Twenty percent said they sold mainly for profit, and the remainder acted as touters. Of the 116 respondents who admitted they were crack users, 89 denied any crack-dealing activity.

Ten of the informants discussed in some detail the process of preparing crack from granular cocaine. Some said they processed as much as 1 or 2 ounces, or as little as half a gram; those who processed larger quantities tended to work toward selling enough "rock" to cover their own use costs. Some entertained ideas of profitable returns on their investment. A popular unit of transaction reported was the "eightball," which is equivalent to between 2.5 and 3.5 grams of powder cocaine. It retailed from $125 to $250 and was expected to yield 45 to 55 "rocks," which could be retailed at prices from $10 to $15.

Currently we have compiled, from the interviews, a list of more than 100 street terms for crack. These terms reflect both generic names (rock, boulder) and brand names ("Schoolcraft," "Troop," etc.). In addition to these descriptive terms, a series of number designations is also used to characterize certain methods of crack consumption. Crack

crushed and sprinkled into a tobacco cigarette is referred to as a "51" or "501" or sometimes a "151."

The popularization of certain terms tells us something of the world view of the drug users and sellers themselves. For instance, the terms may reflect technologies used or believed to be used in processing. Informants have used the terms "ether-based," "synthetic," and "chemical" in describing crack types. A small number of "brand name" designations have been developed and used by particular distribution organizations. Examples of such terms include "eye-opener," "swell up," "speed," "Pony," "Eastside Player," and "Wrecking Crew."(1)

Source

1. Tom Miecykowski, "Understanding Life in the Crack Culture: The Investigative Utility of the Drug Use Forecasting System," *NIJ Reports,* December 1989, pp. 7–9.

Questions for Discussion

1. How can information such as that presented above help police officers and other investigators work to solve the drug problem?
2. How quickly do you think the kinds of data collected for the above report become out of date and useless? Would you expect the crack culture to be relatively stable or in a constant state of flux?

to assaults and homicides, one dealer robs another, informers are killed, their associates retaliate, and bystanders, some of them children, get caught in the crossfire.[33]

The International Drug Economy

The drug problem is a worldwide phenomenon, beyond the power of any one government to deal with.[34] Nor are drugs simply a concern of law enforcement agencies. Drugs influence politics, international relations, peace and war, and the economies of individual countries and of the world. Let us take a look at the political and economic impact of the international drug trade, specifically as it concerns cocaine, heroin, and marijuana. Figure 14.3 shows the sources of these drugs and some shipping routes.

Cocaine. Today the largest cocaine producer is Peru. Annual harvests of 226,000 to 282,000 metric tons of coca leaves yield from 412 to 524 tons of pure cocaine. Cocaine production in Bolivia is not far behind, with a yield of 111 to 153 tons.[35] Colombia, which produces only 25 tons of pure cocaine, exports more than any other country—over half of the world's supply—because it is in Colombia that much of the raw coca of Peru and Bolivia is refined into cocaine. The "cocaine cartel," which controls production and distribution, is said to be composed of no more than 12 families, located principally in Colombia and Bolivia. However, organized-crime interests in other South American countries are establishing themselves in the market.

Each year nearly half of all cocaine seized is shipped to the United States on private planes. Small planes evade controls and land on little-used airstrips or drop their cargos offshore to waiting speedboats.[36] Boats carrying drugs then mingle with local pleasure craft and bring the cargo to shore. Wholesalers who work for the Colombian cartels take care of the nationwide distribution. Some of the estimated 100,000 Colombians living illegally in the United States are thought to belong to the distribution apparatus.

Heroin. "Just five years ago, almost all of the heroin seized came from Asia. Today, 32 percent of heroin seized can be traced to South America, with an estimated 20,000 hectares of opium poppies being cultivated in Colombia alone." This statement, made by the head of the Justice Department's Drug Enforcement Agency, Thomas Constantine, sheds light on the recent expansion in scope of Colombia's cash crop. This diversification is a direct result of simple economics—while 1 kilogram of cocaine sells for between $10,000 and $40,000 on the streets, an equal amount of South American heroin fetches anywhere from $85,000 to $180,000.

Production of heroin in all countries is organized by local warlords, illegitimate traders, and corrupt administrators; it is tending to come increasingly under the control of *triads*—organized-crime families of Chinese origin based in Hong Kong and Taiwan. More and more, heroin in the United States comes from Mexico. Most of the heroin from the Golden Crescent and Golden Triangle enters the United States on commercial aircraft, whereas Mexican heroin comes overland. In Europe and in the United States the traditional Sicilian Mafia families have assumed significant roles in the refining and distribution of heroin.

Marijuana. Because marijuana is bulky, smugglers initially transported it on oceangoing vessels. From January through October 1986, 87 percent of the total volume of marijuana seized was taken from privately owned pleasure craft or charter vessels not engaged in commercial trade. Today, most of the Colombian marijuana—about one-third of all marijuana imported into the United States—is shipped by sea. Mexican marijuana, trucked overland, makes up another third, and the remainder comes in by private plane from such countries as Belize and Jamaica. Hashish, a concentrated form of marijuana that comes predominantly from Pakistan (60 to 65 percent) and Lebanon (25 to 30 percent), is brought in by noncommercial ships.

Money Laundering. The illegal drug economy is vast. Annual sales are estimated to be between $300 billion and $500 billion. The American drug economy alone generates $40 billion to $50 billion in sales. Profits are enormous, and no taxes are paid on them. Because the profits are "dirty money," they must undergo **money laundering.** Typically, the cash obtained from drug sales in the United States is physically smuggled out of the country because it cannot be legally exported without disclosure (Table 14.3).

Smuggling cash is not easy—$1 million in $20 bills weighs 100 pounds—yet billions of dollars are exported, in false-bottomed suitcases and smugglers' vests, to countries that allow numbered bank accounts without identification of names (the Cayman Islands, Panama, Switzerland, Austria, and Liechtenstein, among others).

New methods of "laundering" drug profits, not involving physical transfer of cash, have recently been invented, such as bogus real estate transactions and purchases of gold, antiques, and art. Such transactions permit electronic transfer of drug funds worldwide with minimum chance of detection. Once

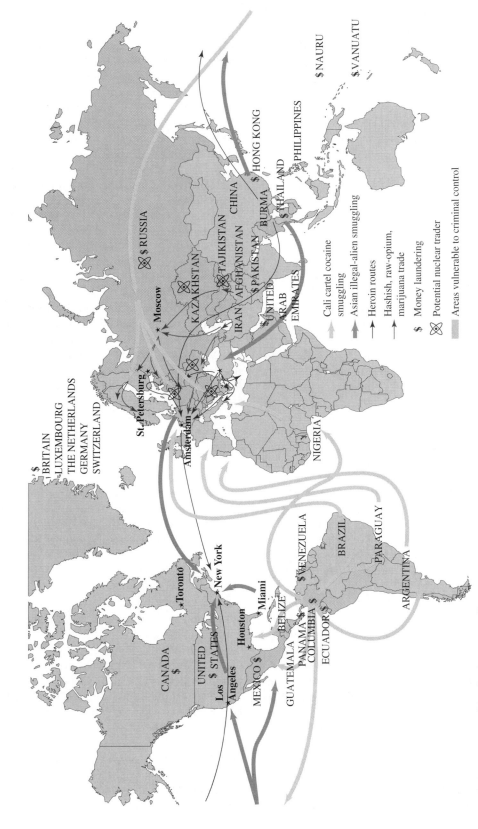

FIGURE 14.3 Worldwide drug smuggling routes, 1993.

TABLE 14.3

La Mina, The Mine, reportedly laundered $1.2 billion for the Colombian cartels over a 2-year period.

Currency from selling cocaine was packed in boxes labeled jewelry and sent by armored car to Ropex, a jewelry maker in Los Angeles.

↓

The cash was counted and deposited in banks that filed the CTRs, but few suspicions were raised because the gold business is based on cash.

↓

Ropex then wire-transferred the money to New York banks in payment for fictitious gold purchased from Ronel, allegedly a gold bullion business.

↓

Ronel shipped Ropex bars of lead painted gold to complete the fake transaction. Ropex used the alleged sale of this gold to other jewelry businesses to cover further currency conversions.

↓

Ronel then transferred the funds from American banks to South American banks where the Colombian cartel could gain access to them.

Source: "Getting Banks to Just Say 'No,'" *Business Week*, Apr. 17, 1989, p. 17, and Maggie Mahar, "Dirty Money: It Triggers a Bold New Attack in the War on Drugs," *Barron's*, **69** (June 1989): 6–38, at p. 7. From the U.S. Department of Justice, *Drugs, Crime and the Justice System* (Washington, D.C.: U.S. Government Printing Office, 1992).

deposited in foreign accounts, the funds are "clean" and can be returned to legitimate businesses and investments. They may also be used for illegal purposes, such as the purchase of arms for export to terrorist groups.

The Political Impact. The political impact of the drug trade on producer countries is devastating. In the late 1970s and early 1980s, the government of Bolivia became completely corrupt. The minister of justice was referred to as the "minister of cocaine." In Colombia, drug lords and terrorists combined their resources to wrest power from the democratically elected government. Thirteen supreme court judges and 167 police officers were killed; the minister of justice and the ambassador to Hungary were assassinated.

The message was that death was the price for refusal to succumb to drug corruption. In 1989 a highly respected Colombian presidential candidate who had come out against the cocaine cartel was assassinated. The government remained fragile and the situation precarious. Over the years, the scandal aroused by liaisons between notorious drug lords and high-ranking government officials has endured. The most recent, and perhaps most injurious to diplomatic relations with the United States, is that involving Colombia's current president, Ernesto Samper. Samper, likened to Nixon by the Colombian opposition leader, received $6 million toward his 1994 campaign fund from the renowned Cali cartel—the leader in cocaine trafficking. Despite his exoneration by Colombia's House of Representatives, the United States government sent an unequivocal message to President Samper by revoking his U.S. visa and decertifying Colombia.

Nor is Colombia alone in its efforts to cope with the drug problem. Before General Manuel Noriega was arrested in a U.S. invasion of Panama to face charges of drug smuggling, he had made himself military dictator of Panama. Seven years later, however, little has really changed:

> President Ernesto Perez Balladares has admitted that his 1994 campaign received $51,000 from a Colombian businessman later jailed on drug charges. Other donations to the President are also under scrutiny. . . . Seven years after the military intervention, Panama's banking system once again is a conduit for drug traffickers laundering their profits. Secret numbered accounts, legal in Panama, prevent prosecutors from putting a name to a number. Lawyers create shell corporations with little more than a stroke of a pen and about $1,000. Those behind the companies remain a mystery. The collapse earlier this year of a Panamanian bank, under investigation in the US for money laundering, with links to two senior aides of the president underscored, for many, the pervasiveness of the problem.[37]

Corruption and crime rule in all drug-producing countries. Government instability is the necessary consequence. Coups replace elections. The populations of these countries are not immune to addiction themselves. Several South American countries, including Colombia, Bolivia, and Peru, are now experiencing major addiction problems; Peru alone has some 60,000 addicts. The Asian narcotics-producing countries, which thought themselves immune to the addiction problem, also became victims of their own production. Pakistan now counts about 200,000 addicts.[38]

One of the more remarkable aspects of the expansion of the drug trade has been the spread of addiction and the drug economy to the Third World and to the newly democratic, formerly socialist countries. Of all political problems, however, the most vicious is the alliance that drug dealers have forged with terrorist groups in the Near East, in Latin America, and in Europe.[39]

Drug Control

In September 1989 President George Bush unveiled his antidrug strategy. On the international level, the president sought modest funding for the United Nations effort to combat the international narcotics drug traffic. He also called for far greater expenditures for bilateral cooperation with other countries to deal with producers and traffickers. This effort extends to crop eradication programs.[40] He singled out Colombia, Bolivia, and Peru for such efforts and immediately sent U.S. Army assistance, including helicopters and crews, to Colombia for use in that country's very difficult battle with the Medellín cartel.

On the national level, the strategy focused on federal aid to state and local police for street-level attacks on drug users and small dealers, for whom alternative punishments such as house arrest (confinement in one's home rather than in a jail cell) and boot camps (short but harsh incarceration with military drill) were started. It also called for rigorous enforcement of forfeiture laws, under which money is confiscated from offenders if it can be established that it came from the drug trade; property purchased with such money is also forfeited.[41] The Bush war on drugs followed a host of federal drug-control initiatives. All of them, like the Bush administration initiatives, have been at best only slightly effective.[42]

The Bush plan continued the American emphasis on law enforcement options for drug control. Treatment and prevention received only a fraction of the money allocated to traditional law enforcement efforts throughout the 1980s and early 1990s. The Clinton administration's approach, unveiled on February 9, 1994, earmarked $13 billion for a national strategy that emphasized antidrug education as well as treatment programs. His 1995 strategy, which targeted four major initiatives, was advanced by the current drug czar, Barry McCaffery. McCaffery placed a decided emphasis on treatment, prevention, domestic law enforcement, interdiction, and international control.

Treatment. The treatment approach to drug control is not new. During the late 1960s and into the 1970s, hope for the country's drug problem centered on treatment programs. These programs took a variety of forms, depending on the setting and modality, for example, self-help groups (Narcotics Anonymous, Cocaine Anonymous), psychotherapy, detoxification ("drying out" in a hospital), "rap" houses (neighborhood centers where addicts can come for group therapy sessions), various community social-action efforts (addicts clean up neighborhoods, plant trees, and so on), and—the two most popular—residential therapeutic communities and methadone maintenance programs.[43]

The *therapeutic community* is a 24-hour, total-care facility where former addicts and professionals work together to help addicts become drug-free. In *methadone maintenance* programs, addicts are given a synthetic narcotic, methadone, which prevents withdrawal symptoms (physical and psychological pain associated with giving up drugs), while addicts reduce their drug intake slowly over a period of time. Throughout the program addicts receive counseling designed to help them return to a normal life.

It is difficult to assess the success of most treatment programs. Even if individuals appear to be drug-free within a program, it is hard to find out what happens to them once they leave it (or even during a week when they do not show up). In addition, it may well be that the addicts who succeed in drug treatment programs are those who have already resolved to stop abusing drugs before they voluntarily come in for treatment; the real hard-core users may not even make an effort to become drug-free.

The latest effort to divert drug offenders (users and purchasers) from criminal careers is a Dade County, Florida, "drug court" program. The drug court judge has the option to divert nonviolent drug offenders to a counseling program in lieu of incarceration. Of the 4500 drug users diverted into the program since 1989, only 11 percent have been rearrested for the commission of any criminal offense in the year following dismissal of the original charges.[44]

Education. While drug treatment deals with the problem of addiction after the fact, education tries to prevent people from taking illegal drugs in the first place. The idea behind educational programs is straightforward: People who have information about the harmful effects of illegal drugs are likely to stay away from them. Sometimes the presentation of the facts has been coupled with scare techniques. Some well-known athletes and entertainers have joined the crusade with public-service messages ("a questionable approach," says Howard Abadinsky, "given the level of substance abuse reported in these groups").[45]

The educational approach has several drawbacks. Critics maintain that most addicts are quite knowledgeable about the potential consequences of taking drugs but think of them as just a part of the "game."[46] Most people who begin to use drugs believe they will never become addicted, even when they have information about addiction.[47] Inner-city youngsters do not lack information about the harmful effects of drugs. They learn about the dangers from daily exposure to addicts desperately searching for drugs, sleeping on the streets, going through withdrawal, and stealing family belongings to get money.[48]

Legalization. Despite earlier increases in government funding for an expanded war on drugs, the goal of a drug-free society in the 1990s is hardly likely to be achieved. There is much evidence that all the approaches, even the "new" ones, have been tried before with little or no effect. Some experts are beginning to advocate a very different approach—legalization. Their reasoning is that since the drug problem seems to elude all control efforts, why not deal with heroin and cocaine the same way we deal with alcohol and tobacco? In other words, why not subject these drugs to some government control and restrictions, but make them freely available to all adults?[49]

They argue that current drug-control policies impose tremendous costs on taxpayers without demonstrating effective results. In addition to spending less money on crime control, the government would make money on tax revenue from the sale of legalized drugs. This is, of course, a hotly debated issue. Given the dangers of drug abuse and the moral issues at stake, legalization surely offers no easy solution and has had little public support. However, the surgeon general of the United States, in 1994, mentioned the option of legalization—only to be rebuffed by the president.

ALCOHOL AND CRIME

Alcohol is another substance that contributes to social problems. One of the major differences between alcohol and the other drugs we have been discussing is that the sale and purchase of alcohol are legal in most jurisdictions of the United States. The average annual consumption of alcoholic beverages by each individual 14 years of age and over is equivalent to 591 cans of beer, or 115 bottles of wine, or 35 fifths of liquor; this is more than the average individual consumption of coffee and milk.[50] Alcohol is consumed at recreational events, business meetings, lunches and dinners at home, and celebrations; in short, drinking alcohol has become the expected behavior in many social situations.

Drinking is widespread among young people. Lloyd D. Johnston, Patrick M. O'Malley, and Jerald G. Bachman asked students at 75 high schools in 7 states how many times during the last month (excluding religious services) they had consumed any beer, wine, or liquor. The responses showed that by age 15 the majority of boys and girls drank on at least one occasion in any given month. Of the male students age 17 or older, one-quarter drank 10 or more times a month. And a significant proportion reported that intoxication was a necessary part of their lives. Yet the authors also reported that alcohol consumption declined during recent years.[51]

The History of Legalization

Alcohol consumption is not new to our culture; in colonial days alcohol was considered safer and healthier than water. Still, the history of alcohol consumption is filled with controversy. Many people through the centuries have viewed it as wicked and degenerate. By the turn of the twentieth century, social reformers linked liquor to prostitution, poverty, the immigrant culture, and corrupt politics.

Various lobbying groups, such as the Women's Christian Temperance Union and the American Anti-Saloon League, bombarded politicians with demands for the prohibition of alcohol.[52] On January 16, 1920, the Eighteenth Amendment to the Constitution went into force, prohibiting the manufacture, sale, and transportation of alcoholic beverages. The Volstead Act of 1919 had already defined as "intoxicating liquor" any beverage that contained more than ½ of 1 percent alcohol.

Historians generally agree that no law in America has ever been more widely violated or more unpopular. Vast numbers of people continued to consume alcohol. It was easy to manufacture and to import. The illegal business brought tremendous profits to suppliers, and it could not be controlled by enforce-

GAMBLING: "INJURIOUS TO THE MORALS"

Since civilization began—and maybe before—people have risked their fortunes on all kinds of chances. They still do in the stock market and in commerce generally. That kind of chance taking has been legal in most parts of the world. But other kinds of risk taking—what we call "games of chance"—have long been considered immoral and prohibited by law.

In England in the early days of the common law, gambling was not illegal. Later statutes made "gaming," including playing billiards or tennis, illegal. In the eighteenth century, the keeping of a gaming house became a "criminal nuisance." But in the American colonies, lotteries, another form of gambling, were perfectly legal. They were used to fund Columbia University (then King's College), Harvard, Yale, Dartmouth, and Williams College. In the nineteenth century, gambling became less and less acceptable, until finally it was prohibited in almost every state.(1)

What is the situation in the United States today? All American states except Nevada prohibit gambling in general, but there are many legal exceptions. Some states have legalized certain forms—for example, dog rac-

ing, horse racing, or (in Nevada, New Jersey, and Puerto Rico) casino gambling—and state lottery programs and church-sponsored bingo also are defined as legal gambling in many jurisdictions. Gambling is now legal in a number of reservations for Native Americans.

Why is gambling sometimes legal and sometimes not? The great English jurist Sir James Fitzjames Stephen wrote in 1877: "Unlawful gaming means gaming carried on in such a manner, or for such a length of time or for such stakes (regard being had to the circumstances of the players) that it is likely to be injurious to the morals of those who game."(2) It appears, then, that the harm in gambling is the threat to players' morals—the idea that the gambler who wins receives an undeserved, unearned reward.

One of the problems in the question of the legality of gambling seems to have economic roots: Gambling is extremely profitable for the operators of games. The 1976 Federal Commission on Gambling reported a turnover of $75 billion per year for American gambling activities; organized crime netted an estimated $7 billion. By now the figures are certainly much higher. So it is possible that states and localities hungry for money and facing budget cuts and

the end of subsidies want some of the vast sums that now are siphoned off into illegal channels. Government, in other words, wants a piece of the action. Antigambling laws may seek less to protect the morals of gamblers, then, than to keep organized crime out of an extremely lucrative business.

Sources
1. Gresham M. Sykes, *Criminology* (New York: Harcourt Brace Jovanovich, 1978), pp. 192–193.
2. Sir James Fitzjames Stephen, *A Digest of the Criminal Law,* ed. 5 (London: Macmillan, 1894), p. 143.

Questions for Discussion
1. Why is the gamble you take when you place your money with a Wall Street futures trader a legal investment, while the off-track bet on the outcome of a horse race may not be legal? Is one less "injurious to the morals" than the other?
2. Do you think gambling should be legal throughout the United States, illegal throughout the United States, or decided on a state-by-state basis? Defend your position.

ment officers, who were too inefficient, too few, or too corrupt. The unlawful sale of alcohol was called "bootlegging." The term originated in the early practice of concealing liquor in one's boot to avoid payment of liquor taxes.

Bootlegging created empires for such gangsters as Al Capone and Dutch Schultz, as we saw in Chapter 13. Private saloons, or "speakeasies," prospered. Unpopular and unenforceable, the Eighteenth Amendment was repealed 13 years after its birth—on December 5, 1933. Except for a few places, the manufacture and sale of alcohol have been legal in the United States since that time.

Crime-Related Activities

The alcohol-related activities that have become serious social problems are violent crime, drunk driving, and public intoxication.

Violence. National surveys of inmates in jails and prisons show the following:

- Almost half of the convicted offenders incarcerated for violent crimes (particularly assaults) used alcohol immediately before the crimes.
- Almost 50 percent of the inmates drank an average of 1 ounce or more of alcohol each day (com-

pared with 10 percent of all persons age 18 and older in the general population).

- Over one-third of the inmates drank alcoholic beverages every day during the year before they committed their crimes.
- From 34 to 45 percent of inmates convicted of homicide, assault, rape, and robbery described themselves as heavy drinkers.[53]

For many decades criminologists have probed the relationship between alcohol and violence. Marvin Wolfgang, in a study of 588 homicides in Philadelphia, found that alcohol was present in two-thirds of all homicide cases (both victim and offender, 44 percent; victim only, 9 percent; offender only, 11 percent).[54] Similar findings were reported from northern Sweden: Two-thirds of the offenders who committed homicide between 1970 and 1981 and almost half of their victims were intoxicated when the crime was committed.[55]

Many other offenses show a significant relationship between alcohol and violence. In the United States, 58 percent of those convicted for assault and 64 percent of offenders who assaulted police officers had been drinking.[56] In about one-third of rapes, the offender, the victim, or both had been drinking immediately before the attack.[57] The role of alcohol in violent family disputes has been increasingly recognized. Among 2413 American couples, the rate of severe violence by the husband was 2.10 per 100 couples in homes where the husbands were never drunk and 30.89 per 100 couples in homes where the husbands were drunk "very often."[58]

Many explanations have been offered for the relationship between alcohol and violence.[59] Some studies focus on the individual. When people are provoked, for example, alcohol can reduce restraints on aggression.[60] Alcohol also escalates aggression by reducing awareness of consequences.[61] Other studies analyze the social situation in which drinking takes place. Experts argue that in some situations aggressive behavior is considered appropriate or is even expected when people drink together.[62]

Drunk Driving. The effect of alcohol on driving is causing continuing concern. The incidence of drunk driving, referred to in statutes as "driving under the influence" and "driving while intoxicated" (depending on the level of alcohol found in the blood), has been steadily rising. Statistics indicate the extent of the problem:

- Driving under the influence (DUI) arrests increased nearly 223 percent between 1970 and 1986, while the number of licensed drivers increased only 42 percent.
- Before arrest for driving while intoxicated (DWI), convicted offenders drink at least 6 ounces of pure alcohol within 4 hours.
- A recent national survey showed that about 7 percent of all persons confined in jails were charged with or convicted of DWI; 13 percent had a current charge or prior conviction for DWI; and almost half of those in jail for DWI had a previous sentence of probation, jail, or prison for the same offense.
- In 1991 there were 398,000 persons injured in alcohol-related crashes.
- In 1989 there were 68,000 alcohol-related traffic accidents resulting in serious injury or deaths.
- The annual cost of drunk driving (property damage, medical bills, and so on) is estimated at $24 billion.
- There were 1,079,533 arrests for driving under the influence in 1994.[63]

Cari Lightner, age 13, was killed in May 1980 by a drunk driver while she was walking on a sidewalk.[64] The driver had been arrested only a few days before on a DUI charge. The victim's mother, Candy, took action almost immediately to push for new legislation that would mandate much stiffer penalties for drunk driving. It was difficult at first to get government to respond, but she did get the attention of journalists. By the end of the year in which Cari died, Mrs. Lightner had organized the Governor's Task Force on Drinking and Driving in California.

And her own advocacy group, Mothers Against Drunk Driving (MADD), was in the national spotlight. MADD's members were people who themselves had been injured or whose family members had been injured or killed in an accident involving an intoxicated driver. The organization has grown to more than 300 chapters.[65] Remove Intoxicated Drivers (RID) and Students Against Drunk Drivers (SADD) have joined the campaign.

The citizens' groups called public attention to a major health and social problem, demanded action, and got it. Congress proclaimed one week each December to be Drunk and Drugged Awareness Week, and the Presidential Commission on Drunk Driving was formed. Candy Lightner was appointed a commissioner. The federal government attached the

Firefighters search for a victim in a drunk driving accident; the Pontiac Fiero was torn in half.

distribution of state highway funds to various anti-drunk-driving measures, thereby pressuring the states into putting recommendations into action. Old laws have been changed, and new laws have been passed.

After the ratification in 1971 of the Twenty-Sixth Amendment to the U.S. Constitution, which lowered the voting age to 18 years, many states lowered their minimum-age requirement for the purchase and sale of alcoholic beverages. By 1983, 33 states had done so; but by 1987, all but one state had raised the minimum drinking age back to 21. Under New York's Civil Forfeiture Law, the government can take any car involved in a felony drunk-driving case, sell it, and give the money to the victims. Texas has a similar law.[66] Tuscarawas County in Ohio places brightly colored orange plates on cars of drivers whose licenses have been suspended for drunk driving.[67]

Other objectives of legislation have been to limit the "happy hours" during which bars serve drinks at reduced prices, to shorten hours when alcoholic beverages can be sold, to make hosts and bartenders liable for damages if their guests or patrons drink too much and become involved in an accident, to limit advertisements, and to put health warnings on bottles. Most states have increased their penalties for

drunk driving to include automatic license suspension, higher minimum fines, and even mandatory jail sentences.

Thus far the results of such legislation are mixed. A study carried out in Seattle, Minneapolis, and Cincinnati found that such meaures did indeed lower the number of traffic deaths, while other investigations did not show positive results.[68] Nevertheless, drunk driving has achieved national attention, and even modern technology is being used in the effort to find solutions: Japanese and American technicians have come up with a device that locks the ignition system and can be unlocked only when the attached Breathalyzer (which registers alcohol in the blood) indicates that the driver is sober.[69] California, Washington, Texas, Michigan, and Oregon have passed legislation authorizing its use.

SEXUAL MORALITY OFFENSES

All societies endeavor to regulate sexual behavior, although what specifically is considered not permissible has varied from society to society and from time to time. The legal regulation of sexual conduct in

Anglo-American law has been greatly influenced by both the Old and the New Testament. In the Middle Ages the enforcement of laws pertaining to sexual morality was the province of church courts. Today, to the extent that immorality is still illegal, it is the regular criminal courts that enforce such laws.

Morality laws have always been controversial, whether they seek to prevent alcohol abuse or to prohibit certain forms of sexual behavior or its public display or depiction. Sexual activity other than intercourse between spouses for the purpose of procreation has been severely penalized in many societies and until only recently in the United States. Sexual intercourse between unmarried persons ("lewd cohabitation"), seduction of a female by promise of marriage, and all forms of "unnatural" sexual relations were serious crimes, some carrying capital sentences, as late as the nineteenth century. In 1962 the Model Penal Code proposed some important changes. Fornication and lewd cohabitation were dropped from the list of offenses, as was homosexual intercourse between consenting adults.

The idea behind these changes is that the sexual relations of consenting adults should be beyond the control of the law, not only because throughout history such legal efforts have proved ineffective but also because the harm to society, if any, is too slight to warrant the condemnation of law. "The state's power to regulate sexual conduct ought to stop at the bedroom door or at the barn door," said sex researcher Alfred Kinsey four decades ago.[70]

Although the Model Penal Code has removed or limited sanctions for conduct among consenting adults, the code retains strong prohibitions against sexual activities involving children. Penalties are severe for **statutory rape** (intercourse by an adult male with an underage female regardless of consent), deviate sexual intercourse with a child, corruption of a minor, sexual assault, and endangering the welfare of a child. Of course, the recommendations of the American Law Institute are not always accepted by state legislatures.

Let us take a close look at three existing offenses involving sexual morality: "deviate sexual intercourse by force or imposition," prostitution, and pornography.

"Deviate Sexual Intercourse by Force or Imposition"

The Model Penal Code defines "deviate sexual intercourse" as "sexual intercourse per os or per anum [by mouth or by anus] between human beings who are not husband and wife, and any form of sexual intercourse with an animal" [sec. 213.2(1)]. The common law called such sexual acts **sodomy,** after the biblical city of Sodom, which the Lord destroyed for its wickedness, presumably because its citizens had engaged in such acts. The common law dealt harshly with sodomy, making it a capital offense and referring to it as *crimen innominatum*—a crime not to be mentioned by name.

Yet other cultures, including ancient Greece, did not frown on homosexual activities. And Alfred Kinsey reminded us that homosexual (from the Greek "same") relations are common among all mammals, of which humans are but one species.[71] The MPC subjects "deviate sexual intercourse" between two human beings to punishment only if it is accomplished by severe compulsion or if the other person is incapable of granting consent or is a child less than 10 years old. To conservative lawmakers, this model legislation is far too liberal; to liberals, it does not go far enough. Generally, liberal thinkers prefer the law not to interfere with the sexual practices of consenting adults at all.

The gay and lesbian rights movements have done much to destigmatize consensual, private adult sexual relationships. Yet legislatures have been slow to respond, and the U.S. Supreme Court has taken a conservative stance as well. In 1986 the Court sustained a Georgia statute that criminalizes consensual sexual acts between adults of the same gender, even if they are performed in the privacy of one's home.[72]

Prostitution

Not so long ago it was a crime to be a prostitute.[73] The law punished women for a status acquired on the basis of sexual intercourse with more than one man. Under some statutes it was not even necessary to prove that money was paid for the sexual act. The Supreme Court ruled in 1962—in a case involving the status of being a drug addict—that criminal liability can be based only on conduct, that is, on doing something in violation of law.[74] This decision would seem to apply to prostitution as well. Therefore, one can no longer be penalized for being a prostitute. But soliciting for sex is an act, not a status, and nearly all states make solicitation of sex for money the misdemeanor of **prostitution.**

The Uniform Crime Reports recorded 97,968 arrests for prostitution and commercialized vice during 1993.[75] The number of arrests continues to fall (Figure 14.4).

The number would be extremely high if we were to include all acts of sexual favor granted in return for some gratuity. Even if the number were limited to straightforward cash transactions (including, nowadays, credit card transactions), there is no way of arriving at a figure. Many persons may act as prostitutes for a while and then return to legitimate lifestyles. There are part-time and full-time prostitutes, male and female prostitutes, itinerant and resident prostitutes, street hookers and high-priced escorts who do not consider themselves to be prostitutes.[76]

Many law enforcement agencies do not relish the task of suppressing prostitution. In some jurisdictions the police have little time to spend on vice control, given the extent of violent and property crimes. Thus, when prostitutes are arrested, it is likely to be in response to demands by community groups, business establishments, or church leaders to "clean up the neighborhood." Occasionally the police find it expedient to arrest prostitutes because they may divulge information about unsolved crimes, such as narcotics distribution, theft, receiving stolen property, or organized crime.

Prostitution encompasses a variety of both acts and actors. The prostitute, female or male, is not alone in the business of prostitution. A **pimp** provides access to prostitutes and protects and exploits them, living off their proceeds. There are still madams who maintain houses of prostitution. And finally, there are the patrons of prostitutes, popularly called "johns." Ordinarily it is not a criminal offense to patronize a prostitute; yet the framers of the MPC proposed to criminalize this act. The section was hotly debated before the American Law Institute. A final vote of the members rejected criminalization.

Researchers have found that many prostitutes come from broken homes and poor neighborhoods and are school dropouts. Yet all social classes contribute to the prostitution hierarchy. High-priced call girls, many of them well-educated women, may operate singly or out of agencies. The television "blue channels" that broadcast after midnight in most metropolitan areas carry commercials advertising the availability of call girls, their phone numbers, and sometimes their specialties. At the next-lower level of the prostitution hierarchy are the massage parlor prostitutes. When Shirley, a masseuse, was asked, "Do you consider yourself a prostitute?" she

FIGURE 14.4 Estimated number of prostitution arrests in the United States, 1970–1993. *Source: Uniform Crime Reports,* 1994.

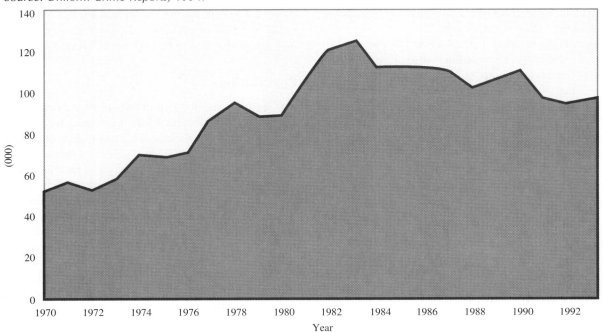

answered: "Yes, as well as a masseuse, and a healer, and a couple of other things."[77] One rung lower on the prostitution ladder are the "inmates" (a term used by the MPC) of the houses of prostitution, locally called bordellos, whorehouses, cathouses, or red-light houses.

According to people "in the life" (prostitution), the streetwalkers are the least-respected class in the hierarchy. They are the "working girls" or "hookers." They are found clustered on their accustomed street corners, on thoroughfares, or in truck and bus depots, dressed in bright attire, ready to negotiate a price with any passerby. Sexual services are performed in vehicles or in nearby "hot-sheet" hotel rooms. Life for these prostitutes—some of whom are transvestite males—is dangerous and grim. Self-reports suggest that many are drug addicts and have been exposed to HIV.[78] Other varieties of prostitution range from the legal houses that a few counties permit to operate in Nevada to troupes of prostitutes who travel from one place of opportunity to another (work projects, farm labor camps, construction sites) and bar ("B") girls who entertain customers in cocktail lounges and make themselves available for sexual activities for a price.

Popular, political, and scientific opinions on prostitution have changed, no doubt largely because prostitution has changed. Around the turn of the century it probably was true that a large number of prostitutes had been forced into the occupation by unscrupulous men. Indeed, it was this pattern that led to the enactment of the "White Slave Traffic Act" (called the Mann Act, after the senator who proposed the bill), prohibiting the interstate transportation of females for purposes of prostitution. There is some evidence that today the need for money, together with few legitimate opportunities to obtain it, prompts many young women and men to become prostitutes.

Sex researcher Paul Gebhard found in 1969 that only 4 percent of U.S. prostitutes were forced into prostitution. More recently Jennifer James found that the majority entered "the life" because of its financial rewards.[79] Whatever view we take of adult prostitutes as victims of a supposedly victimless criminal activity, one subgroup clearly is a victimized class: children, female and male, who are enticed and sometimes forced into prostitution, especially in large cities. Some are runaways, picked up by procurers at bus depots; some are simply "street children"; and others have been abused and molested by the adults in their lives.[80]

Pornography

Physical sexual contact is a basic component of both sodomy and prostitution. **Pornography** requires no contact at all; it simply portrays sexually explicit material. Statutes in all states make it a criminal offense to produce, offer for sale, sell, distribute, or exhibit pornographic (sometimes called obscene, lewd, or lascivious) material. Federal law prohibits the transportation of such material in interstate commerce and outlaws the use of the mails, the telephone, radio, and television for the dissemination of pornographic material.[81]

The Problem of Definition. The term "pornographic" is derived from the Greek *pornographos* ("writing of harlots," or descriptions of the acts of harlots). The term "obscene" comes from the Latin *ob* ("against," "before") plus *caenum* ("filth"), or pos-

A streetwalker waits for a prospective customer on a lower Manhattan streetcorner, June 1993. This was the area where serial killer Joel Rifkin stalked and killed 17 prostitutes.

WINDOW TO THE WORLD

GLOBAL SEXUAL SLAVERY: WOMEN AND CHILDREN

"I thought I was going to work as a waitress," a young Dominican, transported to Greece, told

BBC television, her eyes welling with tears. "Then they said if I didn't have sex, I'd be sent back to Santo Domingo without a penny. I was beaten, burned with cigarettes. I knew

nobody. I was a virgin. I held out for five days, crying, with no food. [Eventually] I lost my honor and my virginity for $25."(1)

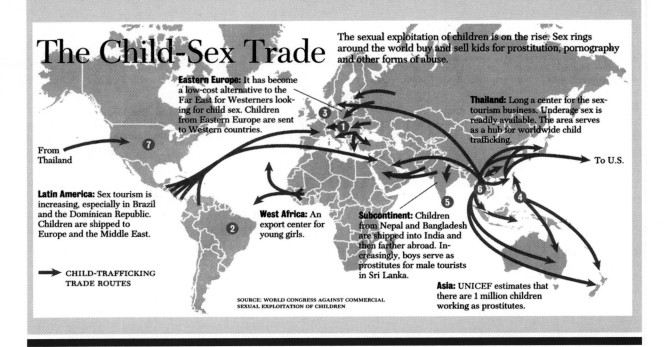

The Child-Sex Trade

The sexual exploitation of children is on the rise. Sex rings around the world buy and sell kids for prostitution, pornography and other forms of abuse.

Eastern Europe: It has become a low-cost alternative to the Far East for Westerners looking for child sex. Children from Eastern Europe are sent to Western countries.

Thailand: Long a center for the sex-tourism business. Underage sex is readily available. The area serves as a hub for worldwide child trafficking.

From Thailand

To U.S.

Latin America: Sex tourism is increasing, especially in Brazil and the Dominican Republic. Children are shipped to Europe and the Middle East.

West Africa: An export center for young girls.

Subcontinent: Children from Nepal and Bangladesh are shipped into India and then farther abroad. Increasingly, boys serve as prostitutes for male tourists in Sri Lanka.

Asia: UNICEF estimates that there are 1 million children working as prostitutes.

➤ CHILD-TRAFFICKING TRADE ROUTES

SOURCE: WORLD CONGRESS AGAINST COMMERCIAL SEXUAL EXPLOITATION OF CHILDREN

---

sibly from *obscena* ("offstage"). In Roman theatrical performances, disgusting and offensive parts of plays took place offstage, out of sight but not out of hearing of the audience.[82] Courts and legislators have used the two terms interchangeably, but nearly all statutes and decisions deal with pornography (with the implication of sexual arousal) rather than with obscenity (with its implication of filth).[83]

Scholars generally agree that the statutes in existence appear to be addressed primarily to pornographic materials.[84] What, then, is the contemporary meaning of "pornography"? The Model Penal Code (1962) says that a publication is pornographic (obscene or indecent) "if, considered as a whole, its predominant appeal is to prurient interests," and if, "in addition, it goes substantially beyond customary limits in describing or representing such matters"

(sec. 251.4). This definition, which is full of ambiguities, was to play a major role in several Supreme Court decisions.

Two presidential commissions were no more successful in defining the term. The Commission on Obscenity and Pornography (1970) avoided a definition and used instead the term "explicit sexual material."[85] The Attorney General's Commission on Pornography (1986) gave no definition.[86] The definition created by a British parliamentary committee in 1979 seems to describe pornography best:

A pornographic representation combines two features: It has a certain function or intention, to arouse its audience sexually, and also a certain content, explicit representation of sexual materials (organs, postures, activity, etc.).[87]

WINDOW TO THE WORLD

This woman's story is a common one. While some women become prostitutes by choice, many are forced into it. The growing sex trade around the world needs a constant supply of bodies, and it is getting them however it can. The statistics are horrifying: For the brothels of Bombay, some 7000 adolescents from Nepal's Himalayan hill villages are sold to slave traders each year. In Brazil the number of girls forced into prostitution in mining camps is estimated at 25,000. Japan's bars feature approximately 70,000 Thai "hostesses" working as sex slaves. Some 200,000 Bangladeshi women have been kidnapped into prostitution in Pakistan.(1)

The numbers of underage prostitutes are equally shocking, whether the children were sold into slavery or are trying to survive in a harsh world by selling their bodies: 800,000 in Thailand, 400,000 in India, 250,000 in Brazil, and 60,000 in the Philippines. Child prostitution recently has increased in Russian and East European cities, with an estimated 1000 youngsters working in Moscow alone.(2) In Vietnam, fathers may act as pimps for their daughters to get money for the family to survive:

> Dr. Hoa, [a] pediatrician from Vietnam, said she asked the fathers of her young patients why they sold their daughters' services. "One father came with his 12-year-old daughter," Dr. Hoa recalled. "She was bleeding from her wounds and as torn as if she had given birth. He told me, 'We've earned $300, so it's enough. She can stop now.'"(3)

The physical wounds suffered by underage prostitutes are part of the terrible irony of the growing market for sex with children. Customers request children under the mistaken belief that they are less likely to be infected with the virus that causes AIDS. In fact, because children are so likely to incur injuries in intercourse, they are more vulnerable to infection.(2)

Experts at a 1993 conference on the sex trade and human rights cited the global AIDS epidemic, pornography, peep shows, and "sex tours" as factors responsible for the increasing demand for child prostitutes.(3) Organized sex tours form a large part of the market for bodies of any age; Taiwan, South Korea, the Philippines, and Thailand have been favorite destinations for sex tourists, and many other places are gaining in popularity.

Sources

1. Margot Hornblower, "The Skin Trade," *Time,* June 21, 1993, pp. 45–51.
2. Michael S. Serrill, "Defiling the Children," *Time,* June 21, 1993, pp. 53–55.
3. Marlise Simons, "The Sex Market: Scourge on the World's Children," *New York Times,* Apr. 9, 1993, p. A3.

Questions for Discussion

1. How would you begin to fight the exploitation of women and children in the sex market?
2. What are some of the forces at work that would make such a fight difficult?

This definition indicates nothing about any danger inherent in pornography. The law will step in only when pornography is exhibited or distributed in a manner calculated to produce harm.

Historically, that harm has been seen as a negative effect on public morals, especially those of children. That was the stance taken by many national and local societies devoted to the preservation of public morality in the nineteenth century. More recently, the emphasis has shifted to the question of whether the availability and use of pornography produce actual, especially violent, victimization of women, children, or, for that matter, men.

Pornography and Violence. The National Commission on Obscenity and Pornography in 1970 and the Attorney General's Commission on Pornography in 1986 reviewed the evidence of an association between pornography, on the one hand, and violence and crime, on the other. The National Commission provided funding for more than 80 studies to examine public attitudes toward pornography, experiences with pornography, the association between the availability of pornography and crime rates, the experience of sex offenders with pornography, and the relation between pornography and behavior. The commission concluded:

> [E]mpirical research designed to clarify the question has found no evidence to date that exposure to explicit sexual materials plays a significant role in the causations of delinquent or criminal behavior among youth or adults. The Commission cannot conclude that exposure to erotic materials is a factor in the causation of sex crimes or sex delinquency.[88]

Between 1970 (when the National Commission reported its findings) and 1986 (when the Attorney General's Commission issued its report), hundreds of studies have been conducted on this question. For example:

- Researchers reported in 1977 that when male students were exposed to erotic stimuli, those stimuli neither inhibited nor had any effect on levels of aggression. When the same research team worked with female students, they found that mild erotic stimuli inhibited aggression and that stronger erotic stimuli increased it.[89]
- Researchers who exposed students to sexually explicit films during six consecutive weekly sessions in 1984 concluded that exposure to increasingly explicit erotic stimuli led to a decrease in both arousal responses and aggressive behavior. In short, these subjects became habituated to the pornography.[90]

After analyzing such studies, the Attorney General's Commission concluded that nonviolent and nondegrading pornography is not significantly associated with crime and aggression. It did conclude, however, that exposure to pornographic materials:

(1) leads to a greater acceptance of rape myths and violence against women; (2) results in pronounced effects when the victim is shown enjoying the use of force or violence; (3) is arousing for rapists and for some males in the general population; and (4) has resulted in sexual aggression against women in the laboratory.[91]

The Feminist View: Victimization. To feminists, these conclusions supported the call for greater restrictions on the manufacture and dissemination of pornographic material. The historian Joan Hoff has coined the term "pornerotic," meaning:

any representation of persons that sexually objectifies them and is accompanied by actual or implied violence in ways designed to encourage readers or viewers that such sexual subordination of women (or children or men) is acceptable behavior or an innocuous form of sex education.[92]

Hoff's definition also suggests that pornography, obscenity, and erotica may do far more than offend sensitivities. Such material may victimize not only the people who are depicted but all women (or men or children, if they are the people shown). Pornogra-

phers have been accused of promoting the exploitation, objectification, and degradation of women. Many people who call for the abolition of violent pornography argue that it also promotes violence toward women. Future state and federal legislation is likely to focus on violent and violence-producing pornography, not on pornography in general.

The Legal View: Supreme Court Rulings. Ultimately, defining pornographic acts subject to legal prohibition is a task for the U.S. Supreme Court. The First Amendment to the Constitution guarantees freedom of the press. In a series of decisions culminating in *Miller v. California* (1973), however, the Supreme Court articulated the view that obscenity, really meaning pornography, is outside the protection of the Constitution. Following the lead of the Model Penal Code and reinterpreting its own earlier decisions, the Court announced the following standard for judging a representation as obscene or pornographic:

- The average person, applying contemporary community standards, would find that the work, taken as a whole, appeals to prurient interests.
- The work depicts or describes, in a patently offensive way, sexual conduct specifically defined by the applicable state law.
- The work, taken as a whole, lacks serious literary, artistic, political, or scientific value.[93]

While this proposed standard is flexible enough to be expanded or contracted as standards change over time and from place to place, its terms are so vague that they give little guidance to local law enforcement officers or to federal and state courts. In 1987 the Supreme Court addressed this problem and modified the Miller decision. In *Pope v. Illinois* the Court ruled that the third aspect of Miller (that the work has "no value") may be judged by an objective test rather than by local community standards. Justice Byron White wrote for the majority:

The proper inquiry is not whether an ordinary person of any given community will find serious literary, artistic, political, or scientific value in the allegedly obscene material, but whether a reasonable person would find such value in the material, taken as a whole.[94]

Whether this test will make juries' tasks easier when they must decide whether a film or magazine is pornographic or obscene is still not clear.

Pornography and the Internet

Warning! This site contains sexually oriented material intended for consenting adults of at least 21 years old.

Any child with basic knowledge of a computer and a minimal amount of curiosity can, with a few clicks of a mouse, open a doorway to the world of cyberporn: pictures of adults having sexual intercourse, adults having intercourse with animals, video clips of adults having sex with children, and guides to bordellos, massage parlors, and various pleasure districts—both local and international.[95]

Censorship of the Internet has been a heavily debated issue in recent times. Almost everyone agrees that access of minors to pornographic material over the Internet should be restricted, but the primary point of contention remains: Who should be responsible for policing access to such material? Parents? Educators? The government? Responding to a nationwide outcry, Congress passed the Communications Decency Act (CDA) on February 8, 1996. This portion of the Telecommunications Decency Act of 1996 made it a felony to "knowingly use a telecommunications device or interactive computer to send an indecent communication to a child or to use a computer to display indecent material in a manner accessible to a child." Violations of this act are pun-

ishable by up to 2 years' imprisonment and a fine of $250,000.

Four months after the passage of this law, however, a federal court in Philadelphia ruled that it is in conflict with the constitutional right to speech. According to the court, blocking enforcement of the CDA was justified because (1) the term "indecent" was found to be impermissibly vague; and (2) while the CDA could restrict Americans from disseminating "indecent" material, it had no jurisdiction over communications originating outside the United States and would thus be ineffective. Existing federal and state laws, however, still ban the sale and possession of child pornography.

In the wake of the continued controversy over "cybersmut," several computer programs have been developed to assist parents and educators in regulating children's access to the Internet. Programs such as Net Nanny, Cyber Patrol, and Surf Watch are designed to block access to sites deemed inappropriate for children.

These programs, however, are far from effective. The software must be continually updated to keep up with the new sites added on a daily basis. If activated by certain keywords, access may also be limited to potentially educational sites (such as those related to sexual harassment). Also, the cost of implementing such programs in a particular school district could run into tens of thousands of dollars.

Anyone with a computer, the right software, and a modem can access the wide world of cyber pornography. Pornography of all sorts—from child pornography to bondage and S&M—is available on binary files in Newsgroups, chat rooms, bulletin boards, and individual websites. The FBI, U.S. Customs Service, Department of Justice, and U.S. Postal Service have committed significant resources to investigate and prosecute distributors and consumers of child pornography.

The Gap between Behavior and Law. When we examine sexual morality offenses, we note an enormous gap between the goals of law and actual behavior. As long ago as the late 1940s and early 1950s the pioneering Kinsey reports brought us evidence about this gap. According to these studies, of the total white male population in the United States:

- Sixty-nine percent had had some experience with prostitutes.
- Between 23 and 37 percent had had extramarital intercourse.
- Thirty-seven percent had had at least one homosexual experience.[96]

Among women:

- Twenty-six percent could be expected to have extramarital intercourse by age 40.
- Nineteen percent had had some physical contact with other females which was deliberately and consciously, at least on the part of one of the partners, intended to be sexual.[97]

Morton Hunt noted that the frequency with which Americans were breaking legally imposed moral standards had increased significantly by the 1970s, yet far fewer American men were buying sex from prostitutes than had done so in the 1940s.[98] This finding raised the question of whether the sexual revolution of the 1960s and 1970s made access to sexual partners more freely available.

REVIEW

Intoxicating substances have been used for religious, medicinal, and recreational purposes throughout history. Lifestyles of people who use them are as varied as the drugs they favor.

Governments have repeatedly tried to prevent the abuse of these substances. The drug problem today is massive, and it grows more serious every year. Heroin and cocaine in particular are associated with many crimes. A vast international criminal empire has been organized to promote the production and distribution of drugs. Efforts of law enforcement and health agencies to control the drug problem take the forms of international cooperation in stemming drug trafficking, treatment of addicts, education of the public, and arrest and incarceration of offenders. Some observers, comparing the drug problem with the wide evasion of the Prohibition amendment and the consequent rise in crime, believe that drugs should be legalized.

Legalization of alcoholic beverages, however, has not solved all problems related to alcohol. The abuse of alcohol has been reliably linked to violence, and the incidence of drunk driving has increased so alarmingly that citizen groups have formed to combat the problem.

The legal regulation of sexual conduct has undergone striking changes in recent decades. Many sexual "offenses" once categorized as capital crimes no longer concern society or government. In this sphere, research has done much to influence public opinion and consequently legislation. Pornography, however, remains a hotly debated issue.

NOTES

1. *United States v. Montoya de Hernandez,* 473 U.S. 531 (1985). The newest ploy used by Colombian drug smugglers is to anesthetize dogs, implant cocaine in small plastic bags between the animal's abdominal wall and stomach, sew the wound, then starve the animal to allow the wound to heal more quickly, and ship the animal to the United States. Upon arrival, the dog is retrieved and the true brutality of these drug runners is realized; the dog is killed and the drugs are taken from the animal's carcass; see Greg B. Smith, "JFK Cocaine Bust's a Shaggy Dog Story," *New York Daily News,* Dec. 6, 1994, p. 8.
2. Richard P. Retting, Manuel J. Torres, and Gerald R. Garrett, *Manny: A Criminal-Addict's Story* (Boston: Houghton Mifflin, 1977).
3. "The Drug Gangs," *Newsweek,* Mar. 28, 1988, p. 20. See also Robert C. Davis and Arthur J. Lurigio, *Fighting Back: Neighborhood Antidrug Strategies* (Thousand Oaks, Calif.: Sage Publications, 1996); Bureau of Justice Statistics, *Guns Used in Crime* (Washington, D.C.: U.S. Department of Justice, 1995); Geoffrey Canada, *Fist Stick Knife Gun* (Boston: Beacon Press, 1995); Susan J. Popkin, Lynn M. Olson, Arthur J. Lurigio, et al., "Sweeping out Drugs and Crime: Residents' Views of the Chicago Housing Authority's Public Housing Drug Elimination Program," *Journal of Research in Crime and Delinquency,* **41** (1995): 73–99; Harvey Rachlin, *The Making of a Detective* (New York: W. W. Norton & Company, 1995).
4. Mark D. Merlin, *On the Trail of the Ancient Opium Poppy* (Rutherford, N.J.: Fairleigh Dickinson University Press, 1984). For a historic account of alcohol consumption, see Harvey A. Siegal and James A. Inciardi, "A Brief History of Alcohol," in *The American Drug Scene: An Anthology,* ed. James A. Inciardi and Karen McElrath (Los Angeles: Roxbury Publishing Company, 1995).

5. Howard Abadinsky, *Drug Abuse: An Introduction* (Chicago: Nelson Hall, 1989), pp. 30–31, 54. For the medicinal benefits of marijuana, see Lester Grinspoon and James Bakalar, "Marijuana: The Forbidden Medicine," in Inciardi and McElrath, *The American Drug Scene.*

6. Michael D. Lyman, *Narcotics and Crime Control* (Springfield, Ill.: Charles C Thomas, 1987), p. 8. See also F. E. Oliver, "The Use and Abuse of Opium," in *Yesterday's Addicts: American Society and Drug Abuse, 1865–1920,* ed. H. Wayne Morgan (Norman: University of Oklahoma Press, 1974).

7. W. Z. Guggenheim, "Heroin: History and Pharmacology," *International Journal of the Addictions,* **2** (1967): 328. For a history of heroin use in New York City, from just after the turn of the century into the late 1960s, see Edward Preble and John J. Casey, "Taking Care of Business: The Heroin Addict's Life on the Street," *International Journal of the Addictions,* **4** (1969): 1–24.

8. Abadinsky, *Drug Abuse,* p. 52.

9. Ibid., p. 56.

10. Lyman, *Narcotics and Crime Control,* p. 10.

11. Public Law 100-690, of Nov. 18, 1988; 102 Stat. 4187.

12. Lloyd D. Johnston, Patrick M. O'Malley, and Jerald G. Bachman, *Drug Use among American High School Seniors, College Students, and Young Adults, 1975–1990,* vols. 1–2, for U.S. Department of Health and Human Services, National Institute on Drug Abuse (Washington, D.C.: U.S. Government Printing Office, 1991). For an early treatment, see James D. Preston and Patricia A. Fry, "Marijuana Use among Houston High School Students," *Social Science Quarterly,* **52** (1971): 170–178. For a look into how teen drug use can influence presidential elections, see Stewart Ugelow, "Drug Use Is Surging among Teenagers, and Dole Makes It a Campaign Issue," *Wall Street Journal,* Aug. 21, 1996, p. A4.

13. U.S. Department of Justice, *Drugs, Crime, and the Justice System* (Washington, D.C.: U.S. Government Printing Office, 1992), p. 31. For an early treatment on the extent of illegal drug use in Britain, see Pierce I. James, "Drug Abuse in Britain," *Medicine, Science, and the Law,* **13** (1973): 246–251.

14. Lyman, *Narcotics and Crime Control,* p. 21. For a German perspective on cocaine use, see Reiner Kaulitzki, "Cocaine Crisis? Myths, Moral Panics and Symbolic Politics," *Kriminologisches Journal,* **27** (1995): 134–158.

15. National Institute on Drug Abuse, *National Household Survey* (Washington, D.C.: U.S. Government Printing Office, 1996), p. 9; see Robert J. Michaels, "The Market for Heroin before and after Legalization," in *Dealing with Drugs,* ed. Ronald Hamowy (Lexington, Mass.: Lexington Books, 1987), pp. 311–318.

16. Mark A. de Bernardo and Marci M. DeLancey, *Guide to Dangerous Drugs: Everything You Should Know about Marijuana, Cocaine, Alcohol, Depressants, Amphetamines, Heroin and Other Opiates, Inhalants and Hallucinogens* (Washington, D.C.: Institute for a Drug-Free Workplace, 1994); Abadinsky, *Drug Abuse,* p. 107; Lyman, *Narcotics and Crime Control,* pp. 33–34. For a description of emerging new drugs and availability, see Dana Hunt, *Pulse Check: National Trends in Drug Abuse* (Washington, D.C.: Office of National Drug Control Policy, 1996).

17. Lloyd D. Johnston, Patrick M. O'Malley, and Jerald G. Bachman, *The National Survey Results on Drug Use from the Monitoring the Future Study, 1975–1993,* vol. 1, National Institutes of Health (Washington, D.C.: U.S. Government Printing Office, 1994). See also Allan L. McCutcheon and George Thomas, "Patterns of Drug Use among White Institutionalized Delinquents in Georgia: Evidence from a Latent Class Analysis," *Journal of Drug Education,* **25** (1995): 61–71; Bruce A. Jacobs, "Anticipatory Undercover Targeting in High Schools," *Journal of Criminal Justice,* **22** (1994): 445–457; Joseph F. Sheley, "Drugs and Guns among Inner-City High School Students," *Journal of Drug Education,* **24** (1994): 303–321; Ken C. Winters, Christine L. Weller, and James A. Meland, "Extent of Drug Abuse among Juvenile Offenders," *Journal of Drug Issues,* **23** (1993): 515–524. For a perspective on drug use among 12- and 19-year-olds living in England and Wales, see Joy Mott and Catriona Black Mirrlees, *Self-Reported Drug Misuse in England and Wales: Findings from the 1992 British Crime Survey* (London: Home Office, Research and Planning Unit, 1995). See, as an early treatment, Lloyd Johnson and Jerald G. Bachman, *Drug Use among American High School Students, 1975–1977* (Washington, D.C.: U.S. Government Printing Office, 1978); Henry Wechsler, "Alcohol Intoxication and Drug Use among Teen-Agers," *Journal of Studies on Alcohol,* **37** (1976): 1672–1677; U.S. House of Representatives, Select Committee on Crime, *Drugs in Our Schools. Hearings, September 21–23, 1972, Chicago, Illinois* (Washington, D.C.: U.S. Government Printing Office, 1972).

18. Lisa Maher, Eloise Dunlap, Bruce D. Johnson, and Ansley Hamid, "Gender, Power, and Alternative Living Arrangements in the Inner-City Crack Culture," *Journal of Research in Crime and Delinquency,* **33** (1996): 181–205; H. Virginia McCoy, Christine Miles, and James A. Inciardi, "Survival Sex: Inner-City Women and Crack-Cocaine," in Inciardi and McElrath, *The American Drug Scene;* Jody Miller, "Gender and Power on the Streets: Street Prostitution in the Era of Crack Cocaine," *Journal of Contemporary Ethnography,* **23** (1995): 427–452; Ann Sorenson and David Brownfield, "Adolescent Drug Use and a General Theory of Crime: An Analysis of a Theoretical Integration," *Canadian Journal of Criminology,* **37** (1995): 19–37. For a summary of psychiatric approaches, see Marie Nyswander, *The Drug Addict as a Patient* (New York: Grune & Stratton, 1956), chap. 4.

19. Richard Cloward and Lloyd Ohlin, *Delinquency and Opportunity* (New York: Free Press, 1960), pp. 178–186. See also Jeffrey A. Fagan, "The Social Organization of Drug Use and Drug Dealing among Urban Gangs," *Criminology,* **27** (1989): 633–669. See also Marcia R. Chaiken, *Identifying and Responding to New Forms of Drug Abuse: Lessons Learned from "Crack" and "Ice"* (Washington, D.C.: National Institute of Justice, 1993).

20. D. F. Musto, "The History of Legislative Control over Opium, Cocaine, and Their Derivatives," in Hamowy, *Dealing with Drugs.*

21. Marsha Rosenbaum, *Women on Heroin* (New Brunswick, N.J.: Rutgers University Press, 1981), pp. 14–15; Jeannette Covington, "Theoretical Explanations of Race Differences in Heroin Use," in *Advances in Criminological Theory,* vol. 2, ed. William S. Laufer and Freda Adler (New Brunswick, N.J.: Transaction). See also U.S. Senate Judiciary Committee, Subcommittee to Investigate Juvenile Delinquency, *The Global Connection: Heroin Entrepreneurs. Hearings, July 28 and*

August 5, 1976 (Washington, D.C.: U.S. Government Printing Office, 1976).

22. Freda Adler, Arthur D. Moffett, Frederick G. Glaser, John C. Ball, and Diana Horwitz, *A Systems Approach to Drug Treatment* (Philadelphia: Dorrance, 1974).

23. Erich Goode, *Drugs in American Society* (New York: Basic Books, 1972); also Ned Polsky, *Hustlers, Beats, and Others* (Chicago: Aldine, 1967).

24. Norman E. Zinberg, "The Use and Misuse of Intoxicants: Factors in the Development of Controlled Abuse," in Hamowy, *Dealing with Drugs,* p. 262.

25. Abadinsky, *Drug Abuse,* p. 53. See also, as an early treatment, Hope R. Victor, Jan Carl Grossman, and Russell Eisenman, "Openness to Experience and Marijuana Use in High School Students," *Journal of Consulting and Clinical Psychology,* **41** (1973): 78–85; U.S. Narcotics and Dangerous Drugs Bureau, *Marijuana: An Analysis of Use, Distribution and Control* (Washington, D.C.: U.S. Government Printing Office, 1971); California Department of Public Health and Welfare, Research and Statistics Section, *Five Mind-Altering Drugs: The Use of Alcoholic Beverages, Amphetamines, LSD, Marijuana, and Tobacco, Reported by High School and Junior High School Students, San Mateo County, California, Two Comparable Surveys, 1968 and 1969* (San Mateo: California Department of Public Health, 1969); Erich Goode, "Multiple Drug Use among Marijuana Smokers," *Social Problems,* **17** (1969): 48–64.

26. Bruce A. Jacobs, "Crack Dealers' Apprehension Avoidance Techniques: A Case of Restrictive Deterrence," *Justice Quarterly,* **13** (1996): 359–381; Bruce A. Jacobs, "Crack Dealers and Restrictive Deterrences: Identifying Narcs," *Criminology,* **34** (1996): 409–431; Bruce D. Johnson, Andrew Golub, and Jeffrey Fagan, "Careers in Crack, Drug Use, Drug Distribution, and Nondrug Criminality," *Journal of Crime and Delinquency,* **41** (1995): 275–295; Abadinsky, *Drug Abuse,* p. 83. See also Jeffrey A. Fagan, "Initiation into Crack and Powdered Cocaine: A Tale of Two Epidemics," *Contemporary Drug Problems,* **16** (1989): 579–618; Jeffrey A. Fagan, Joseph G. Weis, and Y. T. Cheng, "Drug Use and Delinquency among Inner City Youth," *Journal of Drug Issues,* **20** (1990): 349–400; and James A. Inciardi, et al., "The Crack Epidemic Revisited," *Journal of Psychoactive Drugs,* **24** (1992): 305–416. See also B. D. Johnson, M. Natarajan, E. Dunlap, and E. Elmoghazy, "Crack Abusers and Noncrack Abusers: A Comparison of Drug Use, Drug Sales, and Nondrug Criminality," *Journal of Drug Issues,* **24** (1994): 117–141. Smoking crack is certainly not limited to the inner cities of America. For a description of crack use in the tropical paradise of Hawaii, see Gordon James Knowles, "Dealing Crack Cocaine: A View from the Streets of Honolulu," *The FBI Law Enforcement Bulletin,* July 1996: 1–7.

27. *New York Times,* July 13, 1989, pp. A1, B3.

28. James Inciardi, "Heroin Use and Street Crime," *Crime and Delinquency,* **25** (1979): 335–346; Bruce D. Johnson, Paul J. Goldstein, Edward Preble, James Schmeidler, Douglas S. Lyston, Barry Spunt, and Thomas Miller, *Taking Care of Business: The Economics of Crime by Heroin Abusers* (Lexington, Mass.: Heath, 1985); James Inciardi, *The War on Drugs: Heroin, Cocaine, Crime, and Public Policy* (Palo Alto, Calif.: Mayfield, 1986); Eric Wish and Bruce Johnson, "The Impact of Substance Abuse on Criminal Careers," in *Criminal*

Careers and Career Criminals, ed. Alfred Blumstein, Jacqueline Cohen, Jeffrey A. Roth, and Christy A. Visher (Washington, D.C.: National Academy Press, 1986), pp. 52–58.

29. U.S. Department of Justice, *National Institute of Justice Journal* (Washington, D.C.: U.S. Government Printing Office, 1993), p. 32. See also U.S. Sentencing Commission, *Cocaine and Federal Sentencing Policy* (Washington, D.C.: U.S. Sentencing Commission, 1995).

30. For a determination of the causal link between drug use and crime, see Bruce L. Benson and David W. Rasmussen, *Illicit Drugs and Crimes* (Oakland, Calif.: The Independent Institute, 1996); James A. Inciardi, Duane C. McBride, and James E. Rivers, *Drug Control and the Courts* (Thousand Oaks, Calif.: Sage Publications, 1996); Inciardi and McElrath, *The American Drug Scene;* Sybille M. Guy, Gene M. Smith, and P. M. Bentler, "The Influence of Adolescent Substance Use and Socialization on Deviant Behavior in Young Adulthood," *Criminal Justice and Behavior,* **21** (1994): 236–255.

31. George Speckart and M. Douglas Anglin found that criminal records preceded drug use; see their "Narcotics Use and Crime: An Overview of Recent Research Advances," *Contemporary Drug Problems,* **13** (1986): 741–769, and "Narcotics and Crime: A Causal Modeling Approach," *Journal of Quantitative Criminology,* **2** (1986): 3–28. See also Cheryl Carpenter, Barry Glassner, Bruce D. Johnson, and Julia Loughlin, *Kids, Drugs, and Crime* (Lexington, Mass.: Heath, 1988). See also Louise L. Biron, Serge Brochu, and Lyne Desjardins, "The Issue of Drugs and Crime among a Sample of Incarcerated Women," *Deviant Behavior,* **16** (1995): 25–43.

32. James A. Inciardi and Anne E. Pottieger, "Kids, Crack, and Crime," *Journal of Drug Issues,* **21** (1991): 257–270; David N. Nurco, Thomas E. Hanlon, Timothy W. Kinlock, and Karen R. Duszynski, "Differential Criminal Patterns of Narcotics Addicts over an Addiction Career," *Criminology,* **26** (1988): 407–423; M. Douglas Anglin and George Speckart, "Narcotics Use and Crime: A Multisample, Multimethod Analysis," *Criminology,* **26** (1988): 197–233; M. Douglas Anglin and Yining Hser, "Addicted Women and Crime," *Criminology,* **25** (1987): 359–397.

33. Paul Goldstein, "Drugs and Violent Crime," in *Pathways to Criminal Violence,* ed. Neil Alan Weiner and Marvin E. Wolfgang (Newbury Park, Calif.: Sage, 1989), pp. 16–48; *Ebony,* Aug. 1989, p. 99.

34. This section is based on Inciardi, *The War on Drugs.* See also Fernando Cepeda Ulloa, "International Cooperation and the War on Drugs," in *Drug Trafficking in the Americas,* ed. Bruce M. Bagley and William O. Walker III (Coral Gables, Fla.: North-South Center Press, University of Miami, 1996); Ronald Kessler, *The FBI* (New York: Pocket Books, 1993); *United States v. Celio,* 945 F.2d 180 (7th Cir. 1991), where the U.S. Court of Appeals for the Seventh Circuit acknowledged the need for a concerted effort on behalf of various law enforcement agencies to combat international drug-trafficking cartels.

35. *National Drug Intelligence Estimate* (Ottawa: Royal Canadian Mounted Police, 1991), p. 24. See also Kevin Healy, "Recent Literature on Drugs in Bolivia," in Bagley and Walker, *Drug Trafficking in the Americas;* David Scott Palmer, "Peru, Drugs, and Shining Path," in Bagley and Walker, *Drug Trafficking in the Americas.*

36. *The Illicit Drug Situation in the United States and Canada* (Ottawa: Royal Canadian Mounted Police, 1984–1986), p. 19. See also William Gately and Yvette Fernandez, *Dead Ringer: An Insider's Account of the Mob's Colombian Connection* (New York: Donald I. Fine, 1994).

37. Colin McMahon, "Panamas Future Uncertain as Ever; Corruption Persists in Post-Noriega Era," *Chicago Tribune,* Aug. 25, 1996, p. 17.

38. United Nations, "Commission on Narcotic Drugs, Comprehensive Review of the Activities of the United Nations Fund for Drug Abuse Control in 1985," E/CN.7/1986/ CRP.4, Feb. 4, 1986. See also Elaine Sciolino, "U.N. Report Links Drugs, Arms, and Terror," *New York Times,* Jan. 12, 1987.

39. John Warner, "Terrorism and Drug Trafficking: A Lethal Partnership," *Security Management,* **28** (1984): 44–46. See, as an early treatment, U.S. Congress, House Public Health and Environment Subcommittee, *Production and Abuse of Opiates in the Far East* (Washington, D.C.: U.S. Government Printing Office, 1971).

40. For a review of drug enforcement policies aimed directly at the users of illicit narcotics, see Richard Lawrence Miller, *Drug Warriors and Their Prey: From Police Power to Police State* (Westport, Conn.: Praeger, 1996). For a comprehensive guide to state agencies that address drug abuse concerns, see Bureau of Justice Statistics, *State Drug Resources: 1994 National Directory* (Washington, D.C.: U.S. Department of Justice, 1994).

41. James A. Inciardi, *The War on Drugs II: The Continuing Epidemic of Heroin, Cocaine, Crack, Crime, AIDS, and Public Policy* (Mountain View, Calif.: Mayfield, 1992).

42. Even before President Bush's drug initiatives, government agencies recognized the ineffectiveness of narcotic countermeasures during the 1970s; see U.S. Comptroller General, *Gains Made in Controlling Illegal Drugs, Yet the Drug Trade Flourishes* (Washington, D.C.: U.S. Government Printing Office, 1979).

43. See Rae Sibbitt, *The Ilps Methadone Prescribing Project* (London: Home Office, 1996); Paul J. Turnbull, Russell Webster, and Gary Stillwell, *Get It While You Can: An Evaluation of an Early Intervention Project for Arrestees with Alcohol and Drug Problems* (London: Home Office, 1996); Ira Sommers, Deborah R. Baskin, and Jeffrey Fagan, "Getting out of the Life: Crime Desistance by Female Street Offenders," *Deviant Behavior,* **15** (1994): 125–149; Sandra L. Tunis, *The State of the Art in Jail Drug Treatment Programs* (San Francisco: National Council on Crime and Delinquency, 1994).

44. Peter Finn and Andrea K. Newlyn, *Miami's "Drug Court,"* National Institute of Justice (Washington, D.C.: U.S. Government Printing Office, 1993).

45. Abadinsky, *Drug Abuse,* p. 171.

46. David N. Nurco, Norma Wegner, Philip Stephenson, Abraham Makofsky, and John W. Shaffer, *Ex-Addicts' Self-Help Groups: Potentials and Pitfalls* (New York: Praeger Publishers, 1983); Harold I. Hendler and Richard C. Stephens, "The Addict Odyssey: From Experimentation to Addiction," *International Journal of the Addictions,* **12** (1977): 25–42.

47. For a perspective on how corporate America educates employees on the risks of drug abuse, see Mark A. de Bernardo, *What Every Employee Should Know about Drug Abuse* (Washington, D.C.: Institute for a Drug-Free Workplace,

1993); Troy Duster, *The Legislation of Morality: Law, Drugs, and Moral Judgment* (New York: Free Press, 1970), p. 192.

48. Dan Waldorf, "Natural Recovery from Opiate Addiction," *Journal of Drug Issues,* **13** (1983): 237–280.

49. See James A. Inciardi, Duane C. McBride, Clyde B. McCoy, et al., "Violence, Street Crime and the Drug Legalization Debate: A Perspective and Commentary on the U.S. Experience," *Studies on Crime and Crime Prevention,* **4** (1995): 105–118; Steven Foy Luper, Curtis Brown, et al., *Drugs, Morality, and the Law* (New York: Garland, 1994); Robert J. MacCoun, James P. Kahan, and James Gillespie, "A Content Analysis of the Drug Legalization Debate," *Journal of Drug Issues,* **23** (1993): 615–629; Arnold S. Trebach and James A. Inciardi, *Legalize It? Debating American Drug Policy* (Washington, D.C.: American University Press, 1993).

50. James B. Jacobs, *Drunk Driving: An American Dilemma* (Chicago: University of Chicago Press, 1989), p. xiii.

51. Johnston, et al., *Drug Use among American High School Seniors, College Students, and Young Adults (1975–1990).*

52. James Inciardi, *Reflections on Crime* (New York: Holt, Rinehart & Winston, 1978), pp. 8–10. For an even earlier perspective, see Herbert Berger and Andrew A. Eggston, "Should We Legalize Narcotics?" *Coronet,* **38** (June 1995): 30–34.

53. U.S. Department of Justice, *Report to the Nation on Crime and Justice,* 2d ed. (Washington, D.C.: U.S. Government Printing Office, 1988), p. 50.

54. Marvin E. Wolfgang, *Patterns in Criminal Homicide* (New York: Wiley, 1966).

55. P. Linquist, "Criminal Homicides in Northern Sweden, 1970–81: Alcohol Intoxication, Alcohol Abuse, and Mental Disease," *International Journal of Law and Psychiatry,* **8** (1986): 19–37. See also Roland Gustafson, "Is It Possible to Link Alcohol Intoxication Causally to Aggression and Violence? A Summary of the Swedish Experimental Approach," *Studies on Crime and Crime Prevention,* **4** (1995): 22–42.

56. D. Mayfield, "Alcoholism, Alcohol Intoxification, and Assaultive Behavior," *Diseases of the Nervous System,* **37** (1976): 288–291; C. K. Meyer, T. Magendanz, B. C. Kieselhorst, and S. G. Chapman, *A Social-Psychological Analysis of Police Assaults* (Norman: Bureau of Government Research, University of Oklahoma, April 1978).

57. For the role of alcohol consumption in violent episodes against intimates and women, see Christine A. Scronce and Kevin J. Corcoran, "The Influence of the Victim's Consumption of Alcohol on Perceptions of Stranger and Acquaintance Rape," *Violence against Women,* **1** (1995): 241–253; Bureau of Justice Statistics, *Violence between Intimates* (Washington, D.C.: U.S. Department of Justice, 1994); Bureau of Justice Statistics, *Violence against Women: A National Crime Victimization Survey Report* (Washington, D.C.: U.S. Department of Justice, 1994); S. D. Johnson, L. Gibson, and R. Linden, "Alcohol and Rape in Winnipeg, 1966–1975," *Journal of Studies on Alcohol,* **39** (1987): 1877–1894; Menachem Amir, *Patterns of Forcible Rape* (Chicago: University of Chicago Press, 1971), p. 99.

58. D. H. Coleman and M. A. Straus, "Alcohol Abuse and Family Violence," in *Alcohol, Drug Abuse, and Aggression,* ed. E. Gottheil, K. A. Druley, T. E. Skoloda, and H. M. Waxman (Springfield, Ill.: Charles C Thomas, 1983).

59. See Maggie Sumner and Howard Parker, *Low in Alcohol: A Review of International Research into Alcohol's Role in Crime*

Causation (Manchester, United Kingdom: Department of Social Policy and Social Work, University of Manchester, 1995); Klaus A. Miczek et al., "Alcohol, Drugs of Abuse, Aggression, and Violence," in *Understanding and Preventing Violence,* ed. Albert J. Reiss, Jr., and Jeffrey A. Roth (Washington, D.C.: National Academy Press, 1993).

60. K. E. Leonard, "Alcohol and Human Physical Aggression," *Aggression,* **2** (1983): 77–101. See also Matthew W. Lewis, Jon F. Merz, Ron D. Hays, et al., "Perceptions of Intoxication and Impairment at Arrest among Adults Convicted of Driving under the Influence of Alcohol," *Journal of Drug Issues,* **25** (1995): 141–160.

61. C. M. Steele and L. Southwick, "Alcohol and Social Behavior: I. The Psychology of Drunken Excess," *Journal of Personality and Social Psychology,* **48** (1985): 18–34. See also Peter B. Wood, John K. Cochran, Betty Pfefferbaum, et al., "Sensation-Seeking and Delinquent Substance Use: An Extension of Learning Theory," *Journal of Drug Issues,* **25** (1995): 173–193.

62. S. Ahlstrom-Laakso, "European Drinking Habits: A Review of Research and Time Suggestions for Conceptual Integration of Findings," in *Cross-Cultural Approaches to the Study of Alcohol,* ed. M. W. Everett, J. O. Waddell, and D. Heath (The Hague: Mouton, 1976).

63. Uniform Crime Reports, 1992, p. 168; 1989, p. 224; Lawrence A. Greenfeld, *Drunk Driving,* for Bureau of Justice Statistics (Washington, D.C.: U.S. Government Printing Office, February 1988), p. 1; William K. Stevens, "Deaths from Drunken Driving Increase," *New York Times,* Oct. 29, 1987, p. 12. See also Gwen W. Bramlet, "DUI Offenders, Drug Users, and Criminals: A Comparison," *Journal of Crime and Justice,* **18** (1995): 59–78.

64. Joseph R. Gusfield, "The Control of Drinking-Driving in the United States: A Period of Transition," in *Social Control of the Drinking Driver,* ed. Michael D. Lawrence, John R. Snortum, and Franklin E. Zimring (Chicago: University of Chicago Press, 1988).

65. Jacobs, *Drunk Driving,* p. xvi.

66. Faye Silas, "Gimme the Keys," *American Bar Association Journal,* **71** (1985): 36.

67. Atic Press, "The Menace on the Roads," *Newsweek,* Dec. 21, 1987, p. 42.

68. Brandon K. Applegate, Francis T. Cullen, Bruce G. Link, Pamela J. Richards, and Lonn Lanza-Kaduce, "Determinants of Public Punitiveness toward Drunk Driving: A Factorial Survey Approach," *Justice Quarterly,* **13** (1996): 57–79; Stephen D. Mastrofski and R. Richard Ritti, "Police Training and the Effects of Organization on Drunk Driving Enforcement," *Justice Quarterly,* **13** (1996): 291–320.

69. *The Effectiveness of the Ignition Interlock Device in Reducing Recidivism among Driving under the Influence Cases* (Honolulu: Criminal Justice Commission, 1987).

70. Personal communication, 1951. See, as additional early treatments, Dr. Eustace Chesser, *Strange Loves: The Human Aspects of Sexual Deviation* (New York: William Morrow, 1971); David Reuben, *Everything You Always Wanted to Know about Sex: But Were Afraid to Ask* (New York: David McKay, 1969). Contemporary works include Samuel S. Janus and Cynthia L. Janus, *The Janus Report on Sexual Behavior: The First Broad-Scale Scientific National Survey since Kinsey* (New York: John Wiley & Sons, 1993).

71. Alfred C. Kinsey, Wardel B. Pomeroy, and Clyde E. Martin, *Sexual Behavior in the Human Male* (Philadelphia: Saunders, 1948), p. 613. See also Judith A. Reisman and Edward W. Eichel, *Kinsey, Sex and Fraud: The Indoctrination of a People* (Lafayette, La.: Huntington House, 1990).

72. *Bowers v. Hardwick,* 478 U.S. 186; reh. denied, 478 U.S. 1039 (1986).

73. Nickie Roberts, *Whores in History: Prostitution in Western Society* (London: HarperCollins, 1992).

74. *Robinson v. California,* 370 U.S. 660 (1962).

75. Uniform Crime Reports, 1994, p. 283.

76. See Cudore L. Snell, *Young Men in the Street: Help-Seeking Behavior of Young Male Prostitutes* (Westport, Conn.: Praeger, 1995); Sari van der Poel, "Solidarity as Boomerang: The Fiasco of the Prostitutes' Rights Movement in the Netherlands," *Crime, Law and Social Change,* **23** (1995): 41–65; Barbara Sherman Heyl, "The Madam as Teacher: The Training of House Prostitutes," in ed., *Deviant Behavior,* Delos H. Kelly, (New York: St. Martin's Press, 1993); Sari van der Poel, "Professional Male Prostitution: A Neglected Phenomenon," *Crime, Law, and Social Change,* **18** (1992): 259–275; David F. Luckenbill, "Deviant Career Mobility: The Case of Male Prostitutes," *Social Problems,* **33** (1986): 283–296.

77. Jeremiah Lowney, Robert W. Winslow, and Virginia Winslow, *Deviant Reality—Alternative World Views,* 2d ed. (Boston: Allyn and Bacon, 1981), p. 156. For a law enforcement perspective on countering prostitution in New York City, where female undercover police officers are used to seek out the patrons of prostitutes, see Dean Chang, "Dear John, It's a Bust: Cops Target Sex Clients," *New York Daily News,* June 26, 1994, p. 10.

78. Bureau of Justice Statistics, *HIV in Prisons 1994* (Washington, D.C.: U.S. Department of Justice, 1996); Bureau of Justice Statistics, *HIV in Prisons and Jails, 1993* (Washington, D.C.: U.S. Deparment of Justice, 1995); James A. Inciardi, Anne E. Pottieger, Mary Ann Forney, et al., "Prostitution, IV Drug Use, and Sex-for-Crack Exchanges among Serious Delinquents: Risks for HIV Infection," *Criminology,* **29** (1991): 221–236; Joseph B. Kuhns III and Kathleen M. Heide, "AIDS-Related Issues among Female Prostitutes and Female Arrestees," *International Journal of Offender Therapy and Comparative Criminology,* **36** (1992): 231–245; David J. Bellis, "Reduction of AIDS Risk among 41 Heroin Addicted Female Street Prostitutes: Effects of Free Methadone Maintenance," *Journal of Addictive Diseases,* **12** (1993): 7–23; L. Maher and R. Curtis, "Women on the Edge of Crime: Crack Cocaine and the Changing Contexts of Street-Level Sex Work in New York City," *Crime, Law, and Social Change,* **18** (1992): 221–258; Edward V. Morse, Patricia M. Simon, Stephanie A. Baus, et al., "Cofactors of Substance Use among Male Street Prostitutes," *Journal of Drug Issues,* **22** (1992): 977–994.

79. Paul Gebhard, "Misconceptions about Female Prostitution," *Medical Aspects of Human Sexuality,* **3** (1969): 28–30; Jennifer James, "Prostitutes and Prostitution," in *Deviants: Voluntary Action in a Hostile World,* ed. Edward Sagarin and F. Montamino (Glenview, Ill.: Scott, Foresman, 1977), p. 384.

80. R. Karl Hanson, Heather Scott, and Richard A. Steffy, "A Comparison of Child Molesters and Nonsexual Criminals: Risk Predictors and Long-Term Recidivism," *Journal of Research in Crime and Delinquency,* **32** (1995): 325–337;

Dennis Howitt, *Paedophiles and Sexual Offences against Children* (Chichester, United Kingdom: John Wiley & Sons, 1995); Human Rights Watch: Asia, *Rape for Profit: Trafficking of Nepali Girls and Women to India's Brothels* (New York: Human Rights Watch, 1995).

81. See Gerhard O. W. Mueller, *Legal Regulation of Sexual Conduct* (New York: Oceana, 1961), pp. 139–147, tables 9A, 9B. Note, however, that some states have amended their statutes since these data were collected.

82. Donnerstein et al., *The Question of Pornography*, p. 147.

83. For the now famous Justice Potter Stewart comment on pornography, where he couldn't truly define obscenity, but stated he knew it when he saw it, see *Jacobellis v. Ohio*, 378 U.S. 184 (1964). Joel Feinberg, "Pornography and Criminal Law," in *Pornography and Censorship*, ed. D. Copp and S. Wendell (New York: Prometheus, 1979).

84. See Susan M. Easton, *The Problem of Pornography: Regulation and the Right to Free Speech* (London: Routledge, 1994); Donald A. Downs, *The New Politics of Pornography* (Chicago: University of Chicago Press, 1989). See also Donnerstein et al., *The Question of Pornography*, chap. 7; and Gordon Hawkins and Franklin E. Zimring, *Pornography in a Free Society* (New York, NY.: Cambridge University Press, 1988), p. 26.

85. *The Report of the Commission on Obscenity and Pornography* (Washington, D.C.: U.S. Government Printing Office, 1970).

86. U.S. Department of Justice, *Attorney General's Commission on Pornography, Final Report*, vols. 1 and 2 (Washington, D.C.: U.S. Government Printing Office, 1986). For comments on the scientific underpinnings of this report, see Edward Donnerstein, "The Pornography Commission Report: Do Findings Fit Conclusions?" *Sexual Coercion and Assault Issues and Perspectives*, **1** (1986): 185–188.

87. Home Office, *Report of the Committee on Obscenity and Film Censorship* (London: Her Majesty's Stationery Office, 1979), p. 103. See also Dennis Howitt and Guy Cumberbatch, *Pornography: Impacts and Influences: A Review of Available Research Evidence on the Effects of Pornography* (London: Research and Planning Unit, U.K. Home Office, 1990).

88. *The Report of the Commission on Obscenity and Pornography.*

89. R. A. Barron and P. A. Bell, "Sexual Arousal and Aggression by Males: Effects of Type of Erotic Stimuli and Prior Provocation," *Journal of Personality and Social Psychology*, **35** (1977): 79–87. For a more current study, see Scot B. Boeringer, "Pornography and Sexual Aggression: Associations of Violent and Nonviolent Depictions with Rape and Rape Proclivity," *Deviant Behavior*, **15** (1994): 289–304.

90. Dolf Zillman and Jennings Bryant, "Pornography, Sexual Callousness, and the Trivialization of Rape," *Journal of Communication*, **32** (1984): 10–21. See also Berl Kutchinsky, "Evidence Proves That Pornography Does Not Promote Rape," in the Current Controversies series, *Violence against Women*, ed. Karin L. Swisher, Carol Wekesser and William Barbour (San Diego: Greenhaven Press, 1994); Cynthia S. Gentry, "Pornography and Rape: An Empirical Analysis," *Deviant Behavior*, **12** (1991): 277–288.

91. Edward Donnerstein et al., *The Question of Pornography; Final Report of the Attorney General's Commission on Pornography* (Nashville, Tenn.: Rutledge Hill Press, 1986), esp. pp. 38–47. See also Bruno Leone, Bonnie Szumski, Katie de Koster, et al., in the Current Controversies series, *Violence against Women* (San Diego: Greenhaven Press, 1994); Myriam Miedzian, "How Rape Is Encouraged in American Boys and What We Can Do to Stop It," in *Transforming a Rape Culture*, ed. Emilie Buchwald, Pamela R. Fletcher, and Martha Roth (Minneapolis: Milkweed Editions, 1993); Judith A. Reisman, *Images of Children, Crime and Violence in Playboy, Penthouse and Hustler* (Washington, D.C.: Office of Juvenile Justice and Delinquency Prevention, Office of Justice Assistance, Research and Statistics, U.S. Department of Justice, 1990).

92. Joan Hoff, "Why Is There No History of Pornography?" in *For Adult Users Only: The Dilemma of Violent Pornography*, ed. Susan Gubar and Joan Hoff (Bloomington: Indiana University Press, 1989), p. 18. See also Franklin Mark Osanka and Sara Lee Johann, "Pornography Contributes to Violence against Women," in Swisher and Wekesser. *Violence against Women.*

93. *Miller v. California*, 413 U.S. 15 (1973). See also Laura Lederer, Richard Delgado, et al., *The Price We Pay: The Case against Racist Speech, Hate Propaganda, and Pornography* (New York: Hill and Wang, 1995).

94. *Pope v. Illinois*, 481 U.S. 497 (1987). See also Adele M. Stan et al., *Debating Sexual Correctness: Pornography, Sexual Harassment, Date Rape, and the Politics of Sexual Equality* (New York: Dell, 1995); Bill Thompson, *Soft Core: Moral Crusades against Pornography in Britain and America* (London: Cassell, 1994); Catherine Itzen et al., *Pornography: Women, Violence and Civil Liberties* (Oxford: Oxford University Press, 1993).

95. Laura Davis, Marilyn D. McShane, and Frank P. Williams III, "Controlling Computer Access to Pornography: Special Conditions for Sex Offenders," *Federal Probation*, **59** (1995): 43–48; Marty Rimm, "Marketing Pornography on the Information Superhighway: A Survey of 917,410 Images, Descriptions, Short Stories and Animations Downloaded 8.5 Million Times by Consumers in Over 2,000 Cities in Forty Countries, Provinces, and Territories," *Georgetown Law Journal*, **83** (1995): 1849–2008; Great Britain House of Commons, *Computer Pornography* (London: Her Majesty's Stationery Office, 1994). For a perspective on the government's plan to police the Internet's superhighway, see James Aley, "How Not to Help High Tech," *Fortune Magazine*, May 16, 1994, p. 100.

96. Kinsey et al., *Sexual Behavior in the Human Male.*

97. Alfred C. Kinsey, Wardel B. Pomeroy, Clyde E. Martin, and Paul H. Gebhard, *Sexual Behavior in the Human Female* (Philadelphia: Saunders, 1953), p. 453.

Internet Exercise

Drug use among high school students has increased significantly in recent years. Discuss this increase in terms of the numbers and types of drugs.

Your Web Site is: http://www.ojp.usdoj.gov/bjs/

CHAPTER 15
Comparative
Criminology

What Is Comparative Criminology?

The Definition of Comparative Criminology

The History of Comparative Criminology

The Goals of Comparative Research

Engaging in Comparative Criminological Research

Preparatory Work

Comparative Research

The Special Problems of Empirical Research

Theory Testing

Validation of Major Theories

The Socioeconomic Development Perspective

Practical Goals

Learning from Others' Experiences

Developing International Strategies

Globalization versus Ethnic Fragmentation

Review

Notes

Special Features

CRIMINOLOGICAL FOCUS Cross-Cultural Research

WINDOW TO THE WORLD: Transnational Criminality

AT ISSUE: BCCI: International Fraud

Key Terms

comparative criminology
international crimes
international criminal court
transnational crime

In June 1993 the FBI arrested eight "skinheads" who had been plotting to bomb the First African Methodist Episcopal Church in Los Angeles and shoot worshippers. American skinheads have become notorious for their random assaults on blacks, Jews, gays, immigrants, minority groups—anybody they perceive as different and whom they therefore dislike. They revere Hitler and his terror, delight in overt racist music, display swastikas and Nazi flags, and serve as shock troops for more established racist organizations. Between 3300 and 3500 skinheads are scattered in 160 or so groups in 40 states. They have become so dangerous that the FBI had to withdraw some undercover agents who had infiltrated their ranks.[1]

Few people had heard of skinheads prior to May 1985, when groups from Britain, Belgium, Denmark, and France staged a riot at a soccer game in Belgium which left 38 people of color dead and another 200 wounded. Since then, skinheads have become a daily news item in many countries. During the Persian Gulf War, 1990 to 1991, skinheads burned 20 mosques to the ground in the London area.

By 1995, an estimated 70,000 youths, in 33 countries, on 6 continents, adhered to the neo-Nazi skinhead movement, with the largest concentration in Germany, Hungary, the Czech Republic, the United States, Poland, the United Kingdom, Brazil, Italy, and Sweden (listed in descending order).[2]

Hardest hit has been Germany, the birthplace of Nazism, where the homes of Jewish families have been firebombed and hundreds of foreign workers and asylum seekers have been attacked or killed. The skinheads attack with screams of "Heil Hitler," waving their favorite symbol, the old German imperial flag.

> Their ideology, if that is the word, is primitive . . . they know nothing about Hitler, or the war, beyond the fact that Hitler exterminated people who were "different" which is what they like to do themselves. They do not even know about the "ethnic cleansing" going on . . . in Bosnia now. They do not read newspapers. They read killer comic books and listen to Oi music, which is a kind of heavy-metal rock about the pleasures of "genocide."[3]

343

Neo-Nazi groups march in Germany on the anniversary of the death of Rudolf Hess, one of Hitler's best-known associates and one of the few Nazis to serve a long prison term.

In 1990–1991 it had been the mosques of the London region. By 1994–1995 the torch was turned on some 70 African-American churches in the American South, nearly all with the hallmark of hate crime. In France hate has now reversed. The new "enemy" is born of the suburban ghettos, is mostly of African origin, a ragtag subcultural group. Their common language is "hip-hop." Their roots are "in the Bronx and Kingston, Jamaica; in South-Central Los Angeles and Brixton, London; in Dakar and Algiers, in Islam and the N.B.A."[4] Its hallmarks are rage, graffiti, drug dealing, and firearms. For the time being, this movement has been dubbed the "guerrilla renaissance." What has caused the rise of neo-Nazism and the formation of skinhead groups, of torchers of houses of worship, and of "guerrilla renaissance," almost simultaneously, in so many different parts of the world? Who defines the often bizarre ideology of such groups? Do adherents communicate with each other across borders?

To answer these questions, criminologists must engage in comparative research. But so far, there are few answers. For the skinheads, criminologist Mark Hamm has begun this process with his work *American Skinheads—The Criminology and Control of Hate Crime,* which presents the phenomenon in an international perspective. He traces American developments to earlier occurrences in England and to the ideological background of Nazism in Germany.[5] Yet much more comparative research remains to be done

to explain the almost simultaneous occurrence of identical crime problems in many parts of the world.

We begin this chapter on comparative criminology with an attempt to define it. We look next at the history of comparative criminology in order to identify its purpose and goals. Later in the chapter we focus on the prerequisites for comparative criminological research, the process itself, and the challenges globalization is posing to comparative criminology.

WHAT IS COMPARATIVE CRIMINOLOGY?

Comparison is something all human beings do every day. In choosing a home, for example, you compare such elements as number of rooms and price; location; access to transportation, shopping, and recreation; age of the structure; beauty of the surroundings; and so on. This comparison can become a science if it is done in a systematic manner. And so it is with comparative criminology.

The Definition of Comparative Criminology

What is **comparative criminology?** Simply put, it is the cross-cultural or cross-national study of crime and crime control applying the comparative method in the science of criminology.[6]

Many criminologists use comparisons. Just think of a study comparing one group with another group, a control group. But this is not what we mean by comparative criminology; it requires comparison across cultures or nations. A comparative study of victimization rates between Montana and Mississippi is not comparative criminology, because the two states are part of one nation and of one basic culture. But if we were to compare the role of alcohol in the escalation of violence among the Cheyenne nation, in Montana or Wyoming, with that among the people of the rest of the state, we might well have a cross-cultural comparison, because the Cheyenne have a distinct legal system, they have a culture of their own, and they are related to the U.S. government by a treaty.

The History of Comparative Criminology

Comparative criminology is not new. When the Romans had a crime problem in the fifth century B.C., they sent a delegation to the more advanced nation of Greece to learn better techniques for dealing with crime, such as the publication of laws. In the late Middle Ages and during the Renaissance (fourteenth to sixteenth centuries), all of continental Europe became a vast comparative laboratory as laws that had developed in the various principalities and cities were compared against the rediscovered laws of the old Roman Empire.

Unhappily, it was also during this era that crime-control methods became ever more brutal. The situation did not change until the eighteenth century, when—again through comparison, cooperation, and transfer—the work of the classical school (see Chapter 3) began to introduce rationality and humanitarian principles into crime control in Europe and America. In the nineteenth century, as communications improved, policy makers and scholars of criminology compared approaches and introduced into one another's systems what seemed to work. Such ideas as the juvenile court, the penitentiary, the reformatory, probation, and parole gained worldwide acceptance as a result of comparison. Yet the comparisons of the nineteenth and early twentieth centuries lacked scientific rigor; they were impressionistic and often emotional. For example, the juvenile court, first established in Chicago in 1899, seemed such a good idea that it gained acceptance in many parts of the world. But as later experience showed, it did not necessarily work everywhere.

The founders of criminology, including those of American criminology, were, for the most part, comparatists. They would gather at international meetings and trade ideas; they would visit each other and stimulate criminological thought. But truly comparative studies, measuring up to scholarly standards, could not be done until criminology itself became a science. Throughout the first half of the twentieth century internationalism met resistance from isolationism. Comparatists were regarded as dreamers, and the comparative approach was seen as not very practical.

The Global Village: Advantages. Now circumstances have changed drastically. Comparative criminologists have become a necessity, simply because the world has become a "global village." Consider these figures from the U.S. Department of Commerce: In 1960 the United States exported $30 billion worth of goods; in 1994 it exported $838 billion. In 1960 imports were $23 billion; in 1994 they were $954 billion.

World economies have become totally integrated and interdependent. The Japanese car you own was probably manufactured in the United States, and your American car may have parts made in more than 30 countries. Your shirt may come from Hong Kong, your shoes from Italy, and your Swiss watch from the American Virgin Islands. The situation is no different abroad, where Coke and Pepsi and American fast-food chains are only the most visible aspects of economic globalization.

Communications likewise have become global. Sitting in your living room before a TV, you participate in world events as they happen. Phone and fax and computer networking have made instant personal and business communications possible. Transportation advances, especially since the introduction of jumbo jets, together with the easing of frontiers, have made it possible for millions of people to move across oceans within hours. Air-traffic volume increased from 26 billion passenger miles in 1960 to 600 billion in 1992.

Europe is feeling the effects of globalization even more intensely than the rest of the world. The collapse of Communist dictatorships in Central and Eastern Europe[7] and the virtual abolition of frontiers in the European Community countries[8] have brought crime problems until now unheard of in Europe. Consequently, national criminology had to become international criminology. Criminology has in fact been globalized.[9]

The Global Village: Disadvantages. All these developments have been greatly beneficial. Yet they have also brought great problems. Instant communication promotes not only the spread of benefits, in goods, lifestyles, and useful knowledge, but also the dissemination of dysfunctional ideas and values—like the skinhead phenomenon. Economic globalization, as much as it promotes useful commerce, also aids organized crime and fosters the global spread of frauds that were once confined to smaller localities or single countries.

Jet planes transport not just legitimate travelers but also illegal aliens, criminal entrepreneurs, drug dealers, money launderers, and terrorists. Airlines themselves have become the targets of international criminals. Moreover, the industrialization of the world brings not just economic benefits but threats to the world ecology so severe that, unless they are checked, they could compromise the food, water, and clean air supply for all people. It is little wonder, then, that criminologists too must look across borders to study crime and crime-control efforts, and to search for internationally acceptable solutions to common problems.

The Goals of Comparative Research

Before the 1970s there was very little literature on comparative research in criminology. Since then, however, it has been growing rapidly. That is attributable to (1) a realization that we will learn more about crime if we test our theories under diverse cultural conditions and (2) renewed interest in trying to discover what we can learn from the experience of other nations.[10]

Comparative criminology, then, has both a theoretical and a practical goal. It helps us to better understand crime causation and to find successful means of crime control, so that no nation need repeat costly mistakes made elsewhere. Presently, a large number of U.N. and affiliated organizations are engaged in the task of establishing international measures to deal with dangers that threaten people of all cultures. (See Table 15.1.)

Before we discuss the implementation of comparative research, we must look at the methods used by comparative criminologists.

ENGAGING IN COMPARATIVE CRIMINOLOGICAL RESEARCH

Comparative research requires special preparatory work to ensure that research data and information are in fact comparable. Empirical research presents additional obstacles.

Preparatory Work

Studying Foreign Law. Before beginning a comparative study, the researcher must become familiar with the laws of the country or culture to which the comparison extends. Every country belongs to one or more of the world's three great families of law, or legal systems (Table 15.2):

- *The common law system.* Common law originated in England and then spread to the various English colonies. Today it is the legal system not only of the U.K. but also of the United States, Canada (except Quebec), Australia, New Zealand, India, many of the Caribbean islands, and African and Asian countries that were once English colonies. Although common law is now found in written form, it originated from case law, and case precedents still play a determining role.
- *The civil law system.* This system grew out of the Roman legal tradition, was refined by scholars, and was codified under Napoleon in the early nineteenth century. Today it is found in systematic codes of law. The countries of continental Europe belong to this family of law, as do their former colonies in Africa, Latin America, and Asia, including Japan and China, which chose the civil law system when they modernized.
- *Indigenous or customary legal systems.* Among these is the largely written and highly developed Islamic law of countries in the Middle East. This law is also found in a few African and Asian countries. Other societies govern themselves largely by tribal law, tradition, and custom. This customary law is generally unwritten.

Having identified the legal system to which the country under study belongs, the comparatist studies the applicable law and its precise interpretation. Foreign legal systems, just like that of the United States, contain penal codes, codes of criminal procedure, con-

Crime Prevention and Criminal Justice Branch (of the U.N. Secretariat at Vienna, Austria): Reports to the U.N. Commission on Crime Prevention and Criminal Justice and conducts the quinquennial U.N. Congress on the Prevention of Crime and the Treatment of Offenders; provides extensive reports, research, documentation, and technical assistance; responsible for U.N. standards and guidelines in criminal justice; conducts worldwide statistical surveys.

UNICRI—United Nations Interregional Crime and Justice Research Institute (heretofore located in Rome, Italy): Research arm of the U.N. Secretariat in crime prevention and criminal justice; responsible for extensive research and publications.

UNAFEI—United Nations Asia and Far East Institute for the Prevention of Crime and the Treatment of Offenders (Tokyo, Japan): Services the region with training, technical assistance, research, and publications.

ILANUD—United Nations Latin American Institute for the Prevention of Crime and the Treatment of Offenders (San José, Costa Rica): Services the region with training, technical assistance, research, and publications.

UNAFRI—United Nations African Regional Institute for the Prevention of Crime and the Treatment of Offenders (Kampala, Uganda): Services the region with training and technical assistance.

HEUNI—Helsinki European Institute for Crime Prevention and Control. Affiliated with the United Nations (Helsinki, Finland); provides extensive research, training, publications, and technical assistance services on behalf of European countries for both developed and developing countries.

AIC—Australian Institute of Criminology (Canberra, Australia): Under agreement with the U.N., provides research, publication, training, and technical assistance services for Oceania, including Australia and New Zealand.

Arab Security Studies and Training Centre (Riyadh, Saudi Arabia): In close cooperation with the U.N., provides extensive educational and training services, research, publications, and development and technical assistance to Arab countries.

International Centre for Criminal Law Reform and Criminal Justice Policy (Vancouver, B.C., Canada): Newly established, by agreement with the U.N., to provide services within its sphere of expertise.

ISPAC—International Scientific and Professional Advisory Council of United Nations Crime Prevention and Criminal Justice Programs (Milan, Italy): By agreement with the U.N., provides advisory services to the U.N. with respect to data and information, both in general and on specific subjects falling within the mandate of the U.N.

UNCJIN—United Nations Crime and Justice Information Network (Albany, N.Y.): In close cooperation

with *WCJLN*—World Criminal Justice Library Network (Newark, N.J.)—assembles, integrates, and disseminates criminal justice information and data worldwide, with a view to complete electronic accessibility.

NIJ—The National Institute of Justice, of the U.S. Department of Justice: By an agreement with the United Nations signed in 1995, joined the Network of U.N. affiliated institutes to make the services of the National Criminal Justice Reference Service—especially its UNOJUST computer services—available to the U.N. community.

NGOs—Nongovernmental organizations in consultative status with the United Nations Economic and Social Council: International organizations whose expertise is made available to the U.N. They include many major scientific, professional, and advocacy groups, such as:

- International Association of Penal Law
- International Penal and Penitentiary Foundation (special status)
- International Society of Criminology
- International Society of Social Defense
- Institute of Higher Studies in Criminal Sciences
- Centro Nazionale di Prevenzione e Difesa Sociale
- International Association of Chiefs of Police
- International Prisoners Aid Association
- Amnesty International

NGO Alliances in Crime Prevention and Criminal Justice (New York, N.Y., and Vienna, Austria): Made up of the headquarters' representatives of NGOs; provide coordination and research services to the U.N.

U.N. agencies: Concerned with various aspects of crime and justice. The agencies include:

- Centre for Human Rights (Geneva, Switzerland)
- *UNICEF*, United Nations Children's Fund (New York, N.Y.)

The United Nations International Drug Control Programme: Concerned with various aspects of international drug control and drug abuse prevention. The programs include:

- Division on Narcotic Drugs
- International Narcotic Drug Control Board
- U.N. Fund for Drug Abuse Control

Regional intergovernmental organizations: Have organizational units and/or conduct programs concerned with crime prevention and criminal justice. Examples include:

- Council of Europe
- European Economic Community (EEC)
- Organization of American States
- Organization of African Unity
- North Atlantic Treaty Organization

TABLE 15.2   Dominant Criminal Justice Systems

Roman (Civil) Law	Common Law	Customary Law
Law and procedure governed by separate, comprehensive, systematized codes, which are forward-looking, wishing to anticipate all new problems.	Law and procedure governed by laws and precedents, which, if codified at all, simply organize past experiences.	Resembles common law more than civil law, largely relying on precedents transmitted orally or in writing.
Codes based on scholarly analysis and conceptualizations.	Laws reflect experience of practitioners, on a case-by-case basis.	
Supreme courts interpret nuances of law.	Supreme courts develop law.	
Legal proceedings must establish entire truth.	Truth finding strictly limited by pleadings and rules of evidence.	Popular justice, often without trained lawyers.
Judges free to find and interpret facts.	Rules of evidence limit fact-finding process. Parties produce evidence.	
Very little lay participation.	Grand and petit juries play strong role.	
No presumption of guilt or innocence.	Presumption of innocence.	

stitutions, and case reports. But they also include special legislation on such topics as environmental protection and money laundering. In federal countries both federal and state legislation may have to be studied.

Then there is the problem of finding the country's laws. For the English-speaking researcher this need not be an insurmountable task. The laws, court decisions, and textbooks of English-speaking countries, for the most part, are accessible in libraries. The constitutions,[11] criminal codes,[12] and codes of criminal procedure[13] of many other countries are available in English. For a number of non-English-speaking countries there are English-language texts about their criminal law or procedure.[14] But since there is always a gap between the law on the books and the law in action, the comparatist must also consult the criminal justice research literature.

Understanding Foreign Criminal Justice Systems. Laws function within a country's criminal justice system. It is the practitioners of the system who make the laws function. There are reports from around the world based on their experience.[15] There is also a considerable amount of periodical literature and statistical information in English describing the functioning of criminal justice systems in a variety of countries (Table 15.3).[16]

Contemporary cross-cultural texts and treatises contain descriptions of the developments in crimi-

nology and criminal justice for over 50 countries.[17] In addition to the descriptions of entire criminal justice systems, there are accounts of the functioning of subsystems. For example, a five-volume series examines the area of delinquency and juvenile justice in more than two dozen countries and regions throughout the world.[18] Other aspects of criminal justice have been investigated by specialists in such areas as policing,[19] corrections,[20] and the incidence of female criminality.[21]

Learning about a Foreign Culture. Comparatists may have an understanding of their own culture. To do comparative work, they must study a foreign culture: They must become familiar with its history, politics, economy, and social structure. Scholars of comparative criminology—such as Marshall B. Clinard, working in Switzerland as well as India and other developing countries;[22] Louise I. Shelley, working in Eastern European socialist countries and elsewhere;[23] and William Clifford, working in several African countries as well as Japan[24]—have successfully demonstrated that the immersion in the cultures under study that comparative research requires can be accomplished without losing the objectivity of the detached scientific researcher.

Collecting Data. Research, as we emphasized in Chapter 2, requires factual information. Although

TABLE 15.3	**English-Language Periodical Literature for Comparative Criminology**

Abstracting Services

Criminal Justice Abstracts*
Criminology, Penology, and Police Science Abstracts

Periodicals

Crime Prevention and Criminal Justice Newsletter (U.N.)
Criminal Justice International
Criminal Law Forum: An International Journal
Dutch Penal Law and Policy
EuroCriminology
European Journal of Crime, Criminal Law and Criminal Justice
European Journal on Criminal Policy and Research
Forensic Science International
Home Office Research and Planning Unit Research Bulletin
International Annals of Criminology
International Criminal Justice Review
International Criminal Police Review
International Journal of Comparative and Applied Criminal Justice
International Journal of Law and Psychiatry
International Journal of Offender Therapy and Comparative Criminology
International Journal of the Addictions
International Journal on Drug Policy
International Review of Criminal Policy (U.N.)
International Review of Victimology
Japanese Journal of Sociological Criminology
Revue de Science Criminelle et de Droit Penal Comparée†
Revue Internationale de Criminologie et de Police Technique†
Revue Internationale de Droit Penal†
Studies in Conflict and Terrorism
Studies on Crime and Crime Prevention (Norway)
Terrorism
UNAFEI Resource Material Series
Violence, Aggression and Terrorism
Violence and Victims

some countries do not yet have the resources for systematically collecting information on their crime problems,[25] the great majority send statistics to the International Criminal Police Organization (Interpol), which publishes the data biannually,[26] or participate in the United Nations Surveys of Crime Trends, Operation of Criminal Justice Systems and Crime Prevention Strategies. The U.N. surveys, published in 5-year cycles, began with data for the year 1970 and by now include statistics from well over 100 countries on prevalence of crime and the operation of criminal systems.[27]

Several other international data bases are available to the researcher, including the homicide statistics of the World Health Organization;[28] the private-initiative Comparative Crime Data File, which covers 110 sovereignties (published 1984);[29] and the Correlates of Crime (published 1989).[30]

International (or nation-by-nation) crime statistics suffer from the same problems as American UCR statistics, only magnified several times.[31] For this reason, several scholars have recently conducted international victimization surveys. The first major survey, conducted by a team of Dutch, English, and Swiss scholars, covers 17 countries, both developed and developing.[32] To these statistical data bases we can now add self-report studies conducted in several countries, mostly in the Western world.[33] Not surprisingly, these studies exposed the international "dark figure of crime"—the differences between crime reported to the police and crime as experienced by victims or reported by offenders. Consequently, the same caution must be applied to the official crime statistics of foreign countries as we apply to official U.S. statistics.

Comparative Research

Up to this point we have reviewed the general approach to doing comparative criminological research: studying foreign law, criminal justice systems, cultures, and available data. Comparative criminological research begins only after these requirements have been met. It is at this point that the comparatist sets sail for uncharted seas. The comparatist meets two problems right at the outset: the interdependence of all crime and criminal justice phenomena, and culture specificity.

Interdependent Phenomena. Think of an elaborately assembled mobile hanging from the ceiling. All the parts are in perfect balance. If you remove a single part, the whole mobile will completely shift out of balance. It is the same with problems of crime and justice in any society: The existence of each is related to all the others and is explainable by reference to the others. Bicycle thefts may exist in countries like China, Denmark, and the Netherlands—all of which rely heavily on bicycle transportation—as well as in the United States or Mexico. But

CROSS-CULTURAL RESEARCH: SMOKING ONE'S WAY INTO CHEYENNE CULTURE

It was in the summer of 1935 that Karl N. Llewellyn, renowned legal philosopher, and his friend E. Adamson Hoebel, noted anthropologist, visited the northern Cheyennes on the Tongue River Reservation at Lame Deer, Montana. High Forehead of the Cheyennes served as their interpreter. Sitting in a circle with several Cheyennes, a chief filled the pipe and held it to the five directions. After the pipe had been passed around, he asked why the two white men had come.(1)

"To learn of your laws," answered the visitors. There was silence and more pipe puffing. Obviously the term "laws" meant nothing. Llewellyn went on, "For example, your rules on homicide . . .?" More silence, more puffing. "Well," said Llewellyn, making another attempt, "what happens when there is trouble because one of your warriors has killed another man of the tribe?"

At this there was a smile of recognition, and Calf Woman spoke:

Cries Yia Eya had been gone from the camp for three years because he had killed Chief Eagle in a whiskey brawl. The chiefs had ordered him away for his murder, so we did not see anything of him for that time. Then one day he came back, leading a horse packed with bundles of old-time tobacco. He stopped outside the camp and sent a messenger in with the horse and tobacco who

was to say to the chiefs for him, "I am begging to come home."

The chiefs all got together for a meeting, and the soldier societies were told to convene. The tobacco was divided up and chiefs' messengers were sent out to invite the soldier chiefs to come to the lodge of the tribal council. "Here is the tobacco that that man sent in," [the big chiefs] told the soldier chiefs. "Now we want you soldiers to decide if you think we should accept his request. If you decide that we should let him return, then it is up to you to convince his family that it is all right." (The relatives of Chief Eagle had told everybody that they would kill Cries Yia Eya on sight if they ever found him.) The soldier chiefs took the tobacco and went out to gather their troops. Each society met in its own separate lodge to talk among themselves.

At last one man said, "I think it is all right. I believe the stink has blown from him. Let him return!" This view was passed around, and this is the view that won out among the soldiers. Then the father of Chief Eagle was sent for and asked whether he would accept the decision. "Soldiers," he replied, "I shall listen to you. Let him return! But if that man comes back, I want never to hear his voice raised against another person. If he does, we come together."

Cries Yia Eya had always been a mean man, disliked by every-

one, but he had been a fierce fighter against the enemies. After he came back to the camp, however, he was always good to the people.(2)

Llewellyn and Hoebel went on to collect hundreds of anecdotes of Cheyenne "conflict and case law." While they knew that the Cheyennes had structured institutions, they were surprised at the "juristic beauty" that the research revealed. In the introduction to their work on the subject, *The Cheyenne Way*, the authors comment:

Three years of puzzlement went into the analysis of the material before order emerged; and this happened (as it does in modern case law) when the data of sixty or eighty years were arranged not on a flat time-plane, but against the moving time-perspective of the culture and the individual life.(2)

Source
1. As told in class, ca. 1950, by Karl N. Llewellyn, University of Chicago.
2. Calf Woman's story is excerpted from K. N. Llewellyn and E. Adamson Hoebel, *The Cheyenne Way* (Norman: University of Oklahoma Press, 1941), pp. 12–13.

Questions for Discussion
1. What are some of the problems of doing criminological research in other cultures?
2. What are the best ways of ensuring that those problems are overcome?

such theft plays a different role in the various countries, generates different responses, and leads to different consequences.

Is the bicycle theft problem comparable around the world? What could be learned from a comparison,

and what factors must be considered? Would it be more useful to compare the Chinese bicycle theft problem with the Italian automobile theft problem? How do these problems fit in their countries' respective crime and justice mobiles?

The preferred means of transportation during rush hour in the streets of Beijing, China

Culture-Specific Phenomena. The task of a comparative criminologist is like that of a surgeon about to transplant a heart or a liver. The surgeon studies a great variety of factors to be sure the donor's organ is compatible with the recipient's body. If we want to compare Japan's low crime rates with the high crime rates in the United States, we must consider many factors, such as the role of shame in Japanese society. Misconduct brings shame not only on individual Japanese wrongdoers, but also on their families, schools, and companies: Could shaming, as a sanction, play a role in American criminal justice, or is it too culture-specific?

It is easier to ask such questions than it is to answer them, since research experience in comparative criminology is still limited. In fact, the first book entitled *"Comparative" Criminology* appeared as recently as 1965. Its author, the late German-English scholar Hermann Mannheim, relied on his vast cross-cultural experience in criminology but offered no guide to the comparative method.[34] More in the nature of a true comparative exercise—yet also without much guidance regarding the comparative method—is the Polish scholar Brunon Holyst's *Comparative Criminology* (1979), which systematically compares the incidence and causes of crime and the features of criminal justice around the world.[35]

The Special Problems of Empirical Research

Criminologists who cannot find or rely upon comparative data must generate their own, usually by parallel field investigations proceeding more or less simultaneously. They confront three problems: first, the identification of comparable problems; second, the identification of sources of information; and third, the selection of a research method compatible in the countries under comparison.

Identification of Comparable Problems. Researchers of New York University's Comparative Criminal Law Project, in the 1960s, compared the prevalence of delinquency in several cultures. To their surprise, they learned that Egypt had a high rate of delinquency for railroad offenses. Only local assistance could provide a plausible answer: The long railroad line running parallel to the Nile River is a favored haunt for local youths. Their delinquent acts were recorded as railroad offenses, rather than as delinquency.[36] These "railroad offenses" had to be made comparable to nonrailroad delinquencies in both Egypt and the other countries under comparison.

Identification of Sources of Information. The social groups of one society may not be comparable to those of another. American junior high school students may represent American youngsters of that age range as a whole, but Haitian junior high school students would not. What groups are comparable to such favorite research subjects as American college students, blue-collar workers, and self-employed small-business people? What is a fair cross section of any country's population?

Police records may be highly reliable in Belgium, but are they in Mali and Malawi or in Armenia? And if they are not, what comparable substitutes can the comparatist find? Such problems challenge the researcher's ingenuity.

Selection of Compatible Research Methods. Criminologist James Finckenauer, studying attitudes toward legal and other values among American and Russian youngsters, was at first confronted with the reluctance of Russian administrators to ask youngsters to report (even anonymously) their own delinquencies. The Soviet culture had blocked any such initiative. The problem was overcome only by indirect questions to the youngsters, such as: "How wrong would it be (to do this, that, or the other)?" This was followed by further semidirect questions, such as: "Do your peers (parents, and so on) view you as a good kid, bad kid, or something in between?" It was only after the end of communism in 1992 that Finckenauer could administer a self-report delinquency questionnaire.

Certain research methods simply are unknown in many other countries or, if known, are frowned upon. In a study of perceptions of police power in four cultures, for example, the commanding officer of a foreign police department was asked to have some questionnaires distributed to his officers. At first the officer responded: "You don't seem to understand our police! It is we who ask the questions!" Finally he agreed and distributed the questionnaires. After the results were analyzed, the researchers were astonished to find that all the answers were identical. Apparently, all the questionnaires had been reviewed and "corrected" by an attorney to make sure they were accurate.[37]

THEORY TESTING

As we noted earlier, the cross-cultural testing of criminological theories has become one of the major goals of comparative criminology. Recent studies have extended to several of the crime-causation theories discussed in this book. Yet cross-cultural theory testing requires utmost caution.[38]

Validation of Major Theories

After Sheldon and Eleanor Glueck had completed *Unraveling Juvenile Delinquency* (1950),[39] their work was criticized as too culture-specific because it was based on a sample of American children. In response, scholars replicated the Glueck research in different cultural settings—Puerto Rico, Germany, and Japan. As the Gluecks themselves put it, "All these [studies] . . . have provided the most definite of all proofs, that of applicability to other samples by other researchers."[40] These cross-cultural validations of the Gluecks' delinquency-prediction system are some of the earliest empirical, comparative criminological studies.

More recently, criminologist Obi Ebbe has reviewed the Gluecks' studies and found their theories applicable to juvenile delinquents in Nigeria.[41] He has also examined the cross-cultural validity of other American theories, such as differential association, social control, and culture conflict. During the last few years other scholars have tested opportunity theory,[42] situational characteristics of crime,[43] routine-activity theory,[44] differential opportunity theory,[45] social control and strain theory,[46] the synnomie explanation of low crime rates,[47] and Durkheim's anomie theory.[48] Most of these studies have shown the theories to have moderate to significant validity.[49]

The Socioeconomic Development Perspective

Cross-cultural researchers have devoted particular attention to the recently developed hypothesis that modernization and urbanization lead to increases in crime[50] as well as to the general question of whether socioeconomic development necessarily brings an increase in crime.[51] Several have noted a connection between rapid development and an increase in certain types of crime, especially property crime.[52] Other research has demonstrated that sudden urbanization and industrialization have not led to increased crime in some countries,[53] but that unguided socioeconomic and political changes, such as the current transformation from a socialist to a market economy in Central and Eastern Europe, do produce an increase in crime.[54] The complexity of the relation between development and crime has prompted some comparative criminologists to warn that, as yet, there is no universal theoretical framework linking crime and development.[55]

PRACTICAL GOALS

Learning from Others' Experiences

With increasing globalization, the similarity of crime problems increases as well. It is natural that criminologists would look at the experiences of other countries in their search for solutions, especially the experiences of countries that seem to have found workable solutions.[56] For the worldwide drunk-driving problem, for example, comparative research has been done in Australia, Norway, and the United States.[57] One gun-control study investigated the situation in seven nations[58]; another, in twenty-six.[59] Insurance fraud researchers have looked at the situation in eight countries[60]; insider-trading researchers, in three.[61]

A recent symposium compared differential methods of dealing with ecological crime in the United States, Germany, Austria, Japan, and Taiwan.[62] Comparative criminological research has also been done on violent crime, such as homicides of children,[63] spousal homicides,[64] homicides among young males,[65] and urban violence.[66] For the past 25 years, much attention has been devoted to the comparative study of the problem of juvenile delinquency.[67]

By now there is also a considerable body of cross-cultural research on various aspects of crime-control policy. One of the earliest studies in this area examined the perception of police power among divergent population groups in four countries.[68] The perception of law was studied in six cultures,[69] and teenagers' perception of crime and criminal justice was the subject of a more recent two-country study.[70]

Issues in policing[71] as well as sanctions[72] occupy the attention of comparatists in their search for "what works." Victimologists have been particularly active in cross-cultural study.[73]

Developing International Strategies

Comparative criminology reveals that most crime problems are not unique to a single country or a single locality. So we are challenged to develop strategies jointly with other countries. For the sake of convenience, we can group crime problems reaching beyond national borders into three categories:

- Internationally induced local crime problems
- Transnational crime
- International crime

Internationally Induced Local Crime Problems. The skinhead phenomenon is a prime example of the simultaneous appearance of a similar type of crime in various parts of the world.[74] As yet, little is known about what causes such simultaneous appearances, although instantaneous reporting in the mass media may aid the process,[75] and some international organizational connections also may play a role. (Yet neither of these factors was present in another simultaneous occurrence of a crime problem, namely piracy in several widely separated waterways of the world in the mid-1970s, perpetrated in large part by rootless young offenders.[76]) The skinheads are part of the broader problem of crimes of discrimination against minorities, which itself is fueled by vastly increased intracontinental and intercontinental migrations. The appearance of new ethnic minorities within heretofore mono-ethnic communities often results in the victimization of minorities. These population migrations have also resulted in the migration of crime perpetrated by migrants—often against their fellow migrants, but also against the indigenous population. Consequently, criminologists have had to look for new ways to deal with these new forms and dimensions of crime.[77]

Internationally induced local crime problems can be far greater than hate crimes or other forms of crime associated with culture conflict and migration. Consider that drugs produced abroad and distributed locally create a vast problem of crime: Not only is drug dealing illegal, but a considerable portion of street crime is associated with narcotics. Ultimately it could be said that there are very few crime problems that are not associated with persons and events abroad over which we have no direct control. Although the problem is a vast, yet largely uncharted territory, a number of criminal activities with foreign connections have recently been identified and given the title "transnational crime."

Transnational Crime. Criminologists use the term **transnational crime** to refer to criminal activities, transactions, or schemes that violate the laws of more than one country or have a direct impact on a foreign country. Neither individually, nor by type, nor collectively by category, do transnational crimes conform to the definitions and categorizations found in penal codes.

In a recent questionnaire sent to all of the world's national governments, and in a subsequent report on the results, the U.N., for the first time in history, demonstrated the existence and prevalence of transnational crime.[78] Eighteen categories of transnational criminality emerged. While it is conceivable that all these activities could be committed within a single jurisdiction, and/or by individual perpetrators, it is the hallmark of all that they are typically perpetrated by means of transnational activities and by organized groups of perpetrators.[79]

1. *Money laundering.* This category ranks number 1 on the list because of its massive impact on the economy of the entire world. Money laundering is an activity aimed at making illegally obtained funds seem legitimate, so that such funds can be spent or invested in the legitimate economy without arousing suspicion. Consider that a substantial part of the financial gain of the world's citizens is ill-gotten, for example by bribery, by corruption, by black-market activities and transactions outside the tax laws, and especially by dealing in contraband.

The drug barons and others who have illegitimate income have devised many schemes to launder dirty money, including bogus real estate transactions, purchases of gold (many times consisting of lead bars with a coating of gold), and sales (real or fictitious) of art and antiques. But the standard method remains the physical transfer of cash out of the country (by planes or ships or by trucks and trailers with false bottoms), deposit of such cash abroad, followed by a series of international (electronic) transfers, at the end of which the source is untraceable, and the money seems clean and legitimately invested in the economy (Figure 15.1).

The true dimensions of money laundering are largely unknown. Criminologists have just begun to assess this phenomenon.[80] Nevertheless, policy research [especially the Financial Transactions Task Force of the Group of Seven (highly industrialized countries)] has resulted in some remedies.

2. *Terrorist activities.* Americans had been largely unaware of the international scope of terrorist activities, primarily because their homeland had remained unaffected. This naiveté changed with the growing awareness that Americans, and American interests and installations abroad, have become targets of international terrorists. But only the bombing of the World Trade Center in New York City in February 1993 by an organized group of Middle Eastern terrorists alerted Americans to the vulnerability of their own country. The terrorist bombing of Pan Am Flight 103 over Lockerbie, Scotland, in December 1988, and more recently the destruction of TWA Flight 800 (suspected terrorism), in July 1996, unhappily will not be the last such crimes against Americans and American interests.

Much scholarly inquiry has been directed at understanding and explaining international terrorism.[81] And there have been legislative responses. As a matter of fact, a network of international conventions is in place to deal with international terrorism. International judicial and police cooperation have been vastly improved. Yet there is no international machinery in operation to ensure the arrest or adjudication of international terrorists, and criminologists have yet to arrive at theoretically sound explanations that would help to deal with a problem that knows no boundaries.

3. *Theft of art and cultural objects.* This category obtained a number 3 ranking because of its potential for robbing entire cultures and nations of their cultural heritage. Tombs and monuments have been plundered since the time of the pharaohs. But with the development of modern tools and the high demand for cultural objects, as well as the ease of transport, international thieves have developed systems that can strip an entire region or country of its heritage—as well as the work of contemporary artists. There is no country that has not been victimized. An estimated $4.5 billion worth of fine art is stolen every year for sale on the international market. A data base lists 45,000 stolen art objects, with an increase of 2000 items a month.[82] With few exceptions,[83] criminologists have paid scant attention to this phenomenon, though the art industry has endeavored to come up with some practical solutions.[84]

4. *Theft of intellectual property.* Theft of intellectual property includes the unauthorized use of the rights of authors and performers, and of copyrights and trademarks. There is obviously a high temptation to reproduce works of protected originators at a fraction of franchise (or similar) costs, especially in coun-

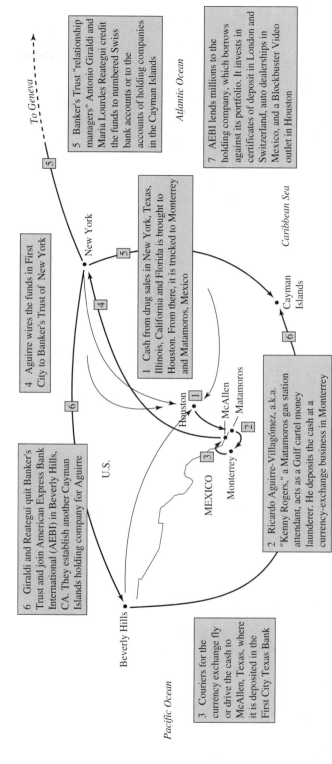

FIGURE 15.1 Wash cycle. Of all the Mexican drug barons, Juan García Abrego may have been the cleverest at money laundering. An indictment brought in 1993, against several of his alleged associates detailed one operation. *Source: Time*, Jan. 29, 1996, p. 51. Map by Paul J. Pugliese.

tries with relatively unregulated economies. Yet the destructive impact on the economies of producing or originating countries is immediately apparent—though hard to assess in monetary terms. One type of theft of intellectual property, namely the illegal copying of software, has been quantified by the U.S. Software Publishers Association: It amounts to an astounding loss of $7.5 billion annually.[85] Despite international agreements, this transnational crime category is a problem without a solution.

5. *Illicit traffic in arms.* Local, regional, or national armed conflicts, which plague us today in every part of the globe, would not be imaginable without an international network of weapons producers and suppliers. This is a shadowy world beyond the reach of statistical assessment. Criminological information on the illegal arms trade is also lacking. Yet the largest portion of the world's homicides is potentially traceable to the illegal trade in arms.

The most lethal part of the world's illegal arms trade centers on the transfer of nuclear materials. It is clear now that during the last few years several relatively small quantities of nuclear material, including pure plutonium, have been diverted from nuclear facilities in former Soviet republics and offered for sale in Germany and other countries west of Russia.

First indications are that the diversions of nuclear material that have occurred so far were carried out by small groups of individuals, rather than organized crime, for motives of individual gain (or possibly to assist in financing totally underfunded former Soviet laboratories and scientists). Most of the efforts were amateurish, and none of the material apparently reached a viable buyer. Indeed, most ended up in sting operations. In several cases the thieves, transporters, and the public have been exposed to radiation hazards—in itself a not insubstantial danger.[86] Criminologists have been caught by surprise. As yet, there have been few criminological responses.[87] At this point, governments have cooperated to control nuclear materials at the source.

6. *Aircraft hijacking.* The system for curbing and responding to the illegal interception of aircraft is in place. Yet at the moment of writing, an Algerian domestic airliner, as well as a Spanish airliner en route to Cuba, have been hijacked. Both episodes ended with all passengers safe.

The airline industry had been plagued by aircraft hijackings in the 1970s and into the 1980s. While a few such incidents were attributable to individuals who demanded ransom, most were political statements with typical terrorist characteristics, seeking to demonstrate the ability of the terrorist organization to strike at vulnerable targets almost anywhere in the world.

Since the entire world community was affected, especially diplomats and politicians, whose mobility depends on air travel, the reaction to the flood of

Police in Mexico City arrest 47 suspects in a major gun smuggling operation.

hijackings was swift and effective. The industry itself reacted effectively by increasing security measures.

The criminological literature on this phenomenon is considerable, centering on the profiles of hijackers, causes, regions, carriers involved, etc., all of which has led to the improvement of controls. Unhappily, the phenomenon of aircraft hijacking has been upstaged by the terrorist destruction of aircraft in flight.

7. *Sea piracy.* Virtually forgotten until the mid-1970s, sea piracy has resurfaced on three fronts since then:

1. The illegal narcotics drug smuggling from South and Central America into the United States initially relied heavily on yachts and fishing vessels captured at sea or in port, after owners and crews were killed. Several thousand vessels were victimized. As the drug trade became prosperous, smugglers began to rely on purchased or illegally chartered vessels.

2. At the roadstead of Lagos, Nigeria, and the narrow shipping channel of the Malacca Straits—as well as in several other comparable sea lanes—the opportunity of deriving some benefit by attacking commercial vessels at anchor or slow speed attracted thousands of marginalized young men in Africa, Southeast Asia, and Latin America. Such piracies (often not piracies in the international law sense, since they occurred in the territorial waters of states) reached a high level of frequency (one a day in the 1980s), but are on the decline now, thanks largely to the research and policy activities of the International Maritime Bureau (London) of the International Chamber of Commerce (Paris), the International Maritime Organization (U.N.), and research by a number of criminologists.[88]

While the problem has been ameliorated, it has by no means ended. Prudent shipping lines order "piracy watches" on their vessels in affected waters. National and regional maritime law enforcement agencies maintain closer watch, and the International Maritime Bureau maintains a special branch office in Kuala Lumpur to monitor developments.

8. *Land hijacking.* The inclusion of land hijacking in the list of transnational crimes was a surprise. At the national level, hijacking of trucks had been well documented as a form of robbery or theft. But the world economy has changed. Long-distance trucking from Eastern to Western Europe, or from the Central Asian republics to the Baltic States, now is a reality, and involves a high percentage of goods transported transnationally. Unhappily, the opportunity to divert such cargos has increased proportionately.

It is telling that only four countries responded to this item on the U.N. questionnaire. At this point the evidence is entirely episodic but seems to point to the involvement of organized groups. Predictably, the problem will increase due to the openness of borders, the growth of organized crime (especially in Eastern Europe), and the lack of data and criminological analysis.

9. *Insurance fraud.* The insurance industry is internationally linked, especially through reinsurance and other methods of spreading risks and benefits. Thus, local insurance fraud ultimately affects all insurers, and all insured, worldwide. The global dimensions of the problem have not been calculated, but for the United States the loss likely amounts to $100 billion annually.[89]

10. *Computer crime.* Just as computers serve legitimate commerce, governments, and researchers, the global Internet is also accessible for criminal schemes, exploitation, and use by organized crime. Current estimates of losses through computer crime range up to $8 billion annually.[90] Unhappily, on this issue we lack information, though criminologists take an increasing interest in the development of legal and other protections.

11. *Environmental crime.* Well into the middle of the twentieth century, harming the environment was regarded as a matter to be controlled by local authorities. It was not until the United Nations Congress on the Environment (Stockholm, 1972) that the global dimensions of environmental destruction, and thus the need for its control, were recognized. In the quarter century since Stockholm, much has been achieved in recognizing environmental dangers, quantifying them, and devising control mechanisms (by treaties, legislation, and ultimately technology) in order to divert these dangers. Criminological research has contributed a great deal in this regard.[91]

12. *Trafficking in persons.* Original forms of trafficking in persons included the slave trade and the white slave trade (traffic in women). While the slave trade may be a matter of the past, the traffic in persons is on the increase, including:

- The transport of illegal immigrants, often resulting in involuntary servitude
- The transport of women for purposes of prostitution
- The transport of migratory laborers to work under slavelike conditions
- The transport of household workers from developing countries
- The transfer of children for adoptions not sanctioned by law

For the most part, laws are in place to prevent the illegal trafficking in persons. Their enforcement is another matter. The problem is bound to increase as the populations of a stagnant Third World press to emigrate to the relatively prosperous countries.

Much of the illegal population flow is controlled by organized crime.[92] The newcomers in the industrialized countries, being largely unemployable, are forming a new marginalized class, likely to be exploited, but also contributing to crime and unrest.

13. *Trade in human body parts.* The first kidney transplant was performed in 1954, the first lung transplant in 1963, and the first heart transplant in 1967. By now close to half a million kidneys have been transplanted. Transplant surgery has become a highly specialized branch of medicine, and the supply of transplantable organs has spawned a very large industry. In the United States, 69 transplant agencies have been established, and federal and state laws seek to control their activities.

Yet, at any given moment, 35,000 people are waiting for a transplant (and the number increases by 14 percent annually); thus, the demand far outstrips the supply. (The number of potential donors in the United States is estimated at about 12,000.) An illegitimate industry has sprung up to provide a service. Recipients are flown to a country where organs can be procured virtually on demand. "Donors" may in fact have been murdered for their organs, or they are children of poor parents sold for their organs, at extremely low prices.

14. *Illicit drug trafficking.* Illicit traffic in narcotic drugs is entirely controlled by organized-crime networks, loosely related with each other geographically, as well as at the various levels of production and marketing and by type of narcotic drugs.[93] The criminological literature exploring this phenomenon from every angle is vast but by no means clear in terms of policy implications.[94] With the Single Convention on Narcotic Drugs (1961), the Convention on Psychotropic Substances (1971), and the United Nations Convention against Illicit Traffic in Narcotic Drugs and Psychotropic Substances (1988), a theoretically perfect international legal structure to control this traffic is in place. Yet its application and enforcement suffers from the following shortcomings:

- The U.N. structure to oversee this treaty scheme is inadequate, primarily due to underfunding.
- Similarly underfunded are comparable national and regional programs.
- Nations differ vastly in their emphasis (interdiction versus repression and control versus tolerance versus treatment approaches).
- Some of the most important countries of origin suffer from corruption at all levels—due to the vast income base of the trade—thus affecting enforcement.
- Corruption similarly affects law enforcement in many countries.
- Most developing and newly democratic countries lack the legal and technical infrastructure necessary to implement the treaties, and a new U.N. assistance program is not yet in place.

No other form of transnational and organized crime is as costly in terms of human and national financial suffering as the illicit trade in narcotic drugs.

15. *Fraudulent bankruptcy.* The internationalization of commerce has turned fraudulent bankruptcy from a local to a transnational crime. The dimensions of the phenomenon are largely unknown. Evidence is anecdotal but includes information that organized crime, after acquiring an enterprise, may subject it to bankruptcy when the gains from bankruptcy exceed the expectations of profit. There is need to strengthen national enforcement efforts and to cooperate these internationally.

16. *Infiltration of legal business.* This is the logical and temporal sequence of money laundering, the principal objective of which is seemingly legitimate investment. At this point the existing information permits no quantitative or qualitative assessment of the phenomenon, but it must be considered that the drug trade alone has between $200 billion and $500 billion to invest in the market. At this rate one could theoretically predict a time at which the world's economy would be controlled by organized crime.[95]

WINDOW TO THE WORLD

TRANSNATIONAL CRIMINALITY: AND NOW THEY DEAL IN HUMAN BODY PARTS!

True to his conviction that the measurement of body and brain is the key to distinguishing between criminals and noncriminals, Cesare Lombroso, the founder of positivist criminology, willed his body to science. Today, many people donate their organs to other human beings who need them to live. Yet the demand for donated organs far outstrips the supply. Where do the donated organs come from? Who are the donors?

In 1988 a German physician attended a medical congress in Rio de Janeiro, Brazil. Unknown perpetrators attacked him from behind and knocked him unconscious. Several days later he found himself on a park bench, awakening from obvious anesthesia. He noticed that he had been professionally bandaged. A medical examination revealed that he was missing a kidney.

THE SCOPE OF THE PROBLEM

In Barranquilla, Colombia, the chief of the University Security Force confessed to 50 murders, committed to obtain organs for transplants. In many parts of Latin America, hospital patients, upon discharge, find out that organs have been needlessly removed; the organs are sold for transplants at exorbitant prices! It has been reported that children's homes in Brazil have been established as "organ farms."(1) President Rafeal Callejas of Honduras has appointed a commission to investigate charges that Honduran children had been sold abroad for illegal adoptions and organ transplants.(2) A member of the European Parliament asked for international police action to stop "barbaric practices" that included "the murder of children whose bodies are butchered for their organs," which are used for transplants in American and European clinics.(3) The Russian parliament (Supreme Soviet) passed legislation in the face of allegations "that organs for transplants are being illegally harvested on a massive scale and that criminal forces are at work in this."(4) The Mexico City weekly *Proceso* revealed the existence of "baby farms" in several Mexican states; the children are used for adoptions abroad and for organ transplants in 17 clinics in Mexican border cities.(5)

The trade in body parts is now worldwide, criminal, organized, and extremely lucrative. An advertisement in a German newspaper offered kidney transplants for $80,000, including cost of the operation and airfare for two persons to an undisclosed clinic in Asia. The "donor" of the kidney will receive little if anything for his or her organ. The risks for recipients are high: Of 130 patients who had traveled to India for a kidney transplant, 8 died on the operating table and another 17 died within a year, mostly of viral and bacterial infections contracted under the unsanitary conditions of the transplant clinics. Less is known about the fate of donors. Yet the poorest inhabitants of the Third World continue to offer skin, an eye, or one or more of their other body parts to transplant clinics catering to foreign recipients.

Sources

1. Britta Buse and Katja Donges, "Illegaler Organhandel," *Magazin für die Polizai,* **203** (1993): 4–7.
2. "Honduran Official Charges Children's Organs Sold," *Orlando Sentinel Tribune,* Apr. 17, 1993, p. A12.
3. "Euro MPs Seek Transplant Laws," *Press Association Limited, Press Association News File,* Sept. 14, 1993.
4. Svetlana Tutorskaya, "Henceforth, Donated Organs Cannot Be Bought and Sold," *Current Digest of the Post Soviet Press,* **45** (1993): 25.
5. "Latin Children Sold in the United States, Study Claims," *Inter Press Service,* Feb. 16, 1993.

Questions for Discussion

1. Based on the examples given above, what laws are violated by those who deal in human body parts or transplant illegally obtained organs?
2. What type of laws or international conventions are needed to stop "barbaric practices" in organ transplants, without hurting those who desperately need a transplant?

---

17. *Corruption and bribery of public officials, party officials, and elected representatives.* While bribery of party officials is not punishable in several countries, all other forms of bribery encompassed by this title are prohibited by penal codes. The problem lies with the enforceability of such laws, in both developed and developing countries, particularly with respect to international investments and trade. Disguised as "commissions," "consultancies," and agency or attorneys' fees, bribes have become a necessary cost of doing business worldwide. Nor is the practice universally condemned. Traders and investors have often proclaimed that it cannot be their business to improve the business or political ethics in countries with which they have commercial relations.[96] A recently established international organization, *Transparency International* (Berlin), has undertaken the formidable task of investigating international business ethics. Among its accomplishments are:

- Publishing a country-by-country bribery index
- Pressing for national legislation abolishing the tax-deductibility of bribes
- Seeking international governmental cooperation in criminalizing the bribing of officials
- Strengthening international cooperation among nongovernmental organizations, such as the International Chamber of Commerce
- Creating independent watchdog mechanisms

18. *Other offenses committed by organized criminal groups.* This catchall category permitted governments to report problems that could not be easily included in the 17 other categories. For example, both North America and Western Europe are experiencing large-scale automobile theft, with the stolen vehicles being transported abroad. These activities are controlled by international organized criminal groups. They affect not just individual owners, but the insurance industry of each country.

This review of the 18 categories of transnational criminality demonstrates the vast impact these criminal activities have on individuals, various branches of the economy, and the world economy itself. Individuals and individual commercial enterprises can do relatively little to protect themselves from these dangers, and increased international cooperation among nations has been recognized as absolutely necessary. But international action must be preceded by research. Thus, comparative criminological research will increasingly focus on transnational crime.

International crime. **International crimes** are the major criminal offenses so designated by the community of nations for the protection of interests common to all humankind. They may be found in precedent (much like the Anglo-American common law of crimes) or in written form in international conventions. They can be tried in the courts of countries that recognize them, or they can be tried by international courts. The war crimes tribunals that tried German and Japanese war criminals after World War II were such courts. In 1993, the U.N. Security Council

Investigators excavate one of many mass grave sites in former Yugoslavia, October, 1995.

ordered the establishment of an international tribunal for war crimes committed on the territory of the former Yugoslavia. This court now holds regular sessions in The Hague in the Netherlands. By mid-1996 the court had issued over 70 indictments, and the number of defendants actually in custody and before the court had grown to seven. The most powerful indicted war criminals are still in hiding, but they cannot leave the small territories under their control, for fear of being taken into custody under outstanding international arrest warrants.

For five decades, the world's governments have tried to reach agreement for the establishment of a permanent **international criminal court,** which would have jurisdiction over the most heinous international crimes. While such an agreement was impossible during the era of the cold war, the governments are now quite close—only a few technical

AT ISSUE

BCCI: INTERNATIONAL FRAUD

"Massive fraud." "World's biggest banking crash." "Financial deception of 'epic proportions.'" Journalists had a field day characterizing the magnitude of the collapse of the Bank of Credit & Commerce International (BCCI), which failed in July 1991. But let's talk numbers instead of adjectives:

- Founded in Pakistan, the international financial institution owed some $2 billion when it folded.
- A senior official admitted to playing a major role in frauds totaling $1.242 billion.
- Thousands of creditors, both businesses and individuals, lost every penny of the money they had deposited.
- In 1991, BCCI agreed to forfeit $550 million to begin compensating depositors worldwide and to salvage institutions the corporation owned secretly in the United States.
- The U.S. investigation that preceded the prosecution of a single person accused of participating in the scandal cost a whopping $20 million.
- In England alone, BCCI had a staff of 1200 and 45,000 customers—personnel who lost their jobs and customers who lost their life savings when the bank failed.

Big numbers! What are the crimes that led to this scandal of "epic proportions"? In the United States, BCCI has pleaded guilty to federal and state charges of racketeering, fraud, and money laundering. Individuals have been charged with withholding information in a scheme to defraud federal and state bank regulators and depositors. In Britain, charges against bank officials include false accounting, the furnishing of false information, and conspiracy to defraud.

HOW IT WORKED

A picture of the corporation's operations has unfolded since the crash:

BCCI's reported profits had been "falsely inflated" by $614 million between January 1983 and December 1985. The misuse of clients' funds by the bank amounted to another $627 million by the end of 1985. . . . By the early 1980s the bank needed to demonstrate its profitability and a healthy balance sheet to maintain the confidence of banking regulators and current and potential investors. In desperation, the bank's founder and his senior officers turned to the trading of commodities as a likely source of funds and began a series of high-risk speculations trading in futures. Most of these were in options on large-scale purchases of silver, which went badly wrong when the price of the metal turned sharply downwards. As money was lost upon money, the frauds became more widespread. The methods involved to maintain the pretense of solidity included filing accounts in which commissions on silver-trading deals that had never taken place were recorded as profits. . . . Accounts were falsified and large sums of customers' money diverted using a financial labyrinth to fool auditors into thinking the bank was solvent when it was actually hugely in deficit.(1)

A HARD LESSON

While the settlement in the United States provided funds for the compensation of some depositors, many more will never see their money again. Some consider this a "school of hard knocks" lesson about the inability of the criminal justice system to deal effectively with international fraud. Gathering the documents needed to provide evidence ranges from difficult to impossible. After one trial in the United States, a *Chicago Tribune* editorial commented: "International financial transactions can be made so complex as to effectively conceal what is really going on; key officials can always flee the jurisdiction and take vital evidence with them."(2) One lawyer summed up his observation of the outcomes of big international cases very succinctly: "No one gets caught but huge sums of money disappear."(3)

Sources
1. Ben Fenton and Sonia Purnell, "Bank Official Admits $750m Fraud, 'Financial Juggler' Was at the Heart of BCCI Scandal," *Daily Telegraph*, Sept. 28, 1993, p. 1.
2. "BCCI Still a Mystery," *Chicago Tribune*, Aug. 27, 1993, p. 23.
3. Peter Blackman, "The BCCI Problem; System's Flaws Stymie Probes of Foreign Banks," *New York Law Journal*, Aug. 26, 1993, p. 5.

Questions for Discussion
1. How could depositors be protected from losing their money in international scams like BCCI?
2. Would an international criminal court be better able to deal with massive international fraud?

issues remain to be resolved. For example, there is the question whether such a court should have primary or exclusive power to try certain crimes, or whether nations should have the option to try persons charged with international crimes in their own national courts.

Which crimes are listed as international crimes? The Draft Code of Crimes lists the following as crimes against the peace and security of humanity:

- Aggression (by one state against another)
- Threat of aggression
- Intervention (in the internal or external affairs of another state)
- Colonial domination and other forms of alien domination
- Genocide (destroying a national, ethnic, racial, or religious group)
- Apartheid (suppression of a racial or ethnic group)
- Systematic or mass violations of human rights
- Exceptionally serious war crimes
- Recruitment, use, financing, and training of mercenaries (soldiers of fortune)
- International terrorism
- Illicit traffic in narcotic drugs
- Willful and severe damage to the environment[97]

These crimes occur in many forms. For example, "systematic or mass violations of human rights" may be organized, large-scale rapes of women in occupied territories, as in Bosnia in 1992 and 1993.[98]

In addition to the listed international crimes, many others are recognized by convention; these include the cutting of undersea cables, the transportation of women for purposes of prostitution ("white slavery"), and fisheries offenses. There is now a considerable body of research and scholarship on international crimes.[99]

Globalization versus Ethnic Fragmentation

Very soon, we will enter the twenty-first century. Comparative criminologists view the new millennium with some uneasiness. Globalization raises great hopes for a better future for all human beings. Yet it brings with it grave dangers in terms of the internationalization of crime. Comparative criminology has a significant role to play in the investigation of new forms of transnational crime. Researchers can apply the methods used when such crimes were strictly local or national, but using the sophistication of the science of comparative criminology.

The new millennium presents additional hazards arising from the trend toward "balkanization." *Balkanization,* the opposite of globalization, is the breakup of nation-states into ethnic entities. Many ethnic groups are striving for the independence and sovereignty denied to them when they were incorporated in larger nation-states, as in the former Soviet Union or Yugoslavia; or when they were joined arbitrarily with other groups in colonial times, as in Africa; or when other accidents of history included them within empires, as in Western Europe. Frequently such ethnic groups had to abide by laws and customs that were not of their own choosing and had to suppress their own languages and cultures. Now they are searching for identities, territories, and criminal justice systems of their own. Unhappily, the struggle has brought with it human rights violations, war crimes, and genocide on a massive scale. This is the latest challenge for criminologists and criminal justice specialists working on the international level.

REVIEW

Comparative criminology, despite its historical antecedents, is a young science, a subspecialty of criminology. In view of the globalization of the world—brought about by recent technological advances and the enormous increase in international commerce, both legal and illegal—comparative studies in criminology have become a necessity. Comparatists are called upon to assist governments in devising strategies to deal with a wide variety of international and transnational crimes.

In this chapter we have traced the history of comparative criminology, sought to define it, and attempted to identify its goals. These goals may be theoretical, like the cross-cultural testing of prominent theories of crime. They can also be very practical, like the search for transplantable crime-fighting strategies or for techniques to deal with specific transnational and international crimes.

There are a number of requirements for successful comparative research: studying foreign law, understanding foreign criminal justice systems, learning about a foreign culture, collecting reliable data, engaging in comparative research, and, when needed, doing cross-cultural empirical research.

We have paid special attention to three dimensions that pose special challenges to comparative criminology: internationally induced local crime, transnational crime, and international crime. There is much research to be conducted before progress can be expected in these three areas.

The accomplishments of criminologists who have engaged in comparative studies form the foundation for further research. The tools of comparative criminology should prove useful in helping both individual nations and the United Nations solve some of their common crime problems. The United Nations and its agencies continue to do very practical work to help nations deal with crime on a worldwide basis.

NOTES

1. Peter Applebome, "Skinhead Violence Grows, Experts Say," *New York Times,* July 18, 1993, p. 25.

2. *The Skinhead International: A World-Wide Survey of Neo-Nazi Skinheads* (New York: Anti-Defamation League of B'nai B'rith, 1995).

3. Jane Kramer, "Neo-Nazis: A Chaos in the Head," *New Yorker,* July 14, 1993, pp. 52–70, at p. 53. See also Marie C. Douglas, "Ausländer Raus! Nazi Raus! An Observation of German Skins and Jugendgangen," *International Journal of Comparative and Applied Criminal Justice,* **16** (1992): 129–134.

4. John Leland and Marcus Mabry, "Toasting the 'Head,'" *Newsweek,* Feb. 26, 1996, pp. 42–43.

5. Mark S. Hamm, *American Skinheads—The Criminology and Control of Hate Crime* (Westport, Conn.: Praeger, 1993).

6. The term "comparative criminology" appears to have been coined by Sheldon Glueck. See Sheldon Glueck, "Wanted: A Comparative Criminology," in *Ventures in Criminology,* ed. Sheldon Glueck and Eleanor Glueck (London: Tavistock, 1964), pp. 304–322.

7. James O. Finckenauer, *Russian Youth: Law, Deviance and the Pursuit of Freedom* (New Brunswick, N.J.: Transaction, 1995); Nanci Adler, "Planned Economy and Unplanned Criminality: The Soviet Experience," *International Journal of Comparative and Applied Criminal Justice,* **17** (1993): 189–201; Wojciech Cebulak, "White-Collar Crime in Socialism: Myth or Reality?" *International Journal of Comparative and Applied Criminal Justice,* **15** (1991): 109–120; Klaus Sessar, "Crime Rate Trends before and after the End of the German Democratic Republic—Impressions and First Analyses," in *Fear of Crime and Criminal Victimization,* ed. Wolfgang Bilsky, Christian Pfeiffer, and Peter Wetzels (Stuttgart, Germany: Ferdinand Enke Verlag, 1993), pp. 231–244; Louise I. Shelley et al., "East Meets West in Crime," *European Journal on Criminal Policy and Research,* **3** (1995): 7–107. As China is undergoing a transformation, mostly economic, changes in that country are noteworthy. See Yue Ma, "Crime in China: Characteristics, Causes and Control Strategies," *Journal of Comparative and Applied Criminal Justice,* **34** (1994): 54–68.

8. Martin Kilias et al., "Cross-Border Crime," *European Journal on Criminal Policy and Research,* **1** (1993): 7–134.

9. William F. McDonald, "The Globalization of Criminology: The New Frontier Is the Frontier," *Transnational Organized Crime,* **1** (1995): 1–12.

10. Piers Beirne and Joan Hill, *Comparative Criminology—An Annotated Bibliography* (New York: Greenwood, 1991), pp. vii–viii.

11. See especially Albert P. Blaustein and G. H. Flenz, *Constitutions of the Countries of the World,* 21 vols. (updated) (Dobbs Ferry, N.Y.: Oceana, 1971 and continuing).

12. The Comparative Criminal Law Project at Wayne State University Law School (formerly at New York University School of Law) has published 21 criminal codes in *The American Series of Foreign Penal Codes,* ed. G. O. W. Mueller, cont. by Edward M. Wise (Littleton, Colo.: Fred B. Rothman, since 1960); G. O. W. Mueller and Fré Le Poole Griffiths, *Comparative Criminal Procedure* (New York: New York University Press, 1969); Albin Eser and George Fletcher, *Justification and Excuse—Comparative Perspectives,* 2 vols. (Freiburg, Germany: Max Planck Institut, 1987); Edward M. Wise and G. O. W. Mueller, eds., *Studies in Comparative Criminal Law,* Comparative Criminal Law Project Publications Series, vol. 9 (Littleton, Colo.: Fred B. Rothman, 1975); Marc Ancel, *Social Defense: The Future of Penal Reform,* Comparative Criminal Law Project Publications Series, vol. 16 (Littleton, Colo.: Fred B. Rothman, 1987). For a historical survey, see G. O. W. Mueller, *Comparative Criminal Law in the United States,* Comparative Criminal Law Project Monograph Series, vol. 4 (South Hackensack, N.J.: Fred B. Rothman, 1970).

13. Seven codes of criminal procedure have appeared in Mueller and Wise, *The American Series of Foreign Penal Codes.*

14. E.g., Shigemitsu Dando, *Japanese Criminal Procedure,* Comparative Criminal Law Project Publications Series, vol. 4 (Littleton, Colo.: Fred B. Rothman, 1965).

15. UNAFEI, 1–26 Harumicho, Fuchu, Tokyo, Japan. There are 47 volumes as of 1996.

16. Kristiina Kangaspunta, ed., *Profiles of Criminal Justice Systems in Europe and North America* (Helsinki: HEUNI, 1995); Matti Joutsen, *Criminal Justice Systems in Europe: Finland* (Helsinki: HEUNI, 1995).

17. Dae H. Chang, *Criminology: A Cross-Cultural Perspective,* 2 vols. (Durham, N.C.: Carolina Academic Press, 1976); George F. Cole, Stanislaw J. Frankowski, and Marc G. Gertz, *Major Criminal Justice Systems—A Comparative Survey,* 2d ed. (Newbury Park, Calif.: Sage, 1987); Richard J. Terrill, *World Criminal Justice Systems,* 2d ed. (Cincinnati: Anderson, 1985); Robert Heiner, ed., *Criminology—A Cross-Cultural Perspective* (Minneapolis/St. Paul: West, 1996); Obi N. I. Ebbe, ed., *Comparative and International Criminal Justice Systems* (Boston: Butterworth-Heinemann, 1996); Charles B. Fields and Richter H. Moore, eds., *Comparative Criminal Justice: Traditional and Non-traditional Systems of Law and Control* (Prospect Heights, Ill.: Waveland Press, 1996).

18. V. Lorne Stewart, *Justice and Troubled Children around the World,* vols. 1–5 (New York: New York University Press, 1980–1983).

19. David H. Bayley, *Patterns of Policing—A Comparative International Analysis* (New Brunswick, N.J.: Rutgers University Press, 1985).

20. Roy Walmsley, *Prison Systems in Central and Eastern Europe* (Helsinki: HEUNI, 1996).

21. Freda Adler, ed., *The Incidence of Female Criminality in the Contemporary World* (New York: New York University Press, 1984).

22. Marshall B. Clinard, *Cities with Little Crime: The Case of Switzerland* (London: Cambridge University Press, 1978).

23. Louise I. Shelley, *Crime and Modernization: The Impact of Industrialization and Urbanization on Crime* (Carbondale: Southern Illinois University Press, 1981).

24. William Clifford, *Crime Control in Japan* (Lexington, Mass.: Lexington Books, 1976).

25. G. O. W. Mueller, *World Survey on the Availability of Criminal Justice Statistics,* Internet-UNCJIN-ftp238.204.33.18WSAYL. See also G. O. W. Mueller, "International Criminal Justice: Harnessing the Information Explosion—Coasting Down the Electronic Superhighway," *Journal of Criminal Justice Education* (Fall 1996), in press.

26. Interpol, located in Lyons, France, has published the crime statistics supplied to it by member states since 1951.

27. First survey: 1970–1975, A/32/199; second survey: 1975–1980, A/Conf. 121/18; third survey: 1980–1986, A/Conf. 144/6; fourth survey: 1986–1990, A/Conf. 169/15 and Add. 1. See the "Window to the World" box in Chapter 2.

28. World Health Organization, "Homicide Statistics," in *World Health Statistics* (Geneva: World Health Organization, annually).

29. Dane Archer and Rosemary Gartner, *Violence and Crime in Cross-National Perspective* (New Haven, Conn.: Yale University Press, 1984).

30. Richard R. Bennett, *Correlates of Crime: A Study of Nations, 1960–1984* (Ann Arbor, Mich.: Inter-University Consortium for Political and Social Research, 1989).

31. Richard R. Bennett and James P. Lynch, "Does a Difference Make a Difference?" *Criminology,* **28** (1990): 155–182; and Carol B. Kalish, *International Crime Rates* (Washington, D.C.: Bureau of Justice Statistics, 1988).

32. Jan J. M. Van Dijk, Pat Mayhew, and Martin Killias, *Experiences of Crime across the World: Key Findings from the 1989 International Crime Survey* (Deventer, Netherlands: Kluwer, 1990); Richard R. Bennett and R. Bruce Wiegand, "Observations on Crime Reporting in a Developing Nation," *Criminology,* **32** (1994): 135–148; Ugljesa Zvekic and Anna Albazzi del Frate, eds., *Criminal Victimization in the Developing World* (Rome: United Nations Interregional Crime and Justice Research Institute, 1995); Gail Travis et al., "The International Crime Surveys: Some Methodological Concerns," *Current Issues in Criminal Justice,* **6** (1995): 346–361.

33. Josine Junger-Tas, Gert-Jan Terlouw, and Malcolm W. Klein, *Delinquent Behavior among People in the Western World* (Amsterdam: RDC Ministry of Justice, Kugler Publ., 1994).

34. Hermann Mannheim, *Comparative Criminology* (Boston: Houghton Mifflin, 1965).

35. Brunon Holyst, *Comparative Criminology* (Lexington, Mass.: Lexington Books, 1979). See also Louise I. Shelley, ed., *Readings in Comparative Criminology* (Carbondale: Southern Illinois University Press, 1981).

36. G. O. W. Mueller, Michael Gage, and Lenore R. Kupperstein, *The Legal Norms of Delinquency: A Comparative Study,* Criminal Law Education and Research Center Monograph

Series, vol. 1 (South Hackensack, N.J.: Fred B. Rothman, 1969).

37. Anastassios Mylonas, *Perception of Police Power: A Study in Four Cities,* Comparative Criminal Law Project Monograph Series, vol. 8 (South Hackensack, N.J.: Fred B. Rothman, 1973).

38. Setsuo Miyazawa, "The Enigma of Japan as a Testing Ground for Cross-Cultural Criminological Studies," *Annales Internationales de Criminologie,* **32** (1994): 81–103; B. Hebenton and J. Spencer, "The Contribution and Limitations of Anglo-American Criminology to Understanding Crime in Central-Eastern Europe," *European Journal of Crime, Criminal Law and Criminal Justice,* **2** (1994): 50–61.

39. Sheldon Glueck and Eleanor Glueck, *Unraveling Juvenile Delinquency* (New York: The Commonwealth Fund; Cambridge, Mass.: Harvard University Press, 1950).

40. Sheldon Glueck and Eleanor Glueck, *Of Delinquency and Crime—A Panorama of Years of Search and Research,* Publications of the Criminal Law Education and Research Center, vol. 8 (Springfield, Ill.: Charles C Thomas, 1974), p. 332.

41. Obi N. I. Ebbe, "Juvenile Delinquency in Nigeria: The Problem of Application of Western Theories," *International Journal of Comparative and Applied Criminal Justice,* **16** (1992): 353–370.

42. Rosemary Gartner, "The Victims of Homicide: A Temporal and Cross-National Comparison," *American Sociological Review,* **55** (1990): 92–106.

43. Gary LaFree and Christopher Birkbeck, "The Neglected Situation: A Cross-National Study of the Situational Characteristics of Crime," *Criminology,* **29** (1991): 73–98.

44. Richard R. Bennett, "Routine Activities: A Cross-National Assessment of a Criminological Perspective," *Social Forces,* **70** (1991): 147–163.

45. Richard R. Bennett and P. Peter Basiotis, "Structural Correlates of Juvenile Property Crime: A Cross-National, Time-Series Analysis," *Journal of Research in Crime and Delinquency,* **28** (1991): 262–287.

46. Sam S. Souryal, "Juvenile Delinquency in the Cross-Cultural Context: The Egyptian Experience," *International Journal of Comparative and Applied Criminal Justice,* **16** (1992): 329–352.

47. Adel Helal and Charisse T. M. Coston, "Low Crime Rates in Bahrain: Islamic Social Control—Testing the Theory of Synnomie," *International Journal of Comparative and Applied Criminal Justice,* **15** (1991): 125–144.

48. Gregory C. Leavitt, "General Evaluation and Durkheim's Hypothesis of Crime Frequency: A Cross-Cultural Test," *Sociological Quarterly,* **33** (1992): 241–263; Suzanne T. Ortega, Jay Corzine, and Cathleen Burnett, "Modernization, Age Structure, and Regional Context: A Cross-National Study of Crime," *Sociological Spectrum,* **12** (1992): 257–277.

49. Christopher Birkbeck, "Against Ethnocentrism: A Cross-Cultural Perspective on Criminal Justice Theories and Policies," *Journal of Criminal Justice Education,* **4** (1993): 307–323.

50. Shelley, *Crime and Modernization.*

51. David Shichor, "Crime Patterns and Socio-Economic Development: A Cross-National Analysis," *Criminal Justice Review,* **15** (1990): 64–78; John Arthur, "Development and Crime in Africa: A Test of Modernization Theory," *Journal of Criminal Justice,* **19** (1991): 499–513.

52. "New Perspectives in Crime Prevention and Criminal Justice and Development: The Role of International Co-operation," working paper prepared by the Secretariat, United Nations, 1980, A/Conf. 87/10.

53. Freda Adler, *Nations Not Obsessed with Crime*, Comparative Criminal Law Project Publications Series, vol. 15 (Littleton, Colo.: Fred B. Rothman, 1983).

54. See Note 7.

55. See Ugljesa Zvekic, ed., *Essays on Crime and Development* (Rome: U.N. Interregional Crime and Justice Research Institute, 1990).

56. V. Lee Hamilton and Joseph Sanders, *Everyday Justice: Responsibility and the Individual in Japan and the United States* (New Haven, Conn.: Yale University Press, 1992); Hans Joachim Schneider, "Crime and Its Control in Japan and in the Federal Republic of Germany, a Comparative Study," *International Journal of Offender Therapy and Comparative Criminology*, **36** (1992): 47–63.

57. Dale E. Berger et al., "Deterrence and Prevention of Alcohol-Impaired Driving in Australia, the United States, and Norway," *Justice Quarterly*, **7** (1990): 453–465.

58. David B. Kopel, *The Samurai, the Mountie, and the Cowboy: Should America Adopt the Gun Controls of Other Democracies?* (Buffalo, N.Y.: Prometheus, 1992).

59. Robert L. Nay, *Firearms Regulations in Various Foreign Countries* (Washington, D.C.: Law Library of Congress, 1990).

60. Michael Clarke, "The Control of Insurance Fraud: A Comparative View," *British Journal of Criminology*, **30** (1990): 1–23.

61. Kenneth Polk and William Weston, "Insider Trading as an Aspect of White Collar Crime," *Australian and New Zealand Journal of Criminology*, **23** (1990): 24–38.

62. Yü-Hsiu Hsü, ed., *International Conference on Environmental Criminal Law* (Taipei: Taiwan/ROC Chapter of the International Association of Penal Law, 1992).

63. Rosemary Gartner, "Family Structure, Welfare Spending, and Child Homicide in Developed Democracies," *Journal of Marriage and the Family*, **53** (1991): 231–240.

64. Margo I. Wilson and Martin Daly, "Who Kills Whom in Spouse Killings? On the Exceptional Sex Ratio of Spousal Homicides in the United States," *Criminology*, **30** (1992): 189–215.

65. Lois A. Fingerhut and Joel C. Kleinman, "International and Interstate Comparisons of Homicide among Young Males," *Journal of the American Medical Association*, **263** (1990): 3292–3295.

66. F. H. McClintock and Per-Olof H. Wikstrom, "The Comparative Study of Urban Violence—Criminal Violence in Edinburgh and Stockholm," *British Journal of Criminology*, **32** (1992): 505–520.

67. Dae H. Chang and Galan M. Janeksela, eds., "Special Issue on Comparative Juvenile Delinquency," *International Journal of Comparative and Applied Criminal Justice*, **16** (1992): 135–170, with contributions by Gaban M. Janeksela, David P. Farrington, Alison Hatch and Curt T. Griffiths, Günther Kaiser, Josine Junger-Tas, Paul C. Friday, James O. Finckenauer and Linda Kelly, Hualing Fu, Michael S. Vaughn and Frank F. Y. Huang, Byung In Cho and Richard J. Chang, Clayton A. Hartjen and Sesharajani Kethineni, Sam S. Souryhal, and Obi N. I. Ebbe.

68. Mylonas, *Perception of Police Power.*

69. Graeme Newman, *Comparative Deviance: Perception and Law in Six Cultures* (New York: Elsevier Scientific, 1976).

70. Russel P. Dobash, R. Emerson Dobash, Scott Balliofyne, Karl Schuman, Reiner Kaulitzki, and Hans-Werner Guth, "Ignorance and Suspicion: Young People and Criminal Justice in Scotland and Germany," *British Journal of Criminology*, **30** (1990): 306–320.

71. Ronald D. Hunter, "Three Models of Policing," *Police Studies*, **13** (1990): 118–124; R. I. Mawby, *Comparable Policing Issues: The British and American Experience in International Perspective* (London: Unwin Hyman, 1990).

72. Leslie T. Wilkins, *Punishment, Crime and Market Forces* (Aldershot, England: Dartmouth, 1991); Dennis Wiechman, Jerry Kendall, and Ronald Bae, "International Use of the Death Penalty," *International Journal of Comparative and Applied Criminal Justice*, **14** (1990): 239–259.

73. See Gunther Kaiser, Helmut Kury, and Hans-Jorg Albrecht, eds., *Victims and Criminal Justice*, **3** vols. (Freiburg, Germany: Max Planck Institut, 1991); Emilio C. Viano, ed., *Critical Issues in Victimology—International Perspectives* (New York: Springer Verlag, 1992).

74. Jack Levin and Jack McDevitt, *Hate Crimes—The Rising Tide of Bigotry and Bloodshed* (New York: Plenum, 1993).

75. See Hans-Dieter Schwind et al., "Causes, Prevention and Control of Violence," *Revue Internationale de Criminologie et de Police Technique*, **43** (1990): 395–520.

76. Gerhard O. W. Mueller and Freda Adler, *Outlaws of the Ocean: The Complete Book of Contemporary Crime on the High Seas* (New York: Hearst Marine Books, 1985); Gerhard O. W. Mueller and Freda Adler, "A New Wave of Crime at Sea," *The World and I* (February 1986): 96–103.

77. Mike King, *Towards Federalism: Policing the Borders of a "New" Europe* (Leicester, United Kingdom: University of Leicester, 1993); H. Lensing, "The Federalization of Europe: Towards a Federal System of Criminal Justice," *European Journal of Crime, Criminal Law and Criminal Justice*, **1** (1993): 212–229; Ethan A. Nadelman, *Cops across Borders: The Internationalization of U.S. Criminal Law Enforcement* (University Park: Penn State University Press, 1994).

78. See Fourth U.N. Survey, 1986–1990, A/Conf.169/15 and Add. 1.

79. See, for example, Jonathan Reuvid, ed., *The Regulation and Prevention of Economic Crime Internationally* (London: Kogan Page, 1995).

80. W. C. Gilmore, *International Efforts to Combat Money Laundering* (Cambridge: Grotius, 1992).

81. Several journals are devoted entirely to terrorism. See *Terrorism* (New York); *Studies in Conflict and Terrorism* (London); *Violence, Aggression, Terrorism* (Danbury, Conn.).

82. From Reuters, "High-Tech Art Sleuths Snare Thieves," *C.J. International*, **9** (1993): 4:6.

83. Truc-Nhu Ho, *Art Theft in New York City: An Explanatory Study in Crime Specificity*, Ph.D. dissertation, Rutgers University, 1992.

84. Ralph Blumenthal, "Museums Getting Together to Track Stolen Art," *New York Times*, July 16, 1996, pp. C13, C15.

85. Natalie D. Voss, "Crime on the Internet," *Jones Telecommunications and Multimedia Encyclopedia*, Drive D:\Studio, Jones Digital Century, 1996.

86. "For Sale—Nukes: Deadly Plutonium from Russia's Vast Nuclear Network Is Turning Up on the European Market. Who Is Buying—and Can They Be Stopped?" *Newsweek,* Aug. 29, 1994, pp. 30–31; Bruce W. Nolan, "Formula for Terror," *Time,* Aug. 29, 1994.

87. Les Johnston, "Policing Plutonium: Issues in the Provision of Policing Services at Nuclear Facilities and for Related Materials in Transit," *Policing and Society,* **4** (1994): 53–72; Phil Williams and Paul H. Woessnar, *Nuclear Material Trafficking: An Interim Assessment* (Pittsburgh: Ridgway Center for International Security Studies, 1995).

88. Eric Ellen, "The Dimensions of International Maritime Crime," in *Issues in Maritime Crime: Mayhem at Sea,* ed. Martin Gill (Leicester, United Kingdom: Perpetuity Press, 1995), pp. 4–11; Martin Gill, *Crime at Sea: A Forgotten Issue in Police Co-operation* (Leicester, United Kingdom: Centre for the Study of Public Order, 1995); Gerhard O. W. Mueller and Freda Adler, "Piraterie: le 'Jolly Roger' flotte à nouveau les Corsaires des Caribes," *Revue Internationale de Criminologie et de Police Technique,* **4** (1992): 408–424.

89. National Insurance Crime Bureau, fax of July 29, 1996.

90. British Banking Association estimate. See Larry E. Coutoria, "The Future of High-Technology Crime: A Parallel Delphi Study," *Journal of Criminal Justice,* **23** (1995): 13–27.

91. E.g., Sally M. Edwards, Terry D. Edwards, and Charles B. Fields, eds., *Environmental Crime and Criminality* (New York: Garland Publishing, 1996).

92. Ko-lin Chin, *Chinese Subculture and Criminality: Non-traditional Crime Groups in America* (Westport, Conn.: Greenwood, 1990).

93. Michael Woodiwiss, "Crime's Global Reach," in *Global Crime Connections,* ed. Frank Pearce and Michael Woodiwiss (Houndmills, United Kingdom: Macmillan, 1993), pp. 1–31.

94. Raphael F. Perl, ed., *Drugs and Foreign Policy: A Critical Review* (Boulder, Colo.: Westview Press, 1994); Günther Kaiser, "International Experiences with Different Strategies of Drug Policy," *EuroCriminology,* **7** (1994): 3–29.

95. See Frederick T. Martens, "Transnational Enterprise Crime and the Elimination of Frontiers, *International Journal of Comparative and Applied Criminal Justice,* **15** (1991):

99–107; Wojciech Cebulak, "The Antitrust Doctrine: How It Was Internationalized," *International Journal of Comparative and Applied Criminal Justice,* **14** (1990): 261–267.

96. See "Crime Prevention and Criminal Justice in the Context of Development: Realities and Perspectives of International Cooperation," in *International Review of Criminal Policy,* **41/42** (1993): 1–19.

97. Draft Articles of the Draft Code of Crimes against the Peace and Security of Mankind, adopted by the International Law Commission on First Reading, United Nations, New York, 1991. For a complete listing, see M. Cherif Bassiouni, *International Criminal Law—A Draft International Criminal Code* (Alphen an den Rijn, Netherlands: Sijthoff & Noordhoff, 1980).

98. Shana Swiss and Joan E. Giller, "Rape as a Crime of War," *Journal of the American Medical Association,* **270** (1993): 612–615.

99. For an analysis of all international crimes, see M. Cherif Bassiouni, ed., *International Criminal Law:* vol. 1, *Crimes* (Dobbs Ferry, N.Y.: Transnational, 1986); M. Cherif Bassiouni, *A Draft International Criminal Code and Draft Statute for an International Criminal Tribunal* (Dordrecht, Netherlands: Martinus Nijhoff, 1987); Farhad Malekian, *International Criminal Law,* 2 vols. (Motala, Sweden: Borgstroms Trycker, 1991); Gerhard O. W. Mueller and Edward M. Wise, *International Criminal Law,* Comparative Criminal Law Project, Publications Series, vol. 2 (South Hackensack, N.J.: Fred B. Rothman, 1965).

■ **Internet Exercise**

How does the United States crime rate compare with that of the world as a whole? You will find this information in the U.N. Survey of Crime Trends and Operations of Criminal Justice Systems.

■ **Your Web Site is:**
http://ravel.ifs.univie.ac.at/~uncjin/uncjin.html

GLOSSARY

A

Accommodate In regard to achieving the American Dream, to adjust noneconomic needs so that they are secondary to and supportive of economic ones.

Accomplice A person who helps another to commit a crime.

Aggravated assault An attack on another person in which the perpetrator inflicts serious harm on the victim or uses a deadly weapon.

Aging-out phenomenon A concept that holds that offenders commit less crime as they get older because they have less strength, initiative, stamina, and mobility.

Anomie A societal state marked by "normlessness," in which disintegration and chaos have replaced social cohesion.

Arson At common law, the malicious burning of the dwelling house of another. This definition has been broadened by state statutes and criminal codes to cover the burning of other structures or even personal property.

Assault At common law, an unlawful offer or attempt with force or violence to do a corporal hurt to another or to frighten another.

Atavistic stigmata Physical features of a human being at an earlier stage of development, which—according to Cesare Lombroso—distinguish a born criminal from the general population.

Attachment The bond between a parent and child or between individuals and their family, friends, and school.

B

Bankruptcy fraud A scam in which an individual falsely attempts to claim bankruptcy (and thereby erase financial debts) by taking advantage of existing laws.

Battery A common law crime consisting of the intentional touching of or inflicting of hurt on another.

Behavioral modeling Learning how to behave by fashioning one's behavior after that of others.

Belief The extent to which an individual subscribes to society's values.

Biocriminology The subdiscipline of criminology that investigates biological and genetic factors and their relation to criminal behavior.

Birth cohort A group consisting of all individuals born in the same year.

Boiler room An operation run by one or more stock manipulators who, through deception and misleading sales techniques, seduce the unsuspecting and uninformed public into buying stocks in obscure and often poorly financed corporations.

Born criminal According to Lombroso, persons born with features resembling an earlier, more primitive form of human life, destined to become criminals.

Burglary A common law felony, the nighttime breaking and entering of the dwelling house of another, with the intention to commit a crime (felony or larceny) therein.

C

Case study An analysis of all pertinent aspects of one unit of study.

Check forging The criminal offense of making or altering a check with intent to defraud.

Chromosomes Basic cellular structures containing genes, i.e., biological material that creates individuality.

Churning Frequent trading, by a broker, of a client's shares of stock for the sole purpose of generating large commissions.

Classical school of criminology A criminological perspective suggesting that (1) people have free will to choose criminal or conventional behavior; (2) people choose to commit crime for reasons of greed or personal need; and (3) crime can be controlled by criminal sanctions, which should be proportionate to the guilt of the perpetrator.

Commitment A person's support of and participation in a program, cause, or social activity, which ties the individual to the moral or ethical codes of society.

Comparative criminology The study of crime in two or more cultures in an effort to gain broader information for theory construction and crime control modeling.

Conditioning The process of developing a behavior pattern through a series of repeated experiences.

Conduct norms Norms that regulate the daily lives of people and that reflect the attitudes of the groups to which they belong.

Confidence game A deceptive means of obtaining money or property from a victim who is led to trust the perpetrator.

Conflict model A model of crime in which the criminal justice system is seen as being used by the ruling class to control the lower class. Criminological investigation of the conflicts of society is emphasized.

Conformity   Correspondence of an individual's behavior to society's patterns, norms, or standards.

Consensus model   A model of criminal lawmaking that assumes that members of society agree on what is right and wrong and that law is the codification of agreed-upon social values.

Consumer fraud   An act that causes a consumer to surrender money through deceit or a misrepresentation of a material fact.

Containment theory   A theory that posits that every person possesses a containing external structure and a protective internal structure, both of which provide defense, protection, or insulation against delinquency.

Corporate crime   A crime attributed to a corporation, but perpetrated by or on the authority of an officer or high managerial agent.

Cortical arousal   Activation of the cerebral cortex, a structure of the brain which is responsible for higher intellectual functioning, information processing, and decision making.

Crime   An act in violation of law that causes harm, is identified by law, is committed with criminal intent, and is subject to punishment.

Crimes against property   Crimes involving the illegal acquisition or destruction of property. *See* Crime.

Crimes against the person   Crimes violative of life or physical integrity. *See* Crime.

Criminal attempt   An act or omission constituting a substantial step in a course of conduct planned to culminate in the commission of a crime.

Criminal careers   A concept that describes the onset of criminal activity, the types and amount of crime committed, and the termination of such activity.

Criminology   The body of knowledge regarding crime as a social phenomenon. It includes within its scope the process of making laws, of breaking laws, and of reacting toward the breaking of laws (Sutherland). Thus, criminology is an empirical, social-behavioral science that investigates crime, criminals, and criminal justice.

Cultural deviance theories   Theories that posit that crime results from cultural values which permit, or even demand, behavior in violation of the law.

Cultural transmission   A theory that views delinquency as a socially learned behavior transmitted from one generation to the next in disorganized urban areas.

Culture conflict theory   A theory that posits that two groups may clash when their conduct norms differ, resulting in criminal activity.

D

Data   Collected facts, observations, and other pertinent information from which conclusions can be drawn.

Deviance   A broad concept encompassing both illegal behavior and behavior that departs from the social norm.

Differential association-reinforcement   A theory of criminality based on the incorporation of psychological learning theory and differential association with social learning theory. Criminal behavior, the theory claims, is learned through associations and is contained or discontinued as a result of positive or negative reinforcements.

Differential association theory   A theory of criminality based on the principle that an individual becomes delinquent because of an excess of definitions learned that are favorable to violation of law over definitions learned that are unfavorable to violation of law.

Differential opportunity theory   A theory that attempts to join the concept of anomie and differential association by analyzing both legitimate and illegitimate opportunity structures available to individuals. It posits that illegitimate opportunities, like legitimate opportunities, are unequally distributed.

Direct control   An external control that depends on rules, restrictions, and punishments.

Displacement   In the event that a crime has been prevented, the commission of a quantitatively similar crime at a different time or place.

Dizygotic (DZ) twins   Fraternal twins, who develop from two separate eggs fertilized at the same time. *See also* Monozygotic twins.

Drift   According to David Matza, a state of limbo in which youths move in and out of delinquency and in which their lifestyles can embrace both conventional and deviant values.

Due process   According to the Fourteenth Amendment of the U.S. Constitution, a fundamental mandate that a person should not be deprived of life, liberty, or property without reasonable and lawful procedures.

E

Ego   The part of the psyche that, according to psychoanalytic theory, governs rational behavior. The moderator between the superego and the id.

Embezzlement   The crime of withholding or withdrawing (conversion or misappropriation), without consent, funds entrusted to an agent (e.g., a bank teller or officer).

Equal protection   A clause of the Fourteenth Amendment to the U.S. Constitution that guarantees equal protection of the law to everyone, without regard to race, origin, economic class, gender, or religion.

Eugenics   A science, based on the principle of heredity, that has for its purpose the improvement of the race.

Experiment   A research technique in which an investigator introduces a change into a process in order to make measurements or observations that evaluate the effects of the change.

Extraversion According to Hans Eysenck, a dimension of the human personality; describes individuals who are sensation-seeking, dominant, and assertive.

F

False pretenses, obtaining property by Leading a victim to part with property on a voluntary basis through trickery, deceit, or misrepresentation.

Federal Witness Protection Program A program, established under the Organized Crime Control Act of 1970, designed to protect witnesses who testify in court by relocating them and assigning to them new identities.

Felony A severe crime, subject to punishment of 1 year or more in prison or to capital punishment.

Felony murder The imposition of criminal liability for murder upon one who participates in the commission of a felony that is dangerous to life and that causes the death of another.

Fence A receiver of stolen property who resells the goods for profit.

Field experiment An experiment conducted in a real-world setting, as opposed to one conducted in a laboratory.

Fraud An act of trickery or deceit, especially involving misrepresentation.

G

General strain theory A criminological theory that posits that criminal behavior can result from strain caused by failure to achieve positively valued goals, stress caused by the removal of positively valued stimuli from the individual, or strain caused by the presentation of negative stimuli.

H

High-tech crime The pursuit of illegal activities through the use of advanced electronic media.

Homicide The killing of one person by another.

Hypoglycemia A condition that may occur in susceptible individuals when the level of blood sugar falls below an acceptable range, causing anxiety, headaches, confusion, fatigue, and aggressive behavior.

Hypothesis A proposition set forth as an explanation for some specified phenomenon.

I

Id The part of the personality that, according to psychoanalytic theory, contains powerful urges and drives for gratification and satisfaction.

Index crimes The eight major crimes included in Part One of the Uniform Crime Reports: criminal homicide, forcible rape, robbery, aggravated assault, burglary, larceny-theft, auto theft, and arson.

Indirect control A behavioral influence that arises from an individual's identification with noncriminals and his or her desire to conform to societal norms.

Insider trading The use of material nonpublic financial information to obtain an unfair advantage in trading securities.

Internalized control Self-regulation of behavior and conformity to societal norms as a result of guilt feelings arising in the conscience.

International crimes The major criminal offenses so designated by the community of nations for the protection of interests common to all humankind.

International criminal court A court that would have jurisdiction over the most heinous international crimes.

Involuntary manslaughter Homicide in which the perpetrator unintentionally but recklessly causes the death of another person by consciously taking a grave risk that endangers the person's life.

Involvement An individual's participation in conventional activities.

J

Justifiable homicide A homicide, permitted by law, in defense of a legal right or mandate.

K

Kidnapping A felony consisting of the seizure and abduction of a person by force or threat of force and against the victim's will. Under federal law, the victim of a kidnapping is one who has been taken across state lines and held for ransom.

L

Labeling theory A theory that explains deviance in terms of the process by which a person acquires a negative identity, such as "addict" or "ex-con," and is forced to suffer the consequences of outcast status.

Larceny The trespassory (unconsented) taking and carrying away of personal property belonging to another with the intent to deprive the owner of the property permanently.

Laws of imitation An explanation of crime as learned behavior. Individuals are thought to emulate behavior patterns of others with whom they have contact.

Longitudinal study An analysis that focuses on studies of a particular group conducted repeatedly over a period of time.

M

Macrosociological study The study of overall social arrangements, their structures, and their long-term effects.

Mafia The entirety of those Sicilian families which, in both the United States and Sicily, are loosely associated with one another in operating organized crime.

Malice aforethought The mens rea requirement for murder, consisting of the intention to kill with the awareness that there is no right to kill. *See also* Mens rea.

Manslaughter Criminal homicide without malice, committed intentionally after provocation (voluntary manslaughter) or recklessly (involuntary manslaughter).

Mass murder The killing of several persons, in one act or transaction, by one perpetrator or a group of perpetrators.

Mens rea (Latin, "guilty mind") Awareness of wrongdoing; the intention to commit a criminal act or behave recklessly.

Microsociological study The study of everyday patterns of behavior and personal interactions.

Minimal brain dysfunction (MBD) An attention-deficit disorder that may produce such asocial behavior as impulsivity, hyperactivity, and aggressiveness.

Misdemeanor A crime less serious than a felony and subject to a maximum sentence of 1 year in jail or a fine.

Money laundering The process by which money derived from illegal activities (especially drug sales) is unlawfully taken out of the country, placed in a numbered account abroad, and then transferred as funds no longer "dirty."

Monozygotic (MZ) twins Identical twins, who develop from a single fertilized egg that divides into two embryos. *See also* Dizygotic twins.

Murder The unlawful (usually intentional) killing of a human being with malice aforethought.

N

Neuroticism A personality disorder marked by low self-esteem, excessive anxiety, and wide mood swings (Eysenck).

Nonparticipant observation A study in which investigators observe closely but do not become participants.

O

Occupational crime A crime committed by an individual for his or her own benefit, in the course of performing a profession.

P

Participant observation Collection of information through involvement in the social life of the group a researcher is studying.

Penologist A social scientist who studies and applies the theory and methods of punishment for crime.

Phrenology A nineteenth-century theory based on the hypothesis that human behavior is localized in certain specific brain and skull areas. According to this theory, criminal behavior can be determined by the "bumps" on the head.

Physiognomy The study of facial features and their relation to human behavior.

Pimp A procurer or manager of prostitutes who provides access to prostitutes and protects and exploits them, living off their proceeds.

Population A large group of persons in a study.

Pornography The portrayal, by whatever means, of lewd or obscene (sexually explicit) material prohibited by law.

Positivist school of criminology A criminological perspective that uses the scientific methods of the natural sciences and suggests that human behavior is a product of social, biological, psychological, or economic forces.

Primary data Facts and observations that researchers gather by conducting their own measurements for a study.

Principals Perpetrators of a criminal act.

Prostitution The practice of engaging in sexual activities for hire.

Psychoanalytic theory In criminology, a theory of criminality that attributes delinquent and criminal behavior to a conscience that is either so overbearing that it arouses excessive feelings of guilt or so weak that it cannot control the individual's impulses.

Psychopathy A condition in which a person appears to be psychologically "normal" but in reality has no sense of responsibility, shows disregard for truth, is insincere, and feels no sense of shame, guilt, or humiliation (also called *sociopathy*).

Psychosis A mental illness characterized by a loss of contact with reality.

Psychoticism A dimension of the human personality describing individuals who are aggressive, egocentric, and impulsive (Eysenck).

R

Racketeer Influenced and Corrupt Organizations (RICO) Act A federal statute that provides for forfeiture of assets derived from a criminal enterprise.

Radical criminology A criminological perspective that studies the relationships between economic disparity and crime, avers that crime is the result of a struggle between owners of capital and workers for the distribution of power and resources, and posits that only when capitalism is abolished crime will disappear.

Random sample A sample chosen in such a way as to ensure that each person in the population to be studied has an equal chance of being selected. *See also* Sample.

Rape At common law, a felony consisting of the carnal knowledge (intercourse), by force and violence, by a man of a woman (not his wife) against her will. The stipulation that the woman not be the man's wife is omitted in modern statutes.

Rational choice   A theory that states that crime is the result of a decision-making process in which the offender weighs the potential penalties and rewards of committing a crime.

Reaction formation   An individual response to anxiety in which the person reacts to a stimulus with abnormal intensity or inappropriate conduct.

Robbery   The taking of the property of another, or out of his or her presence, by means of force and violence or the threat thereof.

Routine activity   A theory that states that an increase or decrease in crime rates can be explained by changes in the daily habits of potential victims; based on the expectation that crimes will occur where there is a suitable target unprotected by guardians.

S

Sample   A selected subset of a population to be studied. *See also* Random sample.

Secondary data   Facts and observations that were previously collected for a different study.

Self-report survey   A survey in which respondents answer in a confidential interview or, most often, by completing an anonymous questionnaire.

Serial murder   The killing of several victims over a period of time by the same perpetrator(s).

Sherman Antitrust Act   An act (1890) of Congress prohibiting any contract, conspiracy, or combination of business interests in restraint of foreign or interstate trade.

Shoplifting   Stealing goods from stores or markets.

Simple assault   An attack that inflicts little or no physical harm on the victim.

Social control theory   An explanation of criminal behavior which focuses on control mechanisms, techniques, and strategies for regulating human behavior, leading to conformity or obedience to society's rules, and which posits that deviance results when social controls are weakened or break down, so that individuals are not motivated to conform to them.

Social disorganization theory   A theory of criminality in which the breakdown of effective social bonds, primary-group associations, and social controls in neighborhoods and communities is held to result in development of high-crime areas.

Social interactionists   Scholars who view the human self as formed through a process of social interaction.

Social learning theory   A theory of criminality that maintains that delinquent behavior is learned through the same psychological processes as nondelinquent behavior, e.g., through reinforcement.

Sociopath   A person who has no sense of responsibility; shows disregard for truth; is insincere; and feels no sense of shame, guilt, or humiliation.

Sodomy   Sexual intercourse by mouth or anus; a felony at common law.

Somatotype school of criminology   A criminological perspective that relates body build to behavioral tendencies, temperament, susceptibility to disease, and life expectancy.

Statutory rape   Sexual intercourse with a person incapable of giving legally relevant consent, because of immaturity (below age), mental, or physical condition.

Stock manipulation   An illegal practice of brokers in which clients are led to believe that the price of a particular stock will rise, thus creating an artificial demand for it.

Strain theory   A criminological theory positing that a gap between culturally approved goals and legitimate means of achieving them causes frustration which leads to criminal behavior.

Stranger homicide   Criminal homicide committed by a person unknown and unrelated to the victim.

Strict liability   Liability for a crime or violation imposed without regard to the actor's guilt; criminal liability without mens rea. *See also* Mens rea.

Subculture   A subdivision within the dominant culture that has its own norms, beliefs, and values.

Subculture of violence   A subculture with values that demand the overt use of violence in certain social situations.

Superego   In psychoanalytic theory, the conscience, or those aspects of the personality that threaten the person or impose a sense of guilt or psychic suffering and thus restrain the id.

Survey   The systematic collection of information by asking questions in questionnaires or interviews.

Synnomie   A societal state, opposite of anomie, marked by social cohesion achieved through the sharing of values.

T

Target hardening   A crime-prevention technique that seeks to make it more difficult to commit a given offense, by better protecting the threatened object or person.

Terrorism   The use of violence against a target to create fear, alarm, dread, or coercion for the purpose of obtaining concessions or rewards or commanding public attention for a political cause.

Theories of crime   Theories that identify conditions under which those who are prone to commit crime will do so.

Theories of victimization   Theories that explain the role that victims play in the crimes that happen to them.

Theory   A coherent group of propositions used as principles in explaining or accounting for known facts or phenomena.

Tort   An injury or wrong committed against a person's property, subject to compensation; an infringement of the rights of an individual that is not founded on either contract or criminal law prohibition.

Transnational crime   A criminal act or transaction violating the laws of more than one country, or having an impact on a foreign country.

U

Utilitarianism   A criminological perspective positing that crime prevention and criminal justice must serve the end of providing the greatest good for the greatest number; based on the rationality of lawgivers, law enforcers, and the public at large.

V

Variables   Changeable factors.

Victim precipitation   Opening oneself up, by either direct or subliminal means, to a criminal response.

Victimization survey   A survey that measures the extent of crime by interviewing individuals about their experiences as victims.

Violations   Minor criminal offenses, usually under city ordinances, commonly subject only to fines.

Voluntary manslaughter   Homicide in which the perpetrator intentionally, but without malice, causes the death of another person, as in the heat of passion, in response to strong provocation, or possibly under severe intoxication.

W

White-collar crime   A sociological concept encompassing any violation of the law committed by a person or group of persons in the course of an otherwise respected and legitimate occupation or business enterprise.

PHOTO CREDITS

2 Anthony Suau/Gamma Liaison; 7 Moe Doiron/AP/ Wide World Photos; 9 Giraudon/Art Resource; 10 From *Cinderella and Other Tales from Perrault.* Illustrated by Michael Hague. Henry Holt & Co., New York, 1989; 13 Evan Agostini/Gamma Liaison; 15 (bottom) Reuters/Archive Photos; 15 (top) Jim Argo/Saba; 18 Atlan/Sygma; 20 Dirck Halstead/ Gamma Liaison; 37 The Image Works; 38 F. Paolini/Sygma; 39 A. Ramy/Woodfin Camp & Associates; 41 Miladinovic/Sygma; 46 Pushkin Museum of Fine Arts, Moscow, Scala/Art Resource; 48 Gerhard Hinterleitner/Gamma Liaison; 58 "Physique and Delinquent Behavior" Hartl, Monnelley, and Elderkin (New York Academic Press, 1982); 68 R. Flynt/The Image Works; 70 Steve Berman/Gamma Liason; 75 Martin Rodgers/Stock Boston; 81 George Widman/AP/Wide World Photos; 97 Thomas Hoepker/Magnum; 101 Paolo da Silva/Sygma; 102 Lennox McLendon/AP/Wide World Photos; 118 Nine Network Australia/Gamma Liaison; 119 Mary D'Anella/ Sygma; 123 Douglas Burrows/Gamma Liaison; 127 Wayne Miles/Gamma Liaison; 136 Greg Mellis/The State Journal Register, Springfield, IL; 143 Beth Keiser/AP Wide World Photos; 147 Miao Wang/ Image Bank; 149 Sygma; 152 Reuters/Archive Photos; 154 Kevin Swank/The Evansville Courier/AP/ Wide World Photos; 156 John Giordana/Saba; 167 M. Siluk/The Image Works; 173 Courtesy Gerhard O. W. Mueller; 174 Haviv/Saba; 181 David Butow/ Saba; 187 Consolidated News/Archive Photos; 192 John Paul Filo; 198 Steven Rubin/The Image Works; 204 Geuorgui Pinkhassov/Magnum; 210 A. Lichtenstein/Impact Visuals; 214 AP/Wide World Photos; 217 AP/Wide World Photos; 218 Bettmann; 223 Culver Pictures; 224 Lacy Atkins/AP/Wide World Photos; 230 David Butow/Saba; 236 AP/Wide World Photos; 244 Mark Le/AP/World Wide Photos; 251 Cynthia Howe/Sygma; 263 Ferdinando Scianna/Magnum Photos; 271 Mike Derer/AP/World Wide Photos; 276 Bonnie Kamin/PhotoEdit; 280 Les Stone/Sygma; 284 John Nordell/The Image Works; 290 John Duricka/AP/World Wide Photos; 296 Baldev/Sygma; 304 Mark Cardwell/Reuters/Archive Photos; 312 Viviane Moos/Saba; 328 Kevin Jacobus/The Image Works; 331 Reuters/Archive; 335 T. Crosby/Gamma Liaison; 342 Kimimasa Mayama/ Reuters/Archive; 344 Chip Hires/Gamma Liaison; 351 A. Ramey/Woodfin Camp; 356 Jorge Nunez/ Reuters/Corbis-Bettmann; and 360 Philip S. Farnsworth/Gamma Liaison.

■ ILLUSTRATION AND TEXT CREDITS ■

Chapter 1

Figure 1.2 From *The Sociology of Deviance* by Jack D. Douglas and Frances C. Waksler, Little, Brown and Company, 1982. Reprinted by permission of the authors.

Table 1.1 Table from Carl Fox, "Some Major Marine Oil Spills, *Albuquerque Journal,* February 20, 1996, p. 6. Reprinted by permission of The Associated Press.

At Issue Excerpts from Tupac Amaru Shakur, "If I Die 2nite," and "Ain't Hard to Find." Death Row Records.

Criminological Focus From Gerhard O. W. Mueller, "The Criminological Significance of the Grimms' Fairy Tales," in *Fairy Tales and Society: Illusion, Allusion, and Paradigm,* edited by Ruth B. Bottigheimer, University of Pennsylvania Press, 1986, pp. 217–227. Reprinted by permission.

Window to the World From Douglas Waller, "Counterterrorism: Victim of Success?" pp. 22–23. From *Newsweek,* July 5, 1993, (c) Newsweek, Inc. All rights reserved. Reprinted by permission.

Chapter 2

Figure 2.1 From *Surveying Victims: A Study of the Measurement of Criminal Victimization, Perceptions of Crime, and Attitudes to Criminal Justice* by R. F. Sparks, H. G. Genn, and D. J. Dodd. Copyright (c) 1977. Reprinted by permission of John Wiley & Sons, Ltd.

At Issue From Cheryl Laird, "Laws Confront Obsession That Turns Fear into Terror and Brings Nightmares to Life," *Houston Chronicle,* May 17, 1992, p. 1. Copyright 1992 Houston Chronicle Publishing Company. Reprinted with permission. All rights reserved.

Chapter 3

At Issue From Ron Rosenbaum, "The Great Ivy League Nude Posture Photo Scandal," pp. 26–31.

(c) 1995 Ron Rosenbaum, which originally appeared in *The New York Times Magazine,* January 15, 1995. All rights reserved.

Criminological Focus From Jim Miller, "The Mismeasure of Man," p. 106. From *Newsweek,* November 9, 1981. (c) 1981, Newsweek, Inc. All rights reserved. Reprinted by permission.

Window to the World Excerpted and adapted from Gerhard O. W. Mueller and Freda Adler, "The Emergence of Criminal Justice: Tracing the Route to Neolithic Times," in *Festskrift til Jacob W. F. Sundberg* edited by Erik Nerep and Wiweka Warnling Nerep (Stockholm: Juristforlaget, 1993), pp. 151–170.

Chapter 4

Table 4.1 Table adapted from *Understanding Psychology* by Robert S. Feldman, 1987, p. 378. Copyright (c) 1987. Reproduced with permission of The McGraw-Hill Companies.

Table 4.2 From Harry F. Waters, "Networks under the Gun," p. 65. From *Newsweek,* July 12, 1993. (c) 1993, Newsweek, Inc. All rights reserved. Reprinted by permission.

At Issue Excerpt from Hanna Bloch and Jeanne McDowell, "When Kids Kill Abusive Parents," *Time,* November 23, 1992. (c) 1992 Time Inc. Reprinted by permission.

At Issue From *Why Kids Kill Parents* by Kathleen M. Heide, Ohio State University Press, 1992, pp. 40–41. Reprinted by permission.

Criminological Focus Table from William S. Laufer, review of "The Jurisprudence of the Insanity Defense," by Michael L. Perlin, in *Journal of Legal Medicine,* 16, 1995, pp. 454. Taylor & Francis, Inc., 1995. Used with permission.

Window to the World From Harry F. Waters, "Networks under the Gun," p. 64. From *Newsweek,* July 12, 1993. (c) 1993, Newsweek, Inc. All rights reserved. Reprinted by permission.

Cartoon, p. 77 Cartoon by Jeff Stahler reprinted by permission of Newspaper Enterprise Association, Inc.

Quote, p. 83 Excerpt from *The Mask of Sanity*, Fifth Edition, by Hervey Cleckley, 1976, 1988, pp. 271–272. Published by Emily S. Cleckley, 3024 Fox Spring Road, Augusta, Georgia 30909. Fifth Edition, 1988.

Cartoon, p. 85 Drawing by Chas. Addams; (c) 1981 The New Yorker Magazine, Inc.

Chapter 5

Figure 5.2 From Jane Gross, "Remnant of the War on Poverty, Job Corps Is Still a Quiet Success," *The New York Times*, February 17, 1992, p. A14. Copyright (c) 1992 by The New York Times Co. Reprinted by permission.

Figure 5.3 From *Theories of Delinquency*, Second Edition, by Donald Shoemaker, p. 82. Copyright (c) 1990 by Donald Shoemaker. Used by permission of Oxford University Press, Inc.

Figure 5.4 Figure from *The City* by Robert E. Park, Ernest W. Bergess, and R. D. McKenzie, 1925, p. 55. Copyright (c) 1925. Reprinted by permission of the Chicago University Press.

Table 5.1 Reprinted with the permission of The Free Press, a division of Simon & Schuster from *Social Theory and Social Structure* by Robert K. Merton. Copyright (c) 1957 by The Free Press; copyright renewed 1985 by Robert K. Merton.

Chapter 6

Figures 6.1, 6.2, 6.4 Figures from *Theories of Delinquency: An Examination of Explanations of Delinquent Behavior*, Third Edition, by Donald J. Shoemaker, 1996, pp. 107, 115, 122. Copyright (c) 1990 by Donald Shoemaker. Used by permission of Oxford University Press, Inc.

Figure 6.3 Figure from pp. 40–41. Reprinted from May 18, 1992 issue of *Business Week* by special permission, copyright (c) 1992 by The McGraw-Hill Companies, Inc.

Table 6.2 Table from John P. Sullivan and Martin E. Silverstein, "The Disaster Within Us: Urban Conflict and Street Gang Violence in Los Angeles," *Journal of Gang Research*, Vol. 2. Summer 1995, pp. 11–30. Courtesy of The National Gang Crime Research Center, Chicago, IL.

Criminological Focus Adapted from *The Girls in the Gang* by Anne Campbell, Blackwell Publishers, Ltd., 1984. Reprinted by permission.

Cartoon, p. 131 Cartoon by Stephen Moore, "Illegitimate Job Center," from *Investigating Deviance*. Published by HarperCollins Publishers, Ltd. Reprinted by permission of Stephen Moore.

Quote, p. 140 From Seth Mydans, "Not Just the Inner City: Well-to-Do Join Gangs," p. A10. *The New York Times*, April 10, 1990. Copyright (c) 1990 by The New York Times Co. Reprinted by permission.

Quote, p. 143 From Robert Reinhold, "In the Middle of L.A.'s Gang Warfare," p. 31. *The New York Times Magazine*, May 22, 1988. Copyright (c) 1988 by The New York Times Co. Reprinted by permission.

Chapter 7

Table 7.1 Table from *Causes of Delinquency* by Travis Hirschi, University of California Press, 1969.

At Issue Excerpts from *Causes of Delinquency* by Travis Hirschi, University of California Press, 1969, pp. 30, 202.

Criminological Focus Excerpts from Barbara Kantrowitz, "Wild in the Streets," pp. 40–47. From *Newsweek*, August 2, 1993, (c) 1993, Newsweek, Inc. All rights reserved. Reprinted by permission.

Chapter 8

Figure 8.1 Figure from *Suburban Burglary: A Time and A Place for Everything* by George Rengert and John Wasilchick, 1985, p. 35. Courtesy of Charles C Thomas, Publisher, Ltd., Springfield, Illinois.

Figure 8.2 Figure adapted from Ronald V. Clarke and Derek B. Cornish, "Modeling Offenders' Decisions: A Framework for Research and Policy," *Crime and Justice*, Sixth Edition, edited by Michael Tonry and Norval Morris, 1985, p. 169. Copyright (c) 1985. Published by the University of Chicago Press.

Table 8.1 Table from Ronald V. Clarke and Ross Homel, "A Revised Classification of Situational Crime Prevention Techniques," in *Crime Prevention at a Crossroads*, edited by Steven P. Lab. (in press) Reprinted by permission of Anderson Publishing Co.

Table 8.2 Table from "Theft Losses of 1992–94 Model Utility Vehicles and Two-Door Cars, Based on an Average Rate of 100," *Injury, Collision, and Theft Losses by Make and Model*, September 1995. Reprinted by permission of Highway Loss Data Institute.

Table 8.3 Figure from Zachary Fleming, Patricia Brantingham, and Paul Brantingham, "Exploring Auto Theft in British Columbia," p. 62. Reprinted with permission from *Crime Prevention Studies*, Vol. 3, edited by R. V. Clarke (1994), published by Criminal Justice Press, Monsey, NY.

Criminological Focus Figure from Ellis Cose, "Drawing Up Safer Cities. Design: How a Community Divided Conquers Crime," p. 57. From *Newsweek*, July 11, 1994, (c) 1994, Newsweek, Inc. All rights reserved. Reprinted by permission.

Window to the World From *Delinquency and Puberty: Examination of Juvenile Delinquency Fad* by Gerhard O. W. Mueller, Criminal Law Education and Research Center.

Cartoon, p. 182 Cartoon by Gary Larson from *The Far Side*. (c) Farworks, Inc./Dist. by Universal Press Syndicate. Reprinted with permission. All rights reserved.

Quote, p. 168 From Marlowe Churchill, "Jury Finds Man Guilty of One-hour Sex Attack," *The Press Enterprise*, July 26, 1996, p. B3. Reprinted by permission of The Press-Enterprise.

Chapter 9

Criminological Focus Excerpted with permission from D. L. Rosenhan, "On Being Sane in Insane Places," *Science*, Vol. 179. 1973, pp. 253–254. Copyright 1973 American Association for the Advancement of Science.

Chapter 10

Figure 10.1 (c) 1962 *The Saturday Evening Post*.

At Issue From Lenore E. Walker, "Self-Defense and the Penal Codes," *The Battered Women Syndrome*, pp. 142–143. Copyright (c) 1984. Reprinted with permission of Springer Publishing Company, Inc., New York 10012.

Criminological Focus Excerpts from *Thirty-Eight Witnesses* by A. M. Rosenthal, 1964. Copyright (c) 1964. Reproduced with permission of The McGraw-Hill Companies.

Window to the World From *Outlaws of the Ocean: The Complete Book of Contemporary Crime on the High Seas* by Gerhard O. W. Mueller and Freda Adler, Hearst Marine Books, 1985, pp. 217–218. Copyright (c) 1985 Gerhard O. W. Mueller and Freda Adler. By permission of William Morrow & Company, Inc.

Chapter 11

Figure 11.1 Reprinted from *The Police Chief*, pages 36–37, March 1988. Copyright held by the International Association of Chiefs of Police, 515 North Washington Street, Alexandria, VA 22314 USA. Further reproduction without express written permission from IACP is strictly prohibited.

Figure 11.2 Table and map from "Crime: a Deadly Neighborhood," *The New York Times*, October 11, 1992, p. 85. Copyright (c) 1992 by The New York Times Co. Reprinted by Permission.

Figure 11.3 Graphic from Gregory L. Vistica, "Extremism in the Ranks." From *Newsweek*, March 25, 1966, (c) 1966, Newsweek, Inc. All rights reserved. Reprinted by permission.

At Issue Quote from Christopher John Farley, "A Nest of Vipers," *Time*, July 15, 1996. pp. 24–25. (c) 1996 Time Inc. Reprinted by permission.

Quote, p. 234 From William Julius Wilson, "Work," pp. 27, 28. *New York Times Magazine*, August 18, 1996. Copyright (c) 1996 by The New York Times Co. Reprinted by permission.

Chapter 12

Figure 12.3 Figure from Peter Kerr, "Ghost Riders Are Target of an Insurance Sting," *The New York Times*, August 18, 1993, pp. A1, D2. Copyright (c) 1993 by The New York Times Co. Reprinted by Permission.

Criminological Focus (c) 1996, Jones Digital Century, Inc. Courtesy of *Jones Telecommunications and Multimedia Encyclopedia*.

Quote, p. 273 From "Citibank Caper: Harbinger of Crimes to Come?" *The News and Observer*, September 28, 1995. Reprinted by permission of Associated Press.

Chapter 13

Figure 13.2 Figure from *Chinese Subculture and Criminality* by Ko-lin Chin, 1990, p. 76. Copyright (c) 1990. Reproduced with permission of Greenwood Publishing Group, Inc., Westport, CT.

At Issue   From *Dangerous Ground: The World of Hazardous Waste Crime* by Donald J. Rebovich, 1992. Reprinted by permission of Transaction Publishers. Copyright (c) 1992 by Transaction Publishers; all rights reserved.

Cartoon, p. 302   Cartoon by Sidney Harris (c) 1997 by Sidney Harris.

Quote, p. 285   From Steve Yozwiak, "Big Fines for Lake Powell Dumping Exceed $1.3 Million," p. A1. *Arizona Republic,* May 13, 1993. Used with permission. Permission does not imply endorsement.

Quote, p. 286   From "Mafia Chief Tied to Crime-Busting Judges Murder." Reuters Information, August 1, 1993.

Quote, p. 295   Excerpt from Jim Mayer, "Confection Maker Indicted in Dumping," *Sacramento Bee,* July 10, 1993. Copyright, The Sacramento Bee, 1996.

Chapter 14

Figure 14.3   Figure from "Crime Goes International," pp. 20–21. From *Newsweek,* December 13, 1993, (c) 1993, Newsweek, Inc. All rights reserved. Reprinted by permission.

Table 14.1   Table from Bruce D. Johnson, Terry Williams, Kojo A. Dir, and Harry Sanabria, "Drug Abuse in the Inner City: Impact on Hard-Drug Users and the Community," in *Drugs and Crime,*

Vol. 13, edited by Michael Tonry and James Q. Wilson, 1990, p. 19. Copyright (c) 1990. Reprinted by permission of Chicago University Press.

Table 14.3   Table from "Getting Banks to Just Say 'No,'" *Business Week,* April 17, 1989. p. 17. By permission of Business Week. (c) 1996. Table also from Maggie Mahar, "Dirty Money: It Triggers a Bold New Attack in the War on Drugs," *Barron's,* 69, June 1989, p. 7. Reprinted by permission of *Barrons,* (c) 1989 Dow Jones & Company, Inc. All Rights Reserved Worldwide.

Window to the World   Figure from "The Child-Sex Trade," p. 11. From *Newsweek,* September 2, 1996, (c) 1996, Newsweek, Inc. All rights reserved. Reprinted by permission.

Chapter 15

Figure 15.1   Map by Paul J. Pugliese, *Time,* January 29, 1996, p. 51. (c) 1996 Time Inc. Reprinted by permission.

At Issue   Quote from Ben Fenton and Sonia Purnell, "Bank Official Admits $750m Fraud, 'Financial Juggler' Was at the Heart of BCCI Scandal," *Daily Telegraph,* September 28, 1993, p. 1. Reprinted by permission of Ewan MacNaughton Associates.

Criminological Focus   Excerpted from *The Cheyenne Way* by Karl N. Llewellyn and E. Adamson Hoebel, 1941, pp. 12–13. Copyright (c) 1941. Reprinted by permission of the University of Oklahoma Press.

NAME INDEX

NAME INDEX

Abadinsky, Howard, 300, 310n., 325, 337n., 338n., 339n.
Abdelaziz, Atiqui, 260n.
Abrahamsen, David, 259n.
Acquino, Benigno, 239
Adams, Reed, 94n.
Adler, Freda, 17n., 40, 41, 45n., 49n., 107, 121n., 145n., 162, 162n., 164n., 166n., 186n., 199, 206n., 223n., 270n., 283n., 337n., 338n., 364n., 365n., 366n.
Adler, Jeffrey S., 206n.
Adler, Jill, 197
Adler, Nanci, 363n.
Ageton, Suzanne S., 41–42, 44n., 45n., 120n., 166n.
Aglipay, Edgar, 309n.
Agnew, Robert, 107, 121n., 153, 164n.
Agusti, Filiberto, 309n.
Ahlstrom-Laakso, S., 340n.
Aichhorn, August, 93n.
Aigner, Stephen M., 45n.
Akers, Ronald L., 79, 94n., 120n., 144n., 193, 206n.
Al-Naif, Abdul Razak, 239
Albanese, Jay S., 302, 310n., 311n.
Albini, Joseph, 310n.
Albonetti, Celesta A., 207n.
Albrecht, Han-Jorg, 365n.
Albrecht, Steve W., 307n.
Alder, Christine, 261n.
Alexander, Shana, 310n.
Aley, James, 341n.
Allan, Emilie Anderson, 44n.
Alomar, Roberto, 7
Ames, M. Ashley, 260n.
Amir, Menachem, 246, 261n., 339n.
Anastasia, Albert, 303
Ancel, Marc, 64n., 65n., 363n.
Anderson, Annelise Graebner, 310n.
Anderson, Bo, 164n.
Anderson, David C., 17n.
Andrews, D. W., 94n.
Anglin, M. Douglas, 94n., 338n.
Appleborne, Peter, 363n.
Applegate, Brandon A., 340n.
Arbuthnot, Jack, 93n.
Archer, Dane, 259n., 364n.
Aristotle, 200
Arlacchi, Pino, 310n.
Arneklev, B. J., 166n.

Arnold, Rolf, 308n.
Arthur, John A., 262n., 364n.
Asahara, Shoko, 253
Athulathmudali, Lalith, 239
Atlas, Randall, 179n.
Aultman, Madeline G., 165n.
Austin, Roy L., 45n.
Austin, W. Timothy, 166n.
Avery, D'Aunn Webster, 185n., 280, 283n.
Avison, William R., 120n., 122n.
Ayat, Mohammed, 242, 260n.

Baarda, B., 94n.
Bachman, Jerald G., 43n., 325, 337n.
Bachman, Ronet, 260n.
Bacich, Anthony R., 260n.
Bailey, William C., 261n.
Bakalar, James, 337n.
Baker, Jake, 278
Ball, John C., 338n.
Ball, Richard A., 146n., 165n.
Ball-Rokeach, Sandra, 145n.
Balliofyne, Scott, 365n.
Balsamo, William, 310n.
Bandura, Albert, 77, 78, 79, 94n.
Barbara, Joseph M., 303
Barnes, Harry Elmer, 50, 64n.
Barnett, W. Steven, 121n.
Baron, Stephen W., 145n.
Barrett, B. J., 121n.
Barron, R. A., 341n.
Barzini, Luigi, 310n.
Basiotis, P. Peter, 364n.
Baskin, Deborah R., 122n., 339n.
Bassiouini, M. Cherif, 366n.
Baucus, Melissa, 306n.
Baudouin, H. de, 96n.
Baumer, Terry L., 261n.
Baus, Stephanie A., 340n.
Bayley, David H., 363n.
Bazelon, David, 219
Beals, Gregory, 34n.
Beatty, David, 30
Beavon, Daniel J. K., 179n.
Beccaria, Cesare, 47, 49, 50–52, 63, 64n., 200
Becker, Ed, 310n.
Becker, Gary S., 185n.
Becker, Howard S., 190, 192, 195, 205n., 206n.
Beeman, E. A., 96n.
Beha, James A., II, 262n.

Beirne, Piers, 64n., 65n., 363n.
Belfrage, Henrik, 229n.
Bell, P. A., 341n.
Bell, Ralph, 186n.
Bellis, David J., 340n.
Bellucci, Charles, 186n.
Bennett, Nathan, 261n.
Bennett, Richard R., 364n.
Bennett, Wayne W., 283n.
Benson, Bruce L., 338n.
Benson, Michael L., 166n., 307n., 310n.
Bentham, Jeremy, 49, 52, 63, 64n., 185n., 200
Bentler, P. M., 338n.
Bequai, August, 307n., 308n.
Berger, Dale E., 365n.
Berger, Herbert, 339n.
Berger, Phil, 308n.
Berk, Richard A., 260n.
Berkey, Martha Lou, 283n.
Berkowitz, David (Son of Sam), 235
Berman, Harold J., 203n.
Bernard, Thomas J., 120n., 121n.
Bernardo, Mark A. de, 337n., 339n.
Berrueta-Clement, John R., 121n.
Bersten, Michael, 306n.
Beseler, P., 311n.
Biaggi, Mario, 290
Biderman, Albert D., 310n.
Bieber, Stephen, 229n.
Binet, Alfred, 87
Binstein, Michael, 306n.
Bintliff, Russell B., 308n.
Birkbeck, Christopher, 364n.
Biron, Louise L., 338n.
Bishop, Donna M., 206n.
Bissel, Barbara, 271
Bjerregaard, Beth, 122n., 145–146n.
Black, Donald J., 149–150, 164n.
Blackburn, Ronald, 93n.
Blackman, Peter, 361n.
Blackmun, Harry A., 216
Blackstone, William, 249
Blane, Howard T., 260n.
Blau, Judith R., 105, 121n., 145n.
Blau, Peter M., 105, 121n., 145n.
Blaustein, Albert P., 363n.
Bloch, Hannah, 76n., 95n.
Block, Alan A., 311n.
Block, Carolyn Rebecca, 186n., 258n.
Block, Richard L., 186n.

Bloom, Joseph, 307n.
Bloomberg, Seth A., 23, 43n.
Blumberg, Abraham S., 282n.
Blumenthal, Ralph, 310n., 365n.
Blumer, Herbert, 205n.
Blumstein, Alfred, 38, 43n., 44n., 146n.
Bock, Alan W., 262n.
Boden, Nancy, 310n.
Boeringer, Scot B., 341n.
Boesky, Ivan F., 3, 289
Bohm, Robert M., 207n.
Bohn, Martin J., 94n.
Boleyn, Ann, 198
Bonfante, John, 145n.
Bonger, Willem Adriaan, 200, 201, 207n.
Bonnano, Joe, 303
Bonnie, Richard J., 228n.
Boostrom, Ron, 306n.
Booth, A., 96n.
Bordua, David J., 144n.
Borduin, Charles M., 93–94n.
Boss, Maria S., 307n.
Bottigheimer, Ruth, 10
Bowden, Charles, 306n.
Bowers, Patricia M., 260n.
Bowers, William J., 262n.
Bowker, Lee H., 45n.
Bowlby, John, 74, 93n., 164n.
Bowman, Cynthia Grant, 260n.
Box, S., 287n.
Boyle, John M., 307n.
Bracton, Henry de, 265
Bradley, Pamela, 94n.
Brady, James, 217, 257
Braithwaite, John, 120n., 121n., 186n., 306n.,
    307n., 308n., 310n.
Bramlet, Gwen W., 340n.
Brantingham, Patricia L., 179n., 182, 184n.
Brantingham, Paul J., 179n., 182, 184n.
Brathwaite, John, 105–106
Bratton, William J., 34
Brennan, P. A., 95n.
Brewer, Victoria E., 262n.
Brewer, Wayne, 311n.
Brewster, Victoria E., 45n.
Brezina, Timothy, 121n.
Briar, Scott, 150, 164n.
Brickey, Kathleen F., 308n.
Brickler, W., 94n.
Brill, William, 183n.
Broca, Paul, 55
Brochu, Serge, 338n.
Brooke, James, 101n., 254n.
Brower, Sidney, 121n.
Brown, Claude, 134–135, 145n.
Brown, Curtis, 339n.
Brown, David, 207n.
Brown, H. Lowell, 228n.
Brown, Teresa D., 164n.
Browne, Angela, 259n.
Brownfield, David, 105, 121n., 145n., 166n.,
    337n.
Brownmiller, Susan, 245, 261n.
Brunk, Molly A., 93–94n.
Bryant, Jennings, 341n.
Buck, Andrew J., 122n.

Buckle, Abigail, 282n.
Buerger, Michael E., 176–177, 185n.
Bukoff, Allen, 262n.
Bumby, Kurt M., 229n.
Bundy, Theodore, 235
Burack, C., 166n.
Burgdorf, K., 260n.
Burger, James de, 259n.
Burgess, Ernest, 79, 94n., 110–111, 111
Burke, Mary Jean, 122n.
Burke, Tod W., 155, 155n.
Burnett, Cathleen, 364n.
Bursik, Robert J., Jr., 122n., 166n., 186n.
Burt, Cyril, 55
Burt, Martha R., 261n.
Burton, Velmer S., Jr., 121n.
Buse, Britta, 359n.
Bush, George, 324
Butterfield, Fox, 34n., 95n., 122n., 145n., 262n.

Caesar, Julius, 239
Calavita, Kitty, 306n., 307n.
Calder, Paul, 236
Caldwell, Charles, 53, 63
Callahan, Charles M., 262n.
Cameron, Mary Owen, 267, 282n.
Campbell, Anne, 22, 43n., 138–140, 139n., 146n.
Canada, Geoffrey, 336n.
Canter, R. J., 166n.
Caplan, Aaron, 164–165n.
Capone, Al, 300, 326
Carey, Gregory, 95n.
Carey, James T., 120n.
Carlen, Pat, 207n.
Carneiro, Robert, 49
Carolin, P. James, Jr., 282n.
Carpenter, Cheryl, 338n.
Carpozi, George, Jr., 310n.
Carrington, Michael D., 261n.
Carrington, Peter J., 262n.
Carroll, John, 283n.
Carter, Timothy, 207n.
Cartwright, D., 165n.
Case, Carole, 311n.
Casey, John J., 337n.
Cassidy, Margery A., 260n.
Castellano, Paul, 303
Castiglia, Francesco, 304
Castillo, Dawn N., 259n.
Catalano, Richard F., 166n.
Catanzaro, Raimondo, 310n.
Catherine II (the Great), Empress of Russia, 51
Cavender, Gray, 308n.
Cebulak, Wojciech, 363n., 366n.
Centerwall, B. S., 94n.
Cernovich, Stephen A., 135, 145n., 164n.
Chaiken, Marcia R., 337n.
Chambers, James A., 121n.
Chambliss, William J., 122n., 193, 201, 202,
    206n., 207n., 282n., 309n.
Chamlin, Mitchell B., 121n.
Chandler, Kathryn, 157n.
Chang, Dae H., 363n., 365n.
Chang, Dean, 340n.
Chang, Richard J., 365n.
Chapman, S. G., 339n.

Chappell, Duncan, 261n.
Chard-Wierschem, Deborah, 145n.
Charren, Peggy, 78
Chayet, Ellen F., 307n.
Cheatwood, Derral, 44n., 65n.
Cheney, Margaret, 259n.
Cheng, Y. T., 338n.
Chesney-Lind, Meda, 40, 45n., 207n.
Chesser, Eustace, 340n.
Chesterman, L. P., 96n.
Chilton, Roland, 233–234, 258n.
Chin, Ko-lin, 130–131, 145n., 305, 366n.
Chirn, Susan, 122n., 166n.
Cho, Byung In, 365n.
Christiansen, Karl O., 85–86, 95n.
Christman, John H., 282n.
Christopher, Thomas P., 44n.
Churchill, Marlowe, 184n.
Clark, Douglas (Sunset Strip killer), 235
Clark, G., 309n.
Clark, John H., 292, 308n.
Clarke, Michael, 283n., 365n.
Clarke, Ronald V., 171, 171, 180, 185n., 186n.,
    268, 283n.
Clear, Todd R., 247, 261n.
Cleckley, Hervey, 82–83, 95n.
Clelland, Donald, 207n.
Clifford, William, 348, 364n.
Clifton, Wayland, Jr., 185n.
Clinard, Marshall B., 162n., 295, 306n., 309n.,
    348, 364n.
Clinton, Bill, 20, 108, 324
Cloward, Richard A., 125, 129–132, 144n., 152,
    337n.
Cochran, John K., 121n., 340n.
Coffee, John Collins, Jr., 309n., 310n.
Cohen, Albert K., 125–126, 128, 129, 138, 142,
    144n., 146n., 152, 205n.
Cohen, Jacqueline, 43n., 44n.
Cohen, Lawrence E., 172, 185n.
Cohen, Mark A., 309n., 310n.
Cohen, Marvin D., 146n.
Cohn, Ellen G., 260n.
Cole, George F., 363n.
Coleman, D. H., 339n.
Coleman, James W., 307n., 309n.
Coll, Vincent "Mad Dog," 300
Collazo, Oscar, 239
Collins, Dean J., 260n.
Collins, Laura, 311n.
Collins, Thomas, 79n.
Comack, Elizabeth, 206n.
Comte, Auguste, 53, 54, 63
Condelle, L., 121n.
Conklin, John, 248, 261n.
Constantine, Thomas, 321
Conyers, John, Jr., 295
Cook, Philip J., 185n., 261n.
Cooley, Charles Horton, 190, 205n.
Coramae, Mann, 234
Corcoran, Kevin J., 339n.
Cornish, Derek B., 171, 171, 185n.
Corrado, Michael Louis, 229n.
Corzine, Jay, 259n., 364n.
Corzine-Huff, Lin, 259n.
Cosby, Bill, 236

Cose, Ellis, 178*n.*, *179*
Costello, Frank, 300, 304
Coston, Charisse T. M., 364*n.*
Cottey, Talbert J., 262*n.*
Cottrell, Leonard S., 121*n.*
Coutoria, Larry E., 283*n.*, 366*n.*
Couzens, Michael, 43*n.*
Covington, Jeanette, 122*n.*, 337*n.*
Crawford, Elizabeth M., 45*n.*
Cressey, Donald R., 80, 94*n.*, 307*n.*, 308*n.*, 311*n.*
Croall, Hazel, 306*n.*
Cromwell, Paul F., 185*n.*, 280, 283*n.*
Croswell, Edgar, 304
Crotty, William J., 239*n.*
Cullen, Francis T., 45*n.*, 121*n.*, 146*n.*, 308*n.*, 309*n.*, 310*n.*, 340*n.*
Cullen, John B., 45*n.*, 309*n.*
Cumberbatch, Guy, 341*n.*
Cummings, John, 311*n.*
Cunningham, Lea C., 145*n.*
Currie, Elliott, 207*n.*
Curry, G. David, 259*n.*
Curtis, Lynn A., 146*n.*
Curtis, R., 340*n.*

Dahmer, Jeffrey, 235
Dahrendorf, Ralf, 197–198, 206*n.*
Dalton, Katherina, 91, 96*n.*
Daly, Kathleen, 206*n.*, 262*n.*
Daly, Martin, 259*n.*, 365*n.*
Damiens, Robert-François, 50
Dando, Shigemitsu, 363*n.*
Daniel, Anasseril E., 259*n.*
Daro, Deborah, 261*n.*
D'Arpa-Calandra, Angela, 135
Darwin, Charles, 53, 54, 57, *63*, 64*n.*
David, James R., 144*n.*
Davies, Elizabeth, 157*n.*
Davies, P., 96*n.*
Davis, Daniel L., 95*n.*
Davis, John H., 311*n.*
Davis, Laura, 341*n.*
Davis, Nanette J., 164*n.*
Davis, Robert C., 336*n.*
Day, James M., 94*n.*
Dean, Charles S., 260*n.*
Deane, Gary D., 122*n.*
Deane, Glenn D., 259*n.*
Decker, Scott H., 145*n.*, 165*n.*, 185*n.*, 259*n.*, 283*n.*
DeKeseredy, Walter S., 207*n.*
DeLancey, Marci M., 337*n.*
Delgado, Richard, 341*n.*
Denno, Deborah W., 88, 96*n.*
Dershowitz, Alan M., 217, 228*n.*
Desjardins, Lyne, 338*n.*
Di Motto, John J., 44*n.*
Diamond, Bernard L., 228*n.*
Dickey, Christopher, 283*n.*
Dietrick, David C., 144*n.*
Dinitz, Simon, 94*n.*, 165*n.*
Dir, Kojo A., *315*
Dixon, Jo, 145*n.*
Dixon, Ronald L., 308*n.*
Dobash, R. Emerson, 365*n.*
Dobash, Russel P., 365*n.*

Dodd, David J., *24*, 309*n.*
Doerner, William G., 145*n.*
Donaldson, Thomas, 308*n.*
Donges, Katja, 359*n.*
Donnerstein, Edward, 341*n.*
Dornfeld, Maude, 260*n.*, 261*n.*
Doto, Giuseppe (Joe Adonis), 300
Douglas, Jack D., 8, *8*, 17*n.*
Douglas, Marie C., 363*n.*
Downs, Donald A., 341*n.*
Drass, Kriss A., 45*n.*
Droegemueller, W., 259*n.*
Drummond, Edward, 218
Duffield, Don W., 122*n.*
Dugdale, Richard L., 59, *63*, 65*n.*
Dunaway, R. Gregory, 121*n.*
Dunford, Franklin, 43*n.*
Dunlap, Eloise, 337*n.*, 338*n.*
DuPont, John, *81*
Durkheim, Émile, 9, 17*n.*, 61–62, *63*, 65*n.*, 99–100, 120*n.*, 195–196, 206*n.*
Duster, Troy, 339*n.*
Duszynski, Karen R., 338*n.*
Dutton, Donald G., 260*n.*
Duyne, Petrus van, 311*n.*

Earle, Beverly, 309*n.*
Easton, Susan M., 341*n.*
Ebbe, Obi N. I., 352, 363*n.*, 364*n.*, 365*n.*
Eck, John E., 184*n.*
Edel, Wilbur, 262*n.*
Edwards, Sally M., 366*n.*
Edwards, Terry D., 366*n.*
Eggston, Andrew A., 339*n.*
Eichel, Edward W., 340*n.*
Eigenberg, Helen M., 43*n.*
Eisenman, Russell, 338*n.*
Eitzen, D. Stanley, 287*n.*
Elderkin, Ronald D., 65*n.*
Elias, Robert, 208*n.*
Elis, Lori A., 307*n.*
Ellen, Eric, 366*n.*
Ellingworth, Dan, 185*n.*
Elliot, David, 186*n.*
Elliot, Delbert S., 41–42, 43*n.*, 44*n.*, 45*n.*, 120*n.*, 121*n.*, 128, 144*n.*, *160*, 161, 166*n.*
Elliott, Frank A., 95*n.*
Ellis, Havelock, 64*n.*
Ellis, Lee, 96*n.*
Ellis, Lori, 45*n.*
Elmoghazy, E., 338*n.*
Engels, Friedrich, 199–200, 201, 207*n.*
Epstein, Ann S., 121*n.*
Epstein, Joel, 261*n.*, 311*n.*
Erez, Edna, 45*n.*, 243, 260*n.*
Erickson, Kai T., 191, 206*n.*
Eriksson, Thorsten, 64*n.*
Erlanger, Howard S., 132, 145*n.*
Ermann, M. David, 308*n.*, 309*n.*
Eron, Leonard D., 77, 94*n.*
Esbensen, Finn-Aage, 145*n.*
Eser, Albin, 363*n.*
Evans, Harold, 308*n.*
Evans, T. David, 121*n.*
Eysenck, Hans J., 81, 83, 93*n.*, 95*n.*

Fagan, Jeffrey A., 34, 122*n.*, 133, 145*n.*, 166*n.*, 260*n.*, 337*n.*, 338*n.*, 339*n.*
Faggiani, Donald, 185*n.*, 186*n.*
Faisal, King of Saudi Arabia, 239
Falcone, Giovanni, 286
Farley, Christopher John, 254*n.*
Farnham, Alan, 270*n.*
Farnworth, Margaret, 105, 120*n.*, 165*n.*
Farrell, Graham, 185*n.*
Farrelland, Ronald A., 311*n.*
Farrington, David P., 43*n.*, 44*n.*, 160, *160*, 165–166*n.*, 185*n.*, 282*n.*, 365*n.*
Fattah, David, 146*n.*
Fattah, Ezzat A., 175, 185*n.*, 186*n.*
Feinberg, Joel, 341*n.*
Feingold, Benjamin F., 90, 96*n.*
Feiring, Candice, 93*n.*
Feldman, M. Philip, 95*n.*
Feldman, Robert S., *73–74*
Felson, Marcus, 172, 185*n.*
Felson, Richard B., 95*n.*, 185*n.*, 241, 259*n.*, 260*n.*
Fenton, Ben, 361*n.*
Ferguson, Colin, 236
Fernandez, Yvette, 310*n.*, 339*n.*
Ferracuti, Franco, 125, 132, 145*n.*, 260*n.*
Ferraro, Kenneth F., 122*n.*
Ferre, M. Isolina, 115, 122*n.*
Ferrero, Gina Lombroso, 64*n.*, 82
Ferrero, William, 40, 45*n.*, 64*n.*
Ferri, Enrico, 54, 56, 57, *63*
Ferri, Gian Luigi, 236
Fielding, Henry, 279–280
Fields, Charles B., 363*n.*, 366*n.*
Figlio, Robert M., 35, 38, 44*n.*, 96*n.*, 145*n.*, 261*n.*
Figueira-McDonough, Josefina, 122*n.*
Finckenauer, James O., 22, 43*n.*, 311*n.*, 352, 363*n.*, 365*n.*
Fine, David, 166*n.*
Fingerhut, Lois A., 365*n.*
Fink, Arthur E., 64*n.*
Finkelhor, David, 261*n.*
Finn, Peter, 339*n.*
Fischel, Daniel R., 308*n.*
Fischer, D. G., 94*n.*
Fish, Albert, 236
Fishbein, Diana H., 92, 95*n.*, 96*n.*
Fisse, Brent, 306*n.*, 307*n.*, 308*n.*
Flegenheimer, Arthur (Dutch Schultz), 300
Fleming, Zachary, *182*
Flenz, G. H., 363*n.*
Fletcher, George P., 229*n.*, 363*n.*
Flowers, R. Barri, 45*n.*
Follain, John, 310*n.*
Forbaugh, Frederick M., 121*n.*
Ford, Gerald, 239
Forney, Mary Ann, 340*n.*
Forssman, H., 96*n.*
Forsyth, Craig J., 261*n.*
Foster, Jodie, 217
Fowles, Richard, 121*n.*
Fox, Carl, 4
Fox, James Alan, 34, 236, 259*n.*, 291, 308*n.*
Frank, Nancy, 310*n.*
Frankowski, Stanislaw J., 363*n.*
Frate, Anna Albazzi del, 364*n.*
Freemantle, Brian, 310*n.*

French, L., 95*n.*
Freud, Sigmund, 62, 71, 93*n.*
Frey, T. S., 96*n.*
Friday, Paul C., 365*n.*
Friedlander, Kate, 93*n.*
Friedrich II, King of Prussia, 51–52
Frisch, Lisa A., 260*n.*
Fromm-Auch, D., 96*n.*
Fry, Patricia A., 337*n.*
Fu, Hualing, 365*n.*

Gabor, Thomas, 308*n.*
Gabrielli, William F., 95*n.*, 96*n.*
Gage, Michael, 364*n.*
Gajewski, Frank, 186*n.*
Gal-Or, Noemi, 261*n.*
Gall, Franz Joseph, 53, *63*
Galton, Francis, 55
Gambino, Carlo, 303, 304
Gambino, Richard, 310*n.*
Gandhi, Indira, 239
Gandhi, Rajiv, 239
Ganson, H., 121*n.*
Ganzini, Linda, 307*n.*
Garbarino, James, 260*n.*
Garcia, Juanita L., 261*n.*
Garcia Abrego, Juan, *355*
Garfield, James A., 239
Garofalo, James, 175–176, 185*n.*
Garofalo, Raffaele, 6, 8–9, 17*n.*, 54, 57, *63*, 65*n.*
Garrett, Gerald R., 336*n.*
Gartin, Patrick R., 176–177, 185*n.*, 260*n.*
Gartner, Rosemary, 259*n.*, 364*n.*, 365*n.*
Gartrell, John W., 120–121*n.*, 259*n.*
Gass, Otto, 300
Gately, William, 310*n.*, 339*n.*
Gault, Robert H., 88, 96*n.*
Gay, John, 280
Gaynor, Jessica, 283*n.*
Gearing, Michael L., 94*n.*
Gebhard, Paul H., 331, 340*n.*, 341*n.*
Gebhardt, Bruce, 254
Geen, Russell G., 94*n.*
Geis, Gilbert, 261*n.*, 286–287, 306*n.*, 307*n.*, 309*n.*
Gelfand, Donna, 282*n.*
Gelles, Richard J., 242, 260*n.*
Gemayel, Bishir, 239
Genn, Hazel G., *24*, 309*n.*
Genovese, Kitty, 213, 214
Genovese, Vito, 300, 303, 304
Gentry, Cynthia S., 341*n.*
George, Barbara Crutchfield, 307*n.*
Gerber, Jurg, 307*n.*
Gertz, Marc G., 363*n.*
Giancana, Chuck, 311*n.*
Giancana, Sam (Momo), 303, 311*n.*
Gibbens, Trevor N., 282*n.*
Gibbs, Jack P., 164*n.*, 206*n.*
Gibbs, John J., 122*n.*, 166*n.*, 282*n.*
Gibson, L., 339*n.*
Gidyez, C. A., 261*n.*
Giever, D., 166*n.*
Gigante, Vincent (The Chin), 304
Gilfus, Mary E., 45*n.*
Gill, Martin, 366*n.*
Giller, Joan E., 366*n.*

Gillespie, James, 339*n.*
Gilligan, Carol, 93*n.*
Gillis, A. R., 45*n.*, 165*n.*
Gilmore, W. C., 365*n.*
Ginsburg, Ruth Bader, 216
Gioe, Antonino, 286
Giordano, Peggy C., 164*n.*, 283*n.*
Glaser, Frederick, 338*n.*
Glass, Clive, 283*n.*
Glassner, Barry, 338*n.*
Glick, Barry, 25, 43*n.*
Glueck, Eleanor T., 40, 45*n.*, 58, 65*n.*, 75, 94*n.*, 352, 363*n.*, 364*n.*
Glueck, Sheldon, 40, 45*n.*, 58, *63*, 65*n.*, 75, 94*n.*, 352, 363*n.*, 364*n.*
Goddard, Henry H., 55, 59–60, *63*, 65*n.*, 87–88, 95*n.*
Goetting, Ann, 260*n.*
Goetz, Bernhard H., 222–225
Goff, Colin H., 309*n.*
Goffman, Erving, 205*n.*
Golant, Susan K., 260*n.*
Gold, Martin, 43*n.*
Goldberg, Jeffrey, 311*n.*
Golden, Reid M., 121*n.*
Goldfarb, Ronald, 310*n.*
Golding, William, 148, 164*n.*
Goldman, Ronald, 242
Goldstein, Paul J., 338*n.*
Goleman, Daniel, 95*n.*
Golub, Andrew, 338*n.*
Gondoli, Dawn M., 260*n.*
Goode, Erich, 338*n.*
Gordon, Corey L., 183*n.*
Gordon, Donald A., 93*n.*
Gordon, Margaret A., 259*n.*
Gordon, Robert, 165*n.*
Gordon, Waxey, 300
Gore, Al, Jr., *20*
Goring, Charles Buckman, 57, *63*, 65*n.*
Gornick, Janet, 261*n.*
Gottfredson, Denise C., 122*n.*, 166*n.*
Gottfredson, Gary D., 122*n.*
Gottfredson, Michael R., 36–37, 44*n.*, *160*, 161, *161*, 166*n.*, 169, 175–176, 184*n.*, 185*n.*, 307*n.*
Gottfredson, Stephen D., 121*n.*
Gotti, John, 304
Gough, Harrison G., 94*n.*
Gould, Stephen Jay, 54–55
Gove, Walter C., 206*n.*
Grabosky, Peter, 306*n.*
Gramling, Robert, 261*n.*
Grasmick, Harold G., 166*n.*, 186*n.*
Green, Gary S., 262*n.*
Green, J. Howard, 228*n.*
Green, Lorraine, 186*n.*
Greenberg, David F., 44*n.*, 144*n.*, 207*n.*
Greenfeld, Lawrence A., 259*n.*, 340*n.*
Greer, Richard, 283*n.*
Gregory, Sophfronia Scott, 118*n.*
Griffin, Roger, 283*n.*
Griffiths, Curt T., 365*n.*
Griffiths, Fre Le Poole, 363*n.*
Grinspoon, Lester, 337*n.*
Griswold, David, 164*n.*
Grosmick, Harold G., 122*n.*

Gross, Jane, *108*, 121*n.*, 164*n.*
Grossman, Jan Carl, 338*n.*
Groves, W. Byron, 309*n.*
Gudjonsson, Gisli H., 95*n.*
Guerry, André Michel, 61, *63*, 170, 184*n.*, 200
Guggenheim, W. Z., 337*n.*
Gusfield, Joseph R., 340*n.*
Gustafson, Roland, 339*n.*
Guth, Hans-Werner, 365*n.*
Guy, Sybille M., 338*n.*

Hagan, Frank E., 23, 43*n.*
Hagan, John, 40, 45*n.*, 105, 121*n.*, 165*n.*, 207*n.*, 307*n.*
Hagedorn, John M., 130, 144*n.*
Hakim, Simon, 122*n.*
Hale, Chris, 121*n.*
Hale, Matthew, 247, 261*n.*
Hall, Jerome, 212, 228*n.*, 282*n.*
Halleck, Seymour L., 81–82, 95*n.*
Hamburg, D. A., 96*n.*
Hamid, Ansley, 337*n.*
Hamilton, Thomas, 236
Hamilton, V. Lee, 365*n.*
Hamlin, John, 165*n.*
Hamm, Mark S., 146*n.*, 307*n.*, 344, 363*n.*
Hammett, Theodore M., 311*n.*
Hampton, Robert L., 258*n.*
Hancock, Lyn Nell, 260*n.*
Hanharan, Kathleen J., 122*n.*
Hani, Chris, 239
Hanlon, Thomas E., 338*n.*
Hansen, Joy, 146*n.*
Hanson, Cindy L., 93–94*n.*
Hanson, R. Karl, 340*n.*
Harding, Richard W., 185*n.*
Hare, Robert D., 95*n.*
Harer, Miles D., 44*n.*
Harrell, Adele V., 179*n.*
Harris, Patricia M., 185*n.*
Hartjen, Clayton A., 122*n.*, 365*n.*
Hartl, Emil M., 65*n.*
Hartmann, Donald, 282*n.*
Hartnagel, Timothy F., 120–121*n.*, 259*n.*
Harvey, William B., 258*n.*
Hatch, Alison, 365*n.*
Hatch, Orrin, 109
Hatcher, Chris, 283*n.*
Hauser, Robert M., 207*n.*
Hawkins, David J., 166*n.*
Hawkins, Gordon, 341*n.*
Hays, Ron D., 340*n.*
Hazelbaker, Kim, 186*n.*
Healy, Kevin, 338*n.*
Hebenton, B., 364*n.*
Hee, Park Chung, 239
Heide, Kathleen M., 76*n.*, 340*n.*
Heimer, K., 122*n.*, 165*n.*
Heimer, Mel, 259*n.*
Heims, Lora W., 283*n.*
Heiner, Robert, 363*n.*
Heinzelmann, Fred, 307*n.*
Helal, Adel, 364*n.*
Helvétius, Claude Adrien, 50
Hendler, Harold I., 339*n.*
Henggeler, Scott W., 93–94*n.*

Hennessy, James J., 43*n.*, 93*n.*, 185*n.*
Henry, Jessica S., 252*n.*
Henry VIII, King of England, 198
Henson, Trudy Knicely, 283*n.*
Hentig, Hans von, 175, 185*n.*, 234, 258*n.*
Hepburn, John R., 282*n.*
Hepburn, R. J., 165*n.*
Herfmann, Donald H. J., 228*n.*
Herrnstein, Richard J., 37, 44*n.*, 59, 59*n.*, 88, 92, 96*n.*
Hersch, Rebecca K., 283*n.*
Hess, Karen Matison, 283*n.*
Heumann, Milton, 262*n.*
Heyl, Barbara Sherman, 340*n.*
Hibbert, Christopher, 64*n.*
Hickey, Joseph, 72
Hill, Gary D., 45*n.*, 121–122*n.*
Hill, Joan, 363*n.*
Hill, Robert, 132, 145*n.*
Hillbrand, Michael J., 95*n.*
Hinckley, John W., Jr., 215, 217–219, 239
Hindelang, Michael J., 29, 44*n.*, 88, 96*n.*, 153, 164*n.*, 175–176, 185*n.*
Hirano, Ryuichi, 309*n.*
Hirschel, J. David, 260*n.*
Hirschi Travis, 29, 36–37, 44*n.*, 88, 96*n.*, 104, 116, 120*n.*, 122*n.*, 128, 130, 144*n.*, 150–155, *151*, 155*n.*, 159, *160*, 161, *161*, 164*n.*, 166*n.*, 169, 184*n.*, 307*n.*
Hitler, Adolf, 212, 343
Ho, Truc-Nhu, 283*n.*, 365*n.*
Hoebel, E. Adamson, 350, 350*n.*
Hoff, Joan, 334, 341*n.*
Hoffer, Abram, 96*n.*
Hoffman, John P., 145*n.*
Hogan, Robert, 94*n.*
Hogg, Russell, 207*n.*
Holcomb, William R., 259*n.*
Hollinger, Richard C., 292, 308*n.*
Holmes, Oliver Wendell, Jr., 60
Holmes, Ronald M., 259*n.*
Holmes, Stephen T., 259*n.*
Holt, Joe, 90
Holyst, Brunon, 351, 364*n.*
Homel, Ross, *180*, 186*n.*
Honeywood, Wesley (Pop), 35–36
Hooten, Ernest A., 57, *63*, 65*n.*
Hoover, J. Edgar, 24
Hope, Susan, 283*n.*
Hope, Timothy J., 185*n.*
Horace, 200
Hornblower, Margot, 333*n.*
Horney, Julie, 44*n.*, 96*n.*, 261*n.*
Horwitz, Allan V., 164*n.*
Horwitz, Diana, 338*n.*
Houston, James, 145*n.*
Howitt, Dennis, 340*n.*, 341*n.*
Hser, Yining, 338*n.*
Hsü, Yü-Hsiu, 365*n.*
Huang, Frank F. Y., 365*n.*
Hubbard, Benjamin J., 252*n.*
Huberty, James, 236
Huesmann, L. Rowell, 94*n.*
Huff, C. Ronald, 146*n.*
Hughes, Michael, 122*n.*
Hui, Boon Khoo, 309*n.*

Huizinga, David, 45*n.*, 120*n.*, 145*n.*
Hull, John D., 146*n.*, 262*n.*
Hume, David, 50
Humphries, Charlie, 185*n.*
Humphries, Drew, 207*n.*
Hunt, Dana, 337*n.*
Hunt, Morton, 336, 341*n.*
Hunter, Ronald D., 186*n.*, 365*n.*
Hutchings, Barry, 95*n.*
Hutchinson, Ira W., III, 260*n.*

Ianni, Francis A., 310*n.*
Iglarsh, Harvey J., 261*n.*
Iguchi, Toshihide, 3
Incantalupo, Tom, 269*n.*
Inciardi, James A., 282*n.*, 310*n.*, 319, 336*n.*, 337*n.*, 338*n.*, 339*n.*, 340*n.*
Innes, Christopher A., 260*n.*
Inoue, Mariko, 309*n.*
Ireland, Timothy, 145*n.*
Ishihara, T., 95*n.*
Itil, Turan, M., 96*n.*
Itzen, Catherine, 341*n.*
Izquierdo, Elisa, *244*

Jackson, Elton F., 122*n.*
Jackson, Howard F., 283*n.*
Jackson, Pamela Irving, 120*n.*
Jackson, Patrick G., 43*n.*, 283*n.*
Jacob, Craig, 308*n.*
Jacobs, Bruce A., 337*n.*, 338*n.*
Jacobs, James B., 252*n.*, 339*n.*, 340*n.*
Jacobs, K. W., 90, 96*n.*
Jah, Yusef, 145*n.*
James, Jennifer, 331, 340*n.*
James, Pierce I., 337*n.*
Janeksela, Galan M., 365*n.*
Jang, Sung Joon, 44*n.*
Janus, Cynthia L., 340*n.*
Janus, Samuel S., 340*n.*
Jarjoura, G. Roger, 44*n.*, 128, 144*n.*
Jaskir, John, 93*n.*
Jeffery, C. Ray, 79, 84, 94*n.*, 95*n.*, 177, 186*n.*
Jeffrey, Richard, 229*n.*
Jeffries, John Calvin, Jr., 228*n.*
Jenkins, E. Lynn, 259*n.*
Jenkins, Philip, 259*n.*
Jennings, William S., 72, 93*n.*
Jensen, Arthur, 88, 96*n.*
Jensen, Gary F., 43*n.*, 45*n.*, 121*n.*, 165*n.*
Jesilow, Paul, 306*n.*, 307*n.*
Johann, Sara Lee, 341*n.*
Johnson, Bruce D., 185*n.*, *315*, 337*n.*, 338*n.*
Johnson, Davey, 7
Johnson, John A., 94*n.*, 206*n.*
Johnson, Lyndon B., 108–109, 115, 142, 302
Johnson, S. D., 339*n.*
Johnston, David, 311*n.*
Johnston, Les, 366*n.*
Johnston, Lloyd D., 43*n.*, 325, 337*n.*, 339*n.*
Jones, Gwen, 166*n.*
Jordan, James, 256
Jordan, Michael, *102*, 103, 155, 256
Joseph, Nadine, 228*n.*
Joutsen, Matti, 363*n.*
Judson, George, 166*n.*

Jukes, Ada, 59
Jung, Sung Juon, 165*n.*
Junger-Tas, Josine, 44*n.*, 364*n.*, 365*n.*

Kagan, Jerome, 87
Kahan, James P., 339*n.*
Kaiser, Günther, 365*n.*, 366*n.*
Kalish, Carol B., 309*n.*, 364*n.*
Kallikak, Martin, 60
Kamin, Leon J., 59, 59*n.*
Kaminer, Wendy, 17*n.*
Kandel, Elizabeth, 95*n.*
Kangaspunta, Kristina, 363*n.*
Kantrowitz, Barbara, 121*n.*, 145*n.*, 157*n.*
Kapardis, A., 308*n.*
Kapardis, M., 308*n.*
Karami, Rashid, 239
Karchmer, Clifford L., 283*n.*
Karpman, Benjamin, 95*n.*
Karpos, Mary Altani, 43*n.*
Karter, Michael J., Jr., 283*n.*
Katel, Peter, 17*n.*
Kaufman, Irving, 283*n.*
Kaulitzki, Reiner, 337*n.*, 365*n.*
Kay, Fiona, 307*n.*
Keane, Carl, 166*n.*
Kellner, R., 96*n.*
Kelly, Linda, 365*n.*
Kelly, Mary, 267
Kelly, Robert J., 261*n.*
Kempe, C. H., 259*n.*
Kemper, Edmond, 236
Kempf, Kimberly L., 164*n.*
Kendall, Jerry, 365*n.*
Kennedy, John F., 115, 142, 199, 239
Kennedy, Leslie W., 145*n.*, 234, 259*n.*
Kennedy, Robert F., 199, 239
Kenny, Dennis Jay, 311*n.*
Kepecs-Schlussel, Laurie, 43*n.*
Kerbo, Harold R., 309*n.*
Kerr, Peter, *274*
Kessler, Ronald C., 338*n.*
Kethineni, Sesharajani, 365*n.*
Keyah, Shah', 145*n.*
Kfita, Najat, 260*n.*
Kieselhorst, B. C., 339*n.*
Kilborn, Peter T., 145*n.*
Kilkenny, Robert, 93*n.*
Killias, Martin, 262*n.*, 363*n.*, 364*n.*
Kindley, Karen, 259*n.*
King, Harry, 282*n.*
King, Martin Luther, Jr., 199, 239
King, Mike, 365*n.*
King, Patricia, 254*n.*
King, Rodney, 112, 222
King, Roy, 95*n.*
Kinlock, Timothy W., 338*n.*
Kinsbourne, Marcel, 96*n.*
Kinsey, Alfred C., 329, 340*n.*, 341*n.*
Kirchheimer, Otto, 200–201, 207*n.*
Kirkham, James F., 239*n.*
Kitsuse, John I., 144*n.*
Kittrie, Nicholas N., 95*n.*, 205*n.*
Klaus, K. A., 95*n.*
Klaus, Patsy, 309*n.*

Klein, Malcolm W., 44n., 144n., 145n., 146n., 259n., 364n.
Kleinfield, N. R., 259n.
Kleinman, Joel C., 365n.
Klinteberg, Britt af, 95n.
Klockars, Carl B., 202, 207n., 280, 283n.
Knightly, Phillip, 308n., 309n.
Knoblich, Guenther, 95n.
Knop, George W., 145n.
Knowles, Gordon James, 338n.
Kobrin, Solomon, 122n.
Koepf, G. F., 95n.
Kohlberg, Lawrence, 72, 93n.
Kopel, David B., 365n.
Koper, Christopher S., 310n.
Korem, Dan, 146n.
Koresh, David, 118, 251–252
Kosberg, Jordan I., 261n.
Koss, M. P., 261n.
Koster, Katie de, 341n.
Kotzer, Sophia, 261n.
Kowlaski, Gregory S., 122n.
Krahn, Harvey, 120–121n., 259n.
Kramer, Jane, 363n.
Krauss, Clifford, 34n.
Kretschmer, Ernst, 58, 63, 65n.
Kreuz, L. E., 96n.
Krisberg, Barry, 202, 207n.
Kroc, Ray, 102–103
Krohn, Marvin D., 44n., 120n., 121n., 128, 144n., 145n., 146n., 164n., 165n., 207n.
Kruttschnitt, Candace, 260n., 261n.
Krzeszowski, Frank E., 283n.
Kuhns, Joseph B., III, 340n.
Kunen, James S., 309n.
Kupperstein, Lenore R., 364n.
Kury, Helmut, 365n.
Kurz, Anat, 261n.
Kutchinsky, Berl, 341n.
Kuttschreuter, M., 94n.

Lacayo, Richard, 34n., 118n.
Lacey, Robert, 310n.
LaFave, Wayne R., 228n., 258n.
LaFree, Gary, 45n., 364n.
LaGrange, Randy L., 122n.
Laird, Cheryl, 30–31n.
LaMacchia, Dave, 278
Lamb, Christina, 101n.
Lander, Bernard, 120n.
Langan, Patrick A., 260n.
Lange, Johannes, 85, 95n.
Langenbahn, Stacia, 261n.
Lanza-Kaduce, Lonn, 120n., 144n., 340n.
Laskey, John A., 144n.
Lasley, James R., 186n., 307n.
Laub, John H., 44n., 65n., 160, 160, 165n.
Lauderback, David, 146n.
Laufer, William S., 80, 94n., 121n., 145n., 166n., 308n., 337n.
Lauritsen, Janet L., 122n.
Lavater, Johann Kaspar, 53, 63
Laws, D. R., 96n.
Laycock, Gloria, 172
Leary, Timothy, 319
Leavitt, Gregory C., 364n.

LeBeau, James L., 261n.
LeBlanc, Marc, 164–165n.
LeBlanc, William G., 179n.
LeCapitaine, J. E., 93n.
Lederer, Laura, 341n.
Ledingham, C. A., 94n.
Ledingham, J. E., 94n.
Leeson, Nicholas W., 3, 41
Leland, John, 363n.
Lemaitre, Andre, 308n.
Lemaitre, Rolf, 308n.
Lemert, Edwin M., 190–191, 205n., 272, 283n.
Lensing, H., 365n.
Leonard, Kenneth E., 260n., 340n.
Leonard, Kimberly K., 165n.
Leone, Bruno, 341n.
Letelier, Orlando, 239
Levin, Jack, 236, 259n., 365n.
Levine, Betti Jane, 165n.
Levine, Dennis, 289
Levine, James, 43n.
Levinson, David, 260n.
Levy, Sheldon G., 239
Lewin, Tamar, 31n.
Lewis, Matthew W., 340n.
Lewis, Michael, 93n.
Lewis, Norman, 310n.
Lewis, Oscar, 102, 120n.
Liazos, Alexander, 144n., 206n.
Lieberman, Alicia J., 93n.
Liebl, Karlhans, 307n.
Lightner, Candy, 327–328
Lilly, J. Robert, 146n.
Lincoln, Abraham, 239
Lindbergh, Charles, 249
Linden, R., 339n.
Link, Bruce G., 206n., 309n., 340n.
Linquist, P., 339n.
Liska, Alan, 165n.
Little, Heather M., 96n.
Littman, R. A., 94n.
Litton, Roger, 308n.
Lizotte, Alan J., 145–146n., 165n., 199, 206n., 257, 262n.
Llewellyn, Karl N., 350, 350n.
Locke, John, 50
Loeber, Rolf, 122n.
Loftin, Colin, 43n., 132, 145n., 259n., 262n.
Lofvers, Jeff, 164n.
Lombness, Michael, 310n.
Lombroso, Cesare, 7, 40, 45n., 54–57, 63, 64n., 359
Looman, Terah, 185n.
Loring, Pamela L., 120n., 122n.
Loughlin, Julia, 338n.
Louis XV, King of France, 50
Lovell, Constance, 80, 94n.
Low, Peter W., 228n.
Lowman, John, 207n.
Lowney, Jeremiah, 340n.
Luciana, Salvatore (Lucky Luciano), 300, 304
Luckenbill, David F., 259n., 340n.
Lucky Luciano, 300, 304
Lunde, D. T., 96n.
Lundman, Richard J., 308n., 309n.
Luper, Steven Foy, 339n.

Lupsha, Peter A., 311n.
Lurigio, Arthur J., 336n.
Lussen, Fredrick M., 214
Lyman, Michael D., 337n.
Lynch, James P., 364n.
Lyston, Douglas S., 338n.

Ma, Yue, 363n.
Maakestad, William J., 308n., 310n.
Maas, Peter, 310n.
Mabry, Marcus, 363n.
McAuley, Finbarr, 228n.
McBarnet, Doreen, 308n.
McBride, Duane C., 338n., 339n.
McCaffery, Barry, 324
McCaghy, Charles, 283n.
McClintock, F. H., 365n.
McConkey, C., 121n.
McCord, Joan, 75, 93n., 94n., 95n., 165n., 260n.
McCord, William, 95n.
MacCoun, Robert J., 339n.
McCoy, Clyde B., 339n.
McCoy, Virginia, 337n.
McCutcheon, Allan L., 337n.
McDevitt, Jack, 365n.
Macdonald, John M., 283n.
McDonald, William F., 363n.
McDowall, David W., 43n., 122n., 257, 262n.
McDowell, Jeanne, 76n.
Macey, Jonathan R., 310n.
McFadden, Robert D., 262n.
McFarland, Bentson, 307n.
McGuffog, Carolyn, 93n.
McKay, Henry D., 111, 113, 114, 115, 121n.
McKenzie, R. D., 111
McKey, R. H., 121n.
McKinley, James C., Jr., 44n.
McKinley, William, 239
MacLean, Brian D., 207n.
McNamara, Joseph, 310n.
McNeil, Richard J., 122n.
Macphail, Daniel D., 93n.
McShane, Marilyn D., 120n., 341n.
McVeigh, Timothy, 253
Madden, Owney, 300
Maddox, Neil, 4
Maestro, Marcello C., 64n.
Magaddino, Stefano, 303
Magendanz, B., 339n.
Magnuson, Dan, 310n.
Magnusson, David, 95n.
Mahar, Maggie, 323
Maher, Lisa, 307n., 337n., 340n.
Maier, Pamela A., 185n.
Major, Victoria L., 43n.
Makofsky, Abraham, 339n.
Malekian, Farhad, 366n.
Mankoff, Milton, 207n.
Mann, Coramae Richey, 45n., 258n., 259n.
Mannheim, Hermann, 64n., 351, 364n.
Marcial, Gene C., 307n.
Marin, Rick, 17n.
Marion, Nancy E., 17n.
Markey, Edward J., 78
Marolla, J., 261n.
Marongiu, Pietro, 64n., 185n.

Marriott, Michael, 13n., 121n.
Marshall, Ineke Haen, 44n.
Martens, Frederick T., 366n.
Martin, Clyde E., 340n., 341n.
Martin, R. D., 94n.
Martone, Mark, 76
Marx, Karl, 200, 201, 207n.
Massey, James L., 164n.
Mastrofski, Stephen D., 340n.
Masuda, Barry, 283n.
Mathers, R., 309n.
Matsueda, Ross L., 122n., 165n., 206n.
Matsueda, T. Ross, 165n.
Matthews, Roger, 179n.
Matza, David, 105, 121n., 145n., 155, 165n., 178, 186n., 206n.
Maudsley, Henry, 60, *63*
Mawby, R. I., 365n.
Mawson, Anthony R., 90, 96n.
Maxim, Paul S., 166n.
Maxson, Cheryl L., 144n., 145n., 146n., 259n.
Mayer, Jim, 309n.
Mayer, Martin, 307n.
Mayfield, D., 339n.
Mayhew, Patricia, 186n., 364n.
Mazerolle, Paul, 121n.
Mead, George Herbert, 190, 205n.
Mednick, Sarnoff A., 85–86, 87, 91, 95n., 96n.
Megargee, Edwin I., 94n.
Meier, Robert F., 45n., 120n., 186n., 309n.
Meland, James A., 337n.
Menard, Scott, 43n., 121n., 164n., 166n.
Mendelsohn, Benjamin, 175, 185n.
Mendelsohn, Gerald A., 94n.
Menninger, Karl, 82, 95n.
Merari, Ariel, 261n.
Mercy, James A., 262n.
Merlin, Mark D., 336n.
Merton, Robert K., 100, 102–107, *103*, 120n., 125
Merva, Mary, 121n.
Merz, Jon F., 340n.
Messner, Steven F., 106–107, 121n., 145n., 165n., 207n.
Metfessel, Milton, 80, 94n.
Meyer, C. K., 339n.
Michaels, Robert J., 337n.
Michalowski, Raymond J., 309n.
Miczek, Klaus A., 340n.
Miecykowski, Tom, 320n.
Miedzian, Myriam, 341n.
Miethe, Terance D., 122n., 186n.
Miles, Christine, 337n.
Milk, Harvey, 89
Milken, Michael R., 3
Miller, Brenda A., 260n.
Miller, Jim, 55n.
Miller, Jody, 146n., 337n.
Miller, Martin G., 45n.
Miller, Richard Lawrence, 339n.
Miller, S. L., 166n.
Miller, Thomas, 338n.
Miller, Walter B., 122n., 125, 134–135, 145n.
Mills, Anne-Marie, 260n.
Mills, Michael, 307n.
Minor, N. William, 165n.
Mirrlees, Catriona Black, 337n.

Mitchell, David B., 260n.
Mitchell, John L., 155n.
Miyazawa, Setsuo, 364n.
M'Naghten, Daniel, 217–218, 219
Modisett, Jeff, 156
Moffett, Arthur D., 338n.
Moffitt, Terrie E., 44n., 95n.
Mohammed, Murtala Ramat, 239
Mokhiber, Russell, 309n.
Monnelly, Edward P., 65n.
Montanino, Fred, 311n.
Montesquieu, 50
Mooney, Warren D., 295
Moore, Elizabeth, 166n., 307n.
Moore, Michael S., 228–229n.
Moore, Molly, 79n.
Moore, Richard, 282n.
Moore, Richter H., Jr., 363n.
Moorehead-Dworkin, Terry, 306n.
Moran, Richard, 228n.
Moran, Thomas Bartholomew, 267
Morash, Merry, 40, 45n., 310n.
More, Thomas, 200
Morganthau, Tom, 157n.
Moro, Aldo, 239
Morse, Edward V., 340n.
Morton, Samuel George, 55
Moscone, George, 89
Mott, Joy, 337n.
Moyer, Sharon, 262n.
Mueller, Gerhard O. W., 10n., 26n., 49n., 64n., 174n., 186n., 205n., 223n., 228n., 258n., 270n., 283n., 309n., 341n., 363n., 364n., 365n., 366n.
Munsterberg, Hugo, 87, 95n.
Murray, Alan, 308n.
Murray, Ellen, 165n.
Muscat, Joshua E., 259n.
Musto, D. F., 337n.
Mydans, Seth, 146n.
Myers, Kenneth D., 308n.
Myers, Laura B., 45n.
Myers, Martha A., 206–207n.
Myers, Norman, 311n.
Mylonas, Anatassios, 364n.
Myrdal, Gunnar, 102, 120n.

Nadelman, Ethan A., 365n.
Nader, Ralph, 295
Nagel, Ilene H., 207n.
Nagin, Daniel S., 44n., 165–166n.
Nash, Jay Robert, 310n.
Natarajan, Mangai, 185n., 338n.
Nay, Robert L., 365n.
Nelli, Humbert S., 310n.
Nelsen, Candice, 259n.
Neustrom, Michael W., 120n.
Newlyn, Andrea K., 339n.
Newman, Graeme R., 64n., 309n., 365n.
Newman, Oscar, 177, 178, 186n.
Newton, George D., Jr., 262n.
Newton, Michael, 259n.
Ngouabi, Marien, 239
Nichols, Terry, 253
Nixon, Richard, 239, 323
Nochajski, Thomas H., 260n.

Nolan, Bruce W., 366n.
Nolen, John T. (Legs Diamond), 300
Nolin, Mary Jo, 157n.
Noriega, Manuel, 323
Norris, Sandra L., 259n.
Norton, William M., 120n.
Nurco, David N., 338n., 339n.
Nye, Francis Ivan, 94n., 120n., 159, 165n.
Nyswander, Marie, 337n.

O'Carroll, Patrick W., 262n.
Oetzi, 48–49
Ohlin, Lloyd E., 125, 129–132, 144n., 152, 337n.
Oliver, F. E., 337n.
Olson, James N., 185n., 280, 283n.
Olson, Lynn M., 336n.
Olson, Virgil J., 120n.
O'Malley, Patrick M., 43n., 325, 337n.
O'Maolchatha, Aogan, 207n.
O'Neill, Eugene, 136, 145n.
Ong, Benny, *304*
O'Rear, Charles E., 155, 155n.
O'Reilly-Fleming, Thomas, 206n.
Ortega, Suzanne T., 364n.
Orvis, Gregory P., 261n.
Osanka, Franklin Mark, 341n.
Osgood, D. Wayne, 43n., 44n., 86, 95n., 96n.
Oswald, Lee Harvey, 239

Page, Brent, 282n.
Pagelow, Mildred Daley, 260n., 261n.
Palendrano, Marion, 213–215
Palermo, George B., 44n.
Pallone, Nathaniel J., 93n., 95n., 185n.
Palme, Olof, 239
Palmer, C., 282n.
Palmer, David Scott, 338n.
Pankan, Edmund J., 283n.
Park, Robert E., 110–111, *111*, 121n.
Parker, Howard, 339–340n.
Parrot, Andrea, 261n.
Pasework, Richard A., 229n.
Passas, Nikos, 121n.
Paternoster, Raymond, 121n., 165n., 185n.
Paterson, E. Britt, 122n.
Patterson, Gerald R., 78, 94n.
Pearce, Frank S., 306n.
Pearson, Frank S., 165n.
Pearson, Karl, 57
Pease, Ken, 185n.
Pease, Susan, 96n.
Peck, Jeffrey, 186n., 283n.
Pedersen, Daniel, 259n.
Peel, Robert, 217–218
Peeples, Faith, 122n.
Pepinsky, Harold E., 206n., 207–208n.
Perkins, Joseph, 164n.
Perl, Raphael F., 366n.
Perlin, Michael L., 228n.
Pervin, Lawrence A., 95n.
Petee, Thomas A., 122n.
Peters, Eric, 269n.
Petersilia, Joan, 45n.
Peterson, Ruth D., 261n.
Pfefferbaum, Betty, 340n.
Phillips, Coretta, 185n.

Piaget, Jean, 154
Pierce, Glenn L., 262n.
Pilchen, Saul M., 308n.
Pileggi, Nicholas, 311n.
Piliavin, Irving, 150, 164n.
Pillsbury, Samuel H., 17n.
Pinel, Philippe, 60, 65n., 82
Pittman, Karen J., 261n.
Pitts, Victoria L., 186n.
Planty, M. C., 121n.
Plato, 47, 64n., 200
Platt, Anthony M., 193, 201, 202, 206n.
Pleck, Elizabeth, 259–260n.
Poel, Sari van der, 340n.
Pogrebin, Mark R., 122n.
Polanzi, C., 309n.
Polk, Kenneth, 144n., 259n., 307n., 365n.
Pollack, Otto, 40, 45n.
Polsky, Ned, 338n.
Polvi, Natalie, 185n.
Pomeroy, Wardel B., 340n., 341n.
Pontell, Henry N., 306n., 307n., 309n.
Poole, Eric D., 122n.
Popkin, Susan J., 336n.
Porta, Giambattista della, 53, 63
Possuelo, Sidney, 101
Potter, Elaine, 308n.
Pottieger, Anne E., 338n., 340n.
Pound, Roscoe, 206n.
Powell, Kevin, 13n.
Power, William, 307n.
Poyner, Barry, 283n.
Prat, Tamar, 261n.
Preble, Edward, 337n., 338n.
Prendergast, M. L., 94n.
Preston, James D., 337n.
Prichard, James C., 82
Prince, Joyce, 282n.
Puig-Antich, J., 95n.
Purnell, Sonia, 361n.

Quételet, Adolphe, 61, 63, 65n., 170, 184n., 200
Quinney, Richard, 201–202, 204, 206n., 207–208n., 306n., 309n.

Rachlin, Harvey, 336n.
Rackmill, Stephen J., 306n.
Rada, R. T., 96n.
Radosevich, Marcia J., 120n., 144n.
Radzinowicz, Leon, 64n.
Rafter, Nicole Hahn, 64–65n.
Rahman, Mujibur, 239
Raith, Werner, 310n.
Rankin, Joseph H., 165n.
Rapp, Doris J., 96n.
Rappleye, Charles, 310n.
Rasche, Christine, 260n.
Rasmussen, David W., 338n.
Ratsimandraua, Richard, 239
Ray, Isaac, 60, 63, 65n.
Ray, Jo-Ann, 282n.
Ray, M., 206n.
Reagan, Ronald, 215, 217, 239, 257, 290
Reasons, Charles E., 309n.
Reaves, Brian A., 43n.

Rebovich, Donald J., 298, 298n., 311n.
Reckless, Walter C., 158, *158*, 159–160, 165n.
Redfern, Allison, 283n.
Reed, Gary E., 309n.
Reichel, Philip L., 207n.
Reichman, Nancy, 307n.
Reige, Mary, 165n.
Reinarman, Craig, 122n.
Reinhold, Robert, 146n.
Reisman, Judith A., 340n., 341n.
Reiss, Albert J., Jr., 88, 95n., 96n., 120n., 122n., 128, 144n., 156–157, 165n., 259n., 309n., 310n.
Renfrew, P., 306n.
Rengert, George, 170, *170*, 185n.
Rennie, Ysabel, 120n.
Reno, Janet, *20*
Retting, Richard P., 336n.
Reuben, David, 340n.
Reuvid, Jonathan, 365n.
Reynolds, Ray, 178
Rhodes, Albert L., 88, 96n., 120n., 122n., 128, 144n.
Rich, Marc, 3
Richards, Pamela J., 340n.
Richardson, Genevra, 310n.
Richardson, John E., 94n.
Richberg, D. R., 308n.
Riedel, Marc, 234–235, 259n.
Rifkin, Joel, 235
Rimm, Marty, 341n.
Ritti, R. Richard, 340n.
Rivara, Frederick P., 262n.
Rivera, Ramon, 145n.
Rivers, James E., 338n.
Robb, George, 308n.
Roberts, Albert R., 260n.
Roberts, Mary K., 164n.
Roberts, Nickie, 340n.
Robin, R. D., 96n.
Robins, Lee N., 75, 94n.
Robinson, Paul H., 228n., 229n.
Rock, Joe, 300
Rodriguez, Orlando, 165n.
Roemer, William F., Jr., 311n.
Rogan, Dennis P., 260n., 262n.
Rokeach, Milton, 165n.
Romilly, Samuel, 52
Roncek, Dennis W., 185n., 186n.
Rook, Karen S., 165n.
Roosevelt, Franklin D., 239
Roosevelt, Theodore, 239, 294
Rose, R. M., 96n.
Rosecrance, John, 282n.
Rosen, Lawrence, 165n.
Rosenbaum, Jill Leslie, 146n., 165n.
Rosenbaum, Marsha, 337n.
Rosenbaum, Ron, 59n.
Rosenfeld, Richard, 43n., 106–107, 121n.
Rosenhan, D. L., 194, 194n., 206n.
Rosenthal, A. M., 214n.
Ross, E. A., 149
Ross, Edward Frank, 168
Ross, Elizabeth, 31n.
Rossi, Peter H., 262n.
Rostenkowski, Dan, 42

Roth, Jeffrey A., 44n., 95n., 259n.
Roth, William, *290*
Rothstein, Arnold, 300
Rousseau, Jean-Jacques, 50
Rowe, David C., 86, 95n.
Ruback, Barry R., 259n.
Rude, George, 64n.
Rumsey, Spencer, 252n.
Rusche, Georg, 200–201, 207n.
Ruth, David E., 310n.
Rutter, Michael, 93n., 96n.
Rzeplinski, Andrzej, 207n.

Sachs, Andrea, 197n.
Sadat, Anwar El-, 239
Sagarin, Edward, 91, 96n.
Sagi, Philip C., 234, 259n.
Salem, Hussein, 239
Salerno, Ralph, 308n.
Salzano, Julienne, 311n.
Samenow, Stanton, 80, 94n.
Samper, Ernesto, 323
Sampson, Robert J., 44n., 45n., 65n., 121n., 160, *160*, 165n., 185n.
Sanabria, Harry, 185n., *315*
Sand, Leonard, 197
Sandberg, A. A., 95n.
Sanders, Joseph, 365n.
Santino, Umberto, 311n.
Savona, Ernesto U., 310n.
Saxon, Miriam S., 309n.
Scarpitti, Frank R., 165n., 311n.
Scarr, Sandra, 88, 96n.
Schaaf, Tim, 168
Schafer, Walter B., 144n.
Schaffer, Richard, 309n.
Schatzberg, Rufus, 261n.
Schlegel, Kip, 306n., 309n., 310n.
Schlossman, Steven, 122n.
Schmeidler, James, 338n.
Schmidt, Janell D., 260n.
Schneider, Elizabeth, 30n.
Schneider, Hans Joachim, 365n.
Schoenberg, Robert J., 310n.
Schoenthaler, Stephen, 89, 96n.
Schott, Ian, 310n.
Schrag, Clarence, 159, 165n.
Schrager, Laura S., 309n.
Schuessler, Karl E., 80, 94n.
Schultz, Dutch, 300, 326
Schuman, Karl, 365n.
Schur, Edwin M., 191, 206n.
Schwartz, Martin D., 186n., 207n., 247, 261n.
Schwartz, Richard D., 193, 206n.
Schweinhart, Lawrence J., 121n.
Schweitzer, Yoram, 261n.
Schwendinger, Herman, 201, 202, 207n., 246, 261n.
Schwendinger, Julia R., 201, 202, 207n., 246, 261n.
Schwind, Hans-Dieter, 365n.
Sciolino, Elaine, 339n.
Scott, Austin W., Jr., 228n., 258n.
Scott, Heather, 340n.
Scott, Peter, 65n.

Scott, Richard O., 262*n*.
Scronce, Christine A., 339*n*.
Scully, D., 261*n*.
Sears, Kenneth C., 283*n*.
Seda, Heriberto (Zodiac Killer), 69–70, 235
Seidman, Robert, 202, 207*n*., 309*n*.
Sellin, Thorsten, 38, 44*n*., 56, 64*n*., 65*n*., 96*n*., 117, 119, 122*n*., 145*n*.
Selva, Lance H., 207*n*.
Sennewald, Charles A., 282*n*.
Serrill, Michael S., 333*n*.
Sessar, Klaus, 363*n*.
Sforza, Daniel, 184*n*.
Shaffer, John W., 339*n*.
Shakespeare, William, 53
Shakur, Tupac Amaru (2Pac), 12–13
Shapiro, Susan P., 306*n*., 309*n*., 310*n*.
Shavelson, Richard, 122*n*.
Shaw, Clifford R., 111, 113, 114, 115, 121*n*., 144*n*.
Shaw, James W., 262*n*.
Shearing, Clifford D., 186*n*.
Shedd, Ed, 310*n*.
Sheldon, William H., 58, 59, *63*, 65*n*.
Sheley, Joseph F., 262*n*., 337*n*.
Shelley, Louise I., 273, 310*n*., 348, 363*n*., 364*n*.
Shelly, Peggy, 282*n*.
Sheppard, David I., 260*n*.
Sherman, Lawrence W., 25, 43*n*., 176–177, 185*n*., 186*n*., 260*n*., 262*n*.
Shichor, David, 287*n*., 364*n*.
Shoemaker, Donald J., *110*, *126*, *129*, *135*, 145*n*., 165*n*.
Short, James F., Jr., 116, 120*n*., 128, 138, 144*n*., 145*n*., 146*n*., 165*n*., 309*n*.
Short, James S., 122*n*.
Shover, Neal, 44*n*., 279, 283*n*.
Sibbitt, Rae, 339*n*.
Sickmund, Melissa, 146*n*.
Siegal, Harvey A., 336*n*.
Siegel, Martin A., 3
Silas, Faye, 340*n*.
Silver, H. K., 259*n*.
Silverman, F. N., 259*n*.
Silverman, Robert A., 234, 259*n*.
Silverstein, Martin E., *138*, 146*n*.
Simon, David R., 287*n*.
Simon, Jeffrey D., 261*n*.
Simon, Patricia M., 340*n*.
Simon, Rita James, 40, 41, 45*n*.
Simons, Marlise, 333*n*.
Simons, Ronald L., 45*n*.
Simpson, John, 45*n*., 165*n*.
Simpson, Nicole Brown, 242
Simpson, O. J., 3, 242
Simpson, Sally S., 45*n*., 185*n*., 207*n*., 306*n*., 307*n*., 310*n*.
Sims, Ronald R., 309*n*.
Singer, Simon I., *35*, 145*n*., 261*n*.
Skolnick, Jerome H., 17*n*., 193, 206*n*.
Skoog, Dagna K., 94*n*.
Sloane, Leonard, 283*n*.
Slovenko, Ralph, 228*n*.
Smith, Brent L., 261*n*.
Smith, Carolyn, 122*n*., 146*n*., 260–261*n*.
Smith, Dietrich, 283*n*.

Smith, Douglas A., 41, 44*n*., 45*n*., 113, 120*n*., 122*n*., 165*n*., 260*n*.
Smith, Dwight, 286, 306*n*., 311*n*.
Smith, Gene M., 338*n*.
Smith, Greg B., 336*n*.
Smith, Jinney S., 65*n*.
Smith, Lynn Newhart, 121–122*n*.
Smith, M. Dwayne, 45*n*., 261*n*., 262*n*.
Smith, Mary S., 186*n*.
Smith, Maurice B., 44*n*.
Snell, Cudore L., 340*n*.
Snider, Laureen, 306*n*., 309*n*., 310*n*.
Snyder, Howard N., 146*n*.
Socrates, 47, 53
Sommers, Ira, 122*n*., 339*n*.
Somoza Debayle, Anastasio, 239
Son of Sam (David Berkowitz), 235
Sophocles, 47, 64*n*.
Sorenson, Ann Marie, 145*n*., 166*n*., 337*n*.
Sorenson, Susan B., 261*n*.
Souryal, Sam S., 364*n*., 365*n*.
South, Steve J., 122*n*.
Southwick, L., 340*n*.
Sparks, Richard F., *24*, 202, 207*n*., 309*n*.
Speck, Richard, 85
Speckart, George, 338*n*.
Spellman, William, 185*n*., 186*n*.
Spencer, J., 364*n*.
Spencer, Margaret P., 309*n*.
Spergel, Irving A., 259*n*.
Spiegel, Ulrich, 122*n*.
Spindler, James W., 203*n*.
Spohn, Cassia C., 261*n*.
Spradley, James P., 206*n*.
Spunt, Barry, 338*n*.
Spurzheim, Johann Kaspar, 53, *63*
Squitieri, Tom, 44*n*.
Sroufe, L., 93*n*.
Stack, Susan A., 95*n*.
Stalin, Joseph, 212
Stan, Adele M., 341*n*.
Stark, Rodney, 121*n*.
Stattin, Hakan, 95*n*.
Stauffenberg, Klaus von, 239
Steele, B. F., 259*n*.
Steele, C. M., 340*n*.
Steffensmeier, Darrell J., 44*n*., 45*n*., 166*n*., 280, 283*n*., 307*n*.
Steffy, Richard A., 340*n*.
Stenning, Philip C., 186*n*.
Stephen, James Fitzjames, 326
Stephens, Richard C., 339*n*.
Stephenson, Philip, 339*n*.
Sterling, Claire, 310*n*.
Stevens, Larry, 235
Stevens, William K., 340*n*.
Stewart, V. Lorne, 363*n*.
Stillwell, Gary, 339*n*.
Stolberg, Mary M., 310*n*.
Straus, Murray A., 242, 260*n*., 339*n*.
Streifel, Cathy, 44*n*.
Strodtbeck, Fred L., 144*n*., 165*n*.
Sullivan, John P., *138*, 146*n*.
Sumner, Maggie, 339–340*n*.
Sunset Strip killer (Douglas Clark), 235
Supancic, Michael, 122*n*.

Sutherland, Edwin H., 6, 7, 11, 17*n*., 22, 43*n*., 61, 79, 88, 95*n*., 115–117, 122*n*., 125, 267, 282*n*., 286, 295, 306*n*., 308*n*., 309*n*.
Swanson, James W., 96*n*.
Swazzi, Vincent, 280
Swift, Carolyn M., 260*n*.
Swiss, Shana, 366*n*.
Sykes, Alan O., 308*n*.
Sykes, Gresham M., 145*n*., 165*n*., 178, 186*n*., 207*n*., 326
Szumski, Bonnie, 341*n*.

Takagi, Paul, 201
Talese, Gay, 311*n*.
Tannenbaum, Frank, 190, 205*n*.
Tappan, Paul W., 17*n*.
Tarde, Gabriel, 61, *63*, 65*n*., 200
Taylor, Ian, 121*n*., 201, 207*n*., 309*n*.
Taylor, Max, 185*n*.
Taylor, Ralph B., 113, 121*n*., 122*n*., 179*n*.
Taylor, Robert W., 283*n*.
Tedeschi, James T., 95*n*., 241, 259*n*.
Teevan, James J., 166*n*.
Tennenbaum, Daniel J., 80, 94*n*.
Tennyson, Ray, 145*n*.
Terlouw, Gert-Jan, 44*n*., 364*n*.
Terrill, Richard J., 363*n*.
Terry, Don, 144*n*., 145*n*.
Tesoriero, James M., 146*n*., 262*n*.
Thomas, Charles W., 206*n*.
Thomas, Evan, 34*n*.
Thomas, George, 337*n*.
Thomas, Jim, 207*n*.
Thomas, Jo, 254*n*.
Thomas, William I., 110, 121*n*., 190, 205*n*.
Thompson, Bill, 341*n*.
Thompson, Carol Y., 44*n*.
Thompson, Dick, 95*n*.
Thompson, Kevin M., 145*n*.
Thompson, Marilyn W., 307*n*.
Thornberry, Terence P., 39, 44*n*., 105, 120*n*., 145*n*., 146*n*., 157, *160*, 160, 165*n*., 261*n*., 262*n*.
Thrasher, Frederick M., 121*n*.
Thurman, Tracey, 243
Tillman, Robert, 309*n*.
Tittle, Charles R., 41, 44*n*., 45*n*., 104, 120*n*., 122*n*., 166*n*., 206*n*.
Titus, Richard M., 186*n*., 307*n*.
Tobias, Andrew, 308*n*.
Toby, Jackson, 150, 157–158, 164*n*., 165*n*., 207*n*.
Toch, Hans, 93*n*.
Tolbert, William R., 239
Tompkins, John S., 308*n*.
Tonry, Michael H., 185*n*., 309*n*.
Tontodonato, Pamela, 243, 260*n*.
Topinard, Paul, 4, 17*n*.
Torres, Manuel J., 336*n*.
Torresola, Griselio, 239
Torrio, Johnny, 300
Toufexis, Anastasia, 228*n*.
Tracy, Paul E., *35*, 38, 44*n*., 261*n*., 291, 308*n*.
Trafficante, Santo, Jr., 303
Trasler, Gordon, 44*n*.
Travis, Gail, 364*n*.
Treaster, Joseph B., 145*n*.

Trebach, Arnold S., 339n.
Tremblay, Pierre, 283n.
Tremblay, Richard E., 94n.
Trickett, Alan, 185n.
Triplett, Ruth A., 45n., 206n.
Tromanhauser, Edward D., 145n.
Truman, Harry S., 239
Tulloch, M. I., 94n.
Tunis, Sandra L., 339n.
Turajilik, Hakija, 239
Turk, Austin T., 197–198, 199, 206n., 207n.
Turnbull, Paul J., 339n.
Turner, J. W. Cecil, 282n.
Tutorskaya, Svetlana, 359n.

Ugelow, Stewart, 337n.
Ulloa, Fernando Cepeda, 338n.
Unisacke, Suzanne, 229n.

Valachi, Joe, 301, 302
Van Bemmelen, J. M., 207n.
Van Dijk, Jan J. M., 364n.
Vaughn, Michael S., 365n.
Verhovek, Sam Howe, 259n.
Verri, Pietro, 50
Viano, Emilio C., 365n.
Victor, Hope R., 338n.
Villar, Roger, 270n.
Villemez, Wayne J., 41, 45n., 120n.
Virgil, 200
Virkkunen, Matti, 90, 96n.
Visher, Christy A., 44n.
Volavka, Jan, 91, 96n.
Vold, George B., 64n., 196–197, 206n.
Volkman, Ernest, 311n.
Voltaire, 50, 51
Voss, Harwin L., 45n., 121n., 128, 144n.
Voss, Natalie D., 283n., 365n.

Waksler, Frances C., 8, 8, 17n.
Walder, Patrice, 282n.
Waldo, G. P., 94n.
Waldorf, Dan, 146n., 339n.
Walker, Lenore E. A., 224, 225n., 260n.
Walker, Samuel, 262n.
Walklate, Sandra, 287n.
Wall, Jose, 254
Wallace, George C., 239
Wallace, Marjorie, 308n.
Waller, Douglas, 16n.
Waller, John B., Jr., 262n.
Wallerstein, James S., 28, 43n.
Wallis, Lynne, 101n.
Walmsley, Roy, 364n.
Walsh, Anthony, 206n.
Walston, James, 311n.

Walt, Steven, 308n.
Walton, Paul, 121n., 201, 207n., 309n.
Ward, David A., 206n.
Waring, Elin J., 306–307n.
Warner, John, 339n.
Warr, Mark, 116, 122n., 144n., 145n.
Warren, Carol, 206n.
Warren, Earl, 189
Washburn, S. L., 65n.
Wasilchick, John, 170, 170, 185n.
Watanavich, Prathan, 309n.
Waters, Harry F., 77, 79, 79n.
Watson, Sylvia M., 93–94n.
Weatherburn, Don, 166n.
Weaver, Frances, 283n.
Webster, Russell, 339n.
Wechsler, Henry, 337n.
Weekart, David P., 121n.
Weeks, Susan L., 307n.
Wegner, Norma, 339n.
Weihofen, Henry, 283n.
Weinberg, Bo and George, 300
Weinberg, Richard, 88, 96n.
Weiner, Neil Alan, 145n., 165n., 259n.
Weis, Joseph G., 29, 44n., 160, 161, 166n., 338n.
Weisburd, David, 165n., 166n., 186n., 306–307n., 309n., 310n.
Weller, Christine L., 337n.
Wellford, Charles F., 165n., 195, 206n.
Wells, L. Edward, 165n.
Wernz, Gerald W., 307n.
Wertham, Frederic, 175, 185n.
Weston, William, 307n., 365n.
Wheeler, Stanton L., 306–307n., 310n.
White, Byron, 334
White, Dan, 89
White, Helene Raskin, 121n.
White, Jacqueline W., 261n.
Wiatrowski, Michael D., 164n.
Widlake, Brian, 310n.
Widom, Cathy Spatz, 93n., 260n.
Wiechman, Dennis, 365n.
Wiegand, R. Bruce, 364n.
Wiegman, O., 94n.
Wiersema, Brian, 259n., 262n.
Wikström, Per-Olof H., 186n., 365n.
Wilbanks, William, 258n.
Wild, Jonathan, 279–280
Wilkins, Leslie T., 23, 43n., 365n.
Williams, Frank P., III, 13n., 120n., 341n.
Williams, J. Sherwood, 145n.
Williams, Phil, 310n., 366n.
Williams, Terry, 315
Williams, Timothy L., 307n.
Wilson, Colin, 310n.
Wilson, Edward O., 84, 95n.

Wilson, James Q., 37, 44n., 59, 59n., 88, 92, 96n., 257, 295, 309n.
Wilson, Margo I., 259n., 365n.
Wilson, Nanci Koser, 45n., 259n.
Wilson, William Julius, 102, 120n., 234, 258n.
Winerip, Michael, 262n.
Wingert, Pat, 121n.
Winslow, Robert W., 340n.
Winslow, Virginia, 340n.
Winters, Ken C., 337n.
Wise, Edward M., 363n., 366n.
Wish, Eric, 338n.
Wisniewski, N., 261n.
Witkin, Herman A., 95n.
Woessnar, Paul H., 366n.
Wolfe, Nancy T., 45n.
Wolfgang, Marvin E., 33, 35, 38, 43n., 44n., 56, 64n., 65n., 88, 96n., 125, 132, 145n., 234, 258–259n., 260n., 261n., 295, 327, 339n.
Wood, Peter B., 340n.
Woodall, Ruth, 283n.
Wooden, Wayne S., 126n., 146n., 283n.
Woodiwiss, Michael, 366n.
Woods, Grant, 285
Wormith, J. Stephen, 94n.
Wright, James D., 262n.
Wright, Richard T., 185n., 283n.
Wright, Stewart A., 262n.
Wyle, Clement J., 28, 43n.

Yeager, Peter Cleary, 295, 306n., 309n.
Yeudall, Lorne T., 96n.
Yllo, Kersti, 261n.
Yochelson, Samuel, 80, 94n.
Young, Jock, 121n., 201, 207n., 309n.
Young, Timothy R., 309n.
Young, Vernetta D., 45n.
Yozwiak, Steve, 306n.

Zahn, Margaret A., 234, 259n.
Zangrillo, Patricia, 260n.
Zawitz, Marianne W., 262n.
Zellman, Goul, 122n.
Zerilli, Joe, 303
Zillman, Dolf, 341n.
Zimring, Franklin E., 262n., 341n.
Zinberg, Norman E., 338n.
Zineb, Khazouni, 260n.
Zion, Sidney, 311n.
Znaniecki, Florian, 110, 121n.
Zodiac Killer (Heriberto Seda), 69–70, 235
Zorza, Joan, 260n.
Zvekic, Ugljesa, 364n., 365n.

SUBJECT INDEX

SUBJECT INDEX

Note: *Italicized* page numbers indicate tables and figures; page numbers followed by *n.* indicate material in notes. This index also includes the names of cases.

Abuse:
  alcohol (*see* Alcohol abuse)
  child (*see* Child abuse)
  drug (*see* Drug abuse)
  sexual (*see* Rape; Sex-related crimes)
  spouse (*see* Spouse abuse)
Academy of Fists (Italy), 50
Accommodation, 106–107
Accomplices, 227
Accusations, false, 192
Acquaintance rape, 246
Acquired Immune Deficiency Syndrome (AIDS), 319, 333
Act requirement, as crime ingredient, 212–213
Adaptation, modes of, 103–104
Addict robbers, 248
Addiction to drugs (*see* Drug abuse)
Adjudication:
  (*See also* Courts)
Adoption studies, 86
Advertising, deceptive, 291
Aesop's fables, 19
Africa, 204, 346 (*See also names of specific African nations*)
African Americans (*see* Blacks)
Age:
  crime and, 28, 35–39, 233, 235, 237, 277
  criminal liability and, 211–212, 221
  (*See also* Delinquency)
Age of Enlightenment, 52
Aggravated assault, 24, 241
Aggression:
  biochemical factors and, 88–91
  genetic factors in, 84–87
  as instrumental behavior, 241
  masculinity and, 246
  neurophysiological factors and, 91
  social learning theory and, 77–80
  (*See also* Violence; Violent crimes)
Aging-out phenomenon, 36–37
AIDS (Acquired Immune Deficiency Syndrome), 319, 333
Aircraft:
  bombing of, 5, 15, 354
  hijacking of, 356–357
Alabama:
  Birmingham, 137
Alaska:
  Exxon Valdez oil spill, 4, 292, 296

Albania, 141, 204
Alcohol, Tobacco, and Firearms, Bureau of, 5, 254, 255
Alcohol abuse, 27, 153, 177, 325–328
  child abuse and, 244
  crimes related to, 326–328
  drunk driving, 215, 327–328, 353
  history of legalization, 300, 325–326
  intoxication defense, 220
  spouse abuse and, 242
Alcoholic robbers, 248
Algeria, 162
Allied Chemical Corporation, 296, 297
Amateur thieves, 266–267
Amazon tribes, 101
America, colonial, 220
American Association for the Advancement of Science, 87
American Bar Association (ABA), 24
American Dream, 106
American Humane Association (AHA), 243
American Law Institute (A.L.I.):
  insanity test, 219
  Model Penal Code (*see* Model Penal Code)
American Skinheads (Hamm), 344
Amish, 109–110
Amphetamines, 319
Anglo-American law (*see* Common law)
Anomic suicide, 100, 101
Anomie:
  Durkheim and, 62, 99–100
  Merton's formula for, 100–103
  strain theory and, 100–103
  suicide and, 100, 101
Anti-Drug Abuse Act (1988), 316
Anti-government fraud, 289–290, 292
Antisocial personality, 82–83
Antitrust violations, 285, 286, 294
Arizona, 105, 254, 285
  Phoenix, 254
  Tucson, 117, 140
Armenia, 203
Arousal, cortical, 81
Arrest:
  for child abuse, 244
Arson, 24, 27, 227, 281–282
Art theft, 268, 354
Assassinations, 199, 232, 239
  attempted, 239

Assault, 24, 27, 237–241, 327
  battery and, 241
  sexual (*see* Rape)
Atavistic stigmata, 54–56, 57
Atlanta, Georgia, 133, 136, 137
  Olympic Park bombing, 5, 15
Atlantic City, New Jersey, 114
Attachment theory, 73–77, 150–151, 153, 244
Attempted crime, 227
  assassination, 239
Attention deficit hyperactivity disorder, 91
Attorney General's Commission on Pornography (1986), 332–334
Aum Shinrikyo, 253
Australia, 346, 353
Austria, 255
Automobiles:
  carjacking, 154–155, 269
  drive-by shootings, 4, 12–13, 138, 237, 256
  drunk driving, 215, 327–328, 353
  motor vehicle theft, 24, 27, 168–169, 179–184, 268, 269
  parking facilities, 182–184
  Volkswagen crest thefts, 173–174
Aversive instigators, 78–79

Baby-boom generation, 31
Babylon, laws of, 9
Balkanization, 362
Baltic nations, 203
Baltimore, Maryland, 143
Bangladesh, 239
Bank of Credit and Commerce International (BCCI) scandal, 361
Bank Secrecy Act, 294
Banking industry:
  BCCI scandal, 361
  check forging and, 272
  credit card crime and, 272–273, 277
  high-tech crime and, 273–274, 275
  money laundering, 321–323, 354, 355, 358
  savings and loan scandal, 286
Bankruptcy fraud, 289, 358
Barbiturates, 319
Battered-child syndrome, 76, 241 (*See also* Child abuse)
Battery, 241
Bayer Company, 316

BCCI (Bank of Credit and Commerce International) scandal, 361
Behavioral modeling, 77
Belarus, 203
Belgium, 29, 61, 250, 343
Beliefs, social bonds theory and, 152–153
Belize, 321
Berkeley, California, 247–248
Bias crimes, 5, 142, 252, 343–344
Bible, 53, 118
Bigotry, 5
Binet scale, 87–88
Biochemical factors, 88–91
    diet, 89–90
    food allergies, 88–89
    hormones, 90–91
    hypoglycemia, 90
Biocriminology, biological determinism, 53–60, 62, 63, 84–92
    biochemical factors in, 88–91
    criticisms of, 92
    inherited criminality, 59–60, 84–87
    IQ tests and, 55, 60, 87–88, 92
    neuropsychological factors, 91
    pioneers of, 53–57, 63
    somatotype school of criminology, 57–59
Birmingham, Alabama, 137
Birth cohorts, 38–39
Blacks:
    civil rights and, 189
    conduct norms, 117–119
    drive-by shootings and, 12–13
    equal rights for, 189
    gangs and, 134, 140
    House of Umoja, Philadelphia, 143
    music of, 12–13
    police brutality and, 112, 222
Blaming the victim, 176
Boat theft, 268–270
Boggs Act (1951), 316
Boiler rooms, 289
Bolivia, 321, 323, 324
Bombings:
    airline, 5, 15, 354
    Oklahoma City, 15, 253, 254
    Olympic Park, Atlanta, Georgia, 5, 15
    World Trade Center, 15, 354
    (*See also* Terrorism)
"Born criminal," 54–56
Bosnia, 16, 239
Boston, Massachusetts, 114, 143, 256
    Coconut Grove disaster, 233
    conflict resolution programs, 117
    Mid-City Project, 115
Brady bill, 257
Brain lesions, tumors, 91
Branch Davidian cult, 118, 251–253
"Brazen theory," 155
Brazil, 101, 333, 343, 359
Breaking of laws (*see* Law-breaking)
Breathalyzer, 328
Bribery, 290, 292, 295, 359–360
Bridgeport, Connecticut, 163
British Crime Survey, 176
Brutality, police, 112, 222
Bulgaria, 162, 204

Burglars and burglary, 24, 27, 170–171, 176, 279
Burundi, 16
Business opportunity fraud, 291
Buy-back programs, for handguns, 257

Cali cartel, 300, 323
California, 105, 128, 131, 140, 150–153, 157, 168, 213, 256, 334
    Berkeley, 247–248
    community response to rape, 247–248
    drunk driving and, 327–328
    "munchkin" case, 211–212, 221
    San Diego, 143, 163
    San Francisco, 140, 236, 257, 319
    (*See also* Los Angeles, California)
California Psychological Inventory (CPI), 80
Cambridge Study of Delinquent Development, 160–161
Canada, 90, 105, 119, 161, 255, 258, 346
Cannabis, 316
Capital punishment, 21, 51, 57, 196, 232–233, 239, 249
Capitalism, 200, 201
Car theft (*see* Motor vehicle theft)
Carjacking, 154–155, 269
Case studies, 22
Caste system, Hindu, 103
Causation requirement, as crime ingredient, 212, 215
Causes of Delinquency (Hirschi), 150
Censorship, 334–335
Census Bureau, U.S., 23, 27
Challenge of Crime in a Free Society, The, 14
Charleston, South Carolina, 163
Charlotte, North Carolina, 29, 32
Cheating (*see* Fraud)
Check forging, 272
Cheyenne culture, 350
Chicago, Illinois, 143, 156–157, 199
    Chicago Area Project, 114–115
    community action projects, 114–115, 163
    conflict resolution programs, 117
    gangs in, 133, 136
    homicide rates in, 233–234
    immigrant population in, 98–99, 110–113, 193
    juvenile courts, 193, 345
    social disorganization studies and, 110–113, 114–115
Chicago Area Project, 114–115
Child abuse, 76, 132, 235, 241, 243–245
    battered-child syndrome, 76, 241
    extent of, 243–244
    nature of, 244–245
    and parricide, 76
Child pornography, 276–277
Children:
    attachment theory and, 73–77, 150–151, 153, 244
    infancy defense, 211–212, 220–221
    juvenile homicide, 37, 38
    prostitution and, 331, 332–333
    statutory rape, 329
    and trade in human body parts, 359
    (*See also* Child abuse; Child pornography; Delinquency; Family)

Chile, 239, 250
China, 4, 26, 78–79, 346
    Tiananmen Square uprising, 79
Chinese triad gangs, 4, 130–131, 141, 300, 305, 321
Choice structuring properties, 171–172
Churning, 289
Cincinnati, Ohio, 328
Citibank, 273–274
Cities (*see* Urban areas)
Civil law, 346
Civil rights:
    high-tech crimes and, 278
    law enforcement and, 189
Civil unrest:
    in the 1960s, 191–192
Class:
    characteristics of, 198
    conflict model of crime and, 9–10, 41–42, 196, 199
    crime and, 41–42, 104–105, 132–133, 277
    delinquency and, 41–42, 124–144, 193
    interest groups versus, 202–203
    lower (*see* Lower class)
    middle (*see* Middle class)
    socioeconomic development and crime, 352–353
    working, 111, 199–200, 246
    (*See also* Conflict theory; Radical theory; Strain theory)
Class, State, and Crime (Quinney), 201–202
Classical school of criminology, 49–53, 345
    Beccaria and, 50–52
    described, 47–48
    evaluation of, 52–53
    free will in, 49–52
    historical context of, 49–50
    time line of, 62, 63
    utilitarianism, 52, 171
Clayton Antitrust Act (1914), 294
Clean Water Act, 295
Cleveland, Ohio, 143
Cloward and Ohlin's theory (*see* Differential opportunity theory)
Coast Guard, U.S., 4
Coca-Cola, cocaine used in, 316
Cocaine, 316, 317, 319, 321, 323, 325
    crack, 317, 319, 320
Coconut Grove disaster (Boston), 233
Code of Hammurabi, 9
Codeine, 316
Cohen's theory (*see* Middle-class, as measuring rod)
College boys, 126
Collusion, 290
Colombia, 250, 300, 305, 313, 321, 323, 324, 359
Colonial America, 220
Colorado, 168
    Denver, 39, 131
    insanity defense, 219
Commerce Department, U.S., 345
Commission on Obscenity and Pornography (1970), 332–334
Commitment, social bonds theory and, 151–152, 153

Common law, *348*
    attempted crimes, 227
    gambling and, 326
    kidnapping and, 249
    larceny and, 265
    legality requirement, 213–215
    origins of, 346
    prevention of crime and, 183
    rape and, 247
Communications Decency Act (CDA) of 1996, 335
Communist Manifesto (Marx), 200
Community action projects, 115, 163, 247–248
Community Tolerance Study, 105
Comparative criminology, 343–363
    crime rate and, 162, 351
    defined, 344–345
    globalization and, 14, 345–346, 362
    goals of, 346, 353–362
    history of, 345–346
    preparatory work for, 346–349
    research process for, 346, 349–352
    theory testing in, 352–353
Comparative Criminology (Holyst), 351
Comparative Criminology (Mannheim), 351
Comprehensive Drug Abuse Prevention and Control Act (1970), 316
Computer network break-ins, 273–274, 275–276, 357
Computers (*see* High-tech crimes)
Concept of crime (*see* Crime)
Concurrence requirement, as crime ingredient, 212, 216
Condition of the Working Class in England, The (Engels), 199–200
Conditioned free will, 92
Conditioning, 81
Conduct norms, 117–119, 134
Confidence games, 272, 291
Confidential information, 292
Conflict gangs, 130
Conflict model, 9–10, *189*, 196
    empirical evidence for, 199
    social class and crime, 9–10, 41–42, 196, 199
Conflict resolution, 117
Conflict theory, 195–199
    conflict model in, 9–10, 41–42, 196, 199
    consensus model in, 9, *189*, 195–196
    criminology and, 196–199
Conformity, 103, 157–158
Congo, 239
Connecticut:
    Bridgeport, 163
Conscience, 71, 81
Consensus model, 9, *189*, 195–196, 199
    (*See also* Classical school of criminology; Positivist criminology)
Constitution, U.S.:
    due process guaranteed by, 49, 189
Constitutional amendments, 189
    First, 334
    Second, 253, 257–258
    Eighth, 213
    Eighteenth, 299–300, 325, 326
    Twenty-Sixth, 328
Consumer fraud, 291

Containment theory, 158–160
    evaluation of, 159–160
    probability of deviance in, 158–159
    tests of, 159
Control theory (*see* Social control theory)
Convenience-store robberies, 171, 181–184
Conventional morality, 72, 73
Conventional society, conventional values (*see* Conformity)
Corn, 88–89, 90
Corner boys, 126
Corporate crime, 285, 292–299
    antitrust violations, 285, 286, 294
    BCCI scandal, 361
    corporate liability and, 293, 297
    curbing, 297–299
    environmental, 4, 292–294, 295–297, 298, 353, 357
    government control of corporations and, 293–294
    insider-related, 289, 292
    investigating, 294–295
    savings and loan scandal, 286
    victims of, 287
Correctional facilities:
    (*see* Jails; Penitentiaries; Prisons)
Corruption, 292, 359–360
Cortical arousal, 81
Cosa Nostra, 286, 299, 301–304, 321
Costa Rica, 162
Course in Positive Philosophy (Comte), 53
Court system, U.S.:
    juvenile, 193, 345
    (*See also* Supreme Court, U.S.)
Courts:
    international, 360–362
    system of (*see* Court system, U.S.)
Crack cocaine, 317, 319, 320
Craniometry, 55
Crank, 319
Credit card crimes, 272–273, 277
Crime:
    age and, 35–39 (*See also* Delinquency)
    alcohol-related (*see* Alcohol abuse)
    attempted, 227, 239
    causes of, 7, 11–12, 20
    characteristics of, 29–34
        crime trends as, 29–31
        high-tech crimes, 274–275
        location and timing, 31–33
        severity, 33–34, *35*, 245–246
    concept of, 8–9
    corporate (*see* Corporate crime)
    defined, 8
    deviance versus, 8
    drug-related (*see* Drug abuse)
    fairy tales and, 10, 19
    gender and, 39–41 (*See also* Female criminals)
    immigration and, 4, 7, 42, 98–99, 130–131, 134, 141, 193, 299
    ingredients of, 212–217
        act, 212–213
        causation, 212, 215
        concurrence, 212, 216
        harm, 212, 215

        legality, 212, 213–215
        mens rea (guilty mind), 212, 215–216, 221, 293
        punishment, 212, 217
    international crime (*see* International crime)
    measurement of, 19–43
        characteristics of crime and, 29–34
        characteristics of criminals and, 34–43
        data collection in, 20, 21–23, 348–349
        ethics and, 23
        international crime, 23, 26, 162, 237, 348–349
        objectives of, 20–21
        police statistics in, 24–27
        self-report surveys in, 23, 27–29, 39–40, 41–42
        victimization surveys in, 23, 27, 176
    natural, 8–9, 57
    nature and extent of (*see* Crime, measurement of)
    against the person, 24 (*See also* Index crimes)
    prevention of (*see* Crime-prevention programs)
    against property (*see* Property crimes)
    sex-related (*see* Sex-related crimes)
    theories of, 169–174
        conflict, 9–10, 41–42, 195–197, 199
        labeling, 189–195
        radical, 199–205
    typologies of, 217, 227
    violent (*see* Violence; Violent crimes)
    white-collar (*see* White-collar crime)
    women in (*see* Female criminals)
    (*See also* specific types of crime)
Crime and Human Nature (Wilson and Herrnstein), 59
Crime and the American Dream (Messner and Rosenfeld), 106
Crime-prevention programs:
    crime prevention through environmental design (CPTED), 177, 178–179, 181–182, 183–184
    cultural deviance theories applied to, 114–115
    delinquency, 163
    differential association theory applied to, 117
    social control theory applied in, 161–163
    strain theory applied in, 107–109
    subcultural theories applied in, 142–144
Crime rate, 25
    comparative, 162, 351
    cross-national comparisons, 23, 26, 162, 237, 349
    differential distribution of, 111–113
    drug-related, 34
    homicide, 237
    in low-crime nations, 162
    police and, 34
    property crime, 282
    social factors and, 61
    trends in, 29–31, 34, 172
Crimes against property (*see* Property crimes)
Criminal and His Victim, The (von Hentig), 175
Criminal attempt, 227
Criminal careers, 38–39
Criminal gangs, 129–131

Criminal justice system:
　adjudication in (*see* Court system, U.S.; Courts)
　courts in (*see* Court system, U.S.; Courts)
　criminology related to, 14
　high-tech crimes and, 277
　juveniles in (*see* Juvenile justice system)
　labeling theory and, 189–195
　police in (*see* Police)
　(*See also* Juvenile justice system)
Criminal liability, 211–212, 216, 221
Criminal Man, The (Lombroso), 54–55
Criminal Personality, The (Yochelson and Samenow), 80
Criminal sexual conduct, 247
Criminality, criminal behavior:
　biochemical factors in, 88–91
　genetic factors in, 59–60, 84–87
　psychological factors in, 62, *63*, 70, 71–84
　sociological factors in, 61–62, *63*, 70–71, 98–120
Criminality and Economic Conditions (Bonger), 200
Criminals, characteristics of, 34–43
　age, 28, 35–39, 233, 235, 237, 277
　criminal traits and (*see* Biocriminology, biological determinism)
　gender, 28, 39–41, 233, 237, 267, 277, 279
　(*See also* Female criminals)
　psychological studies and, 60
　race, 28, 42–43, 105–106, 132–133, 233, 234, 277
　social class, 41–42, 104–105, 132–133, 277
Criminology, 3–17
　classical (*see* Classical school of criminology)
　comparative (*see* Comparative criminology)
　conflict theory and, 196–199
　criminal justice system and, 14
　defined, 6
　Marxist, 199–205, 246
　nature of, 6–7
　positivist (*see* Positivist criminology)
　radical, 201–202, 246
　research in, 14–16 (*see* Crime, measurement of; Data)
　somatotype, 57–59
　theories of crime in, 169–174
　theories of victimization in, 169, 174–177, 334
　(*See also specific theories*)
Criminoloids, 56
Critical theory (*see* Radical theory)
Cross-cultural research, 348, 349–351
　(*See also* Comparative criminology)
Cult of domesticity, female criminals and, 40
Cults, 117–119
　Branch Davidian, 118, 251–253
　MOVE, 117–119
Cultural deviance theories, 99, 109–119
　culture conflict theory, 109, 117–119
　deviance, defined, 109–110
　differential association theory, 79–80, 109, 115–117
　social disorganization theory and, 109, 110–115
　subcultures and, 125

Cultural transmission, 113
Culture:
　of poverty, 102
　(*See also* Subcultures)
Culture conflict theory, 109, 117–119
Curfews, 152–153
Customary law, 346, *348*
Cyber spies, 276
Cyberporn, 278, 335
Cyprus, 250
Czech Republic, 204, 343

Dallas, Texas, 143, 163
Dangerous Ground (Rebovich), 298
Dartmouth, Massachusetts, 156
Data:
　collection of, 20, 21–23, 348–349
　defined, 20
Date rape, 246
Deadly force, 225, *226*
　(*See also* Brutality, police)
Death penalty (*see* Capital punishment)
Deceptive advertising, 291
Decision-making:
　juveniles in (*see* Juvenile justice system)
Defense(s), 217–226
　defense of others, 222–226
　defense of property, 222–226
　duress, 221–222
　guilty but mentally ill, 220
　infancy, 211–212, 220–221
　insanity defense, 82–83, 217–219, 236
　intoxication, 220
　mistake of fact, 221
　mistake or ignorance of law, 221
　necessity, 222, 223
　public duty, 222
　self-defense, 222–226
Defense Department, U.S., 290
Defensible space, 177, 178–179
Defensible Space (Newman), 178–179
Del Webb Corp., 285, 286
Delinquency (juvenile offenders):
　aging-out phenomenon and, 36–37
　arson and, 281
　Chicago Area Project, 114–115
　cultural deviance theories of, 109–110
　in different cultures, 352
　family and, 71–72, 75–77, 163
　female, 22, 39, 40, 138–140
　gangs and (*see* Gangs)
　guns and, 255–256
　"hidden," 23
　IQ and, 88
　labeling and, 193
　longitudinal studies and, 38–39
　Mid-City Project, Boston, 115
　middle-class, 127, 140–142, 193
　moral development and, 72, *73–74*
　prevention of, 163
　psychological development and, 71
　"Scared Straight!" program (New Jersey), 21–22
　self-report surveys of, 23, 29, 41–42
　social class and, 41–42, 124–144, 193
　social control theory of, 99, 148–164

social disorganization theory and, 114–115
　strain theory of, 99, 100–109
　subculture of, 124–144
　(*See also* Crime; Gangs; Juvenile justice system)
Delinquent boys, 126
Delusional instigators, 79
Denmark, 85–86, 87, 343
Denver, Colorado, 39, 131
Depression, 84, 267
Depression, Great, 292–293
Deprivation, maternal, 73–77
Designer drugs, 317
Detention facilities:
　(*See also* Jails)
Detroit, Michigan, 256, 320
Developmental theories, 160–161
Deviance, 7–8
　crime versus, 8
　cultural (*see* Cultural deviance theories)
　defined, 109–110
　labeling theory on (*see* Labeling theory)
　modes of, 104
　probability of, 158–159
　(*See also* Strain theory)
Deviance theory, 99, 109–119
Deviate sexual intercourse, 329
Diet, criminality linked to, 89–90
Differential association-reinforcement, 79–80
Differential association theory, 79–80, 109, 115–117
　evaluation of, 116–117
　policy and, 117
　subcultures and, 125
　of Sutherland, 115–117
　tests of, 116
Differential opportunity theory, 129–132, 142
　evaluation of, 131–132
　tests of, 130–131
Direct control, 159
Direct experience, 77–79
Disney World, 179
Displacement effect, 184, 258
District of Columbia (*see* Washington, D.C.)
Division of Social Labor (Durkheim), 62
Dizygotic (DZ) twins, 85
Domestic violence (*see* Family violence)
"Dramatization of evil," 190
Drexel Burnham Lambert, 289
Drift, drift theory, 155–156
Drive-by shootings, 4, 12–13, 138, 237, 256
Driving under the influence (DUI), 327
Driving while intoxicated (DWI), 327
Dropouts, 128, 157
Drug abuse, 27, 313–325
　child abuse and, 244
　crimes related to, 316–317, 319–320, 321–323, 354, *355*, 357, 358
　drug control and, *314*, 324–325
　drug trade and, 302, *315*, 320–324, 354, *355*, 357, 358
　education and, 324–325
　extent of, 317
　history of, 315–317
　international crime and, 316–317, 320–324, 354, *355*, 358

Drug abuse, *(continued)*
    intoxication defense, 220
    legalization and, 325
    patterns of, 317–319
    political impact of, 323–324
    and retreatism, 104, 130
    spouse abuse and, 242
    treatment and, 324
Drug Enforcement Administration (DEA), 23
Drug Use Forecasting, 319
Drunk driving, 215, 327–328, 353
Drunkenness, 220
Du Pont Plaza Hotel fire (Puerto Rico), 281
Due process, 49, 189
Duress defense, 221–222
Durham rule in insanity defense, 219
Durham v. United States, 219

Early legal systems, 8–10
    Code of Hammurabi (Babylon), 9
    Germanic criminal laws in, 9, 10, 265
    Roman criminal laws in, 9, 265, 345, 346, *348*
    (*See also* Common law)
Ecology:
    defined, 110
    social disorganization theory and, 110–111
    (*See also* Environmental crimes)
Ectomorph somatotype, 58, 59
Education, 106
    drugs and, 324–325
    Head Start, 108, 117
    Perry Preschool Project, 108, 117
    school dropouts and, 128, 157
    (*See also* Schools)
Ego, 71
Egypt, 78, 239, 268, 351
    ancient, 316
Eighteenth Amendment, 299–300, 325, 326
Eighth Amendment, 213
Elderly:
    abuse of, 245
Electroencephalogram (EEG), abnormalities in, 91
Embezzlement, 266, 292
Employee-related theft, 266, 292
Employment:
    Job Corps, 108–109
    job-related illnesses, 287
    unemployment impact on crime, 37
Endomorph somatotype, 58, 59
England, 48, 50, 91, 255, 344
    criminal code of, 52
    fraud and, 271, 272
    insanity defense, 217–218
    larceny and, 265
    London, 199
    Marxist criminology in, 201
    (*See also* Common law)
Enlightenment, Age of, 52
Environmental crimes, 4, 169–171, 292–294, 295–297, 298, 353, 357
    developing legislation, 297
    enforcing legislation, 296–297
    hazardous waste and, 298
    sensitive issues and, 297
Environmental Protection Agency (EPA), 296

Equal protection, 189
Espionage, industrial, 276, 292
Estonia, 203
Ethics, 23, 360
"Ethnic cleansing," 16
Ethnic conflict:
    criminal law and, 203
Ethnic hatred, 5, 16, 142, 252, 343–344
Ethnicity:
    gangs and, 4, 130–131, 134, 140, 141, 237, 305–306, 321
    hate crimes and, 252
    organized crime and, 300–301, 305–306
    (*See also* Blacks; Hispanic Americans; Native Americans; Race)
Eugenics, 55, 59
Europe (*see names of specific countries*)
"Evil, dramatization of," 190
Exasperation, subculture of, 234
Experiments, 21–22
    (*See also* Data, collection of)
Extraversion, 81, 83
Exxon Valdez oil spill, 4, 292, 296
Eysenck Personality Questionnaire (EPQ), 81

Fairy tales, and crime, 10, 19
False accusations, 192
False pretenses, obtaining property by, 271–272
Families First, 163
Family:
    attachment theory and, 73–77, 150–151, 153, 244
    and delinquency, 71–72, 75–77, 163
    maternal deprivation and, 73–77
    violence in (*see* Family violence)
Family violence, 76, 77, 132, 235, 241–245
    abuse of elderly, 245
    and alcohol abuse, 242, 244, 327
    child abuse, 76, 132, 235, 241, 243–245
    mate homicide, 235
    parricide, 76
    self-defense in, 224–225
    spouse abuse, 30, 132, 224–225, 235, 242–243, 327
    and stalking, 30
    stalking and, 30
Fear, 113
Federal Bureau of Investigation (FBI):
    crime statistics and, 23, 24–27 (*See also* Uniform Crime Reports)
    guns and, 255
    National Crime Information Center, 269–270
Federal Bureau of Prisons, U.S., 23
Federal Corrupt Practices Act, 293–294
Federal Election Campaign Act (1971), 294
Federal law enforcement:
    (*See also* Federal Bureau of Investigation)
Federal test, new, in insanity defense, 219
Federal Witness Protection Program, 302
"Felicific calculus," 52
Felonies, 217, 227
    kidnapping, 249
    robbery, 248–249
Felony murder, 232–233
Female criminals:
    black, arrests of, 234

burglars, 279
    delinquency and, 22, 39, 40
    in gangs, 22, 138–140
    male criminals versus, 56
    new, 40–41
Female Offender, The (Lombroso and Ferrero), 40
Feminist movement, 204, 334
Fence (Steffensmeier), 280
Fencing property, 279–281, 289
Field experiments, 21–22
Finland, 29, 90
Firearms (*see* Guns)
First Amendment, 334
First-degree murder, 232–233
Florida, 35–36, 117, 163, 171, 182, 235
    curfew, 152–153
    Miami, 133, 143, 319
    Parrot Middle School, 152
    Tampa/St. Petersburg, 113
Focal concerns, 134–136
Food:
    additives to, 90
    allergies to, 88–89
    dyes in, 90
Forcible rape (*see* Rape)
Forgery, check, 272
France, 48, 49, 50, 51, 61, 62, 169–170, 250
    hate crimes in, 343, 344
    typologies of crime, 227
Fraternal twins, 85
Fraud, 271–273
    anti-government, 289–290, 292
    bankruptcy, 289, 358
    check forgery, 272
    confidence games, 272, 291
    consumer, 291
    corruption, 292, 359–360
    credit card, 272–273, 277
    false pretenses and, 271–272
    insider-related, 292
    insurance, 273, 281, 291, 357
    political, 292
    procurement, 289–290, 292
    securities-related, 288–289
    tax, 291–294
    welfare, 39, 290
    in white-collar crime, 288–292
Free will theory in criminal acts, 49–52, 92, 212
Freedom fighters, 251
Freemen of Montana, 253–255
French Revolution, 49, 50, 51
Funnel of deviance, 8, *8*

Galley slavery, 201
Gambling, 302, 326
Gangs, 136–140
    aging-out phenomenon and, 36–37
    alternatives to, 142–144
    Chinese, 4, 130–131, 141, 305, 321
    conflict, 130
    criminal, 129–131
    delinquent, 141–142
    ethnic, 4, 130–131, 134, 140, 141, 237, 305–306
    getting out of, 144

Gangs, (*continued*)
  girl, 22, 138–140
  guns and, 137–138
  hate, 142, 343–344
  Jamaican, 321
  lower-class, 132–133
  middle-class, 140–142
  motorcycle, 109–110, 305
  murder and, 236–237
  norms of, 134
  retreatist, 130
  satanic, 142
  subculture of violence and, 132–134
  tagger, 127
  violent, 124–125, 132
Gay and lesbian rights movement, 329, 336
Gender:
  crime and, 28, 39–41, 233, 237, 267, 277, 279
  women in gangs, 22, 138–140
  (*See also* Female criminals; Women)
General Electric Company, 285, 286, 297
General strain theory, 107
General Theory of Crime, A (Gottfredson and Hirschi), 161
Genetics:
  adoption studies in, 86
  aggression and, 84–87
  criminality and, 59–60, 84–87
  twin studies in, 85–86
  XYY syndrome and, 84–85
Gentrification, 114
Geography of crime, 177
Georgia, 329
  Atlanta, 133, 136, 137
    Olympic Park bombing, 5, 15
Georgia (Russia), 203
Germanic criminal laws, 9, 10, 265
Germany, 29, 48, 62, 162, 204, 239, 250, 352
  motorcycle helmet legislation, 184
  skinheads in, 343–344
Ghettoes, 113, 114–115, 125, 234
Girls in the Gang, The (Campbell), 139
Global crime (*see* International crime)
Globalization, 14, 345–346, 362
Gods Must Be Crazy, The (movie), 264, 282
Gold mining, and Yanomami suicide, 101
Golden Venture, illegal Chinese immigrants on, 4
Good Samaritan requirement, 213, 214
Government:
  control of corporations, 293–294
  fraud against, 289–290, 292
Graffiti vandalism, 127
Great Britain, 29, 255, 343
Great Depression, 292–293
Greece, 29, 250
  ancient, 53, 286, 329, 345
Grimms' fairy tales, 10
Guilt, 175, 178
Guilty but mentally ill defense, 220
Guilty mind requirement, as crime ingredient, 212, 215–216, 221, 293
Guns:
  delinquency and, 255–256
  drive-by shootings, 4, 12–13, 138, 237, 256
  and gangs, 137–138
  gun control, 257–258, 353

  illicit trade in, 356
  robbery and, 248
  in schools, *137*, 156–157
  (*See also* Assassinations)

Hacking, computer, 275
Hallucinogens, 319
Hammurabi, Code of, 9
Handgun Control, Inc., 257
Handguns (*see* Guns)
Harm requirement, as crime ingredient, 212, 215
Harrison Act (1914), 316
Hashish, 321
Hate crimes, 5, 142, 252, 343–344
Hate gangs, 142, 343–344
Hazardous waste crimes, 298
Head Start Program, 108, 117
Hedonism, 126, 142
Heinz' dilemma, 72
Hell's Angels, 109–110, 305
Heroin, 316, 317–319, 321, 325
"Hidden" delinquency hypothesis, 23
High-tech crimes, 273–278, 357
  characteristics of crimes, 274–275
  characteristics of criminals, 277
  civil liberties and, 278
  as criminal justice problem, 277
  Internet and, 275–277, 278
Hijacking:
  aircraft, 356–357
  carjacking, 154–155, 269
  land, 357
Hirschi's theory (*see* Social bonds theory)
Hispanic Americans:
  anomie and, 102
  community action projects, 115
  gangs and, 140, 141
Home-improvement fraud, 291
Homebuilders, 163
Homicide, 24, 27, 105, 132, 232–237
  assassination, 199, 232, 239
  cross-national comparison of, 237
  extent of, 233–234
  firearms and, 256
  justifiable, 232
  juvenile, *137*, *138*
  manslaughter and, 233
  murder and, 232–233, 235–236
  nature of, 234–237
  negligent, 233
  stranger, 234–235
  types of, 234–237
  without apparent motive, 235
Homosexual activity, 329, 336
Honduras, 359
Hong Kong, 300, 321
Hormones, 90–91, 242
Hot-check artists, 272
House of Umoja Program (Philadelphia), 143
Houston, Texas:
  crime rate and, 34
Human body parts, trade in, 358, 359
Human rights, 16, 362
  United Nations and, 5
Hungary, 204, 323, 343
Hyperactivity, 91

Hypoglycemia, 90
Hypothesis, 20

Id, 71
Identical twins, 85
Illinois, 131, 256, 334
  juvenile courts in, 193, 345
  (*See also* Chicago, Illinois)
Imitation, laws of, 61
Immigration:
  crime and, 4, 7, 42, 98–99, 130–131, 134, 141, 193, 299
  illegal, 4
  social disorganization theory and, 109, 110–115
  sociological impact of, 98–99
  (*See also* Ethnicity)
Incarceration:
  (*See also* Jails; Penitentiaries; Prisons)
Incas, 316
Incentive instigators, 79
Index crimes:
  age of criminal and, 36
  crime rate and, 25
  list of, 24
  race and, 42
  trends in, 29–31
  (*See also* Property crimes)
India, 78, 103, 239, 333, 346, 348
Indirect control, criminality and, 159
Industrial espionage, 276, 292
Infancy defense, 211–212, 220–221
Ingredients of crime (*see* Crime, ingredients of)
Inherited criminality, 59–60, 84–87
Inner containment, criminality and, 158
Innovation as adaptation mode, 103
Insane criminals, 56
Insanity defense, 82–83, 217–219, 236
  A.L.I. test, 219
  Durham or product test, 219
  irresistible impulse test, 219
  M'Naghten test, 217–218
  new federal test, 219
Insider-related fraud, 292
Insider trading, 289
Instigators, behavioral responses elicited by, 78–79
Institute of Juvenile Research, 114
Institutional imbalance, 106–107
Instructional instigators, 79
Insurance fraud, 273, 281, 291, 357
Intellectual property theft, 276, 278, 354–356
Intelligence quotient (IQ) debate, 55, 60, 87–88, 92
Interactionists, social, 190
Interest groups:
  class versus, 202–203
Internal Revenue Code, 291, 294
Internal Revenue Service (IRS), 291
Internalized control, criminality and, 159
International Association of Chiefs of Police (IACP), 24, 25
International crime, 360–362
  assassination in, 239
  child prostitution, 331, 332–333, 357–358, 362

International crime,*(continued)*
  comparative, 14, 345–346, 362
  courts in, 360–362
  drug-related, 316–317, 320–324, 354, *355,* 357, 358
  global approach to law-breaking, 14, 345–346, 362
  high-tech, 273–274, 275, 357
  human rights violations, 5, 16
  intellectual property theft, 276, 278, 354–356
  measuring, 26
  piracy, 357
  statistics on, 23, 26, 162, 237, 348–349
  terrorism, 5, 15–16, 249–255, 354
International criminal court, 360–362
International Criminal Police Organization (Interpol), 349
International drug economy, 320–324
  cocaine in, 321
  heroin in, 321
  marijuana in, 321
  money laundering in, 321–323, 354, *355,* 358
  political impact of, 323–324
International Foundation for Art Research, 268
International Self-Report Delinquency (ISRD), 29
Internet, 275–277, 278, 335, 357
Interpol (International Criminal Police Organization), 349
Intoxication (*see* Alcohol abuse)
Intoxication defense, 220
Involuntary manslaughter, 233
Involvement, social bonds theory and, 152, 153
Iowa, 116, 124–125, 131
IQ (intelligence quotient) debate, 55, 60, 87–88, 92
Ireland, Republic of, 162, 268
Irish Republican Army (IRA), 249
Irresistible impulse test in insanity defense, 219
Islam, 162, 203
Islamic fundamentalism, 15, 249
Israel, 257
Italy, 29, 239, 250, 268, 343
  Mafia, 286, 299, 301–304, 321
  Rome, ancient, 53, 239, 332, 345

Jails, 12–13
Jamaica, 321
Japan, 106, 162, 253, 297, 333, 346, 348, 352
  crime rate, 351
  organized crime, 300, 306
Jersey City, New Jersey, 15, 177
Job Corps, 108–109
Joyriding, *182,* 268
Judiciary (*see* Court system, U.S.; Courts)
Junk-food defense, 89–90
Just-community intervention, 72
Justice Department, U.S., 321
Justice Statistics, Bureau of, 27
Justifiable homicide, 232
Juvenile justice system:
  development of, 193, 345
  juvenile courts in, 193, 345
  (*See also* Delinquency)
Juvenile offenders (*see* Delinquency)

Kansas:
  Kansas City, 256
  Wichita, 144
Kazakhstan, 203
Kefauver Crime Committee, 302
Kent State University killings, 191
Kickbacks, 292
Kidnapping, 249
Kyrgyzstan, 203

Labeling theory, 189–195
  assumptions of, 190–191
  evaluation of, 193–195
  evidence for, 192–193, 194
  in the 1960s, 191–192
  origins of, 190
Labor Department, U.S., 23
Labor racketeering, 302
Land fraud, 291
Land hijacking, 357
Larceny, 24, 25, 27, 168–169, 265–270
  art theft, 268, 354
  boat theft, 268–270
  characteristics of thieves, 266–267
  elements of, 265
  extent of, 265–266
  motor vehicle theft, 24, 27, 168–169, 173–174, 179–184, 268, 269
  shoplifting, 39, 267
  (*See also* Property crimes)
Las Vegas, Nevada, 281
Latin America (*see names of specific countries*)
Latvia, 203
Law, Order, and Power (Chambliss and Seidman), 202
Law-breaking, 7–14
  concept of crime and, 8–9
  conflict theory and, 195–199
  consensus versus conflict models of, 9–10, *189,* 195–196, 199
  deviance and, 7–8
  global approach to, 14, 345–346, 362
  labeling theory and, 189–195
  reasons for, 7, 11–12
  society's reaction to, 12–14
  utilitarianism and, 52, 171
Law enforcement agencies:
  federal (*See also* Federal Bureau of Investigation)
  international, 349
  (*See also* Police)
Lawmaking, 7–10, 50–52
  consensus model of, 9, *189,* 195–196
Laws of imitation, 61
LEAP (Learning, Earning, and Parenting), 117
Learnfare, 163
Lebanon, 239, 250, 321
Left realism, 204–205
Legal system (*see* Criminal justice system)
Legality requirement, as crime ingredient, 212, 213–215
Legalization:
  alcohol, 325–326
  drug, 325
Lesbian and gay rights movement, 329, 336
Lettres de cachet, 49

Liberia, 239
Libya, 5
Life-course theories, 160–161
Life of Mr. Jonathan Wild, the Great (Fielding), 279–280
Lifestyle theory of victimization, 175–176
Lindbergh kidnapping, 249
Liquid Sugars Inc., 295
Lithuania, 203
Lo-Jack, 269
Loan sharking, 302
Lockdown, 113
Lockerbie, Scotland, crash of Pan Am flight 103, 5, 15, 354
London, England, 199
Lone Ranger (char.), 201
Long Day's Journey into Night (O'Neill), 136
Longitudinal studies, 38–39, 153
Lord of the Flies (Golding), 148–149
Los Angeles, California:
  car theft in, 155
  community action projects, 163
  conflict resolution programs, 117, 133
  gangs in, 136–137, *138,* 140, 143
  mens rea requirement, 215–216
  Pioneer Academy of Electronics, 151–152
  police department, 112, 222
  riots of 1992, 112, 136
  Rodney King incident, 112, 222
  smoking laws, 150
Louisiana, 256
  New Orleans, 143, 156, 163
Lower class:
  child abuse and, 244
  crime and, 41–42, 104–106, 132–133
  focal concerns of, 134–136
  gangs in, 132–133
  opportunity theory and, 129–132, 142
  rights of poor and, 197
  welfare fraud, 39, 290
  (*See also* Cultural deviance theories; Strain theory)
LSD, 316, 317, 319

McClellan Committee, 301–302
Mack the Knife (char.), 280
Macrosociological studies, 150
Madagascar, 239
MADD (Mothers Against Drunk Driving), 327–328
Mafia, 286, 299, 301–304, 321
Mail bombings, 277
Maine, 219
Major Fraud Act (1988), 290
Malice aforethought, 232
Manchild in the Promised Land (Brown), 134–135
Mann Act (1910), 331
Manslaughter, 233
  involuntary, 233
  voluntary, 233
Mapping crimes, 61, 169–170
Marijuana, 153, 316, 317, 319, 321
Marijuana Tax Act (1937), 316
Marxist (radical) criminology, 199–205, 246

Maryland, 117, 154–155, 163
  Baltimore, 143
Mass murder, 235–236
Massachusetts, 256 (*See also* Boston, Massachusetts)
  Dartmouth, 156
Maternal deprivation, 73–77
Measurement (*see* Crime, measurement of)
Measuring rod, middle class as, 125–126, 130, 135
Medical Jurisprudence of Insanity, The (Ray), 60
Medicare fraud, 290
Mens rea (guilty mind) requirement, as crime ingredient, 212, 215–216, 221, 293
Mental disorders, 81–84
  guilty but mentally ill, 220
  insanity defense, 82–83, 217–219, 236
  mass murder and, 236
  rape and, 246
Mental retardation:
  child abuse and, 244
Merton's theory (*see* Strain theory)
Mesomorph somatotype, 58, 59
Methadone maintenance, 324
Mexico, 268, 321
Miami, Florida, 133, 143, 319
Michigan, 108, 131, 163, 247, 256, 328
  Detroit, 256, 320
Michigan Militia Corps, 253
Microsociological studies, 150
  (*See also* Social bonds theory)
Mid-City Project (Boston), 115
Middle Ages, 6, 10, 12, 53, 201, 345
Middle class, 111
  delinquency in, 127, 140–142, 193
  gangs in, 140–142
  as measuring rod, 125–126, 130, 135
  protest movements, 191–192
  taggers in, 127
  (*See also* Strain theory)
Millenialism, 251
Miller v. California, 334
Miller's theory (*see* Lower class, focal concerns of)
Milwaukee, Wisconsin, 130
Minimal brain dysfunction (MBD), 91
Minneapolis, Minnesota, 176–177, 267, 328
  Domestic Violence Experiment, 243
Minnesota:
  St. Paul, 136
  (*See also* Minneapolis, Minnesota)
Minnesota Multiphasic Personality Inventory (MMPI), 80
Minority groups (*see* Blacks; Hispanic Americans; Immigration; Native Americans)
Misdemeanors, 217, 227
Mismeasure of Man, The (Gould), 54–55
Mississippi River flood of 1993, 6
Missouri:
  St. Louis, 113, 257
Mistake of fact defense, 221
Mistake or ignorance of law defense, 221
M'Naghten Test, in insanity defense, 217–218
Mobilization for Youth (MOBY) program, 142
Model Penal Code (MPC), 212, 219, 224–225, 227, 248, 286, 293, 329, 330–331, 332, 334

Modeling instigators, 79
Moldova, 203
Money laundering, 321–323, 354, 355, 358
Monopolistic practices, 286, 294
Monozygotic (MZ) twins, 85
Montana, 253–255
  insanity defense, 219
Moral anomalies, 57
Moral development, 72, 73–74
Moral entrepreneurs, 192
Moral insanity, 60
Moral statistics, 61
Morality offenses, 328–336
Morocco, 242
Morphine, 316
Morphing, 276–277
Mothers Against Drunk Driving (MADD), 327–328
Motives:
  for homicide, 235
  for shoplifting, 267
Motor vehicle theft, 24, 27, 168–169, 268
  carjacking, 154–155, 269
  parking facilities and, 182–184
  prevention of, 179–181, 182–184, 269
  Volkswagen crests, 173–174
Motorcycle theft, 184
MOVE (cult), 117–119
Multifactor theories, 160, 161
Multiple victimization, 176
"Munchkin" case, 211–212, 221
Murder, 227, 232–233
  felony, 232–233
  first-degree, 232
  gang, 236–237
  mass, 235–236
  serial, 235–236
"Mushroom" killings, 4
Music:
  violence and, 12–13, 142

National Academy of Sciences (NAS), 87
National Advisory Commission on Civil Disorders, 42
National Center for Juvenile Justice, 137–138
National Center for the Prevention and Control of Rape (NCPCR), 245
National Center on Child Abuse and Neglect, 243
National Commission on Obscenity and Pornography (1970), 332–334
National Crime Information Center (NCIC), 269–270
National Crime Victimization Survey (NCVS), 24, 27, 28, 30, 32, 32–33, 39, 42, 241, 242, 266
National Environmental Policy Act (NEPA) (1969), 296
National Guard, 191
National Incidence Study (NIS), 243
National Incident-Based Reporting System (NIBRS), 25–27
National Institute of Mental Health (NIMH), 117
National Rifle Association (NRA), 257
National Sheriffs' Association, 25
National Survey of Crime Severity, 33–34, 35, 245–246
National Youth Gang Center, 125

Native Americans, 350
Natural crimes, 8–9, 57
Nazism, 175, 200, 239, 343–344
Necessity defense, 222, 223
Negligent homicide, 233
Neo-Nazism, 343–344
Neolithic crime, 48–49
Nepal, 162
Netherlands, 29, 61, 255
Neuropsychological factors, in aggression, 91
Neuroticism, 81
Nevada:
  gambling in, 326
  Las Vegas, 281
  prostitution in, 331
New-company scam in bankruptcy fraud, 289
New Criminology, The (Taylor et al.), 201
New federal test in insanity defense, 219
New female criminal, 40–41
New Hampshire, 219
New Jersey, 116, 256, 326
  Atlantic City, 114
  drug markets in, 177
  Jersey City, 15, 177
  legality requirement, 213–215
  motor vehicle theft in, 168–169, 179–181
  Newark, 143
  prisons in, 21–22
New Mexico, 127
New Orleans, Louisiana, 143, 156, 163
New Phrenology, 59
New theory (*see* Radical theory)
New York (state):
  Civil Forfeiture Law, 328
  organized crime and, 303–304
  police powers, 34, 174
  Rochester, 39, 113, 116, 140, 154–155, 256
  TWA flight 800 crash, 5, 354
New York City:
  Kitty Genovese case, 213, 214
  Bernhard Goetz case, 222–225
  community action projects, 163
  conflict resolution programs, 117
  crime problems, 4, 34, 35, 69–70, 142, 143, 235
  delinquency and guns, 255–256
  gangs in, 4, 130–131, 133, 138–140, 141
  gun buy-back program, 257
  illegal immigrants in, 4
  Mobilization for Youth (MOBY), 142
  police department, 34, 174
  pooper-scooper law, 8
  rights of poor in, 197
  World Trade Center bombing, 15, 354
New Zealand, 29, 346
Newark, New Jersey, 143
Nicaragua, 239
Nigeria, 239, 352, 357
Nolo contendere (no contest) plea, 294
Nonparticipant observation, 22
Norms:
  conduct, 117–119, 134
  gang, 134
North Carolina:
  Charlotte, 29, 32
Norway, 353

Nullum crimen sine lege (no crime without law), 215

Observation, 22
Observational learning, 77
Obtaining property by false pretenses, 271–272
Occupational crime, 287, 288
Ohio, 117, 131, 163, 178, 328
    Cincinnati, 328
    Cleveland, 143
    Kent State University killings, 191
Oil spills, 4, *4*
Oklahoma, 117
Oklahoma City, 161
    bombing in, 15, 253, 254
Old-company scam in bankruptcy fraud, 289
Old Stone Age, 315–316
On Crimes and Punishment (Beccaria), 50
Operation Free Jungle, 101
Opium, 316
Opportunistic robbers, 248
Opportunity theory:
    delinquency and, 129–132, 142
    differential (*see* Differential opportunity theory)
    Mobilization for Youth (MOBY) and, 142
Oregon, 116, 328
Organizational crimes, 227, 285–306
    corporate crime, 285, 287, 292–299
    organized crime, 286, 299–306, 360
    white-collar crime, 3–4, 25, 42, 286–292
Organized crime, 286, 299–306, 360
    business of, 300–301, 304–305, 321, 326, 358
    ethnic diversity of, 300–301, 305–306
    history of, 299–302
Organized Crime Control Act (1970), 302
Organs, trade in human, 358
Origin of Species (Darwin), 53
Others, defense of, 222–226
Outer containment, criminality and, 158
Outlaws of the Ocean (Mueller and Adler), 223

Pakistan, 321, 323, 333, 361
Pan Am flight 103, crash of, 5, 15, 354
Panama, 323
Parricide, 76
Part I offenses (*see* Index crimes)
Part II offenses, 24, *36*
Participant observation, 22
Password sniffers, 277
Peacemaking criminology, 205
Penal institutions (*see* Jails; Prisons)
Penitentiaries, 12–13
Pennsylvania:
    Pittsburgh, 36
    (*See also* Philadelphia, Pennsylvania)
Penny Stock Reform Act (1990), 289
Penologists, 201
Perry Preschool Project, 108, 117
Person, crimes against, 24 (*See also* Index crimes)
Personality, 80–81
    antisocial, 82–83
    criminal behavior and, 80–81
    tests of, 80, 81
Peru, 162, 250, 321, 323, 324

Philadelphia, Pennsylvania, 335
    gun buy-back program, 257
    homicide in, 234, 327
    House of Umoja, 143
    MOVE (cult), 117–119
    study of criminal careers in, 38–39
Philippines, 239, 333
Phoenix, Arizona, 254
Phrenology, 53–54, 59
Physiognomy, 53
Pickpockets, 267
Pilferage, 292
Pimps, 330
Piracy:
    maritime, 270, 357
    software, 276, 278, 356
Pittsburgh, Pennsylvania, 39
Pleas of the Crown (Hale), 247
Pleasure-seeking, 126, 135, 142, 171
Poland, 204, 343
Police:
    brutality of, 112, 222
    crime rate and, 34
    crime statistics of, 24–27
    gun buy-back programs, 257
    hot spots of crime and, 176–177
    international, 349
    powers of, 34, *174*
    repeat victimization and, 176
    Rodney King incident, 112, 222
    spouse abuse and, 242, 243
    (*See also* Law enforcement agencies)
Polish Peasant in Europe and America, The
    (Thomas and Znaniecki), 110
Political fraud, 292
Pooper-scooper laws, 8, 215
Pope v. Illinois, 334
Population:
    survey, 21
Pornography, 302, 331–336
    child, 276–277
    computer, 278, 335
    defining, 331–332
    Internet and, 278, 335
    violence and, 333–334
Portugal, 29, 250
Positivist criminology, 53–62
    biological determinism in, 53–60, 62, *63*
    described, 48
    psychological determinism in, 60, 62, *63*
    sociological determinism in, 61–62, *63*
    time line of, 62, *63*
Postconventional morality, 72, *74*
Poverty:
    crime and, 7
    culture of, 102 (*See also* Lower class)
Powell v. Texas, 213
Power:
    rape and, 246
    spouse abuse and, 243
Preconventional morality, 72, *73*
Premenstrual syndrome (PMS), 91
President's Commission on Law Enforcement
    and Administration of Justice (1967), 14, 302
President's Commission on the Causes and Prevention of Violence, 132

Prevention programs (*see* Crime-prevention programs)
Primary conflict, 119
Primary data, 21–22
Primary deviations, 190
Principals, 227
Principles of Criminology (Sutherland), 115
Prisons:
    penitentiaries, 12–13
    "Scared Straight!" program (New Jersey), 21–22
Probability of deviance, in containment theory, 158–159
Procurement fraud, 289–290, 292
Product (Durham) test in insanity defense, 219
Professional Fence (Klockar), 280
Professional robbers, 248
Professional Thief, The (Sutherland), 22
Professional thieves, 22, 267
Prohibition, 300
Project Follow Through, 108
Project Freedom, 144
Property, defense of, 222–226
Property crimes, 24, 27, 227, 264–282
    arson, 24, 27, 227, 281–282
    burglary, 24, 27, 170–171, 176, 279
    comparative rates, 282
    fencing, 279–281, 289
    fraud, 271–273 (*See also* Fraud)
    high-tech crimes, 273–278, 357
    larceny, 24, 25, 27, 168–169, 265–270
    (*See also* Index crimes)
Prosecution:
    for child abuse, 244
    for rape, 247
Prostitution, 27, 39, 56, 249, 302, 329–331, 336
    child, 331, 332–333
    sexual slavery and, 331, 332–333, 357–358, 362
Protest movements, 191–192
Psychoanalytic theory, 71–72, 80
Psychocriminology, psychological determinism, 62, *63*, 70, 71–84
    attachment theory and, 73–77, 150–151, 153, 244
    intelligence and, 60
    maternal deprivation and, 73–77
    mental disorders and, 81–84, 217–219, 220, 236, 246
    moral development and, 72, 73–74
    personality and, 80–81
    pioneers of, 60, *63*
    psychological development and, 71–72
    rape and, 246
    social learning theory and, 77–80
Psychopathy, 82–83
Psychosis, 81–82, 246
Public duty defense, 222
Puerto Rico, 281, 326, 352
Punishment:
    Beccaria on, 51
    capital (*see* Capital punishment)
Punishment and the Social Structure (Rusche and Kirchheimer), 200–201
Punishment requirement, as crime ingredient, 212, 217

Puritans, 220
Pyromania, 281

Race:
    crime and, 28, 42–43, 105–106, 132–133, 233, 234, 277
    (*See also* Blacks; Ethnicity; Hispanic Americans; Native Americans)
Racketeer Influenced and Corrupt Organizations (RICO) Act (1970), 293, 302
Radical theory, 199–205
    alternative perspectives, 204–205
    evaluation of, 202–204
    feminist, 204, 334
    from 1970s to 1990s, 201–202, 246
    pioneers of, 199–201
Rahway State Prison, New Jersey, 21–22
Random samples, 21
Rape, 24, 27, 32, 168, 245–248
    characteristics of, 246
    community response to, 247–248
    legal system and, 247
    rapists and, 246–247
    statutory, 329
Rape shield laws, 247
Rapists, 246–247
Rational-choice perspective, 171–172, 177–184
Reaction formation, 126
Rebellion, as adaptation mode, 104
Renaissance, 345
Repeat victimization, 176
Republic, The (Plato), 47
Republic of Ireland, 162
Residential therapeutic communities, 324
Retreatism, as adaptation mode, 104
Retreatist gangs, as subculture, 130
Revolution, French, 49, 50
Richmond Youth Study, of University of California at Berkeley, 105
Riots and uprisings:
    Kent State University killings, 191
    Los Angeles (1992), 112, 136
    Tiananmen Square (China), 79
Ritualism, as adaptation mode, 104
Robbers and robbery, 24, 25, 27, 168, 171, 248–249
    characteristics of robbers, 248
    consequences of robbery, 248–249
    convenience-store, 171, 181–184
    (*See also* Property crimes)
Robbery, 248–249
Robin Hood myth, 202, 277
Robinson v. California, 213
Rochester, New York, 39, 113, 116, 256
    Youth Development Study, 140, 154–155
Rodney King incident, 112, 222
Roman criminal laws, 9, 265, 345, 346, *348*
Romania, 204
Rome, ancient, 53, 239, 332, 345
Routine-activity approach, 172–174, 176, 178
Rule of law in law enforcement:
    civil rights and, 189
    due process and, 49, 189
Russia, Soviet Republics of, 51–52
Rwanda, 16

St. Louis, Missouri, 113, 257
St. Paul, Minnesota, 136
Samples:
    defined, 21
    random, 21
San Diego, California, 143, 163
San Francisco, California, 140, 236, 257, 319
Sanity, labeling theory tests of, 192–193, 194
Satanic gangs, 142
Saudi Arabia, 162, 196, 239
Savings and loan scandal, 286
"Scared Straight!" program (New Jersey), 21–22
Schizophrenia:
    labeling of, 192–193, 194
Schools:
    delinquency prevention programs, 163
    dropouts, 128, 157
    social bonds and, 150–153, 163
    weapons in, *137*, 156–157
    (*See also* Education)
Scotland, 5, 15, 236, 354
Sea Empress oil spill, 4
Sea piracy, 270, 357
Seattle, Washington, 163, 178, 235, 256, 328
Second Amendment, 253, 257–258
Second-degree murder, 233
Secondary conflict, 119
Secondary data, 21, 23
Secondary deviations, 190–191
Secondary elaboration, 191
Securities Act (1933), 288
Securities and Exchange Commission (SEC), 288, 289
Securities Exchange Act (1934), 288
Securities-related crimes, 288–289
    boiler rooms and, 289
    churning and, 289
    insider trading and, 289
    stock manipulation and, 289
Self-defense, 222–226
Self-fulfilling prophecy, 193, 194, 252
Self-report surveys, 23, 27–29, 39–40, 41–42
    findings of, 28–29
    limitations of, 23, 29
Sellin Center of the University of Pennsylvania, 38–39
Sentence-enhancement statutes, 256
Sentencing and sanctions:
    (*see* Capital punishment; Prisons; Punishment)
Serial murder, 235–236
Severity of crime, 33–34, *35*, 245–246
Sex chromosomes in criminals, 84–85
Sex-related crimes:
    deviate sexual intercourse, 329
    morality offenses, 328–336
    pornography, 276–277, 278, 302, 331–336
    prostitution (*see* Prostitution)
    rape, 24, 27, 32, 168, 245–248, 329
    sexual slavery, 331, 332–333, 357–358, 362
Sexual assault (*see* Rape)
Sexual intercourse, deviate, 329
Sheriffs, 25
Sherman Antitrust Act (1890), 286, 294
Shoplifting, 39, 267
Similar-name scam in bankruptcy fraud, 289

Simple assault, 241
Singapore, 78
Situational crime prevention, 177–184
Skinheads, 142, 343–344, 353
Slavery, 357–358
    galley, 201
    sexual, 331, 332–333, 357–358, 362
Smoking laws, 150
Social bonds theory, 150–155, 163
    attachment in, 150–151
    belief in, 152–153
    commitment in, 151–152
    empirical tests of, 153
    evaluation of, 153–155
    involvement in, 152, 153
Social class (*see* Class)
Social control theory, 99, 148–164
    containment theory and, 158–160
    described, 149–150
    and drift, 155–156
    evaluation of, 153–155
    integration of theories, 160–161
    international comparisons, 162
    macrosociological studies in, 150
    microsociological studies in, 150
    personal control and, 156–158
    policy and, 161–163
    social bonds and, 150–155, 163
    tests of, 153
Social criminals, 80
Social disorganization theory, 109, 110–115
    Boston and, 115
    Chicago and, 110–113, 114
    evaluation of, 114
    Los Angeles and, 112
    subcultures and, 125
    tests of, 113–114
Social interactionists, 190
Social learning theory, 77–80
    differential reinforcement in, 79–80
    direct experience and, 77–79
    observational learning in, 77
Sociology, sociological determinism, 61–62, *63*, 70–71, 98–120
    anomie theory of, 62, 99–103
    deviance theory of, 99, 109–119
    pioneers of, 61–62, *63*
    social control theory of, 99, 148–164
    strain theory of, 99, 100–109
Sociopathy, 82–83, 236
Sodomy, 329
Software piracy, 276, 278, 356
Solar Temple, 119
Somatotype criminology, 57–59
Son of Sam (David Berkowitz), 235
South Carolina:
    Charleston, 163
South Korea, 239, 333
Soviet Union, former:
    collapse of, 203–204
    ethnic conflict and, 203
    freedom fighters and, 251
    high-tech crime and, 273–274
    immigrants from, 141
    organized crime, 300
    under Stalin, 212

Spain, 29, 250
Spatial crime patterns, 61, 169–170
Spokane, Washington, 267
Spouse abuse, 30, 132, 224–225, 235, 242–243, 327
   extent of, 242
   nature of, 242–243
Sri Lanka, 239
Stalking, 30–31, 213, 214
States:
   criminal justice systems of, 14
   stalking laws, *31*
   (*See also* names of specific states)
Statistics:
   police, 24–27
   (*See also* Crime rate; Uniform Crime Reports)
Status:
   act versus, 212–213, 329
Statutory rape, 329
Stealing (*see* Larceny)
Sterilization laws, 55, 60
Stigmata, atavistic, 54–56, 57
Stock manipulation, 289
Stock market crash of 1929, 100, 288
Stone Age, 48–49, 315–316
Strain theory, 99, 100–109
   anomie and, 102–103
   evaluation of, 106
   general, 107
   institutional imbalance and, 106–107
   modes of adaptation and, 103–104
   policy and, 107–109
   subcultures and, 125
   tests of, 104–106
Stranger homicide, 234–235
Strict liability offenses, 216
Structural-functionalist perspective, 99–100
Subculture of exasperation, 234
Subcultures, 124–144
   cults, 117–119, 251–253
   defined, 125
   delinquency and, 124–144
   differential opportunity theory and, 129–132, 142
   focal concerns and, 134–136
   function of, 125
   gangs (*see* Gangs)
   middle-class delinquent, 140–142
   policy concerning, 142–144
   tagger, 127
   and theories of delinquency and crime, 125–128
   of violence, 125, 132–134, 244
Substance abuse (*see* Alcohol abuse; Drug abuse)
Successful-business scam in bankruptcy fraud, 289
Sugar, 89–90
Suicide:
   among Yanomami, 101
   anomie and, 100, 101
Sunset Strip killer (Douglas Clark), 235
Superego, 71
Supreme Court, U.S.:
   on consensual sexual activity, 329
   on equal protection, 189

   on insanity defense, 219
   on *mens rea* requirement, 215, 216, 221
   on pornography, 334
   on status versus crime, 213, 329
   on sterilization, 60
Surveys:
   defined, 21
   on drug use, 317, *318*
   self-report, 23, 27–29, 39–40, 41–42
   victimization, 23, 27, 176, 241
   of world crime, 23, 26, 162, 237, 349
   (*See also specific surveys*)
S.W.E.A.T. Team, 163
Sweden, 86, 239, 327, 343
Swindling (*see* Fraud)
Switzerland, 29, 104, 106, 119, 162, 257, 348

Tacoma, Washington, 163
Taggers, 127
Taiwan, 321, 333
Tampa/St. Petersburg, Florida, 113
Target-hardening techniques, 178, 268, 269, 273
Task Force on Organized Crime, 302
Tax fraud, 291–294
Team Viper, 254
Telecommunications Decency Act (1996), 335
Television:
   violence on, 77, *78–79*
Tennessee, 128
Terrorism, 5, 15–16, 249–255
   extent of, 250–251, 354
   home-grown, 253–255
   international efforts to control, 251–253
Texas, 176, 213, 236, 328
   Dallas, 143, 163
   Houston, 34
   Waco, 118, 251–253
Thailand, 333
Theft, 24, 27, 173–174
   art, 268, 354
   employee-related, 266, 292
   motor vehicle, 24, 27, 154–155, 168–169, 173–174, 179–184, 268, 269
   (*See also* Larceny; Property crimes)
Theory:
   of crime, 169–174
      labeling, 189–195
   of criminality (*see specific theories*)
   defined, 20
   testing of, 352–353
   of victimization, 169, 174–177, 334
Therapeutic communities, 324
Thieves:
   amateur and professional, 22, 266–267
   (*See also* Larceny)
Third World countries:
   bribery and, 295
   drug abuse and, 324
   pollution in, 297
   (*See also* names of specific countries)
Thurman v. Torrington, 243
Tiananmen Square uprising, 79
Titanic, 267
Torts, 217
Torture, 51
Trade secrets, 292

Tranquilizers, 316
Transnational crime, 353–360
Treasury Department, U.S., 23
Triads, Chinese, 4, 130–131, 141, 300, 305, 321
Trucks, hijacking of, 357
Tryptophan, 90
Tucson, Arizona, 117, 140
Turkmenistan, 203
TWA flight 800, crash of, 5, 354
Twenty-Sixth Amendment, 328
Twin studies, 85–86
"Twinkie defense," 89–90
Typologies of crime, 217, 227
   alcohol-related crimes, 227
   crimes against property, 24, 227, 264–282
   crimes against the person, 24
   drug-related crimes, 227
   organizational crimes, 227, 285–306
   sex-related crimes, 227
   violent crimes, 227, 231–258

Ukraine, 203
Umoja, House of, 143
Unemployment:
   delinquency and, 37
Uniform Controlled Substances Act (1970), 316
Uniform Crime Reports (UCR), 23, 24–27, 105–106, 132–133, 246, 252, 266, 268, 279, 329–330
   compilation of, 24–25
   limitations of, 25–27
   National Crime Victimization Survey (NCVS) versus, 27, 29, *32*
   trends in, 29–31
United Kingdom, 250, 343
   (*See also* England; Ireland)
United Nations (U.N.):
   drug control and, 324
   human rights violations, 5
   organizations and affiliates, *347*
   organized crime and, 300–301
   terrorism and, 249
   World Crime Survey, 23, 26, 162, 237, 349
United States:
   assassinations in, 199, 239
   common law and, 346
   drug abuse in, 316
   firearm-related offenses in, 255
   hate groups in, 343–344
   homicide rates in, 233–234, 237, *238*
   strain theory applied to, 102–103
   terrorism within, 253–255
United States v. Brawner, 219
University of California at Berkeley, 105
University of Chicago, 110–115
University of Pennsylvania, 38–39
Unraveling Juvenile Delinquency (Glueck and Glueck), 352
Urban areas:
   crime rates and, 32
   gangs in (*see* Gangs)
   ghettoes in, 113, 114–115, 125, 134
Utah, 285
Utilitarianism, 52, 171
Uzbekistan, 203

Vagrancy, 27
Vandalism, 127
Variables, 21
Venezuela, 101
Victim(s):
    of corporate crime, 287
    of high-tech crime, 274
    or corporate crime, 287
Victim precipitation, 234
Victimization surveys, 23, 27, 176, 241
    limitations of, 27
    types of, 27
Victimization theories, 169, 174–177, 334
"Victimless" crimes, 27, 196, 313
Victimology, 175
Violations, 217, 227
Violence:
    alcohol abuse and, 326–327
    family (*see* Child abuse; Family violence;
       Spouse abuse)
    gang, 124–125, 132
    genetic factors in, 84–87
    music and, 12–13, 142
    pornography and, 333–334
    social learning theory and, 77–80
    subcultures of, 125, 132–134, 244
    television, 77, *78–79*
Violent crimes, 227, 231–258
    assassinations, 199, 232, 239
    assault, 24, 27, 237–241, 327

family-related, 30, 76, 132, 224–225, 235,
    241–245 (*See also* Child abuse; Spouse
    abuse)
    gun control and, 257–258
    homicide, 24, 27, 105, 132, *137, 138*, 232–237
    kidnapping, 249
    rape, 24, 27, 32, 168, 245–248
    robbery, 24, 25, 27, 168, 171, 248–249
    terrorism, 5, 15–16, 249–255, 354
Virginia, 55, 117, 163
Vitamin deficiencies, and crime, 90
Volkswagen crests, theft of, 173–174
Volstead Act (1919), 325
Voluntary manslaughter, 233

Waco, Texas, Branch Davidian cult in, 118,
    251–253
Wales, 255
Washington (state), 328
    Seattle, 163, 178, 235, 256, 328
    Spokane, 267
    Tacoma, 163
Washington, D.C., 133, 143, 257
WedTech scandal, 289–290
Welfare fraud, 39, 290
West Virginia, 292–293
White-collar crime, 3–4, 25, 42, 286–292
    crimes committed by individuals, 288
    occupational crimes, 287, 288
    types of, 288–292

White Collar Crime (Sutherland), 295
White Slave Traffic Act, 331
Wichita, Kansas, 144
Wisconsin:
    Milwaukee, 130
Women:
    black, arrests of, 234
    as burglars, 279
    delinquency and, 22, 39, 40, 138–140
    domestic violence and, 30, 132, 224–225,
       235, 242–243, 327
    in gangs, 22, 138–140
    men versus, 56
    new female criminal, 40–41
    premenstrual syndrome (PMS) and, 91
    stalking of, 30–31, 213, 214
    (*See also* Sex-related crimes)
Working class, 111, 199–200, 246
World Crime Survey, 23, 26, 162, 237, 349
World Health Organization (WHO), 349
World Trade Center (New York) bombing, 15,
    354

XYY syndrome, 84–85

Yale University, 58
Yanomami, 101
Yugoslavia, former, 5, 141

Zodiac Killer (Heriberto Seda), 69–70, 235